"The Actor" by Pablo Picasso (1881-). Oil on canvas. The Metropolitan Museum of Art; gift of Thelma Chrysler Foy, 1952.

A miniature by Joseph Etienne Blerzy showing acrobatic performances and a theatre of the type used at the French fairs during the eighteenth century (see page 207). Box cover, gold decorated enamel; gouache. The Metropolitan Museum of Art; gift of J. Pierpont Morgan, 1917.

THE THEATRE
AN INTRODUCTION

HOLT, RINEHART AND WINSTON, INC.

New York   Chicago   San Francisco   Atlanta   Dallas
Montreal   Toronto   London   Sydney

OSCAR G. BROCKETT
Indiana University

THE THEATRE

AN INTRODUCTION *Second Edition*

Copyright © 1964, 1969 by Holt, Rinehart and Winston, Inc.
All rights reserved
Library of Congress Catalog Card Number: 69-17648
SBN: 03-080270-9 text edition
SBN: 03-082874-2 trade edition
Printed in the United States of America
1 2 3 4 5 6 7 8 9

COVER
"The Actor" by Pablo Picasso (1881-   ). Oil on canvas. The Metropolitan Museum of Art; gift of Thelma Chrysler Foy, 1952.

ILLUSTRATIONS ON TITLE PAGE
Left to right: Make-up and costume for a porcupine in *Reynard the Fox*; reprinted with permission from *The Mask of Reality: An Approach to Design for Theatre* by Irene Corey, Anchorage Press, 1968.
Scene from Albee's *Who's Afraid of Virginia Woolf?* photograph—Friedman-Abeles.
A Noh actor wearing mask for a production of the play *Hagoromo*: courtesy Kokusai Bunka Shinkokae, Tokyo.

Book design—Pedro A. Noa

TO
MY WIFE

PREFACE

A vital theatre is always sensitive to changes in the society it serves. During the 1960s the theatre has so extensively reflected the numerous challenges to political, social, moral, and esthetic ideals that at times it has appeared merely chaotic. Persistent experimentation has wrought so many changes that the theatre of the 1940s and 1950s now seems increasingly remote. The desire to incorporate the new trends has prompted me to revise this book.

The publisher's decision to redesign the format and to reset the entire text has made many improvements possible. Every chapter has been rewritten in part. Points have been sharpened, new material added, and recent scholarship utilized. Some changes are major. Chapter 3, "Dramatic Structure, Form, and Style," has been thoroughly revised to include much new material on the mixed forms of today. Chapter 15, "The Theatre Since World War II," has been rewritten to show the major trends during the 1960s. A totally new chapter, "The Oriental Theatre," has been added both to include an area not previously treated and to demonstrate one major influence on the contemporary theatre. Many new illustrations have been added throughout the book.

Other less important changes have also been made. In Chapter 2, "The Audience and the Critic," a section on audience psychology has been added. In Part IV, "The Theatre Arts in America Today," many sections have been rewritten to incorporate recent alterations in theatrical practices and in the regulations governing theatrical unions. The final chapter on opportunities for employment (Chapter 23) and the Bibliography have been brought up to date.

Despite these revisions, the basic approach and organization of the book remain unchanged. The favorable reception of the first edition made fundamental changes seem unwise. The main purposes in revising the text have been to make it more up-to-date, efficient, and reliable.

Part I treats the theatre as an art form, discusses critical methods and outlines the elements of dramatic construction, forms, and styles. Thus, it serves as an introduction to the other parts of the book. Part II surveys developments from early Greek drama to the beginning of the modern theatre around 1875. Representative dramatists, forms, styles, and practices are discussed and their significance explored. Part III is devoted to a consideration of the major movements in theatre and drama since 1875. Part IV outlines contemporary American theatrical practice from the writing of the play through performance. Its emphasis is upon principles and techniques rather than upon "how to do it" details.

The book has been organized so that an instructor may select those portions which are most useful for his particular needs. Each section is an integral part of a whole, but each may be used separately or combined in various ways with portions of other sections. For example, a course which concentrates upon contemporary theatrical practice might use Parts I and IV, while a course which emphasizes historical developments might use Parts I, II, and III. Instructors of courses which deal with forms and styles will find that these are treated at some length in Parts I, II, and III.

The volume of plays issued as a companion to the first edition will serve the new edition equally well. *Plays for the Theatre* (edited by Oscar G. and Lenyth Brockett and published by Holt, Rinehart and Winston in 1967) includes ten of the plays discussed at length in *The Theatre, an Introduction: Oedipus Rex, The Menaechmi, The Second Shepherds' Play, King Lear, Tartuffe, The School for Scandal, The Wild Duck, From Morn to Midnight, The Good Woman of Setzuan,* and *Death of a Salesman.* There is no intention of restricting the examination of plays to those discussed in the text. Rather, the discussions illustrate a method of play analysis and emphasize the special considerations which are important for plays of each type or period.

viii

The range of this book does not allow the inclusion of every playwright, actor, director, or other theatrical artist of importance. The intention has been to lay a foundation upon which to build in the future, rather than to attempt an extensive treatment of each topic.

My indebtedness to others is deep. It would be impossible to enumerate all those scholars whose work is reflected here. Some measure of my debt can be gained from the Bibliography. The sources of illustrations are acknowledged in the captions which accompany them. A few persons deserve special mention. Eldon Elder not only supplied many of the illustrations relating to scene design and lighting but generously offered other materials and much of his time. Tomazo Yano of Kokusai Bunka Shinkokai has provided many of the illustrations and helpfully verified information in the section on Japan. Ruth Chapman of Holt, Rinehart and Winston has been untiring in her efforts both in assembling illustrative material and in seeing the book through all of the editorial processes. Undoubtedly, I owe my greatest debt to those teachers and students who, through their response to the first edition, have made this one necessary. My efforts will have been rewarded if they receive this new version as warmly as they did the original.

O. G. Brockett
Bloomington, Indiana
January 1969

CONTENTS

Preface vii

PART I: BASIC PROBLEMS
    1. The Theatre as an Art Form   3
    2. The Audience and the Critic   17
    3. Dramatic Structure, Form, and Style   27

PART II: THE THEATRE OF THE PAST
    4. The Theatre of Ancient Greece   55
    5. Roman Theatre and Drama   88
    6. Medieval Theatre and Drama 102
    7. Spain and Elizabethan England 122
    8. The Italian Renaissance 150
    9. French Classicism 167
   10. The Eighteenth Century 187
   11. Theatre and Drama in the Nineteenth Century 222
   12. The Oriental Theatre 254

PART III: THE MODERN THEATRE
   13. Realism and Naturalism 287
   14. Revolts Against Realism: Symbolism,
            Expressionism, and Epic Theatre 310
   15. The Theatre Since World War II 344

PART IV: THE THEATRE ARTS IN AMERICA TODAY
   16. The Playwright and the Producer 381
   17. The Director 392
   18. The Actor 420
   19. The Scene Designer 439
   20. The Costumer 475
   21. The Lighting Designer 498
   22. Music and Dance 524
   23. The Theatre as a Profession 539

BIBLIOGRAPHY 553
INDEX 573

I

BASIC PROBLEMS

Make-up based on a Byzantine mosaic. For Job in *The Book of Job* as arranged and directed by Orlin Corey. Reprinted with permission from *The Mask of Reality: An Approach to Design for Theatre* by Irene Corey. Anchorage Press, 1968.

Chapter 1 THE THEATRE AS AN ART FORM

It has been said that the theatre dies every night only to be reborn each day, for it exists whenever actors perform before an audience. The ephemeral nature of the theatre makes it difficult to recapture a performance after it has ended, since unlike a novel, painting, or statue, each of which remains relatively unchanged, a theatrical production exists only during a performance. Then it is gone and lives only in the play script, program, pictures, reviews, and memories of those who were present.

Although the theatre is the most ephemeral of the arts — after music — it is one of the most powerful, for while an audience watches, human beings perform scenes which interpret experience as though it were happening at that very instant. In this way, the theatre approximates life as it is lived and felt moment by moment. As in life, each episode is experienced and then immediately becomes part of the past.

The theatre is also the most objective of the arts, since characteristically it presents both outer and inner experience through speech and action. As in life, it is through listening and watching that we come to know individuals both externally and internally. What we learn about their minds, personalities, and motivations comes from what they say and do, and from what others tell us about them. The novel may deal at length with the unspoken thoughts and unexpressed feelings of its characters, but the dramatist can indicate these inner stirrings only through external signs. This limitation, however, serves to give the theatre a lifelikeness which other arts cannot match.

The theatre is also the most complex of the arts, since it requires many creators — the actor, the playwright, the director, the scene designer, the costumer, the light designer, the choreographer, the musician. This

3

Teatro Olimpico, Vicenza. Built between 1580 and 1584 by Italian architect Vincenzo Scamozzi from the basic design by Andrea Palladio. (Inigo Jones later imported Palladio's classical style into England where *Palladian* motifs became popular.) Photograph—O. G. Brockett.

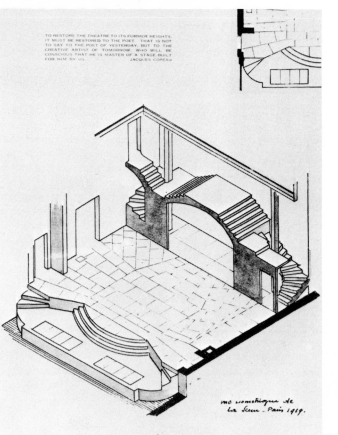

An isometric drawing of Jacques Copeau's stage, the Vieux Colombier, in 1919. From *Theatre Arts*, 1920.

Macbeth as presented by Arthur Hopkins in 1921. Setting by Robert Edmond Jones. The entire production was done in an expressionistic style. Note the three masks suspended above the stage; the arches of the setting tilted ever more precariously as the action progressed. From *Theatre Arts*, 1921.

The 1,140 seat auditorium of the Vivian Beaumont Theater designed by Eero Saarinen. The stage is shown in thrust position. © 1965 Lincoln Center for the Performing Arts (Ezra Stoller photo).

complexity has led many to call the theatre a mixed art since it usually combines the written word of the literary artist, the visual background of the architect and painter, the speech and movement of the actor, the music of the composer, and the dance patterns of the choreographer. Others have called it an impure art because it is not the product of a single creator. These labels imply that several artists cannot achieve a unified result and that the theatre therefore is imperfect and inferior. Certainly the theatre can rarely achieve the purity of form possible in a novel, a poem, or a painting, but it has its own kind of unity. In its very complexity lies much of the theatre's strength, for its varied appeals—action, speech, music, dance, painting—combine in one art product the charms of all the other arts, although in a new and distinctive form.

The number of artists involved in a single production varies widely. In the earliest theatrical performances all artistic functions were served by one person; gradually specialists emerged and the various theatre arts were separated. The actor and the playwright attained recognition first, probably because their functions are basic and closely allied. Since drama tells its story and presents its conflicts entirely through the speeches and actions of characters, it assumes the existence of actors who will lend their bodies, voices, and actions for the time needed to play out the drama.

The actor and the playwright are by necessity complementary, since each needs the other for the completion of his art. The actor may practice his profession without the aid of the playwright, for he may improvise his speech and action—that is, he may become his own dramatist—but unless his improvisation achieves a high degree of excellence, it will not long command attention. To hold interest, a performance must, as a rule, be organized so as to tell a story, to reveal a character, or to illustrate an idea. As the length of the performance increases, so does the need to interweave story, character, and ideas. As these demands are met successfully, the actor approaches more and more the function of the playwright. On the other hand, the person best able to construct an interesting series of events is not necessarily the one most able to enact these events for an audience. Thus, the specialized demands made upon the actor and the playwright have led to separate, though closely related, professions.

The history of the theatre is often treated as though it were synonymous with the history of drama. Although it may distort the truth, such an approach is partially justified, for it is through the written drama that we gain our clearest impressions of the theatre of the past. It is the play script which comes down to us unchanged; we know the other theatre arts only through such secondhand accounts as descriptions of the acting or pictures of single scenes.

The history of the theatre is usually constructed around drama for still another important reason: the play script forms a bridge between our values and those of the past. We are able to appreciate and understand other eras only when we find in them ideas and attitudes which have meaning today, for we remain untouched by that which has no relevance to ourselves. The theatre arts of the past, when viewed in isolation from

Jean Antoine Watteau (1684-1721), "Four Studies of Italian Actors." Red, black and white chalk on gray paper. Courtesy of the Art Institute of Chicago (Gift of Tiffany and Margaret Blake).

Honoré Daumier (1808-1879), "A Clown." Charcoal and water color. The Metropolitan Museum of Art, New York (Rogers Fund, 1927).

A sketch by Philippe Jacques de Loutherbourg for the battle scenes in Shakespeare's *Richard III*. This sketch was made about 1775 when the noted landscape, marine, and battle painter was engaged by David Garrick to superintend scene painting at the Drury Lane Theatre.

drama, may seem totally disconnected from the present, but the great plays of other times create points of contact with the feelings, the thought, the life of these periods. This common bond can then serve as a bridge to understanding the other theatre arts. But while the drama may be a key to understanding what should or did happen in presentation, plays are written to be performed and are not complete until they are filled out by actors, costumes, and scenic background.

The interdependence of the playwright and the actor is clear, but these artists also benefit from the assistance of directors, designers, musicians, and dancers. The need for the director arises as soon as more than one actor is involved, for someone must mediate the differences of opinion which arise as to positions on stage, correct line readings, or interpretations of meaning. But the director is more than a mediator. It is his responsibility to design, edit, and coordinate stage action with the visual background, costumes, lights, music, and dance.

The various elements which go into a production are usually provided by separate artists. The visual background, for example, is the work of the set, lighting, and costume designers, who seek to interpret the qualities found in the script through visual means. The scenic designer not only indicates place and historical period, he supplies the architectural forms, light and shadow, colors, line, and composition which add to and reflect the drama's action. In like manner, the costumer, the lighting designer, and the choreographer seek to embody the mood and spirit of a play through visual means.

It is the interdependent workings of the various arts comprising the theatre which will be pursued in this book.

8

WHAT IS ART?

In the preceding discussion the theatre has been referred to repeatedly as an art form. But what is art? Probably no term has been so widely discussed with so little clear definition.

Until the eighteenth century the term *art* was used almost exclusively to designate a systematic application of knowledge or skills to achieve a desired result. The word is still used in this sense when we speak of the art (or craft) of medicine. During the eighteenth century it became customary to divide the arts into two groups, "useful" and "fine." Into the latter category were placed literature, painting, sculpture, architecture, music, and dance. At the same time, the idea arose that, while the useful arts may easily be learned, the fine arts, as products of genius, could not be reduced to rules or principles which could be taught. As a result, since about 1800 art has often been considered too lofty and esoteric to be fully comprehended and too elusive for close examination.

Although it is perhaps true that no universally accepted explanation of art exists, its nature can be suggested by examining its relationship to other human activities. First of all, and most broadly, art is an aid in understanding the world. As such, it may be compared to history, philosophy, or science, which attempt to discover and record patterns in man's experience. Art may deal with the same subject matter as other approaches, and may even use some of the same methods. For example, history seeks to record the facts of man's past but, since it cannot report everything, it selects those events which seem significant and which

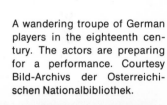

A wandering troupe of German players in the eighteenth century. The actors are preparing for a performance. Courtesy Bild-Archivs der Osterreichischen Nationalbibliothek.

appear to compose a pattern of cause and effect. Thus, history, like art, selects, arranges, and gives emphasis to its materials.

Philosophy seeks to find the truths and principles underlying all being and to relate them to human existence. A play also may suggest answers to this quest. Such branches of science as psychology and sociology seek to determine the causes and probabilities of certain kinds of behavior; a play, too, has some of these concerns. Each approach to man's experience attempts to discover and to put into a communicable form conclusions about man and the world in which he lives.

There are, however, significant differences in the methods used in the various approaches. The historian, philosopher, and scientist attempt to set their conclusions down in logical expository prose: a point of view is expressed, and proof is marshaled to support that view and to gain its acceptance. They direct their appeals principally to the intellect.

The artist, on the other hand, works primarily through direct involvement of the audience's emotions, imagination, and intellect, and by evoking responses more directly. A play, consequently, shows events as though occurring before our eyes; we absorb them in the way we absorb life itself—through their direct operation upon our senses. Art differs from life by stripping away irrelevant details and organizing events so that they compose a significant, connected pattern. Thus, a play illuminates and comments on human experience at the same time that it appears to create it.

Another distinguishing characteristic of art is its manipulation of imagination. Although it may draw upon actual experience, art clearly differs from life. Even historical drama is an imaginative recreation of events; the characters' motivations and dialogue usually must be invented, and certainly the audience knows that what it is seeing is not the historical event itself but a fictional version of it. Just as we do not mistake a statue for a real person, we do not mistake stage action for reality. Rather, we usually view a play with what Coleridge called a "willing suspension of disbelief." By this he meant that, while we know that the events of a play are not real, we agree for the moment not to disbelieve in their reality. One important qualification must be added, however: we are not moved to immediate action by what we see on the stage as we would be by a real event. We watch one man kill another, but we make no attempt to rescue the victim or to call the police. This is a vicarious experience, one we can enter into without the demand for either decision or action. We watch in a kind of suspended animation, a state sometimes called *esthetic distance*, since we seem to be sufficiently removed from the event to view it semiobjectively.

At the same time, however, the distance must not be so great as to induce indifference. Therefore, while a degree of detachment is necessary, involvement is of equal importance. This feeling of kinship is sometimes called *empathy*. Thus, we watch a play with a double sense of concern and detachment, of entering into the experience but without any need for active participation on our part. It is both a removed and an intensified reaction of a kind seldom possible outside an esthetic experience.

10

Hindu dancer. A thirteenth-century carving on a temple in Mysore. Courtesy Information Service of India.

Thus far we have been concerned with art principally as it is embodied in drama. Along with other types of literature, however, drama is the art most apt to have an intellectual content which relates it to areas of knowledge such as history, philosophy, and science. But what of other art forms in which the content is more abstract?

Each art form uses different means and consequently each can best deal with a particular aspect of human experience. Music, for example, makes its appeal through the ear. Using rhythm, melody, and harmony, it organizes sound and time into patterns which can be traced to basic subliminal sensations and feelings. Thus, the universal appeal of music can partially be explained by its rhythmic qualities. Aristotle stated that

11

a sense of rhythm is natural to man; other writers have related all art to the rhythmic patterns of life itself: birth, growth, maturity, decline, and death; the cycle of the year; and the heartbeat. In these ways, the rhythmic element in music is probably related to some of man's most elemental experiences, and the sense of order and harmony which it produces probably stems from its fulfillment of unconscious needs.

The structure of music is also a source of satisfaction. Both melody and rhythm are patterns. Some sound combinations seem harmonious while others seem inharmonious or dissonant: we are pained when unpleasant combinations strike our ears. Each composition has its own patterns—the longer we listen, the clearer the patterns become and the more definite grow our expectations. If a musical phrase is broken off in the middle, we desire to have it completed and sense satisfaction when it is. Thus, structural patterns are an important part of music's effect. They create expectations, which lead to frustrations when interrupted, and to satisfaction when completed.

We value music not so much for what it "says" but for what it "does" to us. It may calm or excite. Whenever it engages our attention, we are bound up in it and respond to its rhythmic patterns. The more completely our attention is engaged, the less we are conscious of other factors outside of the musical experience. While listening we may work or dance without being aware of effort; our energies seem released and we have a sense of freedom and power—of inner harmony. It is only after the music has stopped that we become aware of fatigue and frustration, for during the musical experience, states of feeling, created by organized time and sound, have become the center of our existence.

Painting makes its appeal through the eye, formalizing man's relationship to space. It uses line, mass, and color to create pleasing compositions which are expressive both of order and harmony, of emotions and perceptions. It may represent real objects or it may be totally abstract. Though recognizable subject matter can add another source of pleasure, the appeal of painting does not depend upon its ability to produce exact likeness. Rather, it allows man to experience and understand spatial relationships esthetically.

Each art makes its own distinctive appeal to different senses and through differing means. All art expresses and organizes our perceptions about feeling, emotion, growth, and movement—about life itself. Each art form selects, arranges, and gives emphasis to its elements. Out of this organization, or form, significance emerges.

Significance is a many-faceted concept, however, for it is comprised of all that is communicated or expressed by an art work. Some aspects might be called intellectual significance; others are more closely involved with feelings and emotions.

Intellectual significance may be illustrated by turning once more to drama. In *King Lear*, for example, Lear divides his kingdom between two of his three daughters and gives up all power as ruler. The two daughters cast him out; eventually the formerly great king becomes virtually a beggar and a madman, and further events bring about his death.

12

The 1968 dress rehearsal, Act I, of Giacomo Puccini's opera *Tosca*, based on Victorien Sardou's drama *La Tosca*. Birgit Nilsson—Tosca; Franco Corelli —Cavaradossi; Gabriel Bacquier —Scarpia (left). Conductor— Francesco Molinari-Pradelli; sets and costumes—Rudolf Heinrich. Photograph—P. A. Noa. Courtesy of the Metropolitan Opera, Lincoln Center.

From this series of occurrences we may reach certain conclusions about the relationship of parents to children, about ingratitude, emotional blindness, and so on. Such conclusions are largely intellectual, for they are based upon our perception of a seemingly logical connection between a series of events.

The same sequence, however, has emotional significance of considerable complexity. As the events transpire, expectations, hopes, fears, indignation, and other emotions are aroused; these are thwarted, satisfied, or transformed. With the end of the play comes a feeling of completion, a sense of fulfillment. Although this kind of significance is dependent in part upon the subject matter, it also results from the tempo, rhythm, and structure of the play.

13

The total significance of any work of art is difficult to evaluate. It appeals in varying degrees to different persons, and what the spectator gleans from a work of art depends in part upon his own background and his own sensitivity to emotions and ideas.

Art, then, is one way of ordering, clarifying, and understanding experience. Each art form uses its own special techniques, but each offers both significance and pleasure simultaneously. Of all the arts, the theatre is probably the one most closely related to the patterns of normal experience. It is the art form that most nearly encompasses all of the other arts.

THE PROBLEM OF VALUE IN ART

Art may not appear to be useful. It does not produce the obvious benefits offered by medicine or engineering; it does not promise any advances for civilization; it may seem impractical when compared with business. Its purpose, thus, is vague for most persons; many think of it as a pleasant kind of distraction without fundamental importance. The financially successful artist frequently is honored not because he is effective but because he is successful in the business sense.

Since everyone does not agree upon the worth of individual works of art, many persons question the value of art itself. Even those who profess to like art frequently cast doubt upon its worth; those of conservative taste accuse "modern" art of being an elaborate hoax, while the admirers of modern art reply that conventional forms are shallow and outmoded. Under such a cross fire of argument it is hardly surprising that the general public may develop doubts about art itself.

Furthermore, many persons distrust anything that appeals openly to the emotions. Americans have long been suspicious of their emotional reactions, while the appeal to logic and intelligence has been stressed, if not always followed. Activities that emphasize rationality have been valued, therefore, over those eliciting emotional responses. To many, the display of feeling suggests a lack of control.

There has also been a tendency during the past century to use "art" as a term of praise rather than as a classification. Thus we hear people say, "It may be good theatre, but it isn't art." Not only is such a division of doubtful value, since it fails to clarify adequately how the preferred works differ from those excluded, but it has led the majority of persons to conclude that art has nothing whatever to do with them. Since they do not visit museums or understand the twelve-tone musical scale or Absurdist drama, they do not, according to one view, really appreciate "art." But the man who watches a dramatic program on television, looks at a drawing, or listens to popular music is involved with art, whether or not he calls it by that name. Art is an approach to human experience, it is not a judgment of value. It is part of every person's life, even of those who say they do not understand it or have no interest in it.

This does not mean that all art is equally effective. As in other human activities, it has a range of quality from the excellent to the unsatisfactory, and we are constantly faced with the problem of distinguishing relative value. Is *Hamlet* a good play? Is it better than *Death of a Salesman*? Why? These questions illustrate the problem.

14

Arsenal scene from Bertolt Brecht's *Galileo* as produced at Lincoln Center in the 1966-1967 season. Courtesy of the Repertory Theater of Lincoln Center.

Scene from *Mame* (1966) by Jerry Herman. Angela Lansbury is
seen at center. Photograph by Friedman-Abeles.

It is much easier to pose such questions than to answer them, for no
one can lay down a set of rules for judging art. Nevertheless, approaches
to the problem can be suggested. Since skill in judgment demands experience, the chapters which follow seek to lay foundations for formulating
intelligent and sensitive reactions to the theatre as one form of art.

16

Chapter 2 THE AUDIENCE AND THE CRITIC

In discussing the theatre as a form of art, one important ingredient, the audience, has been ignored. For all arts the existence of an audience is imperative, but for most the audience may be thought of as individuals – the reader of a novel or poem, the viewer of a painting or piece of sculpture – each of whom may experience the art work in isolation. But, for the performing arts – theatre, music, and dance – an audience is assembled at a given time and place to experience a performance as a group.

Although the audience exerts considerable influence, its place in the theatrical experience is not fully understood. Some of the pertinent questions which might be asked about it are: Why does an audience attend the theatre? How does an audience's financial support influence the repertory? What effect does an audience's expectations and demands have on theatrical production? How does the physical presence of the audience affect performances?

WHY DOES AN AUDIENCE ATTEND THE THEATRE?

One of the most powerful motives for going to the theatre is the desire for *recreation* or *relaxation*. Audiences expect to be entertained: this implies suspension of personal cares, relaxation of tensions, and a feeling of well-being, satisfaction, and renewal. Even though everyone may believe that the theatre should provide entertainment, not all agree on what is entertaining. Many would exclude any treatment of controversial subject matter on the grounds that an audience goes to the theatre to escape from cares rather than to be confronted with problems. This attitude is frequently labeled the "tired businessman's" approach, and it is sometimes charged that the Broadway theatre has become merely a place to relax after a hard day's work, or a spot to take prospective clients to put them in the proper frame of mind for business dealings.

17

Other persons look to theatre for *stimulation*. They too desire to be entertained, but argue that the theatre should also provide new insights and provocative perceptions about significant topics. This audience is inclined to view "theatre-as-recreation" as a debasement of art. Both points of view are valid in part but adherents of neither point of view should attempt to limit unduly the theatre's offerings. The whole range of drama should be available to audiences, for the health of the theatre depends upon breadth of appeal.

In America today the success of a play is frequently judged by its ability to attract large audiences over a considerable period of time. But is a play to be considered a failure if it does not achieve financial success on Broadway? Not necessarily. A dramatist has a right to select his audience just as much as an audience selects a play. Actually, he does so when he chooses his subject matter, themes, characters, and language, for, consciously or unconsciously, he has an ideal spectator in mind. Although he may hope for universal acceptance, he desires the favorable response of a particular group. A play may be deemed successful if it achieves the desired response from the audience for which it was primarily intended. Most American theatres, however, have been operated on the principle that public taste is uniform, or that the only valid taste is that of the majority. Little has been done to meet the needs of minority audiences, although off-Broadway, off-off-Broadway, regional and university theatres have done much to diversify the repertory.

FINANCIAL SUPPORT AND THEATRICAL PROGRAMMING

If a theatre is to survive it must be concerned with its ticket sales unless financial support is available from other sources. In America there has been an almost superstitious faith in the box office as the only acceptable means of support on the grounds that if money is accepted from any other source freedom is sure to be lost, since support can lead to control. Advocates of this view admit that a theatre which depends solely upon box office receipts is at the mercy of public whim, but they either see this as healthy or as the best of the alternatives.

Advocates of a more diversified theatre usually point to Europe, where many governments—both national and local—appropriate money each year to subsidize selected theatres. These subsidies have not led to undue interference in the affairs of the theatres (although this is no valid argument that they could not in America). The purposes of a subsidy may be several. First, it relieves the theatre from the necessity of making a commercial success of each production. Second, it enables a theatre to sell tickets at a lower cost and to make productions available to a larger proportion of the population. Third, it normally provides support for a repertory company. (A repertory company usually hires a group of actors for an entire season and produces a number of plays which are performed in rotation. This arrangement allows the company to provide a cross section of drama that appeals to a wide range of tastes.)

In America, subsidies have normally taken the form of grants from philanthropic foundations or gifts from private groups or individuals. In

18

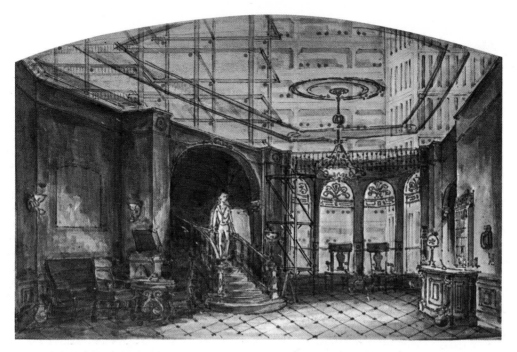

Eldon Elder's design for *Amazing Grace* by Studs Terkel. Watercolor and ink on paper, 1967. (See also page 450.) Courtesy Mr. Elder.

Scene from a multimedia production of Antonin Artaud's *Jet of Blood*. Directed and designed by Richard Mennen and Kenneth Bendel.

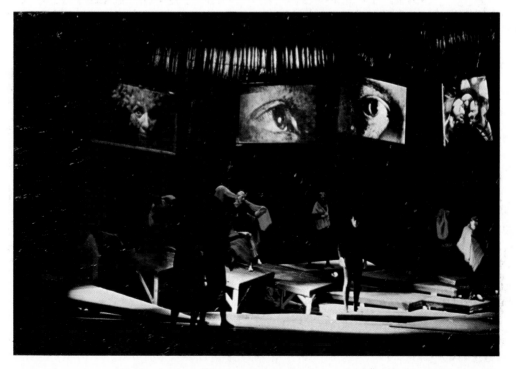

Scene from the Kabuki drama, *Kumagaya Jinja.* Courtesy the Consulate General of Japan, New York.

Make-up based on a Byzantine mosaic. The character is Job in *The Book of Job,* as arranged and directed by Orlin Corey. Reprinted with permission from *The Mask of Reality: An Approach to Design for Theatre* by Irene Corey, Anchorage Press, 1968.

Teatro Piccolo (the small theatre) at Pompeii in 1966. This is the oldest Roman theatre in existence. Photograph—Ella Smith.

"overacting" or "underacting" induced by the audience, productions often take on a tone quite different from that intended.

The "psychology of the audience" is a fascinating but little understood subject. Nevertheless, it plays a significant role in every performance, for not all of the audience's reactions can be attributed to the production. The mood in which it comes to the theatre is important. Since theatre attendance is now something of a special occasion, there may be an atmosphere of festivity which determines initial responses. Conditions which affect the audience's comfort, such as ventilation, lighting, and type of seating, also influence reactions, as do the size of the auditorium, closeness to the performers, and the arrangement of the seating in relation to the stage. Perhaps most important, individuals are transformed into a group by being placed in close physical proximity and by sharing an experience. It has long been known that a small audience scattered through a large auditorium will not laugh as readily as the same number seated together. Community of response, then, influences both the spectators and the actors.

WISE USE OF AUDIENCE INFLUENCE

The average audience member, however, is not aware of exerting any pressure on the fate of the theatre. He is like the voter in a large democracy who finds it hard to believe that his choice can make a difference, or that his actions can in any way influence governmental policy. But the answer to the person who cares about the theatre must be much the same as the answer to one who cares about his country: he does have power and he should learn how to use it.

If an audience member is to exercise his power wisely, he must first try to *understand the theatre* and how it works. Second, he should develop the ability to *judge the relative merits of plays and theatrical performances*. Finally, confident in his understanding and judgment, he should *work for that which seems of value* to him. If all those who like the theatre were to exert themselves in its behalf, a diversified theatre capable of appealing to all levels of taste—a truly healthy theatre— would result. But before anyone can plan intelligently for the future, he must acquire understanding and judgment—he must *seek to become a critic of the theatre*.

THE CRITIC

In a sense everyone who witnesses a play is a critic, since he passes some kind of judgment, however fleeting, upon what he sees. The title of critic is usually reserved, however, for those persons who formulate their judgments for publication. Ideally, the critic should be an experienced and trained audience member who understands plays and theatre well enough to assess effectiveness and the audience well enough to express his evaluations in terms comprehensible to it.

Criticism should be illuminating to both the creators and the audience of a theatre piece. In making explanations or in passing judgments, most critics refer to specific passages in a play, to characterization, structure,

21

Scene from Edward Albee's *Who's Afraid of Virginia Woolf?* Seen here are Arthur Hill, George Grizzard, and Uta Hagen. Directed by Alan Schneider. Photograph by Friedman-Abeles.

acting, or aspects of staging. In this way, critics are of service to the theatre worker as well as to the public, for they point out the reasons for success or failure.

But a single piece of criticism will not serve the needs of all persons, for, just as a playwright selects an audience for his work, so too the critic has an audience or type of reader in mind. The reviews of plays published in the New York daily newspapers are addressed to a general public, and almost no background or knowledge is taken for granted. On the other hand, the criticism written for literary quarterlies is addressed to a more sophisticated and selected audience. Therefore, not all criticism can be read in the same way.

Even when the critic's assumptions are clear, however, there is often a wide range of response to his work. One reader will find a piece of criticism illuminating, while another will find nothing of value in it, for just as one is drawn to certain kinds of plays, one is also drawn to particular types of criticism. As with plays, some of which continue to be acted for generations, criticism may also remain illuminating to readers in widely separated times. Most criticism, like most drama, however, speaks for the moment and is then forgotten.

Not everyone need aspire to be a practicing critic (in the sense of writing and publishing his judgments), but everyone interested in the theatre can become a better judge by acquiring the background necessary for an adequate understanding of plays and theatrical performances.

THE MEANING AND PURPOSES OF CRITICISM

To many, criticism always implies adverse comments, but its true meaning is "the act of making judgments." Evaluation should consider both excellence and failure—the effective and the ineffective—in a play and its production.

Criticism has three main purposes: exposition, appreciation, and evaluation. A piece of criticism is seldom restricted to one of these purposes; usually all are found in conjunction. The purpose of expository criticism is to explain a play or circumstances affecting it. The critic may write about the author, the period in which he lived, the source of the ideas, and similar factors. Using this approach a critic need make no judgment of worth. For example, he might explain how Shakespeare's *Richard III* is constructed, and, although his examination should lead to better understanding of the play, he need not judge its over-all effectiveness.

Appreciative criticism is usually written by the critic who has already decided that a work is good. His principal motive then is to make others feel the power of the play. He may proceed by describing his own responses to the work and then attempt to evoke similar feelings in the reader. He may also analyze the play to show its superior structure, characterization, use of mood, or other elements.

The evaluative critic may employ exposition and appreciation, but his principal aim is to judge effectiveness. As a rule, he begins by analyzing structure, characterization, themes, language, and visual elements. Upon this evidence, coupled usually with information drawn from other sources, he builds his evaluation.

THE BASIC PROBLEMS IN CRITICISM

In pursuing his work, the serious critic is concerned with three basic problems: understanding the play, assessing its effectiveness in terms of its implied aims, and judging its ultimate worth.

In attempting to understand a play, the critic must make sure that all of the important keys to its meaning have been explored. First, he must analyze the play, preferably through a study of the script. (See Chapter 3 for a discussion of dramatic structure.) Before he can fully understand the script, other explorations may be necessary. Sometimes a study of the author and his background is essential. If the play is a work from the past, it may be necessary to examine the dominant religious or psychological beliefs of that period, or the staging conventions in vogue when the play was written. The critic should be content only when he has taken all of the steps necessary for understanding.

While these are methods used by the literary critic, they also are employed by theatre workers in their study of a script prior to its production. Unless the director, the actors and the scenic artists understand a drama, it will be difficult for them to produce it satisfactorily. Although the literary critic and the theatre worker may arrive at the same conclusions in their studies, the theatre worker usually finds that his understanding of the play is modified during the rehearsal period. As the play takes shape on stage, he discovers qualities of which he was previously unaware, for plays do not reveal all of their potentialities on the printed page. Conversely, not all of the implications found in a script can be projected to an audience. Whenever possible a play should be studied both on the printed page and in performance.

Many reviewers write about plays which they have not read and which they know only from a single viewing. Since understanding may be severely limited under such circumstances, most reviewers restrict themselves to reporting impressions without pretending to provide an extensive analysis of the play. The reviewer's grasp of the play depends in large measure upon the quality of the performance he has seen.

After a play is understood, it may be judged in terms of how well it fulfills its intentions. Rarely is intention stated; rather, it must be determined through probing analysis. Intention is indicated by such elements as tone (a play may be humorous, satirical, serious, whimsical, and so on), ideas and their treatment, dialogue, characterization, and conflicts. The critic comes to recognize whether the author is attempting to arouse indignation at some social injustice, deriding a political position, or merely trying to offer an evening of entertainment. Having decided upon the play's purpose, he can then assess how effectively this purpose has been realized.

Assessment of effectiveness can be based entirely upon a study of the script, but it is frequently helpful and always wise to note the response of audiences. It should be kept in mind, however, that while the response may be an accurate measure of the audience's enjoyment, it will not always give a true indication of the play's potential power. For example, the play may not have been well performed. Other factors—such as unfamiliar dramatic techniques or complex ideas—may be responsible for an audience's failure to appreciate a play's power. In such cases, the fault does not necessarily lie with the play, but may indicate shortcomings in the audience. But, if the play has been adequately performed and understood, then audience response is helpful in determining whether the intention of the playwright has been achieved.

Even though a play is understood and judged successful in carrying out its intention, it may still be found unsatisfactory in relation to some larger system of value. Consequently, before passing final judgment, the critic usually asks whether the play's accomplishments are sufficiently significant to merit the highest commendation. It is in making this final judgment that he faces his greatest problem, for there are no universally

24

accepted standards of worth and none can be proven better than another.

To judge a play, it must be surrounded by some larger context which places it in perspective. Disagreements about a play's worth often stem from differences of opinion about the appropriate context. Some critics, for example, argue that the only meaningful context is other plays of the same type; other critics pay little attention to a play's dramatic form but view it within a context of philosophical concepts or of political, social, historical, or economic forces; still others are concerned with psychological forces, ritual elements, or communicative processes. The contexts used by modern critics are numerous and varied.

The battle at the Comédie Française between Classicists and Romanticists on the opening night of Victor Hugo's *Hernani* (1830). The play's triumph signaled French acceptance of romanticism. From Frederic Loliée's *La Comédie Française.* Paris, 1907.

Even though it is impossible to agree upon a single context, judgments must be made. Since a critic cannot force anyone to accept his evaluation, he must rely upon persuasion. Perhaps his first problem is to recognize that his own ingrained convictions and prejudices play an important role in his critical judgments; consequently he should seek to clarify his values both for himself and for his readers. If he first establishes his criteria of worth and then states the evidence upon which he bases his judgment, he may persuade others that his is a dependable evaluation.

Because the theatre itself is a composite art and because each of us is subject to many influences, it is difficult to become a good theatre critic. The qualities for which the would-be critic must strive, however, are these: he must be sensitive to feelings and ideas; he must become as well acquainted as possible with the theatre of all periods and of all types; he must be willing to explore plays until he understands them thoroughly; he must be aware of his own prejudices and values; he must be articulate and clear in expressing his judgments and their bases. Perhaps most important of all, he must be willing to alter his opinion when new experiences and evidence reveal inadequacies in his earlier judgment, for criticism is a continuing process rather than the dogmatic defense of a position.

Chapter 3 DRAMATIC STRUCTURE, FORM, AND STYLE

Broadly speaking, a play is a representation of man in action. But action is not merely physical movement, for it involves, as well, the mental and psychological motivations of external behavior. "Man in action," therefore, includes a wide range of feelings, thoughts, and deeds. Since a single play can depict only a limited aspect of human behavior, the action of each drama is unique in some respect. Nevertheless, all effective plays share common qualities from which we may derive conclusions about desirable characteristics of dramatic action.

Aristotle declared that a play should have a beginning, middle, and end. On the surface, this statement seems obvious and overly simple, but it summarizes a fundamental principle. Basically, it means that a play should be *complete and self-contained*, that everything necessary for its understanding should be included within the play itself. The beginning is the point in the story at which the playwright chooses to start his play, and is itself the foundation upon which the succeeding action is built. The middle develops the potentialities found in the beginning, while the end resolves and completes the action. If the action is not complete and self-contained, it will probably be confusing to an audience.

Dramatic action should be *purposeful.* It should be organized so as to arouse a specific response, such as pity and fear, joy and ridicule, indignation, thoughtful contemplation, laughter or tears. The purpose may be simple or complex, but the events, the characters, the mood, and other elements should be shaped and controlled with a dominant purpose in mind.

Dramatic action should be *varied.* Although the action should be unified, variety (in plot, characterization, or ideas) is also needed if monotony and predictability are to be avoided.

27

Scene from *Phaedra*. Directed by Lael Woodbury. Courtesy Mr. Woodbury.

Dramatic action should *engage and maintain interest*. The characters must command the audience's attention, the situation must be novel enough to arouse interest, or the issues must seem vital enough to warrant concern.

Dramatic action should be *probable* (that is, all of the elements should be logically consistent). Probability is what most persons have in mind when they speak of a play's believability. But probability, or believability, does not depend upon similarity to real life, for a play which depicts impossible events may be called believable if the incidents occur logically within the framework created by the playwright. This point can be better understood by reference to a nonrealistic drama. In Ionesco's *The Bald Soprano* a clock strikes seventeen times as the curtain rises; Mrs. Smith promptly announces that it is nine o'clock and launches into a bizarre speech on virtues of English middle-class life. This opening warns the audience that this play will not follow normal logic. As any play progresses, the guidelines are revealed. The audience then expects the playwright to observe consistently the rules he has established; anything which violates the peculiar logic set up in the play will seem out of place, and, therefore, unbelievable.

METHODS OF ORGANIZING DRAMATIC ACTION

A dramatic action is composed of a sequence of incidents which are organized to accomplish the play's purpose. Organization is ultimately a matter of directing attention to relationships which create a meaningful pattern. The most common sources of unity are thought, character, and cause-to-effect arrangement of events.

28

Traditionally, the dominant organizational principle has been the *cause-to-effect* arrangement of incidents. Using this method, the playwright sets up in the opening scenes all of the necessary conditions—the situation, the desires and motivations of the characters—out of which the later events develop. The goals of one character come into conflict with those of another, or two conflicting desires within the same character may lead to a crisis. Attempts to surmount the obstacles make up the substance of the play, each scene growing logically out of those which have preceded it.

Less often, a dramatist uses a *character* as the principal source of unity. In this case, the incidents are held together primarily because they center around one person. Such a play may dramatize the life of a historical figure, or it may show a character's responses to a series of experiences. This kind of organization may be seen in such plays as Christopher Marlowe's *Doctor Faustus* and *Tamburlaine*.

A playwright may organize his material around a *basic idea*, with the scenes linked largely because they illustrate aspects of a larger theme or argument. This type of organization is used frequently by modern playwrights, especially those of the Expressionist, Epic, and Absurdist movements. It can be seen, for example, in Brecht's *The Private Life of the Master Race*, which treats the rise of the Nazi party in a series of scenes that illustrates the inhumanity of Nazi ideology. Many Absurdist plays, such as Beckett's *Waiting for Godot*, do not develop a story so much as they embroider upon a concept, mood, or apprehension.

All three methods of organizing action may be used in the same play, although one will usually dominate. Regardless of the source of unity, a play normally relies upon *conflict* to arouse and maintain interest and suspense. In fact, the most commonly held idea about drama is that it always involves conflict—of one character with another, of desires within the same character, of a character with his environment, of one ideology with another.

Although overt conflict plays a major role in most plays, there are dramas in which it is of little significance. Thornton Wilder's *Our Town*, for example, makes relatively little use of conflict. Instead, a narrator (the Stage Manager) begins scenes at important moments and interrupts them when his point is made. He shows a typical day in the life of a village, Grovers Corners, and suggests that morning, midday, and evening are related to childhood, maturity, and death. Although momentary conflicts occur within individual scenes, there is no major clash. On the other hand, the concept of conflict may be enlarged until it applies to plays in which there is no obvious clash among characters. For example, in *The Bald Soprano* the events seem to occur aimlessly, and clearly they do not depend upon overt conflicts. Nevertheless, by exaggerating the clichés of everyday conversation, Ionesco forces the audience to question behavior which it normally accepts unthinkingly. Thus, like many plays of its type, *The Bald Soprano* creates a division, a kind of conflict, in the spectator's consciousness.

29

Whether or not conflict is involved, the action of drama is usually *arranged in a climactic order*—the scenes increase rather than decrease in interest. This effect is achieved through the revelation of new aspects of character or idea, by increasing suspense (the decisive moment is felt to be moving nearer and nearer), or by increasing emotional intensity. Although the arrangement is from the lesser to the greater, within this over-all movement there are moments of contrast or repose (such as the comic scenes in Shakespeare's tragedies) which afford a temporary change from the dominant pattern.

Organization may also be approached through the parts of drama, listed by Aristotle as plot, character, thought, diction, music, and spectacle. Although music in the usual sense is no longer an invariable part of drama and will not be treated in this chapter, Aristotle's division is still very useful.

PLOT

Plot is the over-all structure of a play. Although it includes the story line, it refers as well to the organization of all the elements into a meaningful pattern. Although in some plays, both the story and its arrangement may seem vague, all plays have plots, however tenuous they may be. Because the methods used in organizing plays vary widely, the most typical patterns will be emphasized here, although important deviations will be noted as well.

THE BEGINNING. The beginning of a play may establish the place, the occasion, the characters, the mood, the theme, and the level of probability. A play is somewhat like coming upon previously unknown places and persons. Initially, the novelty may attract attention, but, as the facts about the people and the place are established, interest either wanes or increases. The playwright is faced, therefore, with a double problem: he must give essential information, but at the same time create expectations sufficient to make the audience desire to stay and see more.

The beginning of a play requires *exposition*, or the setting forth of necessary information—about earlier events, the identity of the characters, and the present situation. While exposition is a necessary part of the opening scenes, it is not confined to them, for in most plays the background is only gradually revealed.

The amount of exposition required for clarity is partially determined by the *point of attack*, or the moment at which the story is taken up. Shakespeare uses an early point of attack (that is, he begins his plays at the inception of the story and then tells them in a clear chronological sequence). Greek tragedians, on the other hand, use late points of attack, which require that prior events be narrated while the plays show only the final parts of stories.

Playwrights motivate exposition in various ways. For example, Ibsen most frequently introduces a character who has returned after a lengthy absence. Answers to his questions about happenings while he was away supply the needed background information. On the other hand, in a non-

Final scene from Friedrich Duerrenmatt's *The Physicists,* as performed at Indiana University. Directed by Gary Gaiser; designed by Richard Scammon.

realistic play essential exposition may be given in a monologue. Many of Euripides' tragedies, for example, open with a prologue in which a single character summarizes past events and bemoans his present plight.

Attention is usually focused early on a question, potential conflict, or theme. The beginning of most plays therefore, includes what may be called an *inciting incident*, or an occurrence which sets the main action in motion. In Sophocles' *Oedipus the King*, a plague is ravishing Thebes; Oedipus has sought guidance from the oracle at Delphi, who declares that the murderer of King Laius must be found and punished before the plague can end. This is the event (introduced in the Prologue) which sets the action in motion.

The inciting incident usually leads directly to a *major dramatic question* around which the play is organized — the thread or spine which holds events together — although this question may undergo a number of changes as the play progresses. For example, the question first raised in *Oedipus the King* is: Will the murderer of Laius be found and the city saved? Later this question is modified, as interest shifts to Oedipus' own guilt. Not all plays, especially Absurdist dramas, include inciting incidents or clearly identifiable major dramatic questions. Nevertheless, all

31

have focal points, frequently a theme or controlling idea, around which the action is centered. Thus, it is always helpful to identify the unifying principle, whether it be a major dramatic question, a theme, or some other element.

THE MIDDLE. The middle of a play is normally composed of a series of complications. A *complication* is any new element which serves to alter the direction of the action. Complications may arise from the discovery of new information, the unexpected opposition to a plan, the necessity of choosing between courses of action, the arrival of a character, the introduction of a new idea, or from other sources.

Complications usually narrow the possibilities of action and create suspense. At the opening of a play the potentialities are numerous, since the story might develop in almost any direction. As characters and situation are established and as complications arise, however, the alternatives are progressively reduced. As a result, the audience comes to sense the direction of the action. As the possibilities are narrowed, a feeling of approaching crisis develops. Finally, there comes a moment when the alternatives have been so reduced that the next discovery will answer the major dramatic question. This is the moment of crisis or the peak toward which the play builds, after which there is gradual release in emotional tension leading to resolution and the play's end.

The substance of most complications is *discovery*. In one sense everything presented in a play is discovery if by that term is meant the revelation of things not previously known. The term is normally reserved, however, for occurrences of sufficient importance to alter the direction of action. Discoveries may involve objects (a wife discovers in her husband's pocket a weapon of the kind used in a murder), persons (a young man discovers that his rival in love is his brother), facts (a young man about to leave home discovers that his mother has cancer), values (a woman discovers that love is more important than a career), or self (a man discovers that he has been acting from purely selfish motives when he thought that he was acting out of love for his children). Self-discovery is usually the most powerful.

A complication is normally introduced by one discovery and concluded by another. A complication is set in motion by the appearance of some new element which requires a new approach. But the steps taken to solve the new demands give rise to tensions and conflicts which build to a climax, or peak of intensity. The climax is accompanied, or brought about, by still another discovery which serves to resolve the existing complication but which precipitates another. Each complication, thus, normally has a beginning, middle, and end—its own development, climax, and resolution—just as does the play as a whole.

The implications of each discovery are not always followed up immediately. Frequently a playwright is dealing with a number of characters and not every revelation involves all of them. Several complications, therefore, may intervene between the introduction of a discovery and its development. In such cases, the play pursues first one line of action and then another in an alternating or overlapping pattern.

32

Means other than discoveries may be used to precipitate complications. Natural disasters (such as earthquakes, storms, shipwrecks, and automobile accidents) are sometimes used. These are apt to seem especially contrived, however, if they resolve the problem (for example, if the villain is killed in an automobile accident and the struggle is automatically terminated). Sometimes complications are initiated unintentionally by characters acting in ignorance. For example, a father arranges a trip for his daughter without realizing that she has fallen in love and wants to stay at home.

In most complications, the event is not as important as its effect upon the characters involved. The attempts of each to meet the situation give rise to the succeeding action and lead to new complications.

The series of complications usually culminates in the *crisis*, or turning point of the action, which opens the way for the resolution. For example, in *Oedipus the King*, Oedipus sets out to discover the murderer of Laius; the crisis comes when Oedipus realizes that he himself is the guilty person. Not all plays have a clear-cut series of complications leading to a crisis. *Waiting for Godot*, for example, is less concerned with a progressing action than with a static condition. Nevertheless, interest is maintained by the frequent introduction of new elements: Estragon and Vladimir improvise games or plans to pass the time, and the arrival of Pozzo and Lucky creates a diversion. There is no crisis in the usual sense, only the gradual realization that man is to go on waiting, perhaps eternally.

THE END. The final portion of a play, often called the *resolution* or *dénouement*, extends from the crisis to the final curtain. Although often it is brief, it may be of considerable length. It serves to tie off the various strands of action and to answer the questions raised earlier. It brings the situation back to an equilibrium and satisfies audience expectations.

The crisis normally leads to an *obligatory scene* (that is, one which the dramatist must show if the play is to be satisfying to an audience). During much of a play, important facts are hidden or ignored by the characters. The audience senses, however (either consciously or unconsciously), that eventually these facts must be revealed, since the entire action seems to point in that direction. The obligatory scene, then, answers the question: What will happen when all of the facts are revealed? It shows the opposing characters, each now with full knowledge, meeting face to face. Since the final piece of vital information is usually withheld until the moment of crisis, the obligatory scene normally follows close upon it.

The obligatory scene may be extended over a series of complications. For example, a number of episodes may be used to show the tables being turned on a man who has deceived everyone. In such cases, the resolution may be as absorbing as the complications which preceded the crisis. Normally, the resolution creates a sense of completion and fulfillment. The audience can see clearly how the ending has come about, even though it could not have predicted the outcome in advance.

Again, many plays deviate from the typical patterns. At the end of his plays, Brecht often poses questions which can only be answered outside

33

the theatre, for he wishes to stimulate thought and action about real social conditions. Many Absurdist plays are essentially circular and end much as they began so as to suggest that the events of the play will repeat themselves endlessly. This type of resolution is often found in drama organized around thought, for the ultimate purpose is to stimulate the audience to examine its own situation rather than to view the drama merely as a diversion from real life. Nevertheless, all plays clearly have resolutions which bring the action to a close, even if they merely imply a new beginning, and everything in them should contribute to the sense that their endings are appropriate for them.

CHARACTER AND CHARACTERIZATION

Character is the material from which plots are created, for incidents are developed mainly through the speech and behavior of dramatic personages. Characterization is the playwright's means of differentiating one dramatic personage from another. Since a dramatist may endow his creatures with few or many traits, complexity of characterization varies markedly. In analyzing roles, it is helpful to look at four levels of characterization. (This approach is adapted from a scheme suggested by Hubert Heffner in *Modern Theatre Practice* and elsewhere.)

The first level of characterization is *physical* and is concerned only with such basic facts as sex, age, size, and color. Sometimes a dramatist does not supply all of this information, but it is present whenever the play is produced, since actors necessarily give concrete form to the characters. The physical is the simplest level of characterization, however, since it reveals external traits only, many of which may not affect the dramatic action at all.

The second level is *social*. It includes a character's economic status, profession or trade, religion, family relationships—all those factors which place him in his environment.

The third level is *psychological*. It reveals a character's habitual responses, attitudes, desires, motivations, likes and dislikes—the inner workings of the mind, both emotional and intellectual, which precede action. Since habits of feeling, thought, and behavior define characters more fully than do physical and social traits, and since drama most often arises from conflicting desires, the psychological is the most essential level of characterization.

The fourth level is *moral*. Although implied in all plays, it is not always emphasized. It is most apt to be used in serious plays, especially tragedies. Although almost all human action suggests some ethical standard, in many plays the moral implications are ignored and decisions are made on grounds of expediency. This is typical of comedy, since moral deliberations tend to make any action serious. More nearly than any other kind, moral decisions differentiate characters, since the choices they make when faced with moral crises show whether they are selfish, hypocritical, or persons of integrity. A moral decision usually causes a character to examine his own motives and values, in the process of which his true nature is revealed both to himself and to the audience.

34

A multimedia production designed by Josef Svoboda. Scene from Topol's *Their Day* (1959) as presented at the National Theatre, Prague. Photograph copyrighted by Jaromir Svoboda.

A playwright may emphasize one or more of these levels. Some writers pay little attention to the physical appearance of their characters, concentrating instead upon psychological and moral traits; other dramatists may describe appearance and social status in detail. In assessing the completeness of a characterization, however, it is not enough merely to make a list of traits and levels of characterization. It is also necessary to ask *how the character functions in the play.* For example, the audience needs to know little about the maid who only appears to announce dinner; any detailed characterization would be superfluous and distracting. On the other hand, the principal characters need to be drawn in greater depth. The appropriateness and completeness of each characterization, therefore, may be judged only after analyzing its function in each scene and in the play as a whole.

A character is revealed in several ways: through *descriptions in stage directions, prefaces, or other explanatory material* not part of the dialogue or action; through *what the character says*; through *what others say about him*; and, perhaps most important, through *what he does.* It is not enough, however, for a dramatist to assign characteristics to his personages; some action must be motivated, or some idea clarified, by each quality if it is not to be irrelevant or even misleading. The relative importance of each trait, therefore, must be assessed in terms of its function in the play.

35

It is not always easy to perceive a character's true nature, since information about him is usually given in fragments scattered throughout the play. Furthermore, many different or even contradictory images of him may be presented. For example, a character may see himself as a certain kind of person; for one reason or another, however, he may try to project a different image to others; in turn, each of the other characters will see him from a different angle. Because the dramatist builds character through this composite approach, the audience must always watch for clues that indicate which statements and actions are to be accepted as accurate revelations of character.

Characters are defined in much the same way as words: first they are placed in a broad category (typified), and then differentiated (individualized) from other examples of the same type. *Typification* is necessary if characters are to be placed in the context of human experience. If a character were totally unlike any person the spectators had ever known, they would be unable to understand him. Most characters may be placed in a category, such as the doting mother, the bashful young man, or the dumb blonde. But if the playwright goes no further, the audience will probably find the personages oversimplified and will see them as "type" characters. Most dramatists assign several traits which serve to *individualize* characters within the broad categories. Thus, typifying qualities make a character recognizable and familiar, while individualizing traits make him unusual and complex.

A playwright is often concerned with making his characters *sympathetic* or *unsympathetic*. Most frequently, sympathetic characters are created by assigning traits admired in real life, but many modern playwrights have created sympathy for abnormal characters by exploring the reasons behind behavior, showing characters as victims of circumstances and as more worthy of compassion than vilification. Normally, however, sympathetic characters are given major virtues and lesser foibles, while the reverse procedure is used for unsympathetic characters. The more a character is made either completely good or bad, the more he is apt to become unacceptable as a truthful reflection of human behavior.

Acceptability, however, is in part determined by the type of play or the level of probability. Melodrama, for example, oversimplifies human psychology and clearly divides characters and actions into good and evil. Tragedy, on the other hand, normally depicts more complex forces at work both within and without man, and requires greater depth of characterization than does melodrama, which may function very well with type characters. The audience usually expects only that characterization be appropriate for the play's intentions.

THOUGHT

The third basic element of a play is *thought*. It includes the themes, the arguments, the over-all meaning and significance of the action. It is present in all plays, even those which seem to be without purpose, for a playwright cannot avoid expressing ideas, and character and events always imply some view of human behavior. Thought is also one of the major sources of unity in drama, for action may be organized around a central idea. This kind of unity is typical of much modern drama.

In thought, a play is both general and specific. For example, *King Lear* dramatizes the general topic of child–parent relationships, but it does so through the complex story of intrigues among the ruling class in England's legendary past. Thus, the general topic, or theme, serves as a point of focus around which events cluster, while the specific story gives concreteness to ideas which otherwise would be too obscure. Although a play may have a number of themes, one is usually dominant. One key to a play, therefore, lies in its thought. By identifying the major motifs and examining how they have been embodied we can recognize the author's over-all purpose and methods.

The general and specific subjects of a play are related to the concepts of universality and individuality. *Universality* is that quality which enables a play to communicate with audiences, even though centuries may have passed since it was written. To say that *Hamlet* has universal significance does not mean that we should be able to put ourselves in Hamlet's position as a prince or as the avenger of his father's death. The universal elements are to be found in the conflict between a son's duty to his father and his feelings for his mother, between personal integrity and religious faith, between justice and corrupt political power, and in the spectacle of the "underdog" pitted against overwhelming forces. These are situations which might confront human beings of any social class in any period. They provide a point of contact between Hamlet and the audience.

On the other hand, every story must be *individualized* if it is to be believable and interesting. *Hamlet*, therefore, has many elements which depart markedly from normal experience and keep the story from being hackneyed and overly familiar. However, some modern dramatists, such as Wilder and Ionesco, have reversed the normal process. They have chosen the most commonplace events, but have treated them in such a way as to make them seem strange. Thus, they force the audience to view the familiar in a new light.

The significance, or meaning, of a play is normally implied rather than directly stated. It is to be discovered in the relationships among characters, the ideas associated with sympathetic and unsympathetic characters, the conflicts and their resolutions. Sometimes, however, the author's intention is clearly stated in the script. The characters may advocate a certain line of action, point of view, or specific social reform. Sometimes dramas using such methods are called *propaganda* or *social problem* plays, since they aim to persuade an audience to act or think in a particular way.

An author wishing to persuade an audience has two paths open to him. He may subordinate his message and depend upon the implications to be sufficiently persuasive. In this case, he risks being misunderstood. Or, he may make his position quite clear (usually through a direct statement by an admirable character). In this case, while the dramatist leaves no doubt as to his purpose, he may alienate his audience, who may conclude that the play has been an excuse for delivering a sermon. In the hands of

37

the unskillful dramatist this is frequently the result, for the characters seem lifeless mouthpieces for the author. Expert dramatists, however, such as Ibsen and Shaw, have made themselves relatively clear while creating compelling and vital plays.

The dramatist who is intent upon achieving *complete* clarity must restrict the meanings of words and actions and may eliminate those connotations and implications which suggest that the significance of the drama extends far beyond the immediate story. Yet ambiguity is basic to human experience; life does not come equipped with meanings which are unmistakable; we ponder over our experience and try to find significance in it, but we can never be certain that we have solved the riddles. Since human experience is the raw material of drama, the playwright who sees no ambiguities in life may well create a world on the stage which is too simple for an audience to accept. On the other hand, everyone simplifies experience in the process of seeking its significance. Since the dramatist is usually concerned with the patterns behind the infinite detail of life, he must eliminate what he considers to be irrelevant. His selection, nevertheless, must command belief.

Dramatists in different periods have used various devices to project ideas. Greek playwrights made extensive use of the *chorus*, just as those of later periods employed such devices as *soliloquies*, *asides*, and other forms of *direct statement*. Still other tools for projecting meaning are *allegory* and *symbol*. In allegory, characters are often personifications (good deeds, mercy, greed, and so on), and the meaning of the play can usually be reduced to a clear moral statement. Its use can be seen most clearly in a play such as *Everyman*. A symbol is a concrete object or event which, while meaningful in itself, also suggests a concept or set of relationships. For example, the orchard in Chekhov's *The Cherry Orchard* is both a real object and a symbol. As an object, once useful, then admired merely for its beauty, it is finally destroyed to make way for homes which will be occupied by merchants. As a symbol, it represents the Russian aristocracy, which, having lost its usefulness, must make way for the more vigorous middle class. The orchard takes on a double meaning—literal and symbolic—enabling it to comment not only on the characters in the play but on Russian society in general. The symbol has been a favorite device with modern writers, for it allows them to suggest deeper meanings even within a realistic framework.

While some plays, such as farces, may not explore ideas of great significance, all plays comment upon human life in some way.

DIALOGUE

Dialogue is the playwright's principal means of expression. When a play is presented in the theatre, actors, scenery, lighting and other elements are added, but to convey his basic conception, the dramatist must depend upon his skill in writing dialogue and stage directions.

Dialogue serves many functions. First, it *imparts information*. It sets forth the exposition and conveys the essential facts, ideas, and emotions in each scene.

38

Second, dialogue *reveals character*. The speeches of each personage project both emotional and rational responses to situations.

Third, dialogue *directs attention* to important plot elements. Since significant information and responses must be emphasized, dialogue points up conflicts and complications and prepares for further developments. It builds suspense by making the audience aware of potential outcomes, for while scenes always occur in the present, they constantly direct attention toward possible future results and create a sense of forward movement and expectancy.

Fourth, dialogue *reveals the themes and ideas* of a play. It provides clues to significant meanings while it reveals character and develops action.

Fifth, dialogue helps to *establish tone and level of probability*. It indicates whether the play is comic or serious, farcical or tragic. It also suggests the degree of abstraction from reality. Sometimes the use of poetry indicates that the play will not follow ordinary causality. The choice of words, the number of colloquialisms, the length of lines, and other linguistic devices are clues to the level of probability within which the play is operating.

Sixth, dialogue helps to *establish tempo and rhythm*. Tempo is the pace at which a scene is played. The tempo of a love scene is apt to be much more leisurely than that of a duelling scene, for example, and the dialogue should reflect and create the proper tempo. Rhythm is the recurring pattern which results from the flow of speeches. Halting speech gives rise to one rhythmical pattern and animated, excited speech to another. Tempo and rhythm together create a sense of forward movement or of retarded action. When the rhythm of each scene is built to a climax (as is each movement in a symphony), it helps to hold attention and arouse expectancy.

The dialogue of every play, no matter how realistic, is more abstract and formal than normal conversation. A dramatist always selects, arranges, and heightens language more than anyone ever does in spontaneous speech. Consequently, in a realistic play, although the dialogue is modeled after everyday usage, the characters are more articulate and state their ideas and feelings more precisely than would their real-life counterparts. On the other hand, realistic dialogue may retain the rhythms, tempos, and basic vocabulary of colloquial speech.

The dialogue of nonrealistic plays may deviate markedly from normal speech. Sometimes, everyday patterns are reduced to a mere skeleton, as in expressionistic drama where dialogue is often "telegraphic" in its oversimplicity. At other times, the clichés of ordinary conversation are emphasized until they become ludicrous, as in many of Ionesco's plays. More frequently, however, nonrealistic drama employs a larger vocabulary, abandons the rhythms of conversation, and makes considerable use of imagery and meter. A larger vocabulary allows a more precise choice of words, avoids the frequent repetitions of colloquial speech, and permits more forceful expression when characters must transcend the ordinary.

Imagery is always found in poetic drama, but it may appear in realistic prose plays as well. The simile is widely used even in everyday speech ("He was as mad as a hornet," or "She's as nervous as a cat on a hot tin roof"). A simile makes a direct comparison between two qualities or things and helps to point up likenesses which reveal character, situation, or meaning. A metaphor makes an indirect comparison between dissimilarities ("God is my fortress"). There are other kinds of imagery, but all point to comparisons, connotations, or implications which enlarge the literal meaning. Furthermore, the use of a large number of similar images affects the tone of a play. The dark, somber quality of *Hamlet*, for example, is partially explained by the overwhelming number of images concerned with death and decay. Although an audience may not be aware of the images it is unconsciously influenced by them.

Dialogue, like the other elements of a play, uses both the familiar and the unfamiliar, the typical and the individual. Aristotle stated that good dialogue should be both *clear* and *distinctive*. He went on to explain that clarity depends upon the use of ordinary words, but warned that familiar words used alone may lead to dullness. "Diction becomes distinguished and nonprosaic by the use of unfamiliar terms, i.e., strange words, metaphors, lengthened forms, and everything that deviates from the ordinary modes of speech. But a whole statement in such terms will be either a riddle or a barbarism," added Aristotle. Good dialogue, then, should strike a middle ground between overly familiar and overly strange language. The familiar gives clarity, the strange adds variety.

Dialogue should also be *adapted to the stage*. Sometimes a dramatist writes speeches which sound stilted and unnatural when spoken because he has failed to take into account both the possibilities and the limitations of the voice and ear. The good playwright is concerned with how dialogue will sound, and how the human voice will affect the written word.

The basic criterion for judging dialogue, however, is its *appropriateness* to the characters, the situation, the level of probability, and the type of play. Almost any dialogue will be acceptable to an audience if it is in keeping with the other elements in the script.

SPECTACLE

After dialogue, the visual elements of a play are the dramatist's principal means of expression. Unless a reader can envision the action, the characters, the lighting, the setting, the costumes, the properties, and the spatial relationships (all of which are provided by a production), he may fail to grasp the power of the drama.

Many older plays contain almost no stage directions describing the setting, movement and physical appearance of the characters, and the dialogue must be analyzed carefully for clues to spectacle. As the visual background increased in importance during the nineteenth century, stage directions became common and have continued to give the reader considerable help in visualizing the action.

The functions of spectacle are several. First, it *gives information*. It helps to establish where and when the action occurs (a living room, a castle, a prison; the historical period, the time of day, the country), or it may indicate that time and place are irrelevant. Second, spectacle *aids characterization*. It helps to establish such social factors as the economic level, the class, and the profession to which the characters belong. It aids in projecting the psychological aspects of character by demonstrating tastes (in the clothes worn, the rooms in which the characters live, and the like). Psychological factors are also revealed through the spatial relationships among characters (not always apparent in a script but always seen in a production).

Third, spectacle helps to *establish the level of probability*. An abstract setting suggests one level, while a completely realistic setting may indicate another. Costumes, lighting, the actors' gestures and movement all establish the play's level of reality. Fourth, spectacle establishes *mood and atmosphere* by giving clues about the relative seriousness of the action, and by providing the proper environment for tragedy, comedy, fantasy, or realism.

Spectacle, like the other elements of a play, should be *appropriate, expressive of the play's values, distinctive,* and *practicable*. (The problems of transferring the written script to the stage are treated at length in Part Four of this book).

Charles Kean's production of Shakespeare's *Henry VIII* in 1859. The scenery and costumes typify the antiquarian approach in vogue at that time. Courtesy of the Victoria & Albert Museum. Crown Copyright.

FORM IN DRAMA

The parts of drama may be combined in many ways, but recurring combinations have led to the division of plays into dramatic forms. Because it has been used to designate a variety of concepts, form is difficult to define. Basically, however, form means the arrangement of a work of art.

There are three principal determinants of form. First, form is affected by the material being shaped. In actuality, it is difficult, if not impossible, to separate form and matter, since no one can comprehend a formless object or idea. Nevertheless, the matter (the action, characters, mood, and thought) of comedy differs sufficiently from that of tragedy to indicate that one has been shaped to arouse laughter or ridicule while the other is designed to create pity or fear.

Second, the writer (or the maker of an object) is a determinant of form. Each man's view of life and drama differs somewhat from that of others, and his own peculiar talents and intentions show in his work. Thus, while both Sophocles and Euripides wrote tragedies, the forms of their plays show certain differences. Third, the intended purpose of an object helps to determine its form. Just as a chair's shape differs from that of a desk because they are created to fulfill different needs, so the design of a tragedy differs from that of a comedy.

Since no two plays ever have the same material, author, and purpose, each play is unique. On the other hand, plays share many qualities. Because each play is both unique and similar to other works, two major approaches to form have developed: one views form as *fixed* and the other as *organic*. The doctrine of *fixed forms* rests upon the belief that the characteristics of dramatic types can be clearly isolated and defined. Many adherents of this view have also suggested that plays may be judged according to how well they fulfill the requirements of a particular type. The doctrine of *organic form*, on the other hand, depends upon the belief that a play takes shape and grows as a plant does, and that each play must be free to follow its own needs and laws without reference to any pre-existing ideas about form.

Each of these two views is partially defensible. Most plays can be classified according to type, and the major characteristics of each type can be listed. Furthermore, in criticizing a play, it is usually helpful to compare it with other works of the same type, and references to categories may save much time (for example, a term such as *comedy of manners* summarizes many qualities and communicates quickly, provided that a reader understands the meaning of the designation).

On the other hand, each play is unique in some respects and should be appreciated for its individuality. Often it is impossible to classify a play according to form, and the attempt to label it may assume more importance than understanding it. For example, arguments as to whether *Death of a Salesman* can rightfully be called a tragedy have frequently consumed undue attention in discussions. One form is not necessarily better than another, for there are both excellent and poor examples of each and a play is not necessarily defective because it does not fit some

42

abstract idea of form. Thus, while the classification of plays according to form may be helpful, it can be misused.

An almost endless number of forms and subforms have been suggested by critics. Since it would be impossible to discuss all of the labels that have been used, the basic forms will be treated at some length and then deviations will be noted. Almost all divisions into forms can be related to three basic qualities: the serious, the comic, and the seriocomic. In turn, these three divisions are epitomized in three forms: tragedy, comedy, and melodrama.

TRAGEDY. A tragedy presents a genuinely serious action, and maintains a mood throughout that underscores the play's serious intention (although there may be moments of comic relief). It raises important questions about the meaning of man's existence, his moral nature, and his social or psychological relationships.

Most tragedies written prior to the eighteenth century show the interaction between cosmic and human forces: a god, providence, or some moral power independent of man usually affects the outcome of the action as much as do the human agents. Many tragedies imply that the protagonist has violated a moral order which must be vindicated and re-established. Because superhuman forces are involved, the outcome often seems inevitable and predetermined.

In the eighteenth century, the supernatural element began to decline as social and psychological forces were given increased emphasis and the conflicts reduced to strictly human ones. The action no longer involved man's will in conflict with divine laws, but was restricted to conflict among human desires, laws, and institutions. Since man-made problems may be understood and solved, happy resolutions were more probable. Because this later drama has often been concerned with everyday situations and seems less profound than earlier works, many critics have refused to call it tragedy and have substituted the term *drama* or *drame*.

The protagonist of tragedy is usually a person who arouses our sympathy and admiration. In some cases, however, admiration and sympathy may be limited. Macbeth, Richard III, and Medea, for example, are tragic protagonists who have noble qualities and whose indomitable wills we can admire, but whose actions we cannot approve. Normally, the protagonist is ethically superior without being perfect: he is sufficiently above the average to inspire admiration, but is sufficiently imperfect to be believable and at least partially responsible for his own downfall.

Most often, the tragic protagonist encounters disaster through his pursuit of a worthy aim, but, in following one ideal, he violates some other moral or social law which overpowers him. A recurring motif of serious drama is the imposition of a duty, the performance of which will inevitably lead to loss of life, love, reputation, or peace of mind. The protagonist thus is faced with choosing between two lines of action, each of which under other circumstances would be good, but which have been placed in seemingly irreconcilable opposition.

In most tragedies written prior to the eighteenth century the protagonists are members of the ruling class, but in succeeding periods they have been drawn increasingly from the middle or lower classes. Many critics have questioned whether the average man can acquire the stature necessary to a tragic hero. There seems little basis, however, for the assumption that social class has any connection with nobility of character and action. Although most modern serious drama is less powerful than the best tragedies of the Greeks and Elizabethans, the difference is one of degree. (The reverence accorded to tragedy seldom extends to other forms; for example, few critics have even implied that a play should not be called a comedy merely because it is less powerful than certain other comedies or because it differs from the work of other periods.)

The emotional effect of tragedy is usually described as the "arousal of pity and fear," but these basic emotions include a wide range of other responses: understanding, compassion, admiration, apprehension, foreboding, dread, awe, and terror. Pity and fear are rooted in two instinctive human reactions: the desire for self-preservation and concern for the welfare of others. Aristotle, in the *Poetics*, states that pity is aroused by the apprehension of some pain or harm about to befall someone like ourselves, and that were we in the position of the endangered person we would feel fear. Thus, pity and fear are complementary emotions. To feel pity, we must perceive some likeness between ourselves and the tragic character, and we must be able to imagine ourselves in his situation. Aristotle further argues that if we fear too much for ourselves we cannot pity others, for panic drives out altruistic concerns. Fear, then, is an emotion which stems from the instinct for self-preservation, while pity transcends self-concern. Fear enables us to identify with the struggling protagonist, while pity carries us outside ourselves and unites us with man's struggle for integrity. The degree to which these responses are aroused by a particular play depends upon the nature of the protagonist and the action in which he is involved.

COMEDY. The action of comedy is based on some deviation from normality in incident, character, or thought. The deviation, however, must not pose a serious threat to the well-being of the normal, and a comic (or "in fun") mood must be maintained. There is no subject, however trivial or important, which cannot be treated in comedy, provided that it is placed in a framework which exploits its incongruities.

Comedy also demands that the audience views the situation, characters, or ideas objectively. Henri Bergson, in *Laughter*, has stated that comedy requires "an anesthesia of the heart," for it is difficult to laugh at anything with which we are too closely allied either through sympathy or dislike. For example, we might find the sight of a man slipping on a banana peel ludicrous, but if we discover that he has recently undergone a serious operation, our concern will destroy the laughter. Likewise, we may dislike some things so intensely that we cannot see their ridiculous qualities. On the other hand, an audience is not objective about all ele-

44

ments of a comedy, for sympathy is aroused for the norm. Part of comic pleasure comes from witnessing the eventual triumph of normative behavior or ideas over a threat from the abnormal.

Because of its wide range, comedy is often divided into a number of subcategories. All the classifications, however, can be related to three variables: the relative emphasis placed on situation, character, or idea; the degree of objectivity with which the protagonist is treated; and the nature and implications of the action. Consequently, the three basic types are comedies of situation, comedies of character, and comedies of ideas, although each may be related to one or more subtypes.

A *comedy of situation* shows the ludicrous results of placing characters in unusual circumstances. For example, a number of persons are planning to attend a masked ball, but each, for his own reasons, tries to conceal his intentions. The devices for getting rid of each other, the attempts to elude discovery when all appear at the ball, the reactions upon being recognized, and the eventual reconciliation of the characters make up the comic action. In such a play, character and idea are of minor importance.

Many critics treat *farce* as a separate form, although there is little to distinguish it from a comedy of situation. Farce is often used as a classification for those plays, or portions of plays, which rely principally upon buffoonery, accident, and coincidence. Pies in the face, beatings, the naïve or mistaken views of characters, the ludicrous situation arising from coincidence or circumstantial evidence exemplify the devices of farce. Often it seems a kind of inspired nonsense with situations so obviously contrived that a sensible word from any character would resolve the action at once. Farce is sometimes said to have no purpose beyond entertainment. While it is true that some farcical plays seem to be without serious purpose, farce is an important element in many of the world's finest comedies, particularly those of Aristophanes and Molière.

A *comedy of character* grows out of the eccentricities of the protagonist. For example, Molière's best plays show the results of hypochondria, miserliness, or hypocrisy.

Although it may draw some of its characteristics from comedies of situation or idea, *romantic comedy* is most closely related to the comedy of character, for it usually treats the struggles, often those centering around a love affair, of characters who are basically admirable. It is best illustrated by Shakespeare's *Twelfth Night* and *As You Like It*, in which the main characters are lovers pursuing normal and sympathetic goals. A comic response is aroused primarily because of the ludicrous devices the characters use in pursuing success and the misunderstandings which result. The more boisterous action is relegated to subplots and minor characters. Thus, romantic comedy reverses the pattern found in a comedy of character, in which the major emphasis is placed on ridiculous characters.

A *comedy of ideas* develops a conflict over a concept or a way of thought. It is probably best exemplified in the work of George Bernard Shaw and Aristophanes.

While the *comedy of manners* shares some traits with the comedy of situation and of character, it is most nearly related to the comedy of ideas, for it exploits the incongruities which arise from adherence to an accepted code of behavior at the expense of normal desires and responses. As a label, comedy of manners is sometimes reserved for plays about aristocratic and sophisticated characters who indulge in sparkling and witty repartee, attributes which have also given currency to an alternative label, *comedy of wit*.

Social comedy is still another variation on the comedy of ideas, for it explores social values, standards of behavior or accepted ways of thought. If it aims at remedying society or behavior, it may be called *corrective comedy*.

Although most comedies can be placed in one of the categories listed above, almost all have elements which relate them to several types. A comedy of character, for instance, may use devices normally associated with farce, a comedy of manners, or a comedy of ideas. Labels, therefore, need to be used with some flexibility if they are to be helpful.

All comedy seeks to arouse emotions which lie in a range between joy and scorn. At one extreme, Shakespeare's romantic comedies elicit a response which can best be described as a feeling of well-being. They may arouse smiles or quiet laughter, but seldom boisterous laughter. On the other hand, Ben Jonson's *Volpone* at times becomes almost too painful for laughter. These extremes of the gentlest and the bitterest ridicule mark the limits of the comic response.

Comedy seldom raises great moral and philosophical questions, as tragedy does. Rather, it concentrates upon man in his social relationships. It reaffirms the need for a society which allows normal human impulses adequate scope while putting a check on deviations which threaten to destroy what is valuable in it. As normative behavior varies from one era to another, so, too, the scope of comedy changes.

MELODRAMA. Although the term *melodrama* was not widely used until the nineteenth century, the type had existed since the fifth century B.C. In some periods it has been called *tragicomedy*, and today it is often labeled *drama* because the term *melodrama* is in disrepute.

A melodrama deals with a serious action. Its seriousness, however, is only temporary and is usually attributable to the malicious designs of an unsympathetic character. A happy resolution is achieved, therefore, by neutralizing or destroying the power of the villain.

Since melodrama depicts a world in which good and evil are clearly separated, the conflict almost always involves a sharply defined moral issue. There is seldom any question as to where the audience's sympathy should lie.

The characters in melodrama are usually divided into those who are completely sympathetic and those who are completely antipathetic. For the sake of variety, there may also be one or more simpleminded or uninhibited characters who provide comic relief. The unsympathetic characters usually set in motion the complications, while the sympathetic char-

46

acters seek only to free themselves from danger. Thus, the characters do not grow and change, as in tragedy, for the moral nature of each is established at the beginning of the play and remains constant throughout.

The action of melodrama develops a powerful threat against the well-being of a wholly admirable and innocent protagonist. It shows his entanglement in a web of circumstances and his eventual rescue from death or ruin, usually at the last possible moment.

The appeals, therefore, are strong and basic, for the incidents, which seek to build the most intense suspense, create a desire to see wronged innocence vindicated and unchecked evil chastised. The emotions aroused by melodrama range from dread and concern for the protagonist to hatred for the antagonist.

Many variations on melodrama were exploited in the nineteenth century. Among the most popular was equestrian drama, which combined daring horsemanship with melodramatic plots. The illustration above depicts a performance at Astley's Amphitheatre in London in 1815. From *Londina Illustrata*.

Melodrama has a double ending in which the good characters are rescued and rewarded and the evil are detected and punished. Thus, it is related to tragedy through the seriousness of its action, and to comedy through its happy conclusion. It has been a popular form throughout history, for it assures audiences that good triumphs over evil.

Mixed Forms. Although tragedy, comedy, and melodrama are the primary forms, many plays do not fit comfortably into any of these three categories. For example, some works, although basically serious, do not achieve "the sense of high purpose" which we associate with tragedy; thus, we may seek other labels to set them off from plays which are more clearly tragic. Other dramas shift tone frequently from comic to serious and may end either happily or unhappily; consequently, it may be difficult to decide whether they are more nearly comedies or tragedies. Still other works have all of the marks of melodrama until the end, when the failure to reward the good and punish the evil characters raises questions about the play's type.

This mixing of characteristics is probably most typical of modern times, when playwrights have often deliberately departed from the traditional forms. For example, Ionesco has labeled some of his works "anti-plays" or "tragic farces," while Harold Pinter called his early plays "comedies of menace," and Michel de Ghelderode subtitled some of his works "burlesque mysteries" and "tragedies of the music hall." Although these designations indicate significant departures from the conventional forms, most also suggest a connection with them. For example, Ionesco's use of "tragic farce" to describe *The Chairs* indicates his awareness of manipulating comic techniques to make an audience perceive the seriousness behind the semifarcical events. Similarly, his use of "anti-play" to describe *The Bald Soprano* shows his deliberate departure from traditional structural patterns, although, as in *The Chairs*, the dramatic devices are essentially those of comedy.

In reading plays which deviate from the traditional forms, it is probably of little help to insist upon clear-cut type designations. On the other hand, it may be illuminating to note in each the tendencies toward tragedy, comedy, or melodrama, since this may clarify the ways and the extent to which comic, serious, and serio-comic elements have been mingled. Nevertheless, the fact that so much modern drama does not fit into the traditional categories demonstrates the danger of overemphasizing formal classifications. Identifying a play's type is important only because it may help to define its purpose and because it provides a basis for comparing it with other works having similar characteristics. Classification is only one step toward understanding a play and is no substitute for careful analysis.

STYLE

When we categorize plays, we should recognize that even plays of the same type vary considerably. One cause of this variety is style. Like form, style is difficult to define because it has been used to designate many concepts. Basically, however, *style* is a quality which results from a characteristic mode of expression or method of presentation.

48

Eugène Ionesco's *Hunger and Thirst* as presented at the Comédie Française, Paris, in 1966. Courtesy Agence de Presse Bernand.

Style may stem from traits attributable to a period, a nation, a movement, or an author. In most periods, the drama of all nations has certain common qualities which may be attributed to the prevailing religious, philosophical, and psychological concepts, and to current dramatic and theatrical conventions. Thus, we may speak of an eighteenth-century style. Within a period, however, there are national differences which permit us to distinguish a French from an English style. Furthermore, the dramas written by neoclassicists demonstrate qualities which permit us to identify the stylistic features of the movement and to distinguish them from those written by Romantics, Expressionists, or Absurdists. Finally, the plays of individual authors have distinctive qualities which set them off from the work of all other writers. Thus, we may speak of Shakespeare's or Sophocles' style.

Most discussions of style in theatre and drama consider only period and movement. Style is usually divided into such categories as classicism, neoclassicism, romanticism, realism, naturalism, expressionism, symbolism, absurdism, and epic theatre. Since each category is associated with specific periods, it is usually discussed in connection with style as it relates to an age. (The chronological survey of theatre and drama in Parts II and III will treat style more fully as it applies to periods and movements.)

Style in theatre results from three basic influences. First, it is grounded upon assumptions about truth and reality. Dramatists of different movements or periods have all sought to convey truthful pictures of the human predicament, but they have differed widely in their answers to these fundamental questions: What constitutes ultimate truth? By what process can we perceive reality? At times it has been argued that surface appearances merely disguise reality, which is to be found in the inner workings of the mind or in some spiritual realm. At others, it has been maintained that truth can be discovered only by objective study of those things which can be felt, tasted, seen, heard, or smelled. To advocates of the latter view, observable details hold the key to truth, while to the former the same details only hide the truth. Although all attempt to depict the truth as they see it, each playwright's conception of truth is determined in large part by his basic temperament and talents, and the religious, philosophical, social, and psychological influences which have shaped them. Because in each period and movement there are many shared beliefs, we may generalize about the conceptions of truth which provide the raw material of drama and influence style in that period or movement.

Second, style results from the manner in which the playwright manipulates his means of expression. All dramatists have at their disposal the same basic means — language and spectacle — out of which to create plot, character, and thought. Nevertheless, the work of each playwright is distinctive, for each perceives the human condition from a somewhat different point of view and each must find adequate methods of communicating his vision to others. His perceptions are reflected in the situations, characters, and ideas he invents, in his manipulation of language, and in his suggestions for the use of spectacle. Thus, the playwright who believes that truth is embodied in the details of daily existence will probably invent incidents and characters modeled closely upon contemporary life, and his dialogue, settings, and costumes will mirror faithfully the speech, places, clothing, and behavior of daily existence. On the other hand, the playwright who believes that truth must be sought in some psychological or spiritual realm may depart from the standards of observable reality and may deliberately distort or eliminate details in order to force the audience to look behind the surface of things.

50

Third, style results from the manner in which the play is presented in the theatre. The directing, acting, scenery, costumes, lighting, and sound used to translate the play from the written script to the stage may each be manipulated to affect stylistic qualities. (Each of these elements is treated at length in Part IV of this book.) Because so many persons are involved in producing a play, it is not unusual to find conflicting or inconsistent stylistic elements in a single production. Normally, however, unity of style is a primary artistic goal. Each theatre artist, working with his own means, seeks to create qualities analogous to those found in the written text, and the director then coordinates all of the parts into a unified whole. On the other hand, plays are sometimes presented in a manner at variance with the script. Such departures, however, are usually made deliberately and for the sake of some effect considered more significant than that which could be achieved by the typical approach.

Ultimately, then, style in drama and theatre results from the way in which means are adapted to ends. It contributes significantly to that sense of unity and wholeness which is the mark of effective drama.

In many contemporary discussions of the theatre, the term *stylization* is used to indicate any deviation from realism. This terminology is sometimes helpful but it is imprecise, since realism is itself a style and since departures from realism may be in any number of directions. Every play has a style, although, as with form, the specific label to be attached to it may be difficult to determine.

Since structure, form, and style may be combined in infinite variations, discussions of them remain abstract until applied to specific examples. The chapters that follow show how these principles have been put into practice. Each chapter in Parts II and III summarizes briefly the development of theatre and drama in a particular era, and outlines the background needed for understanding the plays of that period. In addition, one or more representative plays are analyzed and treated both as products of a specific time and place and as art works which transcend their age. Pertinent points about structure, form, and style are considered when relevant.

A chronological order has been followed because each period is in part an outgrowth of what has gone before. After following the theatre through history, Part IV examines in detail the working procedures of the contemporary American theatre. Thus, the historical material will provide a perspective from which to view our present situation.

II

THE THEATRE OF THE PAST

Oedipus the King directed by Tyrone Guthrie, 1955. Douglas Campbell as Oedipus. Production photograph by Donald McKague, courtesy of the Stratford Shakespearean Festival Foundation of Canada.

Chapter 4 THE THEATRE OF ANCIENT GREECE

No one really knows how the theatre began, but there are many theories about its inception in Greece. The theory most widely known today is based upon a supposed relationship between theatre and ritual. The argument is developed as follows:

In the beginning, man viewed the natural forces of the world, even the seasonal changes, as unpredictable, and sought, through various means, to control these unknown and feared powers. Those measures which appeared to bring the desired results were then retained and repeated until they hardened into fixed rituals. Eventually stories arose which explained or veiled the rites' mysteries. As man progressed in knowledge, some rituals, such as those involving human sacrifice, were abandoned, but the stories, later called myths, persisted and provided material for drama.

This primitive ritual also contained the seeds of theatre, for music, dance, masks, and costumes were almost always used. Furthermore, a suitable site had to be provided for performances, and when the entire tribe did not participate, a clear division was usually made between the "acting area" and the "auditorium." Since considerable importance was attached to avoiding mistakes in the enactment of rites, priests usually assumed the task for the tribe. Wearing masks and costumes, they often impersonated men, animals, or supernatural beings, and mimed the desired effect—success in hunt or battle, the coming of rain, the revival of the sun—as an actor might. From such dramatic rituals, drama eventually developed as man became sufficiently sophisticated to separate theatrical from religious activities.

This theory has much to recommend it, since it is probably true that primitive people do not distinguish among the various aspects of their lives (work, religion, theatre) as clearly as more advanced societies do.

ritual

totemism ?

The weakness of the theory lies in the fact that all of man's attempts to deal with his world (science, philosophy, art) were in the beginning just as much a part of ritual as was the theatre. It does not explain why the theatre continued to grow in importance after it was divorced from ritual and thus lost its former status as an effective means of influencing man's welfare.

Mimesis

Another clue to the origin of the theatre is suggested by Aristotle, the Greek philosopher of the fourth century B.C., who stated that human beings are instinctively imitative—that they both enjoy imitating others and seeing imitations, for they desire to know how it would feel to be another person or why others act as they do. Furthermore, he added, imitation is one of man's chief methods of learning about his world, as when children learn speech and behavior by imitating adults.

But while most tribes developed rituals and while man may be instinctively imitative, all societies have not produced theatre and drama divorced from ritual. At least two other conditions would also seem to be required: a society which can recognize the artistic value of theatre and drama, and men capable of organizing the theatrical elements into an experience of a high order. For these reasons, the Greeks must be considered the principal originators of theatre, for it was they who first recognized its potentialities.

THE BEGINNINGS OF DRAMA IN GREECE

Although drama may have appeared in Egypt as early as 3000 B.C., the existing references are scarce and unclear, and it is in Greece that we find the first definite information about the theatre and the world's first great drama.

Dionysus

For several centuries Greek drama was presented only in connection with the festivals honoring Dionysus, the god of wine and fertility. Supposedly the son of Zeus (the greatest of Greek gods) and Semele (a mortal), Dionysus was killed, dismembered, and then resurrected. The myths which grew up around him were closely related to the life cycle and to seasonal changes: birth, growth, decay, death, and rebirth; spring, summer, fall, and winter. His worship was designed to ensure the return of spring. As the god of wine and fertility, he also represented many of the world's irrational forces, and his worship was a recognition of man's elemental passions. In the early centuries of Dionysian worship, sexual orgies and drunkenness were accepted parts of the religious impulse, but as time went by these were gradually sublimated, although the basic purpose of Dionysian worship—the inducement of fertility—remained unchanged.

The inclusion of such irrational forces within the sphere of religion illustrates well the Greek belief that the failure to give due honor to any part of nature might lead to destruction. The Greeks constantly sought to achieve harmony among all of the conflicting forces both within and outside themselves.

56

The ruins of the Theatre of Dionysus at Athens today. Evidences of the remodeling of c. A.D. 270 remain. From Ernst Fiechter, *Antike Griechische Theaterbauten*, courtesy Verlag W. Kohlhammer GmbH. *Below:* Ground plan of the Precinct of Dionysus at Athens showing the Theatre and the Temple of Dionysus. From Dorpfeld-Reisch, *Das Griechische Theater*, 1896.

— semi-circular orchestra
— remnant of skene
— 4th c. BC

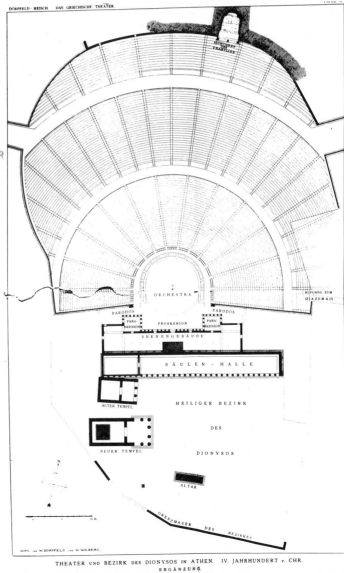

MONUMENT DES THRASYLLOS

AUFGANG ZUM DIAZOMA (?)

ORCHESTRA

PARODOS · PARODOS
PARA-SKENION · PARA-SKENION
PROSKENION
SKENENGEBÄUDE

SÄULEN · HALLE

HEILIGER   BEZIRK

ALTER TEMPEL

DES

NEUER TEMPEL

DIONYSOS

ALTAR

N

GRENZMAUER   DES   BEZIRKES

AUFG. von W. DÖRPFELD   von W. WILBERG.

THEATER UND BEZIRK DES DIONYSOS IN ATHEN.   IV. JAHRHUNDERT v. CHR.
ERGÄNZUNG.

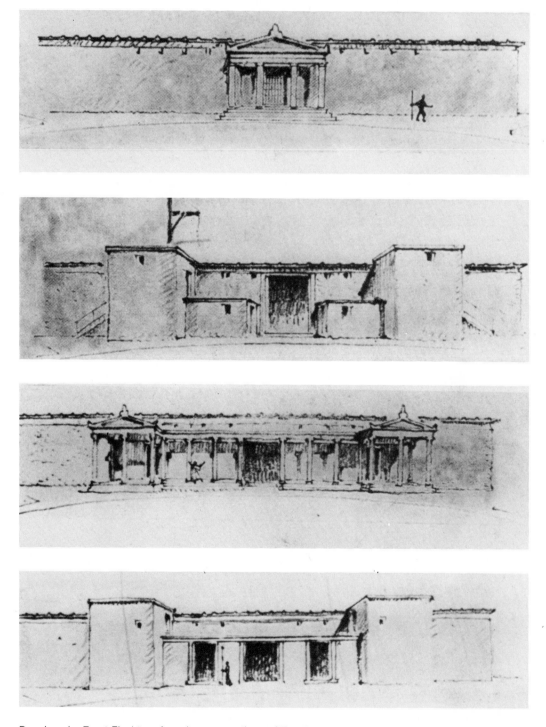

Drawings by Ernst Fiechter of varying conceptions of the stage
house for the theatre of Dionysus in the fifth century B.C. From
Fiechter, *Antike Griechische Theaterbauten,* courtesy Verlag W.
Kohlhammer GmbH, Stuttgart.

The worship of Dionysus was introduced into Greece from Asia Minor around the thirteenth century B.C. By the seventh or eighth century contests of choral dancers were already being held at the festivals given in honor of Dionysus. These dances were accompanied by dithyrambs, or ecstatic hymns, in honor of the god. It is out of these hymns and dances that Aristotle says drama developed.

festivals

dithyrambs

The Greeks did not observe a holy day comparable to our sabbath. Rather they had a series of religious festivals throughout the year honoring various gods. By the sixth century B.C. there were four festivals each year in honor of Dionysus alone: the Rural Dionysia (in December); the Lenaia (in January); the Anthesteria (around the end of February); and the City or Great Dionysia (around the end of March). Plays came to be performed at all of these, with the exception of the Anthesteria. Plays were not given at the festivals in honor of any other god.

The first definite record of drama in Greece is found in 534 B.C. In that year the City Dionysia was reorganized and a contest for tragedy was instituted. It is assumed that drama existed prior to that time, for otherwise a contest would be difficult to explain. The only recorded dramatist of this period was Thespis, who won the first contest. Since he is also the first known actor, performers are often called *thespians*.

The drama of Thespis was relatively simple, since it involved only one actor and a chorus. This does not mean that there was only one speaking character in each play, but rather that all characters were played by the same actor. This single actor used masks in shifting his identity; when he left the stage to change roles, the chorus filled the intervals with singing and dancing. The chorus, therefore, was the principal unifying force in this early drama. Face-to-face conflict between opposing characters, which most later periods have considered a necessary feature of drama, was impossible so long as there was only one actor.

THE FIFTH CENTURY

Although drama was written and performed in Greece for many centuries, plays by only five writers—Aeschylus, Sophocles, Euripides, Aristophanes, and Menander—now exist. Out of the vast number of plays written, only forty-five survive—thirty-two tragedies, twelve comedies, and one satyr play. All but four of these plays were written during the fifth century.

Aeschylus (525–456) is the earliest dramatist whose plays have survived. He began competing in the tragedy contests around 499 B.C., but did not win a victory until 484; after that time he won thirteen contests. The titles of seventy-nine of his plays have come down to us but only seven works remain: *The Persians* (472), *Seven Against Thebes* (467), the trilogy of plays made up of *Agamemnon, Choephoroe,* and *Eumenides* (458), *The Suppliants,* and *Prometheus Bound* (exact dates unknown). *The Persians* is unique among surviving Greek dramas in having been based on an historical event (the Persian war) rather than on mythology, although other plays on historical subjects were written.

59

Aeschylus' major innovation was the introduction of the second actor, which allowed face-to-face conflict for the first time. The increased emphasis upon the actor reduced the importance of the chorus, though it remained a dominant force.

The power of Aeschylus' drama can best be appreciated through his trilogy, usually called the *Oresteia*, one of the great monuments of dramatic literature. Aeschylus was almost always concerned with man's relationship to the gods and the universe. The *Oresteia* demonstrates his interests well, for here he deals with growth in the concept of justice. In the first two plays the characters conceive of justice as personal revenge, but in the final play, private justice is replaced by the impersonal power of the state. This evolutionary process is demonstrated through a powerful story of murder, revenge, and remorse.

Sophocles (496–406) is frequently called the greatest of the Greek dramatists. He is credited with over a hundred plays, of which only seven now exist: *Ajax* (dated variously from 450 to 440), *Antigone* (around 440), *Oedipus the King* (approximately 430 to 425), *Philoctetes* (409), *Electra* and *Trachiniae* (dates unknown, though considered to be late plays), and *Oedipus at Colonus* (written shortly before Sophocles' death). In addition, a substantial part of *The Trackers*, a satyr play, is extant. He won eighteen contests, the first in 468 when he defeated Aeschylus. Sophocles introduced a third actor and thus allowed for still greater dramatic complexity than had been possible with two actors. He was much more concerned with human relationships than with the religious and philosophical issues which had interested Aeschylus. His dramas also place more emphasis upon building skillful climaxes and well-developed episodes than did those of Aeschylus, which were sometimes crude in their structure. The qualities of Sophocles' drama will be explored at greater length in the detailed examination of *Oedipus the King*.

Euripides (480–406) was the last of the great Greek tragedians. He is said to have written ninety-two plays, of which seventeen tragedies have survived. Among these the most famous are: *Alcestis* (438), *Medea*

Sophocles' *Electra*. Directed by George Kernodle.

(431), *Hippolytus* (428), *Ion*, and *Electra* (dates unknown), *The Trojan Women* (415), and *The Bacchae* (produced after his death). In addition, *The Cyclops* is the only complete satyr play which now exists. Although Euripides achieved great popularity in later times, he was not widely appreciated in his own day, winning only five victories in the tragic contests.

Euripides reduced the role of the chorus in his works until its connection with the rest of the play was often vague. His interests were principally philosophical and psychological. He was a skeptic who questioned many Athenian ideals; even the Gods did not escape his probing and were frequently made to appear petty and ineffectual; he examined the motives of his characters and found little to admire. But he also turned toward melodrama and frequently resorted to contrived endings. Thus he has been admired for his ideas and his psychological realism, but has been criticized for faulty dramatic structure. With his death, the great era of Greek tragedy came to an end.

The characteristics of Greek tragedy can best be appreciated through a detailed examination of a representative example. Here, *Oedipus the King* will be used. First, however, it is necessary to describe the theatrical conditions which prevailed about 430 B.C., the approximate date of its first production.

PLAY PRODUCTION IN GREECE

It was at the City Dionysia, one of the great religious and civic occasions of the year, that *Oedipus the King* was first presented. If a tragic dramatist wished to enter plays at the City Dionysia, he applied for a chorus to the principal civic magistrate (the *archon eponymous*). It is not known how this official decided among the applicants, but three tragic writers were granted choruses at each City Dionysia.

The magistrate also appointed the *choregoi*, or wealthy citizens who bore the expense of the choruses. One *choregus* was appointed for each dramatist, and the *choregoi* and playwrights were then matched by lot. *Choregoi* for the next City Dionysia were appointed approximately one month after the conclusion of the preceding City Dionysia. This would have allowed almost a year for planning and rehearsal, although not all of this time may have been used.

The *choregus* paid for the training of the chorus, their costumes, the musicians, the supernumerary actors and their costumes, and perhaps for the scenery. In other words, he was responsible for everything except the theatre and the speaking actors. Since he might be either generous or miserly, the *choregus* could seriously affect the playwright's chances of mounting his play satisfactorily. Usually, however, the *choregus* looked upon the proper outfitting of his plays as a civic duty and as a matter of personal pride.

If a playwright were granted a chorus, he supplied three tragedies and a satyr play. With rare exceptions, the playwright also directed his own works and was in charge of the production as a whole. Until the time of Sophocles the playwright acted in his own plays as well. For his efforts,

61

the playwright was no doubt given some financial remuneration by the state and there was a prize for the winner of the contest, but the amount of money which a playwright might receive for his work is unknown. It is extremely doubtful, however, that any of the Greek dramatists of the fifth century earned a living from work as a writer.

The state paid the actors and supplied their costumes; it also furnished the theatre in which the plays were performed. Dramatic production in the fifth century, thus, was financed either by wealthy citizens or by the state, and was looked upon as a religious and civic function of major importance.

The City Dionysia, at which the plays were produced, was considered so important that during it no legal proceedings were allowed and prisoners were released. It opened with a procession in which the statue of the god Dionysus was taken from his temple at the foot of the Acropolis and carried outside of the city. His entry into Athens was then re-enacted to the accompaniment of much revelry. The ceremony concluded with a sacrifice to the god.

The next principal feature of the festival was the performance of *dithyrambs* (hymns to Dionysus sung and danced by choruses of fifty). There were ten choruses each year, five with men and five with boys. Next came the contest for comedies, five being given on a single day; this was followed by three days devoted to the tragedies. On each of these days, three tragedies and a satyr play were performed. After the festival ended, there was a day devoted to awarding prizes and to considering complaints of misbehavior during the festival.

To this civic and religious celebration everyone was welcome. Admission was probably free originally, but was later set at the small sum of two *obols*. A public fund was established, however, to provide tickets for those who could not afford the price of admission. The theatre was, therefore, considered to be the right of everyone rather than a function for the few.

The audiences took a keen interest in the contests. At each City Dionysia prizes were awarded to the best plays (there was a prize for the best comedy and for the best group of tragedies, the honor being shared by the playwright and the choregus), to the best tragic actor, and to the best dithyrambic choruses. The state supervised the judging, and elaborate precautions were taken to insure that voting would be secret.

THE THEATRE OF DIONYSUS

At Athens the plays were presented in the Theatre of Dionysus situated on the slope of the Acropolis above the Temple of Dionysus. This theatre underwent many changes. In the sixth century it consisted of the hillside on which the spectators stood or sat, and a flat terrace at the foot of the hills for the performers. In the middle of this terrace or *orchestra* (the "dancing place") was an altar (or *thymele*). There was probably no scenic background. Seats, forming an auditorium or *theatron* (the "seeing place"), were gradually added for spectators.

During the fifth and fourth centuries this basic structure was elaborated: a scene house was added and the whole theatre was reconstructed

62

A conjectural reconstruction of the stage of the Theatre of Dionysus remodeled to conform to the Hellenistic ideal about 150 B.C. From Fiechter.

in stone, although this process was not completed until well into the fourth century. The auditorium was the first part of the theatre to assume permanent form, when stadiumlike seating was provided by setting stones into the hillside. The semicircular auditorium, which seated about 14,000 persons, curved around the circular orchestra, which measured about 65 feet in diameter.

The stage house (or *skene*) was late in developing as a part of the theatre. It was the last part to be constructed in stone, and was remodeled many times after that. For all of these reasons, it is difficult to get a clear impression of the scenic background of plays in the fifth century. The *skene* was originally constructed as a place where actors might dress and retire to change roles. Gradually this house came to be used as a background for the action of the play, and its usefulness for scenic purposes was exploited. At the time when *Oedipus the King* was first performed the *skene* was probably a long building which, with its projecting side wings (called *paraskenia*), formed a rectangular background for the orchestra on the side away from the spectators. It was not joined to the auditorium, and the space on each side between the *paraskenia* and the auditorium provided entrances into the orchestra. These entrances were called *parodoi*. (For a plan of the theatre as a whole see the illustration on page 57).

The appearance of the skene is much debated. Most of the plays are set before temples or palaces, but some take place outside of caves or tents, or in wooded landscapes. There is much controversy over the extent to which the background may have been altered to meet these differing demands.

Since it was not entirely permanent, the appearance of the skene could have been changed from year to year or from play to play. A series of holes has been discovered just forward of the foundations, and it has been suggested that upright timbers, to which scenery was attached, were set in these holes. Such a practice would permit rapid alterations in

63

the scenic background. It is impossible to know the truth, but, considering the lack of realistic detail in the plays, it seems unlikely that the Greeks ever attempted to create the illusion of a real place in their theatre. Some indication of a play's setting, however, may well have been given through scenic devices.

It is unclear whether there was a raised stage in the theatre of the fifth century, for there is not enough evidence to settle the question definitely. Since the plays seem to require that the actors and the chorus mingle freely, if a platform were used it was probably low enough to allow free access between stage and orchestra. If there were no stage, both the chorus and actors would have used the acting area composed of the orchestra and the rectangular space formed by the scene house. The roof of the stage house also could be used as an acting area.

Most frequently the actors entered from the stage house, while the chorus used the *parodoi*. There are examples, however, of the chorus entering from the stage house, and of actors using the *parodoi*. Since the number of stage entrances varies from play to play, some difference of opinion has arisen about the number of doorways in the stage house. It is customary to show three doors in the *skene* and one in each of the *paraskenia*, but the number is far from certain.

When the available information about the Greek theatre is assembled, a fairly clear picture of its basic structure emerges, but the details of the scenic background remain uncertain. Some of the many possibilities may be seen in the preceding drawings.

While most of the action of Greek plays takes place out of doors, occasionally interiors are indicated. For example, most deaths occur offstage, but the bodies are frequently displayed afterward. For this purpose the large central doorway seems to have been opened and a wheeled platform moved forward. This device is called an *eccyclema* or *exaustra*.

Another effect frequently demanded in Greek plays is the appearance of gods. These characters may descend to the orchestra level or be lifted up from the orchestra to the roof of the stage house. For this purpose, a cranelike device called the *machina* was used. The overuse of gods to resolve difficult dramatic situations led to the expression *deus ex machina* to describe any contrived ending. The eccyclema and the machina are the only two machines which can definitely be ascribed to the fifth century, and these were not used extensively.

It is possible, however, that *periaktoi* were also in use, although these probably belong to a later period. *Periaktoi* are constructed of three flats put together to form a triangle; the triangle is then mounted on a central pivot. Since each surface can be exposed or concealed as desired, it may be used for sudden revelations or for changes in the background.

THE ACTOR

The number of speaking actors in Greek tragedy seems to have been restricted to three. Although there might be *extras*, these were not considered to be actors. In the second half of the fifth century the state supplied three speaking actors for each tragic playwright competing in the con-

64

tests. A principal actor was assigned to each playwright by lot. The playwright and his leading actor probably chose the other two actors. All were male and all acted in each of the four plays presented by the same dramatist. Since there were only three actors, each might be asked to play a number of roles.

The style of acting is uncertain. The plays themselves call for simple realistic actions (such as weeping, running, and falling on the ground). On the other hand, many elements argue against any marked realism. The fact that the same actor played many roles and that men assumed women's parts suggests that performances could never have been very close to real life. Furthermore, some plays could be performed by three actors only if the same role were played by a different actor in different scenes of the play. The large musical element, the use of dance, and the rather abstract treatment of the story also argue against a realistic style of acting. Nevertheless, the performances should not be thought of as devoid of clearly identifiable human actions. The details of daily life were stripped away, but the audience was still able to sympathize with the characters. The style suggested by the scripts may be characterized as simple, expressive, and idealized.

Left. Terracotta figure of an actor found in an Athenian grave; probably fourth century B.C. Courtesy of the Metropolitan Museum of Art, Rogers Fund, 1913.

Right: The Greek comic actor and his costume. Terracotta statuette from an Athenian grave c. fourth century B.C. The Metropolitan Museum of Art, Rogers Fund, 1913.

COSTUME

A precautionary note seems necessary at this point. Many theatre historians have failed to distinguish between the practices of the fifth century and those of later Greek times. Nowhere is the failure more misleading than in the treatment of costumes. Frequently the tragic actor is depicted as wearing a high headdress, a mask with distorted features, thick-soled boots, and padded clothing. This costume may have been typical of later periods, but has little to do with the practices of the fifth century, the more typical features of which are outlined below and shown in the accompanying illustrations.

All the actors in Greek tragedy wore masks constructed of lightweight linen, cork, or wood. There were several reasons for this practice: each actor played a number of roles; all the actors were male though many of the characters were female; the range of age and character types played by a single actor was great. (There is little evidence to support the argument that the mask acted as a megaphone for the voice.) Although the mouths were open, the features were not exaggerated to any marked degree. Headdresses seem to have followed relatively closely those normally worn during the period.

A variety of clothing was used for stage purposes. A long-sleeved, ankle-length, heavily embroidered tunic, or *chiton*, was worn by certain characters, and some historians have argued that it was used for all the principal roles of tragedy. Since some plays contain references to mourning dress, to ragged garments, and to distinctions in clothing between Greeks and foreigners, however, it seems likely that costumes varied considerably. It may be that the sleeved, embroidered tunic (which was not worn in Greek daily life), was reserved for supernatural and non-

Possible costumes for tragedy. From Furtwängler-Reichold, *Griechische Vasenmalerei*. Series I, 1904.

long sleeves
ornamentation

A redrawing from a vase painting of a type of costume probably used for tragedy in the fifth century B.C.

Greek characters, while native dress was used for others. An ankle-length or knee-length chiton was the usual daily dress in Greece. The selection of the costume was probably determined by its appropriateness to the role. The tragic actor usually wore a high-topped boot, called a *cothurnus*, a soft, flexible footcovering in common use at the time.

While the actor's appearance was somewhat changed from the normal by his costume (largely because of the mask or the embroidered garment), he remained relatively undistorted. His costume allowed for freedom of movement and speech and for the rapid changes of roles.

THE CHORUS, MUSIC, AND DANCE

Although tradition has it that the tragic chorus originally consisted of fifty members, was later reduced to twelve, and then raised to fifteen, there is little evidence to substantiate any of these figures. Nevertheless, it is generally assumed that during Sophocles' lifetime the chorus was composed of fifteen persons. Usually the chorus performed in unison, but at times it was divided into two semichoruses of seven members, which might perform in turn or which might exchange or divide speeches. The chorus leader sometimes had solo lines, but the chorus spoke and sang as a group (though some modern editions of the plays divide the speeches and assign them to individual chorus members).

The chorus usually makes its entrance after the prologue (or opening scene) and remains until the end of the play. It serves many functions. First, it is an actor in the drama. It expresses opinions, gives advice, sometimes threatens to interfere in the events of the play. As a rule, it is sympathetically allied with the protagonist.

Handwritten margin notes:
- circular orchestra remnant of
- stone skene
- stone seating area
- hillside used
- thymele

Greek theatres built after about 325 B.C. are usually called Hellenistic. The ruins of the theatre at Epidaurus are shown here. It is the best preserved of all the ancient Greek theatres and is now frequently used for productions. Photograph—O. G. Brockett.

Second, the chorus often establishes the ethical framework of the play. It may express the author's views and set up a standard against which the actions of the characters can be judged.

Third, the chorus is frequently the ideal spectator. It reacts to the events and characters as the author would like his audience to respond.

Fourth, the chorus helps to set the mood of the play and to heighten its dramatic effects. For example, a mood of foreboding may be created through the chorus' expression of doubts about what is to come; or the chorus may help to achieve more powerful reversals, as when its expression of elation is followed immediately by disastrous events.

Fifth, the chorus adds color, movement, and spectacle. Originally, all the choral interludes were accompanied by music and were both sung and danced. Thus, it offered powerful auditory and visual appeals.

Sixth, the chorus serves an important rhythmical function. This may best be explained through an analogy. A typical Greek temple has columns all around the exterior, without which there would be an uninteresting continuous blank wall. The columns serve to make the eye pause but do not prevent it from moving on. Greek drama without its choral passages would have a similar effect, for the action would move too fast. These retardations—these pauses in which to look backward and forward—contribute enormously to the over-all emotional effect; they are part of the design without which the whole would be incomplete or unsatisfying.

The theatre at Epidaurus during a recent production. Note the modern stage house erected over the ruins of the ancient *skene*.

Oedipus the King as presented at Epidaurus in 1960. Photograph courtesy of the Greek National Theatre.

A performance of *Oedipus the King* by the Greek National Theatre at Epidaurus. Directed by Alexis Minotis. Photograph courtesy of the Greek National Theatre.

The exact nature of Greek music and dance is unknown. Only a few fragments of Greek music have survived, but we do know that the Greeks believed that both music and dance had ethical content—that some types were moral and that others were immoral. Since tragedy displays a strong ethical bias, it is reasonable to assume that in most tragedies the music and dance displayed the qualities which the Greeks associated with stateliness and moral uprightness.

OEDIPUS THE KING

With this background in mind, Sophocles' *Oedipus the King* will now be examined as an example of Greek tragedy.

THEMES AND IDEAS. As in all great plays, there are a number of important themes. One is stated in the final lines of the play:

> let none
> Presume on his good fortune until he find
> Life, at his death, a memory without pain.

The play shows the fall of Oedipus from the place of highest honor to that of an outcast and demonstrates the uncertainty of human destiny.

A second theme is man's limitation in controlling his fate. Oedipus is a man who attempts to do his best at all times; he wants to help his people; he has taken what he considers the necessary steps to avoid the terrible fate predicted by the oracle (that he will kill his father and marry his mother). But man is limited in his vision, no matter how he may attempt to avoid mistakes. The contrast, then, between man seeking to control his destiny and a relentless fate which determines destiny is clearly depicted. But while fate (or the will of the gods) is always the superior force in the play, it works through man. It is Jocasta's attempt to destroy the infant Oedipus, Oedipus' desire to avoid his parents, and Oedipus' search for the murderer, which lead inevitably to the outcome. And at the end,

70

while Oedipus accepts his fate, as he must, he still does not see himself entirely as the instrument of the gods:

> Dear
> Children, the god was Apollo.
> He brought my sick, sick fate upon me.
> But the blinding hand was my own!

It is significant that no attempt is made to explain why destruction comes to Oedipus. It is implied that man must submit to fate and that in struggling to avoid it he only becomes more entangled. There is then an irrational, or at least an unknowable, force at work. This idea is emphasized through the various attempts to communicate with the gods (through oracles) and to propitiate them. The plague is viewed as a punishment from the gods, the exiling of Oedipus is an attempt to placate them, but no one asks why the gods have decreed Oedipus' fate. The truth of the oracles is established, but the purpose is unclear. The Greek concept of the gods, however, did not demand that all the gods be benevolent, since all forces were deified whether good or evil. Therefore, a god might visit evil upon man, and man had to be constantly on guard not to offend any of the many gods.

Another theme, which may not have been a conscious one with Sophocles, is that of Oedipus as a scapegoat. The city of Thebes will be saved if the one guilty man can be found and punished. Oedipus, in a sense then, takes the sins of the city upon himself, and in his punishment lies the salvation of others. Thus, Oedipus becomes a sacrificial offering to the gods. There is a distant parallel here with the crucifixion of Christ, the sacrificial lamb offered up for the sins of all those who believe in Him. This parallel cannot be extended very far, however, since there are more points of difference than of similarity in the two figures.

Another motif—blindness versus sight—is emphasized in poetic images and in various overt comparisons. A contrast is repeatedly drawn between the physical power of sight and the inner sight of understanding. For example, Tiresias, though blind, can see the truth which escapes Oedipus, while Oedipus, who has penetrated the riddle of the Sphinx, cannot solve the puzzle of his own life. When it is revealed to him, he blinds himself in an act of retribution.

These themes indicate that *Oedipus the King* is a comment in part on man's relationship to the gods and on man's attempt to control his own destiny. While the Greek views of these problems may not be ours, the problems and many of the implications are still vital and meaningful.

PLOT AND STRUCTURE. The skill with which *Oedipus the King* is constructed can be appreciated if we compare the complex story (which actually begins with a prophecy prior to the birth of Oedipus) with Sophocles' ordering of the events. In the play there is a simultaneous movement backward and forward in time as the revelation of the past moves Oedipus ever nearer to his doom in the present.

The division of the play into a prologue and five episodes separated by choral passages is typical of Greek tragedy. The prologue is devoted principally to exposition: a plague is destroying the city of Thebes; Oedipus

Scene from *Oedipus the King* as performed at the Landestheater, Darmstadt in 1952. Directed by G. R. Sellner, designed by Fritz Mertz. Photograph by Pit Ludwig. Courtesy of the exhibition, *The New Theatre in Germany,* circulated by the Smithsonian Institution.

promises to help and explains the action already taken; Creon returns from Delphi with a command from the Oracle to find and punish the murderer of Laius; Oedipus promises to obey the command. Thus, all of the necessary information is given in a very brief scene, and the first important question (Who is the murderer of Laius?) is raised. The prologue is followed by the *parodos*, or entry of the chorus, and the first choral song, which recapitulates the plight of Thebes and offers prayers to the gods for deliverance.

The first episode begins with Oedipus' proclamation and curse upon the murderer. This proclamation has great dramatic power because Oedipus is unknowingly pronouncing a curse upon himself. Then Tiresias, the seer, enters. It is important to remember that Oedipus has sent for Tiresias on the advice of Creon, since otherwise Oedipus' suspicion of conspiracy between Creon and Tiresias is not understandable. Tiresias' refusal to answer questions provokes Oedipus' anger, the first display of a response which is developed forcefully throughout the first four episodes. It is his quick temper, we later discover, that caused Oedipus to kill Laius. By the time Tiresias has been driven to answer, Oedipus suspects some trickery. This complication is necessary, for had Oedipus summoned Tiresias, heard his story, and believed him, the play would be over. Sophocles, however, has boldly brought out the truth but has cast doubt upon it, as Oedipus points out, if Tiresias knew the truth why did

72

he not speak out at the time of Laius' murder? The scene ends in a stalemate of accusations.

It is interesting to note that while all of the first four episodes move forward in the present, they go successively further backward in time. This first episode reveals only that part of the past immediately preceding Oedipus' arrival at Thebes.

The choral passage which follows the first episode reflects upon the previous scene, stating the confusion which Sophocles would wish the audience to feel. The chorus ends by declaring that since Oedipus has saved the city in the past it will continue to have faith in him until he is proven wrong.

The second episode builds logically upon the first. Creon comes to defend himself from the accusations of conspiracy with Tiresias. Oedipus, however, is not open to reason. Jocasta is drawn to the scene by the quarrel and she and the chorus persuade Oedipus to abate his anger. This quarrel illustrates Oedipus' complete faith in his own righteousness. In spite of Tiresias' accusation, no suspicion of his own guilt has entered his mind. Ironically, it is Jocasta's attempt to placate Oedipus which leads to his first suspicion about himself. She tells him that oracles are not to be believed and as evidence points to Laius' death, which did not come in the manner prophesied. But her description recalls to Oedipus the circumstances under which he has killed a man. He insists that Jocasta send for the one survivor of Laius' party. Thus, a considerable change occurs within this scene — the self-righteousness of Oedipus is shaken, and the possibility of his involvement creates additional suspense. The scene also continues the backward exploration of the past, for Oedipus tells of his life in Corinth, his visit to the Oracle of Delphi, and the murder of the man who is later discovered to have been Laius.

The choral song which follows is concerned with the questions Jocasta has raised about oracles. The chorus concludes that if oracles are proven untrue then the gods themselves are to be doubted. The song, while reflecting upon the scene immediately past, looks forward to a solution of the question.

Though Jocasta has called oracles into question, she obviously does not disbelieve in the gods themselves, for at the beginning of the third episode she makes offerings to them. She is interrupted, however, by the entrance of the Messenger from Corinth, who brings news of the death of Oedipus' supposed father, Polybus. But this news, rather than arousing grief, as one would expect, is greeted with rejoicing, for it seems to disprove the oracle which had predicted that Oedipus would kill his father. This seeming reversal only serves to heighten the effect of the following events. Oedipus still fears returning to Corinth because the oracle also has prophesied that he will marry his own mother. Thinking that he will set Oedipus' mind at ease, the Messenger reveals that he himself brought Oedipus as an infant to Polybus. The circumstances under which the Messenger acquired the child bring home the truth to Jocasta. This discovery leads to a complete reversal for Jocasta, for the oracles she has cast doubt upon in the preceding scene have suddenly been vindicated. She strives to stop Oedipus from making further inquiries, but he interprets her entreaties as fear that he may be of humble birth. Jocasta goes into the palace; it is the last we see of her, although her actions are later revealed.

This scene not only has revealed the truth to Jocasta, it has diverted attention from the murder of Laius to the birth of Oedipus. It goes backward in time to the infancy of Oedipus. Only one step remains.

The choral song which follows is filled with romantic hopes, as the chorus speculates on Oedipus' parentage and suggests such possibilities as Apollo and the nymphs. The truth is deliberately kept at a distance here in order to make the following scene more powerful. These speculations, however, do serve to concentrate attention on the question while diverting it from the right solution.

This extremely brief choral song is followed by the entry of the Herdsman (the sole survivor of Laius' party at the time of the murder and the person from whom the Corinthian Messenger had acquired the infant Oedipus). The Herdsman does not wish to speak, but he is tortured by Oedipus' servants into doing so. In this very rapid scene everything that has gone before is brought to a climax. We are taken back to the beginning of the story (Oedipus' birth), we learn the secret of his parentage, we see the truth of the oracle, we find out who murdered Laius, we discover that Oedipus is married to his mother. The climax is reached in Oedipus' cry of despair and disgust as he rushes into the palace. The brief choral song which follows comments upon the fickleness of fate and points to Oedipus' life as an example.

The final episode is divided into two parts. A Messenger enters and describes what has happened offstage. The "messenger scene" is a standard part of Greek drama, since Greek sensibilities dictated that scenes of extreme violence take place offstage, although the results of the violence (the bodies of the dead, or in this case Oedipus' blindness) might be shown. It is doubtful, however, that spectators of any age could witness without revulsion the sight of Oedipus jabbing pins into his eyes. Following the messenger scene, Oedipus returns to the stage and seeks to prepare himself for the future.

Oedipus the King is structurally unusual, for the resolution scene is the longest in the play. Obviously, Sophocles was not primarily concerned with discovering the murderer of Laius, for the interest in this lengthy final scene is shifted to the question: What will Oedipus do now that he knows the truth?

Up to this scene the play has concentrated upon Oedipus as the ruler of Thebes, but in the resolution Oedipus as a man and a father becomes the center of interest. By this point he has ceased to be the ruler of Thebes and has become the lowest of its citizens, and much of the intense pathos is due to this change. An audience may feel for Oedipus the outcast as it never could feel for the self-righteous ruler shown in the prologue.

Oedipus' act of blinding himself grows believably out of his character, for it is his very uprightness and deep sense of moral outrage which causes him to punish himself so terribly. Although he is innocent of in-

74

tentional sin, he considers the deeds themselves (murder of a blood relative and incest) to be so horrible that ignorance cannot wipe away the moral stigma. Part of the play's power resides in the revulsion with which people in all ages have viewed patricide and incest. That they are committed by an essentially good man only make them more terrible.

Oedipus the King maintains completely the unities of action, time, and place. There is nothing in the play which is not immediately relevant to the story being told. There are no subplots, and even the main plot is treated as simply as its events will allow. The time which elapses in the play coincides with the amount of time it would take in performance, and all of the events occur in the same place. The play, thus, has a late point of attack and shows only the final stages of the story. Out of very simple means, the playwright has created a drama of concentrated and powerful effect.

CHARACTERS AND ACTING. Sophocles pays little attention to physiological levels of characterization. The principal characters—Oedipus, Creon, and Jocasta—are mature persons, but Sophocles has said almost nothing about their ages or appearance. One factor which is apt to distract modern readers—the relative ages of Jocasta and Oedipus—is not even mentioned by Sophocles, for it is basically unimportant. According to legend, Jocasta was queen of Thebes when Oedipus answered the riddle of the Sphinx. His reward, being made king, carried with it the stipulation that he marry Jocasta. Sophocles, it should be noted, never questions the suitability of the marriage on the grounds of disparity in age.

Scene from Sophocles' *Electra* in Surrealist style. The dark spot at the top center is the face of the dead Agamemnon, whose spirit broods over the action. Directed by Orlin Corey; designed by Irene Corey. Reprinted by permission from *The Mask of Reality: An Approach to Design for the Theatre* by Irene Corey. Anchorage Press, 1968.

Lysistrata as produced by the Moscow Art Theatre in 1923. Directed by Nemirovich-Danchenko; setting by Isaac Rabinovitch.

Although Sophocles does not dwell on the physical attributes of his major characters, he does give brief indications of age for other roles. The Priest of the Prologue is spoken of as being old; the Chorus is made up of Theban Elders; Tiresias is old and blind; the Herdsman is an old man. In almost every case, age is associated with wisdom and experience. On the other hand, there are a number of young characters, none of whom speaks: the band of suppliants in the Prologue includes children, and Antigone and Ismene are very young. Here, the innocence of childhood is used to arouse pity.

On the sociological level of characterization, Sophocles again indicates little. Oedipus, Creon, and Jocasta hold joint authority in Thebes, although the power has been delegated to Oedipus. Vocational designations—a priest, a seer, a herdsman, servants—are used for some of the characters.

Sophocles is principally concerned with psychological and ethical characteristics. For example, we never know how old Oedipus is, but we learn about his moral uprightness, his reputation for wisdom, his quick temper, his insistence on discovering truth, his suspicion, his love for his children, his strength in the face of disaster. It is these qualities which make us understand Oedipus. But even here, a very limited number of traits, only those which are necessary to the story, are shown.

Creon is given even fewer characteristics. He has been Oedipus' trusted friend, his brother-in-law, and is one of the rulers of Thebes. He is quick to defend his honor, and is a man of common sense and uprightness who acts as honorably and compassionately as he can when the truth is discovered. Jocasta is similarly restricted. She strives to make life run smoothly for Oedipus, she tries to comfort him, to mediate between him and Creon, to stop Oedipus in his quest; she commits suicide when the truth becomes clear. We know nothing of her as a mother, and the very existence of the children is not mentioned until after her death.

This treatment of character—the use of few but essential traits—is another sign of Sophocles' economy in writing. To understand his meth-

76

ods, it may help to compare them with those of most modern playwrights who tend to build up characters from a large number of small details.

In the first production of *Oedipus the King*, all of the speaking roles would have been taken by three actors. The most likely casting would be as follows: the first actor would play Oedipus throughout, since he is present in every scene; the second actor would play Creon and the Messenger from Corinth; the third actor would play the Priest, Tiresias, Jocasta, the Herdsman, and the second Messenger. The greatest range is required of the third actor, while the greatest individual power is required of the first. The demands made on the third actor raises questions about the degree to which he differentiated between characters and the importance masks and costumes played in keeping characters separated for the audience. One should remember, however, that no two of the roles played by the third actor closely resemble each other and that the separation in terms of type might make his task simpler than it appears.

In addition to the three speaking actors, a large number of supernumeraries is required, many of whom no doubt appeared in more than one scene. For example, the band of suppliants in the Prologue includes children, two of whom could later appear as Antigone and Ismene. Some who portrayed suppliants probably also later appeared as servants and attendants. To the actors must be added the chorus of fifteen members. The total number in the cast, therefore, was probably not less than thirty-five.

Just as the details of characterization are few, so too the kinds of actions required of the actors are restricted. The physical movement specifically demanded by the script is slight: entering, exiting, kneeling, pouring of sacrificial offerings, torturing of the Herdsman, and displays of anger. The use of masks, the doubling of roles, the fact that Jocasta was played by a man, the relatively small range of action—all these factors suggest that, while the aim was to create moving representations of human actions, the over-all effect would be considerably more abstract than the acting normally seen in the modern theatre.

SETTING, SPECTACLE, MUSIC, AND DANCE. The reader used to all the stage directions given in modern scripts may find a Greek tragedy lacking in spectacle upon first reading. If he tries to envision the action as it unfolds moment by moment, however, quite a different impression results.

First of all, the Greek theatre had no curtain. The play begins, therefore, with the procession of the suppliants through one of the *parodoi*. Oedipus arrives to hear their pleas; then Creon enters. Later the suppliants leave, and immediately the Chorus enters with a song which is accompanied by music and dance. This simple outline of the prologue and *parodos* is indicative of the complexity and variety found throughout the play.

The setting of *Oedipus the King* is simple. The stage house represents a palace; no changes are made and no machinery is needed. Relatively few of the characters enter from the palace: Oedipus, Jocasta, the second Messenger, Antigone, Ismene, and sometimes Creon. Most of the characters, however, enter either through the *parodoi* or from the *paraskenia*. The Chorus and the suppliants would also enter through the *parodoi* and would perform in the orchestra.

There would be an altar in the middle of the orchestra, but there would also be altars near the stage house upon which Jocasta could place her offerings. Since the play was performed out of doors in daylight, no artificial illumination was necessary.

Costumes also would add to both setting and spectacle. Since most of the characters, including the Chorus, are dignified Greek citizens, they probably would wear long *chitons*. But there would also be many distinctions among the characters. Suppliants would carry branches as symbols; the Priest, Tiresias, and the Herdsman would wear garments indicative of their occupations. The rich costumes of Oedipus, Jocasta, and Creon would contrast effectively with the simpler garments of the servants. Each actor also would wear a mask indicative of his age and character.

Choral dancing is an important element of the spectacle. Since dance had ethical connotations for the Greeks, that used in *Oedipus the King* would have been in keeping with the moral position represented by the chorus of the play. Since the Chorus is made up of elderly and wise men, whatever dance they performed must have been dignified and stately, and probably appealed as much through shifting patterns as through dance steps.

The aural appeals were several: instrumental music, singing, and the speech of actors. The Greeks placed great emphasis on effective oral reading. The actors' voices, therefore, must have been trained, and probably created considerable aural beauty. Plays were performed with musical accompaniment. Occasionally, music was used during the episodes, but normally it was reserved for choral passages, all of which were sung and danced to flute music. Not only does music offer an appeal in its own right, it is also helpful in staging choral interludes, for it makes singing and dancing in unison much easier. Furthermore, music, through volume and tempo, aids in building choral passages to a climax. Movement, music, and song were combined to make the choral interludes among the most striking and effective features of Greek tragedy.

When the dramatic, visual, and musical appeals of Greek drama are considered, it becomes easier to understand why these plays, even after the passage of 2500 years, are still powerful and meaningful works of art.

THE SATYR PLAY

During the fifth century B.C., each writer of tragedy was required to present a satyr play, along with three tragedies, whenever he competed in the festivals. A satyr play was comic in tone, usually burlesqued a Greek myth, and used a chorus of satyrs. Following the three tragedies, it formed a kind of afterpiece, since it was short and sent the audience home in a happy frame of mind. Since the actors and choruses were

Actors of a Satyr play. From a vase of the late fifth century, B.C. Note the masks and the various kinds of costume. From Baumeister, *Denkmaler des Klassichens Altertums,* 1888.

those who appeared in the tragedies, the conventions of acting, costuming, and scenery probably resembled those of tragedy, but given a satirical turn.

Only one complete satyr play—the *Cyclops* by Euripides—still exists. It is divided into five sections by four choral odes after the manner of tragedy and is a parody of the serious story—found in the *Odyssey*—of Odysseus' encounter with the Cyclops. A substantial part of one other satyr play—*The Trackers* by Sophocles—is also extant. It deals with Apollo's attempts to recover a herd of cattle stolen from him by Hermes and has the same structural features as the *Cyclops*. Although the satyr play was a regular feature of the Athenian theatre of the fifth century, it has had little subsequent influence and ceased to exist as a form when Greek drama declined.

A greek vase painting depicting satyrs. From Furtwängler-Reichold, *Griechische Vasenmalerei,* 1904.

COMEDY

Greek comedy developed later than tragedy. It was not officially recognized as a part of the festivals—that is, it was not granted a chorus—until about 487 B.C., when it became a regular part of the City Dionysia. After 487, one day of each festival was devoted to the presentation of five comedies. At the City Dionysia, however, comedy was always considered inferior to tragedy; it was to find its true home at the Lenaia—another of the Dionysian festivals—at which it was given official state support beginning around 442 B.C. At the same time, contests for both comic poets and comic actors were inaugurated. The festival arrangement and the production procedures were similar to those for the City Dionysia, though the Lenaia festival was less elaborate. Five comic poets competed at the Lenaia, as at the City Dionysia. After 432, two tragic dramatists provided two tragedies each year as well. Satyr plays and dithyrambs were never presented at the Lenaia.

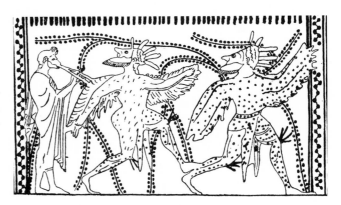

Bird costumes probably similar to those used in Old Comedy. From Dieterich, *Pucinella,* 1897.

Comedy used a chorus of twenty-four members, which like the tragic chorus might be divided into two semichoruses. The chorus also sang and danced and served the same functions as the tragic chorus, but its music and dance were directed, as a rule, toward creating comic effects, although Aristophanes frequently inserted beautiful lyrical choruses into his comedies.

There were fewer restrictions on the number of actors in comedy than in tragedy. Although most comedies could be performed by three actors, occasionally as many as five were required. The acting style was probably based upon everyday behavior but exaggerated for comic effect.

The costume was usually a very tight, too-short *chiton* worn over flesh-colored tights, which created a ludicrous effect of partial nakedness. This effect was further emphasized by the *phallus*, which was attached to the costumes of most male characters. The phallus was both a source of ribald humor and a constant reminder of the Dionysian purpose of the festival. Masks also served to emphasize the ridiculous appearance of the characters. (See the illustrations on pages 65, 80, 82, and 85.)

80

Masks and costumes might also be more specialized in their function. Sometimes portrait masks—that is, masks that depicted actual persons—were used. For example, when *The Clouds* was first produced Socrates is said to have stood up in the theatre so the audience might compare the actor's mask with his own facial features. Many of the plays have non-human choruses—of birds, frogs, clouds, or wasps—and masks and costumes were used to create the appropriate appearance.

Principally, however, comedy differed from tragedy in its subject matter. Most typically it was concerned with contemporary matters of politics or art, with questions of peace or war, with persons or practices disliked by the comic writer. Occasionally the playwright used mythological material as a framework for his satire, but usually he invented his own plots, and often referred to contemporary persons or situations. The allusions were no doubt a source of considerable pleasure to the audiences of the day, but are often obscure to a modern reader.

Numerous authors wrote Old Comedy, as the plays prior to 400 B.C. are called, but only the work of Aristophanes (*c.* 448–*c.* 380) still exists. He wrote about forty plays, of which eleven have survived: *The Acharnians* (425), *The Knights* (424), *The Clouds* (423), *The Wasps* (422), *Peace* (421), *The Birds* (414), *Lysistrata* (411), *Thesmophoriazusae* (411), *The Frogs* (405), *Ecclesiazusae* (392 or 391), and *Plutus* (388). Aristophanes began competing in the contests in 427, and though he may have acted in a few of his plays, he usually depended on others to produce his works.

His comedies mingle farce, personal abuse, fantasy, beautiful lyric poetry, literary and musical parody, and serious commentary on contemporary affairs. *The Clouds* will be examined in some detail as an example of Aristophanes' work. It was produced at the City Dionysia in 423 B.C. and was awarded the third prize. Aristophanes later revised the script, but it is unclear how the present version differs from the original.

THE CLOUDS

THEME AND IDEAS. The basic theme of *The Clouds* is the corrupting influence of the Sophists, in whose teachings Aristophanes saw a danger to Athenian values. The Sophists were interested in rhetoric and argumentation, but, because they were skeptical of absolute values, to Aristophanes they appeared more anxious to win contests than to defend valid positions.

While Socrates was not actually a Sophist, he was probably the most colorful figure among the current teachers. Aristophanes did not pretend to present Socrates' ideas accurately, but used him to epitomize the Sophistic teacher. Nor are the ideas of the Sophists truthfully represented; they too are altered for comic purposes.

The satire is directed at two aspects of the movement: its methods, and its effects. The scenes in the school are concerned with the first of these, while Phidippides' treatment of his father is designed to show the latter.

PLOT AND STRUCTURE. The plot of Old Comedy consists of a "happy idea" and the results of putting it into practice. In *The Clouds*, the idea is

Production photograph of *The Clouds* as presented in 1951 by the Greek National Theatre. Reproduced by permission.

conceived that payment of debts can be avoided by using the "wrong logic" of Sophistic learning. After much ridicule of its methods, the new learning is put into practice with the anticipated results. But while it is effective in ridding Strepsiades of his debtors, it has also taught his son, Phidippides, to beat and abuse him.

The typical structure of Old Comedy is: a *prologue*, during which the happy idea is conceived; the *parodos*, or entry of the chorus; the *agon*, or debate over the merits of the idea, ending with a decision to adopt it; the *parabasis*, a choral passage addressed to the audience and most frequently filled with advice on civic or other contemporary problems; a *series of episodes* showing the happy idea in practice; and the *komos*, or exit to feasting and general revelry. Although all of the usual structural features are present in *The Clouds*, they have been rearranged. The deviations will be noted in the discussion which follows.

In the prologue, Strepsiades sets forth his predicament in a straightforward monologue which gives all of the necessary exposition. He is heavily in debt because of the extravagances of his son, Phidippides. He concludes that the only solution is to send his son to Socrates' school to learn how to avoid paying the debts. When Phidippides refuses to attend school, Strepsiades decides to go himself. The scene shifts instantly from Strepsiades' house to Socrates' school. A number of satirical and farcical jokes about the school and its students concludes the prologue.

The parodos follows. Like many Greek comedies, *The Clouds* takes its title from the chorus, which frequently, as it does here, points up the element of fantasy. The clouds represent the spirit of the new learning which leads men on and then punishes them. The opening song also il-

82

lustrates the element of lyrical poetry for which Aristophanes is noted.

Usually the agon follows the parodos, but in *The Clouds* an episode is introduced to ridicule additional aspects of the new learning. This episode is followed by the parabasis, which denounces the audience for not properly appreciating Aristophanes' merits. He unashamedly praises himself and ridicules his opponents.

The parabasis is followed by still another episode showing Strepsiades' inability to absorb the new learning. It is implied that a man brought up in the old straight-laced ways of Athens cannot really understand the subtleties of the new way. After a choral ode, Strepsiades finally forces Phidippides to attend Socrates' school.

At this point, the long-delayed agon, or debate, occurs. The participants are personifications of Right Logic and Wrong Logic, another example of the fantasy which is typical of Old Comedy. As is usual, at the end of the agon all of the characters agree upon a line of action; here it is decided that Phidippides will be educated in the tradition of Wrong Logic.

This decision is followed by a short second parabasis, directed to the judges of the contest, suggesting that Aristophanes should win the prize. Time passes very rapidly in the next thirty-five lines, for at that point Phidippides re-enters having already completed his training.

A series of episodes showing the results of Strepsiades' plan follows: the creditors appear one by one and are effectively silenced. Strepsiades is overjoyed with his success and leads Phidippides away for feasting and revelry. This exit constitutes the komos and would normally conclude the play.

The joy is short-lived, however, for after a brief choral ode Strepsiades reappears, having been beaten by Phidippides, who then proves by his new learning that it is his duty to punish his father. The play ends as Strepsiades, in a fit of rage and frustration, attempts to burn Socrates' school. Such an ending is atypical of Old Comedy, for as a rule joy and harmony prevail.

The unity of Old Comedy is to be found in its ruling idea rather than in a sequence of causally related events. Its structure, therefore, often seems haphazard. The episodes which show the idea being put into practice are especially apt to seem disconnected. The order could be rearranged and the number of episodes could be increased or reduced without seriously altering the story. They do build in comic intensity, however, and they carry out the author's purpose effectively.

The treatment of time and place in *The Clouds* is dictated by dramatic needs, without any attempt at creating an illusion of reality. Sometimes hours or days are assumed to have passed during one or two speeches, and the place changes at will. Stage illusion is broken frequently: the characters make comments about the audience, and the chorus addresses the spectators directly in the parabasis.

The element of fantasy can be seen in both the personification of the clouds and in the exaggeration of ideas and situations. Thus, while the incidents are related to contemporary affairs, they are treated through the techniques of the "tall story."

CHARACTERS AND ACTING. Aristophanes' plays seem to indicate that all men are governed by physical instincts and are in part corrupt and selfish. That Aristophanes held this opinion of his audience as well is suggested by his frequent practice of implying that the adoption of his point of view will bring monetary and sexual rewards.

Old Comedy puts much more emphasis on the physical aspects of characterization than does tragedy. Aristophanes' major characters are usually drawn from the well-to-do landowners (comparable to the middle class today), while the minor characters are either members of the same class or slaves. Occasionally heroes or gods appear, but they are always brought down to the level of ordinary humanity by emphasizing their physical instincts.

Typically, the main character in a play by Aristophanes is the common man, but one who is worse than the average audience member considers himself to be. Although any comedy may arouse a feeling of superiority, Aristophanes puts this response to special use. Because he wants reform, he makes it seem possible by letting the members of the audience feel that they are wiser than the characters in the play.

Aristophanes' characters are never villainous, merely ridiculous. Rather than focusing attention upon the moral nature of the "idea," he emphasizes the ludicrous or happy results of adopting it. Thus, the characters are usually concerned with expediency—how well a plan can serve their own purposes—rather than with rightness. Strepsiades, for example, never considers the moral implications of cheating his creditors, only the means by which it can be done. But, although the moral issues are never allowed to become the center of his plays, Aristophanes never lets the audience forget that the situations have wider and more important applications. Again, he achieves his purpose in part by allowing his audience to feel morally superior to the characters.

The acting style emphasizes the physical, ridiculous, and ordinary details of everyday life. For example, at the opening of *The Clouds*, Strepsiades and Phidippides, wrapped in blankets, are snoring; Strepsiades awakens and sends for a lamp and his account books. Later the characters catch bedbugs, beat each other, and climb onto the roof.

Old Comedy is as far removed from tragedy as possible; it highlights one aspect of man's life, while tragedy pinpoints another. Thus, comic acting was probably no more realistic than that in tragedy; its deviation from normal behavior, however, was in a completely different direction, for it ridiculed humanity just as tragic acting dignified it.

SETTING, SPECTACLE, DANCE, AND MUSIC. *The Clouds* demands a more complex setting and shows more clearly the facilities of the Greek theatre than does *Oedipus the King*. One interior and two exterior scenes are indicated. The interior was probably suggested by the *eccyclema*, while the two exteriors could be distinguished by the widely separated doors of the *skene*. The *machina* and the roof of the scene house were also used.

Many of the jokes in *The Clouds* are "sight gags." For example, Socrates is suspended in the machine (usually reserved for the gods) to indi-

84

cate the pretentiousness and essential impracticability of the new learning. Other elements of note include the cloud costumes of the chorus, the grotesque and ludicrously obscene appearance of other characters, and the lively music and dance.

Thus, Old Comedy is a theatrical form of varied appeal. It is a strange mixture of fantasy, farce, and poetry which celebrates man's instincts while demanding that he act rationally. It is the reverse side of the coin of which tragedy is the face. Together they indicate the range of the Greek view of man.

Scene from Greek New Comedy. Drawing of a bas relief; from Pougin, *Dictionnaire,* 1885.

LATE GREEK DRAMA

The great writers of Greek tragedy were no longer alive when Aristophanes died around 380 B.C. Consequently, the fourth century saw the decline of Greek drama, although no lessening in the popularity of the theatre.

In the fourth century the Macedonians overran Greece and their leader, Alexander the Great, conquered all of Asia Minor and the northern part of Africa. The Greeks had already established colonies in southern Italy and Sicily, and by the end of the fourth century almost all of the known world was rapidly being Hellenized. The center of learning shifted from Athens to Pergamum (in Asia Minor) and Alexandria (in Egypt), and theatres were built wherever Greek influence was felt.

While the taste for tragedy continued, comedy was the preferred form. But the comedy which satisfied this taste was not that of Aristophanes, for citizens were no longer free to ridicule their rulers or to demand reforms. Athens and other Greek territories were now ruled by despots. The New Comedy (as it is usually called) which amused these people is most intimately associated with Menander (*c.* 342–292 B.C.), a native of Athens. He is said to have written over one hundred comedies of which only one, *The Grouch*, remains in its entirety (rediscovered in 1957). Substantial portions of a few other plays by him also exist.

New Comedy was divided into five parts by four choral interludes. By this time, however, the chorus was of little importance and served merely to break the play into scenes. The major change came in subject

A reconstruction of the Hellenistic theatre at Oropos. Painted panels could be set between the columns below, while some scenic representation may have been used in the alcoves at the rear of the raised stage. From Ernst Fiechter, *Antike Griechische Theaterbauten,* courtesy Verlag W. Kohlhammer GmbH.

matter, which was now drawn from the everyday life of middle-class Athenians. The plays were light in tone and typically showed a son's attempt to marry in spite of his father's opposition. The son was usually aided by a clever slave, who was the major source of humor. Eventually the father was reconciled to the son's choice, frequently because the girl was discovered to be the long-lost child of a friend.

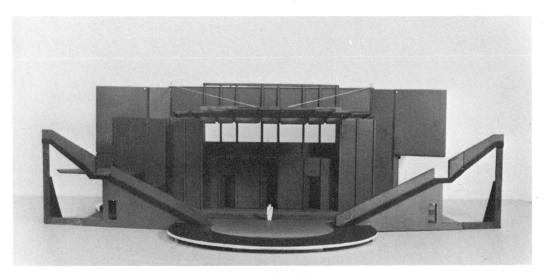

Model of the stage for the proposed Greek Theatre, Ypsilanti, Michigan, designed by Eldon Elder. The intention of the project is to recreate a Greek theatre and stage adapted to modern, enclosed theatre conditions to house an annual Greek Drama Festival. The stage includes the Skene with the three traditional doors, the Proskenion, the Orchestra and the Paradoi. Vertical, wooden stanchions plus interchangeable, removable panels form the construction system of the skene. The ceiling suspended over the playing areas consists of a beam grid and louvered panels to permit lighting from any position. The audience enters the theatre above and behind the stage seeing the orchestra, stage, and theatron through the open wall before circling the stage to enter the theatre and reach the seats.

New Comedy used costumes which were reasonably close copies of everyday garments, and masks which depicted basic character types of the period. Altogether, it marked a movement toward realism in staging, and toward conventionalization in depicting human behavior.

At the same time, the staging of tragedy moved further away from realism. It is to this period (usually called the Hellenistic age) that the distorted masks, high headdresses, thick-soled boots, and padded bodies of tragic actors belong. New theatres were built with stages raised from nine to twelve feet above the level of the orchestra. The actor became increasingly the center of interest as he performed on this new stage high above the orchestra. Plays now ceased to be produced exclusively at the Dionysian festivals and were given on many other civic or religious occasions.

As the fondness for theatrical performances grew, the demand for trained personnel became so great that performers organized the Artists of Dionysus, which furnished actors, trainers for choruses, musicians, and other personnel needed for the production of plays. It set fees for services, and its rights were recognized by international agreement. Many of its members were exempt from military service, had freedom of travel, and frequently served as ambassadors between states.

In the third century B.C. Rome began to expand as a power and came into contact with the theatre for the first time. As it absorbed the Hellenic world it took over the theatre and transformed it in accordance with its own needs. The distinctively Greek theatre had almost disappeared by the second century B.C. and from then until the sixth century A.D. the theatre was to be principally a Roman institution.

Chapter 5 ROMAN THEATRE AND DRAMA

Tradition has it that Rome was founded in the eighth century B.C. At first a small town of little consequence, it did not begin to assume prominence until the third century B.C. But by the beginning of the Christian era it had extended its power over most of the known world.

The Romans were remarkable for their ability to assimilate whatever attracted them elsewhere. Thus, when they found drama in the Greek colonies in Sicily and southern Italy, they imported it to Rome.

Although performances of a theatrical nature may have been given in Rome at an earlier date, the first regular dramas were performed in 240 B.C. These plays were the work of Livius Andronicus, a Greek, and from this time drama was a recognized part of Roman life. Almost every element of Roman theatre and drama was an alteration of some Greek practice. This does not mean, however, that the Romans made no contributions, for their tastes led them to much that was original.

Unfortunately, out of the vast number of Roman plays the works of only three dramatists survive: twenty-one comedies by Plautus, six comedies by Terence, and nine tragedies by Seneca. The comedies of Plautus and Terence date from about 205 to 160 B.C., the tragedies of Seneca from the first century A.D.

ROMAN FESTIVALS

The *ludi*, or festivals, in Rome at which plays were performed, were not associated with the worship of Dionysus, but were of various types. Most were official religious celebrations, but some were financed by wealthy citizens for special occasions, such as the funeral of a distinguished figure or the triumphal entry of a victorious army. Originally (in 240 B.C.), drama was given only at the *ludi Romani*, or Roman Games, and

88

was probably restricted to a single day. But the popularity of dramatic entertainments insured their gradual expansion, and as the number of Roman festivals was increased so were the occasions for presenting plays. By 78 B.C., 48 days each year were devoted to dramatic entertainments at religious festivals. By A.D. 354, there were 175 public festival days of which 101 were devoted to theatrical spectacles.

In the time of Plautus and Terence (the second century B.C.), plays were given principally at four festivals. The *ludi Romani*, held in September, devoted at least four days to drama; the *ludi Plebeii*, established in 220 B.C. and held in November, gave over at least three days to plays; the *ludi Apollinares*, begun in 212 B.C. and held in July, devoted approximately two days to drama; and the *ludi Megalenses*, initiated in 204 B.C. and held in April, had six days of theatrical entertainments.

All state-financed festivals were religious celebrations in honor of the gods, but the Romans were more concerned with the letter than the spirit of the celebration. They believed that each festival, in order to be effective, must be carried through according to prescribed rules and that any mistake necessitated the repetition of the entire festival, including the plays. Since such repetitions were frequent, many more days were devoted to drama than might be supposed.

Scene from a Roman comedy. After a wall painting in Pompeii. From Navarre, *Dionysos*, 1895.

As in Greece, production expenses were undertaken by the state or by wealthy citizens. The Senate made an appropriation for each festival as a whole, and frequently the officials in charge contributed additional funds. These officials normally contracted for productions with the managers of theatrical companies, who then were responsible for all details of production: finding scripts, providing actors, musicians, costumes, and so on. Although each manager was assured of a certain sum of money, special incentives were provided in the form of prizes for the most successful troupes. The manager probably bought the play script outright from the author; it then remained the manager's property and might be played as often as he wished or as audiences demanded.

Admission was free to everyone, seats were not reserved, and audiences were unruly. The programs were lengthy, being composed of a series of plays. No refreshments were available in the auditorium and, since the plays often had to compete with rival attractions, the troupes were forced to provide a kind of entertainment that would satisfy the tastes of a mass audience.

THE THEATRE AND STAGE IN THE TIME OF PLAUTUS AND TERENCE

Besides paying basic production expenses, the state supplied the theatre in which plays were presented. In the time of Plautus and Terence, it was a temporary one, for no permanent theatre was built in Rome until 55 B.C. Since plays were given in connection with religious festivals, each of which honored a specific god, and since each god had his own precinct and temple, it is likely that at each festival a theatre was set up near the temple of the god being honored.

Current ideas of the features of the early theatre are derived largely from the extant stone structures. Most of the surviving theatres, however, date from the first century A.D. or later, and do not necessarily provide an accurate picture of the temporary structures.

The theatre of Plautus and Terence probably included: temporary scaffolds (outlining a semicircular orchestra) which provided seating for the spectators; and a long narrow stage rising about five feet above the orchestra level (the existing stages are over one hundred feet long), which was bounded by the stage house at the back and ends.

The appearance of the stage background, called the *scaenae frons*, is disputed. Some think that it was a flat wall upon which columns, statues, or other details were painted. Others believe that there were three-dimensional niches and porticoes and, for evidence, point to the many scenes in Roman comedy which require one character to remain unseen by others, even though all are on stage at the same time. The back wall of the stage probably contained three openings, each of which might be treated, in comedy, as the entrance to a house. The stage then became a street, and the entrances at either end of the stage were assumed to be continuations of that street. Since windows and a second story are also required by some plays, the background must have provided these as well.

90

Costumes in the Roman theatre varied with the type of play. The works of Plautus and Terence were adapted from New Comedy and retained the Greek setting and garments. Other playwrights, however, wrote of Roman characters, and the costumes varied accordingly. In either case, the costumes were similar to those of daily life, although those of the more ludicrous comic characters were perhaps exaggerated.

Since most of the characters in Roman comedy were "types," the costumes also became standardized. There is evidence to suggest that certain colors were associated with particular occupations, such as yellow with courtesans and red with slaves. This conventional use of color extended to wigs as well. All of the actors wore masks, which made the doubling of parts much easier and simplified the casting of such roles as the identical twins in *The Menaechmi*. Each actor in comedy also wore a thin sandal or slipper, called a *soccus*.

Although there were numerous comic writers in Rome, works by only two—Plautus and Terence—have survived. Titus Maccius Plautus (c. 254–184 B.C.) is the earliest Roman playwright whose works still exist. Innumerable plays have been attributed to him, but the titles of only twenty-one have been agreed upon, all of which survive. The oldest dates from about 205 and the last from about the time of Plautus' death. Some of the most famous works are: *Amphitryon, The Pot of Gold, The Captives, The Braggart Warrior* and *The Twin Menaechmi*.

Publius Terentius Afer, commonly called Terence, was born in 195 (some accounts say 185) and died in 159 B.C. A native of North Africa, he was brought to Rome as a slave, was later freed, and became the friend of many of the great men of his day. He wrote only six plays, all of which still exist: *The Woman of Andros, The Self-Tormenter, The Eunuch, Phormio, The Mother-in-Law*, and *The Brothers*.

All existing Roman comedy is based on Greek New Comedy, although significant changes have been made in the process of adaptation. First, the chorus has been abandoned, doing away with the division into acts or scenes. (The divisions found in most modern editions were made in later times.) Second, the musical elements formerly associated with the chorus have been scattered throughout the plays. In some respects a Roman comedy resembled a modern musical, for certain scenes were spoken, others recited to musical accompaniment, and there might be a number of songs. In Plautus' plays about two-thirds of the lines were accompanied by music, and the average number of songs were three. Although Terence did not use songs, music accompanied approximately half of his dialogue.

Roman comedy, like Greek New Comedy, does not concern itself with political and social problems, but with everyday domestic affairs. Almost invariably the plots turn on misunderstandings of one sort or another:

mistaken identity (frequently involving long lost children), misunderstood motives, or deliberate deception. Sometimes the misunderstanding leads to farce, as in many of Plautus' plays, but it is also used for sentimental effects by Terence, who emphasizes the problems of lovers or parent-child relationships.

Plautus typically employed a single plot and a complicated intrigue. In an expository prologue he explains the dramatic situation, the farcical possibilities of which are developed in the episodes. Terence, on the other hand, uses a double plot, dispenses with the expository prologue, and treats his characters with sympathy and delicacy. His plays may be classified as romantic comedies, whereas those of Plautus are usually comedies of situation.

Roman comedy deals with the affairs of the well-to-do middle class, and the characters fall into clearly defined types: the old man who is concerned about his wealth or children, the young man who rebels against authority, the slaves, the parasite, the courtesan, the slave dealer, and the cowardly soldier. A number of other types appear with less frequency. Of all the characters, the most famous is perhaps the slave, who, to help his master, devises all sorts of schemes, most of which go awry and lead to further complications. Very few respectable women appear in Roman comedy, and while love affairs may be the source of a play's misunderstandings, the women involved are often kept off stage. The number of characters varies from seven to fourteen, although the average is from ten to twelve.

All action takes place in the street. This often leads to the necessity of staging scenes out of doors that would more logically occur inside, and characters must frequently explain what has happened indoors. Occasionally the conventions of Roman comedy strain the modern reader's belief, but they were apparently accepted without question by Roman audiences.

The Menaechmi, probably the most popular of Plautus' plays, will be examined as an example of Roman comedy. In it, the comic possibilities of mistaken identity involving identical twins are handled with especial effectiveness.

THE MENAECHMI

PLOT AND STRUCTURE.   As in most of Plautus' plays, *The Menaechmi* begins with a prologue which clarifies the backgrounds of the dramatic action. All important information is repeated more than once. At the same time, Plautus works in several jokes about the theatre, and tries to put the audience in a comic frame of mind.

Following the prologue, the introductory scenes of the play establish the present conditions out of which the comedy will grow: the dispute between Menaechmus I and his wife; the visit of Menaechmus I to the courtesan, Erotium, his gift to her of a dress stolen from his wife, their plans for a banquet later in the day, and the departure of Menaechmus I to the Forum; the entrance of Menaechmus II and his slave, Messenio. The remainder of the play presents a series of scenes in which the two

Production photograph of Plautus' *The Menaechmi*. Directed by Harrold Shiffler; scenery by Richard Baschky.

Menaechmi are in turn mistaken for each other and accused of acts about which they know nothing. Eventually they meet, and the complications are resolved.

Menaechmus II's failure to guess the cause of his difficulties, inasmuch as he has come to Epidamnus to look for his identical twin, is sometimes said to be a weakness in the play. Indeed, even when he is brought face to face with his brother, he is unable to recognize the truth until it is pointed out by his slave. Plautus has overcome this objection in part, however, by having Messenio warn Menaechmus II that Epidamnus is famous for its swindlers. Messenio even suggests that Erotium, who greets Menaechmus by name, has sent a servant to the docks to seek out information about new arrivals.

Plautus has been less successful in making Menaechmus II's search for his brother believable. Both twins are depicted as completely selfish men, and consequently it seems unlikely that Menaechmus II would devote years to seeking a brother he has not seen since early childhood. But such objections are quibbles in the light of Plautus' main intention—to entertain his audience. In performance the inconsistencies go unnoticed, and it is only on reflection that they become obvious.

Plautus subordinates everything to his main purpose. He brings characters on stage when he needs them and sends them away when the need is gone. Although this is not unusual in drama, Plautus does not always try to hide his contrivances. For example, the wife of Menaech-

93

mus I sends for her father, and he appears four lines later though he lives some distance away; in other cases, Plautus allows characters to see each other only when it suits his dramatic purposes. He also uses eavesdropping as a motivation for a number of complications.

Nevertheless, Plautus has developed his material with great economy. Not only has he eliminated everything that does not contribute to his principal aim, but he has made effective use of such devices as the stolen dress. This garment is a source of unity since it passes through the hands of practically all the characters and is used as evidence to support almost all the charges brought against the two Menaechmi.

Although Plautus' comic sense is everywhere evident, it may be seen at work especially in the reunion, which might have concluded the play on a sentimental note. Instead, the final lines give the story a twist in keeping with the sophisticated tone of earlier scenes: Menaechmus I offers all of his goods for sale—including his wife, if anyone is foolish enough to buy her.

CHARACTERS AND ACTING. The characters of *The Menaechmi* bear a close resemblance to those found in the plays of Aristophanes, for they too are motivated principally by selfish and material interests. With the possible exceptions of Messenio and the father, none of the characters may be considered admirable. Unlike Aristophanes, however, Plautus has little interest in social satire. He concentrates on the ridiculous situation without exploring its significance. Consequently, when his characters indulge in adultery, stealing, or deception, they merely contribute to the over-all tone of good-humored cynicism.

As in most Roman comedy, the characters in *The Menaechmi* are types rather than individuals. Some roles are summed up in their names: Peniculus (or "Brush") suggests the parasite's ability to sweep the table clean; the cook is called Cylindrus (or "Roller"), and the courtesan is named Erotium (or "Lovey"). Each character has a restricted number of motivations: the twins wish to satisfy their physical desires; the wife wants to reform her husband; the father desires to keep peace in the family; and the quack doctor is seeking a patient upon whom he can practice a lengthy and costly treatment. In spite of the restricted number of traits, however, each character is sufficiently delineated for its purpose in the play.

The ten speaking roles of *The Menaechmi* could easily be performed by a company of six actors. In the Roman theatre, all parts were played by men, and extras (used in nonspeaking roles) were employed as needed. The play does not require actors who are skilled in the subtle portrayal of a wide range of emotions. Rather, they must have that highly developed comic technique which produces precision in the timing of business and dialogue. The scenes of quarreling, drunkenness, and madness indicate that physical nimbleness is essential.

SCENERY AND MUSIC. Since *The Menaechmi* is set in a street before two houses, the stage and its architectural background would be suffi-

94

cient to meet the scenic demands. The frequent eavesdropping and the failure of characters to see each other suggest that there probably were alcoves or projections in which the actors could conceal themselves, although this would not be essential.

The costumes were based on those of everyday Greek life, but were conventionalized according to social class, occupation, age, and sex. Each of the characters also wore a mask and wig. Since the performances took place out of doors and during the day, no artificial illumination was required.

Because the music is now lost, it is sometimes difficult for the modern reader to remember that music played an important role in the original production of *The Menaechmi*. Well over half of the dialogue was accompanied by the flute, and a number of the characters probably had "entering" songs on their first appearance. The total effect must have been comparable to that of present-day musical comedy.

Thus, *The Menaechmi* is a farcical comedy designed primarily to divert an audience. It is very successful in fulfilling this aim, and the play's worth is clearly demonstrated by the fact that it has continued to entertain audiences throughout the more than two thousand years which have passed since its first presentation.

OTHER ROMAN DRAMA

The Roman comedy which has survived is of the type called *fabula palliata* (*fabula* means play, and *palliata* designates a Greek garment worn by the characters). There were, however, several other kinds of Roman drama. The *fabula togata*, or comedy on Roman themes, while modeling its form and techniques on Greek New Comedy, drew its material from native life.

Tragedy also played an important role in the Roman theatre. As with comedy, Greece provided the models upon which the Roman playwrights built. Also like comedy, tragedy is usually divided into two types according to whether it used Greek or Roman themes. The former is called *fabula crepidata*, and the latter *fabula praetexta*. Both types featured horrifying plots, totally good or totally depraved characters, melodramatic effects, and bombastic speeches.

The only Roman tragedies which now exist are based on Greek themes and all are the work of Lucius Anneus Seneca (4 B.C.–65 A.D.), a philosopher, satirist, and one of Nero's principal advisers. Nine of his tragedies are extant, of which five are adapted from plays by Euripides. A tenth is sometimes attributed to Seneca, but is undoubtedly the work of a later author.

Seneca was not a professional dramatist and his plays probably were not staged. Nevertheless, he was a major influence on Renaissance tragedy, and therefore the characteristics of his work are of interest.

First, Seneca's plays are divided into five acts by choral interludes. These interludes, however, are largely irrelevant and can be eliminated without serious loss. Although the Renaissance dramatist seldom used a chorus, he was influenced by Seneca's five-act structure.

Second, Seneca wrote elaborately constructed speeches which often resemble forensic addresses, and his work as a whole tends to emphasize rhetorical display. The presence of similar qualities in Elizabethan drama may be attributed in part to his influence.

Third, Seneca, as a moral philosopher, filled his plays with *sententiae* (brief moral conclusions, resembling proverbs, about human behavior). The plays abound with sensational deeds, which illustrate the evils of unrestrained emotion. The characters often lack self-control and set out to perform evil acts from which they cannot be dissuaded. Thus, moral lessons are taught through horrifying examples and sententiae, a practice followed by many Renaissance dramatists.

Fourth, Seneca's plays show many violent actions. In *Oedipus*, Jocasta kills herself on stage by ripping open her abdomen; in another play, a dismembered body is reassembled; and in *Thyestes* the flesh of children is served at a banquet. Such deeds of horror are found also in many plays of the Renaissance.

Fifth, Seneca is preoccupied with magic and death, as may be seen from his frequent use of ghosts and magical rites. This emphasis on the close connection between the human and supernatural worlds may be found in Renaissance drama as well.

Sixth, each of Seneca's main characters is dominated by a single motive which drives him to his doom. Most frequently the motivations, such as revenge, are either evil or obsessive. Again, this practice was to be taken up by writers in the Renaissance.

Seventh, many of Seneca's technical devices were to influence later dramatists. Soliloquies and asides occur frequently, and most of the plays include a *confidant* (a character whose main function is to listen to and advise the principal character).

Today Seneca's plays are almost universally damned but they cannot be ignored, for when Renaissance writers turned to the past, they were attracted by his work rather than by that of the Greek tragedians.

In addition to comedy and tragedy, a number of minor dramatic types were performed in the Roman theatre. After the first century B.C. there is no record of an author making a living from regular comedy or tragedy. Rather, the stage was taken over by minor dramatic forms—the *fabula Atellana*, the mime, and the pantomime.

The *fabula Atellana,* a short farce, was one of the oldest of Roman theatrical forms, having been imported from Atella, an area near Naples. It usually employed a set of stock characters: Maccus, a fool or stupid clown; Bucco, a glutton or braggart; Pappus, a foolish old man who

An ivory statuette of a tragic actor, probably Roman, although the Greek tragic actor of the Hellenistic period probably wore similar costumes and masks. Note the high headdress, distorted features of the mask, and thick-soled boots concealed beneath the robe. The statuette stands on two pegs, by means of which it was attached to a base, now missing. Reprinted from *Monumenti Inediti*, Vol. XI (1879).

The *fabula Atellana* and mime were probably influenced by the *phlyakes* comedy of Sicily and southern Italy. *Phlyakes* comedy dealt primarily with mythological travesty and farcical situations; it flourished c. 400-200 B.C. As this vase painting shows, the costumes were similar to those of Greek Old Comedy. From Dorpfeld-Reisch, *Das Griechische Theater,* 1896.

was easily deceived; and Dossenus, a cunning swindler and glutton, who was probably hunchbacked. Originally, the dialogue was probably improvised. The plots revolved around various forms of trickery, cheating, and general buffoonery in a rural setting. Music and dance also played an important part. After the *fabula Atellana* was converted into a literary form in the first century B.C., the short farce became the most popular dramatic type.

The mime may be traced back to the sixth century B.C. in Greece, but the earliest record of its appearance in Rome is 212 B.C. Many mime troupes traveled widely and performed on makeshift stages. Their plays were short, topical, farcical, and, in the beginning, improvised. While the mime had certain features in common with the *fabula Atellana*, there were also important differences: the female roles were played by women (the earliest record of actresses), no masks were worn, and the subject matter was primarily urban.

Like the Atellan farce, the mime became a literary form in the first century B.C. The subjects of the later mime were often adultery and unnatural vices, and the language was frequently indecent. These characteristics set the rising Christian religion against the mime troupes, who retaliated by ridiculing the sacraments and beliefs of the church. Thus, the mime was more responsible than any other form for the church's opposition to the theatre.

One other dramatic type, the pantomime, was popular in late Rome. This silent interpretative dance was performed by a single actor who played many roles, each of which was indicated by a mask with a closed mouth. A chorus narrated the story, which was usually serious and drawn from mythology, while the action was accompanied by music. Pantomime largely replaced tragedy, being especially popular with the ruling classes.

The degeneration of the theatre under the Roman Empire — which superseded the Republic in 27 B.C. — is further illustrated by the fact that gladiatorial contests were held in the orchestras and on the stages of

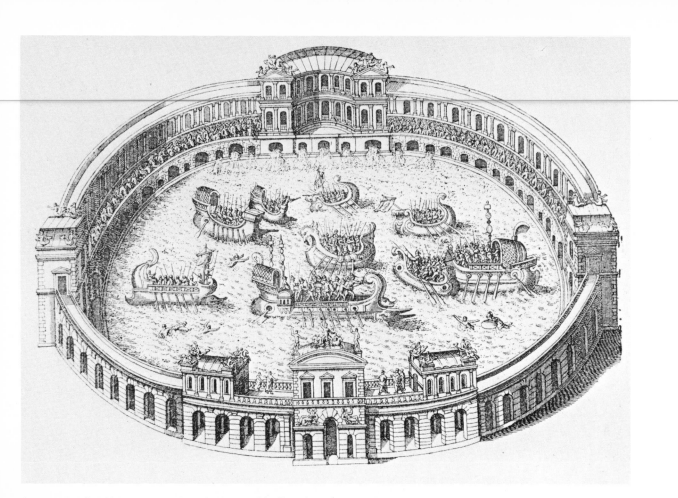

A somewhat fanciful reconstruction of a *naumachia*. From Lau-
mann, *La Machinerie au Théâtre,* 1897.

theatres. Furthermore, in many theatres the orchestras could be flooded
for the presentation of sea battles—called *naumachia*. Spectacular, sensational, indecent, and exotic elements were increasingly emphasized.
The plays of Plautus and Terence were occasionally staged, but during
the Empire the usual fare was mime, pantomime, and nondramatic
spectacle.

THE THEATRE BUILDING
OF THE ROMAN EMPIRE

The permanent theatres of both Greece and Rome were constructed after their great dramas had been written. The first permanent theatre on
the Roman plan was built at Pompeii about 75 B.C., for Rome itself did
not have a permanent theatre until 55 B.C. After this time new theatres
were built wherever Rome's dominance extended and most of the existing Greek theatres were remodeled along Roman lines. The latter structures are often called Greco-Roman theatres, since they display characteristics of both types.

The typical Roman theatre was constructed on level ground—unlike
the Greek, which used a hillside to support its seats. The stage house and
the auditorium were of the same height and formed a single architec-

tural unit. (In a Greek theatre, the scene building and the auditorium were not joined and were, in effect, two separate structures.) The orchestra of a Roman theatre was a half-circle with the front of the stage set on its diameter, and the seats of the auditorium following the lines of its circumference. The auditorium typically seated between ten thousand and fifteen thousand spectators, although some are said to have accommodated as many as forty thousand.

The stage itself was raised about five feet above the level of the orchestra, and measured 100 to 300 feet in length and 20 to 40 feet in depth. It had a permanent architectural background (called the *scaenae frons*) with a minimum of three doors in the rear wall (though frequently there were more), and at least one at either end of the stage. The *scaenae frons* was two or three stories high, was decorated with columns, niches, statues, and porticoes, and, in some cases, was gilded or painted.

A reconstruction of the theatre at Ostia. It is one of the oldest permanent Roman theatres, having been built between 30 and 12 B.C. From D'Espouy, *Fragments d'Architecture Antique.* Volume I, 1901.

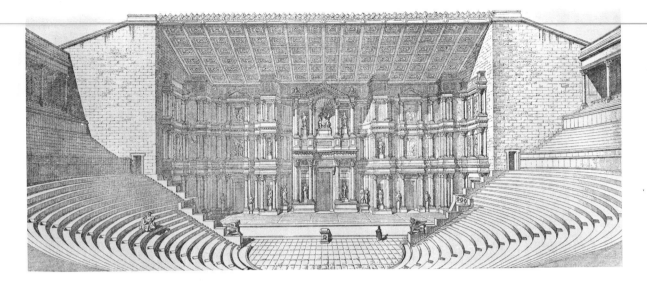

The Roman theatre at Orange is the best preserved in France and is now being used once more for theatrical performances. It was built in the first or second century A.D. Its *scaenae frons* measures approximately 118 feet high and 338 feet long. The illustration above is a reconstruction of the original theatre. The photograph below shows the same theatre in modern times. From Durm, *Die Baustile,* Volume II, 1905.

Two other features distinguish the Roman from the Greek stage. First, some time between 133 and 56 B.C., a curtain was introduced in the Roman theatre. It was dropped into a slot at the front of the stage at the beginning of a performance and was raised at the end. Second, the Roman stage had a roof, which served at least two functions: it protected the elaborate scaenae frons from the weather, and it improved the acoustics.

THE END OF DRAMA IN ROME

The immorality and decadence of the Roman theatre alienated the early Christians of Rome. At first Christianity was of little importance, but after it was recognized as the semiofficial religion of Rome by the Emperor Constantine, who ruled from A.D. 312 to 337, the theatre encountered increasing difficulties. Despite restrictions, however, performances continued to be popular and their eventual abandonment seems to have been due more to invasions from northern tribes than from moral scruples. By 467, Rome itself had twice been sacked. Although festivals were revived for a time, the last recorded performance is found in A.D. 533.

The accomplishment of the Roman theatre is not great when compared with the Greek, but it did produce three playwrights of importance — Plautus, Terence, and Seneca. Furthermore, its drama and theatre were to be major influences on Renaissance writers and theatre artists, and consequently they helped to shape the modern theatre.

Chapter 6 MEDIEVAL THEATRE AND DRAMA

Although it is sometimes stated that theatrical activities were completely suppressed throughout the Dark Ages, numerous contemporary documents attest to the continued presence of *mimes, histriones,* and *ioculatores* (Latin terms for actors). Little is known about these performers, however, for the opposition of the church made it difficult for them to present plays openly. Actors were forbidden the sacraments of the church, and, between the sixth and tenth centuries, religious authorities issued frequent injunctions both against presenting and attending theatrical performances. In addition to surreptitious theatrical activities, many pagan rites and festivals containing dramatic elements also persisted despite Christian opposition. For example, the dance around the Maypole, originally a fertility rite, continued to be performed in many parts of Europe.

The theatre could not develop openly again, however, until the church began to make use of dramatic interludes in its services. This introduction, begun in the tenth century, was the first step in restoring the theatre to a respected place in society, although this was not the church's intention.

DRAMA IN THE CHURCH

It is not clear why the church began to use dramatized episodes, but the most likely answer is that it wished to make its lessons more graphic. Furthermore, since the majority of persons could not understand Latin (the language of the church), spectacle had long been an important means of vivifying church doctrine, and dramatic interludes were merely a further development of this tendency.

102

The organization of the church year around the principal events of the Old and New Testaments also encouraged the development of drama. The calendar begins in November with Advent, a period of preparation for the birth and second coming of Christ; next comes Christmas and Epiphany (the revelation of Christ to the Gentiles); the forty days of Lent, which commemorate the wanderings of both the Israelites and Christ in the wilderness, is followed by the events connected with the death and resurrection of Christ, culminating in Easter; after Easter comes Ascension and Pentecost, or Whitsunday, the traditional time for baptisms. Thus, the church calendar itself suggested the dramatization of incidents appropriate to each season. Easter was the first to be given dramatic treatment in church services, but other events were dramatized later, although the majority of plays always centered around Christmas and Easter.

The oldest existing church playlet is the *Quem Quaeritis* trope, (c. 925 A.D.) reproduced here in its entirety. (A trope means any interpolation into the services.) As the three Marys approach the tomb of Christ, Angels say:

	Whom seek ye in the tomb, O Christians?
MARYS:	Jesus of Nazareth, the crucified, O Heavenly Beings.
ANGELS:	He is not here, he is risen as he foretold.
	Go and announce that he is risen from the tomb.

This simple beginning gradually grew more elaborate as both prior and succeeding incidents were added. For example, on the way to the tomb the women stop at a perfume-seller's stall to buy oils to anoint the body of Christ. After speaking with the Angels, they rush away to tell the Disciples of the Resurrection.

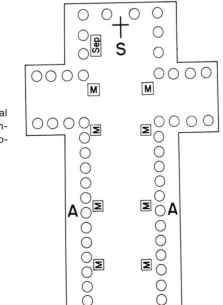

A ground plan of a medieval cathedral. A—aisles. M—mansions. S—sanctuary. Sep—sepulchre.

Drama was not produced in all churches of the period, being confined as a rule to cathedrals and monasteries—in other words, to those churches which had enough clergy to present plays. The actors, and sometimes the audiences, were priests.

Between approximately 950 and 1250 A.D., drama was staged indoors, but in the thirteenth century it began to be moved outside. By that time, staging conventions which were to be used until the sixteenth century had crystallized.

Stage space was divided into two parts: the *mansions*, and the *platea*. The mansions (also called stations, seats, or *sedes*) were simple scenic devices for indicating the location of incidents. For example, a throne might be used to suggest the residence of Pilate. Each place was represented by a different mansion, and all remained in view throughout the play.

Since the action could not be performed in the limited space provided by the typical mansion, the actors used as much of the adjacent floor area as they needed. Often the same space was used in many different scenes. This generalized acting area was called the *platea* (place, or playne). Thus, a series of mansions was arranged around a neutral playing space, and the performers moved from one mansion to another as the action demanded. (See the accompanying illustrations.)

THE REMOVAL OF DRAMA FROM THE CHURCH

Why drama was moved out of doors is not clear. The most likely answers are that plays had begun to interfere with church services and had become too elaborate for proper staging indoors. Although drama continued to be presented in some churches until the seventeenth century, in the majority the shift to outdoor performance came during the thirteenth century.

A page from the manuscript of the Valenciennes Passion Play, with the simultaneous depiction of several scenes. Courtesy of the Bibliothèque Nationale.

After drama was moved outside, secular organizations began to assist in its production, and by the late fifteenth century they had assumed the primary responsibility. In some areas, trade guilds became the principal producers of plays; in others, municipal authorities assumed control; in still others, special societies were formed to present religious dramas.

Many scholars have argued that the church abandoned the drama when it was moved outdoors. Recent studies, however, have questioned the correctness of this older view, for while the church participated less and less in the actual process of production, its approval continued to be necessary. Plays dealt with religious matters, and the church could not afford to ignore such powerful teaching instruments. Furthermore, each trade guild had its own priest, patron saint, and chapel, and was not entirely a secular organization. Thus, it is likely that the production of plays continued to be a cooperative venture, in which the church supplied approval and encouragement while secular groups provided the money and personnel.

Few changes were made in drama during the first century after it was moved out of doors. The plays were still, as a rule, performed in Latin and primarily by the clergy. But in the fourteenth and fifteenth centuries many changes occurred as secular influence increased.

After this time, plays were presented in the vernacular, or local languages, rather than in Latin. The introduction of nonclerical actors enlarged the supply of performers, and secular organizations began to provide considerable sums of money for the production of plays. All of these changes help to explain why the scripts written between the fourteenth and sixteenth centuries gradually increased the size of casts and the number of special effects. This elaboration reached its culmination in a French play at Bourges in 1536 which required forty days to perform.

STAGING TECHNIQUES

When drama was moved out of doors, it was staged at first before the west door of the church. This door usually opened onto a raised porch from which steps led down to the town square. The platform became a stage and the town square provided space for the audience. Later the stage was moved to other locations, but a long rectangular platform against a building remained the most typical arrangement in medieval staging. Many variations, however, were used. In some places the mansions were set up around the town square, and elsewhere the old Roman amphitheatres were used. Perhaps the most drastic departure was the practice of erecting mansions on wagons and drawing them from one place to another.

All of these arrangements, however, shared a number of characteristics. First, all used the staging conventions inherited from the church—a series of mansions and a generalized acting area. Second, the performances were made up of a series of short plays, each of which was more or less complete in itself. The order of the plays was determined by the Bible rather than by any causal relationship among them. Third, every series involved three planes of action—Heaven, Earth, and Hell—which

The stage for the Passion Play produced at Valenciennes, France, in 1547. From the left the various mansions represent: Paradise, Nazareth, the Temple, Jerusalem, a palace, the Golden door, the sea, and Hell's mouth. From a manuscript in the Bibliothèque Nationale; reproduced through their courtesy.

might be arranged either horizontally or vertically. The typical platform stage used a horizontal placement, with Heaven always on the right and Hell on the left (as one faced the audience). The earthly scenes were staged between these two points. On the wagons heaven, earth and hell were often arranged vertically, although a single wagon seldom depicted all three levels.

Fourth, the greatest attention was devoted to special effects, which were made convincingly realistic. Although such efforts may be explained in part by a love of spectacle, an equally important factor was the fear of raising doubts about the miraculous events described in the Bible. Regardless of their motives, medieval producers welcomed the challenge posed by such episodes as Christ walking on the water and being lifted up to the top of a temple. Special pains were also taken in the depiction of Hell and its horrors. The entrance to Hell was often represented as the mouth of a fire-breathing monster (hence the name *hell mouth*), and fire, smoke, and the cries of the damned issued from within.

To achieve these special effects, a considerable amount of stage machinery (called *secrets*) was invented. Much of it was operated from beneath the stage; numerous trap doors also permitted the appearance and disappearance of persons and objects. For the scenes which required "flying," pulleys and ropes were attached to adjoining buildings. The overhead machinery might be hidden by cloths painted to represent clouds or the sky.

106

Such machinery was not the work of inexperienced amateurs. As effects became more and more elaborate, skilled machinists and stage managers emerged. For a play staged at Mons in 1501, technicians were hired to construct the secrets, and seventeen people were needed to operate the hell machinery alone; five men were paid to paint the scenery, and four actor-prompters were employed both to act and to help with the staging. Thus, while the majority of persons connected with a production were amateurs, semiprofessional theatre workers gradually came into existence as productions grew in complexity.

Obviously special effects could be more extensive on a fixed stage than on a wagon. It is not surprising, therefore, that the stationary continental stages had more elaborate stage machinery than did the English pageant wagons.

It was not the sole aim of the medieval stage to produce convincing special effects, however, for these realistic features were coupled with fragmentary scenery and symbolic devices. No place was depicted in its entirety: a small building might represent Jerusalem; a chair under a portico might become the palace of Herod. Moreover, all of the places needed for the play were present simultaneously, thus further preventing the illusion of a real place. Typically, even the wagon stages carried more than one mansion.

The Fool and the Devil. From a woodcut in Sebastian Brant's *Ship of Fools,* published in 1497.

Just as the stage usually included mansions representative of Heaven, Earth and Hell, so too the costumes had to distinguish between the inhabitants of the three realms. God, the angels, the saints and certain Biblical characters wore church garments, often with added accessories. For example, angels wore church robes with wings attached, while God was dressed as a high church official. Each of the saints and important Biblical personages was also associated with a specific symbol. For example, St. Peter was identified by his keys to the Kingdom of Heaven. Since the audience was familiar with such visual symbolism, the mere display of an emblem served to identify the character.

Secular, earthly characters wore the contemporary medieval garments appropriate to their ranks, for there was no attempt to achieve historical accuracy. The greatest imagination went into costuming the devils, who were usually fancifully conceived with wings, claws, beaks, horns, or tails. While Heaven and its representatives were intended to inspire awe and reverence, Hell and its inhabitants were expected to arouse fear and scorn. The human beings who dwelt between were representative of the common man caught between the forces of good and evil.

CONVENTIONS OF THOUGHT AFFECTING MEDIEVAL DRAMA

Since we no longer think in medieval terms, some attempt to recapture the concepts of the Middle Ages is essential; otherwise the drama of the period is apt to seem childish and naïve. Man was said to participate in two kinds of time, eternal and temporal. God, the Devil, and man's immortal soul exist in eternity which has neither beginning nor end, unlike man's physical existence. If man considers only his earthly life, therefore, time may appear to be limited, but if he contemplates God, he sees that life is merely a preparation for eternity, in which his immortal soul participates. When he leaves his earthly existence, he enters into either eternal salvation or damnation. Thus temporal existence is a short interlude, a preface to the ultimate reality, which is eternal. The central part of the stage then—the earthly and temporal realm—was framed by Heaven and Hell, the eternal realms, one of which man must choose.

For the medieval mind, earthly time and place were relatively unimportant. The historical period or geographical location of an event were insignificant when set against the framework of eternity. Consequently, no sense of history is found in medieval plays. Audiences were not offended when ancient Israelites or Roman soldiers were dressed in medieval garments, or when Old Testament characters referred to Christian saints.

The fluidity of time is partially reflected in the structure of medieval cycles, in which a series of short plays dramatized Biblical material beginning with Creation and concluding with the Last Judgment. Although not all cycles were so ambitious, most of them encompassed lengthy segments of time and a variety of events. There was seldom any causal relationship among plays and often not even among the incidents of a single play. Again, however, such techniques are not necessarily signs of poor playwriting. For the medieval mind, Providence played a large part in human affairs, and events were thought to happen simply because God willed them. Since an audience brought this frame of reference to the theatre, it did not demand to see it overtly dramatized in plays.

Another factor which sometimes puzzles the modern reader is the presence of comic elements in religious plays. Our austere view of religion, however, dates only from the Reformation of the sixteenth century. Prior to that time, the church permitted many satirical elements in its festivals. The Feast of Fools, for example, was a kind of New Year's rite during which the minor clergy were allowed to ridicule the mass and the church officials. It is not surprising, then, that comic elements were included in plays. Usually, however, comedy was confined to devils, evil persons, or non-Biblical, lower-class characters.

THE MYSTERY PLAY

The mystery play, which drew its subjects from scripture, was the major form of medieval drama, being produced throughout western Europe. Its name is probably derived from *mystère*, the French word used in the Middle Ages to designate any trade or craft. Thus, "mystery" came to mean those plays produced by the trade guilds. Other names were used elsewhere. In Italy, *sacre rapresentazione* and in Spain, *auto sacramentale* were common designations.

An episode from "The Creation of Noah's Ark;" *The Wakefield Mystery Plays.* Production photograph courtesy of the Mermaid Theatre at Puddle Dock, London.

The dramas most readily available for study are those written in English. Although cycles of mystery plays were produced in over one hundred English towns during the Middle Ages, most of the extant plays are from four cyles: the York, containing forty-eight plays; the Chester, containing twenty-four; the Townley manuscript plays, or Wakefield cycle, containing thirty-two plays; and the Coventry or N_____

_____Town (the blank was to be filled in with the name of the town where the cycle was being performed) cycle (now thought to have originated at Lincoln) containing forty-two plays.

STAGING OF CYCLE PLAYS IN ENGLAND DURING THE FIFTEENTH CENTURY

English plays were usually staged as a part of the Corpus Christi festival (honoring the sacraments of bread and wine, or the *host*), which falls somewhere between May 23 and June 24. The essential feature of the Corpus Christi celebration was a procession of the host through the town. It may be for this reason that several towns in northern England adopted the processional form of staging—that is, the mounting of plays on wagons, and the movement of these wagons to a series of places throughout the town.

Although plays were not given each year, they were presented at reasonably regular intervals, and on those occasions the Corpus Christi festival was extended, since an average of four or five days was needed to perform the cycles. The town council decided whether the plays were to be included, and the guilds assumed primary responsibility for production.

Each trade guild was assigned one play, or, in the case of small guilds, two or more might produce a play together. The master copy of the cycle, which had the approval of the church, was retained by the town council, and each guild was cautioned to stage its play with care and to remain faithful to the text. A fine was imposed if a guild was proven negligent.

No adequate description of the pageant wagons has been preserved. They were probably as large as the narrow city streets would permit and were designed to meet the requirements of specific plays (each guild

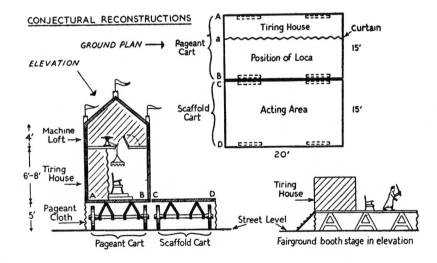

A conjectural reconstruction of an English pageant wagon and stage. From Glynne Wickham's *Early English Stages,* Volume I, 1959. Courtesy of Columbia University Press and Mr. Wickham.

Reconstruction of a medieval pageant wagon. From Sharp's *A Dissertation on the Pageants or Dramatic Mysteries,* 1825.

always presented the same play). A wagon almost always had to carry two or more mansions, and might need machinery for special effects as well. In some plays, places or characters were "discovered" during the action; in others, persons or objects ascended or descended either from above or beneath the stage. The account books of the guilds show sizable expenditures for painted drops, curtains, properties, special effects, and for the pageant wagon itself.

There is much disagreement as to where the acting took place. Some argue that it occurred only on the wagon; others believe that the actors used both the wagon and the street; and still others state that the wagons were pulled up alongside a platform, which served as the acting area, or *platea*, while the wagon provided the mansions. The final argument is a persuasive one, since the action of many plays is too complex to be staged on a wagon which also carried scenery. Furthermore, it appears unlikely that very many scenes were played in the street itself, for the standing spectators would have obstructed the view of much of the audience. On the other hand, the actors did make occasional use of the street, and it is possible that the wagon, a platform, and the street were all used as acting areas.

The actors were primarily amateurs, although they may have received some pay for their services, and account books indicate that they were provided with considerable quantities of food and drink during the rehearsal period. A few actors were paid large sums, however, and it is

Details from Denis von Alsloot's "The Triumph of Isabella," 1615. Although these wagons were not used for play production, they may be similar to those employed in staging the English cycle plays. Courtesy of the Victoria and Albert Museum. Crown copyright.

likely that these were skilled performers who played the leading roles, helped with the staging, and coached the other actors.

Most characters could be costumed from either the ecclesiastical, military, or civil garments of the day, but occasionally special costumes were required for the devils or other exotic figures. Music figured prominently in some dramas and was often used to fill the interval between plays. For the latter purpose, professional musicians were often hired.

Each guild presented its play at several places, the first of which was always the church or monastery. The other locations were chosen by the town council. Thus, audiences gathered at a number of points and the plays were brought to them in a manner which combined a parade and dramatic entertainment.

THE SECOND SHEPHERDS' PLAY

The Second Shepherds' Play is probably the best known of the English cycle plays. It is the thirteenth part of the Wakefield cycle, from which thirty-two plays—ranging from Creation to the Last Judgment—have survived. It is called the "Second" Shepherds' Play because it replaced an earlier segment on the same subject.

112

PLOT AND STRUCTURE. The majority of *The Second Shepherds' Play* is an elaboration of a single sentence from the *New Testament* (Luke 2:8): "And there were in the same country shepherds abiding in the field, keeping watch over their flock by night." This hint has been transformed into a medieval story rich in contemporary details and farcical humor. The number of shepherds is not specified in the Bible, but three are used in the play, probably to suggest a parallel with the three wise men.

Like most medieval dramas, *The Second Shepherds' Play* has an early point of attack. It introduces in leisurely fashion the characters and situation as each shepherd in turn complains about a different problem: general social conditions, marriage, insufficient food and drink. The opening is made even more casual by the inclusion of a song.

Yet this simple beginning serves several purposes which may not be readily apparent. First, through the various complaints, it depicts a world that needs some correction—one that stands in need of Christ's coming. Second, it relates the Biblical story to the contemporary scene and thereby to the audience. Thus, the coming of Christ is placed in the atmosphere of the Middle Ages. Third, the introduction prepares for an unusual occurrence by the third Shepherd's recital of abnormal conditions, concluding with:

> We that walk in the nights our cattle to keep,
> We see sudden sights when other men sleep.

There is little forward movement in the story, however, until Mak appears.

A production photograph of a scene from *The Second Shepherds' Play* at the Mermaid Theatre, London. Courtesy of the Mermaid Theatre.

Mak's reputation as a trickster is established immediately by the Shepherds' concern for their sheep. Soon, however, they all lie down for the night. When the Shepherds are safely asleep, Mak steals a sheep and carries it home to his wife, Gill. As a precaution against discovery, she suggests that they place the sheep in a cradle and pretend that it is a newborn baby. Mak then goes back to the fields and lies down as before.

The Shepherds awake and, with difficulty, arouse Mak, who has been feigning sleep. After Mak takes his leave, the Shepherds discover that a sheep is missing and they immediately suspect Mak. While the Shepherds search the house, Mak protests his innocence and Gill counterfeits post-childbirth pains. As they are leaving, one of the Shepherds remembers the child and insists upon presenting a gift to it; the sheep is discovered and Mak is tossed in a blanket as punishment. This portion of the play is closely related to the medieval farce (to be discussed later) in the characterizations of Mak and Gill, in the comic inventiveness of the plot, and in its resolution. It also shows much greater skill in writing than other parts of the play.

After recovering their sheep, the Shepherds return to the field. A marked change now takes place as the tone of the play becomes serious and devotional. An Angel appears and announces the birth of Christ; the Shepherds go to Bethlehem, worship the child and present their gifts. Christ has appeared within a familiar scene; his promise is not to some forgotten past, but to the immediate present.

THEMES AND IDEAS. *The Second Shepherds' Play* has frequently been viewed as a work composed of two unrelated stories of sharply contrasting tone. A close examination of the work, however, reveals that it is unified through its themes and ideas. The most important of these are man's depravity and the promise of salvation, placed side by side in the form of a demonstration.

The Shepherds symbolize the common man; they are involved first with Mak (the godless man) and then with the Christ child (God incarnate). The many parallels between the two stories suggest that this juxtaposition is intentional. In both there is a father, mother and child; the child is in a cradle; one "child" is a lamb, and the other is Christ, the "Lamb of God"; the Shepherds present gifts to both. The difference between the two stories is to be found in the significance of the events: one shows a world in need of Christ, and the other portrays his arrival. Succeeding plays in the cycle dramatized both the life and the teachings of Christ.

CHARACTERIZATION AND ACTING. There are seven roles—not counting the infant—in *The Second Shepherds' Play*. All parts were played by men, and the same actor could have played both Gill and Mary.

Little is indicated about the physical appearance of the characters. All are adults of unspecified age except the third Shepherd—a boy—and the Christ child—probably represented by a doll. The sociological traits are

114

also limited. The Shepherds, Mak and Gill, are peasants; it is implied that Mak lives by stealing.

Psychological characterization is slight, but effectively drawn. The three Shepherds are differentiated primarily through their opening monologues, in which each is concerned with a different problem. All are generous as may be seen from their reactions to the supposed child of Gill and to the Christ child, and from their decision not to prosecute Mak. (In medieval times, stealing was a capital offense.) A good impulse, the desire to give the "child" a gift, leads to the uncovering of Mak's guilt.

Mak is a clever knave, who is somewhat henpecked and cowardly. Gill is shrewish and clever; it is her idea to put the lamb in the cradle and pass if off as a child. The role of Mak requires more acting skill than any other. The comic plot progresses principally through him, and he must convey a rather wide range of responses, many of which are supposed to communicate one impression to the Shepherds and another to the audience. Since the sheep-stealing scenes are meant to be comic, both Mak and Gill must be able to convey the ludicrous aspects of the situation.

The Shepherds' roles, while longer than those of Mak and Gill, are more nearly serious and demand little exaggeration. They must project the humorous points in the opening speeches and be able to pass from the bantering tone of the first part to the devout tone of the final scene. There is a considerable amount of physical action in the play and, with the exception of the Angel's appearance, all of it is reasonably realistic. Transitional action, however, is indicated only sketchily. For example, the Shepherds lie down and appear to fall asleep instantly. The actors, therefore, must supply many details or the action will seem abrupt. Because they each have only one speech, Mary and the Angel are characterized least and seem especially stiff and stereotyped when compared to the other characters.

Most of the actors must sing. The Shepherds have a song in the introductory scene and another at the end of the play. Mak sings a lullaby to his stolen sheep, and the Angel sings *Gloria in excelsis.*

SPECTACLE AND MUSIC. *The Second Shepherds' Play* calls for three scenes—the fields, Mak's house, and the stable at Bethlehem. One mansion might be sufficient, however, since the fields really require no background, and the other two are so similar in scenic demands that the same mansion could be used in both.

No doubt the mansion used for Mak's house and the stable was equipped with a curtain which could be drawn to reveal the interior. Neither Gill nor Mary is visible throughout the play; rather each is "revealed" at the right moment. Mak's house must have a door (at which he knocks), a cradle, and a bed. All of these would be appropriate items for the stable (the bed for Mak's house need only be made of straw).

It is difficult to imagine this play, being performed on a wagon which would, at the very least, have to be divided into two parts. It is more logical to suppose that the wagon carried only the necessary scenic back-

115

ground and could be pulled up alongside another platform which would serve as the platea, or generalized acting area. Such an arrangement would effectively solve most of the difficulties of staging.

The costume demands for the play are simple: for the Shepherds, Mak and Gill, the everyday contemporary dress of the lower classes; for the Angel, an ecclesiastical garment with wings added; for Mary, an upper-class medieval garment (the traditional way of representing her in art by this time) and the symbols associated with her.

The musical requirements are also relatively simple. The Shepherds' first song and Mak's lullaby would have been contemporary popular songs. The *Gloria*, sung by the Angel, and the Shepherds' final song would have been taken from contemporary church music.

Although the staging demands are simple, *The Second Shepherds' Play* has a considerable range of visual and aural appeals. Its variety makes it an excellent example of that combination of teaching and entertainment which was typical of medieval drama.

COMPARISON WITH GREEK AND ELIZABETHAN THEATRE

Although there are few similarities between medieval and Greek plays, there are striking parallels in the conditions of theatrical representation. In the beginning both were intimately connected with religious observances and gradually became secularized. In both, the theatre was supported by wealthy citizens or organizations and was a combined civic and religious function open to all classes. Although the plays were presented at religious festivals, secular and comic elements were prominent in both.

On the other hand, medieval plays have much in common with Elizabethan drama, although there are few parallels in theatrical organization. By the end of the sixteenth century, the theatre had become a business enterprise and had almost totally ceased to perform religious or civic functions. The physical arrangement of the medieval stage continued to be influential, however, and many characteristics of Elizabethan drama are probably derived from the medieval play. These traits include: an early point of attack; a loosely organized plot which encompasses long periods of time and many places; a mixture of the serious and comic in a single play; and an interest in moral instruction.

OTHER RELIGIOUS DRAMATIC FORMS

Thus far, only church drama (often called *liturgical* drama) and cycle (or *mystery*) plays have been discussed. Actually, however, there are many kinds of medieval drama.

Miracle plays dramatize incidents from the lives and works of saints or martyrs. Although many of the deeds shown in the plays are fictional, all demonstrate miraculous powers at work or divine intercession in human affairs. This type of play was staged in connection with the feast day of the saint by groups especially associated with him. Although it was less extensively developed than the mystery play, it was an important part of medieval theatre.

116

A scene from *The Miracle of Notre Dame,* a French miracle play of the fourteenth century. The episode depicted is about Robert le Diable. From Pougin, *Dictionnaire Historique et Pittoresque du Théâtre* . . . 1885.

Morality plays flourished between 1400 and 1550. They are historically significant, since they dramatize the spiritual trials of the average man, whereas mystery and miracle plays treat Biblical or saintly characters. Thus, they form a bridge between religious and secular drama. Examples of the morality play include: *Pride of Life* (about 1410), *The Castle of Perseverance* (about 1425), *Mankind* (about 1475), and *Everyman* (about 1500).

The plays are allegories about the moral temptations which beset all men. The protagonist (usually called Mankind or Everyman) is advised and cajoled by personifications of good and evil (such as good and bad angels, the seven virtues, and the seven deadly sins), and is surrounded by such characters as Mercy, Good Deeds, Knowledge, Mischief, and Death.

The purpose of the morality play is clarified if the place of the action is considered to be man's soul, for it is the struggle to possess this battlefield which constitutes the drama. In the conflict, man seems to play little active part, because so many of the personifications are human drives and motivations. When these psychological forces are externalized, the protagonist is left with few traits. As a result, he is more apt to resemble a puppet than a human being. The other characters are also one-dimensional, since each personification represents only the essence of a quality, such as pride or wealth. The exception is Vice, a misguided, mischievous, and frequently humorous character sometimes used to satirize contemporary manners.

The most famous morality play is *Everyman*. It is somewhat atypical, however, because of its restricted scope. Whereas many morality plays cover man's entire life, *Everyman* deals only with his preparation for death. Everyman searches to find one among his former companions (Kindred, Goods, Beauty, Strength, Discretion, Five Wits) who will accompany him to the grave; eventually only Good Deeds goes with him. In his search, Everyman comes to understand his past life and its relation to his salvation. *Everyman* is a moving drama which has universal appeal, since all men must face death and must do so alone.

117

A scene from *The Salzburg Everyman,* a modern adaptation of *Everyman* by Hugo von Hofmannsthal, at the Goodman Memorial Theatre. Translated and directed by John Reich; setting — William Ryan; costumes — Sylvia Wintle; lighting — G. E. Naselius. Starring Donald Buka (clasped by Death). Courtesy of the Art Institute of Chicago.

During the sixteenth century the morality play was gradually secularized, and its typical subjects were replaced by such new ones as the proper training of rulers and the content of good education. Then, at the time of the religious reformation in England, it became a vehicle for controversy. For example, John Bale (1495–1563) mixed abstract figures with historical personages in *King John*, which denounced the papacy. Such changes moved the morality play increasingly toward a drama with completely secular subject matter and human characters.

Since morality plays came to be performed by small professional troupes, they are more closely connected with the development of professionalism than are cycle plays. Thus, both in content and presentation, the morality play pointed toward the establishment of a secular and professional stage.

SECULAR DRAMATIC FORMS

In addition to religious and didactic plays, there were a number of secular dramatic forms in the Middle Ages. The first, and probably least important, is the *folk play*, which depicts the adventures of such popular heroes as Robin Hood or St. George. The folk play is noteworthy principally, however, for such elements as sword fights, dances, deaths and resurrections, which are derived from pagan fertility rites. Folk plays were performed by amateurs, who went from house to house, usually at the Christmas season. This type of play, however, had little influence on later drama.

118

The *farce* is probably the most interesting and important of secular forms. It was especially well developed in France, although it also had important exponents in England, the best known of whom is John Heywood (*c.* 1497–1580). The farce is lacking in religious or didactic elements, and shows, rather, the ridiculous depravity of man.

Scene from *Pierre Patelin*. After a woodcut illustration in the first edition of the play printed in 1490. From *L'Ancienne France: Le Théâtre . . . , et La Musique . . .* 1887.

Probably the best example of medieval farce is *Pierre Patelin*, an anonymous French play of the fifteenth century. Patelin, a lawyer, is near financial ruin. He nevertheless persuades a merchant to let him have a fine piece of cloth. The merchant agrees to come to Patelin's house to collect his money and to have dinner. When the merchant arrives, Patelin is in bed, and his wife swears that he has not been out of the house. Patelin pretends madness, beats the merchant and drives him away. This part of the plot is rather loosely joined to a second one. Patelin meets a shepherd and agrees to defend him in court against a charge of sheep-stealing. He cautions the shepherd to answer only with a "baa" no matter what anyone says to him. In court, the accuser turns out to be the cloth merchant, who creates such bewilderment with his alternating charges against Patelin and the shepherd that the judge (in view of the confusion and the shepherd's seeming feeble-mindedness) dismisses the case. When Patelin tries to collect his fee, however, the shepherd runs away, calling "baa." The story shows a series of clever knaves outwitting each other. The final comic twist comes when the master knave is outwitted by an apparent simpleton. *Pierre Patelin* is filled with high spirits and cynicism; it has remained popular with audiences for centuries.

A booth stage such as might have been used by traveling players during the Middle Ages and Renaissance. After a colored design in a fifteenth-century manuscript. From *L'Ancienne France: Le Thèàtre* . . . , 1887.

A final dramatic form is the *secular interlude*, a nonreligious serious or comic play. It began to appear near the end of the fifteenth century, and was performed by traveling players or by troupes employed by noblemen. Such plays were probably called interludes because they were performed between the parts of a celebration (for example, the courses of a banquet). In the sixteenth century, the secular interlude was not always distinguishable from the morality play or the farce. All eventually came closer together and merged in Renaissance drama.

DECLINE AND TRANSITION

Many factors account for the decline of medieval drama. First, the increasing interest in classical learning (to be discussed in a later chapter) introduced many new concepts which affected the writing and staging of plays. Second, changes in the social structure gradually destroyed the feudal and corporate life which had encouraged such community projects as the presentation of cycle plays. Third, and perhaps most decisive, dissension within the church led to the prohibition of religious plays. After the Church of England was officially established in 1536, cycle plays were altered so as to delete any reminders of Rome. Continuing strife, however, caused Elizabeth I to forbid religious plays when she came to the throne in 1558. Although some of the cycles were performed after this date, they were gradually suppressed.

120

A banquet with interlude entertainment. A nineteenth-century reconstruction from Pougin's *Dictionnaire Historique et Pittoresque du Théâtre . . .* , 1885.

On the continent, a parallel movement was under way. The secessionist movements led to a demand for reformation in the Roman Catholic church. The Council of Trent, which was held intermittently between 1545 and 1563, attempted to purify the church of all objectionable practices. One result was the abandonment of dramatic entertainments as a means of religious teaching, except in the case of the Jesuits, who were permitted to have theatres in their schools. In 1548 religious plays were forbidden in Paris, and they were either prohibited or gradually abandoned elsewhere. It was only in Spain, where they were not outlawed until 1765, that plays continued to be an important part of religious festivals. For the most part, however, the drama of the Middle Ages had fallen out of favor by 1600.

121

Chapter 7 SPAIN AND ELIZABETHAN ENGLAND

Two European countries—England and Spain—developed strong popular theatres and major playwrights before the end of the sixteenth century. Although they were affected by the revival of interest in Greek and Roman culture, their theatres were logical outgrowths from medieval practices. Since the English theatre is of greater significance than the Spanish, it will be considered first and in greater detail.

THE EMERGENCE OF THE PROFESSIONAL ACTING TROUPE

Although there were wandering players in England by the fifteenth century, all professional actors were, under existing law, vagabonds and rogues. The only exceptions were those groups attached to the households of the nobility, since such actors were classified as servants. Before the end of the fifteenth century, the ruling family and many noblemen of England were maintaining acting troupes.

Legally, the actor was recognized for the first time in a statute of 1572, which stated that all players must obtain a license either from a nobleman or from two justices of the peace. No other actors were permitted to perform. While this ruling seriously restricted the number of theatrical groups, it did give those able to obtain licenses legal sanction for the first time.

The law of 1572 had allowed local officials (justices of the peace) to license companies, but in 1574 a new law assigned to the Master of Revels (a court official) the duties of examining all plays and licensing all acting companies. This placed the English theatre under the control of the central government.

To receive a license under the new arrangement, a troupe had to be under the patronage of a nobleman, who would allow it to use his name.

122

Equipped with this protection and a license from the Master of Revels, a company had a clear legal right to perform. Usually the nobleman contributed nothing to the financial support of the troupe which bore his name, except on those rare occasions when the company gave private performances at his request. In 1574 the first of these groups, the Earl of Leicester's Men, received a license from the central government. By 1600 there were always at least two companies playing in London, and frequently more.

Without the sanction of Queen Elizabeth and the nobles, the growth of the theatre in England would have been seriously hampered. For, unlike the upper classes who encouraged it, the middle class viewed the theatre with distrust. Many believed that it took people away from their jobs and thereby interfered with honest pursuits, that plays encouraged immorality, and that the theatre was only a camouflage for even more undesirable activities. The powerful town councils, largely composed of middle-class tradesmen, were opposed to professional theatrical activities of any kind.

The royal licensing of acting troupes did not quiet these objections to the theatre. Matters were complicated by the fact that the central government had neither a standing army nor a police force of any size, and had to depend on local authorities to enforce laws. Acting troupes, therefore, were tolerated rather than encouraged, and sometimes town councils paid actors not to perform.

The theatre was centered in London and it was there that the most strenuous objections were raised by local officials. They created so many obstacles that theatre buildings were erected outside the city limits to escape the jurisdiction of the London council. In spite of opposition, however, the protection of the central government permitted the theatre to develop, and by the 1580's it had established a strong foothold.

INFLUENCES ON THE DEVELOPMENT OF ELIZABETHAN DRAMA

The drama which emerged in the late 1580's may be traced to many influences: the schools and universities, the Inns of Court, and the popular theatre.

The revival of interest in classical learning began to be felt in England during the fifteenth century, but was not of major importance until the sixteenth century. As a result of this new interest, plays came to be studied and produced in schools and universities. This development of *school drama* may be divided into three phases: First, the plays of Plautus, Terence, and Seneca were read, studied, and performed in Latin. Second, Englishmen began to write plays both in Latin and English in direct imitation of the Romans. Third, English dramatists injected this classical influence into plays employing English subject matter and backgrounds. In this final phase, the imitation of classical models was largely unconscious, and the plays, although most frequently written and produced at universities, could easily be transferred to the public stage.

Some of the best early English plays were written and produced in the schools. *Ralph Roister Doister* by Nicholas Udall (1505-56) was proba-

123

bly performed at Eton while Udall was headmaster there between 1534 and 1541. *Gammer Gurton's Needle* (by "Mr. S") was acted at Cambridge University sometime between 1552 and 1563. Both of these plays belong to the second phase of development, for they show clearly the influence of Roman comedy.

Thus, schools and universities held a significant position in the development of Elizabethan playwriting, for they acquainted students with classical ideas of dramatic form and structure. Furthermore, English drama blossomed only after such school-trained dramatists as John Lyly, Thomas Kyd, and Christopher Marlowe began to write for the professional theatre.

The Inns of Court—combined residences and training centers for lawyers—were a second influence on the development of Elizabethan drama. Lawyers in this period came primarily from the upper classes, and many were interested in current trends in literature and the new classical learning. Like the schools, the Inns of Court produced plays for themselves and for important guests. The first regular English tragedy, *Gorboduc* by Thomas Sackville and Thomas Norton, was produced in 1561 for Queen Elizabeth. This work, which clearly shows the influence of Seneca's tragedies, is the first English play to be written in blank verse.

Although Elizabethan drama owes much to classical influence, to the schools, and to the Inns of Court, an equal or possibly greater debt is due the medieval drama and the plays produced by the professional troupes in the sixteenth century. The latter plays were a bizarre mixture of elements from all the preceding native drama and often contained a smattering of the new classical learning as well. Perhaps the most famous of these plays was written by Thomas Preston in the 1560's. The full title indicates both its method and contents: *A Lamentable Tragedie Mixed Full of Pleasant Mirth, Containing the Life of Cambises, King of Persia, from the Beginning of his Kingdom, Unto his Death, His one Good Deed of Execution, after that Many Wicked Deeds and Tyrannous Murders, Committed by and through Him, and Last of All, his Odious Death by God's Justice Appointed.* Set in Persia, it mixes local characters with abstractions typical of the morality play (such as Shame, Diligence, Trial and Proof), classical mythological figures (such as Cupid and Venus), and English low-comedy farcical types called Hob, Lob, and Marian-May-Be-Good. Probably no play demonstrates better the chaotic condition of popular drama between 1550 and 1585. It was out of these various influences that a new drama emerged between 1580 and 1642, when England produced many of the world's greatest plays.

PRINCIPAL DRAMATISTS PRIOR TO SHAKESPEARE

Although many dramatists of importance had appeared by the time Shakespeare began to write for the theatre around 1590, the most influential were Thomas Kyd, Christopher Marlowe, and John Lyly.

Thomas Kyd (1558–94) was educated at the Merchant Taylors School, where he studied Roman drama. His *The Spanish Tragedy* (around

1587) shows the influence of Seneca to a marked degree in its sensational subject matter, the motive of revenge, and the use of ghosts and a chorus. It achieved unprecedented popularity and, as a result, was extremely influential. The *revenge play* (of which *Hamlet* is an example) became a popular type of Elizabethan drama, but, more important, Kyd showed his successors how to construct striking situations, startling reversals, and suspenseful plots. Compared to Shakespeare's plays, *The Spanish Tragedy* seems crude, but it represents a remarkable advance in dramatic technique over the English plays which preceded it.

Christopher Marlowe (1564–93) was educated at Cambridge University and began writing for the theatre at about the same time as Kyd. The most important of his plays are *Doctor Faustus, Edward II, Tamburlaine*, and *The Jew of Malta*. Marlowe is generally regarded as the finest English writer of tragedy prior to Shakespeare. His principal contributions to Elizabethan playwriting are the perfection of blank verse as a medium for drama, and the organization of plays around one strong character whose motives are explored thoroughly. Furthermore, with the possible exception of Shakespeare, Marlowe developed the history play to its highest point.

John Lyly (*c.* 1554–1606) is noted principally for his prose comedies, written in an elegant and sophisticated style on themes taken from mythology. The plays have pastoral settings—a kind of "never-never land" where everything is delicate and graceful. They were widely admired and were considered important advances over the rather crude farces of the preceding era. The influence of Lyly can best be seen in Shakespeare's *A Midsummer Night's Dream, As You Like It*, and *Twelfth Night*.

THE ELIZABETHAN THEATRE STRUCTURE

Before considering how Shakespeare built upon the work of his predecessors, it will be helpful to examine the physical theatre and staging conventions for which he wrote between 1590 and 1615. The evidence is not always complete, and practice may have varied from one company or theatre to another, but the probable conditions can be outlined.

Two kinds of theatre buildings—open-air structures (those usually designated "Shakespearean" theatres) and indoor halls—were in use. The former are usually referred to as "public" and the latter as "private" theatres. Both were public in the sense that they were open to any spectator with the admission fee, but "private" theatres were smaller, charged higher prices, and played to a more select audience. Beginning about 1610, the same troupes played in public theatres in summer and in private theatres in winter. Since the public theatres were more characteristic of Shakespeare's day, the following discussion will treat them first.

A note of caution is in order. Since the early 1940's, John Cranford Adams' reconstruction of the Globe Theatre (the theatre used by Shakespeare's troupe) has been accepted by many as an accurate one. This reconstruction, however, is based largely upon conjecture and cannot be regarded as authentic; in fact, it is highly questionable in many of its

125

details. The truth is that we do not know enough about the Elizabethan theatre to make an adequate reconstruction of anything more than the broad outlines.

At least nine public playhouses, not counting remodelings and reconstructions, were built before 1615: The Theatre (1576–97), The Curtain (1577–c. 1627), Newington Butts (c. 1579–c. 1599), The Rose (1587–c. 1606), The Swan (c. 1595–c. 1632) The Globe (1599–1613; 1614–44), The Fortune (1600–21; 1621–61), The Red Bull (1605–63), and the Hope (1613–17). All were built outside the city limits, either in the northern suburbs or on the south bank of the Thames River. It is logical to assume that they differed considerably in details, just as theatres in any period do.

The theatres varied in size, but the most elaborate seated from two to three thousand spectators. They were of differing shapes: round, square, five-sided, eight-sided. Typically, they were laid out in this manner: a large central unroofed space, called the *pit* or *yard*, was enclosed by

Johannes de Witt of the Netherlands visited London in 1596 and made a sketch of The Swan Theatre. De Witt's friend, Arend van Buchell, made a copy of the sketch, which is reproduced here. De Witt's own drawing has not survived. Since this sketch is the only contemporary pictorial evidence, it influences attempts to reconstruct the Elizabethan theatre. From Bapst's *Essai sur l'Histoire du Thèàtre.* Paris, 1893.

three tiers of roofed galleries which formed the outside of the building. At the door to the theatre each person paid the same admission price. This entitled him to stand in the yard; if he wished to sit, he paid an additional fee and was admitted to the galleries. At least one gallery had some private boxes, or "Lords' rooms."

A raised stage (from four to six feet high) extended to the center of the yard. This large platform, sometimes called the forestage or main stage, was the principal acting area. Spectators could stand around three sides, and the galleries also commanded a view from at least three sides.

The greatest disagreement about the Elizabethan theatre concerns the *discovery space* (variously called the "inner below," the "study," and the "pavilion") at the rear of the forestage. In many plays of the period characters, objects, or places must be revealed or concealed. It is generally agreed, therefore, that there was an area at the rear of the main stage for this purpose. Its size and location, however, are disputed. The two major answers have been: (1) that this area was recessed into the back wall with a curtain across the front; and (2) that this area jutted onto the forestage like a pavilion and thus had curtains around three sides. Neither view can be established, though the weight of opinion is shifting toward the second. For our purposes it is sufficient to know that the large acting area jutting into the middle of the yard had two doors at the rear for entrances and exits, plus a space between which could be used for revelations and concealments. It may have been large enough for scenes to be played inside it, or it may have been similar to the medieval mansion (that is, only large enough to indicate a locale, while the forestage served as the *platea*).

Conclusions about the upper stage grow out of those about the discovery space. Those scholars who believe that there was an "inner below" state that there was a similar recessed space on the second level called the "inner above," while those who prefer the "pavilion" argue that there was an acting area on top of this forward projection. In either case, it is clear that there was an area on the second level which could be used by the actors. In addition, there were one or two windows on the second level out of which characters could lean or into which they might climb. The logical place for these would be above the two doors on the main stage. There may have been a third level which was occasionally used by actors in scenes supposed to occur in very high places but ordinarily reserved for musicians.

The basic outlines of the stage, then, are simple: (1) a large platform (at the Fortune Theatre, approximately forty-three feet wide by twenty-seven-and-a-half feet deep) jutting to the middle of the theatre structure; (2) a door on each side at the rear of this stage; (3) a discovery space; (4) an upper acting area on the second level; (5) windows on each side of the upper stage; and (6) possibly a third level.

This stage seems to have been designed for a continuous flow of dramatic action. As the actors left the forestage by one door at the end of a scene, another group might enter at the other door to begin the next scene; or the discovery space might be opened and the stage would be-

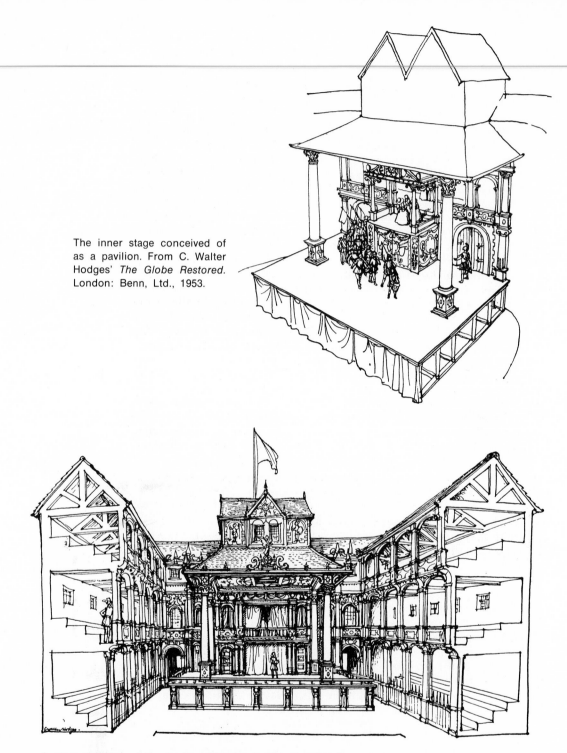

The inner stage conceived of as a pavilion. From C. Walter Hodges' *The Globe Restored.* London: Benn, Ltd., 1953.

A reconstruction of the Fortune Theatre built in London in 1600. The contract, which still exists, for this building is another principal source of information about the features of the Elizabethan theatre. Also from Hodges. Both courtesy Ernest Benn, Limited, London.

come a new place; or a scene on the forestage might be followed by one on the upper level; or more than one level might be used at the same time. One scene flowed into the next without pause. (Most of the plays were not divided into acts; such divisions were made by later editors.)

It is usual today to assume that no scenery was used in the Elizabethan theatre, but the records kept by Philip Henslowe (a businessman associated with the Admiral's Men) list such items as rocks, trees, beds, a hell mouth, and a cloth representing the "city of Rome." It is possible that there were a number of set pieces, or that mansions may have been put up occasionally as on the medieval stage. It is possible that mansions were used in the early years and later were discarded. It seems unlikely, however, that very much scenery requiring shifting was used, as it would have seriously interrupted the flow of scenes.

Machinery was housed both below and above the stage. Trap doors in the floor allowed for grave scenes, for the appearances of ghosts and devils, for fire and smoke, and for other special effects. Typically, a roof (supported by posts at the front of the stage) extended over the stage. Cranes, ropes, and pullies for raising and lowering objects were housed there. Sound effects for thunder, alarm bells, cannons, and fireworks were also operated in this area.

The first private theatre was opened in 1576 in Blackfriars, a fashionable residential area which had formerly been a monastery and which was still under the direct authority of the crown. Remodeled from a large room in one of the monastic buildings, it was used by boys' companies until closed in 1584. The second Blackfriars Theatre was built by James Burbage in 1596, perhaps in anticipation of moving there when his lease

Interior of the second Blackfriars Theatre as reconstructed by J. H. Farrar. Courtesy the Architect of the Greater London Council.

on The Theatre's site expired in 1597. The opposition of local residents put an end to his plans, however, and in 1600 the theatre was leased to the manager of another boys' company, which was extremely successful until 1608 when it was silenced for violations of censorship.

When the boys' company was forbidden, the Burbages resumed possession of the Blackfriars Theatre, which became the winter home of the King's Men after 1610. The success of this innovation led other adult troupes to open private theatres, of which there had been at least six in London by 1642. The private theatres rapidly surpassed the public theatres in prestige and soon the open-air structures were used only during the five summer months.

In basic features, the private theatres differed little from the public ones. Roofed and restricted in size, their seating capacities were only about one-fourth to one-half of that of the outdoor theatres. All spectators were seated in the pit, galleries (of which there were from one to three), or in private boxes. The stage (raised about three feet and without a proscenium arch or front curtain) and the background were similar to those in the public theatres and have been subject to the same scholarly debates. Since companies moved freely from public to private theatres, staging conventions must have been similar at both.

The Elizabethan theatre, with all its originality, included many features similar to those of past structures. For example, it depended primarily on a permanent stage facade for its scenic background, as had the Roman theatre, and the acting area was surrounded by spectators, as

The stage at the Oregon Shakespeare Festival in Ashland, Oregon. Courtesy Oregon Shakespearean Festival Association. Photograph—Dwaine Smith.

The stage of the Stratford Shakespearean Festival, Canada. Although it is an adaptation of many of the features of the Elizabethan stage, it is not an historical reconstruction. Courtesy Stratford Shakespearean Festival Foundation of Canada. Photograph — Peter Smith.

in the Greek theatre. Some features were clearly related to the medieval stage: the generalized acting area, the practice of having spectators stand in the yard, the special effects, and the possible use of mansions — all of these recall medieval theatre. But, the Elizabethan theatre combined these features in a unique structure which was both derivative and original.

LIGHTING AND COSTUMES

In the public theatres no artificial illumination was required, since the performances occurred out of door and in the afternoon. The private theatres probably used candlelight, but little is known of stagelighting practices. In both kinds of theatres, night scenes were indicated by bringing on candles, lanterns, or torches.

While little scenery was used, the Elizabethan stage was certainly not devoid of color and pageantry. Banners and other devices were employed to distinguish between armies or factions; there were many battles, processions, and dances. Most important, costumes were an ever present source of visual pleasure.

The costumes for the Elizabethan stage were of two basic kinds, contemporary clothing and conventional dress. By far the majority of roles were costumed in Elizabethan garments appropriate to the rank or profession of each character. Like the medieval, the Elizabethan mind had little sense of history, and characters from almost any place or time could be dressed alike.

On the other hand, however, certain stereotypes of the period made it necessary to set off some roles. Conventionalized costumes were used principally for: (1) special foreign groups, such as Romans, Turks, or Spaniards, (2) supernatural beings, such as fairies, classical gods, ghosts, and witches, (3) certain professional types, such as clerics, senators, and clowns, and (4) animals, such as lions, boars, and bears.

In spite of this apparent complexity, however, the majority of costumes were basically Elizabethan garments, and most of the conventionalized costumes were created by superimposing a few simple elements on contemporary dress. For example, Roman characters were identified by the addition of drapery to Elizabethan clothing.

131

Nevertheless, a large wardrobe was necessary, since each company changed its program almost daily and had many plays in its repertory. An actor might wear his own clothing in some roles, but the company assumed primary responsibility for costumes.

THE ACTING TROUPES

Adult acting companies included from ten to twenty members, of which approximately ten were shareholders, and the others hired men. After subtracting expenses, the company divided its receipts among the shareholders, while the hired men (the extras, doorkeepers, musicians, and stage hands) were paid a set wage comparable to that received by skilled laborers in other trades. Thus, shareholders had an interest in the financial affairs of the company, and the largest shares were usually allotted to the members most essential to the success of the troupe. Typically, upon the formation of a company, the shareholders agreed to stay together for a stated period of time, and the conditions under which a member might leave or under which new shareholders might be taken in were specified. The hired men were usually engaged for a period of two years.

If a company did not have sufficient capital to build a theatre, to buy costumes and equipment, it usually entered into an agreement with other persons to fill these needs. In return, these "householders" were given half of the gallery receipts, while the company retained the other half and all of the general admission fees.

Besides the adult actors, there were also apprentices (from three to five boys) who performed child and female roles. A boy began his apprenticeship when he was between ten and fourteen and continued until he reached the age of eighteen to twenty-one. At the end of his training, he might be taken into a troupe as a regular member, or he might enter another trade. Each boy was apprenticed to an individual actor who trained him and gave him room and board. The company paid the master for the boy's services.

Each actor probably specialized in a limited range of roles. The playwright, as a rule, wrote for a specific company and thus he could write for the special capabilities of the actors. At times this may have been a limitation, but it could also be advantageous since he knew what could be expected from each actor. The range of Richard Burbage (c. 1567–1619), who played most of Shakespeare's leading roles, suggests that he was one of the great actors of the English stage and he may have inspired Shakespeare to create complex roles.

The adult acting companies performed a large repertory, changing the bill almost daily. A play was repeated several times during a season if there was sufficient demand, and when no longer popular was dropped and a new work added. Each actor had to perform a great number of roles each season and was kept busy rehearsing and playing both new and old pieces.

The children's companies were composed primarily of choir boys at court chapels or cathedrals. Under the guise of training, the choir masters exploited their students' talents by staging plays for which they charged admission. In the children's companies, the masters were completely in charge and reaped the profits, which were considerable, especially from 1576 to 1584 and from 1600 to 1608, when the children rivaled the adults in popularity. The finest dramatists of the day, with the exception of Shakespeare, wrote for them and they were patronized by an elite audience.

Some companies paid dramatists a weekly salary to furnish a number of plays each season, while others bought plays outright. The playwright was expected to assist at the rehearsals of his works. Before a play could be performed, it had to be approved by the Master of Revels. Each actor's part (with cues) was then copied and given to him (he never received a copy of the entire play). A summary of exits, entrances, and the play's story was posted backstage so that actors might consult it during performances. The bookholder (who served as prompter or stage manager) kept the master (or prompt) copy of the play, in which were indicated exits and entrances, properties required for specific scenes, cues for stage hands and musicians. The bookholder probably stood behind one of the doors at the back of the stage and followed the performance through a grating.

On days when plays were to be presented, a flag was raised above the theatre. Performances were given regularly except during plagues, certain religious seasons, or upon the death or severe illness of a ruler or important public official. The audience was composed of all sorts of persons: noblemen, merchants, workmen, and women. No doubt the level of appreciation varied considerably among the members. Some playwrights wrote disparagingly of them, especially the "groundlings" who stood in the yard, while others praised their perceptivity.

SHAKESPEARE

William Shakespeare (1564–1616) is generally conceded to be the greatest of Elizabethan dramatists. Little is known of his early life, but by 1590 he seems to have been established in London, and by 1595 was a shareholder and actor in the Lord Chamberlain's company (later the King's Men). After 1599, he was a householder in The Globe theatre building as well. As householder, actor, director, and playwright, he was the most versatile theatrical figure of his age.

Shakespeare began writing plays around 1590 and completed about thirty-eight. Like most of his contemporaries, Shakespeare borrowed much from novels, older plays, history, mythology, and other sources. The plays have been divided into three groups: histories, comedies, and tragedies. In the histories he dealt with the English past, especially the period of the War of Roses. These plays (*Richard II, Henry IV*, Parts I and II, *Henry V, Henry VI*, Parts I, II, and III, *Richard III*, and *Henry VIII*) show his skill at reducing large masses of historical material to the demands of the stage. His comedies represent a wide range of styles. *The Comedy of Errors* (based on Plautus' *Menaechmi*), *The Taming of the Shrew*, and *The Merry Wives of Windsor* emphasize farce; *A Midsummer Night's Dream, As You Like It,* and *Twelfth Night* are romantic comedies; *All's Well that Ends Well, Measure for Measure,* and *Troilus*

133

Scene from *Macbeth* as presented at the American Shakespeare
Festival (Connecticut) in 1967. Photo by Shirley Herz. Courtesy
American Shakespeare Festival.

and Cressida are plays so nearly serious that they are frequently termed
dark comedies.

But it was in tragedy that Shakespeare displayed his greatest genius,
although here too he used a wide range of subject matter and treatment.
Romeo and Juliet, Hamlet, Julius Caesar, Macbeth, Othello, King Lear,
and *Antony and Cleopatra* must be ranked among the greatest tragedies
ever written. More problematical are *Titus Andronicus*, with its Senecan horrors, and the tragicomedies *Cymbeline, The Winter's Tale,* and
Pericles. Since it is impossible to discuss all of Shakespeare's plays, a
single work, *King Lear*, will be examined in detail.

KING LEAR

THEMES AND IDEAS. A basic theme of *King Lear* is the relationship of
parents and children; it appears in the main plot, concerning Lear and
his daughters, and in the subplot, dealing with Gloucester and his sons.
Since the parent–child relationship is a basic part of human experience,
King Lear has universal significance.

A second theme is appearance versus truth. Both Lear and Gloucester
are deceived (on very little evidence) by an appearance of perfidy and
lack of gratitude in children who are actually loyal and true, and both

134

accept as truth the lies told by their false children. As in *Oedipus the King,* a contrast is drawn between physical sight and spiritual blindness. Gloucester says, after his eyes have been put out, "I stumbled when I saw." In Lear's case, madness is substituted for blindness. The perfidy of his daughters causes Lear to lose his reason, but in this state he grasps the truth more firmly than when he was sane. As Edgar points out, Lear has found "Reason in madness!" Near the end of the play Lear and Gloucester explore the meaning of their experiences.

> LEAR. . . . yet you see how this world goes.
> GLOU. I see it feelingly.
> LEAR. What! Art mad? A man may see how this world goes with no eyes.
> Through tattered clothes great vices do appear;
> Robes and furred gowns hide all. Plate sin with gold,
> And the strong lance of justice hurtless breaks:
> Arm it in rags, a pigmy's straw does pierce it.
> . . . .
> Get thee glass eyes
> And, like a scurvy politician, seem
> To see the things thou dost not.

Both Lear and Gloucester learn the difference between appearance and truth—the difference between those like Cordelia and Edgar and those like Goneril, Regan, and Edmund. In one sense, then, the play dramatizes the results of choices made on the basis of appearance. Through suffering comes wisdom, though in Lear's case it comes too late.

A third theme concerns the degree to which man's fate is determined by forces outside himself. For instance, Gloucester, early in the play, suggests that strange happenings in human affairs are caused by a dislocation in the planets; later he says: "As flies to wanton boys are we to th'gods;/ They kill us for their sport." Fortune also is considered a governor of man's fate.

The opening scene of *King Lear* at the Oregon Shakespeare Festival, 1958. Courtesy Oregon Shakespearean Festival Association. Photograph—Dwaine Smith.

In the Elizabethan period, Fortune was frequently pictured as a goddess with a wheel, who might raise a man to the pinnacle of fame for no demonstrable reason and just as inexplicably dash him down again. It is in this context that Kent says: "Fortune, good night; smile once more; turn thy wheel." On the other hand, there are numerous suggestions that man's fate is determined by his own decisions. It is Lear's first choice which makes all of the later events possible; similarly, it is Gloucester's hasty belief in Edmund's lies that leads to his downfall. In the final scene, Edgar states: "The gods are just, and of our pleasant vices/ Make instruments to plague us."

These opposing views of human destiny are partially explained by the Renaissance conception of the universe. Man, as the final creation of God, was thought to be the center of God's concern, since God had created the earth and all its nonhuman inhabitants for man's use. Furthermore, it was believed that the entire universe revolved around the immobile earth. The planets were said to move in concentric spheres, one inside the other. Because all parts of the universe were connected like the cogs of a machine, the well-being of the whole was affected by each part. Harmony among all created a "music of the spheres," but chaotic conditions in any part were felt throughout the universe. This explains why physical manifestations of disorder play such a large part in Shakespeare's tragedies. The storm in *King Lear*, for example, is a metaphorical indication of the disruption of order.

To Shakespeare, man is not a mere puppet but an intelligent being free to choose his own path. Consequently, he frequently violates the divine order, and, when he does, he suffers accordingly.

No doubt there are other themes in *King Lear*, since the implications of such a great play cannot be easily exhausted. These three—parent-child relationships, appearance versus truth, and the degree to which man is free—are themes, however, which have interested men in all ages.

PLOT AND STRUCTURE. Shakespeare's skill in play construction may be seen by examining the over-all movement of the main plot. The opening scene establishes Lear's position as an absolute monarch. He disposes of the kingdom as though it were his own private property and passes sentence on his daughters and subjects without consulting anyone. He is accustomed to having every whim satisfied: he expects his daughters to express publicly their love for him, and he disowns Cordelia when she will not flatter him; he banishes Kent for presuming to offer advice. In this way Lear's character is established. Furthermore, without this scene it would be impossible to appreciate the extent of Lear's fall. The opening also prepares for later events by revealing the true motives of Goneril, Regan, Cordelia, and Kent.

Between this beginning and Lear's reunion with Cordelia near the play's close comes a series of humiliations for Lear which, though mild at first, lead to his abandonment in a raging storm and culminate in his madness. Although Lear's downfall is not undeserved, the undisguised

136

evil of Goneril and Regan arouse our indignation at his treatment and create constantly increasing sympathy for him. Compassion is aroused when Lear's growing recognition of his mistakes is accompanied by a loss of power to rectify them. In the storm scene he is completely stripped of authority and is forced to face himself as a man, alone, at the mercy of his inward torment just as he is at the mercy of the outward torment of the elements.

The scenes which follow the storm show Lear's attempts to reorient himself. In his powerless state he comes to know the difference between freely offered devotion and that which is pretended for the sake of reward. But the evil forces which Lear has unleashed through Goneril and Regan prevent him from rebuilding a life based upon his new-found wisdom.

Much the same progression is found in the subplot. There are significant differences, however, for while Lear himself sets his destruction in motion when he divides his kingdom, Edmund is the moving force behind Gloucester's downfall. Gloucester's blindness (which parallels Lear's madness) is caused by his loyalty to Lear, and is not inflicted by his own children. Like Lear, however, Gloucester is forced to re-examine himself and experiences a spiritual rebirth.

Perhaps Shakespeare's structural skill can be seen most clearly in the intertwining of the two plots in a number of ways: by having Gloucester and Edmund present at Lear's abdication; by having Gloucester serve as host to Regan and the Duke of Cornwall; through Gloucester's attempts to aid Lear; and through the relationships among Edmund, Goneril, and Regan. Furthermore, the resolutions of the two stories are essentially one: Goneril and Regan kill each other over love of Edmund; Edmund orders the deaths of Lear and Cordelia; the revelation of Goneril's love for Edmund leads to a duel between Edgar and Edmund and to Edmund's death. Thus, while the subplot has its own intrinsic interest, it simultaneously serves to point up the themes found in the main plot and motivates much that happens to Lear. Gloucester's story, therefore, is essential to the main plot and not a distraction.

The unity of action found in *King Lear* is not of the same kind, however, as that in *Oedipus the King*, in which all attention is focused upon Oedipus and his search. Shakespeare uses a much broader canvas than Sophocles and includes more facets of the story, more characters, a wider sweep of time and place. Nevertheless, he has not sacrificed unity, for the various elements have been carefully integrated.

CHARACTERIZATION AND ACTING. The role of Lear is far more complex than any other in the play. It is sometimes difficult to distinguish between such characters as Goneril and Regan because of the few traits assigned each; both have the same motives, and the over-all impression is simply that each is completely depraved. Cordelia, on the other hand, has as little trace of evil as her sisters have of good.

Shakespeare gives little information about the physical and social attributes of his characters and emphasizes psychological motives instead.

137

King Lear at the Old Vic, London, 1958. Scene showing Goneril, Regan, the Fool, and Lear. Directed by Douglas Seale; setting and costumes by Leslie Hurry. Photograph—Angus McBean. Courtesy the Old Vic Company and Angus McBean.

Each of the secondary personages has one dominant drive which is placed in opposition to that of another character. Thus, Cordelia is contrasted with her sisters, Edgar with Edmund, Cornwall with Albany, Kent with Oswald, and France with Burgundy.

Although the secondary characters are not as complex as Lear, they are effectively conceived, for they fulfill well their functions in the dramatic action. Furthermore, each role offers the imaginative actor a challenge to create a characterization of considerable depth. For example, Edgar must assume a series of disguises (madman, peasant, unknown knight), change his speech from poetry to prose and from standard English to an accent, and convey a sense of deep emotional involvement when often his disguise will not permit the open expression of his true feelings. Thus, a basic character type (the good son) is individualized by involving him in a series of unusual events. Nevertheless, the dominant impression created by Edgar is one of simplicity rather than of complexity, and actors who have played the role have sometimes experienced difficulty in making Edgar interesting to audiences. The same is true of Cordelia, but less so of Goneril, Regan, and Edmund, since evil characters always seem to fascinate audiences.

Gloucester comes near to being a copy of Lear. Both are old men, easily deceived, and they undergo many of the same experiences. Lear's role, however, is developed at much greater length and in more depth than is Gloucester's. In the opening scene, both Gloucester and Lear seem vigorous, but by the end of the play both are decrepit and broken. The decline from vigor to debility is dramatically right. Furthermore, visible physical change seems essential to the play's development.

Lear is difficult to interpret because the part encompasses a wide range of action, emotion, and psychological change. In the opening

138

scene, Lear is in complete command; he is easily angered and insists upon having his every wish satisfied. This habitual, and somewhat childish, behavior defeats him when he no longer has the power to enforce his desires. Impotence commences during his first clash with Goneril, and his sense of frustration grows until it leads to madness. Lear's insanity is portrayed with variety. At first he shouts imprecations, and then he becomes quiet and withdrawn; his dialogue shifts to prose, and he becomes preoccupied with sex, devils, and tortures. From this low point, Lear gradually begins a spiritual ascent, though he never regains his physical vigor. His psychological regeneration develops slowly, for he feels undeserving of Cordelia's love and he can comprehend her forgiveness only with difficulty. When he at last understands the extent of her devotion, he determines to make recompense for the past. Their reunion, which reaches heights of happiness only to descend to despair and death, requires consummate acting skill on the part of the actor portraying Lear.

Throughout the play, Shakespeare injects details to humanize Lear. Perhaps the most obvious of these comes in one of the final speeches, into which Lear injects, "Pray you, undo this button." Here, a figure fighting with overwhelming emotions is suddenly reduced to the level of common humanity. It is a simple touch, but one that arouses pathos more effectively than any description of Lear's feelings could.

The part of the Fool is used as a foil for Lear. His privileged state allows him to speak openly what others must leave unsaid, and it is significant that he is present only in those scenes which can profit from such outspokenness. When Lear himself is turned into a simpleton by insanity, he speaks in the same blunt fashion as the Fool. After the storm scene, the Fool does not reappear, for he is no longer needed.

Lear, thus, is the center of concern for Shakespeare. The other characters are well-drawn, but in no sense approach the complexity of the title role.

LANGUAGE. Shakespeare's dramatic poetry is generally conceded to be the greatest in the English language. The basic medium is blank verse, which allows much of the flexibility of ordinary speech while elevating and formalizing it. The final lines in a scene, usually written in rhymed couplets, serve to round off and brake the forward movement of the verse, like a *coda* in music.

This pattern (blank verse ending in a rhymed couplet) is broken frequently by the injection of passages written in prose, which, typically, are spoken by lower-class characters and are often used for comic purposes. In *King Lear*, however, both Edgar and Lear turn to prose in the mad scenes, for though they do not change rank in actuality, they look at life from the standpoint of the simple mind and speak as though they were members of the lower class.

Probably the most important element in Shakespeare's dialogue is figurative language. The principal purpose of a figure of speech in dramatic poetry is to set up either direct or indirect comparisons. Shakespeare's superiority over other writers of dramatic poetry lies in his use

139

of comparisons which enlarge the significance without distracting the attention from the dramatic situation. For example, in the following passage he associates the storm with Lear's daughters and at the same time suggests that the storm is a sign of divine displeasure. Thus, the audience grasps the significance of the immediate event and its larger implications simultaneously.

> *Rumble thy bellyful! Spit, fire! spout, rain!*
> *Nor rain, wind, thunder, fire are my daughters.*
> *I tax not you, you elements, with unkindness:*
> *I never gave you kingdom, called you children;*
> *You owe me no subscription. Then let fall*
> *Your horrible displeasure. Here I stand your slave,*
> *A poor, infirm, weak, and despised old man.*

Shakespeare often combines direct and indirect comparisons in a single passage. For example, both metaphors and similes are used to relate Lear's mental state to that of a tortured soul in Hell.

> You do me wrong to take me out o'th'grave:
> Thou art a soul in bliss; but I am bound
> Upon a wheel of fire, that mine own tears
> Do scald like molten lead.

These examples, which by no means exhaust the range of Shakespeare's figurative language, also illustrate how his poetic devices partially fulfill the same function as the constant visual representation of Heaven and Hell on the Medieval stage. They relate human actions to the divine and demonic forces of the universe; and man's affairs are depicted as significant to all creation.

Shakespeare's language makes special demands upon the actor. Figures of speech are apt to seem contrived and bombastic if the actor does not appear to be experiencing a state of feeling sufficient to call forth such language spontaneously. All too frequently, Shakespeare's plays are damaged in performance when actors do not rise to the emotional demands of the poetry. The very richness of expression can be a stumbling block for both performer and reader.

SPECTACLE AND SOUND. There are many opportunities for visual splendor in *King Lear.* The action occurs in a large number of places, and if all were depicted realistically the stage would present a constantly changing aspect. Our knowledge of the Elizabethan stage, however, suggests that Shakespeare envisioned the spectacle in terms of stage properties, costumes, and the movement of actors.

Although scenery is not important, the frequent change of stage place is. The forestage, inner and upper stages would allow the necessary flow of one scene into the next. For example, the storm scene, which is set consecutively in an open space, before a hovel, and inside a farm house, would require only the forestage and the discovery space.

The relatively bare stage is enlivened by processions, numerous attendants, and constant physical movement. The opening scene, for example, is an important state occasion which would demand an elaborate procession of officials and courtiers, all of whom would be dressed in their finest garments. In later scenes, banners and heraldic devices would be used to distinguish Albany's and Cornwall's forces from those of the French. In almost every scene minor characters enrich the stage picture.

The actors' stage business also creates spectacle. Gloucester's eyes are put out, Kent is seized and placed in the stocks, Edgar and Edmund fight a duel, Lear dies. Nearly every scene offers physical action of this sort. (A comparison of the onstage action of *King Lear* with that of *Oedipus the King* helps to define a principal difference between Elizabethan and Greek tragedy.)

The costumes are an important visual element. In Shakespeare's day, most characters probably wore contemporary garments but the company's large wardrobe would provide much variety in color and line. During the production some characters must change costumes several times. For example, Lear first appears in robes of state; in the following scenes, he wears the garments of a nobleman; after he goes mad he appears in tattered garments entwined with weeds and flowers; and, following his reunion with Cordelia, he is restored to clothes appropriate to his rank. Edgar changes from his gentleman's attire to rags, then to a peasant's garment, and finally to a suit of armor. Although most of the actors probably wore the same costumes throughout the play, the shifting combination of persons on stage would have lent constant variety to the picture.

Such sound effects as the storm, offstage fighting, and trumpet flourishes, are important in *King Lear*. Music is used in a number of scenes. But most important is the sound of the actors' voices speaking Shakespeare's poetry.

King Lear, because of its combination of universal themes, a compelling story, powerful characters, great poetry, and interesting visual and aural effects, is one of the world's greatest plays. Although it embodies the values of its own period, it is timeless in appeal and transcends the limitations of a particular era. Thus, it continues to move audiences today as it has since its first presentation.

SHAKESPEARE'S CONTEMPORARIES AND SUCCESSORS

Shakespeare's greatness diverts attention from his contemporaries and successors, many of whom are also among the world's finest dramatists. Of Shakespeare's contemporaries, Ben Jonson (1572–1637) was the most important. He began his career in the theatre as an actor (around 1597), but did not continue long in that profession. In 1598 he wrote *Every Man in His Humour* (in which Shakespeare acted), and soon became one of the most controversial authors of the day. He often accused his fellow playwrights of failing to understand the purposes and techniques of drama and of catering to the depraved taste of the "groundlings." Of all the authors of the period, Jonson was most attuned to classical ideas, and his work as a poet, playwright, and critic influenced many younger men to work for a more classical "regularity."

Scene from Jonson's *The Alchemist* as produced at Indiana University. Directed by David Wiley; designed by David Gano.

His most famous plays are *Volpone* (1606), *The Silent Woman* (1609), *The Alchemist* (1610), and *Bartholomew Fair* (1614) — all comedies. His tragedies were not well received. Jonson also wrote most of the masques (to be discussed later) presented at the courts of James I and Charles I.

Probably Jonson is best remembered for popularizing the *comedy of humours*. Since classical times it had been assumed that there were four bodily "humours," blood, phlegm, yellow and black bile, and that health depended upon the proper balance among these fluids. Too much of any one was said to lead to illness. The practice of medicine, therefore, consisted of two basic treatments: purging (to eliminate excessive bile or phlegm), and bleeding (to eliminate excessive blood).

A number of Elizabethan authors applied this medical concept to human psychology, and Jonson, in particular, drew upon it in writing plays. He attributed the eccentricities of behavior to an imbalance of humours and created a wide range of character types based upon this scheme. The psychology of humours was much in vogue between 1598 and 1603, and, though it is seldom mentioned in plays after that time, many playwrights continued to base their characterizations on it. This approach to human behavior tended to produce character types rather than well-rounded individuals.

Jonson's most widely admired play is *Volpone*. The main character, Volpone, pretends to be rich and without heirs. Each of several persons is led to believe that he will inherit the fortune if he can stay in favor with Volpone. Consequently, each showers him with expensive gifts. At last,

Volpone tires of his deception, makes a will leaving all his wealth to his servant, Mosca, and pretends to die. Later, when he tries to reclaim his property, Mosca refuses to give it up. Eventually Volpone, Mosca, and the would-be heirs are exposed and punished.

Most of the characters have been given the names of predatory animals, birds, or insects, such as Volpone (the fox), Voltore (the vulture), and Mosca (the fly), which are descriptive of the characters. Into this network of corruption, Jonson introduces two sympathetic figures, Celia and Bonario, who are almost sent to prison through the collusion of the others. This complication threatens to make the play serious, but the truth is revealed in time to prevent injustice and to maintain the high level of comedy.

Jonson frequently used comedy to denounce vice and foolish behavior. His consistent purpose of reforming conduct has led many to describe his plays as corrective comedies.

Francis Beaumont (c. 1584–1616) and John Fletcher (1579–1625), who wrote a number of plays in collaboration, were principally responsible for establishing the vogue of tragicomedy and romantic tragedy. Their chief works are *Philaster, The Maid's Tragedy, A King and No King,* and *The Scornful Lady,* all written between 1608 and 1613.

Tragicomedy and romantic tragedy are similar forms; both are essentially serious but tragicomedy ends happily and romantic tragedy unhappily. The subjects of Beaumont and Fletcher's plays were usually sensational. For example, in *The Maid's Tragedy* a wife tells her husband on their wedding night that she is the King's mistress and that she has married him only as a means of continuing her affair. The rest of the play develops from this sensational revelation.

Both playwrights were particularly skilled in dramatic construction. They built complications to startling climaxes, alternated quiet and tumultuous episodes, and condensed complex material into far fewer scenes than Shakespeare employed. Their plays show more technical proficiency than do Shakespeare's, but their subjects emphasized the shocking rather than the significant. Until well into the eighteenth century, their plays maintained a reputation equal to those of Shakespeare and Jonson and were performed regularly until the nineteenth century.

The work of Beaumont and Fletcher set the standard for the period between 1610 and 1642. Important writers of tragedy during these years include John Webster (?–c. 1630) and John Ford (1586–1639). Webster's *The White Devil* (1612) and *The Duchess of Malfi* (1614) are among the most powerful of English tragedies. Ford is best known for *'Tis Pity She's a Whore* (c. 1625–33), in which a brother and sister are lovers. Since Ford treats this pair sympathetically, his play is frequently used as evidence of the decadence of English drama after the death of Shakespeare.

Other noteworthy playwrights of the time were Thomas Middleton (1580–1627), Philip Massinger (1583–1640), Thomas Heywood (c. 1574–1641), Thomas Dekker (c. 1572–c. 1632), Cyril Tourneur (c. 1575–1626), and James Shirley (1596–1666).

THE COURT MASQUE

When James I came to the English throne in 1603, he brought with him a taste for elaborate theatrical entertainment. He became the patron of Shakespeare's company, which was renamed the King's Men, and all other troupes were placed under the patronage of members of the royal family.

Unlike Elizabeth, who usually contented herself with performances by the public troupes, James also financed private court entertainments, called *masques*, which were performed on special occasions, such as weddings, births, and visits from foreign dignitaries. The English masque was similar in all important respects to the Italian *intermezzo* and utilized Italian staging methods. (See Chapter 8 for a discussion of Italian materials.) Ben Jonson wrote a majority of the masques, which were designed by Inigo Jones (1573-1652), the court architect. Jones had studied in Italy, and it was he who introduced Italian staging methods into England.

Under James I (reigned 1603-25), an average of one masque each year was given, while under his successor, Charles I, two were usually presented annually. Other masques were produced by the Inns of Court and by noblemen. Great sums of money were spent. In 1618, James I expended more on a single masque than for all the professional performances at court during his entire reign.

The masque featured allegorical stories designed to honor a person or occasion through a fanciful comparison with mythological or historical characters or situations. The speaking and singing roles were assumed by professional court musicians, while comic roles were played by pro-

Setting by Inigo Jones for Jonson's *Oberon* (1611). Devonshire Collection, Chatsworth. Reproduced by permission of the Chatsworth Settlement.

Costume by Inigo Jones for Tethys or a Nymph in Daniel's *Tethys Festival* (1610). Devonshire Collection, Chatsworth. Reproduced by permission of the Trustees of the Chatsworth Settlement.

A costume design by Inigo Jones. From Cunningham's *Inigo Jones*. London, 1848.

Costumes by Inigo Jones for antimasque characters in Jonson's *Chloridia* (1631). Devonshire Collection, Chatsworth. Reproduced by permission of the Trustees of the Chatsworth Settlement.

145

fessional actors. The major emphasis, however, was upon the courtier-dancers, who during the masque went into the auditorium to dance with selected spectators. Above all, the masque provided ample opportunity for elaborate spectacle and scenic display, and by 1640, when the last court masque was staged, Jones had introduced almost all of the scenic devices which had been popularized in Italy.

The influence of the masque was soon felt in the public theatres, where processions, music, allegorical scenes and dances were employed with increasing frequency. For example, Shakespeare's *The Tempest* (1611) contains many masquelike elements. But the influence of the masque on scenery in the public theatre was not great until after 1660, when the proscenium arch and perspective settings became standard.

CLOSING OF THE THEATRES

Although the theatre was a thriving institution and was encouraged by the royal family, Puritan opposition to it grew throughout the first part of the seventeenth century. In 1642, the Civil War was used as an excuse for closing all theatres. They were not to be reopened until Charles II was restored to the throne in 1660. Although there were surreptitious perfor-

The frontispiece to Kirkman's *The Wits* published in 1673. The book contains a number of "drolls," or short scenes extracted or altered from longer plays, which were probably performed during the Commonwealth. This illustration was long thought to represent the stage of the Red Bull, a public theatre which was used regularly from c. 1605-42. More recently it has been argued that it represents a composite of the stages used for surreptitious performances during the Commonwealth. Note that the characters are drawn from a number of different plays. From *Londina Illustrata*. Volume II, 1825.

mances during the Commonwealth, the English theatre was virtually nonexistent during these years. When it was revived in 1660, it bore little resemblance to the theatre of Shakespeare, for it now embraced Italian staging ideals and the neoclassical mode.

SPANISH THEATRE AND DRAMA IN THE GOLDEN AGE

As in England, the late sixteenth century brought a burst of activity in Spain. So fertile was the period between 1580 and 1680 that it has been designated the Golden Age of Spanish literature. Both the Spanish theatre and drama of this era have much in common with their English counterparts.

The first permanent public theatre (or *corrale*) was opened in Madrid in 1579. It was remodeled from an already existing courtyard formed by the walls of houses. The balconies and rooms of the surrounding buildings were used to seat spectators, while standing room and benches were provided in the courtyard. The stage was similar to that of the Elizabethan theatre in most respects: back of a large forestage, an inner area could be closed off by a curtain, while a balcony served as an upper stage. Later Spanish theatres were to follow the same basic arrangement.

The connection between the church and the theatre remained close in Spain, and until 1638 the corrales of Madrid were under the control of *cofradias*, or religious and charitable organizations. Even after the city assumed control of the theatres, the revenue was used to support charities. Furthermore, nearly all playwrights of the Golden Age wrote plays (*autos sacramentales*) for religious festivals, while professional troupes performed them. Religious dramas were not forbidden in Spain until 1765.

Although Lope de Rueda (1510–65), a dramatist, actor, and producer, is credited with establishing the professional theatre in Spain, it did not flourish until after 1580. The two great playwrights of the Golden Age were Lope Felix de Vega Carpio, usually called Lope de Vega (1562–1635), and Pedro Calderón de la Barca (1600–81).

Lope de Vega was a prolific playwright. Over four hundred extant works are attributed to him, and some accounts estimate his total output at more than 1800 plays. His subjects were drawn from the Bible, the lives of saints, mythology, history, romances, and other sources. Although he was an inventive and skillful writer, his dramas fail to achieve that profundity which marks Shakespeare's work. Like Shakespeare, he made considerable use of song and dance, and intermixed the comic and the serious. Some of his best known dramas are *The Sheep Well, The Gardener's Dog,* and *The King, the Greatest Alcalde.* Because of his great output and popularity, Lope de Vega influenced almost all subsequent Spanish dramatists. His position in Spanish literature is comparable to that of Shakespeare in English literature.

Although Calderón wrote many kinds of plays, he is best known for those which explore theological or philosophical ideas. He is said to have written more than 200 works, of which about a hundred survive. Of these, the majority are autos sacramentales written for the Corpus

A conjectural reconstruction of a Spanish *corrale* as it might
have appeared about 1660. From Ricardo Sepulveda's *El Corral
de La Pacheca*. Madrid, 1888.

A reconstruction of a *carro* or wagon for an *auto sacramentale*.
From Sepulveda's *El Corral de La Pacheca*, 1888.

Christi festivals of Madrid. Probably the best known are *The Great World Theatre* (c. 1645) and *The Devotion to the Cross* (1633), while his greatest secular play is *Life is a Dream* (c. 1636), a philosophical allegory about the human situation and the mystery of life.

Other important playwrights of the Golden Age were Tirso de Molina (1584–1648), whose play *The Deceiver of Seville* is the first dramatic treatment of the Don Juan legend, and Juan Ruiz de Alarcón y Mendoza (c. 1581–1639). Unfortunately, with the death of Calderón, the Spanish theatre ceased to be a vital force.

Thus, both England and Spain developed strong dramatic traditions before the new Italian ideas of writing and staging were widely known in either country. Their theatres appear to be logical and gradual evolutions from preceding practices. In neither country was there a sharp division between the theatrical entertainment designed for the court and that intended for the common people. Possibly the vigor of Spanish and English drama stemmed from the playwrights' desire to appeal to all classes and not merely to an aristocratic minority.

Chapter 8 THE ITALIAN RENAISSANCE

Even before Spain and England had developed outstanding theatres, Italy, under the impact of the Renaissance, had begun to transform its stage. Although Italy produced little drama of importance in this period, it made innovations which were to influence the theatre throughout Europe.

BACKGROUND

Many forces helped to create the Renaissance. Probably the most important of these was the general secularization of thought, as men ceased to be overwhelmingly preoccupied with the problem of salvation and devoted more attention to present life. Since medieval learning was deficient in most practical subjects, guidance was sought in classical treatises. Rome exerted far greater influence than Greece, since Latin was the language of the educated class and Greek was not widely known until the sixteenth century.

The interest in classical learning soon extended to plays. Although the works of Terence had served throughout the preceding centuries as models of spoken Latin, they had not been studied for their dramatic qualities. In the fifteenth century, however, they became increasingly popular as literary works. Increased attention was also attracted to the plays of Plautus and Seneca. Plautus' reputation was enhanced by the discovery in 1429 of twelve of his plays which had been lost. Greek plays also gradually became known. When Constantinople fell to the Turks in 1453, many scholars fled to the West bringing valuable manuscripts, including those of the Greek dramas. These plays were not widely disseminated, however, until the sixteenth century.

150

The spread of classical learning was aided by the invention of the printing press, which made it possible to reproduce an unlimited number of copies of the same work, reduced the cost of books and made them available to a much wider public. The classical dramas were printed shortly after the printing press was imported to Italy in 1465: Plautus' plays in 1472, Terence's in 1473, Seneca's between 1474 and 1484, Aristophanes' in 1498, Sophocles' in 1502, Euripides' in 1503, and Aeschylus' in 1518.

This new interest in classical drama was accompanied by an inquiry into literary principles. What is the purpose of drama? Are there rules for writing plays? What distinguishes comedy from tragedy? For answers to these and many other questions, Renaissance critics turned to the works of Horace and Aristotle. Horace's *Art of Poetry* (written in the first century B.C.) was published in 1470, and Aristotle's *Poetics* (written in the fourth century B.C.) was published in 1498. The theorizing based on these two works eventually crystallized into those neoclassical precepts which dominated dramatic writing for almost two hundred years. (These precepts will be discussed in Chapter 9.)

The theatre of Greece and Rome also attracted attention. The chief source of information was *De Architectura* by Vitruvius, a Roman architect of the first century B.C. This treatise, rediscovered in 1414, was first printed in 1486 and had had twenty-three editions by 1600.

Interest in plays of the past soon led to a desire to see them staged, and the courts and academies vied for pre-eminence in theatrical production. Italy at this time was a collection of independent states, many of them quite small, each ruled by a Duke or Prince. The maintenance of a sumptuous court at which the arts were patronized became a common means of demonstrating the supposed superiority of one ruler over another.

Many court spectacles were staged in gardens, courtyards, or streets. Here is a scene designed by Buontalenti for a wedding celebration in 1589 and staged in the courtyard of the Pitti Palace in Florence. From a print in the University of Iowa Library.

Another court spectacle, *Das Rossballet,* at the court of Vienna in 1667. From Alexander von Weilen's *Geschichte des Wiener Theaterwesens.* Volume I, Vienna, 1899.

Court theatres, supported by state funds, developed those scenic conventions which were to dominate the European stage until the nineteenth century.

Although less wealthy than the courts, the academies also contributed significantly to the development of the theatre in the Renaissance. An academy was a clublike organization formed for the purpose of studying a specific subject. Those devoted to classical architecture did much to popularize Vitruvius' work; others studied classical drama or literary theory. Some constructed theatres and staged plays. Their greatest influence, however, was exerted through the formulation and dissemination of theories about the physical theatre and drama.

The theatres of both the courts and academies were essentially amateur organizations which performed for select audiences on special occasions. For example, at the courts scenery was designed by court architects, the plays were usually written by authors under royal patronage, and the actors were courtiers. Plays were produced at irregular intervals for such occasions as engagements, weddings, births, or visits by important personages.

ITALIAN DRAMA OF THE RENAISSANCE

Since medieval drama was spurned as formless and old-fashioned, the plays staged by courts and academies were either classical works or close imitations of them. The first comedy written in Italian was Lodovico Ariosto's (1474-1533) *La Cassaria*, staged at the court of Ferrara in 1508. The play with the greatest appeal today is *Mandragola* (c. 1513–20) by Niccolo Machiavelli (1469-1527). It shows how a jealous old man is tricked into approving of an adulterous relation between his wife and a young man. It is an amusing comedy which combines classical form with the cynicism and subject matter of medieval farce. By 1540, a native comedy was well-established in Italy. Although few of the writers are now remembered, they were the first in Europe to master the techniques of Latin comedy and to adapt them to contemporary tastes. After 1575, their plays were read with increasing frequency in England and France, where they exerted considerable influence on the emerging drama in those countries.

The first important tragedy in Italian was *Sofonisba* (1515) by Giangiorgio Trissino (1478–1550), who sought to follow Greek rather than Senecan practices. His influence was greatly diminished, however, by the popularity of Giambattista Giraldi Cinthio's (1504–73) plays. Cinthio's *Orbecche* (1541), a tale of revenge in the Senecan manner, was the first vernacular tragedy to be produced on the Italian stage. Although none of Cinthio's successors achieved his popularity, many were admired both at home and abroad and did much to re-establish the tragic mode which had lain fallow since Roman times.

A third form, the *pastoral*, also came into prominence in the sixteenth century. Although like the Greek satyr play in its use of rural settings and of characters such as nymphs, satyrs, and shepherds, it deviated markedly from the Greek form in its emphasis upon fine sentiments, delicate emotions, and romantic love stories. The most popular of the pastoral plays were *Amita* (1573) by Torquato Tasso (1544–95) and *The Faithful Shepherd* (c. 1590) by Giambattista Guarini (1538–1612).

THE INTERMEZZI AND OPERA

Since the love for spectacle could not always be satisfied by this classically-inspired drama, most of which required only a single setting, the taste for allegorical devices, processions, and miraculous occurrences, a heritage from the Middle Ages, had to be met in other ways. From the late fifteenth century until about 1600, the principal spectacular pieces were *intermezzi*, presented between the acts of regular dramas. Typically, the subjects for intermezzi were drawn from mythology, especially those stories which allowed the use of elaborate special effects, such as Hercules descending into Hades, or Perseus on his flying horse fighting a sea monster. Each character and event was given an allegorical interpretation which related it to the royal patron, his enemies, or friends.

Joseph Furttenbach (1591-1667) studied in Italy from c. 1610-20 and took many of the Italian staging ideas back to Germany. The design here shows clearly the Italian influence. From Furttenbach's *Architectura Civilis,* Ulm, 1628.

Music and dance also were emphasized. Originally the several inter-mezzi performed on a single occasion might have no connection with each other or the main piece, but eventually they came to be related both to each other and the play they accompanied. By the 1580's intermezzi were more popular than the regular drama.

The appeal of intermezzi was undermined by the rise of opera, since most of the characteristics of intermezzi were absorbed into the newer form. Opera received its first impetus from the Camerata Academy in Florence, a group especially interested in Greek tragedy. The members of the Camerata knew that Greek tragedy had had a chorus, that it had in-cluded music and dance, that at least part of the dialogue had been sung or chanted, and that the plots had been drawn from Greek mythology. Out of their efforts to write plays of this kind, opera began to take shape around 1597. By 1650 the new form was popular throughout Italy and was rapidly spreading to all of Europe. After 1600 opera became the fa-vored form and was increasingly important in stimulating experiments with scenery and special effects. It was with opera that Italian theatrical ideas were first imported into most European countries.

DEVELOPMENT OF THE ITALIAN STAGE

Although there were a number of theatrical centers in Italy, those at Florence, Ferrara, Urbino, Mantua, Rome, and Milan were of primary importance. A stage was built in the Vatican as early as 1452, and there are scattered references to temporary theatres during the remainder of the fifteenth century. The major developments, however, had to wait until the sixteenth century.

From the very beginning, two influences were at work: one which stemmed from the architectural treatise of Vitruvius, and another de-rived from the contemporary interest in perspective. Attempts to com-bine these two forces led eventually to the picture-frame stage.

It is possible that the earliest productions utilized a stage similar to that shown in the late-fifteenth-century editions of Terence's plays. In these, a continuous façade, either straight or angled, is divided into a se-ries of curtained openings, each of which represents the house of a dif-ferent character. This stage was first depicted in an edition printed in Lyons in 1493 and was copied or elaborated upon by many later editions. Some scholars have argued that this "Terence stage" was used through-out Europe for productions of school dramas written under classical influence.

But if the Terence stage was used at first, it was soon modified by the addition of perspective painting.

Credit for formalizing the principles of perspective is usually given to the Florentine artist Filippo Brunelleschi (1377–1446), who, although not the originator, integrated previous knowledge into a method which could be taught. Consequently, most Italian artists had mastered it by 1450. It is difficult today to appreciate the reaction of the Renaissance mind to perspective, which was sometimes viewed as a form of magic, since through its use the artist created the illusion of space and distance where they did not actually exist. Perspective gave the artist a power

154

which he had not previously possessed, and he applied it in all possible ways. It is not surprising, then, that he recognized its possibilities for stage scenery. Although perspective settings may have been used as early as the 1480's, the first certain example is that for Ariosto's *La Cassaria* at Ferrara in 1508.

The joint influence of Vitruvius' work and of perspective are evident in the first treatise on staging in the Renaissance: a portion of *Architettura* (1545) by Sebastiano Serlio (1475–1554). In his book Serlio shows how a theatre is to be laid out, how the stage is to be erected, how scenery is to be arranged; he outlines the rules of perspective and discusses a number of additional topics. Since, like most of his contemporaries, Serlio assumed that theatres would be set up in already existing halls, his plan is an adaptation of Vitruvius' description of the Roman theatre to an indoor, rectangular space. Stadium seating is set up at one end of the hall, and a platform is constructed at the other. The space between the stage and the seats is left free in imitation of the Roman orchestra. (See the accompanying illustrations.)

The stage floor is divided into two parts from front to back. The front, which is reserved for the performers, is flat, while the rear, used for scenery, is sloped upward toward the back. The floor is painted in squares, the lines of which diminish in size and converge toward the center back. The upward slope and the diminishing squares help to create a sense of distance in a very limited space.

Left. A cross section of Serlio's theatre. *Below, left.* His ground plan for a theatre, 1545.

Below, right. His design for the comic scene. From Sebastiano Serlio's *Architettura,* 1545.

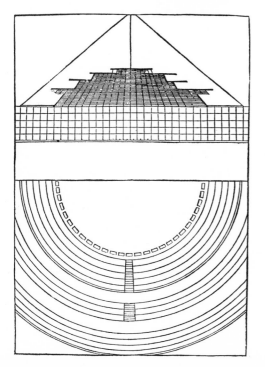

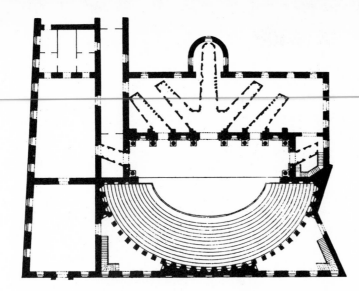

A ground plan of the Teatro Olimpico at Vicenza. From A. Streit's *Das Theater,* Vienna, 1903. A photograph of the interior may be found on page 4.

Houses constructed of canvas stretched over wooden frames are set up on both sides of the stage. The first three houses on either side are three-dimensional, while the fourth is painted on two-dimensional surfaces. The plan is completed by a back-cloth hung at the rear of the stage. All of the scenery is constructed and painted to give the illusion of diminishing size and distance as it nears the back wall of the stage. To help in this illusion the tops of the flats are shaped to slope downward just as the floor slopes upward toward the back.

Serlio envisioned the need for only three settings—one for tragedy, one for comedy, and one for pastoral. His engravings illustrating these settings were imitated by other designers all over Europe. Serlio's scenes for comedy and tragedy are essentially the street scenes of the Roman theatre translated into perspective settings. He does not mention any framing device (or proscenium arch) to cut off the spectator's view at the sides or top. Presumably, the side houses continue until they meet the walls of the hall in which the stage is set up. A valance probably cut off the view at the top.

Serlio and most of his contemporaries who designed stage scenery were court architects who constructed stages and scenery as needed. This may explain why so many of the architectural details of scenery in the sixteenth century were three-dimensional rather than merely painted on flats. It was not until the seventeenth century, when the houses became entirely two-dimensional, that scene shifting was widely practiced.

As the theatre gained a more solid foothold, the need for permanent theatres was felt. Although a few permanent structures may have been built earlier, the oldest surviving Renaissance theatre is the Teatro Olimpico, built between 1580 and 1584 by the Olympic Academy of Vicenza. Founded in 1555 to study Greek drama, the Academy at first used temporary stages but eventually commissioned Andrea Palladio (1518–80) to construct a classical theatre. Palladio died before the theatre was completed, however, and it was finished by his pupil, Scamozzi. First used in 1585, it still stands.

The stage, the stage background, and the auditorium of the Teatro Olimpico more nearly follow Vitruvius' plan of a Roman theatre than any other edifice of the period. But even here the influence of perspective

The Teatro Farnese in Parma. *Below.* The ground plan. *Left.* The stage. *Below, left.* The auditorium. From A. Streit's *Das Theater*, Vienna, 1903.

scenery is felt, for Scamozzi raked the floor upward behind the façade doors and constructed a street in perspective behind each. (See photograph page 4 and plan page 156.) The result is somewhat like a city square into which a number of streets emerge. The street scenes were entirely fixed and could not be shifted. The Teatro Olimpico, therefore, was not in line with the growing demand for more spectacle.

The form which the theatre was to take can be seen clearly for the first time in the Teatro Farnese built in the ducal palace at Parma in 1618. Its importance lies in the fact that it is the first theatre known to have been constructed with a permanent proscenium arch.

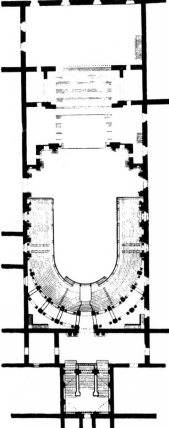

The origin of the proscenium arch is a much-disputed question. Some argue that it comes from the enlargement of the central doorway of the Roman stage façade. Others claim that it is derived from the triumphal arches of the street pageants given for royal entries and processions of various kinds. Still others argue that it is indebted to paintings in which buildings and other objects are used to frame the perspective picture. Any or all of these may be true, since the proscenium arch filled a need felt clearly for the first time in the Renaissance, and it may have been suggested by a number of different sources.

Regardless of its origin, however, the proscenium arch serves two basic functions. First, if perspective is to be effective there must be some means of restricting the view of the audience. For example, if the audience can see the back wall of the stage above the painted cloth, the illusion of place and of distance is destroyed. The proscenium frames the picture and focuses attention upon it. Second, if scenery is to be shifted (and by the seventeenth century there was a growing demand for more spectacle), some framework to hide the machinery and the offstage spaces is desirable. The proscenium helps to maintain the magic of the theatre by concealing the mechanics by which that magic is created.

Some kind of framing device had been used prior to the construction of the Teatro Farnese, but it had been temporary and designed to fit the needs of each play. The Farnese put into permanent form a device which had been evolving over a number of years, and thereby became the prototype of theatres up to modern times.

The new picture-frame stage was unlike any which had preceded it, for it attempted to create the illusion of a single place in its entirety. The medieval stage had suggested symbolically a great number of places all present simultaneously, while the classical theatre had made use of a permanent architectural façade which might serve as any number of places—a street, a temple, or a palace. The desire to create the illusion of more and more complex places in the Rennaissance manner was largely responsible for succeeding developments in the proscenium-arch theatre.

MAIN FEATURES OF THE ITALIAN THEATRE

Although the stage of the Teatro Farnese was the prototype of those which followed, its auditorium was still that of a conventional court theatre. The basis of auditorium design was to stem from the public opera houses, the first of which was opened in Venice in 1637. Although its features were never completely standardized, the public theatre characteristically was arranged in the following manner.

The auditorium was an elongated U-shaped structure. Around the walls boxes were ranged in tiers one above the other. The number of tiers varied from one theatre to another, but there were usually two or more. The boxes contained the most expensive seats, although the view of the stage was not good except from those at the rear of the house, and these were poorly situated for hearing. They were valued, however, for their relative privacy and were especially popular with well-to-do and would-be respectable persons.

158

Above the top row of boxes there was often an undivided gallery which was normally occupied by servants or members of the lower classes. The central floor space (the orchestra or pit) was not popular with the elite until the late nineteenth century. Except in England, there were no seats in the pit until near the end of the eighteenth century, and consequently the spectators stood and moved about freely. This area was usually occupied by fashionable young gentlemen and would-be critics. The price of admission to this part of the house was less than that charged for boxes, but more than that charged for the gallery.

The stage was divided from the auditorium by the proscenium arch. The stage floor was raked upward toward the back. Usually there was considerable space below the stage floor for machinery and trap doors, and space above for painted backdrops, curtains, and additional mechanical devices. There was only a small amount of space at either side of the stage.

Since the theatres were indoors, they required artificial lighting. Candles or oil lamps were the standard illuminants, until around 1825, when gas was introduced. Chandeliers often hung in the auditorium and sometimes over the stage itself. Lights were mounted behind the proscenium arch (both at the sides and above), footlights might be used at the front edge of the stage, and lights might be mounted on vertical poles behind each set of wings. Ordinarily, stage lights were concealed both for greater illusion and to avoid too much strain on the eyes of spectators. Although the stage was sometimes darkened by the use of stovepipe-like devices lowered around the lights, for the most part there was little effective control over intensity, color, or distribution.

Another important feature of this theatre was its scene-shifting devices. Because the Serlian settings, with their three-dimensional details, were difficult to shift, the intermezzi were staged at first by drawing pageant wagons into the space forward of the stage or by carrying portable set pieces onto the platform. Around 1550, periaktoi began to be used for changing the wings. In 1638, Nicola Sabbattini (1574–1654), in

A setting by Furttenbach supposedly using *periaktoi*. From the title page of *Deutsche Schaubuhne,* Strasbourg, 1655.

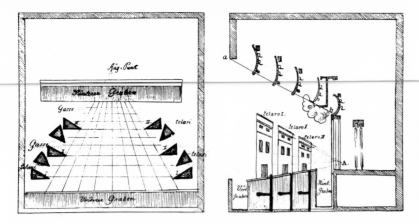

In his *Recreational Architecture*, 1640, Furttenbach shows the use of *periaktoi*. Note the curved borders above the stage right, and the pit for special effects at the rear of the raked stage. From von Weilen. Volume I, 1899.

his *Manual for Constructing Theatrical Scenes and Machines* (a major source of information about seventeenth century practices), listed four methods of shifting scenery. One required periaktoi, while two others were rather clumsy means of changing the angled wings by maneuvering new frames around those already there or by pulling painted canvas over the visible surfaces. The fourth applied only to the flat wings at the rear of the stage.

It was Sabbattini's fourth method which eventually triumphed, as angled wings were replaced by flat wings. The first clear record of a setting composed entirely of flat wings is found in 1606, but by 1650 this arrangement, probably because of its greater mobility, had virtually replaced all others. Using it, flats, or wings, were set up parallel to the front of the stage in a series from front to back. At each wing position, as many different flats were put up (one immediately back of another) as there were scenes to be depicted during the performance. To change from one scene to the next, the visible wings were pulled offstage, revealing others upon which was painted the new scene. The set was enclosed at the back by painted flats which met in the center of the stage. Several backscenes could be set up, one behind the other, and shifted in the same way as the side wings.

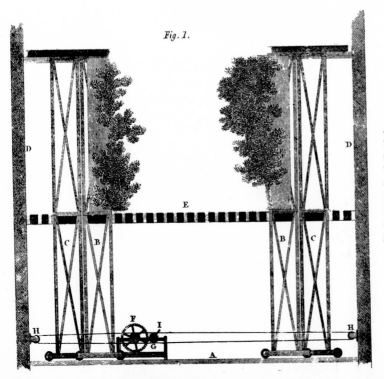

Fig. 1.

A diagram showing the operation of the chariot and pole or "continental" system of shifting scenery. A—the tracks in which the chariot rides; B and C—the chariots; D—stage walls; E—stage floor; F, G, H, and I—the lines, pulleys, and levers which operate the system. From Rees' *Cyclopedia*, XX, 1803.

Borders (two-dimensional framed cloths) hung above each set of wings and continued the scene overhead. The borders might be painted to represent the sky or clouds in an outdoor setting, or the beams, ceiling, or vaulting of an interior scene. Not only did they block the audience's view of the overhead area, but space between them permitted lighting and special effects from above.

Borders, side wings, and back-scene were the three basic elements of every set. To shift them simultaneously and instantaneously was the ideal. At first many stage hands were used to make quick changes, but the results were not always entirely satisfactory since it was difficult to synchronize their movements. The final solution, eventually adopted throughout Europe with the exception of England, was the *chariot and pole* system. At each wing and back-scene position, slots were cut in the stage floor parallel to the front of the stage. At corresponding positions under the stage, tracks were set up. Frames on casters (*carriages*) were placed in these tracks, and to each carriage were attached poles which extended upward through the slots in the floor. In turn, the wings and back-scenes were attached to these poles. Moving the carriages toward the center of the stage thrust a set onstage, while the reverse process moved it offstage.

This basic arrangement was further mechanized by a system of ropes and windlasses. Any carriage or border could be attached by rope to a windlass. When the wings, borders, and the back-scene of a single setting were attached to the same windlass, one man could change the entire set by turning a single crank. The change could be accomplished instantly and all of the pieces of the set moved in unison.

The groove system, used in England, was less complicated. Pieces of wood were attached overhead and to the stage floor to make grooves in which the flats could slide on and off the stage. The scenic elements might be rigged so they could be changed by windlass, but the English normally depended on a number of stage hands for making scene changes. Both systems fulfill the same function and were utilized as long as the *wing and drop* setting dominated the stage.

The man most associated with the perfection of the chariot and pole system is Giacomo Torelli (1608–78). Working in the public opera houses of Venice between 1641 and 1645, he perfected the system of winches for moving all scenic parts simultaneously and created such seemingly magical feats that he won the nickname, "the Great Wizard." In 1645 he went to Paris, where he was largely responsible for transforming the French stage.

By Torelli's time scenery on the Italian stage had become relatively standardized. Behind a proscenium arch a series of side wings and overhead borders terminated in a back-scene. On the flat surfaces of these elements was painted a perspective vista, the vanishing point of which was usually in the center of the back-scene. If the actors moved too far upstage, the perspective effect was ruined by the disparity between the size of the actor and the objects painted on the backdrop. As a result, actors performed principally at the front of the stage. The scenery thus

Alfonso Parigi's (?-1656) setting for Prospero Bonarelli's *Il Solimano. Below.* The same setting with flame effects. From Pougin's *Dictionnaire . . .* , 1885.

became a background rather than an integral part of the characters' environment. This uneasy relationship between actor and stage setting continued until the eighteenth century, when angle perspective was perfected.

Machinery for special effects was also important in the Italian theatre, which merely perfected that which had already been extensively developed during the Middle Ages. The stage floor had a number of trap doors through which special effects could be operated: flames and smoke; the appearance or disappearance of buildings, trees, mountains, or persons; earthquakes and seemingly magical occurrences. Other devices were

A design by Giacomo Torelli for Act II of *Andromède* by Pierre Corneille, 1650. Note the "glories." From a contemporary engraving, courtesy of Alois Nagler.

mounted overhead. One of the favorite effects was the appearance of supernatural beings in clouds, astride mythical animals, or in chariots. These machines, sometimes called *glories*, were usually merely wooden platforms concealed by painted clouds and suspended by ropes, pullies, and cranes. Animals or chariots were made of wooden frames covered with painted canvas. Some of these flying machines were so elaborate that they occupied almost all of the available space.

The front curtain was used only to keep the stage hidden until the play was ready to begin so as to heighten surprise. The changing of scenery was part of the performance and was considered to be a special effect in its own right.

By the mid-seventeenth century all elements of the picture-frame stage had developed: the wing-drop-border perspective setting, the proscenium arch, scene-shifting devices, and machinery for elaborate special effects. The auditorium also had become fixed in its features: the elongated semicircle with pit, boxes, and gallery. This theatre evolved in Italy, spread to all of Europe before 1700, and remained relatively unchanged until the mid-nineteenth century. Many of its elements still dominate the theatre.

COMMEDIA DELL'ARTE

Alongside the drama of the court and academy there grew up another quite different form, *commedia dell'arte*. (*Arte* signified that the actors were artists or professionals in contrast to the amateurs who performed the *erudita* or learned drama.) It was actor-centered, improvised, and adaptable to almost any playing condition.

The actor was the heart of *commedia dell'arte* and almost the only essential element. The script was a scenario which merely outlined the principal action and its outcome. The actors improvised the dialogue and developed the complications as the situation seemed to demand.

163

Pantalone, Illustration by Maurice Sand for his work on actors and types of Italian comedy, *Masques et Bouffons,* 1859.

A set of stock characters appeared in all plays, and the same actor always played the same role. The characters may be divided into three basic categories: lovers, professional types, and servants.

The lovers were straight roles, they did not wear masks and were intended to be handsome and sympathetic. There was always one male and one female lover, and often there was an additional pair. Although the plot often centered around some obstacle to their marriage, the lovers were not usually the center of interest. They provided an excuse for the plot and served as the norm against which other characters could be judged; they were dressed fashionably and frequently spoke elegantly and poetically.

Three professional types appeared most frequently. Pantalone, an old merchant, miser, and often the father or suitor of one of the young women; Dottore, a pedantic bore, and frequently the father of one of the young men or a suitor to one of the young women; the Capitano, a soldier who boasted of his prowess in love and war but invariably proven to be a coward. Each of these characters had his own distinctive mask and costume which he wore in all plays.

The principal comic roles were those of the servants, or *zanni,* who were employed by members of the first two groups. They resorted to all sorts of machinations in helping or thwarting the lovers or professional types.

They varied from the stupid to the clever, and might have marked physical characteristics, such as a large nose or a humped back. Each role had its own mask, costume, and fixed characterization. The most famous of the zanni were Harlequin, Coviello, Pulcinello, Brighella, Scaramouche, and Tartaglia. There were also one or two female servants who attended the women lovers and engaged in intrigues. Fre-

A scene from a *commedia dell'arte* performance. From G. Lambranzi's *Nuova e Curiosa Scuola de Balli Theatrali,* Nuremberg, 1716.

quently they carried on love affairs with the male servants. All female roles were played by women.

These were the basic types. While each play was improvised, the actors, after a time, developed a set of speeches, "sure fire" comic routines, and other dependable aids in holding audience attention. Each troupe had a number of proven *lazzi*, or extended bits of comic business which could be utilized when appropriate or when audience attention wandered.

There are many theories about the origin of commedia dell'arte. Some scholars argue that the commedia was descended directly from the Atellan farce of Rome, and that actors in the Dark Ages preserved traditions which sprang back into prominence when times became more favorable. There are similarities between some of the commedia stock figures and those of the Atellan farce, but no positive evidence of any direct connection between the two forms.

Other historians argue that the commedia is an outgrowth of interest in the plays of Plautus and Terence, which were gradually transformed by the actors. Still another theory sees the commedia as entirely native to Renaissance Italy without any necessary forbears. Any of these theories may be right, for the beginnings of commedia remain obscure.

Regardless of origin, the troupes came into prominence after 1550. The first clear reference to improvisation is found in 1568, and soon afterwards commedia dell'arte troupes were popular throughout Italy, and before the end of the century were playing in France and elsewhere. In the seventeenth century, the commedia spread to all of Europe. It declined after 1750 and was virtually dead by 1800.

Probably the most important troupes were the Gelosi and the Accesi. The Gelosi was probably the most prominent of all the troupes because of the popularity of its leader, Francesco Andreini (1548–1624) and his wife, Isabella (1562–1604). The latter was a favorite with many of the literary figures of the day and was herself a poet. The Gelosi existed from about 1570 to 1604, during which time it played throughout Italy and France. The Accesi troupe flourished between 1590 and 1635. Its leaders were Pier Maria Cecchini (1575–1645), Tristano Martinelli (c. 1557–1630), and Flaminio Scala (active 1600–21), an important composer of scenarios and an actor in the company for a time. The Accesi paid at least two visits to France. Other notable troupes were the Confidenti, the Desiosi, the Fedeli, and the Uniti.

The commedia actors played for all types of audiences and produced a genuinely popular theatre movement. Many of its troupes were invited to play at the courts, but they were equally at home in the market place or at fairs; they at times performed regular drama, but were more famous for their improvised scripts.

After public theatres began to be built in Italy in the seventeenth century, the troupes made use of the kind of theatre which had been developed at the courts, and scenarios were written to take advantage of new scenic possibilities and special effects.

Almost eight hundred commedia dell'arte scenarios still exist. Since they only outline the action, however, it is difficult to get a clear picture

Harlequin. An illustration by Maurice Sand from his *Masques et Bouffons*, 1859.

165

A drawing by Jacques Callot (1592-1635) showing *commedia dell'arte* characters Razullo, left, and Cucurucu, right, and in the background a stage. From Pougin's *Dictionnaire Historique et Pittoresque du Thèàtre . . .* , 1885.

of the actual quality of a commedia performance, although all accounts testify to the great skill of the actors. The popularity of the troupes for a period of over two hundred years also attests to their genuine audience appeal. The commedia exerted considerable influence on a number of later writers, perhaps most notably Molière.

The renewed interest in classical drama, the development of the picture-frame stage, perspective scenery, elaborate machinery for special effects and scene shifting, opera, commedia dell'arte — all of these products of the Italian Renaissance were to have important effects on the theatre in succeeding centuries.

166

Chapter 9 FRENCH CLASSICISM

The French professional theatre had its roots in medieval drama. While trade guilds were staging plays in some towns, special associations were created for this purpose in others. One of these amateur groups, the Confrérie de la Passion, was organized in Paris in 1402 and by 1420 was established in a permanent indoor theatre in the Hôpital de la Trinité. It was virtually the only producer of plays in Paris after this time. Thus, this troupe became the oldest permanent company in Europe and the first to have a permanent theatre.

In 1548 the Confrérie built a new theatre, the Hôtel de Bourgogne, which was to remain in use until 1783. Construction was barely completed, however, when the Confrérie was forbidden to produce religious plays, although its monopoly on theatrical production in Paris was confirmed. Unable to maintain audiences with secular plays, the Confrérie began to rent its theatre to traveling troupes. After 1598 its activities were confined solely to those of a landlord, and each group desiring to perform in Paris had to pay the Confrérie a fee whether or not it played at the Hôtel de Bourgogne.

THE FRENCH THEATRE BETWEEN 1600 AND 1625

Although many companies played in Paris in the late sixteenth century, performances were sporadic until the troupe headed by Valleran-Lecomte (active 1592–1612), the first important French theatrical manager, leased the Hôtel de Bourgogne around 1598. Valleran's troupe dominated the Parisian theatre until 1612, after which the farce actors, Turlupin, Gaultier-Garguille, and Gros-Guillaume, were to be the most popular performers until about 1625.

167

The court of France sponsored many spectacles similar to those of Italy. This illustration depicts *Circe* by Beaujoyeulx in 1581. The settings are by Jacques Patin. Note the galleries for spectators and the mansionlike arrangement of the scenery. The theatre was a hall in the Petit Bourbon and was later converted to conform to the Italian ideal by Torelli in 1645. Molière's company used the Petit Bourbon from 1658-60, when the building was demolished. From Germain Bapst's *Essai sur l'Histoire du Théâtre,* Paris, 1893.

Farce actors at the Hôtel de Bourgogne around 1630. The three male figures at the center are Turlupin, Gaultier-Garguille, and Gros-Guillaume. Notice the *commedia*-like costumes. From a contemporary engraving by Bosse reprinted in Arsène Houssaye's *La Comédie Française*, 1880.

Mahelot's design for *La Prise de Marsilly* at the Hôtel de Bourgogne in the 1630's. Note the simultaneous representation of a number of locales. Courtesy of Bibliothèque Nationale, Paris.

The principal French playwright of the early seventeenth century was Alexandre Hardy (c. 1572–1632), who supplied Valleran-Lecomte with a large proportion of his plays. Hardy is said to have written about five hundred works (of which thirty-four still exist), and was probably the first French author to make a living by writing for the stage. Although his plays were of many types, the majority were tragicomedies. His emphasis was upon a continuous sweep of action similar to that found in novels of chivalry and adventure. Hardy was an extremely popular dramatist, but because his plays lacked depth, he was unable to establish in France a strong tradition of "irregular" drama such as was then current in England and Spain.

The staging of plays at the Hôtel de Bourgogne was quite different from contemporary practices in both Italy and England. From the beginning, the Confrérie had used an indoor stage erected at the end of a rectangular hall. At the Hôtel de Bourgogne the visible stage space was only about twenty-five feet wide (as compared with a typical outdoor stage of over a hundred feet). When the mansions were set up, therefore, they had to be arranged along the sides (one behind the other from front to back) and across the rear of the stage. The resulting picture superficially resembled Serlio's stage, but in Serlio's settings all of the elements were parts of a single location, while at the Hôtel de Bourgogne each structure represented a different place. The space in the middle of the stage was used as a generalized acting area in the manner of the medieval *platea*.

A number of designs by Mahelot for settings of this kind (the *décor simultanée* or simultaneous setting) are still in existence. (See the illustration just above.) Simultaneous settings were used at the Hôtel de Bourgogne until around 1640, when the Italian style began to dominate. The simultaneous stage had been in keeping with Hardy's dramatic method, but was not adapted to the French classical drama which began to appear in the 1630's.

CHANGES IN FRENCH THEATRE BETWEEN 1625 AND 1650

The period from 1625 to 1650 brought sweeping changes because of more settled political conditions, a strong desire to raise the general cultural level of France, the importation of Italian ideas on staging and drama, and the appearance of strong native dramatists.

France was embroiled in civil wars over religion from the 1560's until the 1620's. After Cardinal Richelieu became chief minister of France around 1625, however, the political situation gradually grew more calm as he extended the central government's control over all phases of French life.

In the 1620's Richelieu and many other Frenchmen began to be concerned about France's cultural image and, in seeking to improve the status of literature and the arts, looked to Italy for guidance. Although Italian ideas had been current in France as early as 1550, they were little known except among the educated classes until after 1630.

Until about 1625, the professional theatre had maintained only a precarious footing in Paris. While the Hôtel de Bourgogne had been occupied frequently, no company performed there continuously until 1623. After 1629, however, there were always at least two professional companies playing in Paris.

Both of the public theatres in the 1630's (the Hôtel de Bourgogne and the Théâtre du Marais) still used simultaneous settings. Cardinal Richelieu was not happy with this kind of staging, which emphasized medieval rather than classical ideals, and in 1641 built in his palace a theatre of the Italian type with the first permanent proscenium arch in France. This theatre, called the Palais-Royal after Richelieu's death, was to become the home of Molière's troupe.

When Richelieu died in 1642, Cardinal Mazarin, a native of Italy, succeeded him as prime minister. Mazarin's love of opera eventually brought Torelli to Paris, where by 1650 Italian scenic methods and theatre structures were well understood and had become the ideal.

After the Théâtre du Marais was rebuilt in 1644, it emphasized spectacle in the Italian manner. Since the facilities of the Hôtel de Bourgogne were too limited to allow much scenic display, the unified stage picture had largely replaced the earlier simultaneous settings at that theatre by 1650.

In 1641 Cardinal Richelieu's new theatre contained the first permanent proscenium arch in France. The illustration shows the setting for the first production, *Mirame*. Later this theatre was called the Palais-Royal and was used by Molière's troupe from 1660-73, and after that time was the home of the Opera. From Pougin's *Dictionnaire Historique et Pittoresque* . . . , 1885.

The Italian influence may also be seen in the formation of the French Academy, which came into existence about 1629 when a small group of men interested in literature and language began to meet informally. Richelieu encouraged them to form an official organization, which they eventually did in 1636. This group, whose membership is restricted to forty at any one time (supposedly the outstanding men of French letters), still exists. It has always had considerable prestige, most conspicuously so in the seventeenth and eighteenth centuries, and has exerted a decided influence on French literature and drama. When the French Academy was formed it took as its province the principles and practices of literary composition and the rules of the French language.

THE BASIC PRINCIPLES OF NEOCLASSICISM

The French Academy took its standards of drama primarily from Italian critics. These standards are important to an understanding of the development of drama during the seventeenth and eighteenth centuries, for they are at the heart of what is normally called the neoclassical movement.

Although neoclassical criteria were a synthesis of the ideas of many men in many countries, they were most consistently applied and defended in France. Italian critics of the sixteenth century (especially Minturno, Scaliger, and Castelvetro) laid the foundations upon which French critics of the seventeenth century (notably Chapelain, D'Aubignac, and Boileau) built. While there was, as in all movements, considerable variation in the ideas of individual writers, the basic principles of neoclassicism were consistent enough to allow a general summary.

Neoclassicism was primarily concerned with a number of basic issues: the concept of verisimilitude; purity of dramatic types: decorum; the purposes of drama; the three unities; and the five-act form.

Verisimilitude, "the appearance of truth," is a complex concept. To the Neoclassicist, verisimilitude had three basic aspects: reality, morality, and generality or abstraction. The desire for "reality" required that the playwright rule out those things which could not actually happen in real life. It eliminated fantasy and supernatural occurrences unless they were an accepted part of a story (as in Greek myths or Biblical material). The playwright, however, was encouraged to minimize such features of a story. Such conventions as the soliloquy and chorus were discouraged on the grounds that it is unnatural for characters to speak aloud while alone or to discuss private matters in the presence of a group. To replace these devices, each main character came to be given a trusted companion, or *confidant*, to whom he could reveal his innermost secrets. Violence was placed offstage because of the difficulty of making it convincing.

This demand for faithfulness to reality was considerably modified by the insistence that drama must teach moral lessons. Consequently, the dramatist was asked not merely to copy life but to reveal its ideal moral patterns. Since God was thought to be both omnipotent and just, the pattern should show wickedness punished and good rewarded. Those instances in which injustice seems to prevail were explained as a part of

171

God's plan, which is often beyond human comprehension but inevitably just. Therefore, such apparent aberrations were considered unsuitable subjects for drama, for playwrights should depict that ultimate truth which is inseparable from morality and justice.

Both reality and morality were further modified by the principle of abstraction or generality. Rather than seeking truth in the welter of peripheral details, the Neoclassicist sought it in those attributes which are shared by all phenomena of a particular category. Those characteristics which are variable were considered to be accidental and therefore no essential part of truth. Thus, the truth was defined as those norms which are discoverable through the rational and systematic examination of phenomena, whether natural or man-made. Since these norms were considered the highest form of truth, which remains unchanged regardless of the period or locale, rational men were expected to accept them as the basis for literary creation and critical judgment.

This conception of verisimilitude led to many lesser principles. The idea that truth is to be found in "norms" was extended to every aspect of dramatic composition. Drama itself was reduced to two basic types, tragedy and comedy, with others labeled inferior because they were *mixed forms.*

Tragedy and comedy each had its own normative patterns. Tragedy drew its characters from rulers or the nobility; its stories dealt with affairs of state, the downfall of rulers, and similar events; its endings were always unhappy; and its style was lofty and poetic. Comedy, on the other hand, drew its characters from the middle or lower classes; its stories dealt with domestic and private affairs; its endings were always happy; and its style was characterized by the use of ordinary speech. Such distinctions meant, among other things, that tragedy could not be written about the common man, and that comedy could not be written about the nobility. Each of these rules is somewhat arbitrary, though each bears some resemblance to actual Greek and Roman practice. The neoclassic critic, nevertheless, viewed these demands as necessary and inviolable, and dramatists were denounced when they deviated from them.

In actual practice there were many other dramatic types in the seventeenth and eighteenth centuries. The usual justification of such deviations was that these forms were not serious efforts and were not worthy of critical consideration; they were said to be the products of poorly educated or tasteless writers, and the plays were called *illegitimate* dramas.

Perhaps most important to the dramatist was the belief that human nature has its own governing patterns, which are the same in all places and in all periods. The dramatist, therefore, was expected to confine himself to writing about the permanent aspects of humanity. This meant cutting away all qualities which might be attributed to a particular time, place, or personal peculiarity. In neoclassical plays, therefore, there is little concern with individualizing details and great emphasis upon the more universal aspects of character and situation.

These criteria are most easily seen in characterization. Each age group, rank, profession, and sex was thought to have its own essence. The dramatist was expected to remain true to these norms in creating his characters, and the critic was expected to use them in judging the verisimilitude of the playwright's creations. This principle of character portrayal was termed *decorum*, which in its broadest sense means "fittingness" or "appropriateness." Used in this broad sense, it is a helpful concept; but as employed by the Neoclassicist, it was frequently synonymous with the set of behavioral standards approved at the time. Both verisimilitude and decorum are indicative of the neoclassical attempt to achieve complete universality in drama by cutting away everything that is not true of all men in all times and all places.

The Humanist movement in the Renaissance had had a special problem in justifying literature as a legitimate study. In breaking away from the former preoccupation with theology, the easiest route was to urge the usefulness of drama for teaching moral lessons, and this was the line taken by almost all theorists between 1500 and 1800 (and which many take even today). Most theorists argued that the purpose of drama is twofold—to teach and to please, although precedence was almost always given to teaching. If this teaching were to be clear (as it should be, according to many), the plays should show characters being punished or rewarded for their behavior. (The term *poetic justice* was coined in the seventeenth century to indicate this meting out of justified rewards and punishments to the characters in a play.) Consequently, comedy was expected to ridicule behavior which should be avoided, and tragedy to show the horrible results of mistakes and misdeeds. It was also considered necessary that drama should please, for otherwise teaching would not be possible. This is sometimes called the "sugarcoated pill" function of art—entertainment to sweeten a moral lesson.

Verisimilitude was also said to dictate adherence to the unities of action, time, and place. While unity of action has been demanded in almost every age, critics in the neoclassical period normally interpreted the rule to mean that a play should have only one action, and that there should be no subplots. Neoclassical theorists are the only ones who have placed great emphasis upon the unities of time and place. While Greek and Roman playwrights tended to observe these unities, there was no insistence by critics of the time that they were necessary to good drama. Castelvetro, writing in Italy around 1570, was the first critic to set down the unities as they were to be accepted for the next two hundred years. He argued that since an audience knows that it has been in the theatre for only a few hours, an author cannot convince it that several days or years have passed. Therefore, the time which has passed in the play should be equal to the time the audience has spent in the theatre. Other critics were less severe, but few would allow time to exceed twenty-four hours. Likewise, Castelvetro argued that the audience knows that it has only been in one place and, therefore, that it cannot be expected to accept a change in a play's locale from Rome to Athens, or to other widely separated places. The demand for unity of place was sometimes broadened by other critics to allow more than one location if all could be easily reached within the twenty-four hour time limit. This utter confusion of clock time with fictional time and of actual place with fictional place is characteristic of the period and may be explained by that aspect of verisimilitude which demanded a close correspondence between reality and art.

These, then, are the basic principles of neoclassicism. They may seem artificial and arbitrary today, but to most persons in the seventeenth and eighteenth centuries they were meaningful concepts which seriously affected the writing and staging of plays.

CORNEILLE AND RACINE

The writer most closely associated with the transition to classicism in France is Pierre Corneille (1606–84), who began writing plays in the late 1620's, but did not win great success until 1636 with *Le Cid* (*The Cid*). The production of this play set off a controversy which brought the issues of classicism to a focus, for the play in many ways adhered to neoclassical demands, but in the very observance of them managed to raise serious questions about the validity of verisimilitude, decorum, and the unities.

The Cid is essentially a tragicomedy, for its serious action (centering around the rival demands of love and honor) is resolved happily. The unities are for the most part observed—the action is completed within twenty-four hours, the place is confined to the city of Seville, and there are no important subplots. But so many things happen in twenty-four hours that credibility—or verisimilitude—is strained. Furthermore, at the end of the play Chimène, the play's heroine, has agreed to marry Roderigue, who has killed Chimène's father in a duel less than twenty-four hours earlier. This ending both strains decorum and (since it is a happy one for the main characters) puts *The Cid* outside the neoclassical conception of pure tragedy.

The play was a great success in the theatre, nevertheless, and was both denounced and extravagantly praised. The newly formed French Academy was asked to arbitrate the dispute, and its decision, written by Jean Chapelain, the Academy's acknowledged leader (with Richelieu's help, it is sometimes said), sought to clarify the extent to which the play accorded with the neoclassical ideal. Chapelain decided that *The Cid* was not a tragedy, and that, while it had many things to recommend it, verisimilitude and decorum (the most important requirements) had been severely strained. The whole controversy seems somewhat ridiculous today, but at the time it served to make the public conscious of the new classical ideals which were shortly to dominate critical taste and dramatic writing. Corneille eventually accepted the judgment passed on *The Cid*, and his subsequent plays (the most famous of which are *Horace*, *Cinna*, and *Polyeucte*) adhered to the new demands and helped to establish classicism. In 1647 he was elected to the French Academy, a clear indication that he was by that time acceptable to that group.

The distinguishing characteristic of Corneille's dramas is the hero with an indomitable will. While the hero constantly grows in strength throughout a play, he does not grow in complexity. Since Corneille needs a great number of episodes to demonstrate this increase in strength, his plots are relatively complex while his characters are rather simple.

Although he did not reach the heights that Racine was destined to

174

achieve, it is Corneille who made the important beginning and who marks the transition to the new drama. Corneille gave up writing between 1652 and 1659. Although he resumed his career and continued to produce plays until 1674, his late works never achieved the popularity of the early ones, and he lived to see himself eclipsed in critical esteem by Racine.

The work of Jean Racine (1639–99) marks the peak of French classical tragedy. Racine's first play, *La Thébaïde*, was produced by Molière in 1664, and his reputation was firmly established in 1667 with *Andromaque*. Among his most famous works are *Britannicus* (1669), *Bérénice* (1670), *Bajazet* (1672), and *Phaedra* (1677). Racine's plays contain little external action; most concentrate upon a psychological conflict within a single character, who wants to do the right thing but is prevented either by circumstances or by his own nature. The essential qualities of Racine's plays may be seen by looking more closely at *Phaedra*, usually considered the greatest of French tragedies.

PHAEDRA

Against her will, Phaedra loves her stepson, Hippolytus. Although she is fully aware that this love is wrong, she is powerless to resist it. Racine concentrates principally upon depicting this conflict within Phaedra.

Most plays concerned with the conflict of good and evil have shown goodness at the mercy of some external evil, or as the victim of forces set in motion by some ill-advised decision. In *Phaedra*, good and evil are bound up in the same personality. Herein lies the power of the play, for it shows a person who is thoroughly moral in her convictions but whose willpower has been sapped by irrational emotional drives. Since the conflict is primarily an internal one, Racine needs little external action.

The opening act of the play reveals that Phaedra has been in love with Hippolytus for a long time and that her inner torment has at last driven her to the verge of suicide as the only means of maintaining her moral integrity. She is prevented from carrying out her decision, however, by the news that her husband, Theseus, has died. Oenone, Phaedra's nurse and companion, convinces Phaedra that it is now no longer shameful for her to love Hippolytus.

Phaedra declares her love to Hippolytus, who reacts with disgust. Phaedra is filled with shame at her boldness and is again on the verge of despair. Her hopes are revived by Oenone, only to be completely dashed by the news that Theseus is not only alive but has arrived in Troezen, the scene of the play's action.

When Theseus enters with Hippolytus, Phaedra is faced with a moral dilemma: How can she greet her husband in the presence of his son, to whom she has just declared her love? Her hasty departure arouses Theseus' suspicion, and Oenone, to save her mistress accuses Hippolytus of having made advances to Phaedra. Theseus calls down a terrible curse upon Hippolytus and banishes him.

Phaedra is on the verge of telling Theseus the truth when he unwittingly reveals that Hippolytus is in love with Aricia. Her good motive turns to jealousy, and she refrains from making the revelation which could save Hippolytus' life.

175

Sarah Bernhardt (1844-1923) as Phaedra. The greatest French tragedienne of her time, an actress of immense charm and intensity, in a role contemporary critics considered particularly her own. Courtesy Library and Museum of the Performing Arts, Lincoln Center.

As Hippolytus leaves Troezen, a sea monster (sent by Poseidon, the sea god, in answer to Theseus' curse) frightens Hippolytus' horses and he is dragged to his death. Oenone commits suicide, and Phaedra, driven by grief, remorse, and self-disgust, takes poison. Before she dies, however, she confesses her guilt to Theseus.

As this brief outline shows, the character relationships in *Phaedra* are complex, while the external action is simple. The plot complications are important only because of the emotional reactions they arouse in the characters. The crucial factor at almost every point is Phaedra's uncontrollable passion for Hippolytus; it is this passion which brings misery to all characters in the play, for the deaths of Hippolytus, Oenone, and Phaedra, and the desolation of Theseus and Aricia all stem from this single source.

Racine uses powerful contrasts in story and characters. For example, Phaedra's confession of love to Hippolytus is placed immediately after Hippolytus' similar confession to Aricia. As a result, the innocent love of Aricia and Hippolytus is set against the illicit love of Phaedra, and the sweetness and youth of Aricia serve to point up the torment and maturity of Phaedra.

Each complication sets in motion a chain of events which is irreversible and which leads inevitably to the catastrophe: Phaedra's confession to Hippolytus makes it impossible for her to turn back; Hippolytus' confession to Aricia makes it impossible for him to turn back; Theseus' curse on Hippolytus sets another uncontrollable train of events in motion. Finally, there comes a powerful obligatory scene in which Phaedra forces herself to come face to face with Theseus after both know the full truth. There are no unnecessary scenes; Racine achieves absolute clarity without any superfluous details.

Racine adhered to the neoclassical ideals of drama almost completely, but there is no sense of strain as a result of his remaining within these

176

bounds. The unity of time is clearly observed, a few hours at the most elapse during the course of the play. The place is unspecified (it is in or around the palace), but this is typical of neoclassical drama, since what happens to the characters does not depend upon where it happens. The action is focused almost entirely upon Phaedra's passion and its results. The story of Aricia forms a minor subplot, but it is made a necessary part of the main action.

Racine based his play on Euripides' *Hippolytus*, but he made many significant changes. In Euripides' drama the emphasis is upon Hippolytus' self-righteous vow to remain chaste throughout his life. To punish him for denying her power, Aphrodite sets Phaedra's love in motion. The results are much the same as in Racine's play, but the causes and the implications are entirely different. In Euripides' work, Hippolytus is not in love with someone else, and Phaedra is a more or less innocent tool of the gods.

Racine eliminated the gods from his play and brought events into the realm of verisimilitude by showing only those occurrences which could happen in real life. The monster from the sea is the only supernatural element, and Racine could not omit it since this was an accepted part of a well-known myth. It is subordinated as much as possible, however, by placing the action offstage and by careful preparation before it happens.

Phaedra also departs obviously from its Greek model in eliminating the chorus and substituting *confidantes* for it. Each of the principal characters, except Theseus, has a confidant: Phaedra has Oenone, Hippolytus has Theramenes, and Aricia has Ismene. This is an important device since it realistically motivates the voicing of feelings and intentions. The characters speak very few passages when alone on stage, and these are either prayers or are uttered under extreme emotion. Both the use of the confidant and the elimination of soliloquies show the demand for verisimilitude at work.

Phaedra has always been considered one of the great acting parts in French drama; for a woman, it is a role comparable to that of Lear for a man. It is difficult to perform, for there is little external action, and audience attention must be riveted on Phaedra's internal conflict. The subtleties and changes of emotional states must be clearly portrayed; therefore a wide range in depicting the nuances of emotion is mandatory: her quiet resignation turns to hope in the opening scene; she is overcome by passion for Hippolytus; his rejection fills her with humiliation and rage; Theseus' return arouses abject shame and horror; she is overcome with jealousy when she learns of Hippolytus' love for Aricia; she turns on Oenone with bitterness and recrimination for the advice which has led to such a terrible situation; finally, on the point of death, she performs her duty with firm resolution. But this broad outline does not touch the gradations and subtle shifts of emotion within scenes which lay bare the heart and mind of a woman at the mercy of desires which are in conflict with her moral convictions. It is Phaedra's great capacity for moral feeling in conjunction with her uncontrollable love that makes her both admirable and pitiable at the same time. Her suffering and remorse redeem her in the minds of an audience.

177

A shoemaker's costume (1670) by Jean Berain (1637-1711), the principal designer for the court in the last part of the seventeenth century—said to have created the style associated with the reign of Louis XIV. From Jullien's *Histoire du Costume* . . . , 1880.

While Phaedra is the center of concern, each of the other principal characters is also confronted with a psychological conflict of his own. Hippolytus, for example, is torn in the beginning between his love for Aricia and his duty to his father; later, he is torn between his desire to maintain his father's honor and to vindicate his own. Hippolytus, like Phaedra, loves against his will, so there is no question that he will return Phaedra's love. All the characters desire to act rationally, but each is swayed by irrational forces. Phaedra's is merely the most extreme of the cases.

Almost nothing is said about the age or physical appearance of the characters. The emphasis is entirely upon their psychological and moral states. Decorum of character is observed for the most part, and it is the departure from decorous behavior which brings doom. Broad strokes rather than minute details have been used. The play is permeated with the aim for the universal (for the neoclassical idea of generalization) rather than for the particularities of time, place, and idiosyncrasies of character.

PLAY PRODUCTION IN FRANCE BETWEEN 1650 AND 1675

The tragic hero's costume as it developed during the seventeenth century and persisted through most of the eighteenth. An engraving after a painting by Watteau. From Gillaumont's *Costumes de la Comédie Francaise,* 1884.

The Parisian acting troupes in the time of Racine and Molière were organized on a sharing plan similar to that used by Shakespeare's company. They were democratic organizations in which each member had an equal vote. The French companies also included women, who had equal rights with the men and who received comparable pay.

Since French plays were generally less complicated than Elizabethan dramas, acting troupes were somewhat smaller. A French company was usually composed of from ten to fifteen members. As in the Elizabethan theatre, however, a number of persons were employed by the troupe as supernumerary actors, ticket takers, musicians, scene painters, scene shifters, candle snuffers, and so on.

At the end of each performance the costs of production were deducted from the receipts and the remainder divided among the shareholders. Thus each actor's income depended upon the success of the company rather than upon a fixed salary. All of the leading groups in Paris at the time, however, received some money yearly from the crown although the sum was not large enough to guarantee them against loss.

Plays were selected by a vote of the troupe after hearing a reading of the work by its author. A play might be bought outright, but a more usual practice was to give the author a percentage of the receipts for a limited number of performances, after which the play belonged solely to the troupe. The playwright assisted in the original production of his work, after which the actors were presumed to be ready to perform it upon twenty-four hours' notice.

New plays were cast by their authors, while revivals required agreement among the troupe's members. This process was simplified by the fact that each actor normally played a limited range of roles. Thus, while there were occasional disagreements over casting, in most cases the troupe was in accord about the suitability of each actor to certain kinds of parts. When a new actor came into a troupe he learned his roles from the person he was replacing, or from someone else in the company who

178

was acquainted with the way in which the parts had been played before. Roles came to be played, therefore, in a traditional manner passed on from one actor to another.

While actors might play in both comedy and tragedy, they usually specialized in one or the other. Molière, for example, was never successful in tragedy, although he was considered to be the best comic actor of his day. One additional convention should be noted: ridiculous old women were usually played by men. Molière's brother-in-law, Louis Béjart, specialized in this kind of role.

Actors were expected to furnish their own costumes as a part of their professional equipment. For the most part costumes were contemporary garments, but, as on the Elizabethan stage, there were a number of conventionalized costumes. Classical, Near Eastern, and Indian characters were usually played in elaborate and costly costumes quite unlike those worn in daily life. The typical dress of classical heroes was the *habit à la romaine*, an adaptation of Roman armor, tunic and boots, surmounted by a full-bottomed wig and plumed headdress. (See the illustration lower left, page 178.)

The scenic demands were simple. Ordinarily, the setting represented a single place, and even that was not indicated in detail, because of the neoclassical quest for generality. Since place was not to be depicted with marked individualizing features, the same set (done in the Italian manner with wings, borders, and back-scenes) could be used for a number of different plays. Furthermore, by the second half of the seventeenth century spectators were seated regularly on the stage itself (on chairs or benches at either side), leaving an acting area of only about fifteen feet wide. The actor, therefore, performed in the midst of spectators and in a very confined space. As a result, the majority of plays did not call for very much physical action, and little attention was paid to creating the illusion of a specific place. The stage, auditorium, and scenery followed in all important respects those of the Italian theatre (see Chapter 8).

The best season for plays was from November to Easter. The usual days of performance were Sunday, Tuesday, and Friday, although other days were used at times. Three o'clock was the announced time for performances, but actual starting time was later. The bill for each performance was composed of a long play and a short play (usually a comedy or farce) as an afterpiece.

In his early years Louis XIV was especially fond of the theatre. This engraving shows his costume for "Le Ballet de la Nuit" in 1653 in which he appeared as the "Sun King," an image which he cultivated for the rest of his life. From Bapst's *Essai sur l'Histoire du Théâtre,* 1893.

MOLIÈRE

Jean-Baptiste Poquelin, who assumed the name Molière (1622–73), was the son of a prosperous upholsterer of Paris. He received a good education before entering the theatre in 1643. After his first venture, the Théâtre Illustre, failed, Molière and his companions played in the provinces of France from 1646 to 1658. During those years the group obviously learned much, for when they returned to Paris they rapidly became second only to the Hôtel de Bourgogne troupe and surpassed that group in comedy. Molière was a favorite of Louis XIV, who allowed him to use the theatre which Richelieu had built, now called the Palais-Royal, and protected him in many controversies.

Molière was often called upon to provide entertainment at the court. Shown here is a scene from *La Princesse d'Elide,* a comedy-ballet performed out of doors at Versailles in 1664. The scenery was real shrubbery. From Pougin's *Dictionnaire...,* 1885.

Although Molière is noted today principally for his comedies of character and social criticism, he wrote other kinds of plays as well. Greatly influenced by the commedia dell'arte, many of his plays are farces featuring the commedia character types. He also wrote a number of comedy ballets for the court and tried his hand at tragedy. Throughout his career Molière borrowed as he saw fit from Plautus, Terence, the commedia, and from Spanish and Italian sources. It is almost solely through his efforts that French classical comedy was raised to a level equal to that of French tragedy. Molière's work has retained a more universal appeal than that of his tragic contemporaries; his plays are still to be seen on the stages of almost every country, while those of Corneille and Racine are now seldom produced outside of France.

Molière's most famous works are: *The School for Wives* (1662), *Tartuffe* (1664), *The Miser* (1668), *The Doctor in Spite of Himself* (1666), *The Misanthrope* (1666), *The Would-Be Gentleman* (1671), and *The Imaginary Invalid* (1673). *Tartuffe* will be examined in some detail as an example of his comedy.

TARTUFFE

Tartuffe, or the Impostor was produced in a three-act version in 1664, in an altered form in 1667, and in its present five acts in 1669. It has remained in the repertory almost continuously since 1669 and has been performed more often than any other play by Molière.

THEMES AND IDEAS. *Tartuffe* is obviously concerned with religious hypocrisy. While it is unwise to place too much emphasis upon contemporary conditions, it may be helpful to look at historical events which help to clarify the play.

180

The most likely target of Molière's satire is the Company of the Holy Sacrament, a secret society which had been formed in 1627 and which by 1660 had become influential throughout France. Its purposes included the repression of heresy, the promotion of charity and missionary work, and the improvement of morals. In implementing the last of these aims, the Society offended many, for it maintained "spiritual police" who spied upon the private lives of others. As one critic said of the group: "They had for their agents fanatics who to save souls recoiled from nothing, 'sanctifying by the purity of their intentions' what simple folk would call dirty actions."

Molière read *Tartuffe* to several persons before it was first produced in 1664, and the Society immediately organized an attack upon it. The controversy became so heated that Louis XIV forbade further performances. Molière revised the play in 1667 hoping to remove some of the objections only to have it withdrawn again. By 1669 the opposition was largely gone.

Whether or not Molière had the Society in mind is not of great importance. It is clear that he was thinking of groups like the Society, which feel that they alone can tell true piety from false and who create conditions under which hypocrites can flourish. Molière, through the ending of the play, indicates that France would be better off without such groups, and that the King is able to tell truth from falsehood without their aid.

As in all of Molière's works, the balanced view of life is upheld in *Tartuffe*. To Molière, true piety does not demand the abandonment of pleasure but the right use of it. The truly devout try to reform the world by actions which set a good example rather than by pious speeches, or, as it is put in the play, "They don't espouse the interests of Heaven with greater zeal than does Heaven itself."

Another favorite topic with Molière is the forced marriage. In part, this motif is a convention inherited from past comedy, especially Roman comedy and commedia dell'arte, in both of which plots frequently turn on the attempt of fathers to arrange unsuitable marriages for their children. On the other hand, Molière argues in his plays that most of the evils

Tartuffe's first meeting with Dorine in the production presented at Stratford in 1968. William Hutt as Tartuffe; Pat Galloway as Dorine. Courtesy Stratford Shakespearean Festival Foundation of Canada.

of marriage can be traced to forced unions. In *Tartuffe*, as elsewhere, he suggests that such marriages are apt to result in adultery. But in this play, marriage is an entirely secondary concern. The main theme is hypocrisy.

PLOT, STRUCTURE AND CHARACTERIZATIONS. The plot of *Tartuffe* can be divided into five stages: the demonstration of Tartuffe's complete hold over Orgon; the unmasking of Tartuffe; Tartuffe's attempted revenge; the foiling of Tartuffe's plan; and the happy resolution. There are three important reversals. The first (the unmasking of Tartuffe) brings all of the characters to an awareness of the true situation. The resulting happiness is quickly dispelled, however, when Orgon is shown to be at the mercy of Tartuffe. Since Orgon's credulity has placed him in this position, it would serve him justly to be punished, but innocent members of the family also are involved.

The first two reversals (turning the tables on Tartuffe; Tartuffe turning the tables on Orgon) have been carefully foreshadowed, but the final one and the play's resolution have not. The contrived ending (in which Tartuffe is suddenly discovered to be a notorious criminal) has been the subject of much criticism. It is an emotionally satisfying ending, in the sense that justice triumphs and normalcy is restored, but the contrivance cannot be explained away by accepted criteria of good dramatic construction.

Molière has also been criticized because of the long-delayed appearance of Tartuffe, who does not enter until the third act. This delay is not accidental, however, for Molière himself wrote:

> I have employed . . . two entire acts to prepare for the entrance of my scoundrel. He does not fool the auditor for a single moment; one knows from the first the marks I have given him; and from one end to the other he says not a word and performs not an action which does not paint for the spectators the character of an evil man.

That Molière was attempting to prevent any confusion about Tartuffe's true nature is further borne out by the inclusion in the first act of a lengthy argument by his "common sense" character, Cleante (the character who most nearly represents Molière's point of view), in which true piety is distinguished from false. There is a similar discussion in most of Molière's plays, but as a rule it comes toward the end. The placement of this argument in the first act of *Tartuffe* further indicates Molière's desire to make his purpose clear to the audience.

The structure of *Tartuffe* may also be clarified by examining the use made of various characters. Orgon's is the only role which is of importance in every act (in terms of onstage action). Cleante appears in Act I, where he performs his principal function—to present the common sense point of view. He does not appear again until Act IV; in that act and in Act V he merely re-enforces the ideas set forth in Act I. His presence in the play does not influence the action at all, but merely points up the theme.

While Dorine, the maid, appears in each act, her role is virtually completed after the beginning of Act III, even though she has been a major

Scene from *Tartuffe* as directed by Roger Planchon, one of the most respected of contemporary French producers. Photography by Pic.

character up to that point. Her frankness and openness are used as a foil to show off Orgon's credulity, the lovers' petulancy, and Tartuffe's false piety. It is she, with her wit and common sense who sets their exaggerated behavior in proper perspective. After Tartuffe's entrance, she is no longer needed.

Even Tartuffe is given rather strange treatment when he finally makes his appearance after two acts of preparation. He has one of the most famous entrance lines ever written: "Laurent, put away my hair shirt and my scourge, and pray heaven may ever enlighten you. If any one asks to see me, tell them I've gone to the prison to distribute the charity which others have given me."

But the majority of his role is given over to his two "love scenes" with Elmire. Molière seems to take it for granted that the audience will accept the picture of Tartuffe painted earlier by the other characters and that the play need only show one aspect of his hypocrisy. Tartuffe's first speeches to Dorine (those in which he asks her to cover her bosom with a handkerchief so as not to arouse evil thoughts in him) reveal his sensual nature, and it is this quality that is emphasized onstage.

Tartuffe displays another important side of his character when he is denounced by Damis. Rather than defend himself, he appears to accept the accusations with humility and as the lot of a pious man. This scene more than any other shows how Orgon has come to be taken in by Tartuffe.

While Act V shows Tartuffe's true nature, which has been masked under his hypocrisy, it is still true, nevertheless, that most of what the audience knows of Tartuffe comes from what other characters say about him rather than through what he actually does onstage.

The lovers, Valère and Mariane, appear in Act II and are unimportant thereafter. They serve merely to show how far Orgon has been influenced by Tartuffe, since Orgon is planning to marry Mariane to Tartuffe. The lovers' quarrel is a source of amusement but it is largely unrelated to the rest of the play. As in commedia, the lovers are handsome, upright, and admirable young people who deserve each other's love and who are being kept apart by a muddle-headed and perverse parent.

Elmire is also used when needed and ignored at other times. She appears in Act III (in which Tartuffe tries to seduce her), but she has only a few lines and most of these treat Tartuffe's suggestions with an air of frivolity. The bulk of her lines come in Act IV, where she serves as the instrument for unmasking Tartuffe. This uneven distribution of the role has led to some confusion about her true nature, for some have argued that her moral character is questionable. It seems clear, however, that Molière had in mind a reasonably worldly but upright woman.

It is Orgon's role, however, which is most evenly distributed throughout the play. While the Tartuffes of the world are dangerous, they can exist only because of the Orgons, for the prosperity of the wicked depends upon the gullibility of the foolish. Just as Molière emphasizes Tartuffe's calculated piety, so too, he emphasizes Orgon's impulsiveness and stubbornness. Orgon is not a fool; he is a prosperous merchant with a substantial fortune. He errs in his judgment of Tartuffe largely because he acts without considering sufficient aspects of a question. When Tartuffe is finally unmasked, Orgon's character remains consistent, for failing to see the difference between hypocrisy and piety, he says: "I give up all pious people. From now on I will hold them in utter contempt, and treat them worse than the devil himself." Thus, instead of returning to middle ground he assumes an equally exaggerated, though opposite, position.

Little indication is given of the age or physical appearance of characters. Since Molière wrote with his own company in mind and directed the play, he undoubtedly filled in many of the details left unspecified in the script. The role of Tartuffe was written for DuCroisy, a large man with a ruddy complexion. This, no doubt, was one of the sources of humor. All of Tartuffe's talk about scourges, hair shirts, and fasting were contradicted by his obvious plumpness, rosy health, and lecherousness. Orgon was played by Molière, noted for his expressive face and body, while Elmire was acted by Molière's wife, who was twenty-seven years old in 1669. Since Mme. Pernell was played by a man, the character was no doubt intended to be ridiculous with her exaggerated censure of everyone except Tartuffe, and in her denunciation of pleasure. All of the characters are drawn from the middle or lower classes (in accordance with the neoclassical standard of comedy).

Probably the least challenging roles for actors are those of Cleante and the lovers. Although meant to arouse audience sympathy, they are more nearly cardboard figures than the others. Tartuffe's role is difficult and the actor playing it must be wary of becoming too villainous, if the comedy is not to disappear under too great a threat. Orgon's is probably the best acting role, for not only is it the longest, it requires the greatest comic skill. One indication of the difficulty of the role is the scene in which Orgon conceals himself under the table and overhears Tartuffe's attempts to seduce Elmire. The success of the scene depends in large part upon a highly skilled pantomimic performance by the actor playing Orgon.

The unities of time and place are strictly observed in *Tartuffe*. Only a single room is required and even that needs only a table—under which Orgon can be concealed—and a closet—in which Damis can hide—for no specific use is made of the setting except in these two instances. The action is continuous, or nearly so, and occurs in a single day. All of the episodes, with the possible exception of the lovers' quarrel, are directly related to the main theme of the play. *Tartuffe* is clearly within the classical tradition.

Molière, nevertheless, has let dramatic need, rather than any preconceived notion of form, dictate his technique. In spite of all objections raised to it, *Tartuffe* has remained one of the most popular plays ever written. If it has flaws, it rises above them.

AFTER MOLIÈRE'S DEATH

Molière died in 1673. His life and death illustrate the status of the actor in France at that time, for, while he was highly admired as an author, his acting made him ineligible for many honors. He could not be admitted to the French Academy, and upon his death he was forbidden a Christian burial, since the strictures against actors issued in late Roman times were still in effect. Most actors renounced their professions when death approached so that they might be acceptable to the church, but Molière died suddenly, being taken ill during a performance, and either did not have time or refused to go through the usual formalities. Thus, while the actor's legal and economic status had improved by 1673, he was still in some senses an outcast.

Following Molière's death, French drama rapidly declined. Corneille gave up writing after 1674 and Racine wrote no plays for the public stage after 1677. Thus, the great age of French playwriting was over by 1680. The number of theatres also shrank steadily.

At the time of Molière's death, five theatrical companies were playing in Paris: Molière's, the companies at the Hôtel de Bourgogne and the Marais, a company of Italian actors, and an opera troupe. In 1673, the director of the opera, Jean-Baptiste Lully, gained control of the Palais-Royal, and the Molière's company was forced to move. Soon afterward it was amalgamated with the Marais company and, in 1680 this combined company was ordered to merge with the Hôtel de Bourgogne troupe.

This merger is one of the most important events in French theatrical history, for the new group became the Comédie Française, the first national theatre in the world. This organization is still in existence, and more nearly embodies a continuous theatrical tradition than any other single theatre.

The order which created the Comédie Française also laid down the rules under which it was to be governed. Like its predecessors, it was to be a shareholding company governed democratically by its members.

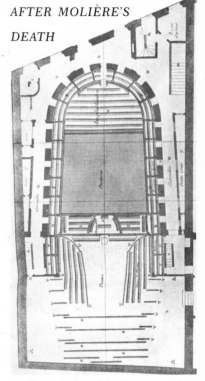

Ground plan of the theatre used by the Comédie Française between 1689-1770. Note the benches on the stage for spectators. From Mantzius' *History of Theatrical Art.* Volume IV, 1905.

The *commedia dell'arte* troupe of the Hôtel de Bourgogne in 1689. From *Almanach de l'An 1689*.

Procedures were established for the admission of actors, retirement, pensions, and all other matters. A yearly subsidy was provided by the state.

After 1680, there were three troupes in Paris: the Comédie Française, the Opéra, and an Italian commedia dell'arte company. When the Italian troupe was expelled in 1697 (after an alleged satirical attack upon Mme. de Maintenon, Louis XIV's second wife), the number was reduced to two.

In 1672, the Opéra had been awarded a monopoly on musical drama and other forms which utilized trained vocalists, more than six musical instruments, or complex dance or spectacle. After the expulsion of the Italians, the Comédie Française achieved a similar monopoly on spoken drama. Thus, by the end of the seventeenth century, the Parisian theatre not only had shrunk but the remaining troupes held entrenched positions which they were to defend against all encroachments throughout the eighteenth century.

The age of French classicism had brought the theatre of France to maturity. It produced three great playwrights, Corneille, Racine, and Molière, who have remained the primary models for French drama since that time. The peak of strength reached in the years between 1650 and 1680 would not be regained for several generations.

186

Chapter 10 THE EIGHTEENTH CENTURY

During the eighteenth century, the theatre expanded rapidly into areas that had not previously had professional troupes. Furthermore, dramatic forms proliferated and theatrical practices underwent many changes, although the neoclassical mode remained dominant. Since the British theatre is of most interest to English-speaking readers, it will be treated first and at greatest length.

ENGLAND

Charles II was restored to the throne of England in 1660 and with him the theatre regained its place in English life. Since then, although theatres have been closed during plagues, at the time of royal deaths, and on other occasions, English theatrical tradition has never been interrupted.

Soon after theatres were reopened, state control was established. At first, control was exercised largely through the patents, or monopolies, which Charles II issued to William D'Avenant (1606–68), who headed the Duke's Men, and Thomas Killigrew (1612–83), who headed the King's Men. For a time George Jolly held a third patent, but the number was soon reduced to two.

Many attempts were made in the first part of the eighteenth century to circumvent the patents, but these violations, coupled with numerous satirical attacks on government officials and policies, led to the passage of the Licensing Act in 1737. This law reconfirmed the patents and further provided that before production all plays must be licensed by the Lord Chamberlain, who thus became an official censor. Under the terms of the law the government came to control both the plays and the number of theatres. Although the enforcement of these provisions was relaxed from time to time, the number of theatres licensed to produce legitimate

The Drury Lane Theatre, one of London's major theatres from the Restoration until the present time, as it appeared in 1792. The present Drury Lane Theatre is used primarily for musicals. From Wilkinson's *Londina Illustrata*, 1825.

Interior of the Covent Garden Theatre in 1794. One of the two main theatres of London from 1732 until 1843, the Covent Garden has been the home of opera since the mid-nineteenth century. From Wilkinson's *Londina Illustrata*, 1825.

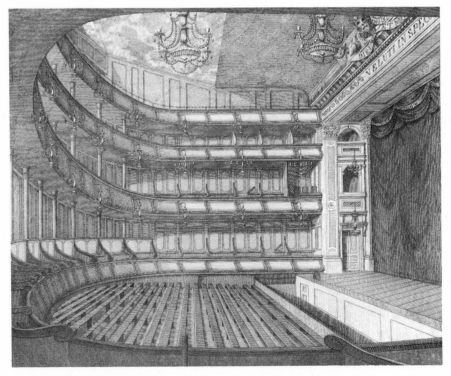

A scene from Elkanah Settle's *The Empress of Morocco* (1673) at the Duke's Theatre in Dorset Gardens, London. Although the forestage is not shown, a portion of the proscenium doors and stage boxes can be seen at the extreme sides. From Wilkinson's *Londina Illustrata*, 1825.

drama in London remained at two until 1843, when the patents were rescinded. The provision for the licensing of plays remained in effect until 1968. Between 1737 and 1843 the two patent houses in London were Drury Lane and Covent Garden. After 1766, the Haymarket Theatre was permitted to present regular drama during the summer months.

THEATRE STRUCTURE

When the English theatre reopened in 1660, performances were given at first in playhouses which had been built before 1642. Soon, however, new structures were erected which differed in only a few respects from those in Italy.

The principal difference was in the size and use of the apron (that portion of the stage which extends forward of the proscenium arch), for while continental theatres had aprons, they were not used extensively and did not have proscenium doors (that is, doors opening onto the apron). During the Restoration, there were sometimes as many as three proscenium doors on each side of the stage, although two were more usual. These doors allowed for great flexibility in staging. For example, an actor might exit through one door and re-enter immediately at another door on the same side, thus indicating a change in place or a passage of time. The apron stage was comparable in many ways to the fore-stage of the Elizabethan theatre and the platea of the medieval theatre.

The apron gradually diminished in depth in the eighteenth century, but both it and the proscenium doors were retained until well into the nineteenth century, when the demand for greater realism led to their gradual abandonment. Because much of the action took place on the apron, the setting was principally a background rather than an environment for the actor, who performed primarily on the apron where he could establish more intimate contact with the audience.

The auditorium, with its boxes, pit, and galleries, was similar to that found on the continent. From the Restoration on, however, all spectators in the English pit were seated. Until 1762, spectators were also permitted to sit on the stage.

SCENERY

The scenery used in the English theatre between 1660 and 1800 differed in no important respect from that of France and Italy. Scenes were painted in perspective on wings, borders and backdrops. Since settings were generalized in accordance with the neoclassical demand for universality, a large number was not needed. Plays were usually set in a palace, a garden, a prison, or another generalized place, and consequently the same setting was used for a number of different plays. Sometimes theatres even used a set of "neutral" wings which remained stationary throughout a play while only the back-scene was shifted to indicate a change in place. The "groove" system of shifting scenery (explained in Chapter 8) was standard in England.

Pantomimes, operas, and a few plays, however, demanded more detailed scenery and elaborate special effects. In these cases, new scenery was specially designed and widely advertised. On such occasions, spectators might also be forbidden to sit on the stage. Until about 1750, theatres did not employ full-time scenic artists, for they commissioned scenery as needed from well-known painters. As the taste for spectacle grew in the last part of the eighteenth century, however, each theatre came to employ one or more scene painters, and new scenery appeared with greater frequency. At the same time, the awakening interest in *local color* led to increased emphasis upon specific times and places.

The most important eighteenth-century English scene designer was Philippe Jacques de Loutherbourg (1740–1812), who began staging spectacular pieces (he seldom designed for legitimate drama) for David Garrick in the early 1770's. He complicated the stage picture by adding ground rows (profile pieces shaped and painted to represent rocks, mountains, grassy plots, fences and similar objects) to the traditional wing-border-drop settings. Since these could be placed almost anywhere on the stage, he increased naturalness and the illusion of greater space and distance.

De Loutherbourg also reproduced likenesses of actual places on stage and thereby helped to create a demand for greater scenic illusion. He improved stage lighting and was able to give the effect of natural light at

190

Left. The closet scene from *Hamlet,* thought to show Thomas Betterton in the role of Hamlet. From Nicholas Rowe's edition of Shakespeare's plays, 1709. *Right.* David Garrick in the storm scene of *King Lear.* Note the eighteenth-century garments. From a contemporary engraving after a painting by Wilson. Courtesy University of Iowa Library.

different seasons, times of day, and in varying weather conditions by utilizing transparent backdrops behind which special lighting devices could achieve the semblance of a rising moon, a volcanic eruption, changes from fair to stormy weather, and similar effects. Such practices were to be more thoroughly exploited in the nineteenth century.

THE ACTOR

When the English theatre was reopened in 1660 its financial structure was considerably altered from that of Shakespeare's day. From the Restoration on, the theatre was to come more and more under the control of businessmen. After 1660 actors often served as managers of theatrical troupes, but most actors withdrew from the business affairs of the theatre. They became employees rather than active participants in management.

Typically, in the English theatre an actor was hired for a stated period, usually one or two years, at a specified salary with the additional guarantee of one or more "benefit" performances each year. At a benefit performance, the receipts (after deduction of operating expenses) go to an actor, author, charitable group, or other designated source. The first benefit performance for an individual actor dates from about 1685, and after about 1710 every performer enjoyed at least one benefit each season. While this practice usually brought the actor additional income, it also offered the manager an excuse for paying him less salary during the rest of the year. Benefits often were occasions for great rejoicing, but they could also be sources of embarrassment if the attendance was small, for they became a test of popularity.

191

Although the English actor did not have the financial security enjoyed by his French contemporaries, his social status was higher. He was never excluded from the church; a number of actresses married into the nobility; some actors were even buried in Westminster Abbey, an honor reserved for persons of great esteem. On the other hand, the moral character of the actor continued to be questioned by the general populace.

Each actor or actress (actresses were introduced to the English stage in the 1660's and were accepted throughout Europe after that time) was usually employed for a *line of business*. This meant that each was trained to play a specific kind of part. If his line of business included the young lover, he usually played such roles regardless of age until he retired from the stage. While this sometimes led to incongruous casting, it also allowed the actor to develop considerable perfection in his specialty.

An actor learned his profession from experience rather than at a school. He might begin in a provincial company and later be taken into a more important troupe, or he might learn a line of business while acting supernumerary roles in a London theatre. Once he was accepted as a full member of a troupe, however, his line of business was usually fixed for life.

Each actor also *possessed parts*. This meant that once he was given a particular role, it remained his until he left the company. An actor might have assigned to him up to a hundred roles, any one of which he could be expected to perform on twenty-four hours' notice.

Many of these practices were determined by the *repertory system* (under which a number of plays are alternated throughout a season). Between 1660 and 1875 the majority of any company's repertory was made up of standard plays from the past. A lesser part was composed of recent plays from previous seasons. Usually these recent plays were not popular enough to justify their continuation for more than a few years. The smallest amount of a company's offerings was made up of new plays. Those sufficiently popular were retained in the repertory, but many new plays were dropped after a single season or even after a single performance.

New plays were usually staged by their writers, while old plays were rehearsed by the stage manager, normally an actor in the company who also performed these additional duties. In any case, "the director" took it for granted that the actor knew his job and probably restricted himself to establishing entrances and exits and suggesting details of characterization or line readings. He probably spent very little time with the blocking (the positioning of actors on stage). Actors learned as part of their training to give the best stage positions to the leading characters and to move around them as inconspicuously as possible. The actor also learned to direct his speeches to the audience as much as to the other characters. The presence of the audience was constantly recognized and emphasized by the practice of leaving the lights on in the auditorium throughout a performance.

Rehearsals for plays not previously in the repertory normally extended from seven to twelve days. Meanwhile the actors were also performing nightly, and a short "refresher" rehearsal was probably held each day for the play that was to be performed that evening. By modern standards rehearsal procedures were perfunctory and great reliance was placed on the actor's stage presence and quick wit.

Acting style was no doubt much more exaggerated than modern taste would approve. The actor was said to base his acting on life, but to idealize what he found there rather than merely to copy it. Thus there was careful selection, arrangement, and considerable exaggeration. Periodically during the eighteenth century, actors supposedly reformed acting in the direction of a more natural style. But naturalism in acting is a relative matter, and these actors probably only eliminated some of the exaggeration. The eighteenth-century actor was always an actor, and it is unlikely that his performance was ever confused with real-life behavior.

The eighteenth-century actor surpassed the playwright as the major artist in the theatre. Audiences in large part went to see a particular actor perform a particular role. The appeal was comparable to that of opera today, for, since it might already know the play, the audience attended to enjoy the skill of a specific actor. After each effective speech or scene the audience applauded as it does today when a singer finishes an operatic aria. This constant interaction between audience and actor made for a more intimate relationship than that encountered in theatres today.

The most famous actors in England between 1660 and 1800 were Thomas Betterton, Colley Cibber, James Quin, David Garrick, and Charles Macklin. Thomas Betterton (*c.* 1635–1710) dominated the English stage from about 1670 to 1710, during which time he played the leading roles in almost all of the plays in the repertory. Colley Cibber (1671–1757) is the best-known performer of the period from Betterton's death until the 1730's. Primarily a comic actor, he excelled in the role of the "fop," or fashionable man-about-town. His autobiography is one of the principal sources of information about the theatre of that period.

David Garrick and Mrs. Hannah Pritchard as Macbeth and Lady Macbeth. From *English Illustrated Magazine*, 1776.

Charles Macklin as Shylock. Macklin supposedly played Shylock as a semiserious character, departing from the earlier tradition of treating Shylock as a low comedy role. From Doran's "*His Majesty's Servants,*" 1897.

Between 1730 and 1740, James Quin (1692–1766), who was noted especially for his declamatory style, was considered the best tragic actor. It was partially due to Quin's acting style that David Garrick (1717–79) was said to have returned acting to a more natural mode when he came into prominence in the 1740's. Garrick was the major actor on the English stage between 1741 and 1776, as well as a manager of the Drury Lane Theatre from 1747 to 1776. Through his sound judgment and taste, both in management and acting, he elevated the English theatre to a position of international esteem. Especially noted for his performance of Shakespearean roles, he is generally thought to have been the greatest of English actors.

Charles Macklin (1699–1797) acted for approximately seventy years and was probably the most realistic actor of the century. He was especially well known for his playing of irascible old men and for his revolutionary portrayal of Shylock, a role which had been performed previously by low comedians.

The actor in an established theatre company in London in the eighteenth century enjoyed a comfortable life, though his counterpart in the provincial company still led a hazardous existence. Even in London, however, there was as yet no pension system (as in France), and many actors ended their days in poverty.

THE PLAYWRIGHT

But the actor's position was more secure than that of the playwright. In the Restoration, writers of plays might be employed by companies on a fixed salary, but this practice was soon replaced by benefits. Under this system, the author received the receipts of the third performance. If a play were especially popular he might also receive benefits on the sixth, ninth, and each additional third night of the initial run of a play. As a rule, however, he was fortunate to receive one benefit. After the initial run, the play belonged to the company and the author received no further payment. The playwright frequently sold the publication rights of his plays for a small sum of money. It was not until well into the nineteenth century that the playwright was able to obtain a copyright and demand a royalty for each performance.

The period from 1660–1700 is noted particularly for heroic tragedy and comedy of manners. The heroic play was written in rhymed couplets, usually concerned the necessity of choosing between love and honor (the relative merits of which were debated in lengthy and bombastic speeches), and abounded in violent action and startling reversals. Today these plays seem totally unreal and absurd, although they were extremely popular in their own period.

Alongside the heroic play another more vital strain of tragedy developed. Written in blank verse and more directly descended from the tragedies of Shakespeare, the outstanding examples are Thomas Otway's (1652–85) *Venice Preserv'd* and *The Orphan*, both of which held the stage until the nineteenth century. Another type of Restoration tragedy can best be seen in *All for Love*, by John Dryden (1631–1700), a rework-

194

ing of Shakespeare's *Antony and Cleopatra* to make it conform to neo-classical ideals.

The Restoration is principally noted, however, for the comedy of manners, a kind of play in which characters and events are subordinated to social values and customs.

There has been much argument over the moral tone of Restoration comedy. Since 1700 most critics have interpreted it as condoning or accepting behavior normally considered reprehensible. It is probably true that these plays waver between accepting and satirizing the age, but they should not be condemned too hastily. Before passing judgment, it is important to understand the basic view behind these plays.

Restoration comedies imply that man is corruptible, but that this fact must be accepted with an attitude of sophistication and tolerance rather than one of indignation and outrage. Restoration writers did not mean, however, that all forms of behavior are justified and that no distinctions are to be made between actions. The admirable man was thought to base his behavior on the maxim, "Know thyself," for this would lead him to assess his own qualities and capabilities and to respect them in his daily life. The plays, therefore, satirize persons who are either self-deceived or who are attempting to deceive others. The humor is directed against the fop, the pretender at wit and sophistication, the old woman who is trying to be young, the old man who marries a young wife, and other similar types. The standard is represented by those characters who are truly witty and sophisticated, who see others and themselves clearly, and who act accordingly. These characters always accept everything with tolerance, however, and for this reason the plays have often given the impression of condoning immoral behavior. In a few plays immoral behavior is accepted, but in the majority the rewards and punishments are meted out in accordance with how well the characters have been able to live up to the ideal of self-knowledge.

Restoration comedy originated with such works as George Etherege's (1634–91) *Love in a Tub* (1664), *The Man of Mode* (1676), and *She Would If She Could* (1668), and it reached its perfection in the plays of William Congreve (1670–1729), especially *Love for Love* (1695) and *The Way of the World* (1700).

The Restoration comedy of manners was not calculated to please the Puritan elements in English society. After the return of Charles II in 1660 Puritan influence, which had dominated England during the Commonwealth, was little felt for some time. Theatre audiences were largely drawn from the upper classes or from the more liberal members of the middle class. A change set in after 1689, however, when William and Mary were crowned rulers of England. Under the patronage of the new rulers, the merchant class came to wield great power, and in the 1690's when it began to attend the theatre, it exerted pressure for reforms.

The rise of the middle class coincided with a resurgence of Puritan ideas, the most powerful statement of which appeared in Jeremy Collier's *A Short View of the Immorality and Profaneness of the English*

A scene from Dryden's *All for Love*. From *The Dramatick Works of John Dryden, Esq.*, 1735.

195

A scene from Farquhar's *The Beaux' Stratagem*. From *The Works of the Late Ingenious Mr. George Farquhar*, 1711.

Stage, published in 1698. In this work Collier attacked current plays, particularly the comedies of manners. While many of the dramatists of the day defended their own works and those of other writers, Collier was sufficiently persuasive that many playwrights reconsidered their views. All of these factors combined to bring about a change in the subject matter and spirit of English drama after 1700.

The transition to the new outlook can be seen most clearly in the comedies of George Farquhar (1678-1707), whose *The Recruiting Officer* and *The Beaux' Stratagem* are among the best English plays of the early eighteenth century. The new drama put a greater emphasis upon a clear-cut set of moral standards, the settings were more frequently placed outside of London, and the characters were less apt to be drawn from fashionable society.

While neoclassical tragedy continued to be written throughout the eighteenth century (the best-known example is *Cato* by Joseph Addison), the most important dramatic types were to be sentimental comedy and domestic tragedy. The appearance of these forms can be explained in part by the desire of the middle class to see itself and its ideals depicted on the stage.

SENTIMENTAL DRAMA

The term *sentimental* is sometimes used to describe almost all of the drama of the eighteenth century. It indicates basically an overemphasis upon arousing sympathetic response to the misfortunes of others.

Even comedy became preoccupied with the ordeals of sympathetic characters, and humorous scenes were reserved for minor characters, usually servants. Plays could be called comedies largely because they

196

ended happily rather than because of subject matter or treatment. The expressed aim of the dramatist was to draw forth a smile and a tear, or, as one writer put it, to produce "a pleasure too exquisite for laughter." Characters were refined, filled with noble sentiments, oppressed by circumstances which they bore bravely, and from which they were eventually rescued and handsomely rewarded.

Today these plays seem highly exaggerated in their depiction of human nature. The characters appear too good and noble and the circumstances too contrived to be convincing. But these plays attracted large audiences, who were reduced to tears and who accepted the works as realistic pictures of human motivations. To understand the plays, therefore, it is necessary to examine the view of human psychology prevalent at that time.

The eighteenth century conceived of man as being good by nature. To remain good, a man needed only to listen to his instincts and to follow their promptings. Evil behavior was thought to result from unfortunate circumstances or the failure to follow dictates of the heart. Consequently, the person who fell into evil ways might be reformed, sometimes even in a moment's time, through an appeal to his basic goodness. The endurance of ordeals was looked upon as the test of true virtue and the rewarding of those who withstood hardships and temptations as a logical and necessary outcome.

One other factor—the attitude toward emotional display—helps to explain the appeal of sentimental drama in the eighteenth century. Man was viewed as subject to all sorts of pressures from without, against which he must exert counteracting pressures from within if he was not to be overwhelmed. The chief form of outwardly directed pressure was considered to be emotion. The display of emotion, then, became both the sign of a healthy mind and a means of maintaining health. Furthermore, the ideal emotions were thought to be those sympathetic responses aroused when witnessing the suffering of innocent beings. Emotional display, therefore, was proof of a virtuous nature (one properly moved at the sight of suffering), and, at the same time, this response helped to maintain health. To weep and to feel deeply, then, were desirable, and playwrights labored to fulfill the needs. Eighteenth-century sentimental comedy received its first full expression in *The Conscious Lovers* (1722) by Sir Richard Steele (1672–1729). Its later development is best exemplified in Hugh Kelly's (1739–77) *False Delicacy* (1768).

Sentimental comedy had its serious counterpart in domestic tragedy, which deliberately avoided the kings and nobility of traditional tragedy and chose its characters from everyday life (principally the merchant class). It usually painted the horrible outcome of giving in to sin, just as sentimental comedy showed the rewards of resisting sin.

George Lillo (1693-1739) established the vogue for domestic tragedy with *The London Merchant* (1731), a play which shows an apprentice who, led astray by a depraved woman, robs his employer and murders his uncle. It is clearly indicated that had the apprentice resisted temptation he could have married his employer's daughter and become a prosperous merchant. The virtues of the merchant class are praised and sin is denounced in the most obvious terms. Today *The London Merchant* seems overly simple, but it exerted great power over audiences throughout the eighteenth century and was a major influence on the drama of France and Germany. Although others tried to follow in Lillo's steps, *The Gamester* (1753) by Edward Moore (1712–57) is the only other notable English play of the type.

Sentimental comedy and domestic tragedy are indicative of the weakening of neoclassical standards. Each represents a considerable departure from the "pure" dramatic forms, mingling elements formerly reserved solely for either comedy or tragedy.

BALLAD OPERA, BURLESQUE, AND PANTOMIME

Other departures from the neoclassical ideal occurred in the eighteenth century as new "illegitimate" forms appeared. The most important of the new forms were ballad opera, burlesque, and pantomime.

The emergence of ballad opera can be explained in part by the popularity of Italian opera. In the early years of the Restoration, opera was imported into England, and for a time there was a struggle between the Italian form and a native English opera. The Italian form triumphed and in the early years of the eighteenth century was enormously popular. The vogue reached its peak with the works of George Frederick Handel (1685–1759), who lived in England after 1710. The ballad opera built upon this enthusiastic response.

The first and most important example of the new form is *The Beggar's Opera* (1728) by John Gay (1685–1732). In *ballad opera*, sections of dialogue alternate with lyrics set to the tunes of popular songs. *The Beggar's Opera* was so popular that the producers were forced to keep it running continuously for sixty performances, one of the first long runs in history. Its popularity led to many imitations between 1728 and 1737.

While *The Beggar's Opera* treated the Italian opera humorously, it did much more, for it also satirized the contemporary political situation in England. At the end of the work one of the characters observes that it is difficult to tell whether the robbers are imitating the ruling classes or whether the ruling classes are imitating the robbers. The moral is said to lie in the demonstration that the lower classes, like the upper, have their vices, but that, unlike the upper classes, the lower orders are punished for their wrongdoings. The ballad opera eventually gave way to the sentimental operetta, or comic opera. The principal writer of this form was Isaac Bickerstaffe (1735–1812), whose most popular works were *Love in a Village* (1762) and *The Maid of the Mill* (1765).

During the 1730's Henry Fielding (1707–54) turned to writing farces which burlesqued much of the drama of the day and frequently satirized the ruling classes more severely than had Gay. Fielding's *The Tragedy of Tragedies, or, The Life and Death of Tom Thumb the Great* (1730) travesties the tragedies of the time, while his *Pasquin* and *The Historical Register for 1736* ridicule contemporary politics and social conditions. The combination of ballad opera and burlesque did much to bring about the passage of the Licensing Act of 1737.

198

A design by Cipriani and Richards for Charles Dibdin's pantomine, *The Mirror, or, Harlequin Everywhere,* at Covent Garden in 1779. From *The Magazine of Art,* 1895.

The most popular new form in the eighteenth century, however, was *pantomime*. It came into being around 1715 and was perfected by John Rich (c. 1682–1761), manager of one of the patent companies. The pantomime was composed of dancing and silent mimicry performed to musical accompaniment and set against elaborate scenery and special effects. Typically, comic and serious scenes alternated. The comic plot usually involved Harlequin, who by some device has obtained a magic wand by means of which he can transform places, objects, and persons at will. Normally, the serious plot was derived from a mythological or historical subject already known to the audience.

Pantomime made its appeal largely to the eye, and great expense and much time was lavished on producing it. But the investment was repaid by increased attendance. It was largely because of the visual requirements of opera and pantomime that stage machinery and scenery became so elaborate in England.

GOLDSMITH AND SHERIDAN

By the 1770's sentimentalism (in the form of comedy, domestic tragedy, comic opera, and pantomime) dominated the English stage. At this time two dramatists, Goldsmith and Sheridan, endeavored to reform public taste.

Oliver Goldsmith (1730–74) through his plays, *The Good-Natured Man* (1768) and *She Stoops to Conquer* (1773), attempted to re-establish what he called "laughing" comedy. His plays are in the tradition of Jonson's more boisterous works or Shakespeare's farces. The plays of Richard Brinsley Sheridan (1751–1816), on the other hand, are in the vein of Restoration comedy but free from its ambiguous moral tone. His most famous plays are *The Rivals* (1775), *The Critic* (1779), and *The School for Scandal* (1777), frequently said to be the greatest comedy of manners in the English language.

THE SCHOOL FOR SCANDAL

THEMES AND IDEAS. On the surface, *The School for Scandal* and *Tartuffe* have striking parallels. These may be seen especially in the unmasking of the hypocrite, and the means used to make the husband realize that he has been deceived.

The differences between Molière's and Sheridan's plays, however, are greater than their similarities. *Tartuffe*, for example, is more restricted in its action and number of characters. But the greatest difference is in tone: *Tartuffe* shows the threat of religious hypocrisy to individual freedom and morality; *The School for Scandal* is largely confined to satiriz-

199

The screen scene from the original production of *The School for Scandal,* 1777. Note the forestage, proscenium doors, stage boxes, clearly defined wings, and the similarity of the actors' costumes to those worn by the spectators. Courtesy Yale University Library.

ing sentimental comedy and scandalmongering. Unlike Tartuffe, Joseph Surface never becomes a serious threat to the welfare of admirable characters, and the "school" of scandalmongers tampers, for the most part, with the reputations of persons never seen by the audience. As a result, Sheridan's play is more lighthearted in tone and seems far less serious in purpose than does Molière's work.

The School for Scandal is a comedy of manners, for it is primarily concerned with depicting the fashions and customs of the day. The main action is set against the background of a "school for scandal" which embodies the contemporary social setting. The shallowness of this group allows hypocrites such as Joseph Surface to flourish, since it cannot distinguish between pious statement and virtuous action. Furthermore, the group's own shallowness prevents its members from perceiving the depths of character in others. Trifling with reputations, consequently, has become a game for those who are unable to distinguish between fashionable behavior and true character.

Sheridan places much of the blame for this state of affairs on the vogue for sentimentalism, and his principal unsympathetic character, Joseph Surface, is made a "man of sentiment"—that is, one who mouths moral maxims. His pious statements are accepted as proof of a virtuous character, while the frank and natural behavior of his brother, Charles, is taken as the sign of a lost soul. Sheridan is ultimately concerned with the distinction between true virtue and pious remarks—between ingrained character and superficial "sentiment." His sophisticated and humorous treatment of this theme, however, never allows its serious aspects to come to the fore, for he concentrates on the comic results of human shortsightedness and frailty. Much of the humor in the play results from the way in which the plans and methods of the rascals serve as traps in which they themselves are caught.

While Sheridan satirizes sentimental comedy, he has not been able to free his own play from many of its traits. His admirable characters are inclined to moralize or fall into "sentiments," as does Maria ("Wit loses its respect with me when I see it in company with malice"), and the play as a whole illustrates the typical lesson of sentimental comedy (true virtue will be rewarded—and with a sizable fortune). Furthermore, characters have been divided into the truly virtuous, who act according to the dictates of their hearts, and the misguided, who behave according to current fashion. Lady Teazle's actions demonstrate at first the results of following fashion; her reform is brought about by listening to the dictates of her heart.

PLOT AND STRUCTURE. *The School for Scandal* has both a Prologue and an Epilogue, as did almost every play written during the Restoration and eighteenth century. The Prologue is used to put the audience in the right frame of mind and to suggest the mood of the play, while the Epilogue contains an appeal for audience favor along with a summation of the play's basic intention. Both Prologue and Epilogue are short and neither is essential for understanding the play.

The School for Scandal is structurally complex since it weaves together the schemes, desires and cross-purposes of so many characters: the underhanded machinations of Joseph Surface and Lady Sneerwell, the cross-purposes of Sir Peter and Lady Teazle, the attempts by Sir Oliver to discover to whom he should leave his money, the desires of Charles and Maria to marry each other, and the rather generalized desire of the scandalmongers to interfere in the affairs of everyone else.

Sheridan has solved his problem in part through the relationship he has established among the characters. All move within the same social circle in London and all know each other well. Furthermore, Sir Peter is the guardian of Maria and has been the best friend of the now-deceased father of Charles and Joseph Surface. These close ties allow Sheridan to maneuver his characters more freely and to motivate their appearance whenever they are needed by the action. They also allow him to bring together logically the various strands of the plot as the play progresses.

The scandalmongers are among the least important characters, but they are used to great advantage in the play's structure. First, Sheridan establishes the social background by showing the school in action. Second, the school is used for expository purposes, for their gossip reveals many important facts and sets up the conditions out of which the conflicts arise. Third, their gossip and intrigues affect the other characters. It is they who have almost ruined Charles Surface's reputation with Sir Peter and Maria, and it is Snake's defection from the group which eventually clears the final obstacle from the path of Charles and Maria. Fourth, the school is one of the principal sources of comedy through its witty and malicious conversations. It is a mark of Sheridan's greatness as a comic writer that the group always remains ridiculous and, while complicating the action, does not seriously threaten the welfare of the sympathetic characters.

201

Sheridan's structural methods often resemble the technique used by Shakespeare. The similarity is especially evident in the way the subplot and the main plot are integrated. In *The School for Scandal* the Sir Peter -Lady Teazle story has little connection with the Joseph-Maria-Charles story in the beginning. As the play progresses, however, the two stories move closer and closer together, and in the "screen" scene the revelation of Joseph's relationship with Lady Teazle leads to the resolution of both the subplot and the main plot. Sheridan, like Shakespeare, also moves the place of action in accordance with the needs of his story. *The School for Scandal* has fourteen scenes which occur in four different houses. This freedom of movement makes the complex plotting much easier, for it would be almost impossible for all of the events to occur believably in a single place.

Sheridan, like both Shakespeare and Molière, constantly strives for clarity in characterization and situation. For example, in the opening scene he makes it quite plain that Joseph Surface is a hypocrite who is attempting to ruin his brother. The situation between Sir Peter and Lady Teazle is made equally clear in the second scene. Asides to the audience are used throughout the play whenever an action or a motivation might otherwise be ambiguous. In addition, many of the characters have been given names which point to their basic natures: Snake, Sir Benjamin Backbite, Lady Sneerwell, and so on.

While Sheridan makes the action completely lucid at any moment, he does not let the audience foresee the way in which it will be resolved. He arouses expectations that Joseph Surface will be unmasked, that the school will be put to rout, that Lady Teazle will be brought to her senses, and that Maria will be made happy, but the play's complications serve to keep the truth sufficiently concealed from the characters to make the outcome doubtful. Thus, Sheridan achieves clarity and suspense simultaneously.

The high point of the play is the screen sequence, which is one of the most skillfully constructed scenes ever written, since it brings to a climax almost all of the preceding conflicts and uses them to build a series of increasingly important comic reversals which culminate in the discovery of Lady Teazle behind the screen. This discovery leads to a obligatory scene that serves to bring Lady Teazle to her senses and to unmask Joseph's hypocrisy. This is the decisive moment in the play, for it makes possible the unwinding of all the complications.

The unities of both time and place are observed, since all action occurs within twenty-four hours and all places are within easy reach of each other. The close connection between the main plot and the subplot creates unity of action also. *The School for Scandal* is a good example of English neoclassicism, which was considerably more liberal than its French counterpart.

CHARACTERS AND ACTING. In accordance with the neoclassical notion of decorum, the characters in *The School for Scandal* are drawn largely as types. Charles Surface is the natural young man who does those things appropriate to youth. He is frank, honest, rash, unthinking, hasty, and fundamentally good-natured. Joseph, on the other hand, pretends to have the characteristics of the older, mature person and thus is unnatural and ludicrous. Except in his marriage to a young woman, Sir Peter observes the proper decorum for a man of his age, and it is for this lapse that he is made to suffer. Maria, Sir Oliver, and Rowley represent the ideal standard of behavior, and their conduct is vindicated in the resolution. On the other hand, the school of scandalmongers and Joseph Surface clearly deviate from the ideal pattern and are punished. Charles, Lady Teazle, and Sir Peter deviate only in a few respects and, at the end of the play, acknowledge their shortcomings and declare their intentions to reform.

Sheridan uses only a few broad strokes to differentiate his characters. For example, the scandalmongers are distinguished from each other principally through age, sex, and methods of gossip. Sir Benjamin and Crabtree differ from each other primarily through age and from the other members of the school by sex. Mrs. Candour is unlike Lady Sneerwell mainly because of her distinctive method of murdering reputations.

All of the characters—except Old Rowley, Moses, and the servants—are drawn from the leisure class. None is concerned about making a living. Charles and his companions worry about getting enough money to live pleasurably, but they do not consider working for it. The characters' world, therefore, is that of the aristocracy. They are preoccupied with such matters as marriages, the making of proper impressions, the maintenance and destruction of reputations. To live life pleasurably is the ideal. Sheridan satirizes those who murder reputations and those who are hypocrites, but he does not raise any doubts about the essential rightness of the social system itself. This restricted concern gives the play a tone of lightness and frivolity which is only slightly modified by the moralizing of Maria and Sir Oliver and by the play's ending.

The actors, therefore, must create a sense of sophistication and urbanity. The members of the school must display an artificiality which contrasts sharply with the down-to-earth qualities of Sir Oliver, Sir Peter, and Old Rowley. Maria's straightforwardness contrasts with Lady Teazle's unthinking behavior, and Charles' frank enjoyment of life with Joseph's pretense of sobriety. All of the roles, with the possible exception of Maria and Old Rowley, and the minor roles of the servants and Charles' companions, offer considerable challenge. Most of the characters are allowed to be delightfully malicious, to undertake a series of disguises, or to undergo experiences which demand a wide range of responses. Maria, however, remains constant throughout the play and serves more than any other character as the ideal against which the others are judged.

VISUAL AND AURAL APPEALS. *The School for Scandal* is set in the London of its own time (1777). This is reflected especially in the costumes, those of the upper classes of the day. The accompanying contemporary engraving of the "screen" scene shows the production's costumes and setting, the theatre's apron stage, proscenium doors, and members of the audience seated in boxes. The actors' dress corresponds closely with that worn by the audience, and the division of the scenery into two sets of wings and a back scene is evident.

By the 1770's spectators had been banished from the stage and more emphasis was being placed on the settings, of which several are required for *The School for Scandal*. Most of the places are not specific in their requirements, however, being designated merely as a room in Sir Peter's house, at Lady Sneerwell's, and so on. More specific settings are required for the scene in which Charles sells the family portraits and for the screen scene. All of the settings would have been changed in full view of the audience.

The School for Scandal contains a considerable amount of rather precisely specified business. For example, at Charles Surface's house a supper is in progress during which toasts are drunk and songs are sung. This is followed by an auction of the pictures. Many other scenes are equally detailed. Much of the action probably took place on the forestage, and many exits and entrances were undoubtedly made through the proscenium doors. The use of the forestage kept the action close to the audience and made the asides more probable.

In the language lies one of the strongest appeals of *The School for Scandal*. Sheridan follows in the tradition of the Restoration by making his characters speak with polish and wit, a kind of idealized conversation in which each turn of phrase seems exactly right, though spontaneous. The dialogue is sophisticated and sparkling; it reflects the same detachment from socioeconomic concerns as does the subject matter; it is English at its best in conversational usage. Sheridan's polished prose demands a precise delivery, which should be a special source of delight for an audience.

The School for Scandal has been more consistently popular than any other comedy in the English language. Its story, its wit, and its comic inventiveness have kept it understandable and thoroughly enjoyable to each generation.

FRANCE

Although today the English theatre of the eighteenth century may seem more interesting than that of other countries, at the time, the French theatre dominated Europe. Throughout the eighteenth century, France was both the political and cultural center of the western world.

By 1700 the neoclassical ideal, as embodied in the tragedies of Corneille and Racine and the comedies of Molière, had become the standard against which European drama was judged. In tragedy the insistence upon remaining true to the ideal established by Racine did much to freeze dramatic invention. The only French tragic writer of note in the eighteenth century was Voltaire (1694–1778), who began writing plays in 1718. After spending a few years in England in the 1720's, Voltaire decided that French drama should be liberalized, and he attempted several innovations, such as the use of crowds and ghosts, more spectacle, greater realism in acting and costuming, and a limited amount of violence on stage. But Voltaire's reforms seem slight today, and his influ-

204

ence operated principally to preserve the ideals of Racine. His best plays are *Zaïre* (1732) and *Alzire* (1736).

But while tragedy remained rather close to the Racinian mold, comedy departed considerably from Molière's pattern as the eighteenth century progressed. The changes parallel rather closely those already noted in England.

The works of Pierre Carlet de Chamblain de Marivaux (1688–1763) are important forerunners of sentimental comedy. Marivaux wrote principally for the Italian players who, after the death of Louis XIV in 1715, were allowed to return to France. This troupe played at first in Italian, but, finding this unprofitable, soon turned to plays in French. It was restricted in the kinds of plays it could do, however, since the Comédie Française had a monopoly on regular drama. The Italians, therefore, performed short plays and "irregular" dramas. Many of Marivaux' plays were written in three acts to conform to this demand, since all regular dramas of the period employed the five-act form.

The dominant theme of Marivaux' plays is the awakening of love. Typically, the main characters are a man and a woman who are skeptical about both love and marriage. Gradual and subtle changes are traced as the characters are brought to a point at which they must confess the love that has overcome them. Earlier comedy had typically treated characters already firmly in love when the plays opened; the complications arose from their attempts to overcome the opposition of parents or some other external force. In Marivaux' plays, however, the obstacles are psychological and internal.

Marivaux's works are written in a polished, carefully wrought, subtle style which has come to be called *marivaudage*. The most famous of the works are *The Surprise of Love* (1722), *The Game of Love and Chance* (1730), and *False Confidences* (1737). Although they contain many sentimental elements, they concentrate primarily upon the revelation of universal psychological states. For this reason, Marivaux' works are today among the most frequently produced in France.

True sentimental comedy appeared first in the works of Pierre Claude Nivelle de La Chausée (1692–1754), whose plays *The False Antipathy* (1733) and *The Fashionable Prejudice* (1735) established the vogue for *comedie larmoyante* (tearful comedy). These plays differed from their English counterparts only by being written in verse, but even this distinction was not maintained by many of La Chausée's successors.

Domestic tragedy had no strong advocate in France until Denis Diderot (1713–84) espoused it in the 1750's. Diderot argued that the traditional classifications of drama into tragedy and comedy should be supplemented by two *middle genres* (which correspond roughly to sentimental comedy and domestic tragedy).

It was the middle genres which interested Diderot most, and he advocated many reforms in contemporary staging to increase the appeal of these dramatic types. He believed that the best drama is that which arouses the greatest emotional response in an audience, and that the degree of emotion aroused is in direct proportion to the illusion of reality created. He argued, therefore, for the use of prose dialogue and for characters and situations drawn from everyday life. Diderot also advocated the "fourth wall" approach, in which the stage is treated as a room with one transparent wall through which the audience looks. The actors then supposedly act as they would in an actual room without taking any cognizance of the audience. To achieve this effect, Diderot argued that the stage picture must be conceived in terms of complete naturalness. Although Diderot's idea of the fourth wall was not to be carried out completely until the late nineteenth century, it is an important landmark in the movement toward realism.

Diderot also wrote an important treatise on acting, *The Paradox of the Actor*. In this work he argues that on stage the actor should feel nothing himself but should render the external signs of emotion so compellingly that the audience is convinced of the reality of the fictional situation. Diderot's ideas are frequently contrasted with those of Stanislavsky, in which it is suggested that the actor should become emotionally involved in the dramatic situation. In their writings both Diderot and Stanislavsky are concerned with arousing the maximum response in the audience, both want the actor to understand fully the emotions to be projected, and both demand a high degree of technical skill from the actor. They differ in the extent to which they wish the actor to be emotionally moved himself. Diderot argues that personal involvement deprives the actor of control over his performance, while Stanislavsky believes that some degree of involvement is essential in achieving spontaneity and is necessary in avoiding a merely mechanical display of skill.

Although Diderot's ideas have remained important, they exerted little influence on his contemporaries. His plays, *The Illegitimate Son* (1757) and *The Father of a Family* (1758), were not successful, although they did help to establish the term *drame* as a designation for serious plays which do not fall into the category of traditional tragedy.

The most important French playwright of the late eighteenth century is Pierre Augustin Caron de Beaumarchais (1732–99), who wrote some *drames* in the fashion of Diderot, but who is remembered primarily for two comedies, *The Barber of Seville* (1775) and *The Marriage of Figaro* (1784). Both center around the character of Figaro. In the first play he is a barber and the epitome of all the clever servants of comedy as he aids Count Almaviva in his plan to marry Rosina, the ward of Doctor Bartholo, who wishes to marry Rosina himself. The scene in which the Count, disguised as a music master, gives Rosina a lesson while Figaro shaves Doctor Bartholo is comparable in quality to the screen scene in *The School for Scandal*.

While social satire plays only a small part in *The Barber of Seville*, it is of considerable importance in *The Marriage of Figaro*. In the later play Figaro is in Count Almaviva's service and on the point of marrying Suzanna, a serving girl in the household. The Count is tiring of Rosina and is attempting to seduce Suzanna. The action of the play is principally taken up with uncovering and thwarting the Count's schemes, which offer many opportunities for comment upon the relative worth of the aristocracy and the lower classes.

206

A scene from Beaumarchais' *The Marriage of Figaro*. An engraving in the original edition of the play, 1785.

Comic opera also developed in France in the eighteenth century. Alain René LeSage (1668–1747), its originator, began his career by writing for the Comédie Française, which produced his great comedy of manners, *Turcaret*, in 1709. A disagreement with the Comédie, left him with no outlet for his plays, since there was no other legitimate theatre in Paris at that time. He turned, therefore, to the small theatres which had been set up at the Fairs. These theatres, which were illegitimate and contrary to the monopoly held by the Comédie Française, managed to remain in operation, nevertheless, throughout the eighteenth century. For them, LeSage wrote short pieces in which spoken dialogue alternated with songs set to popular tunes (just as Gay was to do later in the English ballad opera); the characters were the stock commedia figures and the subject matter was frequently topical and satirical. These short pieces gradually evolved into comic opera.

In the 1740's comic opera came under the sentimentalizing influences of the eighteenth century. The new trend can best be seen in the works of Charles Simon Favart (1710–92), who not only dispensed with commedia characters but also used original music and subject matter similar to that normally found in sentimental comedy. In this new guise, comic opera was taken over in 1762 by the Italian troupe (which had been a state-subsidized company since 1723).

France produced a number of outstanding actors in the eighteenth century, the most famous of whom were Clairon, Dumesnil, and LeKain. Claire Hippolyte Clairon (1723–1803) played in a number of theatres before making her debut at the Comédie Française in 1743 in the role of Phaedra. Her success was immediate and lasting. Diderot thought her the ideal actress, and she was also a favorite with Voltaire, who worked with her in making many of his reforms in acting and costuming. Her acting was the essence of the carefully planned, controlled, "natural" style.

207

Marie-Françoise Dumesnil in Racine's *Athalie*. In spite of the play's Biblical setting, Dumesnil is wearing an eighteenth century court dress. From Pougin's *Dictionnaire Historique et Pittoresque*, 1885.

Henry-Louis LeKain as Orasmane in Voltaire's *Zaïre*. From Loliée's *La Comédie Française*, 1907.

Costume worn by Mlle. Clairon in *The Orphan of China* (1755). This costume supposedly marked a change toward greater authenticity, although from a modern point of view it is still clearly influenced by eighteenth-century taste. From a contemporary print.

Diderot suggests that Clairon's approach was opposite to that of Marie Françoise Dumesnil (1713–1803), who made her debut at the Comédie Française in 1737. Dumesnil excelled in emotional roles but lacked the control of Clairon. She had no interest in reforming the stage and thought the actor should always be magnificently dressed regardless of the part. Her great emotional intensity led many to rank her above Clairon.

Henri Louis LeKain (1729–78) made his debut at the Comédie Française in 1750 and eventually was acclaimed the greatest tragic actor of his age. Although he had a rough voice, was small and not handsome, he overcame these handicaps through diligent work. He was closely associated with Clairon in making reforms in acting and costume.

In addition to championing a more realistic acting style, Clairon and LeKain abandoned the traditional costumes in favor of others which reflected the historical period of the action. These reforms, begun in the 1750's, are symptomatic of innovations which were to undermine neo-classicism. After spectators were removed from the stage at the Comédie Française in 1759, scenic display also increased and began to include elements of local color. Perhaps due to the growing emphasis upon spectacle, the old theatre buildings began to seem inadequate. The Palais-Royal (home of the Opéra) burned in 1763, the Comédie Française abandoned its theatre in 1770, and the Hôtel de Bourgogne was not used after 1783. In their places rose buildings which made better provisions for the audience and provided larger stages and more complex machinery. The effects of the innovations were only gradually felt, however, and were not fully exploited until after 1800.

A setting by Jean-Nicolas Servandoni (1695-1766), one of France's leading designers of the eighteenth century. This setting, done for the Opéra in Paris, dates from about 1730. From Bapst's *Essai sur l'Histoire du Thèatre*, 1893.

The auditorium and stage of the theatre that was to become the home of the Comédie Française in 1799. When this drawing was made in 1789, the theatre was being used by one of the minor troupes. From *L'Ancienne France,* 1887.

At the time of the French Revolution the monopolies held by the Comédie Française, the Comédie Italienne, and the Opéra were abolished. For the first time since the fifteenth century governmental restraints were removed. But the 1790's were a time of chaos in the theatre just as in politics. Order was not restored until Napoleon came to power in 1799, but he soon reinstated governmental control of the theatre and used his influence to encourage neoclassical standards. Not until after 1815 was romanticism to break the hold of neoclassicism, which had dominated the French stage since the mid-seventeenth century.

ITALY

In the eighteenth century, Italy continued to be preoccupied with opera, and as this form spread to other countries, composers, singers, and designers were exported to meet the demand. Largely because of the vogue for opera, Italian theatrical architecture and scenic design continued to dominate Europe.

In the course of the eighteenth century, design underwent a number of significant changes. Of these, perhaps the most important was the introduction of angle perspective. In angle perspective, the vanishing point is placed at either one or both sides. The viewer appears to see the object at an angle, therefore, and a feeling of great space is created by suggesting the continuation of vistas offstage on either side. The backdrop itself may depict relatively close objects, and the actors may move near it without ruining the perspective.

210

The development of angle perspective is usually credited to the Bibiena family, of which at least seven members in the seventeenth and eighteenth centuries were scene designers in the principal theatrical centers of Italy, Austria, Germany, Sweden, Russia, Spain, and Portugal.

The Bibienas were also instrumental in popularizing settings conceived on an enormous scale. During the seventeenth century, the stage had been treated as an extension of the auditorium and the scenery had been proportioned accordingly, but in the eighteenth century the wings near the front of the stage were painted as though they were merely the lower portion of structures too large to be contained on stage. Consequently, settings by the Bibienas often seem so vast that they create a mood of fantasy and unreality.

A design by Vincenzo Mazzi. From Mazzi's *Capricci di Scene Teatrali,* 1776.

A design by Guiseppe Galli da Bibiena. From Bibiena's *Architettura e Prospettiva,* 1740.

211

A palace interior as designed by Antonio Galli Bibiena. Note the encrustation of detail. From Bibiena's *Architettura e Prospettiva*, 1740.

One of Piranesi's engravings for his *Differentes Vues . . . de l'Ancienne Ville de Pesto* (1777-78). Note the ruined architectural detail and the dramatic use of light and shade, features which influenced scene design of the period.

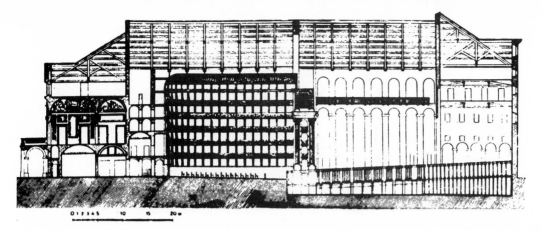

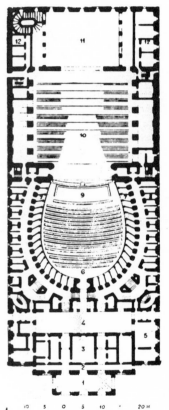

Above. Cross section of La Scala opera house in Milan. Designed by Giuseppe Piermarini, it opened in 1778. Note the seven tiers of boxes. La Scala has long been one of the principal opera houses of the world. *Right.* Ground plan of La Scala. The stage is approximately 100 feet deep; this depth may be further increased by opening the doors at the rear of the stage. From Piermarini's *Teatro della Scala in Milano,* 1826.

The Bibienas also continued the trend toward excessive ornamentation which had begun in the late seventeenth century. Columns were twisted and entwined with garlands, S-curved supports were added to beams and pediments, encrustations abounded everywhere.

During the last half of the eighteenth century still other changes were made. As comic opera developed, domestic and rustic scenes became common, while interest in more specific settings led to the inclusion of "local-color" details. After the rediscovery of Pompeii in 1748 had captured the imagination of Europe, interest was aroused in classical ruins. As a result, classical buildings, formerly depicted in pristine condition, were now represented in a state of decay, often overgrown with vines or shrubs. Under the influence of Gian Battista Piranesi (1720–78), who emphasized extremes of light and shadow in his engravings of prisons and ruins, designers also began to be aware of mood and to depict picturesque places as seen by moonlight or interiors illuminated by only a few shafts of light. Thus, during the eighteenth century scenic design underwent many changes in visual style, although the basic arrangement of wings, drops, and borders continued unchanged.

While the Bibienas were the best known of Italian designers in the eighteenth century, they had many rivals. Among these were Filippo Juvarra (1676–1736), the Mauro family (which flourished from the 1650's until the 1820's), the Quaglio family (which supplied designers from about 1650 until 1942), and the Galliari family (which worked from the early 18th century until 1823).

In addition to opera, interest in Commedia dell'arte continued in the eighteenth century. By the 1730's commedia had become repetitious, somewhat vulgar and decadent, and its emphasis upon farce was out of tune with the new taste for sentimental drama. Two of Italy's playwrights, Goldoni and Gozzi, attempted to reform the commedia and for a time injected new life into it.

213

Scene from one of Goldoni's plays. Note the *commedia* costume at right. From the edition of Goldoni's plays published in Venice, 1789.

Carlo Goldoni (1707–93) began writing plays for a commedia troupe in his native city of Venice in 1734. He soon came to the conclusion that commedia should be reformed and set out to substitute written scripts for improvised action. At first he wrote out only a single part, but soon he was able to persuade the actors to accept plays in which all speeches were written out. Although he continued to use traditional characters, he sentimentalized them and removed all indecency. *The Servant of Two Masters* is a good example of Goldoni's commedia plays.

Had Goldoni's work been restricted to commedia, he probably would not be remembered today, but he also wrote many other kinds of plays, including comedies, comic operas, and tragedies. Today he is considered Italy's greatest comic writer of the eighteenth century.

Goldoni's comedies usually concern women, who are much more sensible than Goldoni's men, and the middle and lower classes, who are almost invariably depicted as superior to the upper class. Sentimentalism pervades most of his work, but a spirit of fun and lightheartedness keeps it from being cloyingly sentimental. Many of his plays are still highly regarded and frequently performed; the most notable are *The Mistress of the Inn* (1753) and *The Fan* (1764). Goldoni's last years were spent in France, and a number of his more than two hundred and fifty plays were written in French for the Comédie Italienne.

Carlo Gozzi (1720–1806) was bitterly opposed to Goldoni's reforms in the commedia and to his satirical picture of the aristocracy. Many of Gozzi's works were calculated to counteract Goldoni's influence; the best known are fairy tales in which imagination is given free rein, and in which many events and practices of the day are satirized. Gozzi wrote out some scenes in their entirety, but others were to be improvised. Because they were incomplete and topical, it is difficult to appreciate his plays today. Neither Gozzi nor Goldoni was long able to stop the decline of the commedia, and by 1800 one of the most interesting of theatrical forms had virtually come to an end.

The most important writer of tragedy in eighteenth-century Italy was Vittorio Amedeo Alfieri (1749–1803) who was born in Turin of a wealthy and noble family. Most of his early life was spent traveling about Europe without any fixed purpose, but in 1775 he turned to writing plays and rapidly became Italy's greatest tragic writer.

His plays are a curious mixture of social consciousness with classical subject matter and form. Most deal with questions of freedom, equality, political consciousness and responsibility embodied in stories taken from classical or Biblical sources. In his attempt to recapture the spirit of Greek drama, he cut away every detail that was not absolutely essential. He employed very few characters, used no chorus, and strictly observed the unities. His *Saul* (1784) and *Mirra* (1786) have great power because they concentrate upon the dilemma of a single individual in a compelling situation.

Saul shows the Biblical character at the end of his life, aware of his decline in power, and jealous of David's strength. He alternates between exerting his authority autocratically and being led by others; in his vacillations between madness and sanity, he is both pathetic and terrifying. The interest of the play is centered in the role of Saul, which is considered in Italy to be the ultimate test of the tragic actor.

But Alfieri was writing at the end of the neoclassical tradition. Although his plays served to revive the national spirit in Italy and continue to be highly regarded, they have had little influence on subsequent writers.

In spite of its great contributions in shaping the European theatre, by the end of the eighteenth century Italy had ceased to develop new ideas. In the nineteenth century it remained the center of the operatic world but played little part in the development of theatre and drama.

NORTHERN AND EASTERN EUROPE

The eighteenth century saw the development of theatre throughout northern Europe and in Russia. Prior to 1750, there were only sporadic theatrical performances in Russia. Although there was some Church drama in the medieval period, a few "school" dramas, and sporadic performances at court, as an institution the Russian theatre dates from the mid-eighteenth century. The first dramatist of note was Alexei Petrovich Sumarokov (1718–77), whose tragedy *Khorev*, written in the neoclassical style, was first performed in 1749 by cadets at the Academy of the Nobility. At about the same time Fyodor Volkov (1729–63) and his brother achieved some success with an acting company in Yaroslavl. Hearing of their work, the Empress Elizabeth summoned them to St. Petersburg in 1752, where they remained to become the core of the state troupe established in 1756. Although the Russian public theatre dates from the 1750's, it was not to produce any outstanding drama until the nineteenth century.

Theatre and drama also came to prominence in Northern Europe for the first time in the eighteenth century. The history of drama in Norway and Denmark are one until the nineteenth century, since they were united from the fourteenth century until 1814 and Danish was the official language of both. No drama of note was written in Norwegian until the nineteenth century. Denmark's drama went through many of the same stages as that of other countries. Although there was religious drama in the Middle Ages (though little evidence remains), and school drama in the sixteenth century, no plays were written in the Danish language until the eighteenth century. The culture of Denmark was largely derived from France. The language of polite society was French, the academic language was Latin, and Danish was used only in business and other daily transactions.

215

The theatre in Denmark at the beginning of the eighteenth century was restricted to a resident French company at the court and to small touring groups from Germany which played at fairs or on special occasions. In 1720 Frederick IV dismissed his French actors, but the leader of the troupe, René Magnon de Montaigu, who had been in Denmark for thirty-five years, petitioned to be allowed to open a public theatre. Permission was granted, but there were no plays in the Danish language. Montaigu commissioned Holberg to furnish him with Danish plays and the theatre opened in 1722. The Danish theatre may be dated from that time.

Ludwig Holberg (1684–1754) was born in Norway, was well educated and widely traveled. He became a professor at the University of Copenhagen in 1718 and in 1719 began writing satires, usually considered to mark the beginning of literature written in Danish. Holberg was thus a natural choice when a need arose for Danish-language plays. He wrote a large number of comedies, the most famous of which are *Jeppe of the Hill* and *Erasmus Montanus.* Although Holberg stated that his models were Plautus and Molière, his plays often seem much closer to medieval farce, although this comparison must be qualified since Holberg used his plays to teach morality. Because Holberg created Danish drama almost single-handedly there is a tendency to praise him too highly. But if he is not a great writer, much of his work still seems fresh in its treatment of Danish types and farcical situations.

Sweden also developed drama in the medieval period, a "school" drama in the sixteenth century, and a professional theatre in the seventeenth century. But it did not produce a dramatist of any stature until Strindberg began writing at the end of the nineteenth century. Sweden's theatre and drama up to that time were primarily reflections of foreign influences, though plays were written in the Swedish language as early as 1550. While there was a public theatre in Sweden as early as 1690, it was not until the reign of Gustav III (1746–92) that the theatre flourished. A national theatre was established in 1773, since then the Swed-theatre has been a relatively vigorous institution.

Gustav III also built a theatre at Drottningholm (a summer residence of the court) which was closed at his death and left unused until it was rediscovered in the 1920's. It is now one of the world's great theatrical museums, since it is one of the few eighteenth-century theatres which have not been altered; even its eighteenth-century scenery and machinery are intact.

AMERICA

The theatre in America is also a product of the eighteenth century. Although there was sporadic theatrical activity from the seventeenth century, the American theatre can be said to date from 1752, when Lewis Hallam (1714–56) brought a company of actors to America. Playing first in Williamsburg, Virginia, they went on to perform in the major cities along the Atlantic seaboard. Many later groups were outgrowths of this company.

216

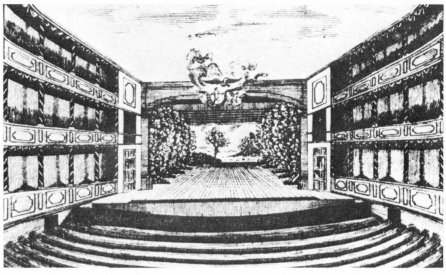

The Chestnut Street Theatre in Philadelphia. Opened in 1794, it was the finest theatre in America at that time. From *The New York Magazine,* 1794.

Although the theatre in America encountered considerable opposition, it was beginning to be accepted when the American Revolution put an end to all theatrical activities in 1774. In the 1780's it was revived and by the end of the century was firmly established from Charleston, South Carolina to Boston. After this time the theatre followed the westward movement of American settlers, and actors soon traveled to any area that could support even a few performances.

The American theatre was a frank imitation of the English system, and most of its early workers came from England. The first important native figure was William Dunlap (1766–1839), playwright and manager, who worked principally in New York and did much to establish a theatre of importance there. His *History of the American Theatre*, written in 1832, has remained an important source of information about the early theatre in the United States.

A scene from Royall Tyler's *The Contrast* (1787), the first comedy by an American to be professionally produced. From the first edition of the play, published in Philadelphia, 1790.

GERMANY

The most striking changes in the eighteenth-century theatre occurred in Germany. In 1700 Germany was composed of many small states divided by religious and political differences. The Thirty Years' War (1618–48) had depleted both Germany's population and its resources, leaving few large cities and little wealth. The theatre was divided between private court productions and public traveling companies, with little connection between the two.

Court theatres arose under the influence of Italian opera. The first opera in German-speaking territories was given at Salzburg in 1618, but it was not until after 1650 that the vogue spread. After 1652 the court at Vienna became one of the major theatrical centers of Europe, and its example was followed throughout Germany, where each court maintained, as well as its financial condition would allow, theatres patterned after those of Italy. Although the courts set a standard for later public theatres, professional touring companies were the true founders of the German stage.

The first traveling players in Germany came from England around 1590. Gradually, the English actors were replaced by Germans, and by 1650 all-German companies existed, although the conditions under which they worked did not change essentially until after 1730. None of the troupes had a permanent home, since no town could as yet support a professional theatre. Touring, therefore, was necessary but costly and time-consuming. Companies varied their programs as much as possible so as to achieve a maximum appeal to the limited audience in each town. For example, one company in 1735 produced seventy-five different full-length plays and ninety-three one-act plays in a period of eight months. The working conditions and the pay were poor, and the troupes were generally scorned by the educated classes. Actors, therefore, were frequently persons who had no other work open to them. The low state of the theatre was reflected in the plays, which were filled with violence, improbable actions and characters, and bombastic dialogue. Hanswurst, a character based on the Harlequin of commedia dell'arte, crept into all plays, even serious ones.

All these factors conspired to keep the German theatre in low repute until about 1725 when Johann Christoph Gottsched (1700–66) and Carolina Neuber (1697–1760) made the first serious effort to reform the German stage. Gottsched, who was interested in improving the level of German literature and in elevating taste and morals, saw in drama one means for reaching the poorly educated classes and as a means of putting his ideas into practice formed a liaison with the acting troupe headed by Carolina Neuber. Gottsched's conception of drama was derived primarily from French neoclassical drama, which was completely unknown to the audience who frequented the popular theatres. Gottsched and his associates, nevertheless, set out to provide a new repertory for the theatre, much of which was to be composed of translations or adaptations of French works.

Carolina Neuber tried to raise the level of acting and the reputation of the theatrical profession by insisting upon careful rehearsals and a high

Hanswurst, the clownish character who appeared in most German plays of the early eighteenth century. From an eighteenth century engraving. Courtesy University of Iowa Library.

level of personal morality. She banished Hanswurst from her theatre and revised her repertory to bring it into closer accord with Gottsched's aims. In none of her attempts was she entirely successful.

Although Gottsched and Neuber never fully achieved their aims, their work marks the turning point in the history of German theatre. From their time there was a steady rise in the fortunes of the theatrical profession and by the end of the eighteenth century German drama and theatre could be compared favorably with that found anywhere in the world.

Germany's first important dramatist was Gotthold Ephraim Lessing (1729–81), who turned attention away from French neoclassicism to English drama as more compatible with German tastes. His own plays influenced later writers and helped to raise the status of German drama in the eighteenth century. *Miss Sara Sampson* (1755), which is set in England, established the vogue for domestic tragedy in Germany. Today, his most popular play is *Minna von Barnhelm* (1767), a comedy which shows how a rich young girl maneuvers an officer into marriage, although he wishes to decline because he has lost his own wealth. It is a romantic play which has much in common with the sentimental comedy of the period, but which, like the works of Goldoni, is saved from the extremes of its type by its over-all good humor and spirit of fun.

Lessing's *Nathan the Wise* (1779) is a dramatic poem not originally intended for the stage, although it has achieved a continuing reputation in the theatre. It brings together Christian, Moslem, and Jewish characters to illustrate that the best religion is that capable of achieving the most humanitarian results. Its testament to religious tolerance has helped to insure its lasting reputation.

Lessing's plays employ a strict cause-to-effect structure in which each event grows naturally out of the one preceding it. He observes the unities

219

Friedrich Ludwig Schroeder as Falstaff. From *Literatur und Theaterzeitung*, 1780.

(except in *Nathan the Wise*) and seeks to return to what he called "true" classicism, as opposed to the "false" classicism of the French.

Lessing's plays and his critical writings, especially the *Hamburg Dramaturgy* (1767–68), turned attention away from French drama, but with results which Lessing did not foresee or approve. Many concluded from his arguments that all rules were meaningless, unnecessary, and contrary to German needs. As a result, much of the German drama of the late eighteenth century is chaotic and difficult to understand. Out of these new experiments and ideas, however, romanticism was to develop.

Just as German drama found a more adequate expression in the works of Lessing, so, too, actors appeared who raised the status of their profession. Johann Friedrich Schönemann (1704–82), originally a Hanswurst actor, performed with the Neuber troupe before forming his own. Into this company he took Ekhof, Ackermann, and Sophie Schroeder, all of whom were to be prominent in German theatre. Konrad Ekhof (1720–78), who joined Schönemann's company in 1740, did more than any other German actor of the eighteenth century to establish a high reputation for the acting profession. He reformed the contemporary acting style in the direction of greater naturalness, ran a short-lived training schools for actors, and influenced most of the other principal performers of the day.

Konrad Ackermann (1710-71) and Sophie Schroeder (1714-92), later husband and wife, began their acting careers in Schonemann's company and then formed their own troupe and played throughout Germany, in Russia and Switzerland. Ackermann's good nature made him a favorite with audiences and his managerial skill kept the company in good financial condition.

Friedrich Ludwig Schroeder (1744-1816), the son of Sophie Schroeder by an earlier marriage, is generally considered the greatest German actor of the eighteenth century and perhaps of all time. He grew up in the Ackermann troupe, but it was from Ekhof that he learned most. Schroeder did more than any other actor to popularize the new drama which came into vogue after Lessing, and it was he who introduced Shakespeare to the German stage. Because of his acting, his managerial skill, and his personal charm, he was for many years considered to be the head of the theatrical profession in Germany.

During the last quarter of the eighteenth century, the prestige of the German theatre grew rapidly. The breach between the court and public theatres was bridged with the formation of subsidized state troupes which served both court and public. The first of the national theatres was formed at Gotha in 1775, and was soon followed by others at Vienna, Mannheim, Cologne, Weimar, Berlin, and elsewhere. By 1800 almost every Germanic capital had a state theatre organized along lines similar to those of the Comédie Francaise.

Thus, by 1800 the German theatre had undergone a revolution. Permanent theatres now housed resident companies, the acting profession was respected, and German drama was beginning to assume international importance. Furthermore, Germany was already in the process of developing a Romantic drama which would overthrow those neoclassical ideals which had dominated the stages of Europe for more than a century and a half.

Chapter 11 THEATRE AND DRAMA IN THE NINETEENTH CENTURY

By the beginning of the nineteenth century a number of earlier trends had coalesced in what is now usually called romanticism. As with most movements, many of the traits of romanticism may be found in other periods as well, most notably in Shakespeare's age. Nevertheless, as a label, *the Romantic movement* is usually reserved for the years between 1800 and 1850.

ROMANTICISM

The forces which led to romanticism were all evident in the eighteenth century. First, there was a growing distrust of reason as the principal tool for achieving man's highest goals. Neoclassicism had been based in large part upon the belief that man can discover, through rational analysis, adequate criteria for everything whether in life or in literature. In the eighteenth century, however, this view was gradually replaced by trust in natural instinct as a guide to right feeling and action.

Second, doubt about the rightness of the existing social and political order increased as the rise of the middle class prompted a reconsideration of the bases of those distinctions which had made most men subservient to an aristocratic minority. Primitive society came to be idealized as a time when man was free to follow the dictates of his conscience without economic and political strictures. The equality of man and freedom of action became battle cries of the new movement. (Both the American and the French revolutions clearly owe much to these ideals).

Third, the notion that truth is to be defined in terms of "norms" was replaced by the conviction that truth can only be discovered in the infinite variety of creation. According to the Romanticists, the universe was created by God out of himself so that he might more easily contemplate himself. Everything in existence, therefore, is a part of everything else, for all have a common origin. To know ultimate truth, then, one must know as much of creation as possible. Rather than eliminate details to arrive at a norm, one must seek to encompass the infinite variety of being.

Fourth, since all creation has a common origin, a thorough and careful study of any part may lead to a glimpse of the whole. Thus trees, grass, rivers, and mountains reflect something about man, just as man reflects something about them. The more unspoiled a thing is—that is, the less it deviates from its natural state—the more suitable it is for use in the search for truth. Romantic writers, therefore, showed a marked preference for poetry about natural objects and landscapes, and for drama about unspoiled men living in primitive times or those in rebellion against restraints imposed by society.

Fifth, since the ultimate source of creation is God, truth is infinite and beyond total comprehension or adequate expression. Therefore, it is impossible ever to grasp all of reality, although one may and should continually seek to do so. Furthermore, no matter how the writer may strive to embody truth, he is doomed to fail, at least partially.

Sixth, the person most capable of grasping and expressing truth is the genius. During the neoclassical period it had at first been implied that if a writer followed the rules he could produce good drama. In the eighteenth century, however, the need for some special, indefinable quality was suggested. In the beginning this quality was called *taste*, but gradually the term *genius* was used to include all the elements of greatness. Originally genius was viewed as supplementing the rules (which were still considered necessary), but eventually it was seen as conflicting with the rules, which were now said to restrict genius to too narrow confines. Genius, therefore, was thought capable of making its own rules and laws.

Design by Alessandro Sanquirico (1780-1849) for *L'Allunno della Giumenta,* a ballet presented at La Scala, Milan, in 1812. Sanquirico was one of Italy's leading designers in the early nineteenth century. From Sanquirico's *Raccolta di Varie Decorazioni Sceniche*. Milan, 1810-28.

In addition, genius was thought to include an innate ability to grasp intuitively the greatness of the universe; this capacity sets off the individual possessing it from his fellow men, who, because they keep their eyes on the material, everyday world, are blind to the true nature of reality. The genius, then, is different from other men, and consequently is at times in conflict with his society, for the true artist is driven to express truth regardless of the consequences. Genius is, therefore, both a gift and a curse.

Seventh, the artist must search for forms which are adequate to the expression of great truths. Given the conceptions of the period, it was only natural that the artist abandoned and denounced the neoclassical rules for writing. New forms were needed which would allow maximum freedom in expressing the infinity of creation. Shakespeare's plays most nearly fit the new conceptions and came to represent the ideal form in the Romantic period, just as Greek and Roman drama had served as models for writers of the Neoclassic period.

The Romanticists frequently saw in Shakespeare's works, however, only a freedom from restraint. As a result, they adopted a loose structure in which the unities (sometimes even of action) were abandoned. Since authors frequently ignored the requirements of the stage, because genius was thought too great to be confined by such practical needs, many of the plays were never produced and others had to be adapted before they could be staged. About much of the work there is an air of impracticality. On the other hand, the new ideas freed writers from the often arbitrary demands of neoclassicism.

Along with the rebellion against the old ideas of form went the abandonment of old subject matter. Greek myths gave way to medieval tales, historical legends, and stories about folk heroes or rebellions against social and moral codes. This subject matter was used to embody themes showing man's attempts to achieve freedom of ideals or behavior, to find personal peace of mind, or the secret of existence. The new forms, subject matter, and themes combined to create a drama quite unlike that of the neoclassical period.

MAJOR ROMANTIC PLAYWRIGHTS

Most of the concepts which made up the Romantic ideal were first set forth in England, but since the philosophical foundations and dramatic forms evolved slowly throughout the eighteenth century, it is impossible to speak of a Romantic "revolution" in England as it is in many other countries. Furthermore, in England the neoclassical ideal was never so firmly entrenched as it was elsewhere and the transition to romanticism was more easily accomplished.

England's Romantic movement led to little significant drama, however, perhaps because a ready-made Romanticist writer was available in Shakespeare. All of the major English Romantic poets—Coleridge, Wordsworth, Byron, Keats, and Shelley—wrote plays and, while many of their works were produced, they were seldom well-received and made little impact in the theatre. The most successful of English Romantic playwrights was James Sheridan Knowles (1784–1862), originally an actor, whose *Virginius* (1820), *William Tell* (1825), and *The Hunchback* (1832) mingle pseudo-Shakespearean verse and techniques with melodramatic stories.

By 1800 a well-defined Romantic movement was under way in Germany and was to prove far more productive than its counterparts elsewhere in Europe. Two of the most important dramatists of the period were Johann Wolfgang von Goethe (1749–1832) and Friedrich von Schiller (1759–1805), both of whom denied being Romanticists and wrote some works in the classical style. Each wrote plays which helped to establish the new drama, however, and the Romanticists often expressed indebtedness to them.

Goethe is to German literature what Shakespeare is to English, for he is universally considered to be the greatest of German writers. His first play, *Götz von Berlichingen* (1773), deals with the attempts of a German knight of the sixteenth century to remain free in the midst of political and religious intrigues. Around him swirls the life of the times presented much in the manner of a modern movie scenario. Goethe did not write with stage presentation in mind, but the play, which contains fifty-four scenes with over forty named characters (in addition to soldiers, peasants, gypsies, judges, jailers, courtiers, and so on), was soon adapted for the theatre, nevertheless, and its enormous popularity established a vogue for dramas of chivalry.

Goethe underwent a change in the 1780's. Concluding that true greatness lies in an idealized art similar to that of the Greeks, he wrote some plays in the classical manner, the most famous of which is *Iphigenia in Tauris*. But Goethe is best known today for *Faust*, a work which in many ways epitomizes the Romantic outlook. It too was not conceived with the stage in mind, although it was soon adapted for theatrical presentation and has been performed frequently. It is a work of enormous scope, about which more will be said later.

Schiller had a much surer feeling for the dramatic than did Goethe. His first play, *The Robbers* (1782), was an immediate success and continued to be performed throughout the world until the end of the nine-

Coronation scene from Schiller's *The Maid of Orleans* as presented at the Royal Theatre, Berlin, in 1801. The setting is by Karl Friedrich Schinkel. About 200 actors appeared in this scene. From Weddigen's *Geschichte der Theater Deutschlands,* 1904.

teenth century. Beginning with *Don Carlos* (1787), Schiller turned for his subject matter principally to moments of crisis in history. *Don Carlos* deals with the awakening aspirations of a Spanish prince to free the Netherlands from Spain and to encourage freedom throughout the world. He is opposed by the court and church, and eventually his father, Philip, gives him up to the Inquisition for punishment. Schiller used English history in *Maria Stuart*, French history in *The Maid of Orleans*, Swiss history in *William Tell*, and German history in his Wallenstein trilogy. Few dramatists have combined such a sweep of historical material with such theatrical power. If he falls short of Shakespeare it is because of his too obvious attempt to set forth philosophical ideas.

Although never a conscious part of the Romantic movement, Heinrich von Kleist (1777–1811) is the best German dramatist of the early nineteenth century. None of his plays was produced during his lifetime; they were not published until 1821 and did not find their way into theatrical repertories until the late nineteenth century. Today Kleist is remembered principally for one comedy, *The Broken Jug* (1811), and two tragedies, *Penthesilea* (1808) and *The Prince of Homburg* (1811). The last play, one of the best of the German Romantic era, concerns a young officer who is so bent upon gaining renown that he defies military orders when he sees the chance of winning a victory. Although successful, he has endangered the entire army, and he is sentenced to die. He is reprieved only after he comes to recognize that his personal ego must be subordinated to that greater good which is to be found in self-renunciation and service. It is a compact and moving drama.

The plays of Georg Büchner (1818–37) illustrate the disillusionment with romanticism which increased steadily after about 1815. The excesses of the French Revolution had called into doubt many of the social and political ideas of the movement, and the doubts increased when Napoleon, who originally had been hailed as the savior of Europe, was crowned Emperor and became as despotic a ruler as those he replaced. As the belief in the possibility of unselfish service to others was shaken, pessimism began to replace the former optimism. Büchner's *Danton's Death* (1835) concerns an idealist who, seeing his highest aims wrecked by the pettiness of his fellow men, comes to question the validity of the ideals themselves. Unable to decide whether life has any meaning, he goes to his death with dignity but still in doubt. *Woyzeck* shows a man who, little better than an animal, is led inevitably to his downfall by the social circumstances under which he is forced to live. Both plays are pessimistic in outlook and peculiarly modern in their views of human psychology.

Like many of his contemporaries, Friedrich Hebbel (1813–63) underwent a serious crisis in belief after first accepting the Romantic view. Unlike Büchner, who never passed beyond pessimism, Hebbel found consolation in a philosophy derived from Hegel. He came to view history as a series of conflicts between old and new ideals through which some absolute spirit works toward perfection. Consequently, in his plays the main characters are representatives of the old and new orders. Since the old has the power of established authority behind it, the new usually suffers, although the suffering foreshadows the triumph of the ideal which has seemingly been defeated. In this way Hebbel reconciled the world's imperfections with a vision of future improvement. His most famous play, *Maria Magdalena* (1844), is now usually read as a forerunner of realism, since its characters are drawn from ordinary life, its dialogue is in prose, and its story ends in the suicide of the heroine, a victim of society's narrow-mindedness. Nevertheless, like Hebbel's other plays, it embodies the conflict of old and new values and suggests that change is on its way. With Hebbel's death in 1863, German drama entered a period of decline from which it was not to recover until after 1890.

The Romantic movements in both England and Germany were already declining before Romantic drama was accepted in France. Although many strictures on the theatre were removed by the Revolution, Napoleon reinstituted censorship in 1804 and openly favored neoclassical drama. In 1807 he issued a decree which established four state theatres (one for major dramatic forms, one for minor dramatic forms, one for comic opera, and one for opera). In many ways, therefore, Napoleon reinstated the conditions which had existed before 1790. There was one important difference, however—Napoleon allowed private theatres, although the number and repertory were carefully controlled. These non-state theatres, located largely on the Boulevard du Temple, are usually called the Boulevard theatres.

In spite of Napoleon's strictures, however, Romantic ideas were in the air. In France they were given currency largely through *On Germany* by Mme. de Staël, an enemy of Napoleon who spent her years of exile in Germany. Published in 1810, her book was suppressed almost immediately, but when Napoleon was overthrown in 1814, it was quickly reissued and widely circulated. But it was not until Victor Hugo (1802–85) published the Preface to his play *Cromwell* in 1827 that the aims and ideas of the French Romanticists were clearly set forth, and romanticism did not triumph in France until Hugo's *Hernani* was produced at the Comédie Française in 1830.

The French plays of the new movement differ considerably from their German counterparts, and in actuality are more closely related to the melodramas of the day. *Hernani* and many other Romantic dramas make use of such devices as disguises, secret panels, hidden staircases, and hairbreadth escapes. They differ from melodramas only in greater depth of characterization, the use of verse, the five-act form, and a preference for unhappy endings.

Hernani concerns a man who has become an outlaw because his father has been unjustly accused of treason and has had his lands confiscated. Hernani loves Dõna Sol, who is also loved by her guardian, Don Ruy Gomez, and by Don Carlos, the future Holy Roman Emperor. Don Carlos comes searching for Hernani while he is a guest in the house of Don Ruy. When he cannot find Hernani, who is hidden in a secret chamber behind a portrait, Don Carlos takes Doña Sol away as a hostage. Before Hernani sets out to rescue Doña Sol, he gives Don Ruy a horn and promises that, if his life is ever needed Don Ruy need only blow the horn. In the final act, which takes place on the wedding day of Doña Sol and Hernani (now forgiven and no longer an outlaw), Don Ruy, filled with jealousy, blows the horn. Hernani drinks poison, as does Doña Sol, and Don Ruy then kills himself. It is a plot in which love and honor are pushed to the extreme, but it is also a play filled with melodramatic devices, suspense, and powerful poetry.

Other important French Romantic dramatists were Alexandre Dumas, Alfred de Vigny, and Alfred de Musset. Alexandre Dumas *père* (1803–70) is remembered today chiefly for his novels, *The Count of Monte Cristo* and *The Three Musketeers*, but in the 1830's he was famous as a dramatist of the new Romantic school. He wrote a number of plays, among them *Henri III and His Court* and *The Tower of Nesle*, which display the same essential characteristics as those of Hugo.

Alfred de Vigny (1797–1863) translated many of Shakespeare's plays into French and helped to popularize them. He is best remembered today for his play *Chatterton* (1835), which depicts a poet who is too delicate and refined in spirit to find happiness in the materialistic world into which he is thrown. He eventually dies rather than compromise his values. In many ways the plot epitomizes the Romantic genius at war with a world which he refuses to accept.

The works of Alfred de Musset (1810–57) are almost totally unlike those of his French contemporaries. Musset was concerned with the psychology of characters, especially lovers. The human ego is the source of complications in most of the plays. Musset frequently writes of two people in love (or who think they are in love), each of whom is so afraid of being hurt that he disguises his true feelings, while this disguise serves only to wound the other person, who strikes back in a way which widens the breach. Sometimes the breach can be healed to permit a happy resolution, but sometimes it cannot and disaster results. Probably because the psychological orientation of Musset's plays have kept them fresh for modern audiences, they are still widely produced in France and are the most universally admired of French Romantic dramas. Musset's best known plays are *No Trifling with Love, A Door Should Either be Shut or Open*, and *Lorenzaccio*.

In addition to England, Germany, and France, many other countries had Romantic movements, although none attained a high level of excellence. Since romanticism was so complex, it is difficult to isolate one work as typical. Goethe's *Faust*, Part I, has been chosen since it embodies so many tendencies, even though Goethe denied any sympathy with romanticism.

FAUST

Faust is usually considered the greatest literary work in the German language. Consequently, it is impossible to do it justice in a short discussion, although its major characteristics can be explored. Goethe worked on *Faust* throughout his life, beginning Part I in the 1780's and not completing it until 1808, while Part II was not published until 1831. It is, therefore, a partial record of Goethe's own growth and change as well as

228

A nineteenth-century setting for *Faust*. From Bapst's *Essai sur l'Histoire du Theatre*, 1893.

a reflection of the attitudes of his age. *Faust* was not written for the stage. A "dramatic poem" conceived on a scale too vast for the theatre, it must be adapted and condensed when it is produced, as it often is.

THEMES AND IDEAS. *Faust* is a play about man's aspirations and capabilities, a hymn to his essential greatness and ability to work out his own salvation. If Part II is included, it is an optimistic work.

The "Prologue in Heaven" establishes the basic theme when God states that man cannot avoid making mistakes in his search for fulfillment, but that continuous striving will lead him to the truth. The scenes that follow dramatize the search itself. Before the search begins, however, Mephistopheles makes a pact to aid Faust in return for Faust's agreement that Mephistopheles can take his soul whenever he finds a moment about which he can say: "O stay! thou art so wondrous fair!" This will be the moment of fulfillment toward which Faust has directed all of his energies and beyond which there will be no point in living.

Part I shows Faust's discontent, his pact with Mephistopheles, and his search for fulfillment in physical pleasures. This is the clearest and most dramatic part of the work. Part II becomes more difficult to understand, but it shows the completion of Faust's striving. Having found sensual pleasure inadequate in Part I, Faust then seeks meaning in ideal loveliness and poetry; eventually he finds the moment for which he has been searching when he renounces his own selfish interests for service to others. But Mephistopheles is thwarted when he comes to take Faust's soul, for Faust has been led to salvation and truth through that very striving for fulfillment in which Mephistopheles has aided him.

229

Goethe is concerned in Part I, however, with only the first phase of this story. The beginning depicts Faust's deep discontent and his longing to encompass the infinite meaning and activity of life. Faust then makes his pact with Mephistopheles, who sets out to show him pleasure. Faust falls in love with Margarete; she is disgraced and dies; Faust and Mephistopheles flee. This rather straightforward story is complicated by a number of seemingly irrelevant scenes. Each scene contributes to Goethe's purpose, however, for his main interest always lies in depicting the philosophical and spiritual development of Faust.

The second scene is an excellent illustration of Goethe's methods and interests. It shows a day of revelry in which a cross-section of humanity participates. Faust's psychological state is delineated through a pointed contrast between Faust, a group of peasants, and Wagner, the scholar. Faust admires the peasants, who are at peace with their world and can find pleasure in music, dance, and drink. But Faust knows that these pleasures are fleeting; he wants to find lasting and complete satisfaction. Wagner, on the other hand, seeks his pleasures in books and in the past. Faust wants to live life intensely as the peasant does, he wants to encompass knowledge as the scholar does, but he is also searching for something more, something indefinable. The scene serves principally, therefore, as a means of outlining Faust's psychological state rather than as a means of forwarding a dramatic action. It is a moment suspended in time and analyzed with care, but it does not arouse the kind of expectations of future developments which are typical of dramatic composition. *Faust* alternates such static scenes with more dynamic ones.

Goethe is also concerned with man's relationship to good and evil. At one point, Mephistopheles says that God lives in eternal light, that the witches and evil spirits live in eternal darkness, and that man lives in both light and darkness. Man thus exists somewhere between good and evil and though he longs for eternal light, his own nature and circumstances keep him in partial darkness. It is not surprising then that many

A scene from Goethe's *Faust,* Part I, at Yale University. Directed by Frank MacMullan; designed by Frank Bevan; lighting by Stanley McCandless. Courtesy Yale University School of Drama.

of the scenes in the play use night and day symbolically. For example, the Walpurgis Night scene points up Faust's dilemma as a man who has given himself up to darkness in his attempt to achieve the light.

Darkness is related to Faust's false search for fulfillment in sensual pleasures, which are part of man's animal nature. Such physical pleasures are also essentially selfish. For example, Faust's love for Margarete is primarily carnal, and he displays no real concern for her welfare until it is too late. He does not talk of marrying her, he only dreams of possessing her. Her death and the dilemma of Faust at the end of Part I show the limitations of sensuality as a way of life. Mephistopheles, furthermore, is the very incarnation of a sadistic sensuality, which Faust accepts as his guide throughout Part I, although he is continually tormented by the difference between the ideal he had set out to find and the actuality.

The Walpurgis Night scene illustrates in part the darker side of man's nature, and in part the range of creation. Everything has been created out of God (it is he who has separated the light and the darkness) and everything is part of his plan. The witches and evil spirits, then, are part of Faust; they represent sensuality without moral standards, unrestrained whim and selfishness.

Goethe shows that sensuality is eventually self-defeating. At the end of Part I, Faust is left more dissatisfied than when he began his search. A higher power can save Margarete, but Faust can only stand by helplessly. He must search elsewhere for the answer.

PLOT AND STRUCTURE. The structure of Faust is extremely loose. Although it bears certain superficial resemblances to Elizabethan drama, it does not have the economy of Shakespeare's plays and it lacks any compelling unity of action. For example, Shakespeare always makes his basic dramatic situation clear in the opening scene, but it is not until the fourth scene of *Faust* that the pact with Mephistopheles sets the play in motion. If the two Prologues are included, almost one fourth of Part I is taken up with introductory material.

The principal dramatic questions raised in the play concern Faust's ability to find completion and to save his immortal soul. These questions hold the play together, but the nature of the first is such that Faust may look anywhere for its answer. Goethe chooses to have Faust seek first for fulfillment in sensual pleasures, but this is not a necessary development out of what has gone before. Any other choice could have been made, though Goethe's is not illogical. Furthermore, any phase of Faust's search could be illustrated at length or briefly.

The only sequence which is developed in terms of a clear cause-to-effect relationship is the Faust-Margarete story. But even this sequence is broken up by the insertion of scenes which illustrate Faust's psychological and philosophical attitudes. Although all of the scenes are thematically related, they are by no means all dramatic. Many could be eliminated without any confusion to an audience, and their removal might actually lead to greater clarity in performance. The major source of unity, then, is thought rather than incident.

Part I does not complete the story of Faust. It concludes the sequence showing Faust's search for fulfillment in sensual pleasure, but the central questions remain unresolved and are continued in Part II. Thus, while Part I reaches a climax and resolution of one phase of the story, it marks only the beginning of Faust's search.

Part I consists of twenty-five scenes (plus two prologues) and requires about sixteen settings. Time and place change rapidly, and many special effects are demanded (such as a dog which grows in size and is transformed into Mephistopheles, the Walpurgis Night scenes, the Witch's Kitchen in which monkeys stir potions, and so on). Its production stretches the demands of the stage as far as they have ever been extended, but these demands are a clear outgrowth of Goethe's aims to encompass as much of life as possible and to dramatize man's search for meaning, his varying states of mind, and the vastness of his aims and abilities. The constant variety keeps the work from becoming boring, but if Goethe's purposes are not understood, *Faust* may appear to be a jumble of disconnected scenes. It is a lofty conception which requires a special effort from the reader for comprehension and a very high degree of interpretive and technical skill from the director.

CHARACTERS AND ACTING. The cast of characters in *Faust*, Part I is too vast to count, for it is made up in large part of crowds, choruses, unspecified numbers of witches, wizards, and spirits. Those given any degree of psychological development are few: Faust, Mephistopheles, Wagner, Margarete, Martha, Valentine, and Lieschen. The rest are types or abstractions. For example, in scene 2 a large number of people are celebrating a holiday outside the city walls, but these are designated only as soldiers, peasants, maids, apprentices, students, and the like.

Goethe is interested in the range of creation but he is not concerned with individuals except in a few cases. His principal effort has gone into Faust, and it is only as the other characters illustrate his condition that they are important to the play. It is evident that the role of Faust is the most difficult one for an actor. This is true not only because of Faust's central position, but because the role consists so much in the expression of longing, of dissatisfaction, of unbounded aims. An actor may easily become bombastic and ridiculous since what Faust wants is so intangible and is expressed in such lofty speeches.

Mephistopheles' role is much easier to encompass. It consists largely of displays of cynicism, cunning, and deprecation. It does offer an actor considerable scope to display his talents, nevertheless, since it must embody the threat to Faust's success.

Margarete is primarily the young and innocent girl brought to ruin by her own too-loving and credulous nature. She is required to display a wide range of emotions, however, for she goes from awakening love, to happiness, to shame, to madness and death. Hers is the most clearly projected and concrete role in the play.

The actors portraying the type characters must bring to the play extensive talents—for movement, dance, song, and pantomime. The "extras"

232

in this play make the difference between a good and bad production, for they supply a background for the action and illustrate the complexity of creation and Goethe's philosophical concerns.

VISUAL AND AURAL APPEALS. There is probably no play which allows designers to utilize their gifts so thoroughly as does *Faust*. The costumer must create suitable garments for will-o'-the-wisps, witches, monkeys, wizards, personifications of abstract qualities and evil spirits, in addition to those for human characters. The lighting designer must suggest the ranges of night and day and the wonders of Walpurgis Night. The scene designer must either provide a single background capable of suggesting the great variety of places or innumerable settings which, at the same time, permit rapid changes of scene.

The audience's senses are assaulted through all possible means: the spoken word, song, music, dance, natural and supernatural visions, witches' frolics, folk festivals, and disembodied voices. There is an almost endless variety of attractions. The proper staging and coordination of all these elements strain the powers of any director, even with the full assistance of choreographer, musicians, costumer, lighting designer, and set designer. The task is stupendous, but if properly done *Faust* shows the theatre in its fullest splendor, for it extends the resources of the stage to their breaking point. In its attempt to embody the infinity of experience, *Faust* is an outstanding example of romanticism.

MELODRAMA

At the same time that Romantic drama was developing, melodrama was also emerging; it was eventually to become the most popular form of the nineteenth century. It appealed to a much wider audience than did Romantic drama and continued to develop and to hold the stage long after the Romantic movement had ended.

Plays have exhibited melodramatic qualities since the earliest times, and examples may be found in every period. But it was not until the eighteenth century that various elements came together to create the conditions out of which a form called melodrama was to emerge.

Perhaps the most important feature of melodrama is its observance of strict moral justice. No matter how horrible the trials of the virtuous characters or how powerful the villainous, the good are rewarded and the evil are punished. The world depicted is one in which deeds and characters are separated by clear-cut moral distinctions. The emotional appeals are basic: the arousal of pity and indignation at the wrongful oppression of good people and intense dislike for wicked oppressors. A melodrama also typically brings in *comic relief* through a minor character, usually a rather simple-minded or severely frank one. The action, which progresses almost entirely through the machinations of the villain, is generally simple in outline, for too many subtleties would confuse the moral distinctions. Normally, it is composed of a series of incidents which show the hero or heroine undergoing superhuman trials at the hands of one or more totally unscrupulous characters. Suspense is em-

233

Setting by Gué for one of Pixérécourt's melodramas. The play is set in Scotland in the sixteenth century. From Ginisty's *Le Mélodrame*, 1901.

phasized and the reversal at the end of the play is extreme (from almost certain death to safety, from near disgrace to complete vindication, and so on). Usually a series of unexpected discoveries or of hairbreadth escapes (frequently utilizing concealed hiding places or disguises) keep the plot moving. Since the characters do not change psychologically or morally, interest is centered upon the manipulation of events. The melodrama of the nineteenth century developed a set of stock characters which appeared in almost every play: the hero, the heroine, the comic character, and the villain. Although specific traits and circumstances differed from play to play, melodrama remained remarkably constant in its handling of characterization and action.

The term *melodrama* means a combination of music and drama, and throughout the nineteenth century this type of play was accompanied by a musical score just as a movie is today. Underlining the emotional qualities of scenes, music helped to achieve the desired response from the audience. Most melodramas included incidental songs and dances as well and, according to the capabilities of the actors, these portions were expanded or contracted from one production to another.

Most of the characteristic features of melodrama were present in such eighteenth-century forms as sentimental comedy, drame, and pantomime, although they had not yet been synthesized. It merely remained for elements to be recombined in a distinct way to create a new form. Credit for the formalization of melodrama goes to two men: August Friedrich Ferdinand von Kotzebue (1761–1819) and René Charles Guilbert de Pixérécourt (1773–1844). Kotzebue, a German, wrote over two hundred plays, the most famous of which are *Misanthropy and Repentance* (played throughout the English-speaking world as *The Stranger*) and *The Spaniards in Peru*. A Kotzebue craze swept the world between 1790 and 1825. Kotzebue was a master of sensationalism, with which he mixed sentimental philosophizing and startling theatrical effects. His success led to many imitations.

234

But it was Pixérécourt, a Frenchman, who first consciously fashioned his plays along lines which have become the accepted marks of melodrama. His first full-length play, *Victor, or The Child of the Forest* (1798), established both his success in the theatre and melodrama as a type. He wrote over one hundred plays, almost all of which were enormously popular, and intended, as he put it, for a public which could not read. He did not labor so much over the dialogue, therefore, as over easily identified character types and startling theatrical effects. His plays brought vast new audiences into the theatre. Although in his own day he was enormously successful, Pixérécourt's fame was not lasting, for others learned to manipulate the same kinds of effects and to invent even more startling stage tricks.

Melodrama soon surpassed all other forms in box office appeal. Its subject matter was drawn from a wide variety of sources: history, lurid or provocative newspaper articles, popular stories and novels, and domestic problems.

The fortunes of melodrama throughout the world cannot be traced here, but, since the basic pattern was much the same everywhere, the English experience can be cited as reasonably typical. Until the 1820's, the majority of melodramas were rather exotic, either because they were set in some remote time or place or because they featured the supernatural or highly unusual. In the 1820's, the form was given a new turn, however, with the introduction of more familiar backgrounds and subject matter: Pierce Egan's *Tom and Jerry, or Life in London* (1821) featured a number of well-known places in London and told a story based on everyday events; J. B. Buckstone's *Luke the Labourer* (1826) helped to popularize domestic themes; Douglas William Jerrold's *Black-Eyed Susan* (1829) started a vogue for nautical melodramas; and Edward Fitzball's *Jonathan Bradford* (1833) was the first of many works based on actual crimes.

Then, in the 1830's, melodrama began to acquire a more elevated tone as well-known writers were attracted to the theatre. Edward George Bulwer-Lytton (1803–73), already famous as a novelist, helped to establish "gentlemanly" melodrama with *The Lady of Lyons* (1838) and *Richelieu* (1839), both of which held the stage through the remainder of the century. From about 1840, melodrama attracted playgoers of all ranks. Probably the most successful of the later English writers was Dion Boucicault (1822–90), whose *The Corsican Brothers* (1852), *The Octoroon* (1859), *The Colleen Bawn* (1860), and *The Shaughraun* (1874) combine sentiment, wit, and local color with sensational and spectacular endings which tax the full resources of the theatre.

UNCLE TOM'S CABIN

The most popular melodrama of the nineteenth century was the American play *Uncle Tom's Cabin*, based on Harriet Beecher Stowe's novel, published in 1852. Mrs. Stowe was opposed to the adaptation of her work for the stage, but was unable to prevent it because of the inadequate copyright laws of the period. Despite their enormous popularity, she never received any financial remuneration from the stage versions.

Eliza crossing the frozen river in *Uncle Tom's Cabin*. Produced by William Brady at the Academy of Music, New York, 1901. Courtesy Harvard Theatre Collection.

A number of dramatizations were made of *Uncle Tom's Cabin*, but that by George L. Aiken, an actor who later became a prolific writer of pulp fiction, was to be the most popular. Aiken's adaptation was produced at Troy, New York, in September 1852. Aiken first constructed a three-act play which ended with the death of Little Eva, and then wrote a second play which continued the story until the death of Uncle Tom. They were soon combined to form the six-act play which was presented after that time. When the six-act version was produced in New York in 1853, it played for 325 performances, a phenomenal run for the period. The play was so long that it was presented without the usual afterpiece, an innovation which helped to establish the single-play entertainment, later to become standard.

THEMES AND IDEAS. Since Mrs. Stowe was principally concerned with the plight of the Negro, her novel was in large part a plea for the abolition of slavery. Much of this is retained in the play. It can best be seen in the story of George Harris and Eliza, which shows how slave owners (even the good ones) parted families by selling members, and how the Negro was forced to become a fugitive if he rebelled against his status as a piece of property. The Negro's plight is also shown in the story of Uncle Tom, who also is parted from his family (although this is not emphasized), and who eventually dies at the hands of the inhumanly cruel Simon Legree.

The rights of slave owners versus the natural rights of man is debated sporadically in the play. The institution of slavery is shown to be evil, even though all slave owners are not. The precariousness of the Negro's position is demonstrated by St. Clare's death, for this good slave owner has planned to free Uncle Tom but fails to do so in time, and Uncle Tom meets a terrible fate under Simon Legree's brutality.

236

Uncle Tom's Cabin is also concerned with religion. (Mrs. Stowe was married to a minister and came from a family famous in religious circles.) Uncle Tom is sustained in his trials by his faith, which is used to explain his trustworthiness and perfection as an individual. He teaches his religion to Little Eva, aids in St. Clare's conversion, and comforts Cassy with his picture of God's love. This emphasis culminates in the final tableau in which Little Eva, riding on a "milk white dove" among clouds bright with sunlight, blesses the kneeling figures of St. Clare and Uncle Tom. This final scene seems to suggest that religious faith, patience, and goodness will bring about eternal salvation. It also serves as a happy ending to what would otherwise be an atypical melodrama.

Along with religion, love plays a large part. Topsy is reclaimed by love, St. Clare reforms because of his love for Little Eva, Eliza and George are made strong by love, and Phineas Fletcher is converted to abolitionism through his love for a Quaker girl. The evil characters are depicted as lacking in love for others.

But the ideas are decidedly subordinate causes for the play's appeal. Ultimately, it is the spectacle of good and evil in conflict that accounts for the strong emotional response which this melodrama elicited from generations of playgoers.

PLOT AND STRUCTURE. *Uncle Tom's Cabin* is composed of a number of loosely connected stories. For example, the subplot dealing with Eliza and George Harris is related to the main plot only because Eliza and Uncle Tom are owned by the same family. The decision to sell Eliza's child and Uncle Tom to a slave dealer initiates both plots, but the two are unrelated thereafter except thematically. The looseness of the plot may also be illustrated in other ways. Even in the main plot Uncle Tom's life with Little Eva and his fate under Simon Legree are connected only through the character of Uncle Tom. Other scenes, such as those between Miss Ophelia and Deacon Perry, have no discernible purpose except as comic relief.

The organization of *Uncle Tom's Cabin*, therefore, is not always that of a cause-to-effect relationship among the various parts (although this kind of organization is often found within the individual subplots), but is largely determined by the play's themes and by a desire for variety. The parts are held together by fortunate coincidences—the characters meet at just the right moment, and their personal lives are manipulated as needed for the story with little attempt to justify the startling fluctuations (for example, apparently Shelby loses and regains his money, and Little Eva and St. Clare die to motivate plot complications).

But the sprawling form and the poorly motivated occurrences obviously did not detract from the play's appeal. The variety was in itself one of the chief sources of attraction: the story of Topsy serves as an antidote to what today seems Little Eva's almost cloying perfection; George and Eliza are suitable contrasts to Uncle Tom in their attitudes toward slavery; and Simon Legree is strikingly different from St. Clare and Shelby as slave owners. Variety is also achieved through the alternation of comic and serious tone, of quiet and bustling scenes, and in the many reversals of fortune.

237

Although the unity of the play is to be found in its themes and characters, the range of appeal is sufficiently wide to reach all segments of the audience. The goodness of Little Eva and Uncle Tom are balanced by the rebelliousness of George and Eliza; the comic and pathetic actions of Topsy and the schemes of Gumption Cute are contrasted with the villainy and punishment of Simon Legree.

The play's six acts are subdivided into thirty scenes, a number of which are tableaux (scenes without words), the most striking of which is the final moment when Little Eva blesses Uncle Tom and St. Clare. (The *tableau* was advocated by Diderot in the eighteenth century, was widely used in minor entertainments by the end of that century, and was especially popular in the nineteenth century, when no play was considered complete without a series of striking tableaux.)

Uncle Tom's Cabin ignores the unities of time and place. It is set in Kentucky, Ohio, Louisiana, and Vermont, and it is obvious that much time has elapsed between the first and last scenes. It shows many of the same characteristics as *Faust*, but in a more accessible form.

CHARACTERS AND ACTING. The play includes approximately twenty-five characters, although a number of additional ones could be used to advantage in such scenes as the slave auction. While this is a large cast, it would be much larger if coincidences did not bring the same characters together frequently, even though the scene may change from Kentucky to Louisiana or Vermont. Since many characters disappear for scenes at a time, roles can be doubled with ease.

All of the characters are types. (The names Uncle Tom and Simon Legree have passed into popular usage as descriptions of types of behavior.) The demands on the actor, therefore, are not great, for each needs to show only a few specific characteristics. Uncle Tom never wavers in his loyalty and convictions; Little Eva is constantly good; George Harris is always rebellious; and, though she becomes less rambunctious, Topsy remains essentially the same. St. Clare is said to reform but, since he is never shown intoxicated on stage, this change has little meaning to an audience.

The character of Simon Legree demonstrates one of the chief differences between nineteenth-century melodrama and that of today. Although the totally brutal Legree shows fear of damnation in one scene, the psychological causes behind his behavior are never explored. In a modern play such a scene would explore the bases for the brutality. This difference in approach to characterization marks the principal change in modern melodrama.

Interesting hints are given about two characters who remain undeveloped in *Uncle Tom's Cabin*. Marie, Little Eva's mother, is petulant, has frequent headaches, and displays other signs of being demanding and childish. After one scene she is completely neglected, however, and no action stems from these characteristics. Similarly, Cassy is shown to be relatively complex. She has abandoned her principles, but still knows the difference between right and wrong. She seems to have some strange power over Simon Legree and torments him, but she remains a minor character, for these hints are never developed. Audiences in the nineteenth century probably supplied missing information, however, since these two characters are developed more fully in the novel.

The characters, then, as is typical of melodrama, are simple. They are characterized physiologically, sociologically, and in terms of basic attitudes. Much is made of physical appearance, and the division into white and Negro is important to the play's theme. Furthermore, the characters have significant "looks" about them—Little Eva is said to have an unworldly appearance; George Harris is spoken of as having a look of courage and conviction; Topsy's comic appearance is an important element in her characterization. Sociological factors are also emphasized, since the division into slaves and free men, owners and overseers, workers and the leisure class is important. The chief concern, however, is with the fundamental attitudes of each character. But these attitudes are confined largely to clear-cut moral stances—either good or bad. No character needs to deliberate about what he should do, for his choice is predetermined by his basic moral nature. The characters remain simple, therefore, because differentiations are restricted to appearance, social position, and habitual attitudes. Although the lack of complexity in the play's personages makes them appear oversimplified, clarity is achieved.

LANGUAGE. By the mid-nineteenth century, prose was being used increasingly in serious drama. Melodrama employed simple, straightforward dialogue in which characters openly state their feelings and motives. The characters seem unduly self-conscious about their own moral qualities—the good people appear self-satisfied and pious, while the bad seem thoroughly aware of their own evil natures. Though the result is clarity of character, such stilted statements of moral purpose make nineteenth-century melodrama easy to parody.

But if the language is simple, it is also capable of arousing intense emotional response. Uncle Tom's death is still touching, and the plight of Eliza and George still arouses indignation and admiration.

The language of melodrama helped to establish the standard of our own time under which everyday speech is imitated rather than idealized. After 1850, poetry was increasingly supplanted by conversational prose.

VISUAL AND AURAL ELEMENTS. Melodrama, like Romantic drama, placed considerable emphasis upon spectacle. The settings for *Uncle Tom's Cabin* range from the comfortable interiors of wealthy homes to rough cabins; from the idealized landscape of St. Clare's garden to the ice-filled river over which Eliza escapes; from city streets to desolate country scenes. The contrast is made more evident by the rapid changes, for no act of the play has fewer than four scenes. Quiet and restrained scenes, such as the idyllic life of Uncle Tom and Little Eva, contrast sharply with the flight of Eliza and George, a slave auction, and the beating of Uncle Tom.

The basic scenic elements were still wings and drops with special pieces added as needed. The illusion of reality was sought, however, and considerable effort was spent in making such scenes as that in which

239

One of the favorite entertainments in America during the nineteenth century was the minstrel show. This sheet music shows some figures associated with one of the best known troupes, Christy's Minstrels. Courtesy University of Iowa Library.

Eliza crosses the ice seem as realistic as possible. The popularity of the play led many companies to mount rival productions in which they competed with realistic stage effects. Mules, horses, and bloodhounds were added in the pursuit of Eliza and George, and the terrible plight of the characters was constantly underlined by spectacle. Melodrama extended the physical demands on staging as far as they could go. Motion pictures eventually built upon this taste and replaced the stage as the principal purveyor of spectacle.

Costuming in *Uncle Tom's Cabin* was adapted from contemporary dress but modified to emphasize the particular qualities of individual characters. Simon Legree was made terrible in part because of his appearance. Little Eva no doubt was costumed as the nineteenth-century idea of perfection.

Uncle Tom's Cabin was accompanied by an orchestral score, and at various points songs were inserted. During the peak of the play's popularity, producers sought to outdo each other in the amount of added incidental entertainment in the form of songs and dances. Undoubtedly, the spectacle, music, and dance of *Uncle Tom's Cabin*, coupled with its strong, simple, emotional story, explains in large part its success as well as that of many other melodramas of the nineteenth century.

Melodrama combined the demands upon staging made by Romantic drama with the simplistic moral outlook of eighteenth-century drama; it popularized most of the trends of the preceding hundred years. While melodrama is frequently thought of principally as a nineteenth-century type, it actually remains the most popular form today, since it includes the majority of motion picture and television dramas. The melodramas of today differ from their nineteenth-century counterparts mainly in their use of up-to-date subject matter and in a greater attention to psychological motivations.

240

During the nineteenth century, the theatre continued to expand, although its growth was at first inhibited by political and economic forces. The Napoleonic Wars, which involved all of Europe in the first part of the century, was followed after 1815 by an economic depression which lasted until about 1840. Despite these obstacles, an ever increasing demand for theatrical entertainment, created primarily by the continually growing urban population, was to lead in the second half of the century to an era of financial prosperity.

MAJOR TRENDS IN THE NINETEENTH-CENTURY THEATRE

The basic producing organization continued to be the resident company performing a large repertory of plays each season. Nevertheless, the system underwent significant changes during the course of the century under the impact of visiting stars and the rise of touring companies.

THE REPERTORY COMPANY

Repertory companies had always had their leading players, and the most powerful companies were able to attract the best actors, but the exploitation of stars was largely an innovation of the nineteenth century. For example, after 1810 English actors with great reputations began to tour America in starring engagements, performing their most famous roles with the resident companies they visited. Originally the star system lifted the level of local productions, since touring actors were those of the first rank, but after 1830 those with lesser talent also began to tour, and as the frequency of visits increased members of the local troupes became merely supporting players. This, in turn, led the better local actors to try their fortunes on the touring circuit. After a time managers found it difficult to maintain a first-rate company. The craze for visiting celebrities was universal and many of the most renowned performers made around-the-world tours.

But while visiting stars may have undermined morale, the number of resident companies continued to grow until about 1870. In America, the thirty-five permanent troupes of 1850 had increased to about fifty in 1870, while in London there were about twenty-one companies in 1850, in Paris about twenty-eight in 1855, and in Germany sixty-five in 1842.

The resident troupes were eventually undermined by the rise of traveling productions, made feasible by the expanding network of railroads. In America, the railroad system extended from coast to coast by 1870 and continued to grow thereafter, offering reasonably dependable transportation to almost any place in the United States. After this time the star system gradually gave way to the *combination company,* in which a star toured with a complete cast, scenery, and costumes. The combination company normally performed only one play rather than a repertory of attractions. By 1886, there were 282 touring companies in America. The impact of the new system is indicated by the rapid decline of resident companies. In America, the fifty companies of 1870 had been reduced to twenty in 1878, to eight in 1880, and to four in 1887. A similar, although less drastic change can be noted elsewhere. In England and France, provincial troupes virtually disappeared, although permanent companies continued in London and Paris. Germany, with its network of state theatres, was perhaps least affected of all countries.

241

Audience at the performance of a melodrama. From Ginisty's *Le Mélodrame,* 1901.

The abandonment of a season of repertory in favor of a single, long-run hit, a principle which most producers had adopted by 1900, meant that actors were now hired to play one role for the run of the play rather than for a line of business. When the play closed, he had to seek a new engagement. Thus, the new arrangement simplified the problems of the producer but greatly complicated those of the actor.

The decline of resident companies did not signal a decrease in theatrical activity, for in quantity productions increased until well into the twentieth century. The change to touring companies, however, created many new problems. In America, New York rapidly became the center of production from which all companies originated. Actors, therefore, had to go to New York to seek employment, just as local managers did to book attractions for their theatres. By the 1890's the booking of productions was extremely chaotic, since a local manager might have to negotiate with as many as forty different producers, each of whom was simultaneously dealing with countless local managers. Often, touring companies defaulted on their contracts, leaving theatres without attractions.

Out of this situation the Theatrical Syndicate grew when six theatre managers and booking agents joined together in 1896 for the purpose of gaining a monopoly on "the road." The Syndicate promised local theatres a full season of plays, complete with stars, on the condition that they book all of their attractions through the Syndicate. Although many local managers welcomed the new stability, others resisted the attempted monopoly. In these cases, the Syndicate bought, rented, or built rival houses and gradually drove the recalcitrant managers out of business. Then, because they controlled a majority of key theatres, the Syndicate could also force New York producers to sign exclusive contracts with them, since otherwise the road companies would find it difficult to obtain enough bookings to make tours profitable. Through such devices, the Syndicate dominated theatrical production in America between 1896 and 1915, when its power was finally broken.

THE AUDIENCE

The eighteenth century had seen the middle classes flock increasingly to the theatre, and to this group the nineteenth century added the lower classes. The Industrial Revolution (which greatly enlarged the urban population), the expansion of public education, the belief in democracy and equality, and other factors served to bring into the theatre many persons who had not previously attended.

242

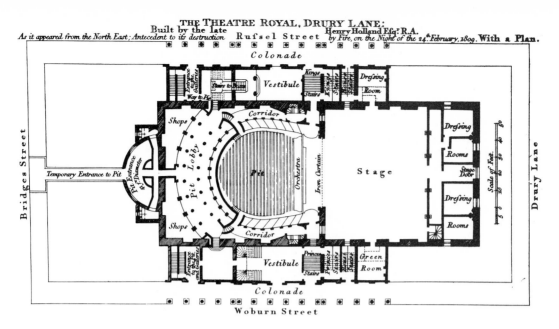

As the audience increased in size, the number of theatres grew rapidly. For example, in London the six theatres of 1800 had grown to twenty-one in 1843. Furthermore, the theatres were enlarged. Both the Drury Lane and Covent Garden seated about 3000 persons and other houses were almost as large; subtlety of playing became increasingly difficult.

The diversity among audiences motivated managers to enlarge the range of entertainment to meet the varied tastes. Since until 1843 the Licensing Act reserved regular drama for Covent Garden and Drury Lane, the new theatres of London were restricted to melodrama, burletta, pantomime, and similar minor forms. The popularity of the lesser houses, however, motivated the managers of Drury Lane and Covent Garden to increase their offerings of incidental entertainment. Programs were extended until they required five or more hours to perform. The decline in quality drove large numbers of sophisticated playgoers away from the theatre after 1815; they were not to return until after 1850.

Ground plan of the Drury Lane Theatre, London, 1808. From Wilkinson's *Londina Illustrata,* 1825.

Interior of the Drury Lane Theatre in 1808. Note the five tiers of boxes. Courtesy Metropolitan Museum of Art, Dick Fund.

In the last half of the century, regular drama was gradually separated from the variety-hall atmosphere. Theatres came to specialize in a particular kind of entertainment and regular drama became again the province of a more sophisticated group, a trend which was accelerated in the twentieth century by the development of motion pictures, which consciously attempted to attract that mass audience which had constituted a large part of the nineteenth-century theatre-going public.

As the theatres turned to greater specialization, the evening's bill became less complex. Theatres offering dramatic entertainment turned more and more to a single play as the sole attraction. The length of performances changed correspondingly, and by 1900 programs lasted only two to three hours.

The changes in programing led to other changes in the auditorium, which continued to be divided into box, pit, and gallery until the late nineteenth century. The increased size of the auditorium, however, made hearing and seeing from the boxes more difficult, and around the middle of the century comfortable armchairs began to be placed in the front rows of the pit. Gradually, the number of chairs was increased and the orchestra replaced the boxes in prestige and desirability. In theatres built after the late nineteenth century boxes were often omitted and the space formerly occupied by them was devoted to mezzanine or balcony seating.

THE STAGE

The developments in staging during the nineteenth century may be attributed primarily to an increasing interest in historical accuracy and illusionism. Prior to the late eighteenth century, history was not considered relevant to art, since universal truth, independent of time and place, was said to be the province of drama. In general, neoclassicism was almost totally antihistorical in outlook. During the eighteenth century, however, a concern for the circumstances of time and place began to appear. As a result, the successive changes and developments of society

A street scene used in a number of Shakespearean revivals at Covent Garden after 1809. This setting is by William Capon (1757-1827), one of the first English designers to be interested in historical accuracy. Some of his scenery remained in use until about 1840. From *The Magazine of Art,* 1895.

became as important as those which had remained constant. Interest began to shift from ideal and universal qualities to the individualizing details of man's existence. National and historical differences in architecture, literature, dress, and social customs began to be studied with enthusiasm. The first history of costume appeared about 1775 and antiquarianism in general came to the fore thereafter.

The interest in time and place extended to the unusual or exotic. Authentic dances and costumes of other countries began to creep into plays, and unusual or picturesque settings became popular. This kind of background detail came to be called *local color*, since it rendered the characteristic and individual features of a specific locale.

At first, historically accurate details and local color were used only sporadically and inconsistently. Charles Kemble's production of Shakespeare's *King John* (produced in London in 1823) was the first in England to claim complete historical accuracy in every detail of costuming, a principle extended to scenery in *Henry IV, Part I* in 1824. Both of these productions were designed by J. R. Planché (1796–1880) who, through his productions and through his histories of costume and other antiquarian studies, did more than any one else in England to forward the movement toward historical accuracy in the theatre.

In Germany, historical accuracy was used as early as 1801 in a production of Schiller's *The Maid of Orleans* presented in Berlin with scenery and costumes by Karl Friedrich Schinkel (1781–1841). The state theatre in Berlin, especially after 1814 under the management of Count von Bruhl, was to be a major force in popularizing antiquarianism throughout Germany. In France, local color was a standard part of melodrama after 1800, but it was the Romantic dramatists, especially Hugo and Dumas *père*, who first insisted upon historically accurate settings and costumes. Nevertheless, throughout the world antiquarianism was inconsistently employed until about 1850, by which time it was becoming a point of pride to offer productions certified to be completely accurate in every detail.

Costume designs by J. R. Planché for Shakespeare's *King John,* produced at Covent Garden in 1823. This production is supposedly the first in England to use historically accurate costumes for all characters. Shown here are costumes for Philip Falconbridge and Hubert de-Burgh. Courtesy Stark Collection, University of Texas Library.

Scene from Shakespeare's *Antony and Cleopatra* at Sadler's Wells Theatre, London, in 1849. Although the men are clad in Roman costumes, the women still wear nineteenth-century garments. From *The Illustrated London News*, 1849.

Quite frequently the historically accurate details and local color were used only as interesting visual embellishments which had no effect upon the action of the play. It did not bother audiences or producers that historical accuracy was most often irrelevant to the spirit of the plays themselves. Nevertheless, it was through such visual details that realism began to enter the theatre. Although realism in subject matter and characterization were not to be exploited until after 1850, the ground work had been laid.

Once realism of spectacle had been accepted as a standard, the wing-and-drop setting began to be replaced by the *box set*. The first steps toward the box set were taken in the late eighteenth century, when flats were set up occasionally between pairs of wings. Gradually the entire setting came to be enclosed, although the precise stages in the development cannot be dated. By the early nineteenth century, the box set seems to have been in use on the Continent but was not introduced in England until the 1830's. It was not to be used consistently anywhere, however, until near the end of the nineteenth century.

The demand for illusionism also led to the leveling of the stage floor, which had sloped upward toward the back since the Renaissance, as it became increasingly difficult to create realistic effects solely through wings and drops, which were normally erected parallel to the front of the stage. As more and more special units were introduced, scenic elements were set up at any angle and at any point on the stage floor. When the old groove and chariot-and-pole systems became too restrictive, they were abandoned in favor of new methods of scene shifting. The most usual substitute was a large number of stage hands to move units manually, but toward the end of the century such devices as the revolving stage, the elevator stage, and the rolling platform stage were tried. (A *revolving stage* is created by mounting a large circular segment of the stage floor on a central pivot. A number of settings may then be mounted on this portion of the stage floor, and scene changes can be effected by merely revolving the stage until a new setting comes into view. On an *elevator stage*, parts or all of the floor may be raised or lowered. Scenery may be mounted on a segment of this floor while it is in the basement and then raised to stage level. A *rolling platform stage* is one mounted on tracks parallel to the front of the stage. Entire settings may be mounted on the platforms in the wings and then rolled onstage. The revolving stage, the elevator stage and the platform stage are only three of the many mechanical devices which have been used to shift scenery since the mid-nineteenth century.)

The trend toward realism also brought changes in other theatrical practices. For example, in the last part of the nineteenth century, the front curtain began to be closed regularly to mask scene changes. Several factors account for this change. The increasing complexity of settings demanded that stagehands do much of their work on stage and their visible presence would have been distracting. Probably more important, however, was the growing demand for illusionism, easily destroyed for most audiences if settings are assembled before their eyes.

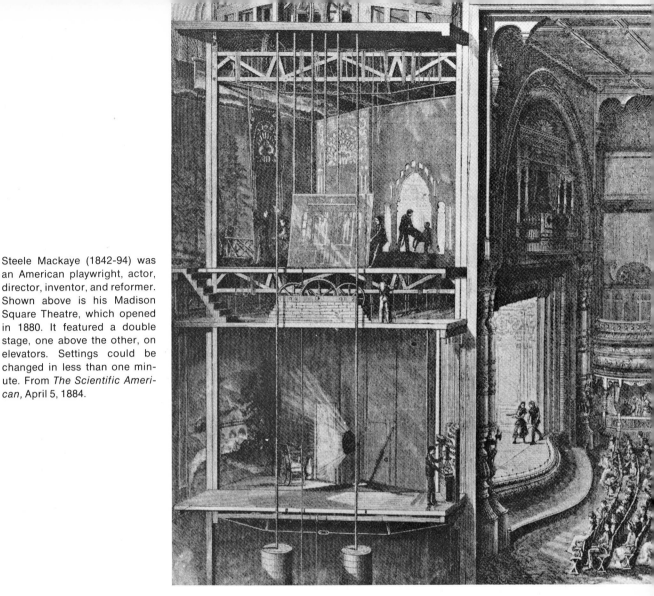

Steele Mackaye (1842-94) was an American playwright, actor, director, inventor, and reformer. Shown above is his Madison Square Theatre, which opened in 1880. It featured a double stage, one above the other, on elevators. Settings could be changed in less than one minute. From *The Scientific American,* April 5, 1884.

Diderot's theory of the fourth wall also began to be applied with some consistency as auditorium lights were extinguished during the performances and actors played more and more inside the proscenium rather than on the forestage, and behaved as though they were in real rooms in real houses. Realism in acting and in staging was not consistently applied, however, although the trend was clearly established.

Innovations in stage lighting also aided the development of realism. By 1820, gas had begun to replace candles and oil lamps and was in use almost everywhere by the 1840's. For the first time since the theatre had moved indoors the stage could be lighted as brilliantly as desired. Furthermore, by 1850 the *gas table*, a central panel of gas valves, permitted complete and instantaneous control over all of the stage lights. This new power led to numerous experiments with realistic effects. The perfection of the lime light and the carbon arc, forerunners of the follow spot, aided in these experiments since with them concentrated beams of light could

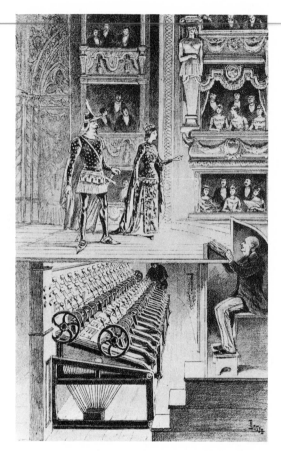

A lighting control board of the late nineteenth century. Note also the prompter at the front of the stage. From Moynett's *La Machinerie Théâtrale,* 1893.

be focused on the stage for the first time. Both were exploited beginning around 1850, at first for such special effects as rays of sunlight or moonlight but gradually for lighting the acting areas as well. After 1880, electricity rapidly replaced gas as the standard illuminant. It offered great flexibility without the constant danger of fire, the chief drawback of gas.

Brighter light, which came with the introduction of gas, emphasized the artificiality of the painted scenery and props, and by the 1830's three-dimensional details began to appear. Door knobs were added to doors, real molding was attached to the walls, carpets were laid over the floors, and artificial fires glowed in fireplaces. Such details began to be demanded by the action of plays, and by the 1860's actors were being required to perform such everyday tasks as boiling water, brewing, serving, and drinking tea.

THE ACTOR

The increased concern for realism carried over into acting as well. Many of the developments can best be seen by surveying briefly the careers of outstanding English actor-managers of the nineteenth century.

248

John Philip Kemble as Cato in Addison's tragedy. From Strang's Vol. I *Players and Plays of the Last Quarter Century.*

Edmund Kean as Othello. From Strang, Vol. I, 1902.

The stage of the early nineteenth century was dominated by the Kemble family, whose most famous members were John Philip Kemble (1757–1823) and his sister, Mrs. Sarah Siddons (1755–1831). Kemble made his London debut at Drury Lane in 1783 as Hamlet, and remained on the stage until 1817. Mrs. Siddons, frequently said to be the greatest English tragic actress, was established in the London theatre by 1782 and retired in 1812. The Kembles aimed at grace, dignity, and beauty in movement, gesture, and voice. Thus, they tended to idealize characters.

By 1820, however, the classical style of the Kembles was being challenged by the Romantic ideal, epitomized in the acting of Edmund Kean (1787–1833), who made his London debut at Drury Lane in 1814, and who remained on the stage until his death. Kean often sacrificed dignity and beauty to the depiction of intense emotion. On the other hand, he sometimes so neglected the quiet moments in a play that he was inaudible. This alternation of intensity with indifference led Coleridge to remark that to see Kean was like reading Shakespeare by flashes of lightning. Nevertheless, Kean could magnetize audiences and his style became so widely accepted that it set the standard for actors who succeeded him.

William Charles Macready (1793–1873) made his debut in 1810 and retired in 1851. His acting style was a compromise between those of Kemble and Kean, since he worked for beauty and dignity combined with

William Charles Macready in the grave-digger scene from *Hamlet*. From *The Illustrated London News*, 1846.

emotional intensity. Furthermore, like the Kembles he planned each detail of his characterizations with care. As a theatre manager, he introduced gentlemanly melodrama, painstaking rehearsals, and mounted new productions with historically accurate settings and costumes.

Mme. Lucia Elizabeth Vestris (1797–1856), after achieving fame in light comedy and musical entertainments, managed the Olympic Theatre in London from 1831 to 1838. With her husband, Charles Matthews (1803–78), she did much to return comic acting to a more natural style and made several other important innovations. She is said to have introduced the box set in England, to have employed real (rather than fake) properties, to have abandoned the practice of costuming comic characters in ludicrous garments, and to have shortened evening programs so that audiences could be out of the theatre by eleven. Most of her changes moved the theatre toward greater realism.

With his wife, Ellen Tree (1806–80), Charles Kean (1811–68), son of Edmund Kean, achieved fame as an actor and manager, principally through his Shakespearean productions at the Princess' Theatre in London between 1850 and 1859. Kean prided himself on the historical accuracy of every detail of his settings, costumes, and properties. His productions mark the triumph of historical accuracy as the standard for English staging. The patronage of Queen Victoria further served to elevate Kean's work in the eyes of the English public and to bring aristocratic audiences back to the theatre again.

250

Squire Bancroft (1841–1926) and his wife, Marie Effie Bancroft (1839–1921), are noted for the many reforms which they popularized at the Prince of Wales' Theatre between 1865 and 1880. They concentrated upon plays of contemporary life, especially those by Tom Robertson (1829–71), to which they applied rigorous standards of realism in every element of production. Just as Charles Kean triumphed with the realism of history, the Bancrofts established the realism of modern life. Their practices helped to popularize the box set, realistic costumes, properties and acting. Furthermore, they gained acceptance of orchestra seating and helped to popularize matinee performances.

Henry Irving (1838–1905) was the first English actor to be knighted, a sign that the acting profession was at last socially acceptable. With Ellen Terry (1847–1928) he achieved great renown during the final decades of the century in his productions of Shakespeare's plays, Romantic drama, and melodrama. Irving was also a theatrical manager, and it was he who abandoned the groove method of shifting scenery. He placed scenic units onstage wherever needed and employed a vast number of stage hands to make the necessary changes. He was the first manager who consistently concealed scene changes from the audience. More than any other producer, Irving synthesized all the trends toward complexity and realism in staging.

Henry Irving's production of *King Lear.* A sketch by Hawes Craven. From the souvenir program.

Francois-Joseph Talma as Titus in Voltaire's *Brutus*. From Jullien's *Histoire du Costume du Théâtre,* 1880.

Edwin Forrest as King Lear. From Strang's *Players and Plays of the Last Quarter Century,* Vol. I, 1902.

Edwin Booth as Hamlet. From Strang, Vol. I.

This survey of English actor-managers by no means exhausts the list of great actors of the nineteenth century. Others include: François Joseph Talma (1763–1826), Rachel (1821–58), Benoit Coquelin (1841–1909), and Sarah Bernhardt (1845–1923) in France; Mikhail Shchepkin (1788–1863) and Prov Sadovsky (1818–72) in Russia; Tommaso Salvini (1829–1916), Adelaide Ristori (1822–1906), and Eleanora Duse (1859–1924) in Italy; Ludwig Devrient (1784–1832), Emil Devrient (1803–72), and Fanny Janauschek (1830–1904) in Germany; Helena Modjeska (1844–1909) in Poland; and Edwin Forrest (1806–72), Charlotte Cushman (1816–76), and Edwin Booth (1833–93) in America.

THE PLAYWRIGHT

The nineteenth century brought the playwright considerable financial security. Previously, he had lost all control over the production of his plays after their initial performances. The *royalty system* of paying authors (a payment either of a fixed sum or of a percentage of the receipts for each performance) was introduced in France in the late eighteenth century, but was not universally accepted until the last quarter of the nineteenth century.

The first copyright law designed to give the dramatist control over the production of his plays was passed in France in 1791. By 1829, the French Society of Dramatic Authors was able to establish the rate of payments to authors, provide a pension system, and secure many additional privileges for dramatists. In England, the first copyright law was enacted in 1833. The laws, however, could not insure the dramatist's rights beyond the boundaries of his own country. Thus, an American might produce an English play without paying its author any fee, or he might translate a play and claim it as his own. More effective protection came after 1887 when under the provisions of an international copyright agreement all countries subscribing to it promised to protect the rights of foreign as well as native authors. With rare exceptions, playwrights throughout the world had been accorded legal protection by 1900. The dramatist might still have difficulty getting his plays produced, but when they appeared, either on the stage or in print, his rights were guaranteed by law.

Typically, the culmination of one trend signals the beginning of another. And so it was in the nineteenth century, for the Romantic drama, melodrama, and the realism of stage spectacle laid the groundwork for that movement, usually called realism, which marks the beginning of the modern theatre. By the last half of the nineteenth century those ideas and practices which characterize the modern era were already emerging and were merely waiting to be exploited.

Chapter 12 THE ORIENTAL THEATRE

While one theatrical tradition was developing in Europe, a quite different one was emerging in the Far East. The two did not make significant contact, however, until the end of the nineteenth century. Although exerting some influence upon each other in the modern period, they have continued along essentially independent lines.

Almost every Asian country has a rich dramatic heritage. Although each deserves extensive treatment, only a few can be considered here. Because the theatres of India, China and Japan have exerted the greatest influence, both upon other Asian countries and upon the West, they have been selected for discussion.

In actuality, the Oriental theatre is almost as old as that of the West. But the review of its history and conventions have been delayed until this point because their treatment must be confined primarily to features which have influenced the modern Western theatre.

THEATRE AND DRAMA IN
INDIA

The origins of the Indian theatre are obscure, for the surviving records are vague about chronology. According to Hindu legend, Brahma taught the art of drama to the sage Bharata, author of *Natyasastra* (*The Science of Dramaturgy*), written sometime between 200 B.C. and 200 A.D. Since this work gives detailed descriptions of acting, dance, costume and makeup, these arts must have been highly developed by that time.

The first important Oriental dramas were those written in Sanskrit. The majority of plays are based upon two epics, *Mahabharata* and *Ramayana*, both dating from sometime between 500 B.C. and 320 A.D. About twenty-five plays written between 320 A.D. and the twelfth century have survived. Thus, Indian drama reached its peak in those years when Western drama was at its lowest ebb.

254

Sanskrit plays differ markedly from their Western counterparts. They are not classified as comedy, tragedy, or melodrama, and are little concerned with characterization or philosophical issues. Rather, they are organized around fundamental moods, or *rasas*. There are nine rasas: erotic, comic, pathetic, furious, heroic, terrible, odious, marvelous, and peaceful. Although a play may employ many rasas, incompatible ones are avoided. All plays end happily, for Sanskrit drama aims to leave the spectator in a state of harmony. Violence and death are kept offstage, good and evil are clearly differentiated, and good is always triumphant.

Sanskrit drama is composed of diverse elements. The plots usually center around one principal story, although to it a number of minor stories, ranging from the serious to the farcical, may be joined. The dialogue is a mixture of prose and verse (which is used in moments of intense emotion or for heightened expression), and of Sanskrit (the learned language, spoken in the plays by Gods, kings, ministers, generals and sages) and Prakrit (the everyday language, spoken in the plays by soldiers, peasants, servants, women and children). Characters range through many social ranks and psychological types. For example, the hero (almost always a ruler or member of the aristocracy) usually has as his companion a dwarfish, gluttonous clown, who serves not only as comic relief in the serious story but also as confidant to the hero.

In many respects, Sanskrit plays resemble epic poems, for narrative passages, alternating with dialogue, establish the situation and relate events which have occurred offstage. As in novels, characters often describe their innermost feelings. Place changes freely. In length, Sanskrit plays vary from one to ten acts. According to the accepted rules, the events shown in a single act should all occur within twenty-four hours, while no more than one year should elapse between successive acts. Bharata lists ten kinds of plays, ranging through monologues, farces, operatic pieces, social plays, and heroic dramas. Of these, the heroic is considered the most important. Based upon history or mythology, it shows an idealized hero defending some righteous cause. Usually there is also a love story, in which the lovers are kept apart by some evil force until the end of the play.

In staging, realism was avoided. Each performance was preceded by a ceremony designed to please the gods and to put both actors and spectators in the right frame of mind. Plays were given only on special occasions (such as marriages, festivals, victories, coronations, and important visits). Performances lasted four or five hours. The majority of the audience was drawn from the aristocracy.

Since there were no permanent playhouses, a temporary one had to be constructed for each performance. Bharata describes how the theatre is to be laid out. He specifies an area about sixteen yards wide by thirty-two yards long; it is then divided into two equal parts, one half for the auditorium, the other for the stage. Seats of honor are to be provided for the patron and his party in front of the stage, the most favorable place for seeing and hearing. The stage area is also to be divided into two equal parts; the front half reserved for acting, the rear for dressing rooms and other offstage space. The stage may have two levels, the lower used for the majority of the action, the upper for scenes set in heaven or other high places.

No scenery was used. The place and situation was established at the opening of each scene through narrative and pantomime. Because there was no scenery, place could shift rapidly to permit a continuous flow of action. Stylized movement and gesture suggested climbing a hill, riding a horse, crossing a stream, driving a chariot, and a myriad of other actions. Through words and pantomime, the actor stimulated the audience to imagine whatever the drama required.

The Hindu theatre depended most upon the actor. Judging by contemporary references, actors did not rank high in social status or in moral esteem. They led a wandering life, moving about seeking engagements. Each troupe worked under a leader, who supervised the construction of the theatre and the over-all production. Both men and women acted.

The actor was considered to have four basic resources at his disposal: movement and gesture, speech and song, costume and makeup, and psychological insight. By the period in which the great Sanskrit dramas were written, movement and gesture had become rigidly conventionalized. Gestures were classified according to the parts of the body and inner feelings. There were thirteen movements of the head, thirty-six of the eyes, seven of the eyebrows, six of the cheek, six of the nose, nine of the neck, five of the chest, twenty-four of each hand, thirty-two of the feet. These were combined according to the situation, mood, and character to create a sign language as complex as the spoken word.

Similarly, speech and music were regulated according to intonation, pitch, and tempo, and were mingled according to the situation, mood, and character. The drama was accompanied throughout by instrumental music played on a drum and stringed instruments. The drum was considered essential, since it followed the speakers' voices closely and underscored rhythms. Through sung passages, especially upon the entrance or exit of characters, the musicians also indicated changes in mood and provided information about situation or character.

Costumes and makeup also followed strictly prescribed conventions. Color was used symbolically: high caste characters were indicated by red, low caste characters by blue; gold was used for the Sun and Brahma, orange for the gods; and so on. Ornaments, such as belts, necklaces, bracelets, and headdresses, differentiated characters within the same basic type. Makeup was so conventionalized that it could indicate a character's place of birth, social position, and historical period. Properties were also used symbolically. For example, if an actor carried a whip it indicated that he was riding in a chariot; a bit indicated that he was on horseback; the presence of an elephant was indicated by a goad.

For purposes of psychological characterization, roles were divided into a number of clearly differentiated categories. For example, the hero might be one of four types: quiet, gallant, impetuous, or sublime. Such classifications extended to a number of other types, each with several subdivisions and prescribed costumes, makeup, and gestures. Furthermore, emotions were divided into nine categories: quietude, wonder, dis-

gust, fear, energy, anger, pathos, laughter, and love. It was the actors'
task to blend these rigidly codified emotions, character types, costumes,
makeup, intonations, gestures, and movements into a totality capable of
arousing the appropriate rasa.

Of the Sanskrit plays which have survived, some of the most famous
are King Harsha's (seventh century, A.D.) *The Pearl Necklace*, *The Lost
Princess*, and *Nagananda*; Bhavabhuti's (late seventh century) *The
Later Story of Rama*, *The Story of the Great Hero*, and *The Stolen Marriage*; and Vishakhadatta's (ninth century) *The Ring of Rahshasha*. By
far the best of the plays are *The Little Clay Cart*, attributed to King Shudraka (probably of the fourth century), and *Shakuntala*. The plot of *The
Little Clay Cart* is entirely invented. It is primarily concerned with the
love of a Brahmin for a courtesan, although there are a number of other
subplots, all of which come together at the end of the ten acts when the
true prince, previously befriended by the courtesan, recaptures his
throne and unites the Brahmin and courtesan, who have narrowly es-
caped death at the hands of the evil prince.

But it is *Shakuntala*, written by Kalidasa in the late fourth or early
fifth century, which is the acknowledged masterpiece of the Sanskrit
drama. *Shakuntala* is divided into seven acts, each separately titled and
each marking an important stage in the story's development. In Act One,
entitled "The Hunt," King Dushanta, following a deer, comes riding into
the forest in a chariot. Upon being informed that he is near a hermitage,
he halts the chase. Entering the hermitage, he sees a number of young
women, among them Shakuntala, daughter of the sage Kanva, and falls

Scene from *Shakuntala* as performed by the Brahman Sabha,
Bombay, in 1954. Courtesy Information Service of India.

in love with her. Much of Act Two, entitled "Keeping the Story Secret," is taken up with the clown's complaints and jokes. The King dissuades his party from hunting and later orders them to disperse the demons who are said to be disturbing the quiet of the hermitage. In Act Three, entitled "The Enjoyment of Love," the King eavesdrops on Shakuntala and her friends, discovers that Shakuntala loves him, reveals himself, and eventually wins her. At the opening of Act Four, called "Shakuntala's Departure," the King has returned to the court, leaving Shakuntala with a ring as a token of their marriage by mutual consent. An ill-tempered ascetic, Durvasas, believing that he has been insulted, places a curse on Shakuntala, declaring that the King will forget her. When he is reproached, he relents sufficiently to say that the King will remember her when he sees the ring. Kanva now discovers that Shakuntala is pregnant and insists that she go to join her husband. Act Five, called "Shakuntala's Rejection," shows Shakuntala's arrival at the court. Unfortunately, while bathing in a river during her journey, she has lost the ring and the King has no memory of her. The King's Chaplain finally suggests that Shakuntala stay at his house until the truth can be investigated, but before the act ends, he reports that a spirit has flown away with Shakuntala. In Act Six, entitled "Separation from Shakuntala," a fisherman is charged with stealing a ring belonging to the King, although he insists that he has found it in the belly of a fish. When the King sees it, his memory returns and he is stricken with remorse. While he is sorrowing over Shakuntala's disappearance, he is summoned to assist the gods in destroying demons. The final act opens with the King flying through the air, the demons now having been destroyed. He lands in a hermitage, where he encounters a young boy, who, through a series of signs, is revealed to be his own son. When the mother is summoned, it is Shakuntala. They are reunited and all ends happily.

As this brief summary indicates, the action of *Shakuntala* takes place over a number of years and in several places. It mingles the natural and the supernatural, the serious and the comic. The basic emphasis, however, is upon the love story, for the majority of the text is devoted to evoking the emotions of awakening love, doubt and yearning, fulfillment, the sorrows of rejection and loss, and the bliss of reunion now tempered with parental love. Thus, the basic rasa is love.

Shakuntala is famous for its powerful evocation of the forest, the fleeing deer, the sense of place and emotion—all through language. Kalidasa, a master of simile and metaphor, has won universal praise for his over-all harmony of style. Despite its sensual charms, *Shakuntala* illustrates well the Hindu search for peace of soul, rest after struggle, and happiness after trial and submission to fate. Its love story and the struggle of admirable characters against unfriendly powers gives *Shakuntala* a universal appeal, even though the Hindu setting and outlook may seem strange to Westerners. As the first Oriental drama known in Europe, it was responsible for stimulating interest in the theatre of the Orient.

Following the Mohammedan invasions of India during the twelfth and thirteenth centuries, Sanskrit drama virtually came to an end. On the other hand, Hindu dance survived. More ancient then drama, dance was well developed by the time Bharata wrote *Natyasastra*, in which he de-

258

scribes 108 dance positions. Dance probably reached its peak during the fourth and fifth centuries A.D. After the Mohammedan invasions, it was preserved primarily by temple dancers in the state of Madras. As Indian nationalism emerged in the late nineteenth century, classical dance came to be highly prized as a heritage of the past. The principal form today, usually called Bharatanatyam, is a solo dance for women noted for its grace. Classical dance has also survived in other forms, most notably the Kathak, characterized by intricate footwork and precise rhythms, and the Manipuri, noted for its swaying and gliding movements.

A dance-drama has also survived in the form of Kathakali, now about 300 years old. Like Sanskrit drama, Kathakali is based upon Hindu epics, but, probably because it is pantomimic, it exaggerates many features subordinated in the dramas. Violence and death are brought on stage; major emphasis is placed upon the passions and furies of gods and demons or upon the loves and hates of superhuman characters. Good and evil engage in desperate struggles, but good always wins.

Performers in a Kathakali dance-drama. Courtesy Information Service of India.

The Kathakali actor-dancers rely entirely upon mime, costume and makeup, although musicians help to tell the story through song and instrumental accompaniment. Gestures are conventionalized into about 500 separate signs. Characters are divided into seven basic types, each with its own costume and makeup, which takes hours to apply. Kathakali is performed entirely by men and boys.

These dance-dramas are presented in a temple courtyard (or other open space) upon a stage about sixteen feet square covered with a flower-decked roof and lighted by torches. Performances last all night. The appeal of Kathakali is so specialized, depending as it does upon a rather thorough knowledge of the conventions, that few attempts have been made to perform it outside of India. In 1967, a troupe was seen in Paris, London, and Montreal, perhaps opening the way for other appearances.

In addition to classical drama and dance, India boasts many other dramatic types, some probably extending back to earliest times. In present-day India, folk plays are important popular entertainments. The folk dramas vary with the region. Some are operatic, others are light farces, dance dramas, or devotional plays. Despite this variety, most folk plays have many common characteristics. A narrator usually sets the scene, summons characters as needed, and describes the events occurring offstage. Music accompanies the action throughout. The plays are performed on open stages surrounded on three sides by spectators. No scenery is used; the acting is stylized. Although differing from one area to another, the conventions are clearly understood by the local audiences. Most performances go on all night.

A western-style drama has also appeared in India, descended from plays brought by the British when they arrived in the eighteenth century. Few Indian authors have had success with the Western forms. In the modern period, Rabindrinath Tagore (1861–1941) has won considerable fame with his blending of Indian and Western conventions in such plays as *The King of the Dark Chamber* (1914) and *The Cycle of Spring* (1917).

India has been hampered in developing a native drama by its lack of a national language. Within India, fifteen major languages and about 500 dialects are in common use. This diversity of speech, combined with differences in local customs, has served to divide the country and to encourage drama with local appeal. Today productions range from ancient Sanskrit drama to folk plays and realistic works in the Western manner. Although the Indian theatre is diverse, its influence on the rest of the world still derives primarily from the Sanskrit dramas written between the fourth and twelfth centuries.

INDONESIAN SHADOW PLAYS

India's influence has also been felt through the shadow play, which spread to both Europe and Asia. This form was especially popular in Java and Bali (now parts of Indonesia).

Perhaps originating as early as the seventh century A.D., the Indonesian shadow plays, like Sanskrit drama, took their subjects primarily

Balinese puppets. Note the sticks for manipulating the figures. Courtesy Embassy of Indonesia, Washington.

from the *Mahabharata* and *Ramayana.* In the Javanese *wayang kulit,* as the shadow plays there are called, flat leather puppets act out the events, while the puppet master chants the story, manipulates the puppets (which are attached to wooden sticks), directs the music and sound effects. Performances often last as long as ten hours, consuming an entire night. They are accompanied by music played by an orchestra composed primarily of percussion instruments. The stories usually center around the struggles between good and evil characters, the good always winning.

There are many variations on the shadow play, each type having its own special name according to the kinds of puppets used and the source of the stories. When plays with live actors appeared in the eleventh century, they also took their inspiration from the puppets. As in the shadow plays, the live actors mimed an action to narrative and musical accompaniment.

Dance also plays a major role in the theatrical life of Indonesia. Supposedly it was the appearance of a Balinese dance troupe in Paris in 1931 which motivated Antonin Artaud to advocate a new Western theatre based on the Eastern model. The dance forms of Indonesia (and those throughout Southeastern Asia) have much in common with those of India, for most take their inspiration from Buddhist traditions. Thus, the drama and dance of India and Southeastern Asia constitute one major strand of the Oriental tradition. Another important strain stems from Chinese practices.

Actors in a dance-drama, an offshoot of the puppet theatre of Indonesia. Courtesy Embassy of Indonesia, Washington.

THEATRE AND DRAMA IN CHINA

As in India, ritual dance in China is of ancient origin, possibly going back to the Shang Dynasty (1766–1122 B.C.). It did not become a form of entertainment, however, until the Han Dynasty (200 B.C.–200 A.D.). Steps toward a dramatic form were not made until the T'ang Dynasty (618–906 A.D.), and a true drama did not appear until the Sung Dynasty (960–1279). The theatre first flourished under the Yuan Dynasty (1280–1368) and reached its fullest expression during the Ming Dynasty (1368–1644). Thus, the first flowering of Chinese drama is roughly contemporary with the medieval period of the West.

The development of the early Chinese drama (extending over several hundred years) is difficult to chart, for no accurate records have been preserved. Broadly speaking, however, two main types—the Southern and the Northern—emerged. The Southern drama used a five-tone musical scale, adhered to strict rules of meter and versification, and employed an elevated dialogue. The basic musical accompaniment was that of the flute. The over-all effect of this drama was one of softness and gentleness. The Northern type used a seven-tone musical scale, was considerably freer in its versification, and was more colloquial in dialogue. The principal musical accompaniment was that of stringed instruments. The over-all effect was one of liveliness and vigor.

262

During the sixteenth century, the Southern school began to dominate, although by this time it had absorbed many characteristics from other types. Plays of this period often run to thirty or more acts, each relatively complete in itself and separately titled. In the first act, a minor character usually explains the situation, which does not begin to develop until the second act. In succeeding acts, many other plots are introduced to give complexity and variety. All are resolved happily. This type of drama was to dominate until the mid-nineteenth century, although many stylistic changes occurred during the intervening years. In performance, acts could be played in various combinations or eliminated without seriously damaging the total effect.

From the sixteenth to the nineteenth century, Soochow was the principal cultural center of China and the major home of drama. Probably because of interference by court dilettantes, the drama had degenerated considerably before the rebellion of 1853 put an end to Soochow's leadership. Although Soochow's theatre had been the most important, many other areas had developed dramas with somewhat different characteristics. After Soochow's dominance ended, many of these variant types merged to create a new style—the Peking Opera. First fully developed during the reign of Huang Hsu (1875–1908), the Peking mode continues to be the major form of classical Chinese drama.

Peking plays are usually divided into two types: civil (dealing with domestic and social themes), and military (based upon the adventures of

A scene from the spectacle of "The Sun and the Moon." The Emperor Chia Ching (1522-60) is shown taking part with his actors. Courtesy the New York Public Library.

A typical Peking opera orchestra. Musical instruments from left to right: *hsiao-lo* (small gong), *nao-po* (cymbals), *ta-lo* (big gong), *tan-p'i-ku* and *pan* (single-skin-drum and wooden-clapper), *san-hsien* (three-stringed banjo), *erh-hu* (second fiddle), *yüeh-ch'ing* (moon guitar), and *ching-hu* (first fiddle). The orchestra is led by the drum player, sitting in the center. Formerly the orchestra was placed downstage left in full view of the audience. Today, it is often concealed behind a stage-left wing or in the orchestra pit. A standard orchestra consists of eight to ten musicians. In some elaborate contemporary productions more than twenty musicians are employed. From Siao and Alley, *Peking Opera* (Peking: New World Press, 1957). Photograph and notes supplied by Daniel S. P. Yang.

warriors or robbers). The two are often mingled. Plays may be based on history, legend, or popular novels. A large number are derived from two novels, *Romance of the Three Kingdoms* (which tells of the exploits of three military leaders during a period of unrest between 220 and 265 A.D.), and *The Water's Edge* (about the adventures of several Robin Hood figures of the eleventh century). An entire Peking play is often no longer than one or two acts of the Soochow type. Today an evening's bill is often made up of portions of plays, or a succession of short pieces, played without intermission. All plays end happily. A Westerner sometimes has trouble following a Chinese play, for the dramas concentrate upon the high points and relegate the development of the story to narrative passages. Thus, interest is focused upon the climactic moments rather than upon a fully dramatized story. A play in the Chinese theatre, however, is essentially the outline for a performance; the audience goes to see a production rather than to hear a literary text.

Although Chinese drama has undergone many changes since its origins, its basic conventions have remained relatively stable. Many traditional practices are best understood in relation to the stage and its equipment. The Chinese stage still preserves features derived from its earliest form—a temple porch with a roof. Thus, the traditional stage is an open, almost-square platform surmounted by a roof supported by columns. Raised a few feet above the auditorium, it is surrounded by a wooden railing about two feet high. The stage is equipped simply. There are two doors in the rear wall (the one on stage right is used for all entrances and the one on stage left for all exits); between them hangs a large embroidered curtain; the floor is carpeted; the permanent furnishings are restricted to a wooden table and two chairs.

The place of the dramatic action may be indicated in a number of ways. The audience may be told through speech or song what the stage represents. Pantomime may be used to establish place or changes of place. For example, actors pantomime knocking at gates, climbing stairs, or entering rooms; a circle around the stage indicates a long journey. Place may be indicated by the arrangement of the table and chairs. Depending upon the arrangement, the stage may become a law court, banqueting hall, or other room; the addition of an incense tripod indicates a palace, an official seal indicates an office, and an embroidered curtain hung from a pole indicates a general's tent, Emperor's chamber, or a bride's bedroom, depending upon the arrangement of the table and chairs and other properties. A wall is created by placing the chairs back to back, a bridge by placing the back of the chairs against the ends of the table; a single chair may stand for a tree or a door; the table used alone may represent a hill, cloud, or some other high place.

Additional properties may be used to indicate place or to clarify the action. A cloth upon which a wall is painted may be used to represent a fort, city gate, or mountain pass; a banner with a fish design indicates water; four pieces of cloth carried by a running actor signifies the wind; a whip symbolizes riding a horse; flags upon which wheels are painted signify a chariot or wagon; a stylized paddle is used to pantomime rowing. Weapons are semirealistic in appearance but are made of bamboo, wood, or rattan.

For full appreciation of the pantomime and properties, a spectator must be familiar with the conventions of the Chinese theatre. The intention is to stimulate the imagination but not to give an illusion of reality. To many commentators, the approach is best exemplified by the *property men*, or stage assistants, who bring on, rearrange, and remove properties as needed. No attempt is made to disguise their presence; they wear ordinary street clothes, often extremely informal ones. But while they are ever present, they are not considered to be a part of the stage picture; they are merely a part of the conventions which they help to create.

The musicians are treated much like the property men. They also remain in full view throughout the performance and are dressed in ordinary street clothes. They come and go freely and are never considered to be part of the stage picture. (In many theatres of present-day China, however, the musicians have been removed from the stage and placed in an orchestra pit.)

Music is indispensable in the Chinese theatre. It establishes atmosphere, controls timing and movement, accompanies the many sung portions, and welds the entire performance into a rhythmical unity. Most of the music for Peking Opera is borrowed from already existing sources and recombined according to the needs of particular plays. It is usually worked out collaboratively among the actors and musicians. Since Chinese musical notation is extremely imprecise, the musicians must memorize their parts.

The instruments used in the Chinese theatre have no exact counterparts in the West. The leader of the orchestra plays a kind of drum, which establishes tempo and accentuates rhythms. Gongs, cymbals, brass cups, flutes, stringed and other instruments complete the orchestra. The entrances and exits of all characters are signaled by deafening percussion passages. Sung portions are accompanied only by flute and strings. Much of the action is performed against a musical background.

The focal point of the Chinese theatre, however, is the actor, for the simplified stage focuses all attention upon him. Acting roles are divided into four main types: male, female, painted face, and comic. The male (or *sheng*) roles range from young to old and from fops to warriors. They include statesmen, scholars, lovers, and other heroic types. The roles are subdivided according to whether they involve acrobatics and fighting or whether they are restricted to singing and dancing. Actors playing these roles wear simple makeup and, with the exception of young heroes, beards. The female (or *tan*) roles are subdivided into six kinds: the virtuous wife or lover; coquettes; warrior maidens; young unmarried girls;

T'an Fu-ying, one of the best *lao-sheng* (old man role) actors on the contemporary Peking opera stage, in the role of Lu Su in *Meeting of the League of Heroes*. The costume and headdress here represent those of a court official. Note the folded "water sleeve" around the hand and the artificiality of the beard—examples of the nonillusionism of a Peking opera production. From Siao and Alley, *Peking Opera* (Peking: New World Press, 1957). Photograph and notes supplied by Daniel S. P. Yang.

The foremost Chinese actor Mei Lan-fang in a *ch'ing-i* (virtuous woman) role. The role can be compared to that of the soprano in Western opera because of its strong emphasis on singing. Peking opera acting is highly stylized, as exemplified here in the delicate pointing of the fingers and the manner of holding a tea tray. From Arlington and Acton, *Famous Chinese Plays* (Peiping: Henri Vetch, 1937). Photograph and notes supplied by Daniel S. P. Yang.

evil women; and old women. Although originally all tan roles were played by women, actresses were banned from the stage from the time of the Emperor Ch'ien Lung (1735–96) until the twentieth century. After 1911 actresses returned to the theatre and have now largely replaced the male tan actors. The "painted face" (or *ching*) roles are distinguished by the elaborate painted facial makeup worn by the actors. The ching roles include gods and other supernatural beings, courtiers, warriors and bandits, but the basic characteristic of all is swagger and exaggerated strength. They are subdivided according to whether they are good or evil or whether they must engage in fighting and gymnastics. The clown (or *ch'ou*) roles are the most realistic. They speak in everyday language and are free to joke and improvise. They may be servants, businessmen, jailers, matchmakers, shrewish mothers-in-law, or soldiers. The clown must be a good mimic and acrobat.

Make-up is an important part of the Chinese theatre. Bearded sheng actors and old women wear little makeup. For most tan roles the face is painted white and the eyes surrounded by a deep red shading into pink. A similar makeup, but with less contrast, is used for the unbearded sheng actors. For the ching roles, the entire face is painted in bold patterns symbolic of the character's traits. Realism is completely ignored. The clown's distinguishing feature is a white patch around each eye. The types of clowns are differentiated by a variety of black patterns painted on the face.

267

General Lien P'u (played by the noted actor Ch'iu Sheng-jung) strikes a magnificent pose in *The Reconciliation between the General and the Minister,* one of the first Peking operas written after 1949. The character belongs to the role of *ching* (painted face). Symmetrically painted facial design of red, black, and white suggest a loyal, straightforward but hot-tempered character. Note the exaggerated length of the beard. From Siao and Alley, *Peking Opera* (Peking: New World Press, 1957). Photograph and notes supplied by Daniel S. P. Yang.

The noted comic actor Ma Fu-lu in the role of Chiang Kan in *Meeting of the League of Heroes.* The role belongs to the category *wen-ch'ou* or "comic scholar." Note the white patch of make-up around the nose and eyes, the trade-mark of a clown on the Peking opera stage. From Arlington and Acton, *Famous Chinese Plays* (Peiping: Henri Vetch, 1937). Photograph and notes supplied by Daniel S. P. Yang.

Typically, costumes are gaudy in color and heavily patterned. There are more than three hundred articles of costume, each designed to indicate the wearer's character-type, age, and social status. Colors, motifs, ornaments, and accessories are combined according to an elaborate system of conventions. Color is always used symbolically: yellow signifies royalty, red loyalty and high social position, dark crimson a barbarian or military advisor. The tiger motif means power and masculinity, the plum blossom long life and feminine charm; the dragon motif is associated with the Emperor. There are more than a hundred varieties of headdress, each symbolic. Almost all costumes are made of rich materials regardless of the character's social position, although clowns and very poor persons sometimes wear linen or cotton garments.

Speech and movement are also highly stylized. Upon entering, each important character describes his own basic attributes and appearance in a half-chanted, half-spoken passage. He may then explain the situation or give other information. In this way, the dramatist may quickly supply essential exposition leaving the majority of the scene for the high point of a situation or emotion.

All stage movement is related to dance, for it is symbolic, pantomimic, and rhythmical. Every word of the text is accompanied by movement intended to clarify or heighten meaning. Thus, stage gesture is completely conventionalized. There are seven basic hand movements, more than twenty different pointing gestures, about twelve special leg movements, many special arm movements, and a great many sleeve and beard movements. The method to be used in walking or running is specified for each role. In creating a part, the actor must combine the prescribed gestures and movements according to the situation, mood, and character.

Vocal delivery is also controlled by rigid conventions. Each role has its own pitch and timbre. Prescribed rhythmical patterns often require that syllables or words be distorted. Even spoken passages must observe conventionalized tempos and rhythms. In addition, chanted or sung passages are freely inserted into spoken portions.

The character of the Chinese theatre also owes much to the audience. Probably because the early theatres were teahouses, the ground floor of the traditional Chinese theatre was furnished with tables and stools at which spectators were served tea as they watched the play. Poorer spectators sat on benches placed on a raised platform which extended along the sides and back of the auditorium. A balcony, divided into sections much like the boxes of Western theatres, was later added; in some periods it was used by wealthy persons, in others it was reserved for women.

Since 1911, this arrangement has been modified. Now most theatres are furnished with Western-style seating. Nevertheless, the audience's behavior has changed little. Spectators come and go freely, eat and drink, carry on conversations. Each member has his favorite passages, to which he attends carefully only to ignore others. Like the dramatists, the spectators seem more interested in the high points of a story or performance than with unified effect.

Setting for a Peking opera. An embroidered satin backdrop and two curtained doorways serve as the basic setting. The door on stage right is used for entrances, that on stage left for exits. The different locales of the action are suggested by the table and chairs, which are arranged by the property man in full view of the audience. This setting was used for *Twice a Bride,* a full-length Peking opera staged at the University of Hawaii in 1963. Directed and designed by Daniel S. P. Yang. Photograph by Camera Hawaii.

Because one needs considerable knowledge of the conventions of the Chinese theatre for a full appreciation of Peking Opera, the uninitiated would probably do well to read annotated versions of the plays. In his *Traditional Chinese Plays*, A. C. Scott has translated and provided extensive descriptions of the costumes, music, and pantomime for two plays, *Ssu Lang Visits his Mother* and *The Butterfly's Dream.* His annotations provide the reader with much that is left unspecified in the Chinese text.

In the West, knowledge of Chinese art and drama has grown slowly since the eighteenth century, when increasing trade precipitated a vogue for Chinese decorative motifs throughout Europe. Nevertheless, it was not until the twentieth century that the Chinese theatre became widely known in the West. Even then, Chinese drama was seen primarily in such adaptations as Benrimo's *The Yellow Jacket* (1913), Klabund's *The Circle of Chalk* (1923), and Hsiung's *Lady Precious Stream* (1938). Since World War II, the appearance of a Peking Opera troupe in Europe and the wide dissemination of a filmed performance have done much to increase direct knowledge. The impact of Chinese drama on the West is best exemplified in the work of Meyerhold, Brecht, and Artaud, who, impressed by the simplicity and anti-illusionistic conventions of the Chinese theatre, have adapted many of its techniques.

Similarly, Western-style drama has made some headway in China. After 1911, when contact with the West increased, many European plays were presented in China. Since 1950, Western-style melodrama has figured prominently, perhaps because it lends itself so well to painting the enemies of communism as villains and the supporters of the regime as heroes. Nevertheless, Peking Opera remains the most influential and most characteristic of Chinese dramatic forms.

THEATRE AND DRAMA IN JAPAN

Today, the Japanese theatre is more widely known in the West than that of any other Oriental country. Since World War II, China has been increasingly isolated from the rest of the world, while India's classical theatre is no longer vital. On the other hand, Japanese traditional forms still figure prominently in the repertory. Because Westerners have become increasingly familiar with Japan and its traditions, to many the Oriental theatre is above all the Japanese theatre.

As in other Asian countries, in Japan the theatre descended from ritual dances. When it emerged, it assumed three major forms: Noh, puppet theatre, and Kabuki.

Although Noh took shape over a long period, it first attained eminence through the work of Kanami Kiyotsugu (1333–84) and his son Zeami Motokiyo (1363–1443). These early playwrights remain the major writers of this form. Of the approximately 240 plays still in the repertory, more than 100 were written by Zeami. It was also Zeami who formulated the principles of Noh acting and production practices. Thus, Noh is rooted primarily in the fourteenth and fifteenth centuries.

To understand the Japanese theatre, one needs to know something of political events in Japan. The period from 1338 to 1590 was one of upheaval and civil strife. With the return of peace, the Emperor was reduced to a religious and ceremonial role, while civil authority passed to the *shogun*, an office which became hereditary. The power of the shoguns was not broken until 1868. Between 1641 and 1868 the shoguns systematically isolated Japan from the rest of the world. At home, they enforced a feudal system under which each trade and rank was carefully regulated. Probably because the limits of freedom were so narrow, the Japanese cultivated elaborate ceremonies and rituals in every aspect of their lives, including the arts. In the theatre, each form was reduced to a system of carefully wrought conventions.

Most of the Noh traditions were fixed by 1650. Although originally Noh had appealed to all classes, it became more aristocratic under the shoguns. In the seventeenth century, Noh actors were granted *samurai* (the highest) status and a stipend raised by a system of national requisitions. Six branches of Noh were recognized and the headship of each was made hereditary. These six schools still exist. After 1868, Noh lost its privileged position and survived primarily under the patronage of special societies. Since World War II it has been recognized as a national treasure and placed on a more secure footing.

Nevertheless, the appeal of Noh is limited, for it is essentially a form of the past. The language, based upon aristocratic speech of the fourteenth

A Japanese Noh stage as it appears today. Reprinted with permission from *The Traditional Music of Japan* by Shigeo Kishibe, Tokyo: Kokusai Bunka Shinkokai, 1966.

century, is unintelligible to most persons today. Many spectators bring scripts so that they may follow the plays. The majority of lines, some in prose and some in verse, are sung or intoned. The few spoken passages — typically fewer than one-third of the text — are recited in a highly stylized manner. Ordinary speech is heard only between the parts of a two-act piece when someone comes on stage to summarize what has happened in the first part.

Noh is essentially a dance-drama in which the script serves to create a setting for choreographic movement. It is not primarily concerned with dramatic action; rather, it seeks to express a situation in lyrical form. All Noh plays reach their fulfillment in a dance; the lines which precede the climactic dance serve primarily to establish the circumstances which motivate it. A chorus sings the actor's lines while he is dancing and narrates much of the story. The script of a Noh drama is usually shorter than that of a Western one-act play.

Noh plays are roughly classified into five types: *kamimono* or *wakinomono*, plays about gods; *shuramono*, about warriors; *kazuramono*, about women; *kuruimono*, about mad persons (often spirits), although this category has a number of divisions such as *genzaimono* "the earthly piece" dealing with contemporary persons realistically treated; and *kirinomono*, about demons. Traditionally, these categories have dictated programming, a total of five plays, in the order listed, making up a program. In recent years, however, it has become common to have programs composed of only two or three plays.

272

One of the most popular of Noh plays is *Atsumori* by Zeami. It includes only three characters, one very minor. It tells of the warrior Kumagai, who has killed Atsumori, a powerful nobleman, in battle. Kumagai is so grieved that he has become a priest, Rensei, so that he may pray for Atsumori's soul. On his way to a shrine, he encounters some reapers. When one of the reapers declares that he is a member of Atsumori's family, Rensei kneels to pray. This ends the first of the two acts. In the interlude between the acts, the events surrounding Atsumori's death are narrated. At the beginning of the second part, the ghost of Atsumori (the reaper of the first act) now appears dressed as a young warrior and identifies himself to Rensei. The remainder of the play is largely a narrative which establishes the background of the battle in which Atsumori perished. The play culminates in the recreation of the fight, a dance to the narrative accompaniment of the chorus. At the climactic moment, the ghost of Atsumori hovers over Rensei, ready to deliver a death blow, but Rensei's prayers have been effective. The play ends with Atsumori saluting Rensei with "pray for me again, oh pray for me again." The entire script consumes only about nine pages in print.

All Noh performers are male. The principal character is called *shite*, the secondary character *waki*. Each may have a companion, although many plays include only two characters. Seldom does a cast extend beyond six characters. Children, or *kokata*, may play young princes or other youthful parts. The shite and his companions wear masks made of painted wood. Other characters are unmasked. Masks may be divided into five basic kinds: aged, male, female, gods, and monsters. These types have many variations and occasionally special masks are required.

Costumes are based upon the ceremonial dress of several centuries ago, although adapted to achieve a sense of grandeur and to increase the performer's apparent stature. Garments are rich in color and design;

A character in the Noh play *Kumano*. Courtesy Kokusai Bunka Shinkokai, Tokyo.

most are made of silk and are elaborately embroidered. They are never gaudy, however, as are the costumes of the Chinese theatre. Articles of dress may be divided into four categories: outer garments; indoor clothing or garments worn without overdress; lower garments, such as divided skirts; and headdresses. Within each category there are many variations, but the same garments may be combined with others for use in several different roles. Thus, costumes are less rigidly conventionalized in color and design than in the Chinese theatre.

Only a few, highly conventionalized hand properties are used. The most important is the fan, which can suggest the rising moon, falling rain, rippling water, and blowing wind, as well as a variety of emotional responses. The meaning of the fan is indicated by the actor's pantomime and the musical accompaniment.

Stage furnishings are also simple. A wooden or bamboo stand may symbolize a mountain, palace, bedroom or other place, depending upon how it is decorated. Usually no more than one or two stage properties are present at once. Each is highly stylized. There is no scenery or stage machinery.

The design of the stage itself has been fixed since about 1615. There are two principal parts: the bridge (*hashigakari*), and the main acting area (*butai*). Both are roofed. The roof over the main stage is supported by four columns, each with its own name. The upstage right pillar is called *shitebashira* ("principal character's pillar"), for here the shite pauses as he enters to announce his name and to give other pertinent information. While reciting, he faces the downstage right pillar (the *metsukebashira*). The downstage left pillar is called *wakibashira*, because of its association with the secondary character (or alternatively the *daijinbashira*, or "minister's pillar," because of the role often played by the waki). The upstage left pillar, beside which the flute player sits, is called the *fuebashira* (or "flute pillar").

The main platform is divided into three areas, although the only architectural barriers are the four pillars. The largest part, used for the main action, is enclosed within the four pillars. It is about nineteen feet square. The floor of this area is specially constructed and sounding jars are placed underneath to make the rhythmic and emphatic stamping of feet, a distinctive feature of Noh, more effective. To stage left of the main area is the *wakiza*, used primarily for the eight- to ten-member chorus, which narrates much of the story. Back of the upstage pillars is the *atoza*, occupied by the orchestra composed of two or three drummers and a flute player.

The principal entrance to the stage is the bridge (hashigakari), a railed gangway extending from thirty-three to fifty-two feet in length and about six feet in width. It joins the stage to the dressing rooms. It is used for all important entrances. In front of it are planted three small pine trees, symbolizing man, earth, and heaven. In the upstage left corner of the atoza is located a second entrance, the "hurry door," used by subordinate characters, stage assistants, chorus, and musicians. It is only about three feet high. Another door, the "noble's door," is located upstage of the wakiza, but nowadays is almost never used.

The rear wall of the stage and bridge are made of wood. On the portion behind the *atoza* is painted bamboo and pine trees, probably representative of the natural setting which formed the background for the original Noh performances. The audience views the stage from two sides. It is seated in front of the main stage, along the stage-right side of the main platform, and in front of the bridge.

The object of a Noh performance is to capture the essence of a situation or emotion. Every episode is drawn out, often to great length. The high points take the form of extremely stylized static gestures or bodily attitudes held for some time. During a performance, every movement of hands and feet, every intonation must follow set rules. The orchestra furnishes the musical setting and establishes the timing of every gesture. Noh is one of the world's most carefully controlled theatrical experiences. The over-all effect is that of an elaborate ceremony or ritual.

The Noh plays on a program are separated by *kyogen*, or short farcical pieces. Kyogen do not use musical accompaniment; all of the dialogue is spoken. Kyogen actors rarely appear in Noh, and seldom wear masks. Most kyogen plays require no more than three actors, although occasionally more are used. Essentially humorous and pantomimic, kyogen plays are, nevertheless, performed according to rigidly controlled patterns.

Puppets have also played a significant role in Japanese theatrical life. Puppet performances may be traced back to the Heian period. (A.D. 781–1185), but the *puppet theatre* did not emerge until the Keicho era (1596–1614). It was given its definitive form by Takemoto Gidayu (1651–1714). Its characteristic plays were written by Chikamatsu Monzaemon (1653–1724), usually considered Japan's greatest playwright, who worked with Takemoto at his puppet theatre in Osaka.

The puppets themselves have undergone many changes. Originally, only a head was used, but by 1678 full figures, with hands and feet, were common. During the eighteenth century, devices were developed to permit the puppets to move their eyes, fingers, eyebrows. They were also enlarged to their present height of three or four feet. Thus, the figures became ever more lifelike. As puppets became more complex, more operators were required. Originally, one operator, completely hidden from view, was sufficient. By the eighteenth century, three men, all com-

A Noh production of *Aoi no Ue* (*The Lady Aoi*) by Zeami Motokiyo. Courtesy Kokusai Bunka Shinkokai, Tokyo.

Kumagai, a noted general of the Genji clan, as portrayed in a puppet theatre production of *Kumagai Jinya.* Courtesy Kokusai Bunka Shinkokai, Tokyo.

pletely visible, were required for each principal puppet. One manipulated the head and right arm, another the left arm, and the third the feet.

The stage also became more complex. Unlike the Noh, scenery was used in puppet theatre, and the desire to change the background motivated the invention of much stage machinery which was to remain largely unknown in the West until about 1900. Elevator traps were introduced in 1727 to raise scenery through the floor and in 1758 the revolving stage was invented.

The conventions of puppet theatre were fixed during the eighteenth century, the peak of its popularity. After this time, it was overshadowed by the Kabuki. Today it survives primarily in one company, the Bunraku of Osaka.

A performance in puppet theatre begins with the appearance of an announcer, clad in black and wearing a hood (the dress of all stage assistants except the principal puppet handlers, musicians, and narrator). He announces the name of the piece, the *samisen* player, and the narrator. The instrumentalists and singers sit on a raised platform at stage left; the *samisen* player and narrator are located at the front edge facing the audience.

The *samisen* is a three-stringed instrument with a drumlike base. It is simultaneously plucked with a large pick and struck with the hand or fingers. Samisen accompaniment is considered essential in puppet theatre, for it follows the rise and fall of the voice and gives special emphasis as needed. Since puppet handlers do not speak, the narrator tells the story, speaks the dialogue, and expresses the emotions of each puppet. He may weep, laugh, draw back in astonishment or fear as he reacts to the changing situation.

The stage is long and shallow. A low partition across the front represents the level upon which the puppets supposedly walk. Back of this, the puppet operators act out the story. All locales are represented scenically and are changed as the story demands. Numerous properties are also used.

The puppets vary somewhat in size and complexity according to their function in the drama. Supernumeraries do not have movable eyes or fingers and are usually operated by a single handler. Female puppets, even major characters, do not usually have feet. Puppets representing important characters are equipped with extremely complex mechanisms. Only the principal handlers are clothed in elaborate costumes, subordinate handlers wear the black dress of stage assistants. The handlers attempt to absorb themselves in the drama and to become one with the puppets they manipulate. The Japanese puppet theatre is probably the most complex puppet theatre in the world.

Today, Kabuki is the most vital of the traditional Japanese forms, for it has remained sensitive to change. But for this reason, many critics consider it debased, since it has borrowed freely from Noh, puppet theatre, and other sources. Perhaps because it has remained sensitive to change, Kabuki is the Japanese form most easily understood by Western audiences.

Kabuki originated around 1600 when Okuni, a ceremonial dancer, began to give public performances in Kyoto. Although it soon attained great popularity, the shoguns, always suspicious of it, sought to restrict its growth. In 1629, women were forbidden to appear on the stage, and in

276

1652 young men's Kabuki was banned. Thus, it was men's Kabuki which persisted. Until the end of the eighteenth century, Kabuki borrowed heavily from puppet theatre, taking over many of its plays, as well as its stage machinery and architecture. After 1780 it eclipsed puppet theatre in popularity. Since the fall of the shoguns, in 1868, it has been Japan's major dramatic form.

Kabuki plays began as simple sketches incorporated into danced performances. The first two-act piece was not given until 1664. The first important writer of this form was Chikamatsu, who worked for Kabuki troupes before turning to puppet theatre. Many of Chikamatsu's puppet plays were later adapted for Kabuki performance. Next to Chikamatsu, the most famous Kabuki dramatist is Takeda Izumo (1691–1756), Chikamatsu's successor as playwright to the Osaka puppet theatre. He is remembered primarily for *Chushingura* (1748), the most popular of all Kabuki plays. Eleven acts long, *Chushingura*, requires a full day in performance. It is based upon an actual event in which forty-seven faithful followers avenged the wrongs done to their master. Only one writer after Izumo, Kawatake Mokuami (1816–93), is of importance, being especially noted for his low-life characters. Today, almost every Kabuki program includes a selection from one of his approximately fifty plays.

A puppet theatre production showing a scene along the road in *Yoshitsune Sembon Zakura* (*Yoshitsune and the Thousand Cherry Trees*). Courtesy Kokusai Bunka Shinkokai, Tokyo.

A Kabuki production of *Gedatsu* (*The Release of Kagekiyo's Soul*), originally produced in 1744 and revised in 1914 and 1953. The scene shows the Todaiji Temple at Kamakura. Courtesy Kokusai Bunka Shinkokai, Tokyo.

Kabuki plays are divided into three types: *jidai kyogen*, or plays with a historical background; *sewamono*, or plays with a domestic or low-life background; and *shosagoto*, or dance plays. Within these categories there is much variety, for the Japanese do not have precisely defined dramatic forms. A Kabuki play often mingles the comic and the serious. There are few purely comic works, however, and these are dance plays in one act. Some longer works are called comedies because they end happily. The majority of plays are essentially melodramas. Kabuki scripts concentrate upon climactic moments rather than upon a clearly articulated story. Thus, there are many strong scenes but the connection between them is sometimes vague. The habit of writing relatively complete episodes probably explains the modern practice of making up programs from parts of plays, or even parts of acts.

Kabuki programs are long. In the eighteenth century, they lasted all day. In 1868, the maximum length was set at eight hours. Since World War II, it has been usual to give two performances a day, each about five hours long.

Many critics consider dance to be the basis of Kabuki, for choreographic movement is a fundamental part of every performance. Kabuki dance distills the essence of real emotions and actions into stylized gestures, movement and postures.

Kabuki roles are divided into such basic types as *tachiyaku*, loyal and courageous men; *katakiyaku*, villains; *wakashukata*, young men, who may be called *nimaime* if they are of mild disposition; *dokekata*, comic roles; *koyaku*, children's roles; and *onnagata*, women's roles, all played by men.

Because Kabuki acting is based upon conventions, it requires long and careful study. The actor usually begins his training at the age of six or seven; he appears on stage in children's roles from the very beginning. Thus, his work combines study and practice. Since acting is largely a hereditary profession, most of the actors come from a few families. Each family has its own system of stage names, some of which are so honored that they can be assumed only by undisputed masters of their art. A Kabuki actor is seldom considered mature until middle age.

278

Kabuki make-up (kumadori) for the play *Shibaraku*. Courtesy Kobusai Bunka Shinkokai, Tokyo.

Kabuki does not make use of masks. Most roles, however, require boldly patterned makeup. Typically, the makeup is composed of a white base upon which patterns of red, black, blue, or brown are painted. The onnagata merely add rouging at the corners of the eyes, leaving the rest of the face white. The makeup of each character is symbolic of his role.

Every role also requires a conventionalized costume. Most garments are based upon historical dress, which is altered for dramatic purposes. Since accuracy is of little importance, several historical periods may be used in the same play. Patterns and colors are usually subdued. Some costumes weigh as much as fifty pounds and must be rearranged frequently with the assistance of stage attendants. The attendants wear black and are considered to be invisible.

Every scene is accompanied by music. Because Kabuki has borrowed from many sources, the placement of the musicians on stage varies: for plays based on Noh, the musicians are placed upstage; for those borrowed from puppet theatre, the musicians are at stage left; for still other plays, the musicians are seated on stage right. In addition to the onstage musicians, others are sometimes placed behind a screen on stage right to provide special effects. As in puppet theatre, the most essential instrument is the *samisen*, which accompanies the singing and narration. The visible musicians are dressed in *kamishimo* (divided skirt, kimono, stiff horizontal shoulder pieces), the formal dress of the nobility in the eighteenth century. When not performing, the musicians sit upright and motionless. There is none of the informality of the Chinese theatre.

Since the Kabuki actor does not sing, a narrator and chorus are often prominent, especially in those plays adapted from Noh and puppet

279

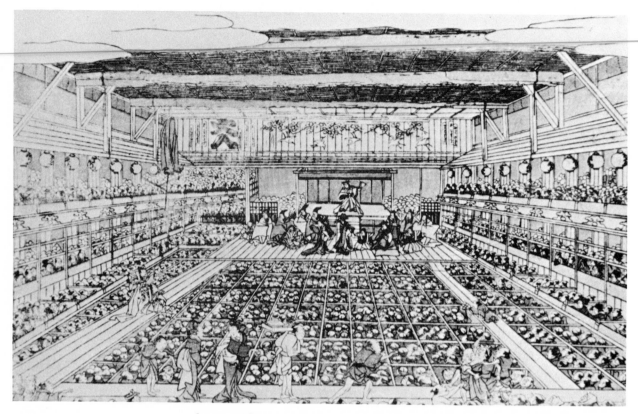

Kabuki stage at Edo as it appeared in 1806. Courtesy Tsubouchi Memorial Theatre Collection, Waseda University, Tokyo.

theatre. The narrator may set the scene, speak part of the dialogue, or comment upon the action. Even in those plays written for Kabuki, the narrator recites many passages, especially during complex dances or strenuous action. Even spoken passages are related to music, for they follow conventionalized intonational patterns.

The visual style of Kabuki lies somewhere between the extreme stylization of Noh and the illusionism of the Western theatre. This compromise can be seen in the stage, scenery, and properties.

Originally Kabuki used the Noh stage. As it came under the influence of puppet theatre, however, it adopted many conventions from that form. Elevator traps were added in 1736 and the revolving stage in 1793. After 1827, the revolving stage was built in two sections, one inside the other, which revolved independently. A forestage was added in the eighteenth century and became the principal acting area. Around 1725, one of the Kabuki's most distinctive features, the *hanamichi*, appeared. A raised gangway leading from a small room at the rear of the auditorium to the stage, the hanamichi is used for all important entrances as well as for many important scenes. This innovation was so popular that a second hanamichi was added in the 1780's.

By the early nineteenth century, the Kabuki stage had reached its characteristic form. The Noh roof had been abandoned and the stage enlarged until it occupied the entire width of the auditorium. The auditorium was divided into numerous square enclosures, or floor boxes, in which spectators sat on mats. After 1868 many changes occurred as Western influence increased. The proscenium arch was introduced in

280

1908 and after 1920 both the proscenium arch and Western-style seating became standard. The second hanamichi was abandoned, although it is still installed temporarily for pieces requiring it. In 1878 gas lighting was introduced and evening performances began. Since the late nineteenth century, the Japanese theatre has welcomed all new developments in stage lighting. Today, Kabuki is noted for its beautiful stage lighting.

Western influence has not altered the basic characteristics of the Kabuki stage, however, for, although the proscenium arch is now used, the proportions are unlike those found in the West. For example, in the present Kabukiza in Tokyo the proscenium arch is ninety feet wide but only twenty feet tall. The auditorium is also proportioned differently. In the Kabukiza, it is only sixty feet deep and about 100 feet wide.

Unlike Noh, Kabuki represents every locale scenically. The scenery is changed in full view of the audience by means of the revolving stage, elevators, grooves, or by stage attendants. Most settings emphasize lateral composition. Perhaps for this reason, no more than two sets are erected on the revolving stage at once; settings are never triangular. Painting is seldom purely representational. For example, the rear of the stage is often enclosed by flats showing a distant view; the painting is not illusionistic, however, for the cracks between the flats show and the top of the view is cut off with black curtains. Sometimes relatively realistic buildings are erected on stage, but they are almost always combined with symbolic pieces. Much scenery is used conventionally. White mats may represent snow, blue mats water, gray mats ground. Different kinds of trees may indicate a change in locale.

A performance at the prewar Kabukiza in Tokyo. Note that both *hanamichi* are in use. Note also the wide proscenium opening and auditorium. From Haar, *Japanese Theatre in Highlight.* Courtesy Charles E. Tuttle and Co., Tokyo.

Similarly, properties range from the symbolic to the realistic. The fan is used, as in Noh, to indicate riding a horse, shooting an arrow, opening a door, the rising of the moon, the falling of rain, and many other actions. Scarves serve equally diverse purposes. Other properties are partially representational. Perhaps the Kabuki horse best summarizes the mixture of realism and convention. A wooden framework, shaped like a horse, is covered with velvet and equipped with saddle and bridle. The upper part is clearly representational. But this framework is mounted on the back of two actors, whose legs clearly show. Other properties, such as armor, swords, human heads, animals, and household goods — are treated in much the same manner. It is this mingling of the conventional with the realistic that makes Kabuki more easily accessible to the Western viewer than any of the other traditional Oriental forms.

Perhaps a short discussion of a Kabuki play will further clarify the form. Since Chikamatsu is universally considered the greatest of Japanese playwrights, his *The Battles of Coxinga* (1715), a history or jidai kyogen play, has been selected. This was Chikamatsu's most popular work, originally playing for seventeen months and being revived frequently thereafter.

The Battles of Coxinga is divided into five acts and twelve scenes; in time, it covers a period of six or seven years beginning in 1644. The basic story may be summarized briefly. The evil minister, Ri Toten, betrays his country (China) to the Tartars, who capture the palace and behead the Emperor. The Empress, about to bear a child, flees but is killed. A faithful minister rips open her womb and rescues the child. The Emperor's sister, cast adrift in a boat, floats to Japan where she is rescued by Watonai (later called Coxinga), the son of an exiled Chinese official. Watonai and his parents decide to return to China and to lead an uprising. After a series of exploits, many magical, Coxinga recaptures the palace and restores the young Emperor to the throne.

Each act develops a different phase of the story and each builds to a high point of action. Act I shows the betrayal, battle, deaths of the rulers, and the escape of the Princess (made possible by a female attendant who fights off an army of pursuers). Act II tells of the arrival of the Princess in Japan, Coxinga's return to China, and his incredible fight with a tiger in the forest. Act III shows Coxinga's attempts to recruit followers, eventually made possible by the suicides of his mother and half-sister, both of whom disembowel themselves on stage. Act IV shows the progress of the struggle and the escape of the child Emperor from the Tartars made possible by a cloud bridge created by the gods. Act V relates the end of the struggle, with the recapture of the palace, the flaying of the Tartar prince and the beheading of Ri Toten. Thus, each act builds to a strong scene allowing the actors to display their special skills.

The characters are divided into the good and the evil. They are differentiated primarily on the basis of age, sex, rank, and degrees of strength or self-sacrifice. The cast includes twenty-three persons and a number of supernumerary characters.

The place shifts often. Locales include the palace, a seacoast in Japan, the exterior of an armed fort, a forest, the mountains, various interiors, and the open sea. At least twelve settings are required. It would be almost impossible to stage this play if illusionism were sought. The task is simplified because the narrator speaks a large part of the text. (This play was originally written for puppet theatre.) The narrative provides exposition, summarizes action which has occurred between scenes, reports the internal feelings of the characters, and describes the action during climactic scenes. Although the actors are assigned many lines, they are more involved in pantomimic dance. Thus, the battles, suicides, beheadings, and other violent deeds are rendered as choreographically ordered movement communicating the essence of deeds without any attempt at realism. Just as the story is larger than life, its rendition lies somewhere between fantasy and reality; its stylized action, speech, and music create a spectacle of great beauty.

In addition to the classic forms, newer styles of drama developed. The earliest of these, *shimpa*, began about 1888 and grew out of the desire to portray contemporary ideas and events realistically. *Shingeki*—new theatre—after 1906 introduced many plays of Western authors such as Shakespeare, Molière, Shaw, Chekhov, and encouraged Japanese dramatists to write in the Occidental mode. Western influence also came through motion pictures, musicals, opera, ballet.

EASTERN INFLUENCE IN THE WEST

Awareness of the Oriental theatre developed only gradually in the West. The first important change came in 1789, when Sir William James translated *Shakuntala* into English. In 1791 this version was translated into German and in 1803 into French. *Shakuntala* made an enormous impression on Europeans, perhaps because it came at a time when romanticism was emerging.

Interest in Oriental drama had little effect upon the theatre until the end of the nineteenth century, for at first there was little appreciation of Asian theatrical conventions, so markedly different from the illusionistic techniques then standard in the West. Not until the revolt against realism began in the 1890's did Oriental theatrical practices begin to attract Western directors.

Considerable interest was aroused by a Chinese troupe which played in Paris in 1895 and by a Japanese group which appeared in London in 1900. During the early twentieth century a number of individual performers toured widely in the West. Nevertheless, it was not until such directors as Lugné-Poë, Meyerhold, Brecht, and Artaud began to champion Oriental practices as antidotes to realism that Eastern conventions had any real impact. Innovations were at first considered merely perverse, but since World War II they have aroused increasing sympathy. Although it is doubtful that many Westerners even now truly understand the Oriental theatre (beyond a few conventions), the Eastern and Western theatres are in closer contact today than at any time in the past. Many developments in the modern theatre are more easily understood if the awakening interest in Oriental conventions is remembered.

283

III

THE MODERN THEATRE

Samuel Beckett's silent play, *Act Without Words, I.* Directed by James Gousseff.

Chapter 13 REALISM AND NATURALISM

By the mid-nineteenth century the Romantic outlook had been modified considerably, for the belief in man's idealistic nature had received many setbacks. For example, after the downfall of Napoleon around 1815, most European countries had reinstated political conditions more oppressive than those of the eighteenth century. The ideals of liberty, equality, and fraternity now seemed doomed. Furthermore, the general misery of a large part of humanity was being emphasized by the Industrial Revolution, as a result of which workers were pouring into urban centers where living conditions were daily more inadequate. Crime and poverty were prevalent.

THE BACKGROUNDS OF REALISM

In the face of such political and economic conditions the Romanticist's emphasis upon the ideal seemed both too vague and too impractical. Many came to argue that dreams must be abandoned for a systematic inquiry into actual conditions and for solutions based upon discoverable facts. Observation, prediction, and control of society became the new goals.

Among the major influences on the new thought was Auguste Comte (1798–1857), whose philosophy came to be called *positivism*. In his writings, published between 1830 and 1854, Comte argued that sociology is the highest form of science and that all knowledge should ultimately be used for the improvement of society. He stated that the key to knowledge lies in precise observation and experimentation, since all events must be understood in terms of natural cause and effect. Comte's philosophy placed primary emphasis upon phenomena which can be experienced through the five senses, and thus focused attention upon observing contemporary events.

287

Positivism attracted a large following and was soon reenforced by Charles Darwin's *The Origin of the Species* (1859). Darwin's doctrine may be divided into two main theses: (1) all forms of life have developed gradually from a common ancestry; and (2) the evolution of species is explained by the "survival of the fittest."

Darwin's theories have several significant implications. First, heredity and environment are made the determinants of existence. Everything that man is or can be is viewed as the result of the physical make-up with which he is born or of the conditions under which he lives. Second, heredity and environment become explanations for all character traits and actions. Furthermore, since behavior is determined by factors beyond the individual's control, he cannot be blamed for it. If blame is to be assigned, it must go to the society which has allowed such undesirable hereditary and environmental factors to exist. While few persons sought to control heredity, many turned their attention to the improvement of environment.

Third, Darwin's theses cast considerable doubt upon the existence of God as traditionally conceived. If He existed, according to the new views, it was as an impersonal force. The idea of immortality was seriously challenged at the same time. If there is no future life, man can reach fulfillment only in the present one, and, to many, science seemed to offer the greatest possibilities of achieving the maximum good.

Fourth, Darwin's theories strengthened the idea of progress. If man has evolved from an infinitesimal grain of being to the complex creature he now is, improvement and progress appear to be inevitable. Nevertheless, it came to be argued that the march of progress can be channeled and hastened by the consistent application of scientific method to social problems.

Fifth, man is reduced to the status of a natural object. Prior to the nineteenth century man had been set apart from the rest of creation and treated as superior to it. Now he lost his privileged status and became merely another object for study and control.

Like most movements, then, realism sought to improve the lot of mankind by coming to grips with truth. The new school, however, limited truth to knowledge gained through the five senses (sight, hearing, taste, smell, and touch). Such a marked change in view inevitably influenced conceptions of art and the theatre.

REALISM IN THE THEATRE

By 1850 a conscious movement toward realism in art was emerging. It developed first in France, and by 1860 had proclaimed the following precepts: the playwright should strive for a truthful depiction of the real world; since he may know the real world only through direct observation, he should write about the society around him; he should strive to be as objective as possible.

Given such an outlook, it was only natural that playwrights came to emphasize the details of contemporary life and to avoid historical subject matter and idealized human motives and deeds. Many writers turned to themes not previously treated on the stage, and conservative critics charged that the theatre had become little better than a tavern or sewer. To such charges of immorality and decadence, the supporters of realism replied that the plays, as truthful depictions of life, were moral, since truth is the highest form of morality, and that to present an idealized picture of life would be to elevate falsehood over truth and to become truly immoral. Furthermore, the supporters of realism suggested, if audiences did not like the pictures of contemporary life being shown on the stage, they should strive to change the society which had furnished the models rather than denounce the playwright who had been fearless in his treatment of what he saw around him.

The visual elements of staging were easily brought into accord with the new demands, for the groundwork had already been laid by Romantic drama and melodrama, both of which had presented with ever-increasing accuracy details of dress and setting. Until after 1850, however, spectacle was used primarily to idealize place, historical period, or characters. It was a simple task to extend these earlier practices to meet the demands of realism.

A suitable dramatic form was also available in the *well-made* play. Although all its elements may be found before the nineteenth century, the well-made play was perfected by Eugène Scribe (1791–1861), one of the most prolific and successful writers of his day. Scribe's plays, numbering over four hundred, are lacking in depth, and are important now primarily because they epitomize the dramatic structure adopted by the new realistic school of writers.

The basic characteristics of the well-made play are: clear exposition of situation; careful preparation for future events; unexpected but logical reversals; continuous and mounting suspense; an obligatory scene; and a logical and believable resolution. This structural pattern was not unique with Scribe, but he reduced it to a near-formula and combined it with absorbing but shallow situations in which character and thought were sacrificed to suspense. Nevertheless, the well-made play was easily adapted by the Realists because of its careful exposition and its clear cause-to-effect arrangement.

While earlier movements supplied dramatic techniques and an approach to spectacle, both of which were readily adaptable to the realistic mode, they did not provide equally helpful guidance in subject matter and characterization. It remained for two French playwrights, Alexandre Dumas *fils* (1824–95) and Emile Augier (1820–89), to direct attention to contemporary social problems as subjects for dramatic treatment.

Dumas *fils* came to the attention of the public in 1847 with a novel, *The Lady of the Camellias*, which he dramatized in 1849. Because of its subject matter, however, the play was not granted a license for production until 1852. One of Dumas' biographers has said of the play:

> Now came a young man who dared to depict not a courtesan of historical legend, not an adventuress surrounded by a halo of poetic symbolism, but a "kept woman" of everyday contemporary life, and this author made his subject even more realistic by writing in ordinary prose.

The play, generally known today as *Camille*, was extraordinarily popular from the first and its heroine, who dies of tuberculosis, has become an

289

almost legendary character. Although the language and subject matter show a movement toward realism, the treatment now seems merely another romanticization of the "prostitute with a heart of gold."

Dumas soon became dissatisfied with his own work and sought to give a more realistic treatment to his subjects. In 1855 he wrote *The Demi-Monde*, which denounces the same kind of characters as those idealized in *Camille*. After this time he attempted to establish a *theatre of social utility* by writing plays about contemporary social problems, such as divorce, unscrupulous business practices, and the plight of illegitimate children. But as Dumas became more and more concerned with social problems he also became increasingly the moralist. As a result, his plays are now usually called *pièces à thèse* (or thesis plays). Dumas' works seem dated because of changes in the society about which he wrote and because of the excessive moralizing in the plays, but they probably did more than any other dramas before Ibsen's to establish a concern for contemporary social problems.

Augier is noted principally for his political and social dramas about contemporary French conditions. Many of his plays deal in a less didactic way with the same problems treated by Dumas: the power of money, the dangers of churchmen in politics, fallen women. The dramatic power of Augier's plays did much to popularize the new style of playwriting.

But it is to Ibsen that credit must be given for the ultimate triumph of the new methods. *Modern drama* is usually dated from around 1875, when Ibsen began to write in the realistic mode.

Henrik Ibsen (1828–1906), Norway's first important dramatist, began writing plays about 1850. His early work, much of which is based on Norwegian legends, is clearly related to Romantic drama, but in 1877 Ibsen turned to the problem play with *The Pillars of Society* and continued in that vein with *A Doll's House* (1879), *Ghosts* (1881), and *An Enemy of the People* (1882). With these plays, Ibsen established his reputation as a radical thinker and controversial dramatist. *Ghosts*, especially,

Scene from *Peer Gynt* (1867), one of Ibsen's poetic dramas, as presented at Christiania, Norway, in 1876. From Blanc's *Christiania Theaters Historie 1827-1877*, 1899.

Scene from *Ghosts,* as produced at the Burgtheater, Vienna, in 1904. From *Bühne und Welt,* 1904-05.

became a storm center, for in it Mrs. Alving, against her better instincts, has remained with a depraved husband out of conformity to traditional morality only to have her son go mad, presumably from syphilis inherited from the father. To audiences and critics of the late nineteenth century, *Ghosts* epitomized the "sewer" into which the drama had sunk. Ibsen soon moved away from social problems, and beginning with *The Wild Duck* (1884) concentrated upon personal relationships in such plays as *Rosmersholm* (1886), *Hedda Gabler* (1890), *The Master Builder* (1892), and *When We Dead Awaken* (1899).

Despite the changes in subject matter and style, Ibsen's basic theme remained constant: the struggle for integrity, the conflict between duty to oneself and duty to others. In his many variations upon this central concern, Ibsen brought together trends which are both the culmination of nineteenth-century movements and the beginning of modern drama.

Much of Ibsen's work contributed to realism. He discards asides and soliloquies and is careful to motivate all exposition. All scenes are causally related and lead logically to the dénouement. Dialogue, settings, costumes and business are selected to reveal character and milieu and are clearly described in stage directions. Each role is conceived as a personality whose behavior is attributable to hereditary or environmental forces.

Ibsen's late plays were to influence nonrealistic drama as extensively as the earlier prose plays did realistic works. In them, symbols enlarge the implications of the action and many of the plays border on fantasy. The sense of mysterious forces at work in human destiny was to be further developed by the Symbolists at the end of the century.

Almost all later playwrights, whether realists or idealists, were to be affected by Ibsen's conviction that drama should be a source of insight, a creator of discussion, a conveyor of ideas, something more than mere entertainment. He gave dramatists a new vision of their role.

The many strands of Ibsen's work are probably brought together most effectively in *The Wild Duck.*

THE WILD DUCK

In *The Wild Duck*, Gregers Werle returns home after an absence of fifteen years, decides that the lives of all his acquaintances are based on lies, and determines to make them face the truth. His efforts lead to catastrophe.

The principal characters are Old Werle (Gregers' father), Hjalmar Ekdal (Gregers' childhood friend), Old Ekdal, Gina, and Hedwig (Hjalmar's father, wife, and daughter). Old Werle is prosperous, while the Ekdals live in comparative poverty, although years ago Werle and Ekdal were business partners. Ekdal was sent to prison for illegal dealings and Gregers suspects that his father let Ekdal accept blame which was partially his. Gregers also believes that Old Werle arranged Hjalmar's marriage to Gina, a former maid in the Werle household, because Gina was pregnant by Werle. Thus, he thinks that Hedwig is not Hjalmar's child.

Gregers takes a room at the Ekdals, in spite of Gina's protest, so that he may force them to face the reality which he believes all are avoiding. Through insinuation and leading questions, Gregers gradually brings his "truth" into the open. After Hjalmar rejects Hedwig, she decides, with a child's simplicity of reasoning, that only some great sacrifice can prove her love for Hjalmar; consequently, she kills herself.

Essentially, *The Wild Duck* is a play about the necessity of illusions. Dr. Relling, another tenant in the Ekdal house, says that most persons need "a saving lie" upon which to base their lives, to enable them to retain a degree of self-respect and a sense of purpose.

All of the play's characters serve to illustrate this theme, but the opposing positions are most obviously represented by Relling (who believes in the necessity of illusion) and Gregers Werle (who believes that everyone must be forced to face the truth). Relling appears more nearly to represent Ibsen's own point of view, for Greger's self-righteous meddling brings only disaster to others.

Ibsen has strengthened his theme through the symbolism of the wild duck. The wild duck is a living creature, but around it are built up a series of relationships and concepts which suggest wider meanings for the

Setting used for *The Wild Duck* by André Antoine. Courtesy Bibliotheque de l'Arsènal, Paris.

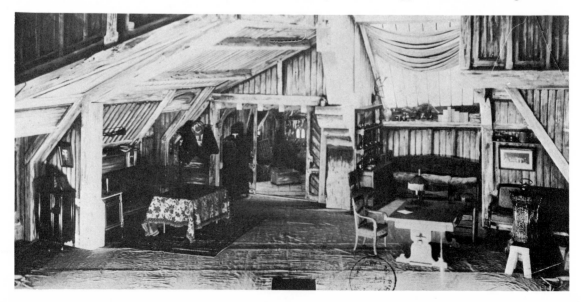

events and characters than would be possible without it. The symbolism of the duck pervades the entire play; to understand it, the stages in the duck's existence should be recalled. First, the duck, happy and carefree, lives in a wild state. Then it is wounded by a hunter. In its pain and desire to hide, the duck dives to the bottom of the sea but is brought to the surface by a dog. The duck survives but does not thrive in the hunter's house. It is given to another family who construct an artificial environment for it, and, though crippled, it now appears to be as happy as in its wild state.

Ibsen seems to suggest that the wild duck's experiences parallel those of mankind. In his early years man may live a relatively carefree existence; then one day, wounded by circumstances, he tries to run away, to hide, or to die because of his feelings of inadequacy and disgrace; but he is forced to return to his daily existence and constructs a set of delusions by means of which he can regain his self-respect and sense of purpose; he becomes relatively happy in this artificial environment. Every major event and character in *The Wild Duck* can be related to this pattern, although exact correspondences are few.

CHARACTERS AND ACTING. The Ekdal family is reflected in the wild duck, while Old Werle corresponds partially to the hunter, and Gregers to the dog. The house in which the Ekdals live is comparable to the ocean depths into which the wounded duck dives, since each of its tenants, with the exception of Hedwig, is seeking to hide within his own particular illusion.

Old Ekdal has lived in an illusory state so long that it has become part of his nature. It is implied that he has always been childish, that when he was in business with Werle he spent most of his time hunting. This neglect of responsibility helped to bring about his disgrace. Since his release from prison he has reconstructed his life around the attic, its "forest," and "wild life." He prefers the safety of this make-believe world to the real one. Like the wild duck, he too has been wounded and now lives in an artificial environment.

Gina is one of the most enigmatic characters in the play, for the truth about her past is unclear. She is the character most capable of accepting her fate and of living life moment by moment. She is the most stolid and down-to-earth person in the play, but she too is one of Werle's victims.

Ibsen has drawn a number of interesting parallels and contrasts between Old Werle and Hedwig. It is possible that Hedwig is the daughter of Old Werle (this is never clarified), both have weak eyesight, both try to make amends to others. But Old Werle has treated life as though it were the sport of hunting, and when he wounds he makes amends with money, arranged marriages, and attempts to rebuild illusions. Hedwig responds to life with her whole being, and, in contrast, kills herself rather than wound others. She is open, frank, without artifice. Unlike Old Werle, who shot the wild duck in sport (just as he had seduced Gina and used others all of his life), Hedwig shoots herself in earnest, for hers is an act of sacrifice performed out of love. Old Werle faces up to his shortcomings at the end of the play, but he still believes that money and material gifts can atone for wounds inflicted on others.

293

Ibsen's principal effort has gone into the roles of Hjalmar and Gregers. Hjalmar speaks as though he were sensitive, ambitious, and idealistic, but his actions show that he is insensitive, lazy, and self-centered. Gina runs the photographic studio, she and Hedwig sacrifice every comfort for Hjalmar. Old Ekdal's disgrace is to Hjalmar an excuse for easy sentiment, just as Hedwig's death will be in the future. But Hjalmar is perfectly happy in his illusions, for he can indulge himself and, at the same time, find excuses for being ineffectual.

That Gregers accepts Hjalmar as a hero demonstrates his own impracticality and lack of experience. He has hidden away from the world for fifteen years, has thought much about life, but has avoided becoming involved in it. Although he never attempts to change his own life, he feels free to meddle in the affairs of others.

Relling is used as a foil for Gregers. His ability to anesthetize the pain of disillusionment is demonstrated in Molvik, the theology student who rationalizes his failures under the belief that he is "demonic." Relling, the doctor, has administered to the psychic wounds of the characters by providing them with "saving lies," while Gregers destroys the illusions that have made life tolerable.

But in spite of the obvious use of characters to illustrate ideas, Ibsen employs realistic techniques in creating roles. Every important characteristic is shown through action. For example, Hjalmar's character is built up through a series of contrasts between actions and statements. The audience sees his awkwardness at the dinner party and then hears his self-glorifying account of it; he leaves the picture retouching to Hedwig in spite of her weak eyes and his previously expressed anxiety about her eyesight. Furthermore, each character's traits are brought out through well-motivated and lifelike speech or action. The audience learns about the characters as it would in a real-life situation; there is seldom any feeling of contrivance.

Ibsen has been careful to fill in the sociological backgrounds of his characters, and each attitude and trait is grounded in particular social circumstances. For example, Hjalmar's selfishness is explained in part by his indulgent upbringing by two maiden aunts.

Ibsen has also made his characters complex personalities by showing both good and bad aspects of each. None is perfect (with the possible exception of Hedwig), but none is villainous. This complexity makes each role challenging to actors, and requires subtlety in playing.

PLOT AND STRUCTURE. In his dramas, Ibsen used many techniques of the well-made play, but was able to overcome the sense of artificiality by avoiding asides, concealed hiding places, overheard conversations, the fortuitous arrival of letters, and similar devices. He retained careful preparation and developed action logically out of previous occurrences and clearly demonstrated character traits. A sense of reality is created by the meticulous selection and arrangement of details.

Ibsen typically used a late point of attack, and in most plays no more than two or three days elapse, for the stage action is the culmination of past events. In *The Wild Duck* the most important antecedent action has occurred at least fifteen years before the play begins. This demands a careful handling of exposition, since the past is essential as an explanation of the present. Ibsen's favorite device for motivating exposition is the return of a character who has been absent for a considerable time. In *The Wild Duck* Gregers Werle has returned home after a fifteen-year absence, during which he has lived in virtual isolation. Thus, he can believably inquire about the past. At the same time, however, Gregers' attitude and his purposeful air arouse curiosity about his motives and create suspicion that the truth is being concealed. Consequently, as the past is revealed, expectations about future developments are also evoked.

Although exposition is scattered throughout *The Wild Duck*, it is especially prominent in the first two acts. Many of Ibsen's plays are written in four acts, but *The Wild Duck* has five, in part because two are required to establish the situation out of which the succeeding three acts grow. Ibsen's need for two acts of preparation is also illustrated by the use of two settings to establish the contrast between Old Werle's and the Ekdals' living conditions. By the end of the second act, both situation and characters have been clarified, the symbolism of the wild duck has been introduced, and Gregers has indicated his intention of rectifying the errors of the past. The final three acts grow logically out of the first two.

Ibsen's skill can be seen in his economy. There are no extraneous scenes and almost nothing could be removed without destroying clarity. At the same time, there is no feeling of haste, for each event seems to develop as it might in real life. Nevertheless, each of the acts is built through a series of complications leading to a high point of suspense near the end of the act, while the play as a whole builds to the climactic scene of Hedwig's death. Ibsen thus achieves great dramatic power (which results from masterful craftsmanship) while giving the effect of naturalness.

Although it might be argued that there are a number of plot strands—perhaps one for each character—all are so woven together that the action is one. It is the effect of each character on all the others that motivates the action and leads to its logical and believable outcome.

VISUAL AND AURAL EFFECTS. Ibsen's realistic technique can also be seen in the visual elements of *The Wild Duck*. Detailed descriptions of the settings are given in stage directions. Furthermore, unlike most earlier plays, the setting plays an important role in the action. The influence of environment upon the characters is made clear in part through an accurate representation of the surroundings. The characters seem to live in the settings, for they do everything there that they would in a real room. In the studio they eat, retouch photographs, entertain friends, and carry on their daily existence in countless ways. The settings, never mere additions, are vital to the action.

Although environment helps to create character, the characters in turn help to create environment. The garret, for example, has been remodeled into an artificial forest to meet the psychological needs of its inhabitants. Unlike a neoclassical play in which settings are generalized, *The Wild Duck* demands a stage environment singularly its own—

295

one determined by the specific action and characters. Instead of merely supplying a typical and normative background, the set designer is now asked to create a clearly individualized environment.

Because the actions performed in *The Wild Duck* are such as might be seen in daily life, the audience is inclined to judge their believability according to how well daily life is recreated. For example, in the third act a table is set, and a meal is served and eaten. Although on stage not everything is done exactly as in real life, it must correspond closely with normal action or much of the play's effect will be undermined. Stage production in such plays as *The Wild Duck*, therefore, must be based in part upon a direct observation of life. The aim is to create an illusion of reality through the accumulation of details.

The same realistic ideal is reflected in the language of *The Wild Duck*. Gina lapses into her lower-class speech in moments of stress, while under similar circumstances Old Ekdal is inclined to express himself more formally. Hjalmar alternates between flights of fancy and mundane expression. Thus, Ibsen has tried to capture an illusion of daily speech colored by individualizing characteristics.

The Wild Duck, with its subject matter drawn from contemporary life, closely observed detail, and avoidance of contrivance, illustrates well the realistic mode.

ENGLAND

The spirit of realism soon spread throughout the world. For example, in England the works of such playwrights as Arthur Wing Pinero (1855–1934), Henry Arthur Jones (1851–1929), John Galsworthy (1867–1933), and George Bernard Shaw (1856–1950) show in varying degrees the influence of the new trend.

Pinero began his career by writing farces and sentimental plays, but turned to realism around 1889. His best-remembered play, *The Second Mrs. Tanqueray* (1893), although it concerns a "woman with a past," helped to break down the strictures against frank subject matter, since it upheld the moral code of conservative audiences. Thus, it was simultaneously daring and reassuring.

Jones started writing plays in the 1870's but made his principal impression in the 1880's and 1890's. He was a didactic and somewhat melodramatic playwright who, along with Pinero, helped to pave the way for more realistic drama with his *Saints and Sinners* (1884), *Michael and His Lost Angel* (1896), and *Mrs. Dane's Defense* (1900).

Galsworthy, who won fame first as a novelist, did not begin writing plays until 1906. His realistic social-problem dramas, especially *Strife* (1909), *Justice* (1910), and *Loyalties* (1922), were among the most powerful plays of the early twentieth century. Galsworthy in many respects follows in the footsteps of Dumas *fils*, for he too, typically, argues from a specific point of view.

George Bernard Shaw was probably the most vociferous and important of Ibsen's admirers. But Shaw's approach differs markedly from Ibsen's, for while his plays are serious in their intention of influencing human behavior, they use comic devices to make serious points. In his treatment of problems, Shaw begins with what he thinks is the audience's attitude and then demolishes it before proposing his own solution. But Shaw is more than a mere propagandist, for his plays remain effective and entertaining even though the problems treated have changed. While he wrote plays from the 1890's until near the time of his death, his major work was over by 1925. Among his most important plays are *Man and Superman*, *Caesar and Cleopatra*, *Candida*, *Major Barbara*, *Pygmalion*, *Androcles and the Lion*, *Heartbreak House*, and *Saint Joan*.

RUSSIA

Another writer of the late nineteenth century, Anton Chekhov (1860–1904), was to be almost as influential as Ibsen. Unlike Ibsen, however, whose plays are clearly related to those of Augier and Dumas *fils*, Chekhov built on the work of such native Russian playwrights as Gogol, Ostrovsky, and Turgenev.

Nikolai Gogol (1809–52) began the movement toward realism with his grotesque and farcical satire on small-town officials, *The Inspector General* (1836). This beginning was developed by Alexander Ostrovsky (1823–86) and Ivan Turgenev (1818–83). Ostrovsky was the first Russian writer to confine himself solely to drama. His forty-eight plays are credited with creating a Russian drama free from west European influence. In his plays about the merchant class and lower aristocracy, Ostrovsky copied the speech and manners of everyday life to create a sense of closely observed reality. He also used symbols in much the same manner as Ibsen and Chekhov were to do later. *The Thunderstorm* and *The Forest* show his work at its best.

As a dramatist, Turgenev is remembered almost solely for *A Month in the Country* (written in 1852 but not produced until 1872). As the title suggests, the action takes place on a remote country estate. Partially out of boredom, Natalya, the protagonist, falls in love with the young tutor of her son. But Natalya's young ward is also in love with the tutor, and another man loves Natalya. The play is a study in jealousy, heartbreak, and compromise. The characters, in no sense heroes, are portrayed with deep understanding, for Turgenev concentrates upon the inner motivations of

Opening scene of Turgenev's *A Month in the Country* as presented at the Moscow Art Theatre in 1909. Stanislavsky appears at the left in the role of Rakitin. From *Moscow Art Theatre, 1898-1917.* Moscow, 1955.

each. In the end, all are disappointed and have made compromises, but each has achieved a measure of self-understanding. It is a quiet but intense drama.

Chekhov began by writing short stories and humorous sketches, and moved on to vaudeville skits and one-act farces. The long plays, which he began to write in 1887, were not successful until the Moscow Art Theatre presented *The Sea Gull* in 1898. This success motivated him to write *Uncle Vanya, The Three Sisters*, and *The Cherry Orchard.* It is upon these four plays that Chekhov's reputation rests.

Many qualities relate Chekhov's dramas to the realistic-naturalistic school. The subject matter and themes, drawn from contemporary Russian life, show how the daily routine gradually breaks the spirit and drains the will. The characters long for happiness and wish to live useful and full lives, but they are constantly thwarted by circumstances and their own personalities. Frustration and compromise are the lot of most of Chekhov's characters.

Chekhov's realism is further seen in his dramatic form, for the plays have an air of aimlessness which matches that of the characters' lives. There is no sense of hurry, of theatrical trickery, or even of normal dramatic structure. Chekhov is nevertheless an excellent craftsman, for each moment is carefully constructed to contribute to the over-all effect. He is so skillful at concealing the machinery of his plays that they create the effect of real and unplanned events.

Chekhov's realism is also seen in the ambiguous tone of his plays. Arguments have raged from the beginning as to whether the plays are comedies or serious dramas, for despite the pessimistic outlook of the characters, humor plays a large part in the action. Chekhov's own point of view is sufficiently subordinated, so that either interpretation of the plays is possible. Actually they are both comic and serious, for mood shifts rapidly. As with life itself, the comic and the serious are not rigidly compartmentalized but occur in close juxtaposition and sometimes simultaneously in the same event.

But Chekhov is not entirely a realistic writer, for like Ibsen, he uses symbolism, especially in *The Sea Gull* and *The Cherry Orchard.* In the latter play, the orchard is a symbol of the Old Russia and of the aristocracy. It is preserved though it no longer yields any fruit; the owners cling to it and fail to sell it even though its sale would save the rest of the estate, which the owners love. In the end, the orchard is bought by a newly rich peasant and is subdivided for a housing development, an action which illustrates the changing social order. The orchard thus enlarges and extends the meaning of *The Cherry Orchard* just as the duck does in Ibsen's *The Wild Duck*.

Chekhov's plays have exerted a strong and lasting influence on succeeding playwrights. Many critics see all modern realistic drama as stemming from the joint influence of Ibsen and Chekhov.

NATURALISM

Thus far only realism has been considered. At the same time that realism was developing, however, another, more extreme movement, naturalism, was also emerging. Realism and naturalism are closely related because both demand a truthful depiction of life and are based upon the belief that ultimate reality is discoverable only through the five senses. The Naturalists, however, insisted that art must become scientific in its methods and must demonstrate that all behavior is determined by heredity and environment.

The major spokesman of the naturalistic school was Émile Zola (1840–1902), who argued that art, if it is not to perish, must become scientific both in its subject matter and method. According to Zola, subject matter might be of two kinds: that taken from scientific findings, or that which faithfully records events observed in real life. Using the first type, the dramatist sets up characters and situation and then lets them interact according to the inevitable laws of heredity and environment. About the second approach, Zola states:

> Instead of imagining an adventure, complicating it, preparing stage surprises, which from scene to scene will bring it to a final conclusion, one simply takes from life the history of a being, or of a group of beings, whose acts one faithfully records.

The dramatist is thus restricted either to dramatizing "scientific" laws or recording case studies.

Zola also argued that the writer should remain detached and never allow his own prejudices to intrude. The dramatist should observe, record, and experiment with the sole aim of demonstrating the truth. Because the dramatist should be objective about his subject matter, he must be free to treat whatever seems most fruitful for arriving at truth. In practice, naturalism tended to emphasize the more degraded aspects of lower-class life. Just as dramatists of the eighteenth century had turned to the middle class for its subjects, so those of the nineteenth century turned to the lower classes. But whereas the life of the middle class had been idealized, the life of the lower classes was most often depicted as debased. As a result, much naturalistic drama was preoccupied with human maladies. Zola was fond of comparing naturalistic art with medicine, and stated that the dramatist should take the same interest in examining and defining human social illnesses as the doctor does in physical ailments.

Zola and his followers also sought a completely objective dramatic method. Selection and arrangement of material, they argued, served only to distort truth rather than to reveal it. "The word *art* displeases me: it contains I do not know what ideas of necessary arrangement," Zola wrote. One member of the movement suggested that a play should be a *slice of life*—that a dramatist should transfer to the stage as faithfully as possible a segment of reality. To avoid distortion, the point at which the story was to be taken up should be selected at random and the point at which it was to end should be equally arbitrary. A concern for complications, crises, and resolutions was to be strictly avoided.

Because of the emphasis upon environment as a determinant of character and action, the stage setting was given greater importance under naturalism than in any previous movement. Every detail was reproduced accurately on stage so as to relate actions to the milieu. Perhaps the most famous setting in the naturalistic vein was Antoine's for *The Butchers* (1888), in which real carcasses of beef were hung on stage to recreate the interior of a butcher shop. Similar care was extended to costumes, furniture, properties, and stage action.

Zola stated that actors should "not *play*, but rather *live*, before the audience." The stage was arranged as much like a room in a real house as possible, and the actors tried to speak and move as they would in real life—to "live" onstage. Sometimes in these attempts the actors became inaudible and their action incomprehensible because of a lack of concern for the audience. While such an approach increased the effect of reality, it also frequently led to confusion.

The extreme demands of naturalism lost sight of the differences between art and life. A dramatist must select, arrange, and heighten his material if he is to hold the interest of an audience. Transferred to the stage, reality is seldom interesting unless it is interpreted. For these reasons, naturalism attracted considerable attention in the late nineteenth century but produced few dramatists of note.

Zola was much more famous as a theorist and novelist than as a playwright, being best known as a dramatist for *Thérèse Raquin* (1873), an adaptation of one of his early novels.

A naturalistic production at the Théâtre Antoine, Paris, in 1902. The play is Menessier's *The Earth*. Note the hayloft in the background and the chickens in the foreground. From *Le Théâtre,* 1902.

A more successful dramatist in the naturalistic vein was Henri Becque (1837–99), remembered chiefly for *The Vultures* (1882), which shows the fleecing of a group of women by supposed friends, and *La Parisienne* (1885), in which a woman justifies her extramarital affairs as an asset to her husband's business career.

Naturalism as a conscious movement was largely ended by 1900. It was instrumental in focusing attention upon the need for accurate, first-hand observation of life, in pointing out relationships between environment and events, and in encouraging greater attention to the details of stage production. In its demands that reality be reproduced onstage, however, naturalism was unsuccessful. As extreme demands were abandoned, naturalism itself was gradually absorbed into the larger and more acceptable realistic movement.

THE EMERGENCE OF THE DIRECTOR

The same forces which produced realism and naturalism also led to corresponding changes in the theatre arts. By 1850, historical realism and local color had already been accepted and the wing-and-drop setting was giving way to the box set. But the realism of 1850 merely added nonessential details to scripts. For example, although Shakespeare's plays were acted in historically accurate settings, this did not make them realistic—it merely added realistic spectacle to nonrealistic dramas. True realism had to wait for plays which made the background a necessary part of the action.

As the demand increased for greater realism in all aspects of theatrical production, so did the need for more careful rehearsals and the better coordination of all elements. As a result, the director gradually assumed authority over production.

The modern director is usually traced from Georg II, Duke of Saxe-Meiningen (1826–1914), the ruler of a small German state, whose troupe came to public attention through a series of tours between 1874 and 1890. The superior quality of his presentations demonstrated the importance of the director to effective theatrical production.

Saxe-Meiningen's troupe performed the same standard plays (such as those by Shakespeare and Schiller) seen in the repertory of almost every company of the day. Nevertheless, this obscure troupe, composed almost solely of unknown actors, gave performances of such electrifying power that it eclipsed the work of the major theatres. It became clear that the unique qualities of the Meiningen troupe were attributable to its staging methods.

The most important elements of the Duke's approach were his complete control over every aspect of production and his long and careful rehearsals. A painter and draftsman, he designed the scenery, costumes, and movements of the actors. Rather than utilizing stars, he subordinated all performers to the over-all effect. Insisting upon absolute obedience, he drilled his troupe in lengthy rehearsals. He paid as much attention to the crowds and supernumerary parts as he did to the principal roles. Furthermore, he designed the scenery and properties to suit the

Antony's oration over the body of Caesar in Saxe-Meiningen's production of *Julius Caesar*. From *Die Gartenlaube,* 1879.

action, and meticulously worked out the total stage picture as it developed moment by moment.

The effectiveness of the Meiningen troupe was largely a result of this careful planning and integration of all theatrical elements. Nothing like it had been seen before, and it stimulated the imagination of several future leaders. Saxe-Meiningen's realism, however, was largely restricted to pictorial elements, for he was not interested in the new realistic plays. Nevertheless, he demonstrated how scenic environment and stage action can be integrated to achieve powerful effects.

Few well-established acting troupes adopted Saxe-Meiningen's methods immediately, however, for they depended upon star actors who were unwilling to subordinate themselves to the demands of a director. Furthermore, the long rehearsals needed for perfection were too costly. It remained for newly organized and largely unknown groups to build upon Saxe-Meiningen's example.

THE INDEPENDENT THEATRE MOVEMENT IN EUROPE

To meet the challenge of the new drama and new theatrical methods, independent theatres began to be established in the late 1880's. Since these organizations were private, being open only to members, they were not subject to censorship, although membership was open to anyone. The actors and other workers were amateurs or little-known professionals who were willing to subordinate themselves to the demands of a director. Independent theatres were therefore able to accomplish what the more important theatres had not, for these newer groups exploited and developed the new staging techniques and gave the new drama its chance to be heard.

302

The first of the independent theatres was the Théâtre Libre, founded in Paris in 1887 by André Antoine (1858–1943), a clerk in a gas company who began his work with amateur actors and with stage furniture taken from his own home. An enthusiastic follower of Zola and Saxe-Meiningen, Antoine sought absolute fidelity to real life. Since he believed that environment determined character and action, Antoine worked out every detail of background and action with great care. He designed interior settings as though they were real rooms, arranged everything as in real life, and only then decided which wall should be removed for stage presentation. He did not always rearrange furniture to accommodate the audience's view, but rather tried to achieve absolute naturalness in the stage picture. He used real properties (such as carcasses of beef, bottles of wine, and running water) and tried to reproduce every detail of an environment. Applying the same standards to the actors' movements and speech, he held long and painstaking rehearsals to achieve the effects for which he was striving.

Many realistic and naturalistic plays were seen in Paris for the first time at Antoine's theatre, and it was to such plays that his approach was most suited. Although his original audience was a special one, the fame of the Théâtre Libre rapidly grew and soon others wished to see productions of this kind. By 1900 most of the old barriers against realistic plays and staging had been broken down and Antoine's methods were being adopted by previously conservative theatres.

Antoine's was only the first of a number of important independent theatres. In 1889 the Freie Bühne was founded in Berlin by a group headed by Otto Brahm (1856–1912). This theatre, like the Théâtre Libre, was formed for the purpose of producing realistic and naturalistic dramas. The Freie Bühne made no significant innovations in staging, concentrating instead upon presenting plays denied a public hearing by the censor. By 1894, when Brahm assumed the direction of a commercial theatre, the new drama was being assimilated into the popular theatre throughout Germany.

In London the Independent Theatre, founded by J. T. Grein (1862–1935), opened in 1891 with Ibsen's *Ghosts*, long banned from the English public stage. The Independent Theatre was organized to produce plays of a "literary and artistic rather than a commercial value," and was not as concerned with the new realistic and naturalistic drama as were most of the other independent theatres. Nevertheless, it paved the way for the new drama, and launched Shaw as a dramatist.

The Moscow Art Theatre was founded by Constantin Stanislavsky (1865–1938) and Vladimir Nemerovich-Danchenko (1859–1943) in 1898, partially under the inspiration of the Meiningen company. Like the German troupe, the Moscow Art Theatre had few experienced actors and tried to compensate for this lack through long rehearsals and careful attention to external detail. As time went by, Stanislavsky became more and more concerned with the problems of the actor, and eventually evolved a method of training which was to be one of the most influential ever proposed. This method has been disseminated throughout the world

Interior of the Moscow Art Theatre about 1910. From *Moscow Art Theatre, 1898-1917,* 1955.

by *My Life in Art* (1924), *An Actor Prepares* (1926), *Building a Character* (1950), and *Creating a Role* (1961).

Although there has been much disagreement over the essence of Stanislavsky's system, basically it consists of the following principles:

(1) The actor's body and voice must be thoroughly trained and flexible so that they can respond instantly to all demands.

(2) The actor must be skilled in the observation of reality so that he can build his role truthfully through the careful selection of lifelike action, business, and speech.

(3) The actor needs to be thoroughly trained in stage technique so that he can project his characterization without any sense of artificiality.

(4) The actor must undergo psychological training of a rather complex nature so that he may imagine himself in the situation of the character he is playing. If he is to perform truthfully, he must develop *emotion memory* (the ability to recall emotional responses comparable to those required in the dramatic situation).

(5) If the actor is not merely to play himself on the stage, however, he must have a thorough knowledge of the script. The actor, therefore, needs to define clearly his character's basic desires and motivations in each scene, in the play as a whole, and in relation to other characters. The character's primary motivation is called the *spine of the role* since the rest of the characterization must be built upon it. The actor must understand his role so thoroughly (every detail of background, feeling, and action) that he can believe in its truth. To make the character thoroughly comprehensible and believable, the actor at times may have to fill in or invent details omitted from the script. A complete understanding of the play should lead the actor to subordinate his own role to the demands of the whole and to cooperate in achieving an ensemble effect for the entire troupe.

(6) All of his work onstage should be welded together through concentration. The actor must focus his entire attention upon the unfolding events moment by moment. He should strive to convince the audience that he is involved in a situation which is occurring spontaneously and

304

for the first time. To do this, he should concentrate upon imagining, feeling, and projecting the truth of the stage situation.

(7) The actor must be willing to work continuously for the perfection of himself as an instrument and for the perfection of his performance in each play.

Stanislavsky's entire system urges the need for devoted and constant effort on the part of the actor. In Stanislavsky's view a performer is successful only when he can convince the audience of the truth of the stage situation, and this conviction results only from intense training and endless striving for perfection.

Although the independent theatres broke down the barriers against the new drama and contributed to the emergence of the director as the key artist of the theatre, most of them produced all plays, regardless of type, in as realistic a manner as possible. In this sense, they continued trends which had begun with romanticism and melodrama.

THE DEVELOPMENT OF ECLECTICISM, OR ARTISTIC REALISM

Around 1900, it began to be suggested that each type of play, and even each individual play, has its own style which demands a distinctive stage treatment. This was a revolutionary idea in many ways, for in each period prior to this time a single standard was applied to all productions. For example, in 1850 a Greek drama, a play by Shakespeare and a melodrama would all have been given the same kind of settings and would have been acted in the same style. Even Antoine approached each play with the same goal – to create scenes as lifelike as possible.

But around 1900, the realistic mode began to be modified toward an *artistic* realism, or the creation of a *stage environment* exactly right for each individual play. Rather than attempting to reproduce scenes from real life, directors emphasized the appropriateness of elements to the style of the particular work. Style, in turn, was said to depend in part upon the theatrical conventions and actor–audience spatial relationships in use at the time when the play was written. Since in stage production the conventions of any period might be adapted, a great variety of production styles came into use. This eclecticism has been one of the distinguishing marks of the twentieth-century theatre. Eclecticism is in some ways a new twist on historical realism, since it often merely uses knowledge of earlier theatrical conventions instead of historically accurate details of architecture or dress as the basis of stage production.

An early phase of the new trend may be seen in the work of William Poel (1852–1934), who founded the Elizabethan Stage Society in 1894 and produced a number of Elizabethan plays on his version of the Shakespearean public stage. After Poel convinced theatre workers that realistic settings only interfered with Shakespeare's true qualities, it became increasingly common to produce Shakespeare's plays on a stage which approximated that for which they were written. Poel, however, worked entirely with plays of a single period.

True eclecticism, or artistic realism, owes most to the work of Max Reinhardt (1873–1943), who began his career as an actor under Brahm

Design by Norman Bel Geddes for Reinhardt's production of *The Miracle*. The theatre was transformed to resemble a cathedral. Courtesy of the Bel Geddes Collection, a gift of the Tobin Foundation, Hoblitzelle Theatre Arts Library, University of Texas.

before turning to theatrical production around 1900. Reinhardt produced plays from all periods and of all types. To him, each play was a new problem demanding a new solution. He constructed or modified theatres to provide the physical arrangement he thought best for each type of play: he transformed a theatre into a cathedral, and built another which approximated ancient Greek structures; he thought some plays required large theatres, and that others fared best in small houses; he experimented with all kinds of stage machinery and theatrical devices in an attempt to create the right atmosphere for each work.

With this eclecticism, Reinhardt coupled the belief that the director is the supreme artist of the theatre. He always made a *Regiebuch*, or prompt book, in which every detail of movement, lighting, scenery, costume, and sound was recorded with exactness. He coached his actors carefully and controlled each element of his productions. A script was for him an outline offered by the playwright for completion by the director.

Auditorium and stage of Reinhardt's Grosses Schauspielhaus (Berlin), a remodeling of the Circus Schumann to simulate a Greek theatre. From Barkhin's *Architectura Teatra*. Moscow, 1947.

Reinhardt contributed many ideas to the modern theatre: the need for a different approach to each play; an awareness of the interdependence of theatre architecture and dramatic styles; the need for a detailed prompt book which has been prepared before rehearsals begin; the acceptance of the director as the supreme artist of the theatre and as the completer of the playwright's work. Reinhardt's continuing influence may be seen in present-day experiments with theatres-in-the-round, open stages, and other audience–actor relationships.

Reinhardt was not committed to realism as such, but in each of his experiments he attempted to achieve an artistic reality. His methods, therefore, frequently had much in common with the nonrealistic approaches that will be treated in Chapter 13.

THE UNITED STATES

The new drama and staging techniques were widely accepted in Europe before they were known in America, partially because until 1915 the conservative Theatrical Syndicate maintained control of theatrical production. Nevertheless, around 1910 the new spirit of the European theatre was beginning to be felt in the United States. The *new stagecraft*, as the European approach was called in America, was imported primarily through the efforts of a few young men who, after traveling and studying in Europe, were determined to transform the American theatre. The most influential were Robert Edmond Jones (1887–1954) and Lee Simonson (1888–1967), major designers after 1915.

The new stagecraft was embraced first by the little theatre movement, which blossomed between 1910 and 1920. Noncommercial organizations more interested in artistic excellence than financial success, the little theatres combined the European notion of an independent theatre with acceptance of the all-powerful director (perhaps because the actors were usually amateurs) and the new staging techniques. The most important of these early groups were: The Little Theatre of Chicago, founded in 1912 by Maurice Brown; The Toy Theatre of Boston, founded by Mrs. Lyman W. Gale in 1912; The Washington Square Players of New York, founded in 1914; The Provincetown Players, founded in Provincetown, Massachusetts, in 1915 but later moved to New York; and The Arts and Crafts Theatre of Detroit, founded in 1916.

Of these groups, The Arts and Crafts Theatre, The Provincetown Players, and The Washington Square Players were to exert the greatest influence. In 1916, Sheldon Cheney at the Arts and Crafts Theatre launched *Theatre Arts Monthly*, which soon became the forum for the new movement in America, popularizing its ideals and keeping Americans abreast

Scene from *Anna Christie* (1922), one of Eugene O'Neill's realistic dramas. Directed by Paul Davee.

of developments both at home and abroad. Until 1948, it was to be one of the major voices of the American theatre. The Provincetown Players sought to encourage new American playwrights. It was this group which first recognized the talent of Eugene O'Neill (1888–1953), generally considered to be America's foremost dramatist. Even after O'Neill achieved popular success with such plays as *Beyond the Horizon* (1920), *Anna Christie* (1921), and *The Hairy Ape* (1922), the Provincetown Players continued to present his works, such as *Welded* (1924) and *The Fountain* (1925), which were unacceptable to commercial producers. The Provincetown Players offered opportunities for experimentation rarely found elsewhere. In 1919, the Washington Square Players became the fully-professional Theatre Guild and set out to produce the best American and European drama. Through its choice of plays and production techniques, it did more than any other company to demonstrate the effectiveness of the new stagecraft. The influence of these groups was reinforced by that of Arthur Hopkins (1878–1950), a commercial producer who, in collaboration with Robert Edmond Jones, championed both the new drama and the new visual mode. The success of these pioneering organizations had by 1925 made the new stagecraft fully acceptable.

Nevertheless, the chief influence of the new movement was exerted upon the visual aspects of stage production. Although the new generation of playwrights, which included Maxwell Anderson (1888–1959), Elmer Rice (1892–1967), Sidney Howard (1891–1939), and Paul Green (1894–   ), was related to its European counterpart in its dedication to a drama which was more than entertainment, none of its members was committed to any particular movement. Thus, its work ranged through many styles.

Probably the most significant American organization of the 1930's was the Group Theatre, which began as a workshop of the Theatre Guild and became an independent troupe in 1931. A repertory company modeled on the Moscow Art Theatre, the Group Theatre attempted to apply the Stanislavsky method to acting and stage production. During the 1930's it produced some of the finest plays seen in New York, being especially suc-

O'Neill's *Desire Under the Elms* as produced in 1924 at the Provincetown Playhouse, Greenwich Village, New York City with Walter Huston (below), Mary Morris, and Charles Ellis. Setting, Robert Edmond Jones. Photograph—Vandamm Collection, courtesy Library and Museum of the Performing Arts at Lincoln Center.

Awake and Sing by Clifford Odets. A scene from the original production of *Awake and Sing* by Clifford Odets. John Garfield, Stella Adler, Phoebe Brand, Art Smith, Morris Carnovsky. Setting, Boris Aronson. Photograph—Vandamm Collection, courtesy Library and Museum of the Performing Arts, Lincoln Center.

cessful with such works of Clifford Odets (1906–63) as *Waiting for Lefty* (1935), *Awake and Sing* (1935) and *Golden Boy* (1937). The Group Theatre also fostered the talents of a number of important directors (among them Harold Clurman and Elia Kazan) and actors (such as Lee J. Cobb, John Garfield, and Morris Carnovsky). Members of this troupe were to be the principal popularizers of the Stanislavsky system of acting in America; some former members such as Lee Strasberg (at the Actors' Studio) and Stella Adler (at her own studio in New York and at Yale University) have continued to teach this method.

REALISM IN THE TWENTIETH CENTURY

Realism has continued to be the dominant mode in the twentieth-century theatre, although its pre-eminence has been seriously challenged in recent years. Since its inception in the late nineteenth century, however, realism has undergone changes which have made it considerably more flexible than in its early stages. The most significant alterations can probably be traced to the influence of Sigmund Freud (1856–1939), whose psychoanalytic theories have provided a scientific explanation for much human behavior which previously had been attributed to instinct or supernatural forces and which had thus been placed outside the scope of realism. Freud's conception of the mind (as a faculty which telescopes experience, sublimates and suppresses desires, and which often works irrationally) made it possible for dramatists to depart considerably from the early techniques of realism without departing from a scientific outlook. These departures, in turn, moved realism in the direction of the many nonrealistic styles which appeared after 1890 (to be discussed in Chapter 14) and made it ever easier to assimilate techniques that had originated in revolts against realism. The eventual results will be reviewed in Chapter 15.

Chapter 14 REVOLTS AGAINST REALISM: SYMBOLISM, EXPRESSIONISM, AND EPIC THEATRE

Although realism continued to dominate the theatre, it was not universally accepted. Revolts against it began in the late nineteenth century and have continued to the present. Each protest, however, has been short-lived, although each has modified realism. The most important of the revolts prior to World War II were symbolism, expressionism, and epic theatre.

SYMBOLISM

Symbolism (sometimes called neoromanticism, idealism, or impressionism) appeared in France in the 1880's and, as a conscious movement, was over by 1900. Symbolism is antirealistic, for it denies that ultimate reality is to be found in the evidence of the five senses or through rational thought processes. It holds that truth is to be grasped intuitively.

Since it cannot be logically understood, ultimate truth cannot be expressed directly. It can only be suggested through symbols which evoke feelings and states of mind, corresponding, though imprecisely, to the dramatist's intuitions. The surface dialogue and action in a Symbolist play, therefore, are not of primary importance. As Maeterlinck put it:

> Side by side with the necessary dialogue you will almost always find another dialogue that seems superfluous; but examine it carefully, and it will be borne home to you that this is the only one that the soul can listen to profoundly, for here alone it is the soul that is being addressed.

310

He went on to say:

> Great drama, if we observe it closely, is made up of three principal elements: first, verbal beauty; then the contemplation and passionate portrayal of what actually exists about us and within us, that is to say nature and our sentiments; and, finally enveloping the whole work and creating the atmosphere proper to it, the idea which the poet forms of the unknown in which float about the beings and things which he evokes, the mystery which dominates them, judges them, and presides over their destinies. I have no doubt that this last is the most important element.

Thus, while a play portrays human actions, its ultimate aim is to convey intuitions about a higher truth which cannot be adequately expressed in words and which can only be suggested through symbols.

Unlike the Realists, the Symbolists chose their subject matter from the past, and avoided any attempt to deal with social problems or to recreate the physical environment of its characters. Like the Neoclassicists, they aimed to suggest a universal truth independent of time and place. Unlike the Neoclassicists, however, the Symbolists did not believe that truth can be logically defined or rationally expressed. A Symbolist drama, consequently, tends to be vague, mysterious, and puzzling.

By far the most famous Symbolist playwright was Maurice Maeterlinck (1862–1949). Born in Belgium, he spent most of his life in France. His most important works are those written in the 1890's during his association with the Symbolist school. His *Pelléas and Mélisande* (1892) is perhaps the best Symbolist drama.

Scene from Debussy's operatic version of *Pélleas and Mélisande* as presented at the Opéra Comique, Paris, in 1902. Note the pictorialized treatment, quite unlike that used in the original production of the play. From *L'Art du Théâtre,* 1902.

*PELLEAS AND
MELISANDE*   On the surface, *Pelléas and Mélisande* is the melodramatic story of a
young wife who falls in love with her husband's younger brother. The
husband kills his brother and the young wife dies of grief. This simple
story of awakening love and its consequences holds the play together,
but it is the ideas and feelings behind this façade which are of most importance to Maeterlinck.

Fate, a sense of presentiment, and an air of mystery dominate each
scene. The characters are puppetlike, for they do not understand their
own actions or motivations. Their backgrounds are never filled in, the
time and place of the action is left unspecified, and events are not causally related. Instead of realistic and logical action growing out of character and situation, the play depicts a fairy-tale world in which inexplic-
able forces control human destinies.

Maeterlinck suggests that life is impenetrably mysterious. Rather than
stating his beliefs directly, he implies them through recurring motifs and
symbols. Because ideas are only suggested, it is impossible to isolate
them definitely. Nevertheless, some of the more obvious motifs can be
examined. Those which recur most often are water, light and darkness,
height and depth.

Water plays a part in almost every scene. Mélisande is first discovered
by a pool; she and Pelléas play by a fountain in which she loses her
wedding ring; later Pelléas and Mélisande declare their love for each
other and Pelléas is killed by the same fountain; they search for her ring
in a grotto, which must be approached by a narrow path between two
lakes; Pelléas and Golaud find bottomless pits filled with water under the
castle; the sea is referred to in almost every scene; and the women try to
wash away the stains on the threshold of the castle with water.

In each scene some important use is also made of light or darkness.
The forests surrounding the castle produce darkness, and light may be
seen only by looking toward the sea; characters sit in darkness or try to
find a pool of light; lamps refuse to stay lighted.

Low and high places are also used symbolically. Mélisande sits in a
tower; Pelléas and Golaud penetrate into the bowels of the castle to investigate the stench which arises; soaring towers or bottomless pits recur in almost every scene.

It is impossible to assign a definite meaning to each of these motifs or
symbols. Rather, the connotations suggested by the context in which the
symbols occur must be examined. The sea, for example, seems to represent the only avenue of escape, unlike the forest which is constantly en-
croaching on the castle. The sea is also associated with light, just as the
forest is with darkness. Light is used to suggest frankness, the known
truth, lightheartedness, and happiness. Darkness, on the other hand,
implies secrets, the unknown, untruths, and unexpressed thoughts and
fears. Throughout the play, love, happiness, and light struggle with fate,
misery, and darkness.

Pools of water are used to suggest many different things. The characters try to see the bottom of the pools, just as they try to peer into the

312

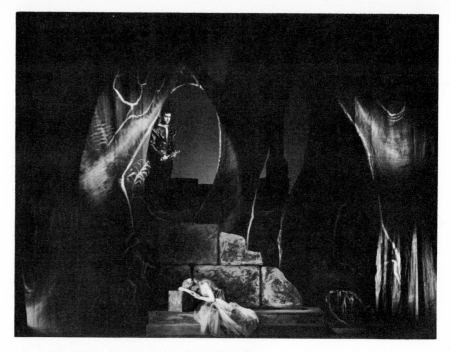

Pelléas and Mélisande at the Belgian National Theatre. Photograph by Carl Hensler, Brussels.

depths of each other's souls; in neither case can they penetrate the mystery. A fountain is also used to indicate the difference between Mélisande's feelings for Golaud and for Pelléas: she has been discovered by Golaud at a fountain in a dark forest; she comes to Pelléas by a fountain in an open park and in full moonlight.

Behind all the happenings, however, there is a sense of mystery and fate. Love comes to Pelléas and Mélisande against their wills, just as the sheep are led to slaughter against theirs; doors will not stay open and lamps will not stay lighted in rooms when Pelléas and Mélisande are alone. They are led by forces greater than themselves.

The powers of love and light are pitted against those of fate and darkness. At the end of the play both the enigma of the human soul and the meaning of life remain as mysterious as when the play began. Arkël, speaking of Mélisande and her baby, makes it clear that this mystery is the essence of life and will continue to be so.

> 'Twas a little being, so quiet, so fearful, and so silent. . . . 'Twas a poor little mysterious being, like everybody. . . . I shall never understand it at all. . . . Come; the child must not stay here in this room. . . . She must live now in her place. . . . It is the poor little one's turn.

Thus, while rebelling against the outlook of the Realists and Naturalists, Maeterlinck, is as deterministic as any of his opponents. His characters are at the mercy of forces just as destructive and far more mysterious than those of heredity and environment. In many ways, Maeterlinck's world is more frightening than that of Zola, for it is both unknowable and uncontrollable.

PLOT AND STRUCTURE. *Pelléas and Mélisande* has sometimes been termed Shakespearean because of its free use of time and place and its lack of specificity about setting. These surface similarities, however, almost exhaust the likenesses between Maeterlinck and Shakespeare, for Shakespeare always told a coherent story in thoroughly understandable terms, while Maeterlinck merely uses a story as a means for suggesting intuitions about life and the soul.

Although *Pelléas and Mélisande* tells a love story, its organization is determined by themes and ideas. Many scenes are only loosely connected with the main story line. For example, the opening scene in which the women try to wash the stains from the castle steps sets a mood of mystery and hopelessness, but has nothing to do with the story's action. Likewise, such scenes as that in which the sheep are led to slaughter are extraneous to the main plot. The mood and theme, therefore, are as important in the play's structure as is the action.

Furthermore, the number of scenes between the first meeting of Pelléas and Mélisande and their deaths could be expanded or contracted without seriously affecting the story. Awakening love is suggested early, but its existence is denied until the moment before Pelléas is killed. Thus, while all the scenes are connected, they do not develop through a clear chain of cause and effect.

Although Maeterlinck has used the five-act form, his act divisions are entirely arbitrary since they do not mark important breaks in the action or high points of suspense. The individual scene is the major structural unit.

Premonition is used to build and maintain suspense. There is a continual hint of some mystery behind the events which will be revealed. The characters seem to be led on inevitably toward an important discovery which is never forthcoming. They meet death but they are not enlightened. Even the audience is led only to the conclusion that life is mysterious and will remain so.

CHARACTERS AND ACTING. The characters are almost as vague as the ideas. They yearn, love, and die without knowing why.

All of the main characters are of the ruling class, but this fact has little effect upon their personalities or the action of the play. Their ages and physical appearance are also of little importance: Arkël is an old man; Genevieve is his daughter and the mother of Golaud and Pelléas; Golaud's hair is beginning to turn gray; Yniold is a child; it is implied that both Pelléas and Mélisande are young and attractive. All of this information is pertinent but slight in amount.

Psychological attributes are vague as well. The compassionate Arkël constantly attempts to look into the depths of being. Genevieve wants everyone to be happy. Golaud is a hunter, a man of action who loves quickly and steadfastly; he has a deep sense of honor which drives him to kill Pelléas. Neither Pelléas nor Mélisande performs any positive action or displays any positive psychological traits prior to the scene in which Pelléas dies. Until that time, they sigh, they resist love and preserve a sense of propriety. None of the characters fully understands his own motivations, and each is driven by forces stronger than himself.

Maeterlinck, therefore, is less interested in portraying lifelike characters than in suggesting states of feeling which come upon characters mysteriously and which lead to mysterious consequences. His concept is further illustrated by the original production of the play in 1893. The actors chanted their lines and used unnatural gestures to emphasize the gulf between everyday occurrences and those presented in the play. It is not the texture of the daily living which is important, but the realm of the spirit which lies beyond physical existence.

VISUAL AND AURAL EFFECTS. In its simplicity and repetitiveness, the language of *Pelléas and Mélisande* suggests a beginner's textbook in reading. But this repetitiveness helps to emphasize the recurring motifs, and the simplicity is designed to prevent too much interest in surface reality. The very lack of complexity suggests that the audience needs to look beneath the surface.

Antirealism was emphasized in the original production through a number of devices. The stage lighting, very low in intensity, came from directly overhead. A gauze curtain, hung at the front of the stage, made it appear that the entire action was occurring in a mist. The scenery was painted in grayed tones to increase the effect of distance and mistiness. The actors wore costumes based on the paintings of Memling, who lived in the fifteenth century. These departures from realism were underscored by a singsong delivery of lines and the use of unnatural gestures. The entire production was designed to remove the action from the world of everyday life; it was as unlike the productions of the Realists as possible.

Scene from Maeterlinck's *The Blue Bird* at the Théâtre Rejane, Paris, 1911. The scenery, by V. E. Egorov, was lent by the Moscow Art Theatre, for whom it was originally designed. From *Le Théâtre,* 1911.

Pelléas and Mélisande, thus, was not concerned with contemporary problems and did not render truth through a depiction of the external details of daily life. Rather, it dealt with such universal (but vague) themes as love, life, and death, and embodied them in symbols and motifs. Because the Symbolists were interested primarily in mysterious spiritual forces, they had to use means quite different from those employed by the Realists. Perhaps because of its lack of concreteness, symbolism appealed only to a limited audience and produced few plays of lasting interest.

Many attributes of symbolism may be found in the work of such later writers as Claudel, Andreyev, Yeats, and Lorca. Paul Claudel (1868–1955) depicted the struggle between the flesh and the spirit, always ending in the triumph of religious faith, in such plays as *Break of Noon* (1906), *The Tidings Brought to Mary* (1912), and *The Satin Slipper* (1930). His fame has grown steadily since Jean-Louis Barrault staged *The Satin Slipper* in 1943. In Russia, the foremost Symbolist playwright was Leonid Andreyev (1871–1919), whose *The Life of Man* (1906) is an allegory of human life and defeat by a cruel and whimsical universe. Peopled with such characters as The Man, His Wife, and Someone in Gray, *The Life of Man* combines the characteristics of a medieval morality play and Maeterlinck's works. In Ireland, William Butler Yeats (1865–1939) embodied simple stories and complex ideas in the unusually powerful poetry of such plays as *Cathleen ni Houlihan* (1902), *On Baile's Strand* (1904), *At the Hawk's Well* (1916), and *Purgatory* (1938). In Spain, Federico Garcia Lorca (1899–1936) blended poetic imagery with primitive passions in such plays as *Blood Wedding* (1933), *Yerma* (1934), and *The House of Bernarda Alba* (1935). But, while the influence of symbolism has continued, as an organized movement it was largely over by 1900.

Final scene from Garcia Lorca's *Blood Wedding.* Directed by Ronald Gee; setting by Joe Zender.

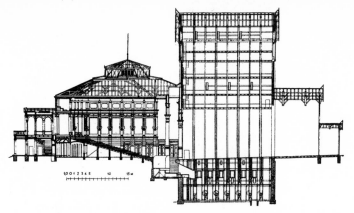

Cross section of Wagner's theatre at Bayreuth which opened in 1876. From Sachs' *Modern Opera Houses and Theatres.* London, 1896-98.

THE SYMBOLIST THEATRE

The revolts against realism also brought new attitudes toward the theatre. The Symbolists drew much inspiration from the work of Richard Wagner (1813–83), who sought to fuse all the arts into a master work: music-drama. Opposed to realism, Wagner argued that music is necessary to the finest drama, for it should be "distanced" from actual life. Furthermore, according to Wagner, music offers a means whereby the dramatist-composer may control the performance of the actor-singer, since music can dictate the pitch, duration, and tempo of the words. Wagner also believed that the master artist should retain complete control over the scenery, costumes, lighting, and all other theatrical elements. Thus, he was one of the first advocates of unified production and the strong director.

Wagner argued that the greatest truths cannot be approached through realism, that the theatre should lift the audience out of its humdrum daily existence through an idealized drama "dipped in the magic fountain of music." To evoke the proper esthetic distance, Wagner used a double proscenium, a curtain of steam, and a darkened auditorium to create a "mystic chasm" between spectators and performers. Because he sought to depict an idealized world, it is not surprising that Wagner should inspire the Symbolists.

Stage and auditorium of the Bayreuth Festival Theatre. Note the steeply raked auditorium, the double proscenium, and the absence of a center aisle and side boxes. From Barkhin's *Architectura Teatra.* Moscow, 1947.

The Symbolists encountered many of the same difficulties in getting their plays performed as had the Realists and Naturalists, and had to establish independent theatres to gain a hearing. The first of these, the Théâtre d'Art, founded by Paul Fort in 1890, was succeeded by the Théâtre de l'Oeuvre in 1892. Under the direction of Aurélien-Marie Lugné-Poë (1869–1940), the Théâtre de l'Oeuvre opened with *Pelléas and Mélisande*. Until 1897 Lugné-Poë staged all plays in a highly stylized manner. Although he later adopted a more eclectic approach, continuing his theatre until 1929, he is remembered primarily for his work with nonrealistic plays. Lugné-Poë did not attempt to create the illusion of reality, seeking instead a unity of mood and style. He summed up his approach with the phrase, "the word creates the decor."

The Symbolists believed that scenery should be confined to draperies or undefined forms which evoke a sense of infinite space and time. Historical detail was avoided because it tied plays to specific periods and places rather than bringing out their timeless qualities. Decor was reduced to elements giving a generalized impression appropriate to the ideas and feelings of a play. Similarly, costumes were usually simple, draped garments of no particular period or place; colors were dictated by the play's mood.

The Symbolists thus advocated simplicity of setting and costume. The physical elements of production were subordinated so that attention might be concentrated upon the words of the playwright. For the most part, Symbolist productions were too determinedly nonrealistic to attract a wide following. Nevertheless, they laid the foundations for several related attempts.

APPIA AND CRAIG

Although not of the Symbolist school, two major theorists, Adolphe Appia (1862–1928) and Gordon Craig (1872–1966) were clearly in the tradition of Wagner and the Symbolists.

Appia's desire to embody Wagner's ideas led him to articulate for the first time many of the now accepted ideals of theatrical production. Appia began with the notion that artistic unity is fundamental, but found it difficult to achieve because of the diverse visual elements: the moving actor, the horizontal floor, and the perpendicular scenery. Appia's search for unity led him to demand many changes in theatrical production. Rejecting painted scenery, he insisted that three-dimensional structures are the only proper environment for the three-dimensional actor if unity is to be attained. To reveal the shape and three-dimensionality of the scenery and the actor, light, from various angles and directions, is required. Furthermore, it must change as action and mood change. Constantly changing light fuses the various elements into a unified whole, for it reveals and reflects shifting emotions and ideas. In this way, light becomes the visual equivalent of music, since it welds the elements together visually just as music does aurally.

Appia suggested that the producer begin with a search for the essential qualities of a script and then for the means to embody them in theat-

Design by Adolphe Appia entitled "Dessin de Rhythmique—l'Ile des Sons." Courtesy Foundation Adolphe Appia, Berne.

rical terms. Since a unified and artistic performance is the goal, the entire production must be conceived by one person—the director. Appia thus re-enforced the trend toward elevating the director to a position of dominance.

Although few of Appia's designs ever reached the stage, his ideas were expressed in a number of books and sketches. His designs are simple, for all unnecessary details have been removed. They use mood, light and darkness, mass and line to interpret the essential character of a scene. His theory and practice have exerted a pervasive influence on modern staging.

Craig believed in many of the same ideas as Appia but was much more militant in his statements and did a great deal more to popularize the theories. Craig had little interest in drama, being primarily concerned with the theatrical product created by the "super theatre artist," who blends action, words, line, color, and rhythm into a unified work, of which the play is only part. Everything is filtered through the eyes of the master artist and must conform to his vision. For this reason, Craig once suggested that the actor should be replaced by the marionette, since the marionette cannot inject its own personality into the work and thwart the director's conception.

Opposed to realism, which he called "the theatre of sermons and epigrams," Craig wanted to create works which would appeal directly to the senses and transform the theatre into "a place for visions." Like Appia, Craig stood for extreme simplicity in scenery, costume, and lighting, and depended upon line, mass, and color for his effects rather than upon historical accuracy or detailed ornamentation. Also like Appia, he helped to promote the director as the supreme theatre artist.

Craig realized that his work would not find immediate acceptance in the commercial theatre and sought other places in which to experiment. He established a school in Italy, at Florence, in 1913, but his work was interrupted by World War I. He also expounded his ideas in his magazine,

Craig's setting for *Hamlet* at the Moscow Art Theatre in 1911. From *Moscow Art Theatre, 1898-1917*, 1955.

The Mask and in a number of books. As with Appia, few of Craig's scene designs were ever carried to completion, but his writing inspired many theatre workers and has had untold influence on the modern stage.

In addition to Appia and Craig, several producers—most notably Fuchs, Diaghilev, Tairov, and Copeau—also encouraged departures from realism in theatrical production.

In two books, *The Theatre of the Future* (1905) and *Revolution in the Theatre* (1909), Georg Fuchs (1868–1949) declared pictorial illusionism outmoded and set out to "retheatricalize the theatre." In 1907, with Fritz Erler (1868–1940) he founded the Munich Art Theatre to implement his ideas. In their theatre, the size of the proscenium opening could be changed by an adjustable inner proscenium; the stage floor was broken into sections, each mounted on an elevator, so that it could be arranged into levels; the acting area was surrounded by four cycloramas, each of a different color, which could be changed electrically; the orchestra pit could be covered over to create a forestage. For decor, Fuchs and Erler depended almost entirely upon levels, a few set pieces, and lighting; they sought to fuse all elements through rhythm, which Fuchs called the "primal" theatrical force. Ultimately they hoped to re-establish that sense of communion between audience and performer which had characterized the Greek theatre and which had been lost with the emphasis upon illusionism. Like Appia and Craig, Fuchs demanded a simplified staging which captured the spirit of a work without regard for surface realism.

In Russia, several groups turned to nonrealistic staging in the early twentieth century. Two of the most important were Diaghilev's Ballets Russes and Tairov's Kamerny Theatre. The Ballets Russes, under the direction of Sergei Diaghilev (1872–1929) and Mikhail Fokine (1880–1942), made an enormous impression in Western Europe after 1909, especially with its pictorial style. Its impact did not come from any new technical devices, for it relied almost exclusively upon painted wings and drops, but from its stylized decor—primarily decorative mo-

320

Design by Gordon Craig for *Elektra*, 1905. From City of Manchester Art Gallery, *Exhibition of Drawings and Models . . . by Edward Gordon Craig*, 1912.

Scene design for *Prince Igor*, as presented by the Ballets Russes, 1909. Setting by N. Roerich. From the souvenir program.

Shaw's *Saint Joan* as presented at the Kamerny Theatre, Moscow. Directed by Alexander Tairov. Note the costumes with their mixture of elements drawn from many periods and sources.

tifs, color, and line—which reflected moods and themes rather than specific periods and places. The costumes also exaggerated line, color and mass. The Ballets Russes' designers, especially Leon Bakst (1866–1924) and Alexandre Benois (1876–1960), were to exert incalculable influence upon the theatre between 1910 and 1930.

Alexander Tairov (1885–1950), director of the Kamerny Theatre in Moscow from 1914 until near his death, argued that there is no relationship between art and life, that the theatre is comparable to the sacred dances of an ancient temple. To him, the text was an excuse for creativity. Like Fuchs, he thought rhythm the most important element in the theatre and orchestrated his productions almost as if they were musical compositions; speech was a compromise between declamation and song; movement always tended toward dance. The over-all effect was nearer to ritual than to the usual dramatic performance. Because of his emphasis upon rhythm, Tairov's settings were composed primarily of steps and levels. Although Tairov was to modify his approach somewhat after 1930, he remained the Russian director most concerned with a theatrical art independent of social or political ideologies.

In France, the movement toward simplicity owes most to Jacques Copeau (1879–1949), a critic who became convinced that the salvation of the theatre lay in the drama rather than in visual reforms. Copeau argued that the director's primary task is to translate faithfully the dramatist's script into a "poetry of the theatre." Furthermore, he stated that the actor, as the "living presence of the author," is the only essential element and that the rejuvenation of the drama can best be served by a return to the bare platform stage. In 1913, he founded the Théâtre du Vieux Colombier, where he removed the proscenium arch to create an open platform. At the rear of the stage he erected an alcove surmounted by a balcony reached by steps. This basic structure, which could be altered somewhat by the addition of curtains and set pieces, was used for all productions. Forced by World War I to close his theatre, Copeau reopened it in 1919 and continued until 1924, when he retreated to the provinces to perfect his art and to train actors.

Copeau's single-minded devotion to excellence, in which scenic investiture is subordinated to acting, was to dominate theatrical production in France between the two world wars. With variations, his work was carried on by Louis Jouvet (1887–1951), Charles Dullin (1885–1949), Georges Pitoëff (1884–1939), and Gaston Baty (1882–1951), the most prestigious of French directors in the 1920's and 1930's. In 1927 they formed an association, usually called the Cartel des Quatre, to assist each other and to promote common ideals. While no member of the Cartel used as simplified a stage as Copeau, all were opposed to realism and all but Baty accepted Copeau's view of the director's function.

Thus, several men in the early twentieth century encouraged the movement toward simplicity and sought to substitute decor appropriate to mood and theme for that copied from real life. All believed that art should depend upon implication and suggestion rather than direct statement. They contributed much to that eclecticism which has weakened the hold of realism on the modern theatre.

EXPRESSIONISM

The second significant revolt against realism was *expressionism*. Although similar elements may be found in earlier art, expressionism emerged as a movement in Germany around 1910. The name was first applied to the paintings of men who modeled their work on that of Van Gogh and Gauguin. Soon, however, the term was extended to include other art forms. The first important success in the theatre came with Walter Hasenclever's *The Son* in 1914. After reaching the peak of its popularity during World War I, expressionism disintegrated as post-war disillusionment grew. As a conscious movement it was over by 1925.

Because almost any departure from realism in Germany came to be called expressionism, the movement is difficult to describe. Nevertheless, its basic premises may be summarized.

Man is always the center of the Expressionist's interest. He is seen as capable of nobility and as striving for greatness; but an industrial and scientifically-oriented society has reduced him to a machinelike creature by subordinating him to ideals of mass production and conformity of behavior. Furthermore, the Expressionists argued, realism accepts this machinelike state as fixed truth and seeks to understand man through a study of external details. Although like the Symbolists in rebelling against realism and naturalism, the Expressionists were opposed to the Symbolists' preoccupation with the past and with mysterious forces outside of man. Most Expressionists were concerned with the present and many were even more militant than the Naturalists in their desire to change society. But the Expressionists sought their fixed truths within

323

man's nature rather than in any mysterious outside force or external appearance. They wished to begin by understanding man's soul or spirit and then to transform society so that man's greatness might be fully realized.

Since to the Expressionists truth was primarily subjective, it had to be expressed through new artistic means. Distorted line, exaggerated shape, abnormal coloring, mechanical movement, and telegraphic speech were devices commonly used to lead the audience beyond surface appearances. Often everything was shown through the eyes of the protagonist, whose view might alter emphasis and impose drastic interpretations upon the events.

The Expressionists saw their world as having been distorted by inhuman forces, and sometimes argued that man's soul itself has been twisted. Thus, they tended to employ two differing approaches in depicting man's plight. First, much of the drama concentrates upon the negative aspects of the present. It attempts to show how false ideals have distorted man's spirit and transformed him into a machine. Second, a smaller proportion of the drama looks forward to the transformation of society and to harmony between man's environment and his spirit. Most Expressionist plays are structurally episodic, their unity deriving from a central idea or argument rather than from a causally related action.

EXPRESSIONISTIC DRAMATISTS

Among the major influences on Expressionist drama are the works of Strindberg and Wedekind. August Strindberg (1849–1912), the first Swedish playwright to achieve international fame and one of the major dramatists of the modern world, wrote over fifty plays, in addition to novels and nonfictional works. Up to about 1895 his writing belongs to the realistic school, and his plays *The Father* (1887) and *Miss Julie* (1888) are among the best works of the time. But when personal crises drove Strindberg to the edge of insanity, his outlook on life and art underwent profound changes. In the late 1890's he began to write a number of plays which are forerunners of expressionism. These include *The Dream Play* (1902) and *The Spook Sonata* (1907). In his Preface to *The Dream Play*, Strindberg states:

> The author has tried to imitate the disconnected but seemingly logical form of the dream. Anything may happen; everything is possible and probable. Time and space do not exist. On an insignificant background of reality, imagination designs and embroiders novel patterns: a medley of memories, experiences, free fancies, absurdities and improvisations.

In other words, in *The Dream Play* Strindberg tries to destroy the limitations of time, place, and logical sequence by adopting the viewpoint of the dreamer. One event flows into another without logical explanation, characters dissolve or are transformed into other characters, and widely separated places and times blend.

Franz Wedekind (1864–1918), like Strindberg, moves between starkest realism and symbolic abstraction. Sometimes he paints the world as we know it, but at others he depicts the most subjective nightmares. His

Scene from Strindberg's *The Dream Play*. Directed by Philip Benson; lighting by David Thayer.

Spring's Awakening (1891) tells the story of two adolescents' struggles with sexual awareness; much of the play is straightforwardly realistic, but the final scene passes over into pure fantasy. One boy has committed suicide and his ghost urges the other to do likewise but is thwarted by the symbolic Man in the Mask. This mixture of styles and the preoccupation with sexual themes continued throughout Wedekind's work, seen at its best in *Earth Spirit* (1895) and *Pandora's Box* (1904). It was to Wedekind and Strindberg that the Expressionists turned for many of their dramatic techniques.

The most widely known Expressionist playwrights are Ernst Toller (1893–1939) and Georg Kaiser (1878–1945). Toller's first play, *Transfiguration* (1918), written while he was in prison for pacifism, is an antiwar drama. Among his later works the most important are *Man and the Masses* (1921) and *The Machine Wreckers* (1922). *Man and the Masses* shows how the machine and factories have come to dominate men's lives. Toller realizes that the machine is here to stay, but argues that the soul of man must conquer the factories so that the machine may become the servant of man rather than man being subservient to the machine. More importantly, *Man and the Masses* shows a heroine, who stands for the expressionistic ideals, betrayed by the workers, who are not yet ready for the new vision. It points out the great gap between the ideal and actuality, and between the Expressionists and the masses, whose lives the Expressionists hoped to transform. But while the play is pessimistic in its outcome, it still looks forward hopefully to the day when the workers will be ready for a better life.

Kaiser began writing in 1911, but his early work is principally satirical and without any strong conviction. World War I, however, made him question the whole foundation of a society which could generate such acts of destruction. In the process of questioning he wrote some of the most powerful of expressionistic plays.

His best-known works are *From Morn to Midnight, Gas I* (1918), and *Gas II* (1920). In *Gas I* the Expressionist view is treated much as in Toller's *Man and the Masses* (it is defeated, but hope is expressed). By the time he wrote *Gas II*, however, Kaiser had abandoned his belief in the ideal and was predicting man's ultimate destruction. Kaiser's *From Morn to Midnight* will be examined in detail as an example of Expressionistic drama. Written in 1912, it was published in 1916 and first produced in Munich in 1917.

FROM MORN TO MIDNIGHT

From Morn to Midnight has much in common with medieval drama. Some critics have stated that it shows the "stations of martyrdom" in the life of modern man. The play's central character, the Cashier, may be viewed as an Everyman of the modern world, and the time of the action, from morn to midnight, suggests the span of human life.

The play is also related to *Faust*, since both are concerned with man's search for meaning and fulfillment. Like Faust, the Cashier ultimately finds an answer, but unlike Faust, he becomes a martyr because of the debasement of modern man.

From Morn to Midnight shows man reduced to a machinelike existence, devoid of any purpose except material gain. The Cashier is jarred out of this pattern by the exotic and sensual appeal of the Lady from Italy. He realizes for the first time that he has been dehumanized and sets out to find some meaning in existence. Along the way he makes several stops: one involving home and family, another symbolic of society and the state (the race track scene), another of sensual pleasure, and one of religion. He ultimately recognizes the rightness of the soul's claims, but the debasement of the masses is such that they are not ready for his answer.

While the ending is pessimistic, it suggests that since "the new man" has emerged in the Cashier, it might also emerge in the masses. Were this to occur, a rebirth of society would ensue.

PLOT AND STRUCTURE. The seven scenes of *From Morn to Midnight* are held together by the presence of the Cashier in each and by themes and ideas. Everything is focused upon the central character's search for fulfillment.

The first two scenes are primarily preparatory and expository. Scene I establishes the dehumanizing effects of materialism and demonstrates the system of values which underlie the action. The bank is symbolic of society, since the accumulation of wealth is the primary goal of materialism. The Stout Gentleman and the Bank Manager, representatives of the established order, are convinced that in money lies the answer to all of man's problems.

The effect of such values on the common man is seen in the Cashier. He does not speak until the end of the first scene, but functions like a robot: he raps when he wants attention, he takes in and pays out money, he enters sums in a book. For all practical purposes he has become a soulless machine.

But this routine is broken by the appearance of the Lady from Italy. Her strangeness jars the Cashier out of his machinelike state and, in his

Scene 3 of *From Morn to Midnight* as presented by The Theatre Guild in 1922. Note the tree which has turned into a skeleton. Directed by Frank Reicher; settings by Lee Simonson; photograph by Francis Bruguiere. Courtesy Lincoln Center Library of the Performing Arts.

desire to possess her, he responds as his society has conditioned him to act—since money is the key to success, he steals an amount which should be sufficient to accomplish his aim, the possession of the Lady.

Scene 2 shows that the Cashier's view of the road to happiness is erroneous. The Lady is respectable, and the Cashier has irrevocably lost his old place in society.

Scene 3 marks the major transition from the old to the new life. The Cashier cannot go back, and therefore must decide upon a course of action. For the first time he realizes the emptiness of the past, and he is eager to explore what he has been missing: "I have reason to expect great discoveries." He still believes that his stolen money will be the key to success.

Scene 3 also prepares for those to follow, for it is out of his decision to search for the meaning of life that each of the succeeding scenes grows. The scheme of the play is seen further in the appearance of Death. The Cashier declines Death's invitation to go with him by saying, "Call me up around midnight," and, "Before nightfall, I'll have to meet a number of obligations." In the scenes that follow the Cashier makes several visits, and then at midnight re-encounters Death.

Although Scene 4 shows the first of his stops, it is still related to the past since it involves the Cashier's own home and family. But the home, which might satisfy man's search for happiness, has been as completely mechanized as the bank, for here even sentiment has been thoroughly standardized. The Cashier's decision to leave the house before he eats lunch seems such a disruption of order that his mother dies. It is not surprising then that the Cashier decides that the home "does not meet the final test."

Scene 5 shows the Cashier's attempt to find meaning in the political and social structure of society, symbolized in the race track. Here the people assemble to watch the contestants, who, no matter how tired they may be, race whenever a monetary prize is offered: the higher the prize the more exciting the race becomes. All eyes in the stadium (except those of the Cashier) are on the races and the prizes. The race becomes a symbol of the drive for monetary gain.

From Morn to Midnight. Scene 5, the first gallery, as staged by the Theatre Guild. Photograph — Brugueire. Collection of the Library and Museum of the Performing Arts at Lincoln Center.

The stadium, however, is also segmented in terms of the social classes. "In three rings placed on top of each other, bursting with spectators – the magic works. In the first gallery, discipline is maintained by the higher class audience . . . . Higher up, the bodies begin to move. Exclamations are heard. Second gallery. At the very top, all restraint is abandoned. Fanatic shouts. Naked screams. The gallery of passion." The Cashier sets out to break down all the barriers of class and feeling by offering the highest prizes ever heard of. "Fusion of all rings. Utter dissolution of the individual results in the densest core: passion. To reach that point is the greatest experience."

At this stage in his search, then, the Cashier is attempting to break down class barriers and to achieve a universal brotherhood of man. By inducing the fullest expression of emotion, he thinks that he can break down the regimentation of society. But just as the Cashier is about to succeed, the ruler arrives and the spectators resume their conditioned responses. The Cashier has still been using the lure of money as the key to happiness. He has not yet been able to rid himself of the values of his society.

Scene 6 explores the search for happiness through sensual pleasures. The most exotic foods, plus the suggestion of sexual orgy, are used to represent this goal. This road, too, proves to lead nowhere. When the Cashier lifts the mask of one of the women she is so ugly that he is repulsed, and another proves to have a wooden leg. The anticipated joys of the flesh turn into disgust and the Cashier rushes out. Kaiser emphasizes the emptiness and soullessness of material pleasure through the complete selfishness of the cabaret's customers. Since they steal the money left by the Cashier, the poor and tubercular waiter must pay the bill himself.

Scene 7 brings the Cashier to the end of his journey, as he searches for fulfillment in religion. He has been brought to a Salvation Army hall by the same Salvation Lass who has appeared fleetingly in Scenes 5 and 6, in both of which she has gone about her business as mechanically as the Cashier did in Scene 1. It is not surprising, therefore, that she too turns out to be as corrupt as the rest of society.

328

The Cashier has come to the Salvation Army hall because he has lost all sense of purpose. In the meeting which follows, the testimonials of repentant sinners sum up the Cashier's experiences in the play and each makes the Cashier see himself more clearly.

Finally, he realizes that the call of the soul is the true road to happiness. But when he repents of his past and scatters his stolen money about him, the materialism of society is reconfirmed. The supposedly repentant sinners become beasts striving to tear the money from each other. Since the Salvation Army Lass does not enter the fight, the Cashier thinks that he has found his true mate. But she is merely more cunning than the others, for she turns him over to the police for the reward.

In the darkness of the hall a tangle of wires outlines the skeleton of Death, whom the Cashier had eluded in Scene 3. "From morning till midnight I race in a circle. Now his finger shows a way—toward what goal?" He dies with his arms outstretched on the Cross and his dying sigh echoes words associated with Christ, *Ecce Homo* (Behold the Man). The lamps explode, and the Policeman says, "We've had a short circuit" —a remark which the audience should interpret as referring to society.

Although the Cashier has seen the way to truth, the people (as in the history of Jesus) are blind to his values and prefer materialism to his spiritualism. He has changed nothing, but he has shown the way. Kaiser expected his audience to see the difference between two sets of values, and to prefer those of the Cashier.

CHARACTERS AND ACTING. Each of the characters in *From Morn to Midnight* is given only a social designation or "type" name. Each is intended to embody the characteristics of a group rather than an individual. Most speeches are made up of clichés and the characters perform only stereotyped actions. This machinelike quality, essential to Kaiser's attitude toward modern life, should be reflected in the acting.

Only the Cashier (beginning in Scene 3) and the Lady escape stereotyping. The Lady is from another world, and it is her unusualness which jars the Cashier out of the mold into which he has been forced.

The play centers around the Cashier. He is the only truly articulate character and the only one who is able to escape from that machinelike existence which dominates the lives of the others. His speech and action must undergo a change beginning in Scene 3, therefore, and must contrast with those of the other characters. He should grow in humanity and strength as his search comes nearer and nearer to fulfillment. Only if his role is made sympathetic and his search meaningful can Kaiser's intentions be realized. A mechanical quality must be achieved with all characters except the Lady and the Cashier. On the other hand, the Cashier's universal qualities must be brought out, for he represents mankind seeking to escape the stultifying results of modern life.

VISUAL AND AURAL FACTORS. The mechanical qualities of action and speech should be reflected in the scenery, lighting, and costumes, and each of these must represent modern life in its most stereotyped form. Scene 3 offers a clue to the proper approach to spectacle. In that scene a

329

tree turns into a skeleton and then reassumes its normal appearance. The visual elements, therefore, are intended to express the Cashier's vision of reality, rather than to reflect the everyday appearance of objects.

In their efforts to find visual counterparts for their themes, the Expressionists frequently used fragmentary rather than full-stage sets. The scenic elements might be given jagged lines, the walls might tilt or lean, unnatural color might be used; details might be enlarged or diminished in size to emphasize the relative importance of each to the play's ideas. Appearances, thus, were distorted to express feelings and ideas.

Costumes, lighting, and stage properties were treated in similar fashion. Many characters might be dressed identically so as to emphasize the uniformity of modern man. (See, for example, the treatment of the Jewish Gentlemen in the race track scene of *From Morn to Midnight.*) Unnatural color, angle, or intensity in lighting might be used to parallel the distortion of human values depicted in the scripts.

From Morn to Midnight attempts to express the playwright's personal vision of modern man: the mechanization of feelings and activities and the subjugation of the human spirit. It demonstrates the results and suggests a way out of the dilemma. As with much modern art, *From Morn to Midnight* requires a special intellectual effort for comprehension. Once the scheme is understood, the play appears relatively clear. Today it seems oversimplified in its analysis of human ills and in its recommendations for a better future.

THE DECLINE AND LATER INFLUENCE OF EXPRESSIONISM

Two German directors, Leopold Jessner (1878–1948) and Jurgen Fehling (1890–1968), were especially associated with expressionism in production. Jessner, working in Berlin after 1919, won international fame for his imaginative use of flights of steps (*Jessnertreppen*) as a major scenic and compositional device. He also manipulated color and lighting to reflect the inner feelings of characters and reversals of situation. Jessner worked primarily with older plays, to which he gave new life through his visual approach. Fehling, on the other hand, made his reputation by staging Expressionist plays. He experimented with a wide range of devices to reflect the emotional qualities found in the scripts. As the work of Jessner and Fehling became widely known, their practices were adopted elsewhere. Expressionism reached the height of its popularity during and immediately following World War I. Its desire to transform the world into a place where man's highest spiritual potential might be realized raised high hopes, which were soon dissipated by the wranglings over peace settlements and the aftermath. As optimism gave way to the suspicion that man is basically selfish and destructive, the foundations of expressionism were undermined and the movement had ceased to be productive by 1925.

Although primarily a German movement, expressionism exerted considerable influence elsewhere. American dramas indebted to this movement include Elmer Rice's *The Adding Machine*, Eugene O'Neill's *The Hairy Ape* and *The Great God Brown*, and Marc Connelly and George Kaufman's *Beggar on Horseback*, all written in the 1920's.

330

Trial scene from Elmer Rice's *The Adding Machine.* Directed by Gregory Foley.

The later influence of expressionsim is to be seen largely in a freer treatment of visual elements, the introduction of dream sequences into otherwise realistic plays, and in other devices which permit free manipulation of time, place, and appearance. Its dramatic and staging techniques have been absorbed into the general eclecticism of the twentieth-century theatre.

THE THEATRE OF SOCIAL ACTION

Although the Expressionist movement came to an end, its intention of revolutionizing society did not. Rather, it was absorbed by new theatrical trends which combined features of both naturalism and expressionism.

The Naturalists had recorded the details of life as faithfully as possible, since they believed that environment determined character and action. Therefore, they envisioned transforming and controlling environment as the key to change in society and the individual.

The Expressionists, on the other hand, believed that a recording of the externals of existence only prevented man from perceiving the deeper reality which lay embedded in the human soul. They distorted external reality, therefore, in order to reveal inner reality. They looked forward to social reform stemming from a prior change in man's conception of himself and the human spirit.

Thus, while both Naturalists and Expressionists desired change, they disagreed about the sources and the methods for bringing it about. But after World War I another trend emerged which combined elements of both. There is no generally accepted name for this movement as a whole, but here, for the sake of convenience, it will be called the *Theatre of Social Action.* It has been most thoroughly exploited in Soviet Russia, but has also been developed elsewhere, most notably in the *Epic Theatre* of Bertolt Brecht.

Typically, advocates of a theatre of social action have accepted the idea that man's behavior is in large part determined by economic and political forces. They have abandoned the Expressionists' mystical belief in the human soul while retaining their faith in the possibilities of human greatness. Also like the Expressionists, they have tended to seek reforms by moving audiences to recognize the need for change.

331

André Gide's and Jean-Louis Barrault's adaptation of Franz Kafka's expressionistic novel, *The Trial.* Directed by F. C. Strickland; settings by Wendell Cole; costumes by Lenyth Brockett.

Although proponents of a theatre of social action have seen themselves as "realistic and down-to-earth," they have abandoned the Naturalists' demand for objectivity and the faithful recording of reality. Instead, they have adopted a partisan view of subject matter and have taken over many theatrical devices associated with expressionism (such as fragmentary scenery and the distortion of visual elements). They seek to entertain, to teach and, most of all, to move the spectator to practical action outside the theatre. Thus, while they have viewed society in much the same light as the Naturalists, they have sought to depict reality and to work for its transformation through means associated with the Expressionists. They have also been attracted by many conventions of the Oriental theatre.

THE RUSSIAN THEATRE AND MEYERHOLD

The most concerted attempt to use the theatre in transforming society is found in Russia after the Revolution of 1917. The theatres, which had been frequented principally by the privileged classes, were now thrown open to the workers, many of whom had never seen a performance. Because the new audience and the new political structure created new problems, many argued that new methods were needed. Consequently, a number of experimenters sought to create a *People's Theatre.*

Much of the so-called "new" theatre was merely realistically mounted melodrama in which opponents of the Revolution were depicted as villains seeking to thwart heroic Communists. This type of drama was to dominate the Russian stage after 1934, when it received official sanction as *socialist realism.* Many of the older theatre workers, such as Stanislavsky, attempted to meet the needs of the new audiences by making plays as psychologically real as possible. Stanislavsky's methods eventually triumphed and have had the official support of the Soviet regime since the 1930s.

On the other hand, there were many who felt that the political and economic revolution demanded a comparable theatrical revolution. The most influential exponent of this view was Vsevolod Meyerhold (1874–1942), who began his career as an actor in Stanislavsky's company. In 1905, Stanislavsky appointed him director of an experimental group seeking alternatives to the realistic methods of the Moscow Art Theatre. But Meyerhold's dehumanization of the actor led to friction and he soon left the troupe. Between 1905 and the Revolution Meyerhold worked with many groups exploring the limits of the theatre as an artistic medium. In many ways his work parallels that going on in painting at the time, especially the movement toward abstraction.

After 1917 Meyerhold tried to use his methods in the service of the Revolution. In the 1930's he was declared too *formalistic* (that is, not sufficiently attuned to the masses) and was removed from his post as a theatre director. By that time, however, his work had become famous and influential throughout the world.

Three concepts are normally associated with Meyerhold: biomechanics, theatricalism, and constructivism. First of all, however it is necessary to understand that to Meyerhold the director was the only true artist of the theatre. He rewrote or adapted plays to fit his own conceptions and shaped every element in accordance with his own vision. His was a director's theatre.

Meyerhold devised a system for training actors which he called *biomechanics*. Not interested in psychological realism, Meyerhold wished each of his actors to have a body as efficient as a machine in carrying out the orders of its operator. The actors, therefore, were trained in ballet, gymnastics, and circus techniques until they were capable of responding instantly to the needs of the director. (In performance they were frequently asked to swing from trapezes, to turn somersaults, or shoot up through trap doors.)

Meyerhold worked to achieve *theatricalism*. Instead of striving for the illusion of real life, he wished the audience to remain conscious that it was in the theatre. He believed that, since the theatre is an art, all its means should be used self-consciously and to their fullest capabilities. Consequently, he removed the front curtain from the stage, placed lighting instruments in full view of the audience, used a "gymnastic" approach to acting, juxtaposed many contrasting dramatic elements, and used totally abstract settings called *constructions*. Meyerhold never allowed his audiences to confuse the theatre with real life, but sought to comment upon social, political, and economic situations, to stir up thought, and to incite the audience to desirable social action outside the theatre.

Meyerhold's work is sometimes referred to as *constructivistic*. The name constructivism was first applied around 1912 to Russian sculptures which were merely *constructions* composed of intersecting planes and masses. Meyerhold adopted many ideas from these artists, especially in his stage settings, completely nonrepresentational platforms, ramps, trapezes, and other elements which formed a structure upon which the actors might perform efficiently. Ultimately, the stage, the actor, and all theatrical elements were viewed by Meyerhold as a single, complex machine to be used by the director. His was a dictatorial approach. Although his methods proved too abstract for many theatregoers, Meyerhold's use of nonrealistic techniques to comment on real social problems has exerted continuing effect upon the theatre.

Design for one of Meyerhold's constructivist productions.

Meyerhold's set during production.

Another influential but less radical post-Revolutionary director was Eugene Vakhtangov (1883–1922), who began as a faithful follower of Stanislavsky and then sought to blend Stanislavsky's and Meyerhold's approaches. From Stanislavsky he preserved the emphasis upon concentration, the exploration of each character's biography, and the search for hidden meanings; with this he combined stylized movement and scenic elements not unlike those used by the Expressionists. Vakhtangov was not so preoccupied with politics as was Meyerhold, and his theatrical methods always remained comprehensible to the general public. For these reasons, and because so many of his co-workers and pupils became leading directors, Vakhtangov's influence has remained strong.

BRECHT AND EPIC THEATRE

Perhaps the most successful attempt to create a theatre of social action was that of Bertolt Brecht (1898–1956), who began his work in the German theatre at the time when the Expressionists were at the peak of their popularity. Much of his early writing is obviously influenced by that school, but he went on to develop distinctive theories which he continued to refine until his death.

Brecht called his work *epic* theatre to distinguish it from the *dramatic* theatre against which he was in revolt. He stated that the old theatre has outlived its usefulness since it reduces the spectator to a role of complete passivity. In it, according to Brecht, events are presented as fixed and unchangeable, since even historical subjects are treated in present-day terms; this approach encourages the audience to believe that things have always been the same. Furthermore, realistic staging gives the ac-

334

tion an air of stability which contributes to the idea that an entrenched position cannot be altered. The spectator, therefore, can only watch in a hypnotized and uncritical way; his senses are lulled, and he cannot participate "productively" in the theatrical event.

In the place of this old theatre, Brecht envisioned a new theatre in which the spectator would become a vital part. To bring about this change, Brecht sought to alter both drama and theatrical production. In describing his ideal theatre, Brecht used three key terms: *historification, alienation,* and *epic.*

Unlike the Realists, Brecht thought that the theatre should not treat contemporary subject matter in a lifelike manner. Rather, the theatre should "make strange" the actions it presents. One avenue to strangeness lies in *historification,* which ordinarily means using material drawn from other times or places. But contrary to old theatrical practices, which depict historical material in today's pattern, Brecht argued that the dramatist should emphasize "pastness"—the removal of events from the present. The playwright should make the spectator feel that, if he had been living under the conditions shown in the play, he would have taken some positive action. The audience should then go on to see that, since things have changed, it is possible to make desirable social reforms in the present.

Historification is a part of the larger term *alienation.* (Although alienation is not a precise translation of Brecht's original term, *verfremdungseffekt,* it is the one which has been popularized in America. More accurately it means "to make strange.") In addition to historification, the playwright may use other means for making things strange. He may deliberately call the audience's attention to the make-believe nature of the work (rather than trying to convince the audience of the play's reality). Songs, narrative passages, filmed sequences, and other devices may be used for this purpose. The audience should never be allowed to confuse what it sees on the stage with reality. Rather the play must always be thought of as a comment upon life to be watched and judged critically.

Although Brecht always insisted that the theatre should bring pleasure, he thought that the greatest pleasure comes from "productive participation," in which the spectator actively judges and applies what he sees on the stage to conditions outside the theatre. If he is to watch productively, the spectator must be alienated from the play's events.

Alienation does not mean that the spectator should not become emotionally involved with the characters and the action; if he is to respond as Brecht desired ("If I had lived than I would have done something"), emotional response is essential. This emotional response, however, is always part of the larger, critical response.

Each element of production should contribute to alienation. Brecht did not envision, as have most twentieth-century theorists, a synthesis of all the arts in the theatre, but rather the independence of each. Music, for example, should make a comment upon the action rather than merely underscoring the meaning of the words. For example, in *Mother Courage* the satirically bitter words of a song which tell of the gradual moral

Scene from Brecht's *Mother Courage* as presented at the Berliner Ensemble. Photograph by Berlau. Courtesy Berliner Ensemble.

335

degradation of a character are set to a consciously "pretty," light-hearted tune. The contrast between words and music achieves alienation, for it forces the spectator to consider the song's significance.

Likewise, scenery is not intended to create the illusion of place. It may suggest a locale, but it does not depict it in detail. Brecht advocates the use of projections, fragmentary set pieces, and similar devices for indicating the location of action, but in each case the elements comment upon the action as well.

As a further aid in alienation, Brecht wishes to let the mechanics of the theatre remain visible. He suggests mounting the lighting instruments where they may be seen, changing the scenery in view of the audience, and placing the musicians on stage. Such devices prevent a production from lulling the audience into a feeling of security and timelessness, and engage the spectator's judgment in such a way as to arouse his social consciousness.

Brecht calls his plays *epic* because he thinks they resemble epic poems more than traditional drama. The epic poem, composed of alternating sections of dialogue and narration, presents a story from the viewpoint of a single storyteller. The epic also may freely change place and time; it narrates some scenes and shows others; it bridges passages of time with a single sentence or a brief passage; it may easily cover the sweep of a historical period. (It is easier to understand Brecht's point if such a work as *The Iliad* is compared with traditional dramatic works.)

As with other examples of theatre of social action, epic theatre envisions the ultimate effect of drama occurring outside the theatre. By stirring up thought and inciting the spectator to act for desirable social reforms, a play escapes becoming an opiate and assumes a vital and productive role in men's lives.

Many of the staging techniques used by the epic theatre were first employed by Erwin Piscator (1893–1966) in Berlin in the 1920's. The most famous of his productions, *The Good Soldier Schweik* (1927), is a bitter satire on the German war machine. In it, the experiences of the common soldier, Schweik, are depicted through a swirl of events that occur in an enormous number of places and over a lengthy stretch of time. Piscator used treadmills, projections, scenic fragments, giant caricature drawings, and many other devices to adapt the action to the stage

Scene from Brecht's *The Caucasian Chalk Circle.* Directed by John Terfloth.

and to comment upon it. Like Brecht, Piscator did not intend to be objective in his stage presentations; he wished to comment upon society and to arouse the critical faculties of his audience.

Among Brecht's more important plays are *The Three-Penny Opera, The Caucasian Chalk Circle, Mother Courage, Galileo,* and *Mahagonny. The Good Woman of Setzuan* will be examined as representative of epic theatre.

The Good Woman of Setzuan, written between 1938 and 1940 and first produced in 1943, is a parable which has been historified by placing it in China, although the time is more or less contemporary.

In this play Brecht is concerned with the possibility of goodness. Shen Te, the heroine, wants and tries to be good, but as she points out:

> *When we extend our hand to a beggar, he tears it off for us*
> *When we help the lost, we are lost ourselves*
> *And so*
> *Since not to eat is to die*
> *Who can long refuse to be bad?*

Two factors have created this situation — society and human nature. It is difficult to know which of these Brecht thinks most responsible. Much of his nonfictional writing suggests that society is the culprit, and that a different economic system (presumably some form of socialism) would remove many of the incentives for immoral behavior which exist under capitalism. In *The Good Woman of Setzuan* the capitalist class is represented by Shu Fu, Mrs. Mi Tzu, and Shui Ta, who exploit the others. The methods of this class are most graphically illustrated through Shui Ta, the disguise Shen Te assumes to protect herself from her relatives.

THE GOOD WOMAN OF SETZUAN

Scene from Brecht's *The Good Woman of Setzuan,* as presented at the University of Texas. Directed by Francis Hodge; setting by John Rothgeb; costumes by Paul Reinhardt.

But this is not the whole picture, for the capitalists are no less admirable than the proletariat. Shen Te's relatives are liars, thieves, and parasites. While they may have been forced into such behavior by social conditions, their vindictiveness and cruelty (for example, the enjoyment they get from seeing the Carpenter deprived of pay for honest work) make them as callous as the others. Ultimately Brecht shows human nature as consistent regardless of social class—all are ready to tear off the hand that is extended in help.

The exceptions are to be seen in Shen Te and Wong, and even here they are more a matter of desire than of accomplishment. Although Shen Te wants to be good, she is eventually driven to disguise herself as Shui Ta. When Shen Te sins, however, it is out of love for others and not out of self-love.

So much evil set against so little good gives the play a sense of hopelessness, and makes it difficult to believe in the possibility of change outside the theatre (as Brecht would desire). Herein lies one of the basic contradictions in Brecht's work as a whole. Brecht felt deeply man's inhumanity to his fellow creatures and deplored the failure to live in love and harmony; he longed for a better existence; but, at the same time, he implies in his plays that such ideals are hopeless because of man's essential selfishness.

Brecht is not entirely pessimistic. He always suggests that man is partially responsible for his own fate and is not entirely at the mercy of hereditary and environmental forces. He insists that if an audience can be made to watch critically, it can reach conclusions about contemporary society and can take steps to alter what it does not like. Thus, the pessimism found in his plays is modified by Brecht's optimism about the possibilities of action outside the theatre. Nevertheless, a sense of ambiguity always remains.

PLOT AND STRUCTURE. The "epic" nature of *The Good Woman of Setzuan* is established by the prologue, in which narration and dialogue are freely mingled and in which time and place are considerably telescoped. The irony which permeates the whole work is also established by the disparity between Wong's assurances to the Gods that everyone is waiting to receive them and the fact that they must accept lodgings with a prostitute.

The prologue also establishes the basic situation: the Gods find the good person for whom they have been searching and enjoin her to remain good. At the same time, however, they refuse to be concerned about how such a difficult assignment is to be carried out—they "never meddle with economics." Herein lies the basic conflict, for economic factors are the very ones which stand in the way of goodness. Thus, the Gods' demand that man be good and their refusal to be concerned with the determinants of morality are clearly at odds. By this means Brecht implies that the solution to human problems is not to be sought in divine injunctions.

The Good Woman of Setzuan alternates short and long scenes. The short scenes serve two main purposes: to break up and to comment on

338

the action. Both contribute to Brecht's aim of forcing the audience to think by giving it clues about the significance of what it has seen and time in which to reflect upon it.

The long scenes are devoted to the conflict between good and evil as seen in the two aspects of the "good woman." Her true self is shown in the person of Shen Te, while her evil self is embodied in Shui Ta. She assumes the disguise of Shui Ta whenever her goodness has brought her to the edge of destruction. At first the impersonation is for brief periods, but, as the play progresses, she must become Shui Ta for longer periods. Brecht uses this device to show the progressive deterioration of morality. The play ends in a stalemate, for the Gods leave Shen Te with the same message as in the prologue, "Be Good." She is still no nearer to knowing how this is to be accomplished, and they are still unconcerned over such practical matters.

The long scenes have been broken up by the insertion of songs and speeches delivered directly to the audience. The songs are ostensibly about subject matter different from that of the scenes they accompany; some are parables in themselves. Nevertheless, all comment, directly or indirectly, upon the action.

Brecht makes no attempt to create the illusion of real happenings. For example, when Wong says that he will find a place for the Gods to spend the night, he suggests the attempt, although the various houses are not represented on stage. The action, thus, is outlined, but many of the details are omitted.

This approach allows Brecht to telescope events and to eliminate transitions. For example, in the prologue the Gods are taken into Shen Te's house and the lowering of stage lights designates the passing of night. This device is analogous to the narrative technique in which a writer bridges a transition with, "The next morning— —." This technique can be seen more clearly in the scene in which Shen Te meets Yang Sun and falls in love with him. There has been no preparation for this turn of events, and again it is much as if a storyteller had said, "One day when Shen Te was out walking in the park she saw a young man trying to hang himself." The need to motivate her presence or to show the connection of this scene with those which preceded it is ignored.

Again, however, Brecht's structural techniques are explained in part by his belief that scenes should be clearly separated as part of the alienation process. They are further explained by his insistence that the basic social content of each scene should be capable of expression in one simple sentence (for example, scene three of *The Good Woman of Setzuan* might be expressed by "Shen Te falls in love with a young aviator"), and that all parts of a scene should be clearly related to this simple statement. Brecht is not concerned with inner psychological truth but concentrates upon what he calls "social gestures"—or the embodiment of attitudes in social behavior. The clear depiction of a "gesture," then, is the aim of each scene.

Although Brecht desires simplicity and clarity, his techniques have puzzled many, for they deviate from normal dramatic conventions. The introduction of songs, the failure to make clear connections between

339

scenes, and other devices designed to achieve alienation frequently conflict with traditional conceptions of effective dramatic structure. For these reasons, Brecht's hoped-for clarity has become only obscurity for many spectators.

Given some understanding of Brecht's aims, however, the same devices which some find distracting become effective sources of contrast and vigor. The alternation of long and short scenes, of narration and dialogue, of song and speech, of direct appeal and oblique reference—all of these serve to increase interest and to depict those social gestures with which Brecht is concerned.

CHARACTERS AND ACTING. Brecht considerably oversimplifies characters, for he is principally concerned with social relationships. He is not interested in total personalities or the inner lives of his characters. Instead of names, the majority of speakers in *The Good Woman of Setzuan* have been given social designations, such as Gods, Wife, Grandfather, and Policeman. All represent types of behavior more than they do individuals. Their desires are also stated in terms of social action: Shen Te wishes to treat all persons honorably, to make it possible for Yang Sun to become a pilot, to provide proper food for the children, and so on. Social and economic facts are most important in each characterization.

These social factors are modified by Brecht's basic belief that all men are selfish. In the social situations, therefore, the actions are in large part determined by each character's attempt to better his own situation at the expense of others. Brecht has not been accused of distorting human psychology as much as he might since his view of humanity is basically in keeping with modern psychological theories and with determinism. The modern world has accepted the idea that everyone is basically selfish and that even good deeds fulfill some need within the individual. Thus, Brecht's picture of humanity has not offended as it would had his exaggeration been in the direction of showing the goodness of men. Nevertheless, Brecht's characterizations are based on only a few traits and are confined principally to social factors and a limited number of psychological attitudes.

Brecht, however, did not intend to portray well-rounded individuals. He set out to present an interpretation of social reality, and his characters are important only insofar as they forward that presentation. The action does not exist to display character, but character to demonstrate social action.

The only character who rises to the level of moral decision is Shen Te. The plot progresses in large part through the series of choices which she makes: to accept the God's injunction to be good; to become Shui Ta in order to preserve her well-being; to help Yang Sun; and so on. These choices are necessary to demonstrate one of Brecht's basic concerns: the moral dilemma of man under the existing economic conditions.

Brecht's ideas on acting are in keeping with his general approach to the theatre. The actor should not impersonate a character so much as present the behavior of a person in a specific situation. Brecht wishes actors to avoid identifying with the characters or trying "to live the part."

340

He suggests that the actor should analyze the basic social qualities of his role and concentrate upon "presenting" these to the audience in a kind of demonstration which comments upon the action and the characters. The actor, thus, aids the alienation effect and arouses a critical response in the audience.

The actor performing in Brecht's plays should be familiar with Brecht's ideas on acting, although it is doubtful that they can always be carried out. The members of Brecht's own acting troupe have stated that they did not approach the roles in his plays differently from those in other plays, and that Brecht himself was not insistent upon the acceptance of his ideas. Nevertheless, his intentions are important to an understanding of his over-all approach to the theatre. The more introspective approach of Stanislavsky is of limited value in acting Brecht's plays.

VISUAL AND AURAL ELEMENTS. Brecht once characterized his use of visual elements as naïve and added, "The opposite of a naïve approach is naturalism." He strives for a childlike simplicity, a make-believe quality: "The natural must be made to look surprising."

The sweep of events and the rapid changes of time and place would in themselves prevent the full-stage representation of all the locales indicated in any of Brecht's plays. But Brecht desires neither historical accuracy nor the accumulation of naturalistic details in his settings; he wants only those elements which aid in the alienation effect. Scenery and costumes, therefore, remain only outlines or suggestions. Fragmentary settings, projections, and captions are his favorite devices. Costumes may use some historically accurate elements but others may be modern or merely expressive of social factors rather than of a historical period.

The Good Woman of Setzuan is set in ten different places. Each of these, however, can be indicated by a few scenic elements. For example, Scene 4 is set in a square onto which three shops open. Each shop may be suggested by a single flat and these may be carried on stage by the actors in full view of the audience. As Brecht wrote:

> *. . . let the spectator*
> *Be aware of busy preparations, made for him*
> *Cunningly; he sees a tinfoil moon*
> *Float down, or a tiled roof*
> *Being carried in; do not show him too much,*
> *But show him something!*

While little scenery is needed, that which is used should be designed with great care so that it makes a definite contribution to the play's effect. In Brecht's theatre it is not enough to copy reality; reality must be clarified by transforming it and by making it strange. The right kind of scenery allows the spectator to view reality critically and to understand it—something which would not be possible were it presented in its everyday and familiar guise. With every aspect of drama, then, Brecht seeks to transform the old theatre into a new one in which the spectator can participate rather than merely observe passively.

All of Brecht's major works were written before the end of World War II. Living in exile throughout the Nazi regime, Brecht was little known

341

until after 1945. Since that time, however, his plays and theories have assumed increasing importance, being one of the most pervasive influences on recent dramatic and theatrical techniques.

RELATED FORMS

One of the forms most obviously related to Brecht's Epic Theatre is the *Living Newspaper* which grew out of the Federal Theatre project in America. During the economic depression of the 1930's, the United States government authorized a Federal Theatre as part of its Works Progress Administration programs, designed to relieve unemployment. In operation between 1935 and 1939, the Federal Theatre had units in various parts of the country but was most active in New York, where unemployment in the theatre was most serious. While the New York branch of the Federal Theatre produced many kinds of plays, it is best remembered for its Living Newspaper productions. The Living Newspaper, as the title indicates, aimed at achieving in the theatre something similar to the printed newspaper. In actuality it was more closely related to the documentary film, for each play treated a single problem. The most famous examples are *One Third of a Nation* (on slum housing), *Triple-A Plowed Under* (on the farm program), and *Power* (on public utilities and flood control). The plays alternate scenes illustrating social conditions with narrative sequences; statistical tables, still photographs, and motion pictures were projected on screens; offstage voices, music

Setting for a Living Newspaper, *One Third of a Nation* (1938), at the Federal Theatre, New York. Setting by Howard Bay. From *Theatre Arts,* 1938.

and sound effects were used freely. The plays were written by many authors in collaboration and took a definite point of view (in favor of social reform and corrective legislation). This political and social bias eventually led to the discontinuance of the Federal Theatre, for in 1939 Congress refused to appropriate funds to support it. It marks the United States government's first attempt at subsidizing the theatre.

The Living Newspaper used many of the same devices and upheld points of view similar to those advocated by Brecht and Piscator. This "epic" approach did not attract many imitators in the United States until the 1960's, however, and most plays dealing with social problems continued to be cast in the form popularized by Ibsen. The theatricality of epic staging, nevertheless, served, in conjunction with other movements, to turn staging away from illusionism.

Symbolism, expressionism, and the theatre of social action each sought to replace the realistic ideal which had dominated the theatre since the nineteenth century. While they were not able to overthrow realism, they called attention to its shortcomings and altered its outlook and methods. Some of the results will be examined in the chapter which follows.

Chapter 15 THE THEATRE SINCE WORLD WAR II

The theatre since World War II can best be described as eclectic. It has borrowed, combined, and modified elements from various modern movements, has adapted staging devices from many earlier periods, and has explored new techniques in both writing and staging. Its diversity can be illustrated by examining some of its most representative forms: modified realism, musical drama, the "theatre of the absurd," Brechtian drama, and "happenings."

MODIFIED REALISM

Realism probably remains the most common theatrical style, although it has been modified considerably since the nineteenth century. The various modern movements have conditioned audiences to accept simplification, suggestion, and distortion as basic techniques in art. In the theatre the result has been a greater emphasis upon theatricality, less dependence upon illusionism and more willingness to recognize that art is different from reality.

Stage settings, for example, now usually rely more upon suggestion than upon detailed representation of period and place. Although locales may be indicated pictorially, many details are eliminated. Similarly, play structure has become freer and less dependent upon the techniques of the "well-made play" than in the late nineteenth and early twentieth centuries. There has been a trend toward a large number of scenes and away from the division into acts. Experimentation with dramatic techniques is now common.

These modifications have been brought about in part by changes in our view of the world. In the late nineteenth century, the discoveries of science were hailed as liberators from irrational explanations of social

344

The final scene of O'Neill's *A Long Day's Journey into Night,* one of the most effective plays of the 1950s. Directed by Lael Woodbury.

phenomena. But such advances as control over atomic energy (with all of the potentialities for good and evil) have re-emphasized the need for moral and spiritual values capable of guiding such power. With the realization that science cannot provide moral answers has come a lessening of faith in the scientific method as the only source of truth.

Furthermore, psychology has shown increasingly that many of man's most powerful motivations are subconscious ones which cannot be reduced to purely external signs. Reality, then, is no longer thought to be so simple as in the late nineteenth century, and the means for representing it in the theatre have consequently become much more flexible. As the realistic outlook has absorbed irrational elements, dramatic and theatrical techniques have been borrowed from nonrealistic movements.

CONTEMPORARY REALISTIC DRAMATISTS

The fusion of modern movements is probably seen most clearly in the works of Tennessee Williams (1914–   ), who came to prominence in 1945 with *The Glass Menagerie* and who has contributed regularly to the theatre since that time with such plays as *A Streetcar Named Desire, Summer and Smoke, The Rose Tattoo, Suddenly Last Summer, The Night of the Iguana,* and *Slapstick Tragedy.*

Williams uses many nonrealistic devices. Symbolism, of the type employed by Ibsen and Chekhov, is found in almost every play and the titles of his works indicate their deeper symbolic meanings. Normally, Williams also demands fragmentary settings, although each fragment is usually realistic. Frequently his sets combine interiors and exteriors to allow fluidity without scene changes. A good example is found in *Summer and Smoke,* which shows two interiors and a park simultaneously.

Tennessee Williams' *Summer and Smoke.* Directed by David Schaal; scenery by Arnold Gillette.

William Inge's *Picnic* with the original (1953) cast: Arthur O'Connell, Eileen Heckatt, Ralph Meeker, Janice Rule, Ruth Mc-Devitt, Betty Lou Holland. Director, Joshua Logan. Setting, Jo Meilziner. Produced by the Theatre Guild and Joshua Logan. Photograph—Alfredo Valente, courtesy of the Library and Museum of the Performing Arts, Lincoln Center.

Time is also fluid in many of Williams' plays. *The Glass Menagerie* is especially noteworthy for its use of memory as the motivation for calling up scenes from the past. In this respect, the play resembles the works of Strindberg.

But while Williams' plays may be extremely theatrical, they are intensely real in their treatment of character. Williams is concerned principally with inner psychological realities which can best be projected through the manipulation (rather than the mere recording) of external elements. Complex Freudian motivations underlie most of the plays.

The conflicts in Williams' plays are frequently representative of larger human issues; spirituality and materialism are almost always at odds and the resolution of a dramatic action depends upon how well the characters can reconcile the demands of these two sides of human nature. For example, in *A Streetcar Named Desire*, Blanche's desires for beauty and love are eventually defeated by Stanley Kowalski's materialism and lust. Some of Williams' plays make the conflict too abstract and allegorical, but in others it is embodied in intensely powerful and lifelike portraits.

Another aspect of Williams' realism is seen in his juxtaposition of comic and serious elements. Like Chekhov, Williams is able to depict multiple character traits and differing moods simultaneously. Amanda in *The Glass Menagerie*, for example, is admirable, pathetic, and ridiculous, and the scenes in which she appears shift mood rapidly. Williams' portrayal of human limitations in conjunction with high aspirations produce both pathos and humor. His plays, consequently, are at once compassionate and bitter.

These characteristics show both the continuing power of realism and its modification by other approaches. In many ways, Williams' plays sum up twentieth-century movements.

The works of William Inge (1913–   ), such as *Picnic*, *Bus Stop*, *Come Back, Little Sheba*, and *The Dark at the Top of the Stairs*, show many of the same characteristics as those of Williams, although they are more limited in range and depth. Inge is concerned with internal anxieties—with facing "the dark at the top of the stairs." The resolutions of his plays are more optimistic than Williams', for Inge seems to indicate that to achieve happiness one need only face up to psychological realities. Since he is much less interested in the wider implications of psychological conflicts and with theatrical devices, Inge remains more clearly in the main stream of realism than does Williams.

The Ibsenian tradition has been continued by Arthur Miller (1915–   ), who came to prominence with *All My Sons* (1947), and went on to write such plays as *The Crucible*, *A View from the Bridge*, *After the Fall*, *Incident at Vichy*, and *The Price*. But it is *Death of a Salesman* (1949) that has insured Miller's position, for many consider it the finest American play of the postwar era. It will be examined in detail as an example of modern American drama and of modified realism.

DEATH OF A SALESMAN

Death of a Salesman explores Willy Loman's obsessive desire to succeed. Willy wants to be recognized, liked, and admired. It is his perplexity over the gulf between his accomplishment and his ideal that precipitates the play's action. Success as Willy conceives it, however, is largely material, for to be well liked and to be materially successful are inextricably linked in his mind.

Because material success seems so necessary to Willy, he believes that his sons cannot love him if he is not successful. Love becomes an item to be bought rather than something to be freely given. Willie has also conditioned his sons to believe that they do not deserve respect unless they are successful on his terms. It is only when Willy understands that Biff loves him, even though both are failures, that he achieves a degree of insight. It is too late to change the course of events, but he goes to his death more nearly at peace than at any time in the play.

The conflicts, then, arise from tensions between the passion for success and the need to be loved and understood. Miller has used two characters to represent the poles between which Willy is pulled. Uncle Ben, Willy's brother, epitomizes material success, while Linda, Willy's wife, represents love given without question or conditions. Willy's dilemma grows out of his unconscious assumption that success is necessary before love is possible.

Many have seen in *Death of a Salesman* a condemnation of American business. Miller has stated that he did not have such a purpose in mind and the play largely bears him out. Charley, a businessman, is one of the most admirable characters in the play and the one who has most nearly achieved success in both private and business life. Charley has never

347

Scene from the first production of *Death of a Salesman*. Directed by Elia Kazan. Setting by Jo Meilziner. Courtesy Graphic House, Inc.

worried about being "a success," however, while Willy has thought of little else. Willy has condoned petty stealing, lying, and cheating so long as they lead toward his goals. His failure, therefore, does not result from being a salesman, but from the means he has used to get ahead. His failure in business is important only because it reflects his failure as a father, husband, and human being.

PLOT AND STRUCTURE. Miller has said that he originally conceived the action of *Death of a Salesman* within Willy's mind and that Willy's psychological state dictated the structure of the play. This is only partially true since Willy does not participate in several scenes and could know nothing of them. These exceptions, however, take place in the present; those scenes which go backward in time invariably grow out of Willy's psychological associations.

The present action occurs during a twenty-four hour period (with the exception of the funeral), but the scenes from the past range over twenty years. Past and present flow together as Willy tries to find the answers to his questions: Why have I failed? Where did I go wrong? What is the secret of success?

348

It is interesting to compare Miller's play with works from earlier periods. Both *Death of a Salesman* and *Oedipus the King* involve a search into the past to find the roots of present evils. The scenes in *Oedipus the King*, however, are all drawn from the present and the past is revealed only through narration; *Death of a Salesman*, on the other hand, uses Willy's anxieties to transport the audience backward in time to witness scenes. As in *Faust*, there is a search for the meaning of life, but whereas Faust goes forward in time to find fulfillment, Willy goes backward in time to seek the causes of his failure. *Death of a Salesman* also recalls medieval drama in its use of a simultaneous setting and in the complete fluidity of time.

The only unusual structural feature of *Death of a Salesman* is the *flashback* technique, for otherwise it is organized conventionally in terms of exposition, preparation, complications, climax, obligatory scene, and resolution. Each flashback is carefully introduced by wandering talk, offstage voices, sound effects, music, or some similar cue. Most productions of the play have also used changes in lighting to lead the audience from the present to the past. The flashbacks are carefully engineered so that each reveals only a small part of the past. The outline gradually emerges but is incomplete until the climactic moment.

In *Death of a Salesman* psychological realism has replaced external realism and a greater freedom in dramatic structure has resulted. Although many of the scenes materialize out of Willy's mind and are treated only in fragmentary form, the aim remains much the same as that which moved Ibsen—to depict with fidelity a contemporary situation.

CHARACTERS AND ACTING. By far the most important character in *Death of a Salesman* is Willy Loman. Biff serves as a strong secondary interest, since the major issues of the play are worked out between him and Willy.

Willy, now sixty-three years old, is on the verge of a physical and psychological breakdown. All his life, he has been trying to sell himself; he has lied both to himself and to others out of a desire to believe that he is a success. Recent developments, however, have forced him to see that actually he is a failure. Yet he cannot see where he has taken the wrong path.

Willy is tired, puzzled, touchy, quick to get angry, ready to hope; he cajoles his sons, offers advice when it is unwanted; he is always looking for the secret that will "open doors." Above all, he is dominated by the ideal of success, which he tries to instill in his sons as well.

Uncle Ben personifies success, and in many ways is merely an extension of Willy's personality. He represents the mystery of success, for he has gone into the jungle and come out rich; he has been to far-away and dangerous places and thus he gives a romantic aura to success. Ben also implies that success is bound up with the "law of the jungle," with shady deals and quick-wittedness.

Willy, however, wants to triumph on his own terms—as a salesman who is liked by everybody. Therefore, he can never completely accept

349

Ben's advice just as he can never give up Ben's ideal. This division is at the root of Willy's character and is seen even in his death, which is a final attempt to achieve material gain and the gratitude of his family simultaneously. He is both a pathetic and a powerful figure.

Biff is thirty-four years old but still adolescent in his attitudes. He is irresponsible, a wanderer, and incapable of happiness because of the sense of guilt aroused in him by Willy. From Willy he learned early that the way to success lies through lying, stealing, and powerful acquaintances. But the lure of success has been short-circuited in Biff by his disillusionment with Willy, dating from the discovery of his father's unfaithfulness to his mother. Consequently, Biff rebels against success, flouts authority, and enjoys hurting his father.

Biff has his admirable side, nevertheless, for he tries to face the truth, and he has a sense of moral responsibility which his brother, Happy, is totally lacking. It is Biff who finally makes his father see the truth as they both come to understand that love is a gift freely bestowed rather than something earned through material success. Miller gives no indication of what the future holds for Biff, but it will no doubt be more peaceful than the past.

Linda understands from the beginning what Willy and Biff learn during the play: love has no conditions. She knows all there is to know about Willy, but she loves him, accepts him, and fights fiercely for him, even against her own sons. Her sense of decency and rightness makes her put Willy above everyone, for to her it is not a question of whether Willy has earned love and respect—his right to them is unquestioned. Because she loves so unconditionally, Linda cannot understand why Willy commits suicide or why the boys have turned out as they have. Success holds no magic for Linda. She fears Ben and his lures. It is only because of Biff that Willy eventually begins to see the appeal of Linda's view.

Happy has inherited the worst of Willy's traits without the saving possibility of love. He is entirely selfish and unfeeling; lying and cheating are integral parts of his nature. He is a materialist and sensualist beyond redemption, but devoid of Ben's vision and strength.

Charley and Bernard have succeeded where Willy and Biff have failed; thus, their principal function in the play is to serve as contrasts. Charley says that he has succeeded because he has never been passionately dedicated to anything. Yet the play shows that Charley is dedicated to being a good man, as opposed to being a success in Willy's terms. Although unaware of his dedication, Charley's unconscious commitment to *human* above *material* factors is the key to his happiness, just as the reverse is the key to Willy's failure.

Many have seen in Howard an indictment of the "businessman's morality." Miller has denied this and has said that Howard is a man of common sense and that he acts as he must. More importantly for the play, however, Howard spurs Willy on in his search for an answer. In real-life terms it might have been more humane for Howard to find a place for Willy in the home office, but in terms of dramatic action his decision is necessary to make Willy face himself more completely. In constructing his characters, Miller has concentrated upon sociological and psychological attitudes; other details have been cut away. Miller's success in creating convincing figures is indicated by the general tendency of audiences to see in the play a clear reflection of modern society.

SPECTACLE AND SOUND. Miller's ideas about staging *Death of a Salesman* are clearly indicated in the script. The continuous presence of the house helps to establish the convention that the flashbacks are fragments of the past and to make clear the simultaneity of the past and the present in Willy's mind.

Miller has stated that the motion picture version of *Death of a Salesman* was not successful in large part because of the overly realistic depiction of the settings used for the flashback scenes. He believes that in this way the emphasis was shifted from the psychological conflict in Willy's mind to the physical background. The fragmentary and schematic setting specified by Miller eliminates many illusionistic details. It is entirely in keeping with the dramatic techniques used in the play.

Sound has also been used effectively. Music helps to set the mood and to mark transitions to flashback scenes. Ben has his own special music, played each time he appears; honky-tonk music accompanies Willy's scenes with the Other Woman; music helps to set the locale of the restaurant scene. The method by which Willy commits suicide is made clear only through the offstage sound of a car driving away.

Although audiences have accepted as realistic the fragmentary setting and novel staging conventions and have never been puzzled by them, the realism of *Death of a Salesman* has been modified by cutting away the surface so that the inner reality may be seen more clearly. Miller's methods are representative of the way in which realism is practiced in present-day theatre.

THE CONTINUING TRADITION

Largely because of Miller and Williams, American drama seemed especially vital in the years immediately following World War II. By the late 1950's, however, the vigor had disappeared as the older playwrights ceased to develop and few new writers emerged. Of the later dramatists, Edward Albee (1928–   ) continues to be the most promising. After several short plays in the Absurdist vein, such as *The American Dream* and *The Zoo Story*, Albee turned to studies of tortured family relationships, as in *Who's Afraid of Virginia Woolf?* (1962) and *A Delicate Balance* (1966), or to symbolic, pseudophilosophical exercises, as in *Tiny Alice* (1964). Combining characteristics of Williams' and O'Neill's dramas, Albee's plays demonstrate his considerable gift for characterization, striking situation, and literate dialogue.

The production style which dominated the American theatre from the 1940's until the 1960's was established by Elia Kazan's (1909–   ) and Jo Mielziner's (1901–   ) productions of such plays as *A Streetcar Named Desire* (1947) and *Death of a Salesman* (1949). *A Streetcar Named Desire* also popularized a new style of acting with Marlon Bran-

351

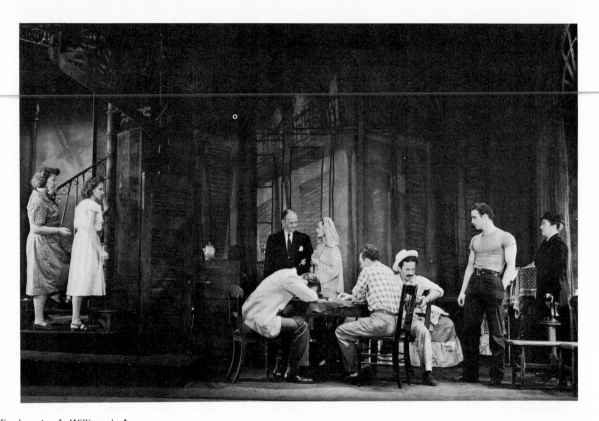

The final act of Williams' *A Streetcar Named Desire.* This production, directed by Elia Kazan, designed by Jo Mielziner, and starring Marlon Brando, did much to establish the dominant postwar style of the American theatre. Courtesy Graphic House, Inc.

do's (1924–   ) characterization of the inarticulate, uneducated, and assertive Stanley Kowalski. The novelty of serious acting based upon substandard speech, untidy dress, and boorish behavior captured the public imagination and soon became associated with the Actors' Studio, at which Brando had worked. In the popular view, the Actors' Studio, established in 1947 by Lee Strasberg, Elia Kazan, and Cheryl Crawford to permit selected actors to work and develop according to the Stanislavsky system, soon came to be a place where actors were encouraged to explore their psyches without regard for skills needed to project a characterization. Although this image is a mistaken one, the major emphasis in training was upon the "inner truth" of characters. The Kazan-Mielziner-Brando style (earthy realism in acting and directing combined with simplified backgrounds) was not seriously challenged until the 1960's, when the turn away from psychological preoccupations made it seem too limited.

The rejuvenation of English drama also owes much to realism. After World War II, the British theatre had settled into a repertory composed primarily of drawing room comedy and poetic drama, both remote from postwar anxieties. Many critics pronounced the English theatre dead. Then, in 1956, George Devine's (1910–65) production of John Osborne's (1929–   ) *Look Back in Anger* signaled a revolution. Osborne's attack upon class distinctions and the complacency of all classes captured the discontent of his generation so well that they came to be called *angry young men.* Although not all new British plays followed the realistic style of *Look Back in Anger*, most breathed a new spirit of protest and a dislike for false values. By the 1960's, British drama had regained its position as one of the most vital in the world.

352

The original production of Osborne's *Look Back in Anger* at the Royal Court Theatre, London, in 1956. Directed by George Devine. Photograph by Houston Rogers.

THE MUSICAL PLAY

The musical play is probably the most popular form of entertainment in today's theatre. The modern musical is a descendant of many minor theatrical forms of the nineteenth century, most notably extravaganza, variety, burlesque, and vaudeville.

The *extravaganza* depended upon music, dance, and lavish scenic display for its appeal; its subject matter was most frequently drawn from myths or fairy tales. It was a favorite form with nineteenth-century audiences. The *variety show*, as the name suggests, was composed of short acts of various types, most of which involved singing, dancing, or comic routines. Although no attempt was made to link the parts through a connected story, the various kinds of entertainment were similar to those of a musical.

Burlesque has had a long and complex history. Originally a parody of some well-known play, literary work, or social custom (for example, Buckingham's *The Rehearsal* (1671) and Sheridan's *The Critic* (1779) parodied the drama and theatrical conventions of their times), in the nineteenth century burlesque was converted into a travesty (or a farcical retelling) of well-known plays, theatrical conventions, or contemporary affairs. It was not until around 1870, however, that modern burlesque emerged. Taking its inspiration from an extravaganza, *The Black Crook* (1866), which became notorious because of its scantily clad dancers, burlesque had soon become a collection of monologues, comedy sketches, songs, and dances featuring a female chorus. The emphasis upon beautiful women and jokes with sexual implications rapidly made it an entertainment for male audiences, but not until about 1929 did the striptease become its main feature. Since that time it has existed on the fringes of legality and in many places has been banned. Nevertheless, it is one of the forerunners of the musical because of its use of chorus numbers, comic acts, music, and dance.

353

Like burlesque, *vaudeville* has had a long and varied history. Originally vaudeville meant a satirical song and later designated a play which contained songs set to well-known tunes. In the nineteenth century, *comédie-en-vaudeville* indicated a comic play interspersed with incidental songs. Vaudeville in the current sense developed in the late nineteenth century when Tony Pastor (1837–1908) altered the newly popular *Black Crook* form of burlesque into entertainment suitable to mixed audiences. Beginning around 1880, he was successful in turning the emphasis away from sex and the off-color joke to a family entertainment with many characteristics of the variety show. The transition had been made successfully by the 1890's. The decline of vaudeville in the 1930's is usually attributed to the rise of the sound motion picture which could furnish the same kind of entertainment at lower admission prices. Vaudeville and burlesque were training grounds for numerous great comedians of the twentieth century: Jack Benny, Jimmy Durante, George Burns, Bert Lahr, and many others.

In the nineteenth century it was also usual to introduce songs and dances into plays, especially melodramas. Furthermore, singing and dancing were used as *entr'actes* in almost every theatre until the late nineteenth century, when the movement toward greater realism and the one-play bill gradually eliminated incidental entertainment in legitimate theatres. It was at this time that many elements from older forms were combined to create musical comedy.

The origin of musical comedy is usually traced to the work of George Edwardes at the Gaiety Theatre in London. In the 1890's, his productions, in which farcical plots provided excuses for songs, dances, and chorus-ensemble numbers, proved so popular that a number of imitations soon appeared. Most of these early musical comedies were set in mythical places where Barons and Counts abounded. The stories, having little to

The original production of Rodgers and Hammerstein's *Oklahoma* in 1943. Setting, Lemuel Ayers; costumes, Miles White; choreography, Agnes de Mille. Photograph — Vandamm Collection, courtesy Library and Museum of the Performing Arts, Lincoln Center.

do with everyday life, emphasized the romantic and exotic appeals of faraway places and unusual happenings.

Around World War I the vogue for ballroom dancing and ragtime music turned attention to more familiar characters and surroundings. The plots remained unimportant, however, and served principally as excuses for spectacular settings, songs, dances, and beautiful chorus girls. In the late 1920's another important change occurred when more concern began to be paid to plot and psychological motivations. The new stature of the musical is indicated by the awarding of a Pulitzer Prize to *Of Thee I Sing* in 1931. The new direction can also be seen in *Lady in the Dark* and *Pal Joey*, psychological studies of characters. The new trend was completed in the 1940's in the works of Oscar Hammerstein II (1895-1960) and Richard Rodgers (1902-   ), especially *Oklahoma*, *Carousel*, and *South Pacific*. Innumerable fine musicals have been written since World War II. They include *Guys and Dolls*, *Pajama Game*, *Damn Yankees*, *West Side Story*, *The Music Man*, *How to Succeed in Business without Really Trying*, *Hello, Dolly*, and *Mame*. One of the most successful writing teams has been Alan Jay Lerner (1918-   ) and Frederick Loewe (1904-   ), with *Paint Your Wagon*, *My Fair Lady*, and *Camelot*. *My Fair Lady*, one of the most popular musicals ever written, will be examined as an example of the modern musical.

MY FAIR LADY

My Fair Lady (1956) is adapted from George Bernard Shaw's *Pygmalion* (1912), "A Romance in Five Acts." It is a retelling in modern terms of the legend of Pygmalion, a sculptor, who falls in love with Galatea, one of his statues. After praying the goddess of love to bring the statue to life, his wish is granted and he marries Galatea.

Shaw uses this legend only as a point of departure, for his principal interest lies in showing that differences in speech undergird the class structure of England. He argues that if everyone were taught to speak English properly the mainstay of the class system would be destroyed. To make his point, he shows how a flower girl can be passed off as a duchess by changing her speech. Other factors (how she dresses and walks, her topics of conversation) are also changed, but Shaw argues that these alterations would be useless unless her speech patterns were changed.

Although Shaw's points are relevant to Europe, where the class structure is more rigid than in America, it is doubtful that the social message has contributed to the play's success. Most audiences have seen in it only the romance which the title indicates — a Cinderella story. To *Pygmalion* Shaw eventually added a postscript in which he denies that Higgins marries Liza (Eliza in *My Fair Lady*). In spite of this denial, however, most audiences have interpreted the play more sentimentally, and Shaw's association of it with the Pygmalion legend invites such a view. *My Fair Lady* changes the story of *Pygmalion* chiefly in making the love story more definite. The ending of the musical seems as much in keeping with the over-all tone of the play as does Shaw's postscript.

PLOT AND STRUCTURE. Although *My Fair Lady* follows Shaw's play closely in basic outline, many structural changes have been made. *Pygmalion* is written in five acts, while *My Fair Lady* divides eighteen scenes into two acts. The musical breaks up the acts into short scenes, dramatizes events only talked about in the play, and condenses Shaw's speeches to allow time for songs and dances.

In actuality, the musical is much closer to the motion picture version of the play than to the original work. For example, while the stage play does not show any of Eliza's voice lessons, both the movie and the musical use a series of short scenes to dramatize her training; likewise, unlike the play, both show the ball at which Eliza triumphs.

Well over half of the eighteen scenes of the musical have no direct counterpart in Shaw's play, although almost all are based upon material in the play. Many of the additions create variety and spectacle. For example, the slums from which Eliza comes are shown and offer opportunities for choral numbers. Some additions emphasize the love story. A new final scene has been added, and the part of Freddy, who falls in love with Eliza, is built up to show Eliza's desirability and to create a threat to Higgins.

Some scenes are also added to create suspense. For example, the break between the two acts follows a scene not shown in Shaw's play. At the ball, Karpathy, an expert on speech, repeatedly questions Eliza's identity and the authenticity of her title. He vows to find out the truth and as the curtain falls he is seen dancing with her. Thus, the act ends on a note of suspense which contrasts markedly with the exultation of the opening scene of Act II.

The division of *My Fair Lady* into two acts also marks a change in the plot. Act I is concerned with the decision to pass off a flower girl as a duchess. This purpose has been accomplished when Act II begins. The last half of the musical shows Eliza's refusal to be used and then abandoned.

Many departures from the original play have been dictated by conventions of the musical. In its original form the play requires almost as much playing time as does the musical. Changes had to be made, therefore, to allow for the addition of music, song, and dance. Since a chorus is an accepted feature of the musical, occasions had to be created for its use. In *Pygmalion* only Act I (outside the Covent Garden Theatre) readily allows for a chorus. In *My Fair Lady*, slum and ballroom scenes are added and a race track is substituted for a drawing room. In Act III of Shaw's play Higgins takes Eliza to his mother's home for tea, at which only seven persons are present. In the musical the same purpose (to allow Eliza a trial appearance in the fashionable world) is served, and most of Shaw's dialogue preserved, but the change in setting to a race track allows more scope for spectacle and the full use of the chorus. This change led to one of the most admired scenes in *My Fair Lady*, the Ascot Gavotte.

Thus, while the differences between *Pygmalion* and *My Fair Lady* are numerous, the musical has maintained the essence of Shaw's play while transforming it to meet the demands of the musical stage.

356

Opening scene of *My Fair Lady,* showing Rex Harrison as Professor Higgins and Julie Andrews as Eliza Doolittle. Courtesy Friedman-Abeles, Inc.

CHARACTERS AND ACTING. The writers of a musical face a dilemma, since excellence in both acting and singing are seldom found in one person. They are frequently forced, therefore, to subordinate one demand to another. In *My Fair Lady* the decision in most cases was made in favor of the actor. Only four of the major characters (Higgins, Eliza, Doolittle, and Freddy) are required to sing alone and only two of these (Eliza and Freddy) need to be trained singers.

The songs written for Higgins and Doolittle lie within so limited a range that almost anyone can sing them. On the other hand, those written for Eliza and Freddy demand considerable vocal ability. Since Freddy's acting is of only secondary importance, only the role of Eliza demands outstanding ability in both acting and singing.

In terms of the action, *My Fair Lady* has only five roles of importance: Higgins, Eliza, Pickering, Doolittle, and Freddy. Of these, Higgins and Eliza are of primary importance, while Pickering, Doolittle, and Freddy are of secondary importance.

Higgins has been made more polished and urbane in the musical than he is in Shaw's play, where he was inclined to be unfashionable in his dress and unconventional in his behavior. The Higgins of the musical is still an individualist, but the rough qualities are gone. Nevertheless, he is still self-confident, selfish and unfeeling where others are concerned.

357

Throughout the musical he is passionately devoted to his work and blind to the needs of others. It is only at the end that Eliza is able to force him to recognize the power of love. His last line indicates, however, that he will not change very much, for instead of rising to embrace her he merely says, "Eliza? Where the devil are my slippers?"

The greatest range in acting ability is required of Eliza. She must be able to give a convincing portrayal of a cockney flower girl and must be able to transform herself gradually until the audience is willing to believe that she might pass as a duchess. Her emotions are varied: outrage, defiance, frustration, dejection, longing, triumph, love, and so on. Eliza's principal motivation is the desire to be loved and respected. This drives her in the beginning to accept Higgins' offer to transform her, and later to leave Higgins because he has merely used her for his own purposes instead of considering her feelings as a human being. Ultimately it is her personal integrity that forces Higgins to see himself more clearly and to recognize his need for Eliza. When he comes to respect and love her, both have reached a new basis for future action.

Although he is onstage during a large part of *My Fair Lady*, Pickering serves principally as a foil for Higgins. It is he who bets with Higgins that he cannot pass Eliza off as a duchess; it is he who treats Eliza as a lady and points up Higgins' indifference to her as a human being. Pickering has as his principal characteristic acting as a gentleman would at all times. While he aids in advancing the plot, the events have no effect upon him personally and he plays little part in the last act.

Doolittle is almost the opposite of Pickering. He is a wastrel, a near-drunkard, and an avoider of responsibility. He represents lower-class morality and attitudes, but eventually falls victim to respectability. His complete lack of conventionality and his frankness have made the character a favorite with audiences.

Freddy serves as another contrast to Higgins, for he sees Eliza almost completely from a sentimental point of view. He offers Eliza love and respect in large part because she has the strength which he lacks. Higgins on the other hand has the strength that Eliza wants in a man, but is lacking in the love and consideration which Freddy offers. It is only when Higgins can make some compromise that the possibility of happiness for Eliza materializes.

The other characters have little effect upon the outcome of the play and serve principally to supply the background of the action. Most are played by members of the singing or dancing choruses. Thus, while *My Fair Lady* has great variety and dramatic strength, it requires only a few outstanding actors. The lesser members of the cast are obviously still of importance, but need not be performers of the first rank.

LANGUAGE AND MUSIC. Shaw has long been recognized as a master of the English language. The speeches in his plays are sharply outlined, clear and graceful. Much of the dialogue in *My Fair Lady* is taken directly from *Pygmalion*; the rest has been written with Shaw's style in mind and successfully blended with the original. Shaw was not afraid to make his characters express themselves clearly and at length. He believed that good speech is an essential part of the theatre, and had little patience with playwrights who make their characters inarticulate mumblers. Shaw's relish for the English language is carried over into *My Fair Lady*. Higgins, especially, is a sophisticated and urbane master of the well-turned phrase.

Nevertheless, much of Shaw's dialogue has been eliminated so that songs and dances may be included. The songs, therefore, must supply much that has been left out. For example, the first three solos (Higgins' "Why Can't the English Learn to Speak?"; Eliza's "Wouldn't It Be Loverly"; and Doolittle's "With a Little Bit of Luck") establish the basic traits of the characters who sing them.

Much time is saved in the musical by capitalizing upon the audience's ready acceptance of forthright statements of feelings and intentions in song, for in a more realistic kind of drama the revelation of motivations must be carefully prepared for. Thus, the song is comparable to the soliloquy or aside in its ability to convey a great deal of information in a brief amount of time. When good use is made of songs, then, the time which they take away from the spoken episodes is more than made up.

Music also makes the condensation of time more acceptable. For example, the lesson scenes in *My Fair Lady* are run together, with the entire sequence building to the song of triumph, "The Rain in Spain," based upon a phrase which has formed the motif of the lessons. Time may also be saved by the effective use of the reprise (the repetition of a song or musical phrase). Such repetitions associate events separated in time and establish connections without the need for lengthy or explicit statement.

Music also establishes moods and builds expectations. Even before the curtain opens the overture has given some idea of the general mood and the melodic qualities of the work to follow. Music also helps to establish the mood of individual scenes and to create audience expectation.

Music further aids in achieving variety. *My Fair Lady* contains musical numbers of widely contrasting types: songs of delight, such as "The Rain in Spain" and "You Did It"; love songs, such as "On the Street Where You Live," "I Could Have Danced All Night," and "I've Grown Accustomed to Her Face"; songs of rage and defiance, such as "Just You Wait," "Show Me," and "Without You"; songs of boisterous enjoyment of life, such as "Little Bit of Luck," and "Get me to the Church on Time"; of longing, such as "Wouldn't It Be Loverly"; descriptive musical numbers, such as the "Ascot Gavotte," and the "Embassy Waltz."

Although effective, the music in *My Fair Lady* is relatively small in amount, for while many musicals include over thirty numbers, *My Fair Lady* has only twenty-one. Its superior effectiveness in underlining, adding to, and supplementing the drama is clearly attested to by the play's great and lasting popularity.

SPECTACLE. The musical almost always offers great scope to designers. The mingling of song and dialogue usually places a production outside

The Ascot Gavotte from the race track scene of *My Fair Lady.* The original production. Courtesy Friedman-Abeles, Inc.

the restrictions of realism and indicates the need for an imaginative use of pictorial elements to match the musical and dramatic qualities of the script.

A listing of the settings needed for Act I of *My Fair Lady* indicates some of the demands made on the set designer: outside the opera house; the tenement section; Higgins' study; the tenement section; Higgins' study; near the race at Ascot; inside a tent at Ascot; outside Higgins' home; Higgins' study; promenade at the Embassy; the ballroom. Not only is a wide variety of places indicated, but the alternation and frequent repetition of some indicates that they must permit quick changes so that the flow of one scene into another will not be impeded. The designer's problem is simplified somewhat by the fact that some sets need accommodate only a few persons, while others are used by the entire cast. Some sets may be small, therefore, while others must occupy the entire stage.

The costumes are also numerous and equally a source of great visual variety and beauty. The time of *My Fair Lady* is 1912, a period noted for elegance. Cecil Beaton, who designed the costumes for the original production, made effective use of the period. Upper-class characters appear in the Ascot race scenes and at the Embassy Ball, while lower-class characters are seen in the flower market and tenement scenes. Not only did Beaton distinguish between the two classes but he also used great imagination in commenting upon the scenes. In the Ascot setting, for example, all characters were costumed in shades of black and white, thereby emphasizing the uniformity of the characters. On the other hand, for the flower market he took his inspiration from the paintings of Renoir, and through subtle gradations of pastel colors made the characters themselves resemble bouquets.

360

Since *My Fair Lady* covers a period of over six months, many costume changes are needed. The transformation of Eliza is indicated in what she wears as well as in how she sounds. Furthermore, the chorus changes its identity often and therefore needs a great variety of costumes: sometimes they represent slum dwellers, at others they are dancers at the Embassy Ball or loungers outside the opera house.

Dance adds to the visual effectiveness of the musical play. Like the music, it too comments upon the action and forwards the plot. It is not used extensively in *My Fair Lady*, but in other musicals it has played an extremely important part. Here, nevertheless, it is a source of considerable charm and visual beauty.

My Fair Lady combines an extremely effective story with interesting and unusual characters, memorable music, and charming and colorful spectacle. It is both a representative and a superior example of the musical today.

MOTION PICTURES AND TELEVISION

Most contemporary popular entertainment is cast in the realistic or musical modes. While both may be used for serious purposes, in recent times realistic and musical plays have been exploited for their mass appeal. With them, producers have sought to attract the same kind of audiences to which motion pictures and television cater.

Motion pictures have grown steadily in popularity since penny arcades began to show miniature films soon after Thomas A. Edison demonstrated his kinetoscope in 1894. Only one person at a time could view a program, however, until George Eastman invented flexible film and Thomas Armat perfected the projector. The first motion picture theatre was opened in McKeesport, Pennsylvania in 1905; by 1909 there were 8000 others. These early theatres seated only about 100 persons and showed only short films.

In 1914 the Strand Theatre in New York, with its 3300 seats, began the trend toward larger houses, and in 1915 D. W. Griffith's *The Birth of a Nation* inaugurated the full-length film. Two other events—the addition of sound to motion pictures in 1927 and the economic depression of 1929 —gave the film such increased appeal that the legitimate theatre rapidly declined.

The weakened theatre was dealt another serious blow after World War II with the introduction of television. In 1948 there were only 48 stations, but by 1958 there were 512 stations and 50 million receivers. Television affected motion pictures almost as much as the theatre, for audiences were now loathe to pay for entertainment of the kind to be seen free in their own living rooms. Thus, television did much to make both film and theatrical producers reconsider the potentialities of their media. As a result, film makers became increasingly conscious of the motion picture as an art form, and theatrical producers sought to revitalize the theatre by offering plays which television, controlled by its advertisers, was reluctant or unable to broadcast. Although most films and theatrical productions are still designed for the mass audience, new techniques and subject matter have been increasingly exploited since about 1950. Perhaps the best known of the new approaches in the theatre is absurdism.

THE THEATRE OF THE ABSURD

The Absurdists assume that the world is entirely neutral, that facts and events do not have meanings, but that it is man who assigns meanings to them. Thus, when we regard an action as immoral, it does not denote that the act is immoral, but only that we have chosen to label it such. The concept of morality itself is said to be a human fabrication without logical foundations.

The Absurdist finds ultimate truth in chaos, formlessness, the welter of contradictions and inanities which make up everyday existence. Truth is the lack of logic, order, and certainty. Since there is no objective truth, each man can only seek a set of values by which he can live, but he must be willing to recognize that his values are as absurd as any others.

The Absurdist movement is a logical extension of the nineteenth-century scientific outlook. The Naturalists argued that the only truths are those that can be apprehended through the five senses and verified by the scientific method. But thus far the only fields that have yielded consistently to scientific treatment are the physical and biological sciences, which are applicable to only a very small part of daily existence. Man's most difficult decisions normally involve moral questions (that is, the rightness or wrongness of possible courses of action) which are not subject to scientific verification. From a strictly naturalistic point of view, therefore, morality lies outside the realm of objective truth.

The Naturalists never stated this view, for in spite of their attempts to restrict truth to scientific fact, for the most part they still believed in objective standards of morality. Nevertheless, the implication of a strictly scientific outlook is that, since it has no objective foundation, morality is based merely upon a set of accepted conventions—on conformity to a code of behavior which is convenient rather than truthful.

The Absurdists choose to see all aspects of human existence in this light, for to them all ideas about man's significance, knowledge, and behavior are equally fictitious and illogical. Man, adrift in a chaotic universe, constructs whatever fictions he can to help him survive.

FORERUNNERS OF THE ABSURDISTS

While absurdism has gained prominence only since 1950, its roots go back to the late nineteenth century. It is now usual to label *Ubu Roi* (1896) by Alfred Jarry the first absurdist drama. While this play, with its inversion of conventional values and its determinedly nonrealistic techniques, certainly anticipates many later works, it had no immediate successors. The first organized movement with an essentially Absurdist outlook was dadaism, launched in 1917 by Tristan Tzara. The name dada (French for "hobbyhorse"), chosen because of its irrelevance, indicates the negative view of men more interested in denying the validity of older views than in affirming a positive position. Much of their work was satirical, illogical, and irrational. They championed automatic writing (that is, setting down thoughts as they came into the mind regardless of connection or relevance), the formless nature of which was said to be a truthful expression of the writer's subconscious mind. Dadaism soon faded, for it seemed more a fad than a serious artistic movement.

362

Jarry's *Ubu Roi* as performed at the Théâtre Antoine, Paris, in 1908. A sketch published in *Le Figaro,* Feb. 16, 1908.

Dadaism gave way to surrealism, which reached the peak of its popularity in the 1920's. Surrealism took its name from Guillaume Apollinaire's *The Breasts of Tiresias* (1917), subtitled a *drame surréaliste.* Purporting to be a plea for the repopulation of France, the play concerns Thérèse, who (after releasing her breasts, balloons, which float away) is transformed into Tiresias, soon the parent of 49,049 children.

For the Surrealists the principal source of truth lies in the subconscious mind, at its freest (that is, least subject to control by the conscious mind) when man is dreaming. Thus, the dreamlike state, in which the subconscious mind reorganizes everyday reality and evades the normal processes of thought and perception, is said to be the road to truth.

In 1924 André Breton, the movement's principal spokesman, defined surrealism as "pure psychic automatism, by which is intended to express, verbally, in writing, or by other means, the real process of thought. Thought's dictation in the absence of all control exercised by the reason and outside all esthetic or moral preoccupations." Truth, then, is to be sought by freeing the mind from rational control and by activating the subconscious mind through a dreamlike state.

Neither dadaism nor surrealism produced a substantial body of drama. Both are important primarily as forerunners of other schools and as influences on other movements. Their relevance to current practices, however, is indicated by the frequent designation of Absurdist drama as surrealistic.

Another important pioneer of absurdism is Luigi Pirandello (1867–1936), one of the major dramatists of the twentieth century. His plays, such as *Right You Are, if You Think You Are* (1918), *Six Characters in Search of an Author* (1921), *Henry IV* (1922), and *As You Desire Me* (1930), rest upon the idea that truth is a matter of one's point of view. Typically, in a play by Pirandello, although all of the principal characters have been involved in the same event or with the same person, each has a quite different version of what has happened and each is convinced that he is right. Pirandello does not settle these arguments, since to him

363

Scene from Pirandello's *Henri IV* as presented at the Theatre de l'Atelier, Paris, in 1951. The kneeling actor is Jean Vilar, one of the major directors of postwar France, as well as a fine actor. Courtesy Agence de Presse Bernand.

there is no objective truth. Out of such ideas Pirandello fashioned powerful plays that achieved worldwide renown. Although his plays do not depart markedly from traditional structural patterns, Pirandello's view of reality is clearly similar to that of the Absurdists.

The most significant forerunner of the Absurdist school, however, is existentialism. Many of the plays now labeled Absurdist were originally called Existentialist, and the beginnings of absurd drama are clearly associated with existential philosophy.

The central problem in existential philosophy is the meaning of "existence." (What does "to exist" mean? What are its implications for action?) Although this problem has concerned philosophers since the beginning of time it attracted many new adherents after World War I and especially during and following World War II. With its concern for moral values in a civilization which has engendered two world wars and produced the atomic and hydrogen bombs, existentialism seemed particularly relevant after 1945.

The best known dramatists of this school are Jean-Paul Sartre (1905–   ) and Albert Camus (1913–1960), although Camus denied allegiance to any particular philosophical position. Sartre, a major spokesman for existentialism, has stated that all of his work is an attempt to draw logical conclusions from a consistent atheism. He argues that there are no universal and absolute moral laws or values, that man

364

The Condemned of Altona by Jean-Paul Sartre. Directed by Herbert Blau; setting by Robin Wagner; 1965-1966 season. Courtesy Repertory Theater of Lincoln Center.

is adrift in a world devoid of purpose. Therefore, each man is free (since he is not bound to a god or to a set of verifiable principles governing behavior) and is responsible only to himself. It is each man's duty to find his own values and to act in accordance with them. This viewpoint, set forth in a number of essays and philosophical treatises, forms the basis for such plays as *The Flies* (1943), *No Exit* (1944), *The Devil and the Good Lord* (1951), and *The Condemned of Altona* (1959).

Camus, the first theorist to use the term *absurd*, states that absurdity arises from the gulf between man's aspirations and the meaningless universe into which he has been thrust. Man's problem, then, is to find his way in a world of chaos. Camus' plays, illustrating this position, include *Cross-Purposes* (1944), *Caligula* (1945), and *The Just Assassins* (1949).

Both Camus and Sartre, however, emphasize the necessity for each man to find a set of values capable of ordering an otherwise chaotic existence. Thus, they see man as determining his own course rather than being at the mercy of heredity and environment. In their plays, both dramatists adhere rather closely to traditional structural patterns.

The Absurdists who succeed Camus and Sartre differ from them in two important respects: the later writers emphasize the absurdity of existence rather than the necessity of bringing order to absurdity; and they embody their chaotic subject matter in equally chaotic dramatic form. It is these later dramatists, especially Beckett, Genet, and Ionesco, who are normally called the Absurdists.

The popularizer of absurdism was Samuel Beckett (1906–   ) with *Waiting for Godot* (1952), now translated into over twenty languages. Beckett, Irish by birth, has never acknowledged his allegiance to any formal school of philosophy and *Waiting for Godot* has as many religious as Absurdist connotations. In it, two tramps improvise diversions while they wait for Godot, who never appears. Although it depicts waiting and hope, it is also a play about the nonfulfillment of hope. Some critics find in it an argument that the hope of salvation gives meaning to life, while others see in it a comment upon the absurdity of hope.

Beckett's work as a whole suggests that it is impossible to be certain about anything, an attitude reflected in his subject matter and dramatic

Beckett's *Waiting for Godot*. Directed by William Reardon.

techniques. Beckett's works are rich in implications about the nature of human existence, but, as with Symbolist drama, the essential mystery which lurks behind the action remains unexplained. Beckett leaves it up to the audience to find its own meaning in the dramatic events. Among Beckett's later plays are *Endgame, Krapp's Last Tape, Happy Days*, and *Back and Forth.*

Jean Genet (1910–   ), whose major dramas are *The Balcony, The Blacks, The Maids*, and *The Screens*, sees existence as an endless series of reflections in mirrors. Each image may for a moment be mistaken for reality, but upon examination it always proves an illusion. Truth (or the beginning of the set of reflections) can never be found. Genet's characters assume roles, but when the disguises are removed the true persons are never discovered, for each appearance is only a new disguise. Genet, who has spent much of his life in prison, suggests that deviation is essential to society, for nothing has meaning without its opposite — law and crime, religion and sin, love and hate. Consequently, deviant behavior is as valuable as accepted virtue. He transforms life into a series of ceremonies and rituals which give order and an air of importance to what would otherwise be nonsensical behavior.

Eugene Ionesco's (1912–   ) first play, *The Bald Soprano*, was produced in Paris in 1950. To indicate his attempt at writing something as unlike conventional drama as possible, Ionesco called it an *antiplay*. In it no action is developed, many of the characters are so alike that they may be interchanged, and the dialogue is made up almost entirely of clichés. The meaninglessness and repetitiousness of the subject matter is paralleled in the dramatic techniques, for the plot does not progress to a climax and the dialogue degenerates until the characters merely repeat the letters of the alphabet.

Ionesco has continued to write in much the same vein. Among the more important of his later plays are *The Chairs, The Lesson, Victims of Duty, The New Tenant, The Killer, Rhinoceros, The King Dies*, and *Hunger and Thirst. The Chairs* will be examined as an example of Ionesco's work and of Absurdist drama.

366

THE CHAIRS

Ionesco labeled *The Chairs* "a tragic farce," and elsewhere has said that the theme of the play is nothingness—reflected in the empty chairs, the empty stage, and the emptiness of the life portrayed. The play also suggests the impossibility of communicating anything about experience to others, for the speech of the deaf-mute orator is as specific about the meaning of life as one can be. The inanities of everyday conversation, the repetitiveness of daily existence, the thwarted hopes and ambitions of mankind are depicted. The play sums up the Absurdist view of the human condition. Ionesco does not offer any solution or plan for change; he is content merely to set forth the situation.

PLOT AND STRUCTURE. The principal thread holding *The Chairs* together is the promise of a revelation about the meaning of life. The delay of the message until the end of the play arouses and maintains expectation and suspense.

The majority of the play, however, is taken up with an exploration of different aspects of human experience, ranging from childhood to old age. The Old Man sits on the Old Woman's lap and becomes a child, while she assumes the role of a mother. Later they talk about their courtship and marriage; events from their past married life are suggested, as when one of the invisible characters tries to seduce the wife and the husband conceives an idealistic attachment to one of the invisible women. The Old Man and Old Woman also illustrate many facets of old

Scene from Ionesco's *The Chairs*. Directed by James Clancy.

age, and death itself comes with their suicides. The play explores a wide range of human emotions and attitudes. The characters laugh uncontrollably, cry, become dreamily forgetful, angry, or outraged; they cajole and fawn, make love, greet visitors, and do obeisance to the emperor; they juxtapose discussions of the significance of existence with the sale of programs. The universal desire to discover the meaning of life is demonstrated through the vast crowd that inundates the couple when the Old Man announces his intention of revealing the secret.

One key to the play's structure is found in the chairs. When the play begins there are only two chairs on stage. Into this setting other, invisible characters begin to appear. Each arrival is matched on stage by an empty chair. The first arrivals are treated at some length and are rather clearly individualized, but after a time the pace quickens as more and more people enter. The later arrivals are identified only by a name or a professional designation and many are not identified at all. Chairs eventually take up so much of the space that the old people must elbow their way about.

In several of Ionesco's plays objects grow and multiply. In this way, he suggests that men are dominated by material objects. This use of objects has led many critics to call Ionesco a Surrealist. The nightmarish quality of *The Chairs* is created in part by the fact that, although the chairs are real, the people remain invisible. Objects, thus, have greater reality than people. Although the multiplication of chairs seems to be pointing toward some goal, the goal is never reached.

It is significant that the Old Man hires someone else to deliver his message about the meaning of life since he cannot articulate it himself—a sign that he does not know what it is he wants to say. Ionesco has specified that the Orator should be costumed as a caricature of the nineteenth-century poet. He undoubtedly meant in this way to satirize the idealistic Romanticist playwright who believed that he understood the meaning of existence.

This expected message never comes. As in *Pelléas and Mélisande*, life remains an enigma, but while Maeterlinck implies that a mysterious force presides over the universe, Ionesco merely derides the notion that life has any significance. Ionesco's ridiculous and pathetic treatment of human attempts to resolve the riddle leads here to a dramatic form corresponding to his view of existence as chaotic and meaningless.

CHARACTERS AND ACTING. The Old Man and the Old Woman in *The Chairs* represent mankind. Ionesco has made them old to emphasize the idea that they have experienced all of life. At the same time, he parodies the custom of asking old people to what do they attribute their long lives and for advice to others.

Equally important, the Old Man and the Old Woman serve as mirrors in which the audience sees everything else. Their reactions create the invisible characters and people the stage. The play is a *tour de force* for two actors, for it demands excellence in pantomime and in the portrayal of a vast range of human emotions and attitudes. While all plays need to

368

be skillfully performed, *The Chairs* is especially dependent upon good acting for its effectiveness.

Ionesco has little interest in consistency of character and does not attempt to explain his characters' reactions. Rather, he shows them responding in typically human ways to a series of commonplace situations. Their typicality is manipulated to point up the uniformity of existence and to comment upon human experience in general.

The actors must shift rapidly from one kind of situation or emotion to another, although in the script no logical explanations are offered for the changes. Again, this points up the essential lack of logic in life. The rapidly shifting moods and situations are held together principally by the play's theme and by the presence of the same actors throughout.

The dialogue of the characters is made up largely of clichés, emphasizing the conformity and repetitiveness of life. It satirizes man's illusion that he is communicating with others when in fact he is only repeating meaningless banalities.

Although Ionesco's ultimate aim is to show the absurdity of existence, he has provided two actors with extremely rewarding roles. The theatricality of the play is only heightened by the demand that the actors give convincingly lifelike portrayals of a wide range of human attitudes.

VISUAL AND AURAL EFFECTS. Ionesco places so much importance upon the staging of *The Chairs* that he has found it advisable to furnish a diagram of the setting. A close study of his floor plan and a careful reading of his stage directions in relation to it is extremely helpful in understanding the spirit of the work. He has indicated a number of doors and one window on each side of the stage. During the play the Old Woman frequently goes out a door on one side and reappears with chairs through another door on the opposite side. Yet in the script the house is said to be surrounded by water and the old people commit suicide by jumping out the windows into the water. The Old Woman, then, would have had to go through the water in order to get to the other side of the stage. The action, thus, contradicts the logic of the setting and Ionesco uses this contradiction deliberately to show his lack of concern for illusionistic stage conventions. By this means he is able to comment upon theatre and at the same time achieve a comic effect. Consequently, his use of the stage, itself absurd, parallels the play's action.

Other visual effects contribute to the play's power. The multiplication of chairs is extremely important. The actors must create the feeling that every inch of stage space has been usurped by the invisible crowd—the invisible must seem visible. This need is emphasized by the final stage directions which specify that, after the old people have committed suicide and the orator has failed to communicate his message, noises of the invisible crowd (laughter, murmurs, coughs) should become audible.

Ionesco has thus been able to achieve a union of content and form. His subject, the absurdity of human existence, is paralleled in dramatic techniques. Although *The Chairs* is in many ways distinctive, it is representative of the outlook and methods of the Absurdists.

369

RELATED DRAMATISTS

Although the Absurdist movement has been centered in France, it has gained many adherents in other countries. In England, the early plays of Harold Pinter (1930–   ), especially *The Room* (1957), *The Dumb Waiter* (1957), and *The Birthday Party* (1958), which Pinter called "comedies of menace," display many Absurdist characteristics. Since 1959, in such works as *The Caretaker* (1960) and *The Homecoming* (1965), Pinter's method has become more direct as his interest has shifted to conflicts among characters and away from mysterious outside forces. Nevertheless, ambiguities remain, and the plays seem nightmarish at times because the motivations behind behavior are unclear. In Poland, Slawomir Mrozek (1930–   ) has emerged as one of Europe's leading dramatists. His *Tango,* an Absurdist fable of modern life, tells of a young man who, after using force to bring order to his family's chaotic existence, is himself destroyed. In Czechoslovakia, Vaclav Havel, in *The Garden Party* (1963) and *The Memorandum* (1965), has employed Absurdist techniques to satirize bureaucracy.

Absurdism has now been accepted in almost every country. Because the plays no longer seem especially strange, Absurdist devices have now been adopted by dramatists who do not share the Absurdists' view of reality. Thus, absurdism is being assimilated into other movements.

Scene from Pinter's *The Homecoming.* The actors are Vivian Merchant and Ian Holm. Photograph by David Sim. Courtesy Royal Shakespeare Company.

Absurdist drama has also popularized new productional approaches, many inspired by Antonin Artaud (1896–1948). Entering the theatre as an actor in 1921. Artaud worked for several well-known directors and managed his own company, the Théâtre Alfred Jarry, before formulating his theories. Supposedly under the stimulus of a Balinese dance troupe which he saw in 1931, Artaud reshaped his view of the theatre. The result was *The Theatre and Its Double*, published in 1938.

Artaud states that men may be divided into two groups, the primitive and the civilized; in the Western world, civilized men have entirely dominated the theatre, with the result that it has become increasingly "a theatre of words" seeking merely to solve a conflict or elucidate a character. Artaud concludes that the "true" theatre, the Eastern (for which the Western is merely a "double"), is based upon prelogical, nonverbal, and incantatory experience. To replace the Western pattern, Artaud envisions a "theatre of cruelty," which will disrupt the spectators' logically controlled equilibrium and free their subconscious minds so that they may glimpse once more the mysterious sources of existence. He wishes to create a theatre of magic and myth which will ruthlessly expose man's inner anxieties so that they may be expelled and allow him to commune more deeply both with himself and his fellow beings.

Artaud argues that reform must begin with the *mise-en-scène*, in which he includes all visual and aural elements. The production itself is to be the work of art, for which the verbal text serves merely as a scenario. By insisting that all theatrical elements play significant roles, Artaud seeks to arrive at *total theatre* rather than an embellished text. Because Artaud is concerned with expanding human consciousness, his theories have become increasingly relevant in recent years.

Although Artaud had little immediate effect upon the theatre, his theories have been applied in varying degrees by many postwar directors, perhaps most notably by Barrault, Blin, and Brook. Jean-Louis Barrault (1910–   ), France's most prestigious actor-director, owes much to Artaud, with whom he worked in the 1930's. Barrault's production of Claudel's *The Satin Slipper* in 1943 is often said to be the first important example of total theatre. Actually, Barrault owes as much to Copeau as to Artaud, for he has declared that the text of a play is like an iceberg, since only about one-eighth is visible; it is the director's task to complete the playwright's text by revealing the hidden portions through an imaginative use of all the theatre's resources. At the Comédie Française, the Théâtre Marigny, and the Théâtre de France, Barrault has produced plays ranging from the classics to Absurdist drama, to all of which he has imparted distinction. Roger Blin (1907–   ), a disciple of Artaud, brought the Absurdist movement to public attention with his staging of Beckett's *Waiting for Godot* in 1953, and has continued to use Artaud's methods in his numerous and increasingly popular Parisian productions. In England and America, Peter Brook's version of Weiss' *Marat/Sade* did much to popularize the concept of total theatre, although many other directors had been utilizing its techniques for several years.

The Living Theatre's production, *Mysteries and Smaller Pieces.* This troupe has experimented persistently with theatrical forms and audience-performer relationships. Photograph © 1968 by Fred W. McDarrah.

Scene from LeRoi Jones' *Home on the Range,* as performed by the Spirit House Movers. The growth in awareness and pride of black Americans has led to greatly increased theatrical activity among black playwrights, actors, and producing groups. Photograph © 1968 by Fred W. McDarrah.

Scene from Duerrenmatt's *The Visit.*

Like most concepts, the original meaning of total theatre has now been obscured, for today almost any effective use of the theatrical medium is apt to be labeled total theatre. Nevertheless, Artaud's intention that every theatrical element be explored for its expressive power and that all should be combined so as to disrupt the audience's habitual complacency continues to be one of the most pervasive influences on the contemporary theatre. To it may be attributed the experiments with nudity, profanity, and other "shock" techniques which have become so numerous in recent productions.

POSTWAR BRECHTIAN DRAMA

Unlike the Absurdists, who have for the most part portrayed the anxieties of individuals, another school of postwar dramatists has emphasized the social and political implications of moral dilemmas. For most of these dramatists Brecht has been a major inspiration.

Although all of Brecht's principal works had been written by 1945, many had not yet been produced. Thus, after the war his plays and theories found a wide audience for the first time. His fame was confirmed by the Berliner Ensemble, Brecht's own company, formed in 1949 and since the mid-1950's recognized as one of the world's finest troupes.

Because new German dramatists were slow to appear, until about 1960 the major postwar German-language playwrights were the Swiss authors, Max Frisch (1911–   ) and Friedrich Duerrenmatt (1921–   ). Frisch's reputation rests primarily upon *The Chinese Wall* (1946) *Biedermann and the Firebugs* (1958), and *Andorra* (1961), all posing questions of guilt. In each, as the past is reviewed the characters construct elaborate rationalizations to justify their cowardly actions. Durerrenmatt's fame is based primarily upon *The Visit* (1956) and *The Physicists* (1962). Like Frisch, Duerrenmatt is concerned with moral responsibility. He has stated that plays should frighten audiences and make them face up to the grotesque world in which they live. Such an experience he hopes will make men attempt to find some order, although he seems to have little faith in the possibilities of positive action, for he has said, "The universal for me is chaos." The most that men can hope for, therefore, is the courage to endure.

In the late 1950's, promising new German dramatists began to appear. Of these, Weiss and Kippardt are perhaps the best. Peter Weiss (1916–   ) achieved world fame with *The Persecution and Assassination of Jean-Paul Marat as Performed by the Inmates of the Asylum of Charenton under the Direction of the Marquis de Sade* (1959), which contrasts de Sade's anarchistic views with Marat's dream of a superior world order. Weiss has stated that the traditional theatre is outmoded and must be replaced either by the documentary or by happenings. That he has chosen the documentary is illustrated by his later works, *The Investigation* (1965), put together from testimony given during the official inquiry into the Auschwitz extermination camp; *The Song of the Lusitanian Bogey* (1967), about Portuguese colonialism in Angola, and *Discourse on the Previous History and the Course of the Long Continuing*

373

Scene from Weiss' *Marat/Sade* as performed by the Royal Shakespeare Company. Directed by Peter Brook; Ian Richardson as Marat; Patrick Magee as de Sade. Photograph by Morris Newcombe. Courtesy Royal Shakespeare Company.

War of Liberation in Viet Nam as an Example of the Necessity of an Armed Struggle which Crushes its Suppressors Despite the Attempt of the United States of America to Destroy the Foundations of the Revolution (1968).

Heinar Kippardt (1922–   ) has also turned to the documentary with *The Oppenheimer Case* (1964), the dialogue of which is taken from the U. S. Senate's investigations into the loyalty of J. Robert Oppenheimer, and *Joel Brand* (1965), about the middleman who sought to convince the Allied powers that Adolf Eichmann was serious in his offer to exchange one million Hungarian Jews for 10,000 trucks.

Because the majority of significant postwar German drama has dealt with questions of guilt in relation to larger political and social issues, it differs considerably in tone from the French Absurdist drama. It has gained steadily in prestige during the 1960's as interest in public morality has grown.

Brecht's theories of staging have also been widely adopted, both in Germany and elsewhere. In England, Joan Littlewood, director of the Theatre Workshop, has advocated Brechtian techniques to make the theatre a place where spectators can feel as much at home as in a "fun palace." Her productions combine didacticism with earthy entertainment to create a style probably best exemplified in *Oh, What a Lovely War* (1963), which used the musical revue as a vehicle for a biting satire on World War I. In France, Roger Planchon (1931–   ) has popularized Brechtian techniques with his productions at the Théâtre de la Cité (located in a working-class suburb of Lyon), in Paris, and at the Avignon Festival.

The postwar era has seen many attempts to alter traditional patterns (such as the repertory calculated not to offend, the restriction of theatre to a few cities, the rigid spatial arrangements, the atmosphere of middle-class respectability, the intimidating routine of checkrooms, ushers, and so on) blamed by some critics for alienating numerous potential theatre-goers.

In New York, the desire to enlarge the repertory gave rise around 1950 to the off-Broadway movement. Believing that financial conditions forced Broadway producers to cater almost exclusively to mass audiences, the new groups sought out-of-the-way buildings where rent was sufficiently low that they might offer short runs of plays of limited appeal. Off-Broadway, and its younger, more experimental descendant, off-off-Broadway, now offer a repertory ranging through domestic and foreign classics to new works, and through styles ranging from starkest realism to improvised, free-associational fantasy. Among the off-Broadway and off-off-Broadway groups, the best have been the Circle-in-the-Square, the Living Theatre, and the LaMama Experimental Theatre Club.

There have also been many attempts to decentralize the theatre by establishing permanent companies outside the few large cities to which the theatre was restricted at the end of World War II. In the United States, there are now about thirty-five resident companies outside of New York. In France, the government has established Centres Dramatiques in a number of cities outside of Paris, and in England, many local authorities outside of London are now subsidizing resident troupes.

Scene from *Birdbath* as presented by the LaMama Experimental Theatre Club. Photograph by James D. Gossage.

Shakespeare's *Taming of the Shrew* as produced at the Arena Stage, Washington. Photograph by George de Vincent. Courtesy Arena Stage.

This expansion has been accompanied by experimentation with audience-performer spatial relationships. Many off-Broadway groups were forced to work in buildings without stages or traditional seating. As a result, plays came to be staged in-the-round, on open platforms, and in a variety of other arrangements. Furthermore, as illusionism declined after World War II, many new theatres were built with open stages thrusting into the auditorium and surrounded by seating on at least three sides. Good examples of the new architecture are to be seen at the Tyrone Guthrie Theatre in Minneapolis and the Vivian Beaumont Theatre in New York.

Some groups have concluded that any theatre building carries with it too many associations with outmoded middle-class attitudes about the theatre. Consequently, they have sought to arouse interest in the theatre by playing in streets, parks, subways, cabarets, and other places where unsophisticated audiences may be found. In this way, they hope to bring the theatre to persons who otherwise would remain untouched by it and to rejuvenate the theatre by creating new audiences. This approach is sometimes called *environmental theatre*.

Probably the most extreme rebellion against the theatre as an institution came with *happenings*, which took their name from Allan Kaprow's *Eighteen Happenings in Six Parts* (1959). Although advocates of happenings have not always agreed upon the basic ingredients, some of the original premises were: (1) the creator consumes his product rather than making art objects for others; (2) all those present participate, thus eliminating any distinction between performers and spectators; (3) since only a restricted number can participate, a happening cannot become a mass-oriented art; (4) a true happening can occur only once, since the activity rather than the completed work is the end.

The happening is essentially a nonverbal art. There are no rehearsals (although there may be lengthy preparations or detailed plans of action), no professional performers, and no auditorium or stage in the usual sense. Essentially, the happening aims to break down the barriers between art and life.

376

The lively experimentation in the off-off-Broadway theatre is demonstrated here in *Dionysus in 69,* a production of Performance Group. Photograph by Fred McDarrah.

As with most experiments, happenings have lost much of their original identity. The name is now applied to almost any kind of experience in which improvisation and chance are encouraged. The fusion of spectator and performer is no longer always followed. Nevertheless, happenings are significant because of their concerted attempt to break down almost all of the traditional ideas of a theatre — the distinctions between audience and performer, between stage and auditorium, between the process of play production and the completed work.

In recent years several attempts have been made to enlarge the expressive powers of the theatre through the combination of media. Perhaps the best known experiments are those of the Czech designer, Josef Svoboda (1920-   ), who has sought to combine projected film, stereophonic sound, music, and live actors. Svoboda maintains a studio (comparable to a research organization with its permanent staff of architects and electronic engineers) to explore the potentialities of new devices.

In a multimedia production, close-ups, fragments of scenes, or panoramic views may be projected simultaneously on screens to provide a background; or cameras may pick up and project portions of the onstage action so as to show several dimensions of a single event. Directional sound can be used to make the audience feel that it is in the midst of the action. Although multimedia productions are still in the experimental phase, their potentialities are considerable.

377

THE CURRENT SITUATION

The theatre of today is so diverse that only a few of its aspects have been considered here. In the complexities and seeming contradictions, however, may be read many signs of things to come. Old taboos have been broken, illusionism has been routed and experimentation encouraged. Although the divisions in the world are still too numerous to warrant a prediction that a common style will soon emerge, many of the postwar experiments growing out of absurdism, Brechtian drama, and happenings now seem to be moving toward a synthesis.

Regardless of what the future holds, it is safe to predict that the theatre of our day will give way to new movements reflecting man's changing conceptions of himself and his world. The passing of the old conventions should cause no concern, however, for it is by responding to the needs of its time that the theatre forever renews itself.

IV

THE THEATRE ARTS
IN AMERICA TODAY

Robert Joffrey's *Astarte* was the first multimedia production by a major American ballet group. Maximiliano Zomosa and Trinette Singleton of the New York City Center Joffrey Ballet Company. Photograph—Herbert Migdoll.

Chapter 16 THE PLAYWRIGHT AND THE PRODUCER

Since the script is normally the starting point for any theatrical production, the work of the playwright is of primary importance in any consideration of the contemporary theatre. The playwright's means have already been discussed in Chapter 3, but more needs to be said about his working methods.

THE PLAYWRIGHT'S WORKING METHODS

There are many ways to write a play. Sometimes a writer starts with an idea. For example, he may be struck by the difference between professed ideals and actual behavior. He may then work out an action, either comic or serious, illustrating his perceptions.

Another writer may start with a character. His interest in an unusual, amusing, or abnormal person may lead him to speculate about the potentialities for conflict in human peculiarities. Still other playwrights may be stimulated by stories. A newspaper article, a personal experience, or an anecdote may set the dramatist to thinking about the significance of events, or the possibilities of comedy or tragedy in a particular situation.

Regardless of the original impetus, the effective playwright is seldom content merely to set forth an idea, to outline characters, or to tell a story. In most cases he does all of these things simultaneously, for it is difficult to reveal characters except through an action that tells a story. Similarly, incidents and characterization inevitably create implications, profound or trivial, and suggest ideas. The initial interest which gave rise to the play is not always evident in the finished work, and writers themselves do not always remember how they first became interested in writing a particular play. Since the possibilities for drama are ever present, any event may stimulate the dramatist to write a play.

Scene from Jean-Claude van Itallie's *Motel*, a segment of *America, Hurrah!* as presented by the Open Theatre, New York. Photograph © 1968 by Fred W. McDarrah.

382

Just as plays stem from various impulses, so, too, methods of writing vary. Some dramatists prefer to work from a scenario. This involves making an outline of the story prior to writing the dialogue and then elaborating on this plan. There are many variations on this procedure. Some writers prefer a brief sketch which merely indicates the major developments, while others prefer a detailed outline which includes all details of plot and characterization so that writing merely involves the invention of dialogue. The use of a scenario, however, requires the playwright to have in mind what he wishes to do before he begins writing. While most playwrights do know their goals, some do not.

Many writers find a scenario too inhibiting, since it seems to direct thought along a rigid channel. They frequently find that their interests shift as they go along. A minor character may take on such stature that the playwright decides to shift the focus to him. In such a case the entire scenario will probably need to be reworked. Therefore, the scenario must remain flexible until the play is finished.

Another procedure which has worked well for many dramatists is to write the scene of crisis first and then to work out those scenes which precede and follow it. The justification offered for this method is that, since the crisis is the scene toward which the entire action builds, all the rest must be constructed to make it convincing and effective. Having written this scene, then, the dramatist can more clearly see what must precede and what must follow it. Again, however, as the play takes shape the dramatist may change his mind about his over-all purpose; if a different crisis is needed, the whole process will have to be repeated.

Other writers prefer to make a large number of notes about characters, situations, and ideas. These notes may be read over and over until the play gradually evolves from random jottings. The actual writing may not start until the whole play has taken shape in the author's mind.

A favorite method, especially with beginners, is to "think on paper." That is, the writer begins composing with only a vague idea of how he wishes the play to conclude, and lets the characters and situations develop as he goes along. This is one way of thinking through situations, but it is apt to be a lengthy process, since it may necessitate a great number of attempts and may never result in an organized story.

In recent years, some plays have been written with the aid of group improvizations. Supposedly van Itallie's *America, Hurrah!*, Terry's *Viet Rock*, and the Living Theatre's *Frankenstein* took shape over a period of time as a group of actors tried out and perfected ideas and devices. Since few have acting troupes at their disposal, however, most playwrights find this method to be outside the range of possibilities open to them.

No doubt there are many other ways in which playwrights work. The central purpose of all, however, is to organize and reduce to an effective form the many elements which go into a play. It is possible that every dramatist must "feel his way" toward the final product: he may not be entirely clear himself what it is he is trying to capture until he does it. This may be true even of those who start with a clear-cut scenario, since a play is a great deal more than the bare outline of its plot.

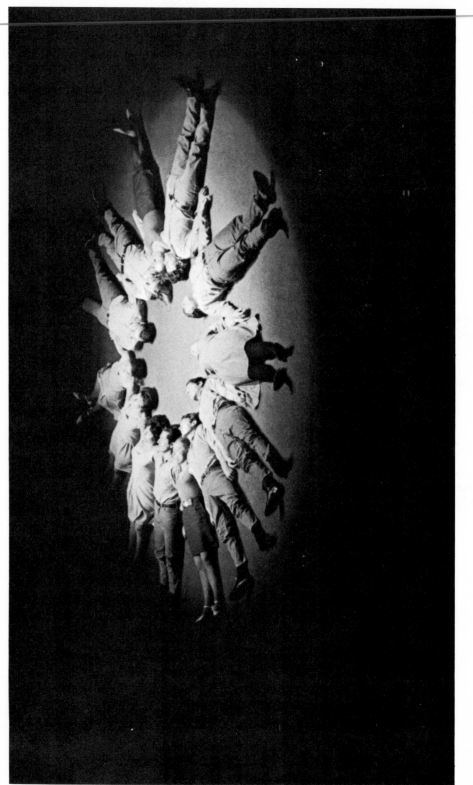

Megan Terry's *Viet Rock* as
presented at Yale University
in 1966. Courtesy Yale University School of Drama.

Seldom does a playwright arrive at the final version of his play in the first draft. Most finished works represent many revisions, sometimes made over a period of years. Furthermore, since plays are intended for the stage, most writers need to see their works in performance before they can be sure that no further revisions are needed.

Although there is a constant demand for good scripts, a playwright seldom finds it easy to get his work performed. The goal of most playwrights is professional production, which has become increasingly difficult to achieve because of the great financial risks involved.

If the dramatist wishes a Broadway production, a producer must be found. Negotiations with potential producers have become so complex that most writers work through agents, who understand the market and who can devote a great deal of time to selling a play.

If a producer is interested in a work, he may take an option on it. This means that a sum of money is paid to the playwright for the possibility of performing the play and to prevent others from doing so. A time limit is specified; if the play is not produced during that period or if the option is not renewed, all rights revert to the playwright, who is then free to negotiate with other producers. An option is never a guarantee of production, for the same play may be optioned many times without ever being presented.

Usually, before his play is produced on Broadway an American playwright becomes a member of the Dramatists Guild of the Authors League of America. Anyone who has had a play optioned for professional production may join the Dramatists Guild. The purpose of the Guild is to protect the author and to secure for him the best possible contract.

If a producer decides to present a play, the dramatist is given a contract specifying the amount of his royalties and the limit of the producer's control over the play (most of the provisions in a contract are specified in a standard form used by the Dramatists Guild). The playwright seldom relinquishes television, motion-picture, or foreign rights to the producer. The playwright's contract usually specifies that he must be available for consultation and to make revisions throughout the rehearsal period. His duties are over only when the play opens in New York. His contract also states that his is the final decision on any proposed changes in the script. Legally, he does not have to make any revisions in his work after the contract is signed.

On the other hand, the playwright is constantly under pressure to make changes. Even before a producer sees a play, a dramatist's agent may suggest a number of alterations. A producer may express an interest in a script if certain revisions are made. The financial backers (*angels*) may suggest certain alterations. Frequently a well-known actor will agree to appear in a play if it is rewritten to show off his abilities to greater advantage. Rehearsals may show up real or imagined weaknesses in the script, and rewriting may continue until opening night in New York.

It has been customary to have a series of out-of-town (that is, out of New York) tryouts. This means that plays are opened in such cities as

Philadelphia, New Haven, Washington and given a short road tour. Critical notices and the responses of audiences are carefully studied, and after each performance the play is reworked in accordance with these reactions. The process is continued until the production is considered ready for New York. Sometimes a play is almost completely rewritten during this time. In recent years, some producers have replaced the out-of-town tryout with a number of preview performances in New York. The purpose remains the same—to use audience response as a basis for revision before the formal opening.

Such a procedure dismays many, who feel that the playwright is reduced to the status of a hack writer; that is, that he is forced to rewrite for the sole purpose of achieving popularity and financial success. Whether this is true or not, it is certain that the playwright is subjected to pressures from many sources. If anyone knew what makes a successful play, there would not be so many failures in the New York theatre. Yet the playwright is bombarded with advice and demands from many sources—all of which claim to have the answer which will turn the playwright's work into a successful venture. Consequently, his ability to assess the validity of each suggestion is of prime importance.

The penalties for failure (both financial and artistic) are so great that everyone strives to avoid them at any cost. Regardless of the source of the failure in a New York production, the blame is almost always placed on the playwright.

This pressure on the dramatist is more pronounced in the United States than in any other country. Since the costs of production are not nearly so high elsewhere, the pressure to achieve commercial success is not so great. Where theatres are subsidized, a failure is absorbed. Repertory companies do not expect to survive or fail upon the basis of one production but select a series of plays which complement each other; losses on unpopular works are then offset by the income from more successful pieces. On Broadway, a playwright is always under extreme pressure to succeed. One failure, even after a series of successes, raises doubts about a dramatist's future and makes producers somewhat wary of his plays.

In spite of all these factors, most playwrights refuse to let any nonprofessional group present their works so long as there is any hope for professional production. Most of the original plays produced by nonprofessional companies are written by students, local residents, or the winners of playwriting contests. While these may be good plays, as a rule experienced authors do not even enter contests unless they have been unable to interest an agent in their work.

This situation is in many ways unfortunate. A dramatist needs to see his plays performed if he is to progress. Frequently the nonprofessional theatre offers more freedom for experimentation than the professional, and certainly the pressures are fewer. Playwrights seem to feel, however, that any incompetence in production will make their work appear so bad that all chances for commercial production will be ruined. It is certain, however, that many nonprofessional organizations in America

The Living Theatre's free interpretation by directors Julian Beck and Judith Malina of Mary Wollstonecraft Shelley's *Franken-stein*. Photograph © 1968 by Fred W. McDarrah.

could produce original plays effectively and could offer the playwright an opportunity to see his work on the stage. This is only one area in which the professional and nonprofessional theatre have failed to achieve a mutually rewarding relationship.

THE PRODUCER

The ultimate fate of a play depends much upon the producer, who is concerned primarily with its financing and sale. It is the producer who options the play and secures a director, theatre, and the necessary financial backing; it is he who publicizes the production, sells tickets, and makes other arrangements of this kind. While he is not directly responsible for the artistic aspects of a performance, he exerts considerable influence on all theatre workers. The producer, therefore, is one of the most important persons in the theatre.

The producer's methods vary according to the type of organization—professional, repertory, summer stock, community, or educational theatre. The responsibilities are most clearly defined in the professional theatre.

The producer of a play in New York may be a group, such as the Theatre Guild, or an individual, such as David Merrick. If a producer has been in business for some time, he may maintain a permanent office and staff, but many producers are concerned with only one show at a time and many maintain no office except when they have a play in production. In most cases, a special corporation or partnership is formed for each play to protect the investors in the production. In this way, no investor is responsible for debts beyond a specified amount.

Before money can be raised, the producer must have a play under option. The majority of plays performed in New York are new plays or foreign plays not previously seen in America. New plays are normally secured by the producer through a playwright's agent, although some will read scripts which have been submitted directly by the author. If he is sufficiently interested in a script, the producer takes an option on it. With a play in hand, he then seeks to raise money for its production. The cost of producing a play on Broadway has become exceedingly high; even a simple show requires about $100,000 to meet all expenses up to the opening performance, and a musical may run to $500,000. Since few individuals could afford to invest so much money in such a risky venture, it is usual for a producer to solicit funds from individuals or groups. One of the producer's first jobs, then, is to interest others in the script and to convince them that the play will be a worthwhile investment.

If the author is well known, or if the producer has a reputation for wise choices, or if actors of enough box office appeal are secured, raising money may not be difficult. But it is frequently necessary to send out brochures, along with copies or summaries of the play, to prospective investors. Sometimes readings are arranged. The producer must submit to prospective investors a proposed budget for the play up to its Broadway opening and a statement as to how profits are to be divided. (The producer usually receives from one-third to one-half of the net profit, regardless of how large or small an amount of money he has invested personally.)

388

After the money has been raised, the producer may then proceed with the actual business of preparing the play for performance. He usually needs a considerable number of secretarial, financial, and legal assistants, since the details of production may become extremely complex. He must negotiate contracts with all of the persons involved in the production: the director, the actors, the designers, the stage manager, and so on. He must rent space for tryouts and rehearsals and must lease a theatre for performances (which is not always easy since the number of New York theatres is relatively small). The producer arranges for out-of-town tryouts (including theatres, transportation, and publicity). He must keep financial records, which are submitted to all investors at regular intervals. He handles the payroll and closes down the show at the end of its run.

The producer must give his approval to all changes in plans made after the contracts are let. He may participate in conferences about alterations in the script, settings, costumes, lighting, music, and dance – any factor which affects the show as a financial investment.

The producer's job is made difficult in part by the fact that he may have to deal with at least eleven different unions representing the following groups: playwrights (though some deny that the Dramatists Guild is a union); directors and choreographers; actors; musicians; stagehands; wardrobe attendants; press agents and managers; treasurers; ushers and doormen; porters and cleaners; and engineers. Each has its own minimum demands which the producer must meet.

The League of New York Theatres, the producers' organization, requires that each production have a company manager and a theatrical press agent (who must belong to the Association of Theatrical Press Agents and Managers). The company manager works with the producer in carrying out the provisions of the budget. He aids in letting the contracts and is usually in charge of the payroll; he makes arrangements for rehearsal space, a theatre, the out-of-town tryouts, and similar matters.

The press agent is concerned principally with selling the show. He is responsible for all news releases (though these must be approved by the producer) and advertisements; he makes sure that pictures of actors and of scenes from the play are available to the press; he works with the newspapers in those towns in which the show is tried out. He must decide upon the most strategic time for the major drive to sell tickets. He arranges for the playbills which are given to all customers and any souvenir programs which are to be sold. He must know the order of billing for the stars and must see that everyone is given proper credit. After the show opens, he chooses the quotations from the reviews which appear in the ads and does all that he can to keep the public interested in the play.

The producer's work, then, is largely concerned with the financial aspects of play production. It has become fashionable in recent years to blame the producer for the state of the American theatre and to argue that he has turned it into a business venture. Given the handicaps under which he works, however, it is remarkable that anyone attempts to stage a play in New York, and it is certain that a sound business sense is required to keep the theatre alive under the present conditions.

389

In resident companies, summer stock, community and educational theatres, the position of the producer is not so clearly defined, although his responsibilities must be assumed by someone. Such groups normally perform a number of plays each year rather than being organized to produce only one play. Many of the problems, therefore, are simplified. For example, a group may use the same theatre for several years and will not need to rent one for each play. The producer's work is also frequently divided among several members of the permanent group.

Most of the resident companies and summer stock groups use variations on the procedure outlined above. Although they too must raise money from investors, as a rule the sum is less than that needed to produce a play on Broadway and the investment is made in the organization rather than in a specific play. The financial pressures on resident and summer groups are not usually so great since most are not subject to the demands of so many unions as are New York producers. Since they also tend to produce plays already proven elsewhere, resident companies avoid some risks, and they may use the previous success of plays advantageously in publicity.

Similarly in community and educational theatres, the group is the producer and the duties may be divided among many persons. As a rule, a community theatre hires only a director (and sometimes a designer-technician). All other work is done by volunteers under the supervision of the director or of unpaid, elected members of the group (such as the board of directors, the president, or a committee).

In the educational theatre, the responsibilities are divided in still other ways. Frequently the director of a play must take primary responsibility for choosing the play, working out a budget, and arranging for publicity. Since his salary is usually paid by the school and since most of the other work is done by students or by faculty members, the expenses are confined to such items as royalties, publicity, programs, and the materials for building costumes and scenery. Furthermore, the use of the theatre building does not normally cost the group anything.

Most permanent organizations present from three to twelve plays each year. In planning a season, a group may consider: (1) the need for variety in the type of plays to be presented; (2) the available actors; (3) the requirements of each play in terms of scenery, costumes, and lighting; (4) the total cost; and (5) the taste of local audiences. The amount of weight given to each of these factors varies from group to group.

The majority of plays done by resident and nonprofessional groups fall into two categories: (1) plays recently produced in New York, and (2) the classics, or plays from the past thought to be still meaningful. Relatively few original plays are done by these groups, although educational theatres are more apt to present original plays than are community theatres.

If a nonprofessional group produces an original script, the arrangements are usually made directly with the author or his agent. The amateur-production rights to previously produced plays are handled by agencies (such as Samuel French and Dramatists Play Service), which collect a royalty fee for each performance of the play. Older plays may not require a royalty payment if the copyright has expired. Translations and adaptations of older plays may be copyrighted by persons other than the author, however, and a producing group should determine the copyright status of each script before presenting it.

THE AGENT

Many theatre workers—playwrights, director, designers, choreographers, musicians, dancers—have agents. The agent's function is to sell his client's services to the producer. An actor (and to a lesser extent other theatre workers) may have difficulty in securing a tryout or an interview if he does not have an agent who is known to the producer.

An agent may work alone or he may be employed by an organization. There are a few large organizations which represent hundreds of persons in various branches of the theatre. Most agencies, however, are small and maintain close contact with their clients.

An agent is usually unwilling to accept a client unless he has seen his work. Since the agent's own earnings depend upon the talents of his clients and upon the reliability of his recommendations, he does not wish to represent anyone who does not have the talent to fill a job satisfactorily. For his services he is paid a percentage of his clients' earnings on each contract negotiated.

Like other careers in the theatre, the agent's has come under progressively stricter regulations as more attempts have been made to protect theatre workers from unethical practices. Today an agent must normally be approved by the client's union (in other words, an actor's agent must be approved by Actors' Equity, and so on). In the complex world of the professional theatre, a good agent is well worth his fee and frequently makes the difference between employment and unemployment.

The playwright, producer, and agent have usually done much of their work before the actual process of play production begins. It is upon this foundation that other theatre workers build when they translate the written script into a staged performance.

Chapter 17 THE DIRECTOR

Just as the producer is the person most concerned with the financial aspects of play production, the director is the one most responsible for the artistic elements. He must decide how the script is to be interpreted, and he must coordinate the efforts of all the other theatre artists into a unified performance. An effective director, therefore, is of primary importance in the success of any play.

There are two basic conceptions of the director. One sees him as an interpretive artist whose purpose is to serve the playwright by translating the script as faithfully as possible into theatrical form. The other views him as a creative artist who uses all the elements of the theatre, of which the script is merely one, to fashion his own art work. Exponents of the latter view argue that the director may alter a play in any way he sees fit, just as he is free to shape scenery, costume, lighting, and sound to suit his goals. For them, the director is the master artist, to whom all others are merely contributory. Although this second view is the less common one, it has had many powerful supporters—among them Craig, Meyerhold, and Artaud—and has gained new adherents in recent years. In such an approach to directing, much of the material covered in Chapters 16 through 22 would be applicable. It is more usual, however, to view the director as one of several interpretive artists. It is from this standpoint that he is treated here, for it would be almost impossible to outline the working methods of a director of the second type.

Although the director's exact duties may vary from one organization to another, ordinarily he performs these functions: (1) he decides upon the interpretation to be given the play, (2) he casts the actors, (3) he works with the playwright, designers, and technicians in planning the production, (4) he rehearses the actors, and (5) he coordinates all of the elements into the finished stage performance.

The length of time available to a director for the study and analysis of a script varies greatly. Each spring most educational theatres select their bills of plays for the following school year. A director then may have several months in which to prepare. On the other hand, many organizations choose plays one at a time, and in the professional theatre a director may be hired at the last moment. In these cases the director has little time in which to study the script. Regardless of the time available, the director must familiarize himself as thoroughly as he can with the play if he is to cast and rehearse the actors intelligently, and if he is to assist the designers and technicians in their interpretation of the script.

The kind of analysis undertaken varies from director to director and with the complexity of the play. The principal elements of play structure, characterization, thought, language, and spectacle have already been outlined in Chapter 3, and will be reviewed only briefly here.

The director should thoroughly understand the play's structure. He may begin by examining the over-all pattern of preparation, complication, crisis, and resolution. As he progresses to more detailed study, he may wish to divide the play into short scenes, determined by the entrance or exit of characters (since each entrance or exit usually alters character relationships). Each short scene may then be examined in terms of its major functions. What are the motivations of the characters in the scene? What is the predominant mood? How is the scene related to those that precede and follow it? What is its significance in the play as a whole?

Answers to these and similar questions will help the director to understand the play and to see why it is constructed as it is. He will become aware of both the strengths and weaknesses of the script and of the problems he must solve.

The director must also understand each character, both in terms of its function in the play and the demands made upon the actor who will play the part. He must be aware of the physical characteristics, dominant qualities (such as wistfulness, strength, or cunning), emotional range, and the vocal qualifications needed for each character so that he can cast and rehearse the play intelligently.

The director must analyze a script in terms of the scenic, costume, and lighting requirements. He must try to envision the stage setting in terms of its mood and atmosphere, its arrangement for the proper flow of action, and as an appropriate environment for the characters and events. He must be able to talk intelligently and persuasively with the designers and technicians about any factors that influence design.

In addition to analyzing the script, the director may need to acquire considerable information about the author, the period of the play (if it is not modern), and the environment depicted (if it is one unfamiliar to the director); he may wish to read what critics have said about the play, about other productions, and about the response of audiences to the play. Each of these inquiries should help the director to understand the play more fully so that he may decide what approach he wishes to take in his production.

Adaptation of the stage conventions of a past period are seen here in *Noah*, a medieval cycle play, as performed at the Mermaid Theatre, London.

The problems of interpretation vary with the kind of play. The director may encounter special problems when he undertakes a play from the past, for he must ensure that it will be comprehensible and moving to a present-day audience. He may decide that the script would benefit from alterations. He may substitute current words and phrases for those that have become obsolete. He may omit subplots, cut speeches, rearrange or combine scenes. He may decide that a play can be made more meaningful by transposing the time and place. As examples, *Hamlet* has been done in modern dress and *Much Ado About Nothing* has been set in the southwestern part of the United States. A director may alter emphases in a play to give a new interpretation to a character. For example, the comic aspects of Shylock in *The Merchant of Venice*, usual in productions until the eighteenth century, have often been subordinated to the role's sympathetic qualities in recent times. *Hamlet* has been played as a man of action and as one too paralyzed to act.

A production of *Hamlet* in which the world was conceived as a prison from which Hamlet is seeking to escape. Each cell-like compartment could be used in isolation or in combination with other units. Presented at the Mayakovsky Theatre, Moscow, in 1954.

A director may also seek to make a play more comprehensible by building his interpretation around a central visual image or symbolic device. For example, a production of *Hamlet* has been built around an image of the world as a prison. The setting was divided into a series of compartments, each resembling a cell, in which the action transpired.

The style and period of a play can sometimes be made more understandable to a modern audience through the adaptation of the staging methods—the acting techniques, the costumes and scenery, and the stage—in use at the time when the play was written. For example, the stage of the Elizabethan public theatre is often adapted for Shakespearean productions.

The director may encounter even greater difficulties with certain kinds of new plays than with classics, for much of contemporary drama is so novel in outlook and technique that it puzzles or repels audiences. Although spectators, having been faced with radical experiments since the 1950's, now accept more departures from the traditional modes, the director still must often serve as a mediator between playwright and viewer. To be effective, he may need to read widely until he understands the views which have shaped the scripts and may need to experiment with theatrical techniques capable of projecting the ideas.

Recent popular successes offer fewer problems. In working with such plays, the director will usually find that the printed version supplied by the play agency contains a floor plan of the setting, a property list, clear indications of the actors' movements, and many suggestions for interpretation. Most of this information has been taken from the prompt copy of the Broadway production (that is, it describes what happened in the New York production). Some directors follow these suggestions closely, but most prefer to reinterpret the play for their own audience rather than merely to copy the New York production. Even if he does follow the acting edition, however, a director must add much, since it is impossible for stage directions to specify all of the subtleties which go into a competent production.

In producing a new play, the director may work closely with the playwright. Frequently the script is being revised up to the opening night. Sometimes only transitions or individual lines are reworked, but entire acts may be rewritten.

In working with the new play, the director should look upon himself as an adviser to the playwright and should avoid being autocratic in his requests for changes. If the director and the playwright are too much at odds, either the director or the production will have to be dropped.

In arriving at an understanding of a new play, the director is usually aided by the dramatist, who can clarify doubtful points. On the other hand, the director must not accept the playwright's word that qualities or ideas are in the script which the director cannot see. The playwright's ideas must be expressed in a form which can be projected to an audience, and when they are not the director must work with the playwright to overcome inadequacies.

THE DIRECTOR AND THE DESIGNERS

Usually before rehearsals begin, the director meets with the designers to discuss his approach to the play. They, too, should have read and studied the play by this time and should be able to discuss it intelligently. They may not have arrived at the same interpretation as the director, however, and the first task for all will be to reach an agreement about the basic treatment to be given the script. The director should be willing to listen to ideas and suggestions, some of which may alter his previous conceptions of the play. Ultimately, however, the director must decide on the interpretation to be used, and the designers must work within these limitations.

If the director has any specific requests, he should make them at this first meeting. For example, the floor plan of a setting does much to determine the movement pattern of the actors. Therefore, the director may desire to have a setting of a particular shape, or to have a door, desk, or sofa located at a particular place. He may also have specific suggestions about costumes and lighting. The director's needs should be made clear to the designers before they begin work.

After deciding upon the basic approach and requirements, the designers must be allowed time in which to visualize the production and to make sketches. There may be a series of meetings among the designers and the director in which proposals are talked over and revisions are made.

Before giving final approval to plans, the director must be sure that he has anticipated all needs. He must assure himself that the proposed setting is suitable to the action, mood, theme, style, and characterization of the play. He must be convinced that it will be functional for movement. If there are to be scene changes, he needs to know how long each will take. He must believe that the proposed costumes will enhance the actors' movement, and that they will reflect sufficiently the attributes of each role. The director must also know the kind of lighting he desires; he must be specific about the size, shape, and general appearance of properties.

Royall Tyler's *The Contrast* (written in 1787) as performed in a modern production using wings and drops to simulate the stage conventions of the eighteenth century. Directed by William D. Coder.

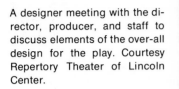
A designer meeting with the director, producer, and staff to discuss elements of the over-all design for the play. Courtesy Repertory Theater of Lincoln Center.

Sketches and drawings of various kinds are mandatory, since words are inadequate for communicating about visual elements. Every designer must be capable of demonstrating the color, shape, and stage appearance of each item he proposes, and the director usually insists upon this demonstration as a way of assuring himself that everyone has the same conceptions in mind. Unless the designers are specific, the director may discover at the dress rehearsal that a number of elements do not function as he had envisioned. Last-minute changes not only are costly, but sometimes impossible because of insufficient time.

Although the director must be in a position to make the final decision on all elements of his production, he should not assume the role of dictator. Each designer has important contributions to make and should be allowed as much freedom as possible. Too many restrictions may discourage an artist rather than bring out his best work.

After all plans have been approved, the designers and technicians execute the scenery, costumes, and properties, while the director turns more and more to his work with the actors. There may be conferences at regular intervals throughout the rehearsal period, but the work of the designers and of the director and actors progresses more or less independently until dress rehearsal.

CASTING

By far the greatest amount of a director's time is devoted to working with the actors. Normally, one of his first tasks is the casting of roles. Occasionally, a director must accept a cast which has been selected by someone else. Some producing organizations employ a casting director to select actors for its various productions. Sometimes even before a director is hired a star is employed and casting must be worked around him. Usually and ideally, however, the director sets out to find the actors who seem most capable of embodying his conception of the characters.

Various methods are employed in casting. One of the most usual is the

397

open tryout, the purposes of which are to have as wide a choice as possible and to give all interested actors a chance. Since 1964, Actors' Equity Association has required Broadway producers to use a modified version of open casting. Under the present rules, a producer must send to Actors' Equity a list of the roles he will be casting, along with instructions about the time and place for interviews. This information is posted on a bulletin board, to which all members of Equity have access. The producer is required to devote a minimum of eight hours to these interviews. In meeting these provisions, producers often establish a list of specifications and let assistants eliminate those actors who do not fit the basic requirements. The tryouts themselves are usually limited to actors who have survived this process and to those already known to the producer or who have been recommended to him by trusted agents. Since time is limited, each applicant may have only a few minutes in which to display his talents. Under such circumstances, much casting is done on the basis of personal qualities and physical attributes rather than on demonstrated acting ability. Open tryouts in the nonprofessional theatre usually proceed at a more leisurely pace and there are normally fewer candidates for roles. Even here, however, decisions may be made on the basis of very limited knowledge about the acting abilities of those trying out.

A variation on the open tryout makes initial sessions open to all but restricts final sessions to those who have been specifically invited to return. In this case, the early periods are used to eliminate unlikely candidates.

Another common practice is the closed or invitational tryout. Many educational and community theatres assemble card files which indicate the experience, personal characteristics, and estimated acting ability of candidates. These records are usually compiled at a large open tryout held early in each theatrical season. In casting each play thereafter, the directors invite to tryouts only those persons whose records show them to be likely candidates for roles. Some educational institutions restrict casting to those who are majors in theatre or who are enrolled in theatre courses. Many community theatres restrict casting to their members.

The way in which tryouts are conducted also varies widely. Sometimes actors are able to read and study a play in advance; at other times, they may be asked to read material at tryouts which they have not previously seen. Some directors ask that actors memorize scenes from plays and perform them. Sometimes actors are requested to prepare pantomimes so that imagination, inventiveness, and movement may be tested. Sometimes a director gives detailed explanations of characterization and situation and then asks the actors to read a scene with these explanations in mind. He may stop the reading to give further instructions or to suggest changes in characterization or emphasis. In such a case, the director is attempting to find out how flexible the actor is, or how easily he can assimilate criticism.

Since the director seldom finds actors who are ideally suited to the play, he must make many compromises. Some parts are more important than others, however, and the director usually casts the major roles first and then selects the remainder of the cast.

Many factors determine the final casting. Some roles demand specific physical characteristics in terms of height, weight, handsomeness, or a particular quality of voice or accent. This may limit the choice considerably. Another important consideration in casting is an actor's potentiality for growth in a role. Sometimes an actor has the right qualities for a part but may be unable to move well or to accept criticism. Another actor, who may not seem as well suited to the role, may be quick to respond and may show greater likelihood of developing a convincing characterization. Some actors give very good readings at tryouts but never develop beyond that point. The director, therefore, must assess the potentialities of each candidate to give finished performances.

The director must also consider the range of characteristics which each actor will have to portray. Although each role will have a dominant quality, it also has other attributes which give it subtlety and variety. A great tragic role, such as Lear, has many facets and the director must seek an actor who is capable of portraying as many of them as possible.

In casting, the total effect must be considered. Sometimes a tall girl must be rejected because of the necessity of using a short man in another role. Two actors may not work well together and one may have to be eliminated. The director also tries to avoid casting too many persons of the same physical type or with the same vocal qualities, since contrast is needed. Therefore, he seeks actors who are both right for particular roles and who combine to make up a balanced ensemble.

Casting may be further complicated by the necessity of designating *understudies*. An understudy normally plays a minor part in the play but also learns a larger role so that he may play it in case the usual performer becomes ill or must miss a performance. When an understudy takes over a larger role, the part which he has vacated must be filled; therefore, many productions have an elaborate scheme of understudying designed to avoid disruption of performances. This policy is almost always used in the professional theatre, where productions are usually planned to run indefinitely and where the producer cannot afford to cancel performances because of the unexpected absences of actors. Since most non-professional productions are performed only a few nights, understudies are seldom used.

Many professional productions also employ *standbys*. This means that a well-known actor is paid to be available in case the star is unable to go on. A standby does not perform in the play at other times.

Some theatres also use a system of *double casting* (that is, two actors alternate in performances of a role). This practice has been used especially for musical shows in which the vocal demands are great. Some educational theatres use double casting to give opportunities to more actors.

Understudies, standbys, and double casting all complicate rehearsing a play, since each actor must be given a reasonable amount of time in which to perfect his role. They also complicate casting, since an effort must be made to find two actors for each part who can keep the quality of performances reasonably even and the over-all pattern of the show unchanged.

399

Casting is almost always a difficult task for the director, and he is seldom able to assemble an ideal cast. Out of the actors available to him, the director chooses those whom he believes most capable of projecting the qualities he sees in the script.

WORKING WITH THE ACTOR

While the director acts as a guide and interpreter to all members of the production staff, he works most closely with the actors. He supervises rehearsals, explains the script, criticizes performances, and makes suggestions for improvements. He attempts to create an atmosphere free from unnecessary tensions so that the actors may explore and develop their roles.

The director should recognize that each actor has his own working methods and problems. For example, some actors accept criticism gracefully in the presence of others, while public comments make other actors self-conscious or argumentative. Some actors feel the need to work first on the psychological aspects of a role, while others prefer to begin with lines and movement. Some actors need to be handled firmly, others gently. The director must be flexible, therefore, if he is to get the best performance out of each member of his cast.

The director must also remember that the actor's ego is unusually involved in his work. In creating a role, the actor uses his own body, his own voice, his own mind and emotions. He can never put his creation at a distance and look at it as can most other artists. Since the inadequacies of a performance are often attributable to the actor's lack of understanding or to his own personal inadequacies, any criticism of his work may be interpreted as a personal affront. The director, therefore, must be tactful and understanding.

The director must assume the role of the ideal audience. Since an actor can never see his own performance from the point of view of the audience, the director must try to do this for him. The director attempts to assess the probable effect of the performances, both individually and as a whole. He seeks to alter, correct, or intensify characterizations wherever necessary so as to achieve the proper emphasis. But a director is not infallible, and must be willing to listen sympathetically to the actors' ideas. Although as an efficient executive he must make all important decisions, he should seek always to avoid a dictatorial approach. Much of the success of a production depends upon the director's ability to win the respect and cooperation of the actors. He must be a critic, a teacher, a leader, a friend, and a disciplinarian.

THE DIRECTOR'S MEANS

The means available to the director in staging a production include the entire resources of the theatre: the script; the voice, speech, and movement of the actor; the stage space, scenery, and properties; the costumes and makeup; the lighting; the music and sound. Since each of these elements is discussed elsewhere in this book, the primary emphasis here is on the director's use of actors for interpreting the script. Three major

400

Scene from Wilder's *Our Town*. Note the variety of bodily positions and the use of focus. Directed by Lewin Goff.

problems will be considered: (1) the creation of the stage picture; (2) the use of movement, gesture, and business; and (3) the use of voice and speech.

THE STAGE PICTURE. Each moment of a performance may be thought of as a picture capable of communicating with the audience apart from speech or movement. If this ideal is to be put into practice, the director must carefully arrange the visual elements available to him at each instant. He must embody pictorially the situation, the dominant emotion, and the character relationships. Furthermore, he must arrange the picture with due regard for composition, mood, style, period, and type of play.

In creating the stage picture, the director must focus attention on the significant elements and subordinate the unimportant ones. Therefore, he must be especially aware of devices for achieving emphasis. One of the most important is the bodily positions of the actors in relation to the audience, for, all other factors being equal, the actor most nearly facing the audience will be the most emphatic. The director, then, may manipulate the actors' positions to achieve emphasis. (Various bodily positions are explained in greater detail in Chapter 18.)

A second source of emphasis is height. All other factors being equal, the tallest character will be the most emphatic. To vary height, the director may have actors sit, stand, kneel, sit on the floor, lie down, stand on steps or platforms. The range of possibilities depends in part upon the setting and the type of play. Some settings contain no furniture, others may have no steps or platforms; actions, such as lying on the floor, may be inappropriate to tragedy but quite acceptable in modern domestic comedy.

A third device for achieving emphasis is the use of specific stage areas. It is generally believed that an actor becomes more emphatic by moving closer to the audience or the center of the stage, and that he becomes less so when he moves away from the audience or to the sides of the stage.

Scene from Anderson's *Elizabeth the Queen*. Here the protagonist must be seated, but emphasis must shift often. Note the use of various levels (both in the setting and the actors' positions seated, kneeling, and standing) and the use of lighting to focus attention on the central areas. Directed by E. C. Mabie; setting by Charles Elson; lighting by Hunton Sellman.

Therefore, the director may shift emphasis by manipulating the actors in relation to the audience or the stage space. (One division of the stage into areas may be seen in the chart below.)

Emphasis may also be gained through focus. If all of the actors look at the same thing or person, so will the audience. In this way attention may be shifted rapidly from one character to another or from one part of the stage to another. It is one of the easiest methods of changing emphasis.

Emphasis may result from spatial relationships. If a number of actors are grouped on one side of the stage and a single actor is placed on the other side, attention will be directed to the isolated character. This is an extreme example, but any change of spatial relationships may aid in focusing attention upon a character. Contrast may also be used. If all of the actors except one face in the same direction the contrast will direct attention to the one who is different.

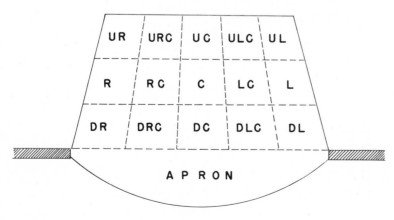

To facilitate positioning actors, the director usually speaks of the stage as though it were divided into many small areas. The diagram shows typical subdivisions.

402

Obey's *Noah*. Here the scenic elements divide the stage into a number of areas, while the line of actors leads the eye to the kneeling figure. Directed by Sidney Spayde; setting by Charles Elson.

Other ways of gaining emphasis include the use of costume (a brilliantly colored garment in the midst of drab clothing will become a center of interest); lighting (contrasting colors or a spotlighted area may create a point of emphasis); and scenery (placing a character in a doorway or against a piece of furniture may put a frame around him or strengthen the visual line sufficiently to call attention to him). In addition to these visual means of gaining emphasis, a number of others are available to the director, although they are not directly related to creating the stage picture. These include movement, gesture, business, voice, and speech — all of which will be discussed later.

A light or bright colored costume in the midst of drab clothing will focus attention upon a character. Scene from *Danton's Death* by George Büchner. Direction, Herbert Blau; scene design, Jo Mielziner; costumes, James Hart Stearns. Courtesy of the Repertory Theater of Lincoln Center.

Seldom does a director depend upon a single device for gaining emphasis. He may use several simultaneously and he should avoid repeating the same device too often. Furthermore, since emphasis often needs to be divided between two or more persons, several devices may have to be combined to achieve the proper effect.

Emphasis automatically implies that some elements are subordinated just as others are brought out. After the focal point of a picture is determined, therefore, all of the characters can be arranged according to their relative importance in the scene. To subordinate characters, all of the devices used for emphasis may be reversed. For example, a subordinate character may be seated while the focal actor is standing; the lowering of height thus reverses a device used to gain emphasis.

Since emphasis and subordination are important only insofar as they clarify situations, character relationships, or mood, the stage picture should be composed with these elements in mind. For example, in a love scene nearness in space may be used to indicate the emotional relationship of the characters; bodily attitudes may indicate the internal state of each character; bodily position may indicate which character's response is the most important at the moment; and so on.

The stage picture should also be arranged with due consideration for composition. It should be balanced in terms of line, mass, and proportion, and should create a harmonious effect. A concern for pleasing composition often leads the director to adjust the positions of the actors onstage. For example, an actor may be directed to move from one place to another merely for the sake of the composition, which would otherwise become unbalanced because another actor has left the stage or changed his position.

Many directors feel that too much attention to composition will lead to the self-conscious posing of actors and will draw attention to the stage picture rather than to the dramatic situation. Others feel that if the actors understand the dramatic situation sufficiently well they will group themselves properly and that only rarely does attention need to be given specifically to composition. Obviously, it is possible to overemphasize composition, but the director should not leave the pictorial aspects to chance.

The stage picture depends to a large degree upon the setting and costumes. The placement of doors, windows, and furniture allows some compositional patterns and impedes others. The absence of furniture in many period plays (such as Greek and Shakespearean tragedies) rules out certain kinds of pictures which would be normal in modern plays set in living rooms. The costumes of some periods do not lend themselves to kneeling or lying down; in others, skirts may be so large that they do not allow close physical contact. In discussing plans with the designers, a director must be conscious of the kind of stage picture he would like to achieve and the limits imposed by the proposed designs. Picturization is also affected by the type of play. For example, tragedy will not normally permit the ludicrous arrangements which are entirely appropriate to farce.

Although a properly composed stage picture will not in itself insure success for a play, no director should be unaware of its importance. A good visual sense is a basic part of the director's equipment.

MOVEMENT, GESTURE, AND BUSINESS. So far, the stage picture has been treated as though each moment were frozen in time, but in performance an impression of movement, rather than of stillness, dominates. Movement blends one stage picture into another and creates a sense of flow, change, and development. It is one of the director's most powerful means of expression.

Movement may be divided into three main types: *movement from place to place, gesture,* and *business.* Each type of movement may be dictated by the script or may be invented by the director or actors. Many movements (such as entering and exiting, ringing for a servant, closing curtains, lighting lamps) may be specified by stage directions or dialogue. Frequently they are so clearly indicated that a failure to perform them would contradict the sense of the scene.

Many scripts, however, indicate no action beyond the arrival and departure of characters. Since a completely static stage picture would soon become boring, the director seeks motivations for physical action. Even in plays which specify a considerable amount of movement, the director may arbitrarily move characters to balance the stage picture or to create interest.

Regardless of the true reason for a movement, the director seeks to make it appear motivated rather than aimless by taking his cues from the play. For example, every scene involves character relationships and emotional connotations which may motivate movement. Surprise, anger, and eagerness normally make persons move closer to each other, while disgust, fear, and reluctance separate them. Thus, the director may use movement to illustrate the inner responses of characters.

Several factors help the director to determine which characters should move and how they should move. First, movement can be used for emphasis. Since it catches the eye of the spectator, it directs attention to that actor whose movement is strongest; it almost always attracts more attention than speech. Since all of the participants in a scene need to react visibly, however, movement must be controlled so as to create the proper focal point. For example, after a surprising announcement, the focal actor may rise, while a subordinate actor may show his response merely by sitting more erect. All actors must respond appropriately and all may use some movement, but the amount and type must be selected so as to direct attention to the actor requiring most attention.

Second, movement should be appropriate to the characters. An elderly person normally uses fewer and slower movements than a young person; the nervous or angry person has a different pattern of response than the casual or relaxed person. Sometimes a character must attempt to appear relaxed when he is not, and his movement should clarify this point. Movement, then, becomes an important part of characterization.

Third, movement should be appropriate to the situation. Highly emotional scenes normally demand more movement — and it is apt to be more rapid and sharply defined than in others. Conversely, a casual atmosphere may call for slower and more curved movement. Guarded, careful movement may be needed in a scene in which characters are trying to outwit each other, while movement which conveys an air of spontaneity is appropriate in scenes of relaxed family life.

Fourth, movement must be appropriate to the type of play. The movement for *Oedipus the King* should be more stately and formal than for *The Chairs*. Furthermore, certain kinds of movement may be associated with a given period. For example, *The School for Scandal* deals with a society noted for its elegance of dress, walk, and gesture. Other plays, such as *From Morn to Midnight* and *Pelléas and Mélisande*, deliberately distort or stylize movement in their conscious departure from realism.

Fifth, movement may be used for building scenes to a climax, for achieving contrast, and for rhythmical effects. An increase in the amount and size of movements helps to achieve a sense of growing confusion or conflict, of development and change. The effect of rapidity is greatly increased if one group of actors moves across the stage in one direction while another crosses in the opposite direction. A sense of confusion can be created by having actors run, stop, change direction, and run again. Even in a production with a small cast, the feeling of growth and development toward a high point of interest may be achieved by a steady increase of movement. Since scenes also need to be clearly differentiated from each other, a contrast in movement from one scene to the next can point up differences in mood and situation and can provide variety as well.

The handling of large numbers of characters poses a difficult problem. In this scene from Aeschylus' *Agamemnon,* the mass of figures contrast with the woman at the right; her position is further emphasized by the column against which she leans. Directed by F. C. Strickland; scenery by O. G. Brockett.

Much stage action does not require movement from place to place. Of this kind of movement, *gesture, facial expression*, and *bodily attitude* are of special importance in achieving subtlety and clarity.

Although gestures normally involve the hands and arms, they may also be movements of the torso, head, feet, or legs. Gesture is especially important as a subtle means of gaining emphasis, since a gesture preceding speech is usually sufficient to shift attention to an actor at just the right moment.

Gesture may also be used effectively in scenes where the situation must be clear to the audience, but obscure for the characters. For example, in a crucial scene in which one character questions another, the interrogator may be placed upstage of the actor he is questioning. The downstage actor may be facing the audience with his back to the questioner. Upon being asked a particularly revealing question, a slight movement of a hand held in front of the body (such as upward toward the throat) can tell the audience that a deep impression has been made, though the questioner may not be aware of any reaction.

Gesture can be indicative of basic psychological traits. A large number of spontaneous gestures can create the impression of an uninhibited, extroverted personality, while few and awkward gestures may bring the opposite response. Gestures that are appropriate to the particular character must be sought, therefore, even when their primary purpose may be emphasis and clarity.

Bodily attitude and facial expression are especially useful means for displaying emotional states and for indicating immediate reactions. Bodily attitude refers to the over-all tone and configuration of the human figure—stiffly upright, slumping, relaxed, and so on. When not obscured by a costume, bodily attitude is one of the most telling indexes to the actor's relative tension or relaxation (so much so, in fact, that the actor frequently has difficulty in demonstrating the character's, rather than his own, states of feeling). Although facial expression is not always visible to the entire audience, especially in a large auditorium, it should not be overlooked as a supplementary aid in projecting emotion. By themselves, facial expression and bodily attitude are insufficient to convey the substance of a scene, but they support and clarify other means.

Scene from Synge's *The Playboy of the Western World*. Note the variety in bodily positions and the S-curve composition with the principal focus on the figure at the left. Directed by James Haran.

407

Another kind of movement is *stage business* (those detailed actions, such as filling and lighting a pipe, arranging flowers, wrapping packages, eating and drinking, dueling and fighting). Business should be carefully rehearsed, since the actors normally must carry on a conversation or react to other characters while performing it. Each step in the business must be timed to make appropriate points and coordinated with dialogue to avoid distracting attention from more important action or lines.

Much of the business in a play is prescribed by the script, but much of it may be invented by the actors or the director, for carefully chosen business may clarify and enrich characterizations left somewhat vague by the playwright. Although business should never be allowed to interfere with the build of a scene or with important lines, when properly used it can do much to indicate basic traits and inner emotional states.

Since movement encompasses the total physical action, it is one of the most powerful means of affecting the audience. The director, therefore, must know how to use it effectively.

VOICE AND SPEECH. Although the director frequently uses sound and music, his most typical means of audible expression are the actors' voices and the playwright's words. Although voice and speech are usually associated with the actor, the director must understand and know how to use these elements for his purposes.

The variable factors in voice are *pitch, volume*, and *quality*. Each may be used for characterization and as an indicator of changing emotions and relationships. For example, in moments of stress, the pitch and volume of the voice normally rise and the quality becomes strained. Thus, the trained voice may be used effectively for projecting varying psychological states and dramatic situations.

A director should understand vocal factors and their potential effects on audiences so that he can decide which are desirable for each character and so that he can aid those actors who are incapable of determining the proper vocal attributes for their roles. Since an actor can improve his vocal skills only over a long period of time, however, directors must usually cast their plays with those actors who already most nearly have the vocal attributes required by the roles.

The variable factors of speech are *articulation, pronunciation, duration, inflection*, and *projection* (or audibility); each of these may be manipulated to achieve specific results. Articulation involves the production of sounds, while pronunciation involves the selection of sounds. A person may articulate sounds clearly, but mispronounce words. A well-trained actor should understand both articulation and pronunciation and should be able to utilize both in the production of standard stage speech. But he also should be able to alter articulation and pronunciation to suit the demands of character and situation.

Poor *articulation* is caused by careless use of tongue and lips in forming sounds; it connotes lack of education or regionalism. *Mispronunciation* has many of the same associations, but it sometimes indicates na-

408

ïveté or inexperience (a person may never have heard certain words pronounced). A knowledge of the International Phonetic Alphabet symbols (I.P.A.) can be of great help in describing how sounds should be altered for dramatic purposes.

Duration refers to the length of time assigned to any sound, while inflection refers to rising and falling pitch. Both duration and pitch may be used to emphasize some syllables and to subordinate others. Stress on one or more syllables is usually necessary if the audience is to recognize a word. For example, in *probably* the first syllable is normally stressed through duration; if the stress is shifted to the second syllable, the word becomes almost unrecognizable.

Duration also refers to the number of words spoken per minute. Slowness and speed in speaking have definite value in characterization. For example, slow speech may help to create the impression of laziness, sickness,or weakness, while a rapid rate may suggest tension or vivacity.

Inflection is one of the principal indicators of meaning. Surprise, disgust, indifference, and other reactions are frequently indicated by tone of voice. The sense of many speeches can be completely altered by changing the inflections. Dialects are distinguishable in part by their pitch patterns. That of the southern United States, for example, is characterized in part by a stress on the verb and by a rising inflection at the end of sentences.

In working with voice and speech, the director must strive above all for audibility (projection) and intelligibility, for unless the audience can both hear and understand the actors the play will have little chance of success. For this reason, dialects frequently need to be altered to make them understandable (a completely accurate rendering of the Irish dialect is often gibberish to an American audience). Some actors mumble lines out of a desire for greater naturalness. The director must decide when the competing demands for naturalness and communication have been satisfactorily resolved, but he should never accept speech which is unintelligible to the audience (unless it is part of the effect being sought).

The director must also seek variety in voice and speech. Nothing is more monotonous than the delivery of all lines at the same speed and with the same emotional intensity. Each scene usually has a dominant tempo and emotional tone, but these dominant patterns need to be broken up if monotony is to be avoided. Many devices may be used for variety. Among the most powerful is contrast. For example, a character who has delivered an emotional, rapid, and loud speech may pause and then, in a quiet, slow, and controlled manner, go on to his next lines. The pause may also be used with great effect to mark transitions in thought, changes in emotion, a shift in tempo, and so on. Pauses, however, must be made meaningful to an audience, for unless the significance of the pause is clear the effect will be merely one of slowness or a suggestion that the actors have forgotten their lines. All of the variable factors in voice and speech—pitch, volume, quality, articulation, pronunciation, duration, and inflection—may be manipulated for the purpose of achieving variety.

409

The director must make sure that the dominant ideas and emotions of each scene are reflected in voice and speech. Some ideas and emotional responses need to be stressed and other subordinated. Solutions to this problem can normally be found by working with the actors until each understands his character's motivations and relationship to the other characters, the significance of each moment in the particular scene and of the play as a whole. From such understanding, proper emphases usually result, although the director may need to give some technical aid in phrasing, intensity, and inflection, especially when working with inexperienced actors.

The director must strive for believability in voice and speech, for actors may sound false and unconvincing. Shortcomings often may be corrected by working on motivations. Sometimes difficulty arises from the failure of one or more actors to respond "in key." (That is, the response may seem inappropriate to the stimulus.) Overacting and underacting are usually judged according to the adequacy of a response. The director must help the actor to find the right "key." Sometimes an actor's speech may seem too artificial and studied. In such cases, the director must help the actor to achieve a sense of spontaneity or a more conversational tone. Conversely, for Shakespearean and other verse plays a director may need to help actors get away from the phrasing of everyday speech and into the sweep of the poetic lines.

The director may also use voice and speech in building a scene or the entire play toward a climax. A crowd scene may be structured in part through the increasing volume and intensity of vocal sounds. While large groups offer the most obvious opportunities, voice and speech may be used advantageously in all plays to establish progression, to build climaxes, and to create a sense of resolution.

The devices available to the director are many and varied. Regardless of which he uses, he must strive for clarity and harmony of effect through emphasis and subordination, and through a progression from beginning to middle to end. He should be both a sound technician and an impeccable critic.

REHEARSING THE PLAY

Rehearsals can seldom be held in surroundings which approximate those used in performance. As a rule, the scenery, costumes, lighting, and properties are not available until dress rehearsals, and the place where rehearsals are held is seldom the stage upon which the play will be presented. The director and the actors must rely heavily upon imagination in working toward a finished performance.

One of the first problems which must be solved is that of adequate rehearsal space. A room at least as large as the stage setting is required, although more space is desirable. The ground plan of the set is usually marked out on the floor with chalk, paint, or adhesive tape. If there is more than one set, each must be indicated (lines of different colors may be used to distinguish different settings). Chairs, tables, and other improvised furniture may be brought in to help the actor become familiar with

410

the floor plan and the stage space in which he will be performing. Difficulties are greatest when the setting has a number of levels and steps upon which the actors must move. It is sometimes impossible to duplicate these levels in the rehearsal space, and the actor must keep himself aware of the demands of the setting by forcing himself to go through the motions of climbing stairs, by standing on chairs to simulate raised platforms, or by similar devices.

Further problems arise with stage business. If actors must serve tea, wrap packages, or perform other complicated actions, it is usually necessary to find temporary properties which approximate those to be used on stage, for such complex business cannot be put off until dress rehearsals. Comparable difficulties occur with costumes in those plays in which clothing differs markedly from modern dress. The convincing use of long skirts, trains, complicated headdresses, swords, and similar articles requires considerable practice. Many theatres maintain a supply of rehearsal garments to aid the actor in becoming accustomed to unfamiliar dress. Without such help the actor may be awkward and self-conscious if he dons his costume for the first time at dress rehearsal.

Rehearsing plays under these conditions creates a number of additional problems. In a small space, it is difficult to judge the degree to which a play is being projected adequately for a large auditorium. For this reason, it is important to have as many rehearsals as possible in the theatre where the play will be performed.

The director must know approximately how much rehearsal time he will have. In the nonprofessional theatre, actors are usually available for rehearsals only in the evenings or on week ends and for periods not exceeding three or four hours. It is typical to restrict rehearsals to five evenings each week over four to six weeks. In the professional theatre a rehearsal period of about four weeks is usual, but actors are available approximately eight hours each day.

Knowing how much rehearsal time he will have, the director must then work out a schedule which will utilize the available time to maximum advantage. A number of factors must be considered in constructing a schedule. First, the director should strive to make the most efficient use of his actors. It is unfair to ask an actor to attend a number of rehearsals in which he is never used. If the director breaks the play down into short scenes, he will usually find that he can schedule all scenes using crowds on the same day and that other periods may be devoted entirely to the principal characters. If a script is complex, the director may use assistant directors and schedule more than one rehearsal simultaneously. He may also plan to allow actors to go over difficult pieces of business or lines elsewhere while he is rehearsing another scene on stage.

Second, since the director cannot work on all problems simultaneously, the schedule should be broken down in terms of objectives. For example, the actors cannot work on detailed pieces of business until they have learned the lines well enough to dispense with the script. For this reason, the director usually divides the rehearsal schedule into phases each concerned primarily with a specific objective.

The first phase is usually devoted to reading, analyzing, and understanding the script. The amount of time reserved for study of the text varies from director to director, with the complexity of the script, and with the experience of the cast. During this period the director is principally concerned with making sure that each actor understands his role and its function in the play; he seeks to make clear his own interpretation of the script and to clarify the objectives toward which everyone must work. The director may also strive to stimulate the actors' imaginations by raising questions about the motivation of characters, by pointing out the relationship between scenes or characters, by clarifying symbolic devices, and by indicating key speeches. Some directors give the actors specific directions for the reading of lines at this time, but most prefer to defer such details until later in the rehearsal schedule.

The next period of time is usually reserved for *blocking* (that is, with indicating movement from place to place on the stage and with the position of each actor moment by moment). For example, an actor may be directed to enter up center, to cross slowly to the sofa down left, and to stand facing front. Normally the director is concerned at this point only with the gross patterns of movement; subtleties and refinements are left until a later time.

Directors disagree about how much planning should be done prior to blocking rehearsals. Some argue that the director should have every movement planned and charted. Blocking rehearsals then consist merely of relaying directions to the actors, who perform the prescribed movements and note them in their own scripts. Others argue that it is impossible to decide with any accuracy what movements are needed until the actors are present, and that movement should evolve out of the actors' feelings rather than from a mold imposed by the director. The latter method usually involves considerable trial and error with fixed patterns developing only after many rehearsals.

The majority of directors use a method somewhere between these two extremes. Much thought has usually been given to blocking before rehearsals begin and much will remain exactly as planned. On the other hand, most directors find it necessary to make many adjustments as inadequacies become obvious and as the actors suggest improvements. Although time can be saved by preplanning, rigidity should be avoided.

Scene from Sherwood's *Abe Lincoln in Illinois*. The woman at center remains dominant in spite of her profile position because of her spatial relationship to the other characters, her stage position, and focus. Directed by E. C. Mabie.

221

ТРИГОРИНЪ. Красивая птица. Право, не хочется уѣзжать. Вотъ уговорите-ка Ирину Николаевну, чтобы она осталась [записываетъ въ книжку].

НИНА. Что это вы пишите?

ТРИГОРИНЪ. Такъ записываю... Сюжетъ мелькнулъ... [пряча книжку]. Сюжетъ для небольшого разсказа: на берегу озера съ дѣтства живетъ молодая дѣвушка, такая, какъ вы; любитъ озеро, какъ чайка, и счастлива и свободна, какъ чайка. Но случайно пришелъ человѣкъ, увидѣлъ и отъ нечего дѣлать погубилъ ее, какъ вотъ эту чайку.

НИНА [вздрагивая]. Не надо такъ.

[пауза].

[Въ окнѣ показывается Аркадина].

АРКАДИНА. Борисъ Алексѣевичъ, гдѣ вы?

ТРИГОРИНЪ. Сейчасъ! [идетъ и оглядывается на Нину; у окна, Аркадиной]. Что?

АРКАДИНА. Мы остаемся.

[Тригоринъ уходитъ въ домъ].

НИНА [подходитъ къ рампѣ; послѣ нѣкотораго раздумья]. Сонъ!

ЗАНАВѢСЪ.

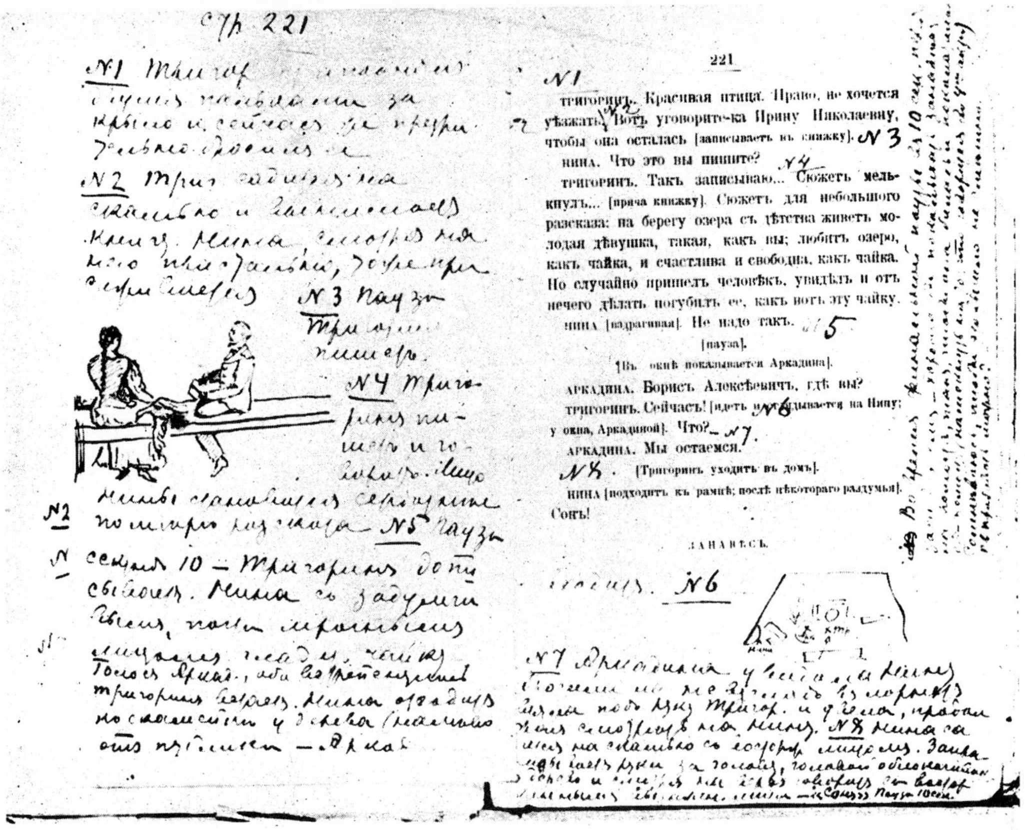

A page from Stanislavsky's prompt book for Chekhov's *The Sea Gull.* Note the floor plan of the setting at bottom right and the sketch at left. From *Moscow Art Theatre, 1898-1917,* 1955.

Regardless of how the blocking is arrived at, the patterns of movement should be rehearsed until they are entirely clear to all the actors. It is usual to block an act or a few scenes at a time. When the blocking for a segment is clear, the director moves on to the next part and repeats the process until the entire play is finished. One or more rehearsals may be devoted to blocking each act.

The next period is normally devoted to dialogue. At this time the director is concerned with the actors' ability to repeat their lines without the aid of a script or a prompter. The director normally sets a date by which the actors must know their lines; usually he designates a deadline for each act. Lines should be learned early, for it is extremely difficult to work for subtlety and polish if the actors must consult their scripts for blocking or speeches.

Once the actors are sure of movement and lines, the director may proceed to the next phase – detailed work on characterization, line readings, business, transitions, progression, and ensemble playing. The director may need to spend much time exploring with the actors their motivations for certain actions or speeches; he must see that the timing is right; he may wish to question the interpretation of certain lines; and so on. It is frequently necessary to go over and over the same piece of business to ensure that it is integrated precisely with the lines and that it is being used to make the appropriate points. He may have to repeat the same scene many times to get the proper build in intensity. He must make sure that there is variety; he must work for ensemble playing, as opposed to a series of isolated individual performances.

In any phase of the rehearsal schedule the director may stop the cast frequently to comment, criticize, or to repeat a scene partially or wholly. He must allow the actors to play entire scenes or acts through as often as possible, however, so that they develop a feeling for the continuity of scenes, the shifts in mood, and the build of each scene and of the play as a whole. The director must avoid letting too many days elapse between rehearsals of the same scene, for if actors forget too much, valuable time must be spent in accomplishing all over again the gains of a previous rehearsal.

The final phase of the rehearsal schedule is devoted to integrating all of the elements of production. For the first time the actors are able to rehearse in their costumes and make-up and with the scenery, lighting, sound, and music which will be used in performance. Frequently these rehearsals also mark the first time that the actor has rehearsed on the stage. Consequently, many changes may need to be made at this time.

The process of integration will be eased considerably if proper planning was done at the early conferences between the director and the designers. Further steps may also be taken to ease the tensions of final rehearsals. For example, a dress parade, at which all of the actors appear together in their costumes, will allow the director to see how the actors look individually and when grouped by scenes. It also allows the actors to become familiar with their costumes, to try out movements, to discover the possibilities and problems in their garments. Problems may be discovered at this time which can be corrected without taking valuable time at dress rehearsals.

In addition, a technical rehearsal—the purpose of which is to work out problems of scene changes, lighting cues, costume changes, sound, music, and properties—may be scheduled. All necessary adjustments cannot normally be made during this rehearsal, but difficulties can be noted and often can be corrected before dress rehearsals begin.

Lighting and sound are apt to present the greatest problems of integration. While the lighting may be planned in advance, it cannot be finished until the scenery is in place and until the actors use the stage area. It is not always possible to know exactly how large an area a lighting instrument will cover, or exactly what level of intensity is desirable until all other elements are present. Much time is normally spent, therefore, in adjusting the lighting instruments, in setting the exact intensity in recording light cues, and so on. Sometimes this process takes more than a full day. Likewise, sound must be adjusted in terms of other elements. It is impossible to know exactly how loud it should be, exactly when it should begin, how it should build and fade away until it is tried out in the auditorium which will be used for performances.

Dress parades and technical rehearsals, thus, can minimize difficulties. When these rehearsals are not used, dress rehearsals must also serve these additional functions. Regardless of when the various elements are introduced, the process of integration must take place, and it is almost always a time of stress.

414

Most directors attempt to have two or three dress rehearsals. These are intended to approximate the conditions of performance as nearly as possible. Difficulties are noted and corrected. The wise director uses the crises which arise as a means of preparing his cast for coping with the emergencies which may occur during public performances. Some directors invite a number of people to the dress rehearsals as a way of getting some indication of probable audience response and as a way of preparing the actors for a larger audience. Some adjustments may be made as a result of this response.

In the professional theatre, the out-of-town tryout may function as a series of dress rehearsals, after each of which changes are made. The alterations are then tried out on other audiences until the play is opened in New York.

Although as a rule there are no further rehearsals after the play is opened officially, there are many exceptions. The stage manager of a professional company may call a rehearsal whenever he feels one is needed. The understudies are rehearsed regularly in their alternate roles throughout the run, and touring companies may have run-throughs at each stop in order to acquaint the actors with the particular stage and auditorium. In the nonprofessional theatre, the director may discuss each performance with the actors and may make suggestions for improvements. Sometimes such groups play only on week ends so several days elapse between performances. In such cases, refresher rehearsals may be held. Normally, however, the director's work is over and his responsibilities are completed with the opening performance.

SPECIAL PROBLEMS

The director is often faced with special problems. For example, his work is considerably complicated if he is staging a musical. In this case, a choreographer normally designs the dance movements and rehearses the dancers; the musical conductor rehearses the singers and chorus. The director, however, must integrate song and dance into the whole and devise the transitions from spoken lines into song, and from stage movement into dance. Many of these problems will be dealt with in Chapter 22.

So far directing has been discussed primarily in terms of the proscenium stage. More and more, however, arena and open stages are being used. It should be obvious that, if the audience is to view the action from three or four sides (rather than one), adjustments must be made in picturization, movement, voice and speech. What is near one part of the audience will be far away from another; an actor, while facing one group of spectators, will have his back to another. Therefore, the director must turn his actors often so that no segment of the audience is deprived. Furthermore, the actor must use his entire body more expressively, so that the back, side and front views communicate effectively. While the same devices for achieving emphasis suffice, several must be used in combination because of the altered audience-actor relationship.

415

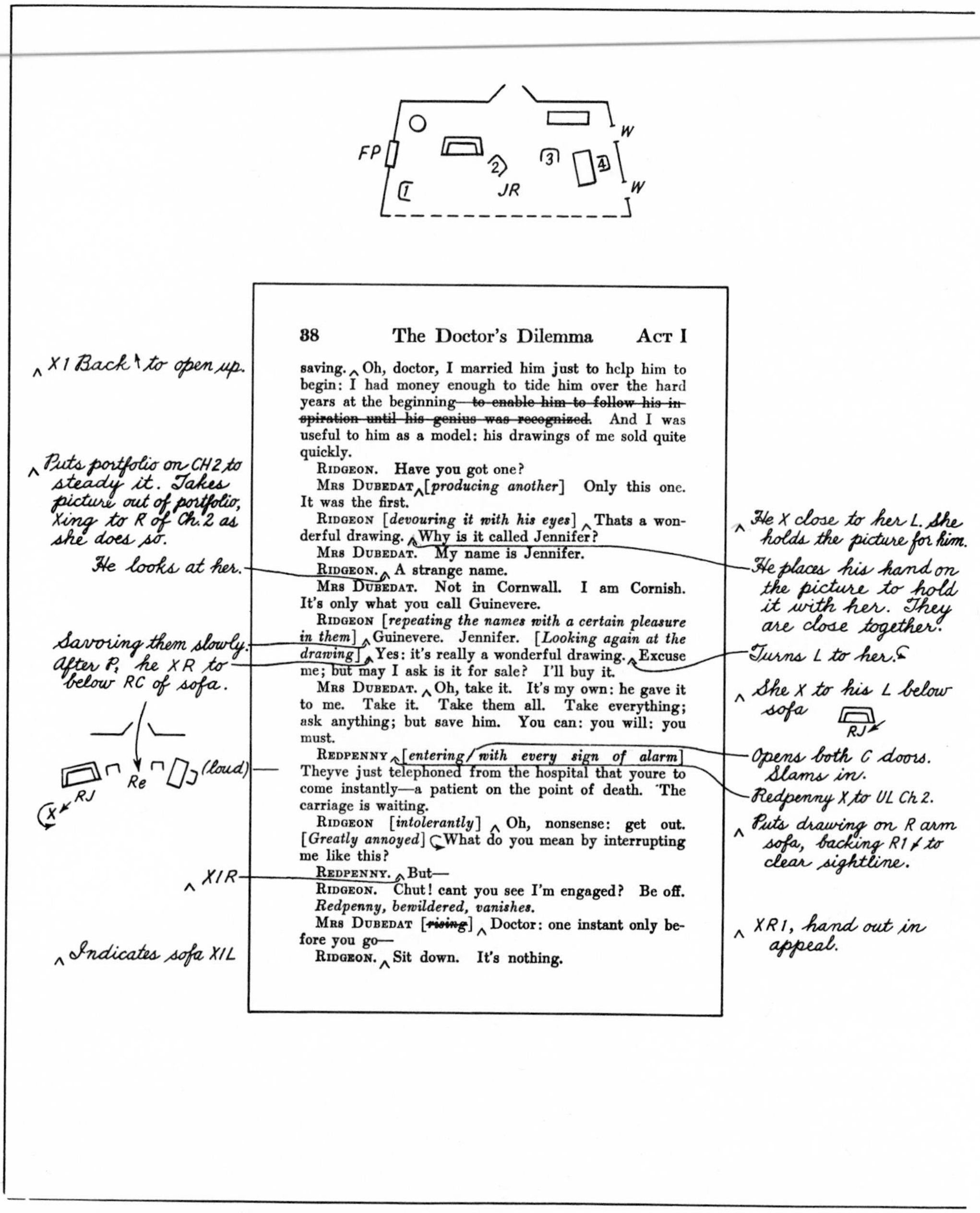
38 The Doctor's Dilemma **Act I**

saving. Oh, doctor, I married him just to help him to begin: I had money enough to tide him over the hard years at the beginning ~~to enable him to follow his inspiration until his genius was recognized.~~ And I was useful to him as a model: his drawings of me sold quite quickly.

RIDGEON. Have you got one?

MRS DUBEDAT [*producing another*] Only this one. It was the first.

RIDGEON [*devouring it with his eyes*] Thats a wonderful drawing. Why is it called Jennifer?

MRS DUBEDAT. My name is Jennifer.

RIDGEON. A strange name.

MRS DUBEDAT. Not in Cornwall. I am Cornish. It's only what you call Guinevere.

RIDGEON [*repeating the names with a certain pleasure in them*] Guinevere. Jennifer. [*Looking again at the drawing*] Yes: it's really a wonderful drawing. Excuse me; but may I ask is it for sale? I'll buy it.

MRS DUBEDAT. Oh, take it. It's my own: he gave it to me. Take it. Take them all. Take everything; ask anything; but save him. You can: you will: you must.

REDPENNY [*entering with every sign of alarm*] Theyve just telephoned from the hospital that youre to come instantly—a patient on the point of death. The carriage is waiting.

RIDGEON [*intolerantly*] Oh, nonsense: get out. [*Greatly annoyed*] What do you mean by interrupting me like this?

REDPENNY. But—

RIDGEON. Chut! cant you see I'm engaged? Be off.

Redpenny, bewildered, vanishes.

MRS DUBEDAT [~~*rising*~~] Doctor: one instant only before you go—

RIDGEON. Sit down. It's nothing.

FP
W
JR
W
X1 Back to open up.
Puts portfolio on CH2 to steady it. Takes picture out of portfolio, Xing to R of Ch.2 as she does so.
He looks at her.
Savoring them slowly. After P, he XR to below RC of sofa.
Re
RJ
(loud)
X1R
Indicates sofa X1L
He X close to her L. She holds the picture for him.
He places his hand on the picture to hold it with her. They are close together.
Turns L to her.
She X to his L below sofa
RJ
Opens both C doors. Slams in.
Redpenny X to UL Ch 2.
Puts drawing on R arm sofa, backing R1 to clear sightline.
XR1, hand out in appeal.

A page from a prompt book showing the ground plan, script cuts, and blocking notes. From Curtis Canfield's *The Craft of Play Directing.* New York: Holt, Rinehart and Winston, Inc., 1963. Courtesy of the author.

Since the arena theatre can use little scenery, the director must find other ways of communicating. Properties and costumes may take on greater significance, and, since they are normally seen at much closer range than on the proscenium stage, may need to be selected and executed with greater care. Facial expression, subtle reactions, and business can be used with greater effect. While the director may be unable to use some of the devices which work well on the proscenium stage, he will find that others which are of little value in the proscenium theatre assume considerable importance. The basic problems and the basic techniques remain the same; the selection of the specific means differ with the situation.

EMPLOYMENT

In the professional theatre, the director is employed by the producer. If he is well known, he may be put under option early so that the producer may use his name as an inducement to investors. On the other hand, a director is sometimes employed after the show has been cast (although this is unusual). Since many producing organizations have a permanent casting director, the director of a particular play may have far less control over casting than does his counterpart in the nonprofessional theatre. Nevertheless, the director in the professional theatre may request that an actor be replaced if he does not find him competent. (The conditions under which an actor may be replaced are clearly specified by Actors' Equity.)

Until recently the professional director did not belong to a union. The Society of Stage Directors and Choreographers was formed in 1959 and was recognized in 1962 as the bargaining agent for its members. As a result, the director's rights and working conditions are now clearly out-

Scene from *The Trespassers* by Ralph Arzoomanian performed in the round. Directed by Philip Benson.

lined by union contracts. It is customary for the director to be paid a part of his fee when the contract is signed and the rest during the rehearsal period. It is also customary for the director to receive a percentage of receipts throughout the run of the play. The director's responsibilities normally end with the opening of the play in New York, although he may be called upon periodically to approve replacements and to make sure that performances remain reasonably close to his original intention. He may also be asked to direct road companies of the play (although this is entirely optional).

In resident companies and summer stock, directors are usually employed to direct a specified number of plays within a stated period of time. In such organizations the director's duties are apt to be less precisely stated than in the Broadway theatre, and, if there is more than one director, each may have other responsibilities when he is not actively directing a show.

In the community theatre it is typical for one director to be responsible for all productions. He must either direct all of the plays himself or find other competent persons to do so (frequently without pay or for a nominal fee). In many groups, the director is the only paid member of the staff and must assume primary responsibility for all aspects of the theatre's operation. If there is also a designer-technician, the director's duties are usually restricted to directing, business management, and publicity.

In the educational theatre, directors normally are also teachers. Directing may be considered as part of the teaching load, or it may be looked upon as an extracurricular activity. The position of the director varies widely in educational theatre. Occasionally a single faculty member must bear the burden of the entire theatre program; on the other hand, he may be one of a large and specialized staff and may have no production duties other than directing.

THE DIRECTOR AND HIS ASSISTANTS

The director may have a number of assistants. The most important of these are a *rehearsal secretary*, an *assistant director*, and a *stage manager.*

The *rehearsal secretary* sits near the director at rehearsals and takes down whatever notes and comments he wishes to have recorded. Sometimes the director may see the need for a particular prop; he may wish to be reminded of a weak point in the script, or some deficiency in the acting. At the end of a scene or a rehearsal he may ask the secretary to read these notes to him and he may relay his comments on acting directly to the performers. Sometimes he may ask the secretary to type out the notes and give them to the persons concerned.

Sometimes the duties of the rehearsal secretary are combined with those of the *assistant director*, whose over-all responsibilites are difficult to define since he may be called on to do almost anything. Sometimes he is asked to rehearse specific scenes or to coach actors. He may act as an intermediary between the director and the designers; he may attend all conferences and be given specific tasks. On complex productions, there may be a number of assistant directors, each with his own area of responsibility.

The duties of the rehearsal secretary, assistant director, and the stage manager may all be combined into a single job (although this is not usual). The *stage manager's* is the most important executive post after the show has opened, for it is his responsibility to see that each performance proceeds as planned. Because of his great importance to the proper running of a show, he is selected with considerable care.

In the professional theatre, the stage manager is hired by the producer and must be a member of Actors' Equity. A large show may have one or two assistant stage managers, each with a specific area of responsibility (such as the chorus in a musical). An assistant stage manager may also act in the production, but a stage manager may not. In the professional theatre the stage manager helps to organize and run tryouts; he attends all rehearsals and records all changes in lines, blocking, and cues in the master copy of the play; he posts the rehearsal schedule and keeps all notices up to date; he may be asked to notify the designers of any changes in plans which affect their work. If the company goes on tour, he must see that all belongings are shipped and received. Since the stage manager is in charge of the performance, he must know as much as possible about every aspect of the production. As a guide, he compiles a prompt book, which records everything that affects the performance (all cues for lights, scene changes, sound, actors' entrances, curtains, and so on), and he must see that all directions are carried out. After the show has opened, he rehearses the understudies each week and may call a rehearsal of the entire cast if he believes that performances are deviating too far from the director's conception. If replacements in the cast must be made, the stage manager may, in consultation with the casting director or director, employ them.

In the nonprofessional theatre the stage manager's job is much less demanding, since the director usually remains on the job and can take care of many of the problems which arise, although the stage manager is still responsible for running the show during each performance. In some theatres he does not attend rehearsals from the beginning, but comes in a few days before the first technical or dress rehearsal (that is, just in time to familiarize himself with the problems of running the show). Regardless of when he assumes his post, however, the stage manager is one of the most important persons for assuring the proper running of a performance.

While this discussion has not covered all of the problems and responsibilities of the director, the nature of his duties should be clear. A director cannot make bad or inferior acting good, nor can he entirely overcome the handicaps of inappropriate scenery, costumes, and lighting, but only the director can create a truly integrated performance in which all elements are utilized to maximum advantage. His job requires artistic insight, taste, tact, organizational ability, leadership, and perseverance.

Chapter 18 THE ACTOR

Of all theatre workers, the actor most nearly personifies the stage for the general public, for he is the only one an audience sees. It is the actor who lends his body and voice to the character and makes it live and breathe. Except in rare cases, however, the actor's fame does not outlive him, for new interpreters are always ready to step into the roles he has vacated.

The actor's problems are in many ways unique. He is one of the few artists whose means of expression cannot be separated from himself, for he must create with his own body and voice out of his own psychological and mental endowments. The director, designers, and playwright may sit in the auditorium and watch their work, but the actor can never completely separate himself from what he creates. Only through a filmed performance can he see himself from the viewpoint of others, and even then the experience of working in a theatre before a live audience cannot be duplicated.

Since the actor must attempt to evaluate his own work, he develops a kind of double view of himself—as the creator of a role, and as the embodiment of a character. In performance, he must be attuned to the response of the audience as a measure of effectiveness, but at the same time he must seem thoroughly absorbed in his character. Like any artist, if he is to grow and mature in his profession, he must develop a capacity for assessing his own accomplishments, although for him the task is extremely complex.

It is often difficult to separate an actor's talent from his personality. Stage presence (being at ease on the stage), tricks that please or amuse an audience, and attractive personal traits are often confused with acting. While it may make use of all these, good acting is ultimately distinguished by the ability to embody and project the essence of a role regardless (or in spite of) the actor's own personal endowments.

420

It is sometimes assumed that there are no prerequisites for success in acting beyond a few striking personality traits. Acting is an art, however, and as with any art there are three components—native ability, study, and practice. Native ability is essential; although it cannot be taught, it can be cultivated and developed through study and constant practice.

THE ACTOR'S TRAINING AND MEANS

The actor's means of expression are his body and voice, the role, and the stage environment. These means were discussed in the preceding chapter from the standpoint of the director. Here many of the same topics will be considered from the actor's point of view.

THE BODY. Since it is one of the actor's principal means of expression, the body should be flexible, disciplined, and expressive. Flexibility is needed so that the actor may express physically a wide range of attitudes, traits, and reactions. If he is to use this flexibility effectively, the actor must also be able to control it, and control comes only through practice and discipline.

Some actors can achieve physical control with comparative ease, but for others it remains troublesome. An actor may receive much help from courses in stage movement, dancing, fencing, and acrobatics, and by participating in activities which demand physical control and coordination. Dancing and fencing may be of special help, not only because of the gracefulness and discipline they promote, but because the actor who can also dance has many additional opportunities open to him in musical drama, while fencing is a skill demanded in many period plays.

Regardless of his training or skill in movement, the actor must meet the problem of embodying a role physically. The actor with a well-trained body has mastered the principal means for doing so.

THE VOICE. In training the voice, the same ideals—flexibility, control, and expressiveness—apply. The actor should understand how the vocal instrument functions, and should strive for maximum control over pitch, volume, and quality. He should learn how to breathe properly, how to achieve variety, how to insure that he will be audible and intelligible. He should train himself to speak standard American speech habitually, and should acquire a sound knowledge of phonetics as an aid in recording and learning dialects and other deviations from normal stage speech. To develop flexibility, control, and expressiveness constant practice is necessary. Training in oral reading, acting, and singing may be of help, but years of drill are usually required. Changes cannot be wrought overnight and normally an actor without a good foundation in voice training can do little to transform his vocal characteristics during the four to six weeks of the typical rehearsal period. In every role the actor has a greater chance of success if his voice can be manipulated to achieve the desired results.

OBSERVATION AND IMAGINATION. While the body and voice are the actor's principal means of expression, other faculties—observation and imagination—help him determine how they should be used in a particular situation. Except in rare cases, the characters an actor is asked to portray are recognizable human types (occasionally an actor may be asked to assume the role of an animal, flower, or inanimate object; such nonhuman roles, however, are still assigned human traits). To portray a role well, then, the actor should understand human emotions, attitudes, and motivations, and know how they are manifested externally.

In understanding others the actor must rely principally upon observation. Therefore, he must develop the habit of observing and remembering the behavior of others. For example, if an actor must play an old man, observance of the behavior of old men may be the best preparation for the role. Since the actor cannot observe all aspects of behavior at once, he should study one detail at a time. In looking at old men, he should analyze the walk, the posture, the use of the hands and arms, the manner of sitting and rising, and so on. Furthermore, it is not sufficient as a rule to observe only one person of a type, for that person may be an exception to more normal behavior. The actor should observe many examples and try to find what is typical.

This type of observation may also be extended to the display of emotions (the way in which people respond when they are happy, grieved, surprised, terrified, and so on). While the results of such observation cannot always be transferred directly to the stage, it can form the foundation for characterizations; through such means believable, lifelike portrayals develop.

Observation of others must be restricted to external behavior. The actor, however, does have his own internal states of feelings, emotions, and attitudes and he can, in effect, observe these. In a given situation, he can analyze his emotions, motivations, and behavior. As a rule, the actor assumes that his own reactions are normal and typical, and that he may utilize on the stage what he has learned through self-analysis. He may strive to develop emotion memory so that he may easily recall how he felt in a given situation (presumably one similar to that in the play) and utilize this memory in building character motivations and reactions. Since the actor is usually faced with *feeling* himself into the place of another, the solution will probably be easier if he can recall how he has felt under like circumstances. The actor, thus, comes to know others by knowing himself, and he embodies roles in part by calling upon his knowledge of himself.

Since the actor is asked to create fictional rather than real-life situations, however, he must develop his imagination. In utilizing observation and emotion memory, he must keep in mind the circumstances dictated by the play. He must be able to project himself imaginatively into the situation and make it believable to himself. Unless he can imagine himself as the character in the situation, it is unlikely that he will be able to convince an audience.

CONCENTRATION. If the body and voice are to be directed by understanding and imagination in the creation of a believable stage per-

Scene from Williams' *A Street-car Named Desire*.

formance, concentration is also needed. Concentration refers to the actor's ability to immerse himself in the action and to shut out all distractions.

Many actors, because of overfamiliarity with the lines and movement of a play, seem mere automatons. They respond on cue, but it is clear that they have not actually been listening or watching. The good actor, on the other hand, creates the illusion of the first time, no matter how often he has performed the role. To give such performances he must concentrate on what is happening around him, not in a general sense but upon the specific phrases, intonations, gestures, and movements, and must respond in the appropriate key and at the appropriate moment. Concentration is a difficult skill to develop, but it is a necessary one for the actor.

TECHNIQUE. Experience has shown that some ways of doing things on the stage are more effective than others, and over the years many of the actor's routine tasks have become standardized. These mechanics of acting are normally referred to as technique.

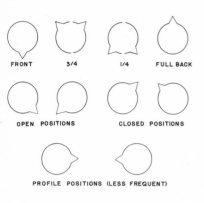

FRONT   3/4   1/4   FULL BACK

OPEN POSITIONS   CLOSED POSITIONS

PROFILE POSITIONS (LESS FREQUENT)

Diagram showing bodily positions. See page 402 for a diagram of stage areas.

Scene from Fry's *The Lady's Not for Burning* showing considerable variety in bodily position and level. Directed by Henderson Forsythe.

Sometimes all actors are separated into two broad categories: those who depend primarily upon technique, and those who depend primarily upon feeling or instinct. The *technical actor* understands what devices will achieve the desired results and applies them systematically. The *instinctive actor* is said to depend upon the sincerity of his own responses or the inspiration of the moment to arouse belief in the audience. The best actors probably draw upon both approaches. At any rate, a thorough knowledge of technical devices should never be disparaged. Every director hopes that his actors will know the basic mechanics of acting, many of which are elementary.

The actor needs to be thoroughly familiar with stage areas, since directions are usually given in relation to them. *Upstage* means away from the audience; *downstage* means toward the audience; *right* and *left* refer to the actor's right or left as he faces the audience. The stage floor may also be spoken of as though it were divided into squares, each with its own designation: *up right, up center, up left, down right, down center, down left,* and so on. The actor's knowledge of this terminology is usually taken for granted and it is assumed that he will know what to do if he is told, for example, to enter up right and cross to down center.

The actor should be familiar with body positions. *Full front* means facing the audience; the *one-quarter* position means turned approximately 45 degrees away from the audience; *one-half* or *profile* means turned 90 degrees away from the audience; *three-quarter* means turned 135 degrees away from the audience; and *full back* means turned completely away from the audience.

Other terminology may supplement designations of area and bodily position. *Open up* means to turn slightly more toward the audience; *turn in* means to turn toward the center of the stage; *turn out* means to turn toward the side of the stage. Two actors are sometimes told to *share a scene*, meaning that both should play in the one-quarter or profile posi-

tion so that they are equally visible to the audience. *To give a scene* means that one actor gives the dominant stage position to another by changing his own bodily position to face more away from the audience than the other actor. In most scenes, emphasis shifts frequently from one character to another, and the actors may constantly be giving and taking the scene according to which needs to be most emphatic at that moment.

An actor may be told to *dress stage,* which means that he should move so as to balance the stage picture. This usually involves moving to a position just vacated by another actor. Experienced actors make such movements almost automatically and without being obtrusive. To *focus* means to look at or to turn toward a person or object in order to direct attention to it. Since stage terminology, such as that given here, summarizes a large number of the technical devices which the actor must know, it serves as a kind of shorthand in communications between the director and actors.

Although other technical problems cannot be reduced to such basic terminology, solutions to them must be learned. Many of the mechanics of stage technique have been devised to keep the actors as visible to the audience as possible. For example, the actor normally gestures with his upstage hand so as not to cover his face; he learns to kneel on his downstage knee so as to keep his body more visible to the audience; he opens doors with whichever hand is on the offstage side as he faces the audience; he stands upstage of doors and windows if he must call through them.

Other technical devices emphasize or subordinate actions. For example, a letter which is to be important later may be *planted* in an earlier scene. While its placement needs to be emphasized, its handling must not seem unnatural. The actor, therefore, might hesitate, or start to put it somewhere and then change his mind, before selecting the final spot. On

Even in moments of stress the actor usually seeks to remain "open" to the audience. Note how the kneeling actor keeps his face visible. Scene from Lope de Vega's *The Sheep Well.* Directed by Francis Hodge.

Scenes of eating pose difficult problems for both the actor and the director. Here some solutions are shown in a scene from Garcia Lorca's *The House of Bernarda Alba*. Directed by Shirley Ahern. Also see illustration page 309.

the other hand, many actions need to be masked from the audience. Eating, for example, must be faked to a large degree since actors can seldom eat the amount or the actual kind of food designated in the script. Scenes of violence (such as stabbings, shootings, and fist fights) must also be faked. They require careful planning and rehearsal so that they appear convincing although the details are hidden from the audience.

Furthermore the actor normally strives to be graceful, since gracefulness is usually unobtrusive, while awkwardness is distracting. The actor must learn to sit without looking to make sure that he is in front of a chair; he must rise without effort, be able to turn without seeming awkward, and avoid calling attention to anything unless emphasis is desired. For example, if an actor turns and looks at a chair before sitting in it, the chair and the act of sitting receive an emphasis which is normally inappropriate.

The actor must learn to make his movements precise and clear. Vagueness of movement creates the impression of indefiniteness. If the actor understands the purpose of his movements and gestures, he can usually make the purpose clear to an audience by selecting those actions which are expressive and by executing them with precision.

Only a few of the most common technical problems have been touched upon here. Every actor should acquire the soundest technical training possible, however, for technical devices are always needed to project a characterization.

SYSTEMS OF ACTING. No matter how well trained the actor is in basic skills, he will be unable to use them adequately unless he has a consistent method of working. Without system, results are spotty and accidental. A person cannot set out merely to become a good actor; he must define his objectives and then seek means for achieving them. Only in this way will his work have focus and will he be able to measure his progress and accomplishments.

426

There are many systems of acting. No actor should adopt a method, no matter how highly recommended by others, until he has given it a thorough trial. He should try as many different approaches as possible and adopt those elements from each which most effectively aid him.

While each actor must find that method which best fits his own needs, systems of acting tend to have many elements in common. The two poles are usually called the *psychological-internal* and the *mechanical-external*. The controversy which has raged between the advocates of the two extremes is centered around the question: Must the actor be emotionally moved himself in order to act convincingly?

Exponents of the *external* school argue that the actor need not feel anything himself and that, in fact, feeling may interfere with his acting since it may cause him to lose control. The principal sources of good acting are said to be observation and technique, and the actor is advised to study human behavior to see how each emotion is typically manifested. When called upon to portray an emotion, then, he need merely recreate all of the external signs, since the audience can not know whether the actor is feeling anything.

Believers in the *internal* school argue that it is only through feeling that an actor can project himself into the situation of the character, and that the ability to re-create states of feeling through emotion memory is the only way to avoid mechanical performances.

In their extreme forms, both of these schools are of questionable value. While Stanislavsky's name is popularly associated with the internal school, in actuality his theory represents a middle ground between the two extremes. It gives equal stress to the actor's psychological and technical training. In his system, feeling gives force and meaning to technique, while technique allows the clear and expressive projection of feeling. But like others, Stanislavsky's system must be judged by the degree to which it works for a given actor.

ADDITIONAL SKILLS AND TRAINING. Ultimately the actor applies all of his skill in the creation of a specific role. To be effective, therefore, he must be able to analyze plays, since he may apply his skills to advantage only if he understands the motivations, attitudes, and function of the character he is to portray.

Since he must create within a stage (rather than in a real-life) environment, the actor should also seek to understand all aspects of theatrical production. The more he knows about the possibilities and limitations of scenery, costumes, and lighting, the better he will be able to utilize them in his work.

CREATING THE ROLE

Regardless of his experience and training, the actor must solve a number of specific problems each time he undertakes a new role. Some of the typical problems can be treated under the following headings: analyzing the role; psychological and emotional preparation; movement and pantomime; vocal characterization; memorization and line readings;

427

conservation and build; ensemble playing; and dress rehearsals and performances.

ANALYZING THE ROLE. Before the actor begins work, he should understand his role thoroughly. Since a character must be approached in part through its function in the play, the actor should seek first to understand the script as a whole. Not until then should he concentrate upon the study and analysis of his own role. Play analysis has been discussed in Chapter 3, and only the most pertinent points about characterization will be reviewed here.

First, it is helpful to look at a role in terms of levels of characterization. What does the playwright reveal about the character's physical make-up; his profession, social class, economic status, and family background; his basic attitudes, likes, dislikes, and general emotional make-up; his ways of meeting crises and conflicts? Which characteristics are most important? How is each used in developing the story? Some traits will be of primary importance, while others may scarcely affect the play at all. The actor should strive to embody as many of the characteristics as possible, but he should emphasize those which are most essential to the story.

At times, the actor may find that the script fails to provide enough details to create a well-rounded characterization. In fact, the actor is almost always forced to invent much. For example, if the character's physical appearance is not specified, the actor must decide upon appropriate physical characteristics. In working on psychological characterization, many actors find it essential to reconstruct the life of the character prior to the beginning of the play, although the playwright may have given little information about it. In filling in missing details, the actor must be careful to take his cues from the script and to invent nothing contradictory to the author's portrait. Some actors become so engrossed in inventing business and details that they lose sight of a character's dramatic function.

Second, the actor must define the goals of the character he is to play. He should seek to isolate the over-all goal first, and then see how it is manifested in each scene, how it evolves and changes. In defining the character's goals, it is usually helpful to break the play down into short units or scenes and to isolate the character's principal motivation in each. This will help the actor to find the right focus for each scene, while an examination of individual scenes in relation to the whole play will show him how his characterization must build or grow.

Third, the actor should study character relationships. He must determine how his character is viewed by all the others. What a character thinks of himself may not be the same as the image he tries to create for others (he may try to mask his true self); each of the other characters may have differing conceptions of him. The actor also must analyze his character's feelings and attitudes about each of the other characters. Fourth, the actor must examine how his role relates to the play's structure, ideas, and themes.

If the play is from a past period, involves an unfamiliar environment, or deviates from the realistic mode, the actor may need to make a special effort at understanding the script and his role. He may need to study the period or place and determine the proper acting style.

Some period plays make special demands on movement. For example, men in the eighteenth century usually wore swords, carried walking sticks, snuff boxes, lace handkerchiefs, and other accessories which most modern men would find embarrassing to use. Therefore, a satisfactory and convincing performance may depend upon the actor's ability to project himself imaginatively into the past. The actor should find out what functions these accessories filled in the life of the eighteenth century, how they were used, and how they affected movement and gestures.

Most actors have been trained to perform primarily in a realistic style. Nevertheless, at times they are confronted with a role in an expressionistic, epic, or other nonrealistic style. In most cases, understanding of nonrealistic acting styles must come from reading and experimentation, for seldom do actors see specific nonrealistic styles on the stage often enough to learn them through direct observation.

While the actor must seek to understand his role, his interpretation must be adjusted to that of the director. If the actor and the director disagree, they should discuss their differing conceptions. Each should be willing to listen carefully to the other, but ultimately the actor must subordinate his interpretation to that given the play as a whole. The actor may have to change his interpretation or, if this is impossible, give up his part, for a satisfactory performance is unlikely if there are basic disagreements between director and actor.

PSYCHOLOGICAL AND EMOTIONAL PREPARATION. While through analysis the actor may come to understand a play, he must still be able to project himself imaginatively into it—the situation, the environment, and any conditions laid down by the director—before his preparation is complete.

Scene from Congreve's *Love for Love*. Note the cane, lace, wigs, fan, and other accessories which affect the actors' movements. Directed by Peter Arnott; costumes by Pat Crawford.

429

Sometimes an actor finds it difficult to imagine himself as the character and may need to experiment with ways of inducing belief in himself. The use of emotion memory and observation of similar persons and situations are the most common aids. When these do not work, improvisations based upon more familiar circumstances may help the actor to get the right feeling for a role. With this foundation, he may then enter more fully into the less familiar circumstances of the script.

Although not all actors prepare in this way, a good performance usually depends upon the actor's ability to understand the character's every motivation. Although the actor may never actually feel anything himself, he should at least know how the character would feel.

MOVEMENT, GESTURE, AND BUSINESS. As a rule, blocking is done early. Although the director may indicate a position for each moment, the actor should feel that all his movements are justified and should speak out whenever he finds a direction contrary to his understanding of the role. Conflicts over movement can frequently be resolved by discussing the character, since disagreements usually stem from the actor's feeling that certain actions are inappropriate.

Even when the director specifies stage and bodily positions, the actor must fill in many details—the character's walk, posture, bodily attitudes, and gestures. Since the kinds of movement and their purposes have been discussed in Chapter 17, they need be reviewed only briefly here.

Movement is either specified by the script or invented. In either case it may be used for several purposes: to tell a story; to establish character; to clarify motivations, attitudes, and emotional responses; to establish mood and style; to create variety; to secure and hold attention; and to compose a stage picture. While some of these purposes are not directly related to characterization, all movement is executed by actors and, therefore, should be performed in a manner appropriate to the character and the play's style. The better the actor understands the purpose behind each movement, the more he will be able to make effective use of it.

Scene from Anderson's *Elizabeth the Queen.* Note the effective use of gesture.

The actor's physical characterization proceeds on at least three levels. First, a role must be approached in terms of its physical attributes. While some roles require marked changes between the initial and final appearances, as a rule the broad outlines (habitual ways of walking, sitting, and gesturing) remain unchanged.

Second, out of basic attributes the actor must be able to select and use those appropriate to any given moment. It is sometimes helpful to think of the play as though it had no words. The actor then must decide how the situation, character relationships, emotional responses, and motivations can be expressed visually. Much of what he would do under such circumstances would have to be discarded when words are added, for it would be redundant, but this approach may stimulate the actor's imagination and help him to find helpful devices for physical characterization.

Third, within the limitations imposed by the script and role, the actor should work for distinctiveness. While a characterization should always be clear, good acting usually seems orginal and free from clichés. The actor can achieve this effect only after considering the various ways in which a given point might be made and by choosing one which is both clear and unusual.

Although no rules can be laid down for physical characterization, the broad criteria of appropriateness, clarity, expressiveness, and distinctiveness should be kept in mind.

VOCAL CHARACTERIZATION. The actor's analysis of his role should also involve appropriate vocal qualities and mannerisms. For one role, a high-pitched voice might be helpful; another might profit from a jerky delivery; another might require loudness and boisterousness; another may demand a dialect.

The actor cannot always change his own voice sufficiently to give an ideal vocal characterization. For this reason, directors normally cast actors who already possess the vocal qualities they are seeking. The actor with a well-trained voice, however, can certainly modify his own vocal patterns.

Every actor should be thoroughly familiar with his own voice and speech (a tape recorder will help in this analysis). When he undertakes a role, he can decide what vocal changes are desirable and which are possible. The actor must be careful not to put undue strain on his voice, however, for serious damage can result if changes are incorrectly made.

Not only should the actor analyze the over-all vocal demands of a role, he should also examine each scene for its requirements. Some scenes are relaxed, others are emotionally high-keyed, and still others are varied in tone. A scene can be clarified through well-thought-out vocal patterns. For example, tension, typical of high-keyed scenes, may be manifested in raised pitch, greater volume, and faster tempo. A clear understanding of the function and the emotional content of each scene will tell the actor what he should work for vocally.

Voice is also an important element in clarifying ideas and emotions. Any change of thought or feeling may be indicated by a change in vol-

431

Scene from Sherwood's *Abe Lincoln in Illinois.* Here level, bodily position, and focus all "give" the stage to the standing actor.

ume, pitch, or quality. The voice should, of course, be used in character and be entirely appropriate to the situation.

Much of his vocal characterization may come naturally to an actor if he understands his role thoroughly and if he has been able to project himself into the situation imaginatively. Such automatic characterization should never be taken for granted, however, and the actor should try to assess the degree to which his use of voice is appropriate to the role.

MEMORIZATION AND LINE READINGS. One of the technical problems facing every actor is memorization. It is usually helpful to memorize speeches and action simultaneously, for lines help to recall movement and movement to recall lines. It may be difficult to coordinate these two elements in the beginning, but, since blocking is always made in relation to specific speeches, their conjunction ultimately becomes fused in the actor's memory.

In solving the problem of memorization there are a few simple rules. First, since it is impossible to memorize everything at once, it is necessary to divide the play into sections and to master them one at a time. Second, since it is extremely difficult to memorize disconnected words, the actor should begin by familiarizing himself with the sequence of ideas and motivations—the sense of each scene. After he is able to recall this sequence, he may then proceed to the memorization of actual words. This contextual approach is also an aid to the actor in performance if he forgets the specific wording of a speech, for he can improvise its sense. Furthermore, it enables him to assist other actors should their memories fail. Third, the actor should be familiar with the lines of all the other actors in his scenes, and he must memorize *cues* (the words or action of others which precede each of his own lines) as thoroughly as he does his own speeches.

There is some difference of opinion about the best time to memorize. The sooner the actor learns his lines, the earlier he will be able to polish and work for subtlety. On the other hand, if an actor memorizes his lines before he is clear about his interpretation of the role or the significance of speeches, he may be unconvincing. Nevertheless, it is better to learn

432

lines too early than too late, for nothing more quickly destroys the believ-ability of a performance than shakiness in lines.

In addition to knowing his lines, the actor must be concerned with stress, intonation, and duration. A thorough understanding of all the implications of a line is necessary before it can be properly delivered. The good actor normally concentrates upon the over-all thought and emotion rather than upon individual words. He knows where one idea ends and another begins, and he makes transitions with care so that each thought is clear.

To indicate progressions and transitions, the actor uses changes in pitch, volume, and duration so as to set off one unit or idea from another. This is especially important in long speeches where both monotony and confusion of thought or feeling are most apt to occur.

In the majority of plays, the actor must work for the effect of spontane-ity, for his speeches should appear to arise from the situation and emo-tion and without forethought. Falseness in line readings or in tone makes the audience question the sincerity of the actor or of the charac-ter. Spontaneity and believability depend upon the type of play (*King Lear* differs from *Death of a Salesman* in part because of dissimilarities in language and phrasing). Regardless of the type of play, the actor should strive for: clarity of ideas and emotions, spontaneity, believabili-ty, variety, distinctiveness, and audibility.

CONSERVATION AND BUILD. The actor must learn to conserve his pow-ers and build his role in a climactic order. Every play progresses from the less to the more interesting as it builds in intensity or suspense. Similar-ly, an actor's performance should grow and progress. Sometimes an ac-tor fails because, while individual scenes are well-played, his perform-ance as a whole does not develop in intensity and complexity.

The need to sustain and build a part is most clearly seen in highly emo-tional roles. If the actor begins at an emotional pitch which is too high, he may soon find that he can build the intensity no farther. The rest of the performance, then, remains on a level and becomes monotonous. Therefore, the actor must learn to judge his power and plan performance so that it builds throughout the play.

ENSEMBLE PLAYING. No acting performance (except in those rare plays written for one character) is complete by itself. It is only one of many characterizations, and its effectiveness must be judged in part according to how well it is integrated with the other performances. An actor must therefore be able to relate himself convincingly to all the characters on stage. The sense of artistic wholeness which results from the cooperative efforts of the entire cast is frequently called *ensemble playing*.

Ensemble playing is the result of a number of factors. First, it comes only when each actor is willing to subordinate himself to the demands of the play. Each must be able to fade into the background when unimpor-tant, refrain from trying to steal scenes, and put the good of the produc-tion above winning plaudits for himself.

433

In ensemble playing the actor must refrain from trying to steal scenes, must concentrate and appear really to listen, must respond with properly timed reactions so that the action seems to be unfolding spontaneously. A scene from *Danton's Death*, Alan Bergman (foreground) as Danton. Courtesy of the Repertory Theater of Lincoln Center. Photograph—Peter Daness.

Second, ensemble playing depends in part upon each actor's awareness of the working methods, strengths, and weaknesses of his fellow actors. He learns what he can expect of the others, where he needs to compensate for their shortcomings, and how they may help him. Such cooperative acting is one of the distinctive marks of a company whose members have worked together over a long period of time. While such awareness is limited in a cast working together for only one play, it should be developed as far as possible.

Third, the most important factor in ensemble playing is the ability to concentrate. It is the actors who appear really to listen, see, and respond with subtle and properly timed reactions who seem most believable. No matter how often they have played the same role, they create the illusion of the first time. The best performances come when all the actors concentrate so completely on the stage events that the action seems to be unfolding spontaneously.

DRESS REHEARSALS AND PERFORMANCES. As a rule, it is not until dress rehearsals that an actor is able to work with all properties, settings, costumes, make-up, and stage lighting. The surer he is of his performance by this time, the less distracting the new elements will be. He can do much to ease the transition from rehearsal to performance if he has taken time earlier to familiarize himself thoroughly with the stage environment. The visual background will seem less strange if the actor will take time to study the sketches and models made by the designers. Through rehearsals he should have become familiar with the floor plan of the scenery. Of special importance is his costume. He should find out everything he can about it — what movements it enhances, which it restricts, its possibilities for business, and so on. A costumer is usually delighted when an actor takes a genuine interest in his costume and is willing to help him explore its intricacies and potentials. If stage garments are significantly different from those which the actor normally wears, he should be provided with a rehearsal costume which simulates the clothing to be worn in performance.

The actor should also have given considerable thought to his make-up before dress rehearsal. He should know what effects he wishes to create and should have experimented with achieving them if they are in any way unusual.

If the actor has business with swords, guns, packages, food, or other items which may create difficulties, he should rehearse frequently with reasonable facsimiles of those which will be used in performance.

Performance, of course, is the goal. The better rehearsed the actor is, the more certain he will feel when opening night comes. It is a rare actor, however, who does not experience some stage fright. And this may be beneficial, for it keeps the actor alert and ready to meet any emergency.

If all goes well on opening night, actors tend to relax and to give poorer performances on the second night. Actors playing in long-run shows find it difficult to maintain interest in their roles and the quality of performance suffers. The actor must remember, however, that each performance is the first for the audience to which he is playing. The ability to maintain a reasonably even quality depends ultimately upon the actors' ability to concentrate.

The actor finds it easier to maintain interest if he seeks to assess the effectiveness of his acting in each performance and if he looks upon each night as an occasion for improvement. Performance offers the actor his greatest opportunity for learning, since the ability to affect an audience is the ultimate test of skill. Each audience should be viewed as a new judge of his strength.

After a show has closed, the actor should take stock of his abilities and achievements. He needs to re-evaluate his goals and his working methods. The development of acting ability is a never-ending process and only the conscientious actor succeeds in perfecting his art.

THE ACTOR'S EMPLOYMENT

In America today, most actors enter the theatre after attending colleges, universities, or professional schools. This is a major change from past practice. Previously the actor was trained on the job. He entered a company at an early age, learned his trade as he played minor roles, and eventually graduated into a line of business which he filled for the rest of his life. This kind of training was possible, however, only so long as there were many permanent companies. When the repertory system began to die out in America near the end of the nineteenth century, new ways had to be found to train actors. As early as 1884, the American Academy of Dramatic Art had begun to provide professional training and other professional theatre schools soon sprang up. About 1915, theatre training began to be offered in colleges, and became especially widespread after World War II.

Today the majority of colleges and universities in America offer at least one course in acting. These courses usually introduce students to the principles, techniques, and goals of acting. The student often wrongly views such course work, however, as sufficient to equip him for a professional career. Few colleges and universities offer enough work to train the actor adequately for the professional stage.

In the educational theatre, the actor with real talent seldom finds it difficult to be cast in plays, although the supply of available actors is often greater than the demand. The actor who has been trained in college and who does not wish to work in the professional theatre can almost always find an outlet for his talent in a community theatre after he has left school.

Professional schools, most of which are located in or near New York, give the actor intensive training in his craft. They also allow him to become familiar with the professional theatre at close range (although the degree to which this is true is often exaggerated). Unfortunately, however, completion of a professional program carries little more guarantee of employment in the professional theatre than does any other training.

Since the 1920's, summer stock companies have flourished in the United States, and many actors have found them good sources of training and employment. All companies approved by Actors' Equity pay scaled salaries, and many accept apprentices for training. Unfortunately most summer theatres have so few rehearsals that the actor is more apt to learn tricks for covering up inadequacies than the solid foundations of acting. Because of its intensive schedule and its tendency to mingle learners with experienced actors, summer theatre can serve as a bridge, even if not an entirely satisfactory one, between the educational and the professional theatre.

Regardless of training, the young actor who wishes to work in the professional theatre almost invariably goes to New York, although there may be somewhat longer but more promising roads to success. An increasing number of professional theatres now operate outside of New York, and the aspiring actor might well consider them. They include The Alley Theatre in Houston, The Cleveland Playhouse, The Tyrone Guthrie Theatre in Minneapolis, and the Arena Theatre in Washington, D.C. As long as New York remains the center of theatrical activity, however, the majority of would-be actors will flock there, even though 85 percent of the members of Actors' Equity are frequently unemployed.

The unknown actor without an agent has little chance of being cast in a New York production, although theoretically he has an opportunity each time a play is produced. Since 1964 Actors' Equity has required producers to hold open interviews in connection with each play. Before he begins casting, the producer must supply Equity with a list of the roles and information about the time and place for interviews. This information is posted on a bulletin board in the Equity building so that all members can have access to it. The producer must devote a minimum of eight

436

hours to interviews. The number of actors seen depends upon the length of time spent with each and the number of persons conducting interviews. If only one person sees actors, even if only five minutes is spent with each, fewer than 100 applicants are seen during an eight-hour period. Consequently, while Equity rules make it mandatory that casting be open to all of its members, only a fraction of the 15,000 can be considered under these conditions.

Not all of those interviewed are permitted to tryout for roles. Those who meet certain basic requirements may be admitted to the tryouts, but others are also admitted on the basis of the producer's knowledge of their previous work or because they have been recommended by agents whose judgment the producer trusts. When he is about to begin casting, a producer notifies actors' agents who then seek hearings for clients suited to the roles. Even off-Broadway producers now depend heavily on agents. Thus, the actor with an agent has a much better chance of being cast than one who does not.

It is not easy for an actor to obtain an agent, for few agents are willing to represent clients whose work they have not seen. A role in a nonprofessional or summer stock production is frequently used by an actor to display his ability to an agent. The actor, on the other hand, should make sure that his agent is on the approved list maintained by Actors' Equity to protect its members from unethical agents.

Employment opportunities are so restricted in New York that many actors work at other jobs, often at night so as to be free for interviews and tryouts during the day, while awaiting a break. Persistence pays off frequently enough to encourage the hundreds of would-be actors who flock to New York each year, most of whom are destined for disappointment.

Before an actor can perform in a Broadway production he must become a member of Actors' Equity Association. (He may be cast without being a member, but he must join before he can be given a contract.) Actually, there are a number of unions to which actors may belong. Sometimes they join more than one so as to increase the possibilities of employment. These unions comprise a larger organization, the Associated Actors and Artistes of America, an affiliate of the American Federation of Labor. The AAAA is composed of the following groups: Actors' Equity Association; American Federation of Television and Radio Artists; Screen Actors Guild; Hebrew Actors Guild; Italian Actors Union; American Guild of Variety Artists; Screen Extras Guild; and American Guild of Musical Artists.

Actors' Equity controls most contracts in the legitimate theatre. (Actors' Equity classifies acting companies according to production conditions; the percentage of the company which must be Equity members and the minimum wage scales are determined by a company's classification. Non-Broadway companies are usually governed by different regulations than those applying to Broadway productions.) Actors' Equity specifies minimum wages and working conditions and maintains a legal staff to advise its members on deviations from standard contracts.

There are three basic kinds of contracts in the New York theatre: standard minimum; run of the play; and conversion. The normal contract is the *standard minimum,* which specifies that an actor may leave the show after giving two-weeks' notice and that he may be let go under similar conditions. *Run of the play* contracts are most often used for stars, who agree to remain with a production for a given length of time. The contract also specifies financial arrangements should the play close or the star leave the show before the stated period has expired. The *conversion* contract contains an option for converting a *standard minimum* contract to a *run of the play* contract; it is used when the producer has reservations about a star's abilities. If the contract is converted, the actor's salary must also be increased; after the conversion, the contract is governed by all the conditions of a *run of the play* contract.

Any contract may have special clauses which indicate additional duties (such as understudying a role), privileges, billing, and so on. No Equity contract may be made, however, which violates the minimum standards established by Actors' Equity.

Most touring shows are also cast in New York. It is probably easier to obtain a role in a touring company than in any other kind because of the reluctance of so many actors to leave New York. A number of resident and summer stock companies also seek their actors in New York. For these reasons, New York and the American professional theatre have become synonymous for the aspiring professional actor.

Acting is one of the most glamorous professions in the world, but it is also one of the most exacting and one of the most difficult in which to secure a foothold. Yet the actor is the artist most necessary for the existence of a theatre. Given the conditions under which he must work in America today, he not only needs great talent but unflagging perseverance and dedication.

Chapter 19 THE SCENE DESIGNER

While the director and actor use the stage environment in their work, they normally depend upon others to design the scenery, costumes, and lighting which compose the environment. The designers are concerned with the visual embodiment of the mood and atmosphere, theme, style, period, place, and socioeconomic background of the play.

All theatrical design has common aims and uses similar means; frequently the same person designs all of the visual elements. Since scenery, costumes, and lighting each has its own distinctive features, however, they will be discussed separately so that each may be more fully clarified.

The scene designer is concerned principally with defining and characterizing the stage space. Through the placement of scenic elements he outlines the areas which will be used by the actors and limits the view of the audience to that portion of the stage which is needed for the production. He determines the desirable visual characteristics of each scene and of the play as a whole. He dresses the setting with appropriate furniture, draperies, pictures, or other properties. He makes sure that all of his plans are properly executed and that his settings function as envisioned during the performance of the play.

The various aspects of the scene designer's work will be considered under the following headings: the purposes of design; the elements and principles of design; working procedures and plans; standard scenic pieces; assembling scenery; painting scenery; shifting scenery; furniture, decoration, and properties; rehearsals and performances.

THE PURPOSES OF SCENE DESIGN

The two basic purposes of scene design are: to aid understanding, and to project artistic qualities. As an aid to understanding, the stage setting

Designer's sketch for Goldoni's *The Mistress of the Inn*. Note the asymmetrical balance; the variety in line, shape, decoration, and texture; the pleasing proportions; and the floor plan, which encourages an easy flow of movement. Design by Alexandre Benois. From *Moscow Art Theatre, 1898–1917,* 1955.

may define the time and place of the action, it should clarify the relationship of the offstage and onstage space, and it should assist in establishing characterization.

The amount of emphasis placed on period and place varies considerably from one work to another. Some plays (such as *The Wild Duck* and others in the realistic mode) specify many details drawn from a particular period or place. The designer may need to create, through furniture, pictures, and other properties, an environment similar to that found in real life at the time of the action. Other plays, such as those by Molière and Sheridan, indicate time and country but do not emphasize these details. In such cases, the designer may use decorative motifs of the period, or a wing-and-drop setting similar to those used in the seventeenth and eighteenth centuries, but make no attempt to create the real-life environment of the time. In other cases, such as in Shakespeare's plays, time and place are of so little importance that the locale may be left indefinite. In this case, the stage setting should tell the audience immediately that the place of the action is of little consequence. Regardless of the importance of period and locale, the designer depends primarily upon architectural forms, painted details, and properties to define time and place as they will be used in each production.

The physical arrangement of the setting should aid understanding in a number of ways. Whenever characters enter or exit, the script usually implies the place from which they are coming or to which they are going. The floor plan of the setting, therefore, should help to clarify both the onstage and the offstage space. In designing a realistic living-room, the arrangement of the rest of the house must be kept in mind (the location of the main entrance, the kitchen, and the bedrooms is usually important). In other plays, the nature of the offstage space may not be specified, but the designer must make sure that his set allows clarity of action (for example, if one character must enter the stage immediately after another has left, and if the two are not supposed to see each other, the design must clearly permit this action if the audience is not to be confused).

The stage space can also aid understanding by allowing variety in the grouping of actors. Platforms and steps permit the director greater scope

440

Setting for Maeterlinck's *The Blue Bird*, a symbolic drama about the search for happiness, as performed at the Moscow Art Theatre in 1908. From *Moscow Art Theatre, 1898–1917*, 1955.

than does a single-level setting for creating emphases and compositions which clarify character relationships and situations. Furthermore, since the floor plan of any setting allows certain patterns of movement and restricts others, it can be arranged to encourage the smooth flow of action. For example, the setting required by *Death of a Salesman* includes three different rooms and an exterior. This arrangement permits one scene to flow smoothly into the next while defining clearly the location of each scene. The use of nonlocalized settings in the staging of Shakespeare's plays has arisen from the desire to keep the action moving uninterruptedly.

The stage setting must also be expressive of the play's basic artistic qualities. It should help to create and heighten the proper mood. It should help to answer the question: With what kind of world are we in contact (a reasonable facsimile of everyday existence; a world like our own but one in which all except the essential details have been stripped away; a world of fantasy; an absurd world)? The setting should give some indication of the type (tragedy, comedy, melodrama), the style (expressionism, naturalism, epic, and so on), and the theme of a play. It should embody the essential qualities of the play through line, color, form, and spatial relationships, just as the actor seeks to embody the play's qualities through his use of body and voice. A good setting is a visual statement of the script's artistic characteristics.

Steps and platforms used to create numerous playing levels. A scene from Webster's *The Duchess of Malfi*.

THE ELEMENTS OF
DESIGN

All visual design uses the same basic elements—line, shape, space, color, texture, and ornament.

Line defines boundaries. Although in reality a tree, for example, does not have lines (it occupies a given space), in a drawing its shape is indicated by a series of lines. A line should be distinguished from the shape or form it outlines, for a line has only one dimension—length—whereas form can create the impression of two- or three-dimensionality.

While a line has only one dimension, it may go in any direction. There are two basic kinds—straight and curved. They may be combined or altered to form zigzags, scallops, or other variations. The dominant lines in most stage settings are horizontal (the stage floor and ceiling) and vertical (the upright scenery). This basic pattern is varied by furniture, draperies, foliage, and other scenic elements.

Line is normally thought to elicit emotional responses. Straight lines may give a quality of stability, curved lines of grace. The inherent opposition of zigzag lines creates a dynamic quality. Two lines which move farther apart as they rise vertically can generate a feeling of openness, while those that come close together may create a sense of oppression because they seem to be falling inward. Although emotional value depends in part upon the context, line is an important device for creating mood and atmosphere as well as for defining shape.

Shape and space are closely related concepts and are frequently treated together as a single element—mass. While line has only the dimension of direction or length, mass involves three dimensions. It identifies the shape (square, round, oblong) and the size (height, width, and thickness) of objects.

Each part of the setting, each piece of furniture, and each prop has a shape and occupies space. Therefore, mass must be considered in relation to each individual element and to the entire setting, which also has a dominant shape and occupies a given space.

The setting may be thought of as a hollow cube, the inside of which can be organized in a variety of ways. By altering the shape and size of the individual elements and their relationship to each other, almost any effect may be achieved. Thick, horizontal forms (for example, a room with a low ceiling and thick beams) may create an effect of compression, while narrow, vertical, and pointed forms (such as a room with thin, tall columns and high Gothic arches) may create a sense of airiness, openness, and grace.

The shape and size of objects may be emphasized by sharp distinctions between planes and surfaces (for instance, one side of a cube may be very dark, another very light). Such sharp definition gives a quality of harshness. On the other hand, if the differentiations between planes and surfaces are subtle, a feeling of softness or diffusion results.

Mass, then, involves the shape and size of the total setting and its various elements, and the organization of the stage space. It can be perceived in such factors as the height of a setting in proportion to its width and depth; the thickness of door frames and beams; the size and shape

442

of furniture, trees, platforms and stairs. It creates impressions of openness or compression, of heaviness or lightness, of great space or of confinement.

In addition to line and mass, color is an important element in design. Color may be described in terms of three basic qualities, dimensions, or properties: hue, saturation or intensity, and value. Hue is the name of the color. Saturation or intensity refers to the relative purity of a color (its freedom from gray or its complementary hue). Value is the lightness or darkness of a color—its relation to white or black. A color which is light in value is usually called a tint, while one dark in value is called a shade.

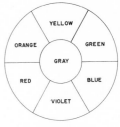

COLOR WHEEL

Colors may be classified as *primary*, *secondary*, or *intermediate*. The *primary* colors are those which cannot be created by mixing other colors, but from which all other colors are derived. The primary colors in pigment are yellow, red, and blue. The *secondary* colors—orange, violet, and green—are those created from equal mixtures of two primary colors. The *intermediate* colors are mixtures of a primary with a secondary color. They are yellow-orange, red-orange, red-violet, blue-violet, blue-green, and yellow-green. The various colors may be arranged around a wheel to indicate their relationships. Those opposite each other on the wheel are called complementary colors, while those next to each other are called analogous colors. Colors may also be described as warm or cool. For example, red, orange, and yellow are warm colors, while green, blue, and violet are cool colors.

Almost any combination of colors may be used together if saturation, proportion, or value are properly controlled. Two colors which seem to clash when used in their full intensity or in equal quantity may be made harmonious by graying one or both of the colors (that is by lowering the saturation), by lightening the values, or by using a small amount of one color in proportion to the other.

Color schemes may be monochromatic, analogous, or contrasting. The simplest is the monochromatic scheme. This means that a single hue is used, and variety is gained by combining differing intensities and values. An analogous color scheme is one in which all of the hues have one element in common. For example, blue-green, green, and yellow-green all have green in common. The most obvious contrast is to be found in complementary hues: orange and blue, yellow and violet, blue-green and red-orange. If such a color scheme is not to be unpleasant, it must be used with considerable attention to proper saturation, value, and proportion. Sometimes a split-complement is used. This means that, instead of using the hue directly across the color wheel, those which lie on either side of the complementary are selected. For example, instead of using yellow and violet, as one might in a simple complementary arrangement, a split-complement would use yellow with red-violet and blue-violet. Another common color scheme is called the triad; that is, three colors which are equidistant from each other on the color wheel are used together (for example, yellow-orange, red-violet, and blue-green).

The three properties of color may be manipulated in many different ways to achieve the effects desired by a scene designer. Mood and at-

443

mosphere, for example, depend much on the use of color. Many persons believe that light, warm colors are much more likely to evoke a comic response than are dark, cool colors. Furthermore, colors are sometimes associated with specific emotions. Red and orange may connote heat and passion, whereas green and blue may suggest coolness and restraint. The response which will be elicited by any given color is difficult to predict, for much depends upon the context in which it appears. Nevertheless, color does affect audiences emotionally, and the designer must use it accordingly.

Other effects also utilize color. A hue of light value can help to create a feeling of openness and space, while a dark color may aid in arousing the sense of oppression and confinement. Dark objects seem bulkier and heavier than those which are light in value. Some color combinations are garish, while others are sophisticated. The designer, therefore, may use color to create the right mood and atmosphere and to establish the taste of the characters who inhabit the settings.

Texture is another element of each design. In stage settings, texture is often used to indicate the supposed material of which the setting is made. In actuality, the visible surface of most scenery is painted canvas. Nevertheless, in most cases it must appear to be of some other material (brick, stone, rough or smooth plaster, wood) or to be some natural object (a tree, the ground, outcroppings of rock). Most frequently a setting makes use of more than one texture. The walls of a room may appear to be plaster, while the doors and windows appear to be wood and glass. Other textures are brought in through rugs, upholstery, draperies, and pictures.

Texture may be used for many purposes. It may help to establish a period. For example, Elizabethan houses are often depicted as half-timbered (that is, made of heavy timbers and plaster or stucco). Texture may help to establish the appropriate feeling. Adjectives such as smooth, rough, shiny, soft, and grained are often applied to texture and such descriptive words frequently seem equally applicable to the qualities inherent in a script. Some plays seem to demand rough textures, whereas others may call for smooth textures. The qualities of sleaziness, fragility, or richness depend in part upon the textures used. Texture, thus, may be chosen and manipulated by the designer to achieve his purposes.

Ornament is also an element in design. It includes the pictures on the walls, decorative motifs, wallpaper patterns, molding, and similar items. Ornament is one of the chief means for achieving distinctiveness in a setting, for it is used principally to add the touches which complete the picture. For example, even if all the other elements of design have been used skillfully, the walls of a living-room setting will appear barren without proper ornament. This ornamentation, however, must clearly distinguish the living room of a wealthy person from that of a person of modest means, of the person of good taste from that of the person devoid of taste. Ornament, thus, is a subtle but important element of design.

The scene designer must be thoroughly familiar with each element of design and with what may be accomplished with each. Through his manipulations of these elements he externalizes the qualities inherent in the script.

444

In applying the elements of design, certain artistic principles must be used if the results are to be pleasing and effective. The principles of design are *harmony, balance, proportion, emphasis,* and *rhythm.*

Harmony creates the impression of unity. All of the elements of each setting should be harmonious and the various settings for the same play should be related so that all are clearly parts of an ordered whole. If monotony is to be avoided, however, variety is required both in a single setting and among the various settings. The elements of design may be manipulated so as to accomplish this double effect of unity and variety.

Balance is that sense of stability which results from the apparent equal distribution of weight on either side of a central axis. The stage may be thought of as a fulcrum with the point of balance at the center. The scenic elements placed on each side of that line should appear to be equal in weight; if they are not, an uneasy response may be aroused. Apparent weight has no direct relationship to actual weight. It is perceived in such factors as color, size, placement, and texture. A large, light-colored object may appear to weigh no more than a small, dark-colored object. Furthermore, the placement of elements on stage has much to do with the sense of balance. A small object near the outer edge of the set may be used to balance a large object near the center of the stage. A small object which appears to be made of stone may balance a larger one which appears to be made of wood. Thus, each of the elements of design may be manipulated to achieve a sense of balance.

There are two basic kinds of balance: symmetrical and asymmetrical. Symmetrical balance means that each side of the stage is a mirror image of the other (that is, the same elements are repeated on each side of the center line). Obviously symmetrical balance can be easily achieved, but it is not always desirable since it creates an impression of formality and often seems contrived. Asymmetrical balance uses a more random placement of elements and creates the effect of informality. It requires a more subtle manipulation of the elements of design, however, for it must give the appearance of being unplanned while being perfectly balanced.

Proportion involves the relationship between the parts of a design: the shapes (squares, rectangles, free-form, and so on); the scale of each element in relation to the others; and the division of the space (for example, if a wall is to be painted two colors, how much space should be devoted to each?). Proportion can be manipulated to elicit a wide variety of responses. It can help to create the impression of stability or of instability, of grace or awkwardness. Furniture that is too large in proportion to the size of a room may give a cramped feeling, whereas furniture that is too small in scale may appear meager and poor. Each element of the stage setting must be properly proportioned both in itself and in relation to each of the other elements, for the beauty or ugliness of the whole depends in large part upon the proportions of the individual items.

A design must also have a focal point, or center of *emphasis.* A well-composed design will direct the eye to the most important point immediately and then to each of the subordinate parts in the order of their importance to the whole. Although there may be a number of focal points in the same design, one should be dominant.

A drawing by Ferdinando Galli da Bibiena (1657–1743) to demonstrate perspective drawing for his students. At the bottom, the floor plan is shown reversed in relation to the drawing. Note the perspective points at either side. From Bibiena's *Direzioni a'Giovani studenti nel disegno*. Bologna, 1731–32.

Emphasis may be achieved in several ways. Line may be used. For example, a triangular platform with its apex at center stage will lead the eye to that point. The lines of walls, furniture, steps, and decorative motifs may all be utilized to create focal points.

Emphasis may be achieved by the grouping or placement of objects. For example, a sofa may become an emphatic object through its position on stage, or a series of similar objects may be used to lead the eye to the last in the series or to contrast with an unlike object.

Color may be used effectively for achieving emphasis: a brighter saturation, a hue which contrasts with others around it, or a difference in value may direct the eye to a point of interest. Unusual texture or decoration may also gain emphasis.

Rhythm is that factor which leads the eye easily and smoothly from one part of a picture to another. All of the elements of design may be used to achieve a sense of rhythm. Lines and shapes may be repeated; the size of objects may be changed gradually so as to give a sense of progression; gradations or alterations in hue, saturation, and value may lead the eye easily from one part of the composition to another; changes in texture and ornament may give a sense of flow and movement.

The ways in which the elements and principles of design can be utilized are inexhaustible. The scene designer should be aware of many possibilities so that he may vary his means to create the effects he wishes. A mastery of the elements and principles of design is part of the scene designer's education and is assumed when he begins work on a show.

446

Like other theatre workers, the designer should first attempt to under-stand the script. He should make as thorough an analysis of the play as does the director or actor. He should begin by studying the play in terms of its action, characters, themes, language, and spectacle. Only then should he proceed to an analysis of its scenic demands, for the more thoroughly he understands the play the better are his chances of providing an appropriate visual rendering of its values.

The designer analyzes the script with several points in mind: the number of settings required; the kinds of settings (interior, exterior, living room, courtyard, prison, and so on); the space needed for the action; the physical arrangement of the settings (number and placement of doors and windows, the furniture, the need for platforms and steps); indications of period, place, social and economic background; indications of type and style (tragedy, melodrama, comedy; symbolism, expressionism, realism).

The designer may need to do research into the manners and customs, the principal decorative motifs, the common architectural forms, the typical furnishings and household equipment, the materials normally used in buildings, and the uses made of color in the period of the play's action. He may wish to explore the staging conventions for which the play was written. Although he may not use all of this information, it can stimulate the imagination and will provide accurate knowledge when authenticity is desired.

Before the designer makes sketches and plans, he should meet with the director and the other designers. These conferences may be attended also by the producer, playwright, choreographer, conductor, and principal actors. The purpose of the initial conference is to clarify the interpretation and the kind of production being given the play. Differences of opinion should be resolved, but when they cannot, the director's point of view should be adopted.

At the initial conference, the scene designer should also note any specific requirements of the director. For example, must the entrances and exits be at particular places on the stage? How much floor space does the director envision using for each scene? Are there pieces of business which will demand a specific property or which will require a given arrangement of the set or furniture? If he does not already know, the designer must also find answers to such questions as: How much money is available for the scenery? Upon what stage is the play to be performed? What are the physical characteristics of the stage? With what equipment is it provided?

His knowledge of the script, of the director's interpretation, and of the financial and physical arrangements provide the limitations within which the designer must work. With these in mind he can proceed to make sketches.

Since the designer's principal means of communication are pictorial, he must put his ideas into visual form before they can be assessed. In the early stages of his work the designer may make numerous sketches be-

447

Designer's sketch for Studs Terkel's *Amazing Grace*. Eldon Elder's wash drawing shows the lobby of a once-elegant hotel that is to be demolished and replaced by a skyscraper. Near the stair is the first scaffolding. Through the scrim ceiling, when the lights are behind it, may be seen the steel girders and form of the building going up next door. Produced at the Mendelssohn Theatre, Ann Arbor, by the Professional Theatre Program of the University of Michigan, 1967. Reproduced courtesy Eldon Elder.

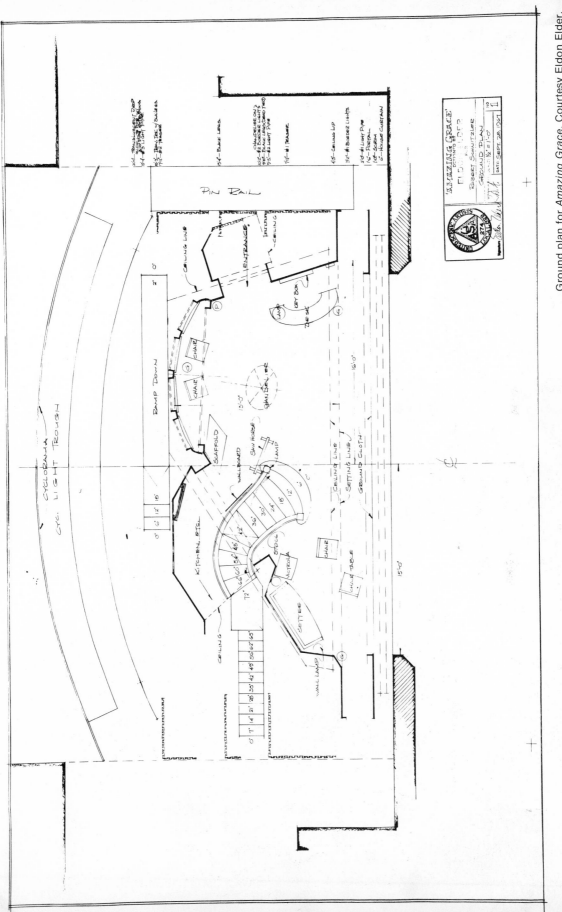

Ground plan for *Amazing Grace*. Courtesy Eldon Elder.

fore he arrives at one which pleases him. These "idea" sketches may be line drawings. After he has settled upon designs which he thinks right for the play, his ideas are discussed at other conferences with the director and designers. Some suggestions may have to be abandoned and new ones made. Before final approval can be given, the designs must be rendered in color and drawn in perspective to show how the finished settings will look on stage when lighted. Since sketches can be deceptive, the designer must also, as a rule, supply floor plans which show the arrangement of each setting, and he may be asked to construct three-dimensional scale models which show in miniature each set as it will appear when completed. Revisions are made until agreement is reached. The plans for scenery should not be approved until the lighting and costume designs are available, since the total stage picture includes all these elements.

After his visual conception of the scenery has been accepted, the designer must make working drawings. The number depends in part upon who is to execute them. If the designer also builds and paints the scenery, few drawings may be made. If other persons must carry out the plans, however, numerous drawings may be needed. Working drawings are instructions that show what is to be done and the materials and methods to be used. Complete plans greatly diminish the likelihood of errors.

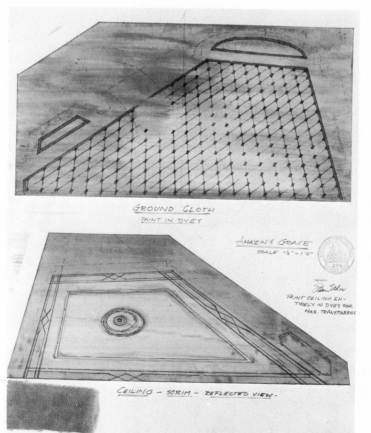

Detail of ground cloth, *above. Below*, ceiling scrim, reflected view. Note attached swatch of material used for ground cloth. Courtesy Eldon Elder.

Skyscraper design for translucent muslin backdrop. Courtesy Eldon Elder.

Color elevations of finished woodwork and upstage flats. Instructions for finishing desk and window. Courtesy Eldon Elder.

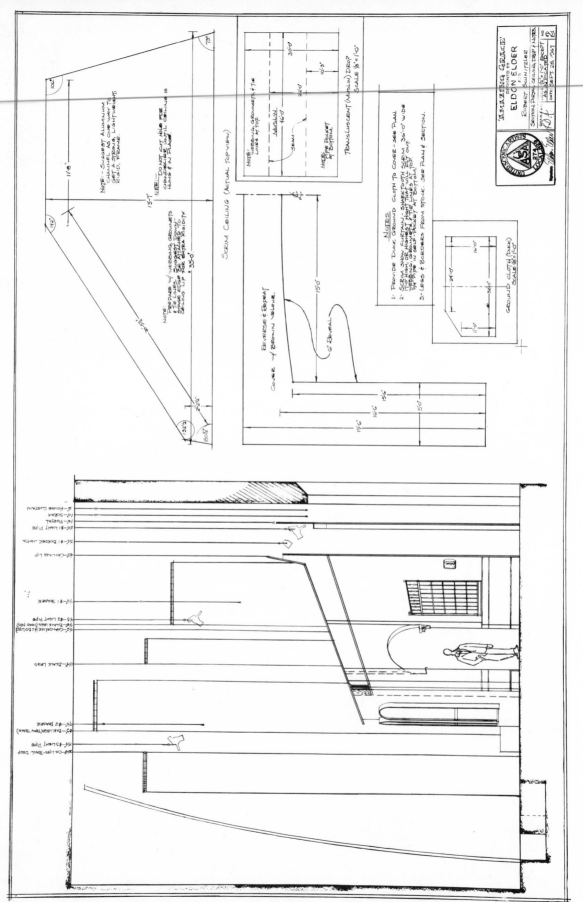

Section, portal, ceiling, and drop drawing with notes for *Amazing Grace*. Courtesy Eldon Elder.

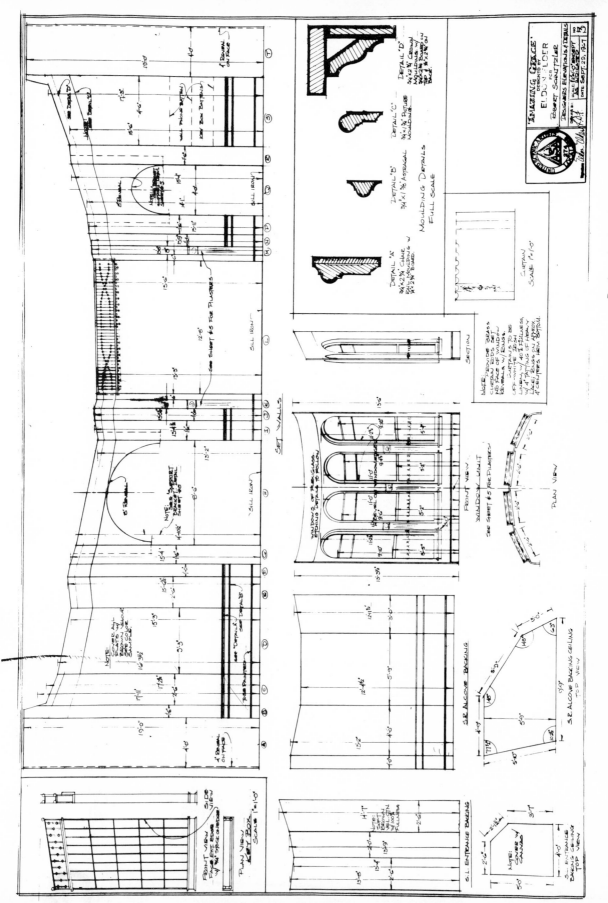

Designer's elevations and details. Courtesy Eldon Elder.

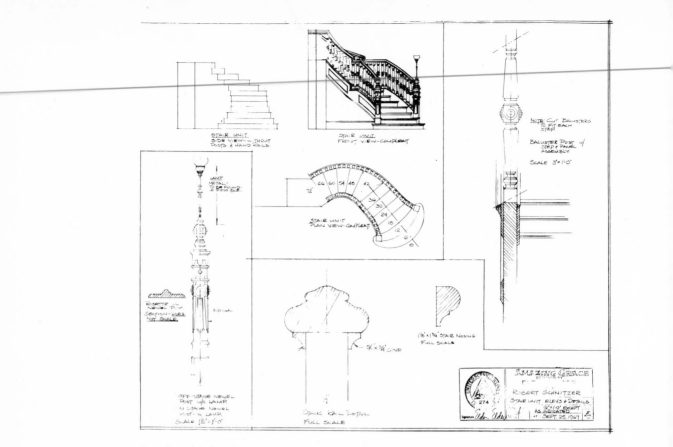

Drawing of stair unit, elevation, and details by Eldon Elder for *Amazing Grace.*

Cathleen Nesbitt and Victor Buono in *Amazing Grace.* Photograph shows the detail of the stair unit. Courtesy Eldon Elder.

In the professional theatre, scenery is built by scenic studios and every detail of construction, assembling, and painting must be indicated. The designer's plans are used much as are an architect's blueprints. Any expenses caused by errors or omissions in the plans must be paid by the designer. In the nonprofessional theatre, organizations may own a large amount of scenery which is used over and over. Under these circumstances, construction drawings may be made only for new pieces.

Although the number and type of drawings vary from one organization to another, the following is a list of the drawings and plans which a designer may be asked to provide: (1) perspective sketches in color showing the finished settings; (2) a floor plan of each setting; (3) a scale model of each setting; (4) rear elevations, which indicate the construction, materials, and methods to be used in assembling each unit of scenery (a rear elevation shows the unit from the back and in two dimensions only); (5) front elevations, which show each unit in two dimensions from the front with indications of any features (such as molding, baseboards, or platforms) which would be seen when looking at each unit straight on; (6) side elevations, which show units in profile and indicate the thickness and shape of each unit as viewed from the side; (7) detailed drawings, which show the methods by which such units as platforms, steps, trees, columns, and similar objects are to be built (some may be so complex that a separate drawing, possibly on a larger scale, is needed to clarify details of construction); (8) painter's elevations of each unit, showing the color of the base coat and any overpainting to be used. With the exception of the perspective sketches, all of the plans are drawn to scale so that the exact size of any object may be determined. In addition to the drawings listed above, the designer may also need to provide special plans showing how the scenery is to be shifted and stored when not in use. Ultimately the designer must be able to answer by means of sketches or drawings any question about the size, shape, construction, assembly, painting, rigging, and operation of his settings.

The designer, therefore, must have many skills. He must be familiar with the elements and principles of design, he must have facility in sketching, he must be able to make accurate scale drawings, he must know materials and be able to give exact specifications, he must understand how each item is to be built, assembled, painted, and operated. The designer must have both artistic talent and specialized practical knowledge.

After the plans are completed, the process of execution begins. While he may not be directly involved in carrying out the plans, the designer must approve all work, for it is his responsibility to see that the finished settings conform to his specifications.

BASIC SCENIC ELEMENTS

To implement his plans, the designer utilizes a number of basic scenic elements. These may be divided into standing units (those that rest on the floor or on other parts of the set) and hanging units (those suspended from above).

Eldon Elder's model (scale: ¼ inch = 1 foot) for *The Affair*,
an adaptation of C. P. Snow's novel. Produced at the Henry
Miller Theatre, New York, by Bonard Productions. Directed by
John Fernald. Courtesy Mr. Elder.

A working model for Arnold Sundgaard's *Of Love Remembered*.
(Scale ½ inch = 1 foot.) Produced at the ANTA Playhouse, 1967,
by Arthur Cantor. Directed by Burgess Meredith. Setting and
model by Eldon Elder and reproduced with his permission.

STANDING UNITS. The basic standing unit is the flat (that is, a frame, made of white pine or similar wood, over which canvas or muslin has been stretched). Flats of almost any width or height may be made, but if they are too large they become unstable. Therefore, the typical height of flats ranges from eight to sixteen feet, and the normal widths range from one to six feet. In the professional theatre and television, flats have been standardized at 5 feet 9 inches in width by 10 feet in height, since this is the maximum size which can be fitted into a railroad car (most shows do some touring even if it is only for out-of-town tryouts).

The most common piece of scenery is the plain flat—a rectangle without an opening. Other types of flats include: the door flat (one with an opening into which a door frame may be set); the window flat (with an opening into which a window frame may be set); a fireplace flat (against which or into which a mantelpiece and fireplace frame may be set); and arch flats (variations on the door flat, with openings shaped to simulate Roman, Gothic, or other kinds of arches).

There are many variations on these basic types of flats. For example, for a setting with double doors, two flats with one half of the opening in each are constructed. These two flats may then be hinged together to complete the full-sized opening. Similar procedures may be used for extra-wide windows or arches. Flats may also be constructed with slanting sides, with edges shaped to simulate trees, foliage, rocks, ruined walls, decaying arches, and so on.

Flats are used in almost all settings, but they are of special importance for interiors. A living-room set, for example, is normally assembled by hinging together a number of flats. Since flats are made in various widths, walls of any length may be constructed and the door and window openings placed exactly where needed by selecting flats of the right type and size.

Other standing units, in addition to flats, are: door frames, with doors; window frames, with windows; fireplace units; platforms; steps and staircases; rocks; built-up ground; tree trunks; and columns. While there are accepted methods for constructing each of these units, the procedures vary according to the intended appearance and use. For example, windows may be hinged to open outward or inward, they may slide up and down, or may be fixed. Doors may vary in appearance from the intricately-paneled to the rough-hewn; they may stand open throughout the play or they may be slammed or forced open. Rocks may be used merely as a place behind which characters may hide, or a large number of actors may stand on them. Size, shape, and use, then, determine in part how each of these units is to be constructed. It is not within the scope of this book to indicate how scenic units are built; the process is described in detail in a number of books on stage scenery.

Another typical standing unit is the ground row. It is used, as a rule, to show in profile such objects as walls, rocks, mounds of earth, distant hills and mountains, rows of buildings, and shrubbery. Ground rows are flats placed on their sides, with the tops and ends shaped according to the object being represented; details are painted on the flat surface. Although ground rows may be placed anywhere on the stage, most often they are set up near the back of the setting, since they usually represent

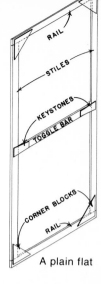

A plain flat

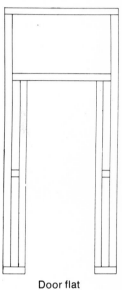

Door flat

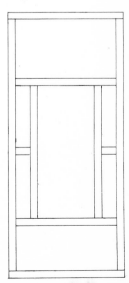

Window flat

distant objects. They break up the line of the stage floor, create the effect of depth and distance, and mask the bottom of the cyclorama, drops, and lighting instruments.

HANGING UNITS. Hanging units include ceilings, drops, curtains, borders, and cycloramas. Ceilings are usually constructed in two parts approximately equal in size. Each of these parts is a rectangle with the length approximately equal to the width of the proscenium opening (that is, large enough to cover the widest set which will be used on the stage), and its width equal to one half of the deepest set to be used on the stage. These two rectangles are then covered with canvas, in the same manner as a flat, and hinged together on the face. The hinges are then covered with a muslin strip and the whole surface painted. The ceiling is suspended above the setting and let down on top of the flats which compose a room. The hinges allow the ceiling to be folded and drawn up out of sight when not in use. Ceilings may be made in other ways as well, but that described here is the most typical.

Ceilings are used with interior settings to limit the overhead view and to create the illusion of a real room. Other devices may be used with interior settings, however, and are typical in exteriors, where a ceiling would be out of place. The most common substitute for a ceiling is the border—a short curtain or piece of painted canvas. Borders are hung parallel to the front of the stage and in a series from the front to the back of the stage. They may be made of black cloth or may be painted and shaped to represent foliage, the beams of a ceiling, or other objects.

For almost three hundred years, drops were a basic part of all stage settings and they still appear regularly in exteriors. Drops are made by sewing together enough lengths of muslin or canvas to create an area of the desired size. This piece of cloth is then attached at the top and bottom to wooden battens which support the cloth and keep it free of wrinkles. This cloth surface can be painted to represent any scene.

Draperies and curtains of various sorts are standard parts of scenery. Draperies may be hung parallel to the proscenium on either side of the stage in a series from front to back to mask the sides of the stage in the manner of flat wings. They are used at times to divide the stage into parts. They also may be an integral part of the scenic background.

The scrim is a special kind of curtain. It is made of net or theatrical gauze and appears opaque when lighted from the front only, but becomes transparent when light is placed behind it. It is used for sudden appearances and disappearances, for showing first the outside and then the inside of a building or other object, for creating effects of fog or mist, and for a number of purposes. In recent years designers of musicals have made considerable use of scrims on which plastic is sprayed. The plastic-covered areas can be painted to represent any object, and parts of the scrim may be cut away. In this way, settings of great delicacy and apparent depth can be achieved with materials of very light weight.

One of the most useful of hanging units is the cyclorama. Technically, a cyclorama is any arrangement of curtains or other materials which surround the stage area on three sides. For example, it may be composed of draperies or a plaster dome. Most typically, however, the cyclorama is

458

A scene from Giraudoux's *Ondine* in which the cloud effect on the cyclorama aids the mood of the play. Directed by Willard Welsh.

a continuous, tightly-stretched curtain suspended on U-shaped battens which curve around the back and sides of the stage. It is usually neutral or grayish blue so that its apparent color may be changed through lighting. It is employed to represent the sky, to give the effect of infinite space, and to allow the maximum use of stage space without the necessity of masking units.

In addition to the standard scenic units, scripts demand highly specialized pieces. For example, children's plays call for such objects as giant toadstools on which a character may perch. How such an object is to be constructed depends upon its use, but most special demands can be met through variations on standard construction practices. As a rule, however, the basic scenic units meet the needs of most plays.

ASSEMBLING SCENERY

The designer must decide not only what scenic units to use in his design, but also how these units are to be assembled. The method will depend in large part upon how the scenery is to be transported from the scene shop to the theatre, and whether or not it needs to be shifted. Sometimes, scenery must be transported from one town to another by truck or train and, therefore, must be assembled in units small enough to permit easy handling. If the scenery is to be shifted manually, it may need to be in smaller units than if it is to be moved by other methods.

The typical methods of assembling scenery are hinging, permanent joining, and lashing. Hinges are used most often to join flats. Almost every interior wall is composed by joining two or more flats to create a continuous surface. After the flats are hinged together on the face, the hinges and cracks between flats are covered with strips of muslin (called *dutchmen*). The wall is then ready for painting. Wooden battens may be attached to the rear surface of the assembled units to make them rigid and to prevent folding. These battens or stiffeners may be attached permanently, or they may be removable so that each wall may be folded for easy storage when not in use. The hinging is permanent, since the units remain joined throughout the production. Other units may be held together temporarily by hinges when the sets are in use and then taken apart for shifting and storage. Temporary hinging requires loose-pin hinges (in which a removable pin holds the two halves of a hinge together); when the pins are lifted out of the hinges the two pieces of scenery may be separated. Temporary hinging is often used where two units meet at ninety-degree angles, for joining platforms and steps or attaching them to other units.

Permanent joining is done with screws, bolts, and nails. This kind of assembly is used for heavy units which do not need to be shifted, or for those that are shifted by means which do not require that the units be taken apart. Permanent joining gives stability to a setting and is used whenever possible.

Lashing is a method of joining scenic units (especially the walls of an interior setting) with lines or ropes. A line is permanently attached to the top, outer edge of one unit; this line is drawn around cleats attached at intervals to the outer frames of the units being joined; the line is pulled tight and tied near the bottom of the units. Lashing and unlashing, which may be done quickly, allows the rapid assembly and dismantling of settings during a performance.

Technicians, or the employees of scenic studios, assemble the basic units of each setting in the scene shop. The scenery is then ready for painting.

PAINTING SCENERY

Scene shops normally stock dry pigment in a wide range of colors, from which any hue, saturation, and value may be mixed. When the desired color has been achieved, the dry pigment is combined with a binder—that is, a liquid solution which allows the paint to be applied to the scenery and which binds the pigment to the surface after it is dry. The most common binder is a glue and water solution, but others may also be used.

For a number of reasons, a mixture of dry pigment and glue *size* has become the standard medium for painting scenery. It is relatively economical in cost; it has a low gloss when dry; its colors are easily duplicated if touching up or repainting is needed; and it may be easily removed with warm water, which loosens the glue.

New flats are first painted with a solution of glue and pigment to stretch and seal the cloth. This process is called *sizing*. After sizing, a prime coat, near in color to the final coat, is applied. It is usually mixed from cheap pigments to keep down the cost. A prime coat is not always used but it is desirable since it insures a reasonably uniform surface for the base coat.

The base coat is applied after the prime coat is thoroughly dry. The result should be a uniform color of smooth texture. The final step is usually the modification of the base coat through overpainting designed to simulate texture (such as those of plaster, brick or wood), or to alter the flat appearance of the surface. Overpainting may also be used for other purposes: to shade the upper portions of settings so as to decrease their prominence; to emphasize the shape and form of objects by giving emphasis to corners or curves; to counterfeit three-dimensional details, such as molding, paneling, the bark of trees, and mortar.

Painting may be done with a variety of techniques. The prime and base coats are normally done with a technique called *flat painting*, since the

460

Techniques used in painting scenery. *Top, left,* wet blending or scumble. *Center,* dry scumble. *Right,* spattering. *Below, left,* combing or dry brushing. *Center,* rag rolling. *Right,* spraying. From W. Oren Parker and Harvey K. Smith, *Scene Design and Stage Lighting,* 2nd ed. Holt, Rinehart and Winston, 1968. Courtesy Mr. Parker.

purpose is to give an even surface. It is usually done with a large brush or with a spray gun. *Overpainting* requires more specialized techniques than flat painting, since it aims to add texture, shading, or details. The colors used in overpainting, therefore, must contrast with the base coat. The degree of contrast depends on the purpose. For example, the texture of relatively smooth plaster may be achieved by "spattering" (that is, by

461

flicking small drops of paint from a brush onto the base coat) with one color which is slightly lighter and a second which is slightly darker than the base coat itself. This creates the effect of raised and receding surfaces.

On the other hand, rough plaster may be simulated through *rolling*. This involves the use of a rolled-up piece of ragged burlap or other rough-textured cloth. The cloth is dipped into paint, partially wrung out, and then rolled over the surface of the base coat in irregular patterns. It may be repeated with a variety of shades or tints.

Other common painting techniques include *sponging* and *scumbling*. In *sponging* a natural sponge is dipped into the paint and patted onto the surface of the base coat. It may be used to achieve a variety of patterns and effects. *Scumbling* involves the simultaneous application and blending of more than one shade of paint on the same surface. This gives a mottled effect and may be used for foliage, or to simulate walls on which the paint is fading, mildewing, or crumbling.

The appropriate painting technique must be specified by the designer on his painter's elevations. The designer, as a rule, must be able to do the painting himself or to supervise the work of others. In all cases, he must approve the finished job.

THE ASSEMBLY AND SHIFTING OF SCENERY ON STAGE

After the scenery has been painted, it is transported to the stage upon which it will be used. In the nonprofessional theatre and in most summer stock organizations, this may merely mean moving the scenery from one part of the building to another. In the professional theatre, however, transportation by truck or train is usually involved. The typical New York production has an out-of-town tryout which requires that the scenery be moved from one city to another and that it be used on a number of stages before it is assembled on the one for which it was intended.

How scenery is to be assembled on stage depends upon the method of shifting to be employed. A single setting can be set up permanently, whereas multiple settings may require much planning so that the individual units can be assembled and disassembled quickly and quietly, moved easily, and stored economically.

There are many methods of shifting scenery, of which the most common are: by hand, flying, on wagons, jackknife stages, elevators, and revolving stages.

The simplest procedure (in the sense that no mechanical devices are needed) is to change all of the scenic elements manually. In this case, each part of a set is moved by one or more stage hands to some prearranged storage space offstage, and the elements of a new setting are brought on stage and assembled. Parts of almost every setting must be moved manually, even when the major shifting is accomplished by complex mechanical devices. Since manual shifting can be used on any stage, however simple or complex, a designer can always rely on it, though a large crew may be required to carry it through efficiently. Its drawbacks are its relative slowness and the necessity for breaking the setting into units which are small and light in weight.

The second most common method of shifting scenery is flying. In this case, the elements are suspended on battens or lines over the stage and are raised and lowered as needed. With an adequate gridiron and strong lines, entire settings can be flown. It is extremely unusual to do so, however, and flying is normally reserved for such elements as drops, curtains, ceilings, borders, cycloramas, and small units of flats.

A number of problems arise in connection with flying: (1) in most theatres scenic pieces can only be flown parallel to the front of the stage, since the battens to which they are attached are permanently installed in that position; (2) the flying of extremely heavy units may be too dangerous unless the apparatus is in excellent condition; (3) the stage space above the top of the proscenium opening must be at least one and a half times as great as the height of the proscenium arch if full-sized scenery is to be flown completely out of sight (for example, if the proscenium arch is twenty feet high, there should be an additional space of thirty feet above that).

Most stages provide some means for suspending short curtains and lighting equipment overhead, but this space may be inadequate for shifting scenery. When the overhead space is not sufficient to allow drops to be flown out of sight *tripping* is sometimes used. This means that the top and bottom of a drop are attached to adjacent sets of lines. When both are raised, the drop is folded in the middle and drawn up. In this way, only half as much overhead space is required. Drops may also be rolled up if there is not sufficient flying space overhead, but this is time consuming and is apt to damage the painting on the drop.

For proper flying, a gridiron (that is, a network of steel girders) is installed at the top of the stage house to serve as the weight-supporting structure. The lines for flying scenery are normally attached to steel pipes or battens which extend across the width of the stage (three or four lines are needed to support each batten). The scenic elements to be flown are attached to these battens. For maximum efficiency, battens should be installed at regular intervals from the front to the back of the stage, so that scenery may be flown at any spot.

The lines (usually steel cables) which support the battens run up to the top of the stage house where they pass over pulleys resting on the gridiron; after passing over these pulleys they continue to one side of the stage house where they pass over another set of pulleys; they then turn downward and are attached to the top of a cradle or frame; into this cradle, weights in sufficient amount to counterbalance the scenery are placed. To the bottom of the cradle are attached ropes which continue downward to the fly rail, where stage hands can raise and lower the battens on which scenery is being flown. The ropes may be tied off securely when not being used. This method of flying scenery is called a counterweight system, since it allows the even balancing of offstage and onstage weight. With a good counterweight system, a single stagehand can easily raise and lower scenic elements of any size.

A somewhat out-of-date variation on the counterweight system is the rope and sandbag arrangement. Here the lines are hemp ropes and the weights are bags filled with sand. This is a cumbersome method, howev-

Scene from Paul Green's *The House of Connelly* mounted on a wagon stage. Note the use of foliage and other real objects. It is difficult to shift such a setting except on a movable platform. Setting by Lewis McFarland.

er, and most modern theatres have abandoned it. Its purpose and basic principle of operation, however, is the same as the counterweight system.

Some recent experiments with flying systems have utilized electronically controlled winches without counterweights, and a more flexible arrangement of lines which allows scenery to be flown at angles rather than parallel to the front of the stage. This method, however, is still in the experimental phase.

The rolling platform, or wagon, is another common device used to shift scenery. Platforms of almost any size may be placed on casters and rolled on and off stage. The larger the platform the more scenery may be placed on it and the less dependence need be put on manual shifting. On the other hand, wagons require a considerable amount of offstage space for maneuvering and storage. Many stages do not have enough wing space to allow the use of large wagons. The top surface of a wagon is normally raised off the stage floor from six to twelve inches—about one step—so that actors may step on and off it easily.

Most commonly, wagons are freely maneuverable and may be moved to any spot on the stage. But some stages have permanently-installed tracks in which the casters of the wagons move. This guides the platforms on and off stage with precision, but does not permit flexibility in the positioning of wagons on stage.

The jackknife stage is a variation on the wagon. It normally requires a platform approximately as wide as the proscenium opening. When the wagon is in position on stage (that is, set up facing the auditorium), it is attached to the stage floor at a single point—one of the downstage corners—to provide a pivot. It may then be rotated on and off stage much as a jackknife blade is opened and closed. Normally two jackknife stages are used in conjunction—one attached to each side of the stage—and are especially useful in productions where two complex settings alternate. This arrangement, however, requires a considerable amount of wing space on each side of the stage.

464

It is also possible to mount the supporting braces of walls and heavy pieces of scenery on casters and to roll them on and off stage. These devices—which include the tip jack, the lift jack, and the outrigger—are not platforms but devices by which a scenic unit can be lifted off the floor sufficiently (an inch or so) by means of braces and casters to allow the units to be rolled about. Any book on stagecraft will show the methods of constructing and operating these rather complicated devices. The basic principle is much the same as that of a wagon without the platform surface.

The revolving stage and the elevator stage are among the less common devices for shifting scenery. Each is costly and complex.

A revolving stage may be either a permanent or a temporary part of the theatre. In the case of the permanent revolving stage, a circle of the stage floor (normally larger in diameter than the width of the proscenium opening) is mounted on a central supporting pivot, so that the entire circle may be rotated. Since the weight of this circle is considerable,

A continuous setting for Claudel's *The Tidings Brought to Mary* mounted on a revolving stage. Note that the stage is surrounded by a cyclorama, the bottom of which is masked by low flats.

Setting for *The Tidings Brought to Mary* as it appeared in performance. Setting by Arnold Gillette.

Each segment of this stage floor is mounted on an elevator. The segments may also be joined to form revolving stages. The Red Army Theatre, Moscow. From Barkhin's *Archetect. Teatra,* 1947.

it is normally rotated electrically. A temporary revolving stage may be constructed by mounting a low circular platform on casters and attaching it at the center to the stage floor. One or more small revolving units may also be used at almost any place on the stage.

The revolving stage allows a number of settings to be erected simultaneously; the individual sets are placed so that each faces outward toward the circumference of the circle. To shift scenery, the stage is revolved until the desired setting faces the audience.Settings may be changed on the backstage part while another setting is being used onstage.

The elevator stage is the least common method of shifting scenery in America. In this arrangement, sections of the stage floor may be raised and lowered like an elevator. In some theatres, portions of the stage may be lowered to the basement, where scenery may be mounted and then raised to the stage level. Each segment may also be moved in tracks up- and downstage. In other words, as that part of the floor at the front is lowered, the upstage part may move forward with another setting and a third portion may rise from the basement to occupy the position just vacated by the upstage part.

In some theatres each segment of the stage floor is mounted on lifts which allow that section to be raised, lowered, or tilted. This permits the creation of ramps, platforms and levels without the necessity of building

466

and shifting them in the usual ways. A number of recently constructed theatres have orchestra pits on lifts. Since the pit can be set at any level, it may be raised to form a forestage, or it may be used for audience seating or for musicians. Such an arrangement allows great flexibility in the use of an area often wasted.

All of these shifting devices may be combined in various ways, and seldom is one means used alone. The designer must know what methods are available to him and must decide how each unit is to be moved. His scenery must be designed, constructed, and assembled with these requirements in mind.

SET DECORATION, PROPERTIES, AND FURNITURE

When the scenery is assembled on stage, the set decoration, properties, and furniture are added. Although these are all part of the basic design, with the exception of certain props, they are not normally built in the scene shop, since they are not structural parts of the setting.

Set decoration and properties include such items as banners, pictures, draperies, books, vases, and lamps — anything which completes a setting. Properties are frequently subdivided into *set props* and *hand props*. A *set prop* is one that is attached to the setting or which functions as a part of the design. A *hand prop* is principally used in the actor's stage business. Sometimes a set prop is used in business, but it is classed as a set prop if it is a part of the setting and remains on stage.

The designer is always responsible for the selection of set properties. He may also choose the hand props, but more frequently hand props are left to the director since they are so intimately connected with acting. In the nonprofessional theatre, the responsibility for obtaining properties of both types may be assigned to a property crew.

The set decorations, properties, and furniture may be obtained in a variety of ways. Since they must be appropriate to the setting, style, and period of the play and may need to meet other demands, it is not always possible to find props of the ideal shape, size, or general appearance. In such cases, properties or furniture may have to be made. For most productions, however, appropriate pieces may be bought, rented, or borrowed.

In the professional theatre, since the designer must plan for a long run, it is usually necessary to purchase all items to be used in the show. In the nonprofessional theatre, or for short-run shows, it may be possible to rent or to borrow props.

Regardless of how properties and furniture are obtained, the settings are not complete without these decorative and practical features.

TECHNICAL REHEARSALS, DRESS REHEARSALS, AND PERFORMANCES

Many organizations regularly schedule technical rehearsals for the purpose of checking the scenery, costumes, lighting, and sound. Other theatres make this a part of dress rehearsals. Regardless of when it is done, provision must be made for determining whether the settings function as planned and for establishing the procedures to be used in running the show.

467

It is extremely difficult to make major changes in settings after dress rehearsals begin. A costume may be altered with relative ease, lights may be adjusted, and even the movement of actors may be changed, but alterations in the size and basic appearance of a setting are difficult to make because of the rigidity of scenic units and of stage space. Nevertheless, at times entire settings are abandoned and new ones are constructed and painted at the last moment. In the professional theatre, the designer receives extra pay for making any changes in the settings which are not due to his own mistakes.

The designer must be available for consultation and changes until the play opens. If the play has a long run he may be consulted occasionally about the replacement of elements which are becoming shabby. He may also be asked to redesign the show for touring. Usually, however, responsibility for the scenery passes to the stage crew and the stage manager on opening night.

THE DESIGNER'S EMPLOYMENT

In the professional theatre the scene designer is placed under contract by the producer. He must be a member of the United Scenic Artists Union, the most exclusive of all theatrical unions. The applicant for membership must pay an examination fee and if accepted must pay a sizeable initiation fee ($1000 for full membership in 1968). His rather severe examination involves the ability to paint, to make sketches, working drawings, costume and lighting designs. While the requirements are rigorous, they insure the capability of members.

The allied fields of television, motion pictures, opera, ballet are also controlled by this union. Membership now enables the designer to have wider, more constant employment by participating in one or all kindred fields.

Many beginning designers work as assistants to well-established designers to gain experience. Some off-Broadway theatres and summer stock companies employ nonunion designers, but this is becoming less common.

In the community theatre, a designer-technician is often responsible for all areas of design and construction. It is not unusual, however, to find the director, as the only salaried worker, in charge of design. In such cases, he normally attempts to secure the services, free or at a nominal fee, of a competent person in the community.

In the educational theatre, situations vary from those in which one person is responsible for all aspects of the theatre program to those in which there are separate and specialized designers for scenery, lighting, and costumes. Since some educational theatres employ more than one person in each of these areas, a staff member, often called the Artistic Director, may be appointed to supervise the work of this large staff and to insure continuity and high quality.

The working conditions of the designer, thus, vary considerably from one type of organization to another and even within the same kind of organization. His basic responsibilities as a scene designer, nevertheless, remain constant.

468

THE DESIGNER'S ASSISTANTS AND CO-WORKERS

In carrying out his duties, the designer is aided by a number of persons: the assistant designer, the technical director, the master carpenter (or the heads of the scenery, property, and rigging crews), the stagehands, and the property crew.

In the professional theatre, well-established designers usually employ one or more assistants. These assistants are for the most part younger members of the United Scenic Artists Union. They may be asked to do almost anything: make working drawings, search for furniture and properties, act as liaison between the designer and the scenic studios—anything the designer may request. Designers outside the professional theatre may at times have an assistant, but such a position is not typical outside of New York.

In the nonprofessional theatre, the technical director may perform many of the functions of the designer's assistant. In many theatres, however, the technical director's job is considered to be quite independent of the designer and of equal status. Nevertheless, the technical director, as a rule, merely assumes part of the duties which are performed by the designer in the professional theatre. Usually, he is responsible for constructing, assembling, rigging, and shifting the scenery—in other words, he carries out the designer's plans. In many organizations he is also in charge of lighting. The technical director's position has been created in many educational theatres because the tasks performed by the professional scenic studios in New York must be done in the theatre itself. When a theatre produces a large number of shows each year the designer's job may become too great for one person. In this case, it may be divided into its artistic and its practical aspects. A designer then assumes responsibility for the conception and the technical director for the execution of the designs. The technical director may also be asked to purchase all materials and to supervise the backstage operation of the theatre.

The scenery is built, assembled, and painted in a scene shop (or another work space which fills that function). In the professional theatre, all persons involved must be union members, and the painters must have passed an examination given by the United Scenic Artists Union. In other types of organizations, the workers may be paid but are not always union members. Much of this work is done by apprentices in summer stock companies, while in community and educational theatres assigned or volunteer helpers work under the supervision of the designer or technical director.

When the scenery is delivered to the stage for rigging and shifting, scenery and property crews are brought in. In the professional theatre, all such persons must be members of the International Alliance of Theatrical Stage Employees. A master carpenter travels with the show on tour and makes sure that the scenery is kept in good condition. In the nonprofessional theatre, scenery and props are usually handled by volunteers or assigned crews. Some organizations pay the persons in charge of the scene and property crews a small fee. In all types of theatre organizations, the head of the stage crews must operate under the supervision

469

of the stage manager. Regardless of how these crews are secured or paid, their duties include the efficient movement and accurate placement of the scenery and properties during performances and the upkeep of material throughout the run of the show.

The designer's helpers frequently go unnoticed by the public since little is done to draw attention to them. They are, nevertheless, important members of every theatrical organization, since they make possible the efficient execution of the designer's plans.

ARCHITECTURE AND THEATRICAL PRODUCTION

One of the major influences on theatrical production is the theatre building. Thus, theatre architecture probably merits a separate chapter. Since space does not permit such a full treatment, an abbreviated discussion has been placed here because architecture is more closely related to scene design than to any of the other theatre arts. Nevertheless, it is important to remember that the size of the auditorium, the relationship of the audience to the acting area, and the equipment of the stage affect every aspect of theatrical production.

Every theatre has three basic parts: that intended for the audience; the stage; and the work areas. Facilities designed for the audience include the box office, lobby, coat-check rooms, rest rooms, corridors, entrances and exits, and refreshment stands. Not all of these are found in every building, but the most complete theatres normally provide maximum comfort for the audience.

From the standpoint of theatrical production, the auditorium is the most important of audience facilities. It should be designed to insure optimum conditions for seeing and hearing. Unfortunately these needs are frequently subordinated to others, the most common of which are: that a certain number of removable seats be included because the theatre must also be used as an assembly hall, a gymnasium, or cafeteria; that the seating capacity be as great as possible so as to bring in the maximum boxoffice receipts; that the auditorium be fitted into an already existing structure or into a space of a particular shape.

Auditoriums vary widely in their basic characteristics. They may be large or small; all seats may be on the same level (although normally the floor is raked to allow for better sightlines), or there may be one or more balconies; the audience may view the acting area from one side, or it may be seated on two, three, or four sides; the distance of spectators from the acting area may vary from one or two feet to hundreds of feet; sightlines may be such that all members of the audience may see practically all of the acting area, or they may prevent some members of the audience from seeing large portions of the stage.

Today there are in wide use three basic types of stages: the proscenium stage, the open (or platform) stage, and the arena (or theatre-in-the-round) stage. Each creates a different audience-actor relationship, each has different facilities, and each demands a different approach to production.

The proscenium stage is designed to be viewed from the front only. Since the action is oriented in one direction, the designer may utilize

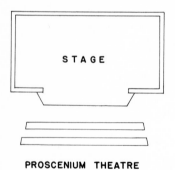

PROSCENIUM THEATRE

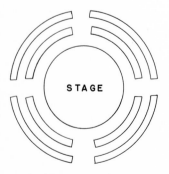

ARENA THEATRE

three sides of the stage for the scenery, entrances, and exits. The scenery may be as tall as the designer wishes and he may use few or many units. There is only one basic restriction: the view of the audience must not be blocked from the front.

The proscenium stage is equipped with a curtain which may be used to conceal or reveal the stage. It ordinarily has a counterweight system, wing space, and other features which allow for a wide variety of scene-shifting methods. There may also be trap doors in the floor for special effects or for entrances and exits from beneath the stage.

In the proscenium theatre, the action and scenery are usually removed a greater distance from the audience than in other types of theatres. There may be an orchestra pit or forestage between the first row of seats and the point at which scenery begins. Therefore, the scenery is not seen at close range, and may permit a different treatment than were it viewed from a distance of a few feet. The work of the designer in the proscenium theatre is a cross between that of the architect and the painter, for although the scenery is created in three dimensions, it is viewed from only one direction.

With an open stage, the seats are usually arranged around three sides of a raised platform which juts into the auditorium. (A good example may be seen on page 131.) Less frequently, an open stage is viewed from only one side, but in this case it is essentially the traditional stage without its proscenium arch.

Most open stages permit only a restricted use of scenery (usually small units) and sometimes a shallow cyclorama. Some have a permanent architectural façade at the back, as in an Elizabethan theatre, which can be altered slightly to meet the demands of the action.

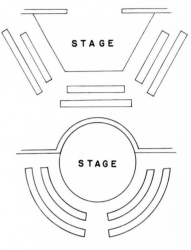

TYPES OF OPEN STAGES

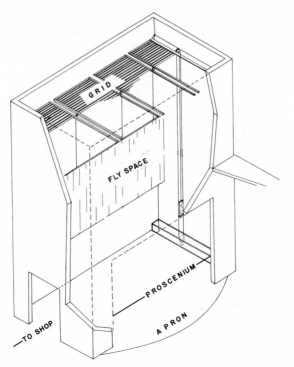

Isometric drawing of a proscenium stage.

The open stage has no proscenium arch. There may or may not be a curtain; if there is one, it is usually mounted in the ceiling on a recessed track, shaped to follow the contours of the stage. The ceiling of the stage is normally continuous with that of the auditorium. Often there is no provision above the stage for flying scenery, drops, or curtains (with the possible exceptions already noted of a front curtain and a backcloth of some kind). Lighting instruments are mounted in recesses in the ceiling.

The acting areas and the auditorium of the open-stage theatre are more unified than in the proscenium theatre, for the basic purposes of the open stage are to bring the audience and the actors into a more intimate relationship and to do away with the trappings of realism. Consequently, there are fewer provisions for the use of traditional scenery. Since three sides of the stage are usually surrounded by seats, even if the auditorium is large the audience members can be brought closer to the actors than in a proscenium theatre with the same seating capacity.

Since the open stage is usually seen from three sides, it is in most respects a more three-dimensional medium than is the proscenium stage. The acting, the scenery, and all the elements of theatrical production must be designed to project in three directions simultaneously. On the other hand, the designer cannot use large units of scenery except near the back. Any scenery used at other points must be low enough not to interfere with the audience's view of the stage. Furthermore, as a rule, scenery is shifted manually. Occasionally a revolving stage may be installed and there may be a number of trap doors, but scenery is usually kept relatively simple. The designer, therefore, must compensate for the restrictions upon his means by greater ingenuity.

In the typical theatre-in-the-round, there is no stage as such (that is, there is no raised platform). Rather, an open space is left at floor level in the middle of the auditorium. The seats for the audience are set up in a bleacherlike arrangement around all four sides of the acting area. Since as a rule in theatres of this type the acting area and the seats are not permanently installed the arrangement may be varied at will. The seats may be placed around three sides (thereby creating a variation on the open stage), or they may be placed on two sides. In the latter case, the seats may be set up so that the two halves of the audience face each other across the acting area, or they may be arranged in the shape of an L with the acting area located in one corner of the auditorium. Arena theatres with fixed stages and permanent seating arrangements are becoming more common. In some cases, raised stages have also been installed. Since the theatre-in-the-round typically has a small seating capacity, the relationship between the actors and the audience is intimate.

An arena theatre restricts the scene designer considerably in the amount and kind of scenery he can use. In the true theatre-in-the-round (that is, one in which the audience is seated on all four sides), all scenery must be kept low enough to allow the entire acting area to be seen from every angle. The designer, therefore, must rely principally upon furniture and properties, or flats no more than two or three feet high placed around the outer edge of the acting area. Since there is no curtain, all changes must be made either in darkness or in full view of the audi-

472

An open or thrust stage. From W. Oren Parker and Harvey K. Smith's *Scene Design and Stage Lighting,* 2d ed. Holt, Rinehart and Winston, 1968. Courtesy Mr. Parker.

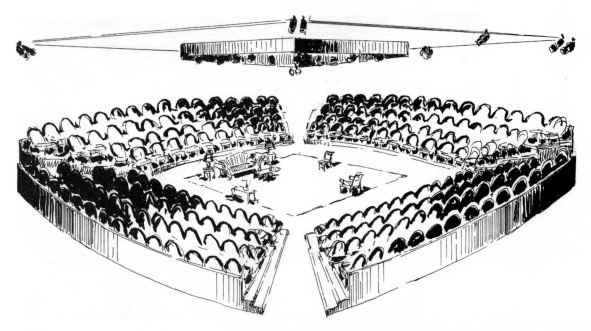

An arena stage. Note the actor-audience relationships and the use of lighting. From Parker and Smith's *Scene Design and Lighting,* 2d ed. Courtesy Mr. Parker.

ence. All shifting, as a rule, must be done manually and units must be moved through the aisles of the theatre. While lighting instruments are suspended overhead, no provision is usually made for hanging scenic elements.

The designer, therefore, may suggest a locale, period, mood, and style, but he must do so with a few set-pieces or properties. This enforced economy makes it necessary that the designer choose each element with great care, since each must suggest much that cannot be shown. Furthermore, because of the closeness of the audience to the acting area, the units must be built and painted carefully. Above all, the scenery, like the actors, must be expressive when viewed from any angle.

A few attempts have been made to create a completely flexible theatre that can be altered to permit proscenium, open, or arena staging. With all seats in place and facing front, the structure may be used as a conventional proscenium theatre. For arena staging, a section of seats near the center of the auditorium may be removed to provide a playing area, while other sections of seats may be mounted so they can be turned to face this central area. For open staging, the seats near the proscenium may be removable and that portion of the auditorium floor mounted on an elevator which permits it to be raised to create a platform stage. Such flexibility is rare, however, and most theatres are designed with one dominant type of staging in mind.

The amount of work space in theatres also varies widely. A well-designed, self-contained theatre (that is, one which has facilities for preparing productions as well as performing them) will include the following: a scenery construction shop (with space to store equipment and materials), painting facilities, an area for assembling scenery, sufficient offstage space for the storage and shifting of scenery during performances, and provisions for the permanent storage of scenery when not in use; a property room near the stage, and another area for the permanent storage of furniture and bulky props; a costume shop; laundry, dyeing, cleaning and pressing facilities, and an area for the permanent storage of costumes; a work space for lighting personnel, a storage area for lighting equipment, a large room designed to house the remote-control lighting board, and a lighting booth for the control-board operator during performances (ideally with full view of the stage); a number of large rehearsal rooms; a number of dressing rooms, each with make-up facilities (unless a separate make-up room is provided); adequate showers and rest rooms for the actors and crews, and an area where all of the actors and crew members can assemble to receive instructions or to relax (usually called the *green room*); space to house sound equipment and from which to operate it; adequate office space for supervisory personnel.

Not all theatres are ideally equipped, but all make some provision for each aspect of production. Unfortunately, theatre workers must often function in cubbyholes within the theatre or in improvised quarters in buildings totally unsuited to theatrical needs. Fortunately, theatre workers seem to make do with whatever facilities they have, and sometimes the necessity of rising above difficulties leads to amazing results.

474

Chapter 20 THE COSTUMER

While the scene designer creates the stage environment in which the actors perform, the costumer is concerned with the visual appearance of the actors themselves. At times, the same person serves as both scene and costume designer, but costumes and scenery can be separated profitably for clarification.

Costumes and scenery fulfill many of the same purposes and utilize the same elements and principles of design. They employ entirely different materials, however, and are completely different products.

THE PURPOSES OF COSTUME DESIGN

The purposes of costume design are the same as those of scene design: to aid understanding, and to interpret the play. Each purpose may be achieved in a number of ways.

Costumes may aid understanding by identifying the period in which the action occurs—ancient Greece, Elizabethan England, or present-day America. If the period is unimportant or unspecified, the costumer (with the approval of the director) usually selects a period which seems most appropriate to the themes, characters, and action.

Costumes may establish the locale. For example, they can distinguish a farm from a city, one part of the country from another (southern California from New England), and may indicate a particular nation. Costumes may identify the time of day and clarify the occasion: an informal morning at home with the family, a party, or a formal dance.

Costumes may establish the social and economic status of the characters by distinguishing between the lower and upper classes, between rich and poor, or between decaying and affluent members of the same class. Costume often identifies an occupation: maid, nurse, milkman, office worker, soldier, and so on.

475

Costumes may establish the age of the characters, since some garments are appropriate to the young and others to the old. In some cases, garments may show that characters are trying to appear older or younger than they actually are.

Costumes may help to clarify character relationships. For example, in many of Shakespeare's plays, warring factions may easily become confusing to an audience because of the difficulty of identifying individuals. One common solution is to use the same color scheme for all members of a faction and to contrast two groups. Similar devices may be used to show either a sympathetic or an antipathetic relationship among characters in other kinds of plays. Likewise, changes in costume may be used to indicate an alteration in relationship among characters, or in the psychological outlook of an individual. For example, increasing dishevelment in dress may parallel the growing disillusionment of a character.

Through emphasis and subordination, costume may indicate the relative importance of characters in the play's action. For example, if a woman dressed in black enters a scene in which all the other characters are clothed in pastel colors, she is immediately emphatic. The costumer may use a number of similar devices to distinguish major from minor roles.

In addition to clarifying points which are primarily factual, the costumer must seek to express a number of intangible qualities, such as mood, style, and theme.

Costume and make-up based on medieval sculpture. Note the partial mask with extended forehead, and the hair and beard made of rolled organdy. The character is St. Paul in *Romans by St. Paul* as arranged and directed by Orlin Corey for the Everyman Players. Reprinted with permission from *The Mask of Reality: An Approach to Design for Theatre* by Irene Corey. Anchorage Press, 1968.

Costume design by J. R. Planché for Shakespeare's *King John* as produced at Covent Garden, London, in 1823.

King John 1st dress.

Costumes should be expressive of the over-all mood of a play, and, whenever possible, of individual scenes. A somber play will probably fare best if the costumes are of grayed, subdued colors, while the mood of a farce may benefit from bright hues.

Costumes should be expressive of a play's style. For example, a play such as *The Wild Duck* demands a closer fidelity to life than does *Pelléas and Mélisande.*

Costumes should be indicative of the play's themes and ideas. This goal is accomplished largely through emphasis and subordination, through revelation of character relationships and psychological traits and through the embodiment of mood and style.

Each costume should be expressive of the psychological nature of its wearer. (Is he extroverted or introverted? Is he fastidious or careless? Is he open and frank, or is he concealing something?) The costumer must try to project the truth about a character while allowing him to wear clothing that he would choose himself.

Fanciful and unusual costumes for *Alice in Wonderland.* Costumes by Aline Felton.

The costumer must also see that the play's structure is paralleled in the costumes. If the same costumes are to be worn throughout, they must be designed with the needs of each scene as well as the play's over-all qualities in mind. Furthermore, if the same costumes are to be used throughout, they must be capable of sustaining interest for a long period of time, unlike the costume which is to be worn in only one scene. If changes are required, costumes should build in interest.

*THE ELEMENTS OF
COSTUME DESIGN*

Like the scene designer, the costumer utilizes the basic elements of design—line, mass, color, texture, and ornament—and combines them in various ways.

Line has direction only. It may be curved, straight, or a combination (scallops, zigzags, or other patterns). In costume, line is manifested primarily in the silhouette of garments, and to a lesser extent in darts, ornamentation, seams, and other features which create visible lines.

Mass involves the shape and size of objects—their over-all configuration and the amount of space they occupy. Since they are so intimately connected in costuming, line and mass will be considered together.

Each period has its own distinctive silhouette. For example, the Greek woman wore a garment that fell in loose folds about the body, whereas the mid nineteenth-century woman wore a tight-fitting bodice and a bell-shaped skirt. In describing the silhouette of a period the characteristic lines of each part of the body should be considered: head, arms, the upper body, lower body, feet, and legs.

Hair styles and head coverings vary markedly from one period to another. For example, the man of the 1950's had little in common with his late-seventeenth-century ancestors, who wore plumed hats and full-bottomed wigs hanging in curls about the shoulders. In considering the head, beards and mustaches should not be forgotten.

Two costumes designed by Lodovico Burnacini in the late seventeenth century. From von Weilen's *Geschichte des Wiener Theaterwesens*, 1899.

Arms may be uncovered, partially covered, or fully covered with close-fitting sleeves, with puffed sleeves, or with sleeves as full as those of an academic gown. The covering of the upper body may be tight or loose. Shoulders may be bare or covered; the bust and waist may be emphasized or masked. In many periods, corsets have altered considerably the natural shape of the body.

The appearance of the lower body may be changed more easily than that of the rest. Tights or bathing suits may reveal the form, while garments of various shapes and lengths may mask it. For example, skirts may be hung over variously shaped foundation garments to make them resemble bells, barrels, or a variety of other objects.

Foot and leg coverings have also varied widely through history. Men have worn high-heeled shoes, sandals, and wide-topped, knee-length boots. At times the legs have been revealed and at others covered.

Although the foregoing discussion emphasizes the differing silhouettes of various periods, it also illustrates that the natural lines of the human body may be altered in many ways. The costumer, therefore, can select those lines, shapes, and masses that convey the qualities he thinks most appropriate.

Since the basic properties of color—hue, saturation, and value—have been discussed in the preceding chapter, only the costumer's uses of color will be considered here.

All the colors of the spectrum are available, but, if the designer is to achieve unity, he must limit his palette. He may decide to costume a play in the style of a particular painter. He will then use the favorite hues, the characteristic saturations and values found in that artist's works. The costumer may choose a particular color scheme (such as green, blue, and orange). By combining these colors in differing amounts, saturations, and values, he can achieve considerable variety while remaining within the unifying limits he has established. Several other methods could be used equally well.

Scene from Molière's *Don Juan* showing costumes from a period seldom used on the stage because the fashionable male garment called "petticoat breeches" (worn by Don Juan at center) may be considered too effeminate. Costumes by Elizabeth Parsons.

Scene from Destouches' *The Married Philosopher* at the Comédie Française in 1732. From Loliée's *La Comédie Française*, 1907.

Color is one of the most powerful means for expressing mood and character. Although it is difficult to specify connotations, different colors can arouse different responses. Hues that are grayed in saturation and dark in value aid in establishing a somber mood, while those light in value suggest a mood of gaiety, delicacy, or frivolity. The colors of each costume should be expressive of the traits of its wearer. A character's lack of taste may be indicated through the inharmonious colors. A defiant nature may be suggested by clothing of a color at odds with the occasion; the relative conservatism of an individual can be implied by subdued tones.

Color can point up relationships among characters. Those closely related through sentiment or politics may be costumed in the same basic color scheme, while antipathy may be indicated through contrasting colors.

Line, mass, and color are abstractions, however, until embodied in materials, each with its own texture and weight. The appearance and behavior of velvet and taffeta, for example, are very different. Velvet has a pile that gives depth and low sheen; bulky, it hangs in large folds; only with difficulty can it be shaped into intricate pleats or compressed into a small space; its qualities are associated with opulence and solidity. Taffeta, on the other hand, has a light, crisp, somewhat glossy surface; it may be shaped with relative ease; it connotes brittleness and femininity.

Materials with heavy threads and loose weaves have a homespun quality associated with the working classes, whereas the smooth texture of silk suggests the upper classes. Each material has its own texture, which the designer can use to capture desired effects.

Ornament includes such items as ruffles, buttons, fringe, feathers, lace, and piping. It may not be essential to good design, but in most cases ornament adds a special touch that brings the whole to life. For example, it is the white collar and cuffs which give variety and distinction to the dress of the Puritan. A red rose on a black mourning dress not only sets off the black, but may indicate that the wearer is not totally engrossed in

480

grief. Feathers may give a dashing appearance to an otherwise uninteresting hat and transform it into a symbol of gaiety and high spirits.

Ornament can also be used to indicate a lack of taste. Too many ruffles, too much ornamentation of any kind, indicates a person without restraint. Likewise, too many kinds of ornament may create a cluttered and disorganized effect. Ornament, thus, gives variety, sharpens effects, and helps to characterize. It must be used with considerable discrimination and taste if it is to be effective.

Costumes are complemented or completed by accessories, such as canes, swords, purses, and jewelry. In many cases, accessories perform the same function as ornamentation. Accessories, like the costumes themselves, combine line, mass, color, texture, and ornament. They must be entirely appropriate to the character and the accompanying costumes. Frequently, the design of accessories is dictated by their use since they normally serve as properties for the actor as well as part of a costume.

PRINCIPLES OF DESIGN

The costumer also utilizes the principles of design — *unity, balance, proportion, emphasis,* and *rhythm. Unity* means the harmonious relationship of all the parts; it is that factor which makes a garment seem a complete whole, rather than a collection of disparate parts. Each of the elements of design may contribute to unity. As with other artistic products, however, monotony must be avoided. Not only should unity and variety be attained in individual costumes but in the total collection of costumes for a production.

The principle of *balance* is relatively easy to apply in costuming since in most cases garments are symmetrical — that is, both sides are alike. Not all clothing is symmetrical, however, and the costumer may use asymmetrical balance effectively. As examples, a drapery may hang down only one side of the back, and ornamentation or accessories may alter an otherwise symmetrical arrangement.

Costume and set design by Filippo Juvarra (1684-1735) for the opera *Giunio Bruto overa la Caduta de Tarquinii.* From von Weilen's *Geschichte des Wiener Theaterwesens,* 1899.

Proportion is of great importance in the design of clothing. The amount and distribution of color, the length of the bodice in comparison to that of the skirt, the width of the shoulders in relation to the hips, bust, and waist are some of the factors involved in proportion. Through the manipulation of proportion much can be done to change an actor's normal appearance. By emphasizing vertical lines (that is, by increasing apparent height in proportion to width) a plump actor may be made to appear more slender, while emphasis on width may make an actor seem stocky. Grace and beauty in large part result from right proportions, whereas awkwardness and ugliness derive from poorly proportioned elements.

As with all artistic objects, a costume needs a *center of interest*—a point to which the eye is directed first. It may be created by a patch of color, by converging lines, by a change in texture, or through ornament or accessories. The skillful costumer can direct attention to an actor's good points and disguise his poor features. He can also lead the audience to perceive each character's basic psychological qualities. Furthermore, when the costumes are viewed together, some should be more important than others, since attention should be directed to the principal rather than to the subordinate actors.

Finally, the parts of a costume should be related in such a way that the eye travels easily from one part to another from the major point of interest to subordinate ones. *Rhythm* is closely related to unity and emphasis since the easy flow of vision depends in large part upon the relationship of elements.

As with the scene designer, the costumer should have a thorough knowledge of the elements and principles of design before he sets out to create costumes. In the actual process of design, he organizes the elements (line, mass, color, texture, and ornament) in accordance with the principles (unity, balance, proportion, emphasis, and rhythm) in such a way that the purposes of costuming (to aid understanding, and to express the play's values) are accomplished. The process and the final product (the costumes) vary with each production, since they are adapted to meet the demands of the script and the limitations imposed by working conditions.

WORKING PROCEDURES AND PLANS

As with other theatre workers, the costumer should make an analysis of the script in terms of plot, character, thought, language, and spectacle, for not only should the costumes be appropriate to the individual characters, they should project the over-all traits of the script. Only after he has analyzed the play as a whole should he proceed to a study of costuming demands. The costumer's study of a play should most resemble the actor's, since his designs, like the actor's performance, must be expressive of the characters. But whereas the actor seeks to embody his understanding of character through movement and voice, the costumer uses line, mass, color, texture and ornament to create a visual counterpart of the action.

482

Rough sketch of costumes by Inigo Jones. From Cunningham's *Inigo Jones,* 1848.

The costumer may also need to do considerable research. He must be thoroughly familiar with the garments worn in the period of the play's action—the characteristic silhouettes, typical textures and materials, favorite colors, ornamental motifs, and the usual accessories. He should know as much as possible about the manners and customs of the day so that he understands how each garment and accessory was used.

Before he begins to design costumes, a conference should be held with the director, scenic designer, lighting designer, and possibly the producer, playwright, and some of the actors. The play should be discussed at length and its interpretation clarified.

If he does not already know, the costumer should find out how much money is available for costumes, how many costume changes are envisioned for each character, and any special demands which must be met (for example, actors sometimes refuse to wear certain colors, or the director may have specific business in mind which requires a costume of a particular cut). The costumer must know the kind of theatre in which his work will be seen, since small details may be used to advantage in a theatre-in-the-round but be totally ineffective in a large, more conventional auditorium. He must find out as much as he can about the plans of the other designers, since the scenery, costumes, and lighting should be unified.

When he understands the limitations under which he must work, the costumer is ready to make sketches. Like the scene designer, he may begin with idea sketches in pencil or ink, and he may need to do many before he arrives at designs which he considers right. After he is reasonably well satisfied, additional conferences are held with the director and other designers. The sketches are discussed, revisions may be requested, and still other conferences may be needed before final agreement is reached. In any case, before the designs can be approved, they must be rendered in color and in such a way that they convey a clear impression of the final product.

Alexandre Benois' costumes for Miran-dolina in Goldoni's *The Mistress of the Inn.* From *The Moscow Art Theatre, 1898-1917,* 1955. (See set design page 440.)

The designer is then asked to provide working sketches and plans. The costumer's basic working drawing is the color sketch showing the basic lines and details of each costume. If there are any unusual features, details are shown in a special drawing (usually in the margins of the color sketch). It is also necessary at times to show more than one view of the costume if the front, back, or sides have distinctive features. Samples of the materials to be used in making the garment are attached to each drawing. The sketch, then, shows the lines and cut of the garment, clarifies any unusual details, and shows the materials from which it is to be made.

A costume chart is also needed. This chart is made by dividing a large sheet of paper, or cardboard, into squares. Down the side the name of one character (and that of the actor playing the role) is listed in each square. In like manner each scene (or act) is listed across the top. Thus, there will be one square for each actor in each scene of the play. In each square the designer indicates the costume items (including accessories) to be worn in that scene, and may attach color samples of each garment. The range of colors and the over-all color scheme, thus, can be seen at a glance, and the list of costume items can be used as a guide for dressing the actors and for keeping the costumes organized for efficient running of the production. A sample costume chart is printed on page 485.

484

OTHELLO

ROLE	I-7 (184 Lines)	I-2 (99)	I-3 (410)	II-1 (321)	II-2 (12)	II-3 (394)	III-1 (60)	III-2 (6)	III-3 (479)	III-4 (201)	IV-1 (293)	IV-2 (252)	IV-3 (106)	V-1 (129)	V-2 (371)
DUKE OF VENICE			Duke 1 Red												
BRABANTIO	1 Change to 2 add Jerkin, Hat, Gloves	Bra.	Bra.												
GRATIANO														Grat. 1 Black Gown	Grat.
LODOVICO											Lodovico 1 Gown Boots		Lod.	Lod.	Lod.
OTHELLO		Othe. 1	Othe. White & Gold	Othe. 2 Armor		3 Brown Dressing Robe		Othe. 4 Armor	Othe. 5 White Doublet	6 Dark Brown Doublet-Jerkin	Othe.	Othe.	Othe. Jerkin Off	Othe.	Othe.
CASSIO		Cas. 1	Cas. Olive & Gold	Cas. 2 Armor		Cas. Stripped of Rank	Cas.		Cas.	Cas.	Cas.			Cas.	Cas.
IAGO	Iago 1 Black Cape	Iago	Iago Black & Green	Iago 2 Armor		Iago	Iago	Iago	Iago	Iago	Iago	Iago		Iago in Shirt	Iago
MONTANO				Mont. 2 Armor		Mont.									Mont.
RODERIGO	Rod. 1 Black Cape	Rod.	Rod. Brown & Coral	Rod. 2 Armor		Rod.						Rod.		Rod.	
CLOWN				Clow.		Clow.	Clow.			Clow.					
DESDEMONA			1 Brown with Red Trim	1a Blue Gown over Brown		2 Tan Negligée			3 Rose with Tan Jacket	Des.	Des.	Des. Remove Jacket	Des.		Des. 4 Nightgown
EMILIA			Emi. 1 Green Dress	Emi.		2 Negligée	Emi.		Emi.	Emi.		Emi. Remove Over-sleeves	Emi.	Emi.	Emi.
BIANCA										1 Bian. Dk.Red & Brown	Bian.			Bian.	

INTERMISSION *(between III-3 and III-4)*

A costume chart for *Othello*.

CARRYING OUT THE DESIGNS

Costumes may be borrowed, rented, assembled from an existing wardrobe, or made new. When costumes are borrowed, the designer attempts to find already existing garments which fit his conceptions. Often, however, he must accept clothing which is not ideal.

Borrowed clothing can be altered only slightly, since, as a rule, its owner will wear it again after the performances are over. Much can be done, however, through the imaginative use of accessories or through the addition of ornamentation without altering the basic garment.

The practice of borrowing clothing is restricted almost entirely to the nonprofessional theatre and to short-run productions. Because older garments are not available for borrowing, this practice is also restricted to twentieth-century clothing in most cases. Male actors in the professional theatre often are asked to provide their own wardrobes in modern, realistic plays. This is not the same as borrowing costumes, however, since in such cases the actor's contract specifies that he will wear his own clothing.

Costumes from rental houses fall into a number of categories. Some of the larger agencies buy the costumes of a Broadway or road show when it closes and rent these costumes as a unit. The fact that the costumes from the original production are available is often used as an inducement to rent them. At other times, a house has a staff designer (all major costume agencies employ at least one) who creates costumes for frequently produced plays. In such cases, the costumes are designed according to the agency's conception of the period and style most likely to be used in the greatest number of productions. In still other cases, costume houses merely assemble a large variety of costumes for each period. From this stock, the most appropriate garments are selected to make up the wardrobe for any given show.

When costumes are rented, the costume house assumes the function of designer. The director or costumer may write at length about his interpretation of the play, may request specific colors and kinds of garments, but eventually he must accept what is sent, for rental agencies often make substitutions. Sometimes a costume agency is near enough to the producing organization that the costumes can be selected or approved on the spot. Rented costumes normally arrive at the theatre in time for one or two dress rehearsals, but there is seldom time to secure replacements, or to do more than make minor changes.

The better costume houses provide good service, but seldom can the work of even the best rental agency provide adequate substitutes for garments designed and made with the needs of the specific production in mind. It should be added, however, that even groups which normally make their own costumes sometimes rent articles which are extremely difficult to construct, such as uniforms, male clothing of the nineteenth century, animal costumes, and other unusual items.

Permanent theatre organizations which make their own costumes usually maintain a wardrobe composed of items from past productions. In this way, a large stock of garments is built up over a period of time.

The justification for such a practice is that the costumes can be reused in a number of future productions. The organization, in effect, becomes its own rental agency.

There are important differences between reusing costumes from one's own wardrobe and renting them from another source, however, for when garments are taken from the theatre's own stock, the costumer designs the play with this in mind. He knows what is available and can choose in advance. Furthermore, existing costumes can be remade or altered to fit new conceptions. As a rule, some costumes are taken from stock while those to be worn by the principal characters are made new.

The procedures and working conditions for creating new costumes vary from one kind of organization to another. In the professional theatre, the designer's sketches are turned over to a costume house which executes the designs under a contract with the producer. The designer must approve the finished costumes but has little to do with the actual work itself beyond supervising the fitting of garments.

Unlike the scene designer, the costumer does not have to furnish technical working drawings which show how his designs are to be carried out (that is, the costumer does not have to supply patterns, or cutting, sewing, and fitting directions). He depends upon the costume house to fill in this information.

In the nonprofessional theatre, the designer most frequently supervises the construction of his own costumes and must know as much about pattern drafting, draping, and fitting as he does about design. Every costumer should understand the techniques for carrying out his designs so that he will know what effects can be accomplished and by what means. Furthermore, such knowledge permits him to speak with authority and to give guidance to those who aid him in carrying out his plans.

Regardless of who actually makes the costumes, however, a number of standard procedures are involved. First, accurate measurements must be made of all the actors. (The stage manager or assistant director usually makes appointments for measurements and fittings.)

Second, the necessary materials must be bought. While it is expected that the designer will specify materials, it is not always possible to find precisely the same cloth or color. Either the designer, or some authorized person, may need to search at length for the right materials.

Next, patterns must be drafted as guides for cutting and shaping the material. Many books print patterns for garments of various periods. These must be adapted to fit the particular actor, but in some cases patterns must be made without the help of existing diagrams. It is at this point that the technical knowledge of the tailor and seamstress is of greatest value.

Patterns are needed for most garments, especially those tightly fitted or intricately shaped, but some costumes are more easily draped. For example, the typical Greek garment hangs from the shoulders in folds and is not fitted to the body. It is easier, therefore, to drape the material on the actor or on a dress form. In this way, the folds may be arranged as desired, and many possibilities can be tried out.

Eldon Elder's design of Baby Doe's wedding dress, Act I, Scene 6 (worn by Doris Yarick), Santa Fe Opera Company's production of *The Ballad of Baby Doe. Opera* by Douglas Moore, libretto by John La Touche. Director, Henry Butler. *The costume was made of dull white satin with silk-tassel fringe, white-lace overlay, marabou, hidden rhinestones.*

After the patterns are completed, the material is then cut and the parts are basted together. Before sewing is completed, the first fitting occurs. Each garment is put on the actor who is to wear it and its fit and appearance is checked by the designer. It is easy to make many alterations or changes at this point which will be impossible (or extremely troublesome) after the garment is entirely finished.

After the preliminary fittings, the garment is finished, and ornamentation and accessories are added. Another fitting is arranged at this time to assure that the costume looks and functions as planned.

THE COSTUME PARADE, REHEARSALS, AND PERFORMANCES

When all of the costumes are finished, it is wise to hold a dress parade. At this time, each scene of the play is covered in sequence so that the actors may appear in the appropriate costumes under lights which simulate those to be used in performance. The actors may be asked to perform characteristic portions of each scene.

The dress parade, which is attended by the director and the other designers (as well as the producer and the playwright in the professional theatre), allows everyone to see and evaluate the costumes without the distractions of a complete performance. Difficulties can be noted and corrected before dress rehearsals.

In the professional theatre, the dress parade is held at the costume house, while in other organizations it usually occurs on stage. It is normally supervised by the costumer.

After difficulties have been corrected, the costumes are moved to the dressing rooms in the theatre where the performances are to take place. If no dress parade is held, its functions must be accomplished during the dress rehearsals.

Dress rehearsals allow the costumes to be seen under conditions as near as possible to those of performance. Changes at this time should be few, but those which are necessary must be made speedily so that the actor is not confronted with new details on opening night.

Once dress rehearsals begin, a wardrobe mistress (or costume-crew head) usually assumes responsibility for seeing that costumes are in good condition and that each actor is dressed as planned. In the nonprofessional theatre, the costumer frequently assumes these duties. Technically, the costumer's work is over after opening night. In the professional theatre, he may be asked to supervise the replacement of costumes when they become shabby, and he may be asked to redesign the costumes for road companies.

THE COSTUMER'S EMPLOYMENT

The costumer's function may be performed by persons who are employed in other capacities as well. A very large number of nonprofessional organizations do not have a special costume designer. Sometimes his duties are filled by the director; more often, however, a designer-technician assumes responsibility for all the visual elements of a production. On the other hand, many organizations have a costumer who has no other responsibilities, and some have more than one customer.

489

Even in the professional theatre, however, the scene designer may also design the costumes. In fact, scene designers who belong to the United Scenic Artists Union must be able to design costumes. In recent years, however, it has become common for one person to design the costumes and another the scenery. Like the professional scene designer, the costumer must also belong to the United Scenic Artists Union, although he is not required to pass those parts of the examination dealing with scenery unless he wishes to be certified in that field as well. His entrance examinations and his responsibilities are otherwise the same as those for the scene designer.

Union rules forbid a designer to submit any designs for a prospective production until he has signed a contract (he may, however, show previous work). His fee is based on the number of costumes required. His contract specifies his billing and any special arrangements. He must be available for consultation throughout the rehearsal period and must accompany the show on its out-of-town tryouts if the producer desires.

Off-Broadway theatres, summer stock companies, and professional companies outside of New York sometimes employ nonunion costumers. It is difficult to specify with any exactness the working conditions in such organizations, since the situation varies so widely.

THE COSTUMER'S ASSISTANTS

In carrying out his work, the costumer needs a number of helpers, the most important of which are: an assistant costumer; cutters, fitters, and seamstresses; the wardrobe mistress; the dressers.

The costumer's assistant does whatever is asked of him. He may make sketches, seek out appropriate materials, supervise fittings, or act as liaison between the costumer and other theatre workers. He must be as versatile as the costume designer himself, but he must be prepared to perform the less exciting tasks.

Cutters, fitters, and seamstresses make the costumes. Skilled workers at this stage can save time and make the difference between ill-fitting and correctly fitting garments. Furthermore, if the designer is not to make the patterns and supervise the sewing himself, he must depend upon workers who have sufficient knowledge to carry out his plans. In the professional theatre, such workers must be union members. In the nonprofessional theatre, much of this work is done by volunteer or student labor, although occasionally a paid seamstress may be hired, either on a permanent or temporary basis, to sew and to supervise the work of others.

When the costumes are finished, a wardrobe mistress takes charge. She is assisted in her work by a crew of dressers. It is the responsibility of the wardrobe mistress to see that costumes are ready for each performance. They may need to be mended, laundered and ironed, or cleaned and pressed. She must see that garments are replaced when they begin to look shabby so that the show will continue to look as it did on opening night. She is directly responsible to the stage manager during performances. Some permanent producing organizations employ a full-time

490

wardrobe mistress to supervise the upkeep of the stock as well as to supervise the preparation of costumes and the running of particular shows.

The number of dressers needed for a production depends upon the size of the cast and the complexity and rapidity of costume changes. Sometimes actors need very little help, but quick changes and complicated garments may require more than one dresser to aid a single actor. There must be a sufficient number to keep the show running smoothly during performances and to keep the costumes in shape at all times.

In the professional theatre, both the wardrobe mistress and the dressers must be union members. In the nonprofessional theatre, the costumer may serve as wardrobe mistress, or a paid or volunteer assistant may serve in this capacity. Dressers are normally students or volunteers.

THE COSTUMER AND THE ACTOR

The costumer must work very closely with the actor, for many of their problems are shared. First, the costumer should consider the strengths and weaknesses of each actor's figure when designing costumes. It is possible to design an appropriate and expressive costume without considering the actor who is to wear it, but this leads to questionable results when the onstage effect is destroyed by the performer's physical appearance. Thus, if an actor's thin legs are out of keeping with the role he is playing, the costumer can conceal this shortcoming. Boots, a cape, or some flowing garment can cover the legs or draw attention away from them. Although there are limits to what the costumer can do for an actor, he should strive to make him look as nearly as possible the embodiment of the role he is playing.

The costumer should also keep in mind the physical actions demanded of the actor. For example, it is difficult to climb steps in a tight skirt, and fencing may be dangerous if an actor wears billowing sleeves. On the other hand, these same garments can enhance movement in other situations.

Almost any unfamiliar garment will seem awkward to the actor until he becomes familiar with its possibilities. Every costume, except one that is skin tight, allows some movements and restricts others. The characteristic features of clothes in each period emphasize qualities which were admired at the time, and allow movements which were socially useful, beautiful, or desirable. For example, the sleeves on a fashionable man's coat in the eighteenth century will not allow the arms to hang comfortably at the sides; rather, the arms must be bent at the elbows and held away from the body. On the other hand, the modern suit coat is cut so that the arms are most comfortable when hanging at the sides, while outward and upward movement is restricted. Each of these coats is adapted to the needs of its period. The costumer should understand the relationship between the cut of garments and movement. If he makes garments from authentic period patterns, the costumes will help the actors to get the feel of the time.

The costumer should also aid the actor by proper attention to shoes and undergarments. The height of the heel on shoes is of great importance to

491

stage movement. A high heel throws the weight forward onto the balls of the feet, while heelless shoes bring the weight back. The right kind of footwear, therefore, can aid the actor in achieving appropriate period movement.

Undergarments also affect movement. Corsets, for example, are of various kinds and each is designed to force the body into a specific shape. By doing so, it encourages some actions and makes others impossible. A hooped, crinoline underskirt will not allow the same kind of movement as modern underwear.

If the costumer encourages suitable movement with the clothes he designs, he can be of enormous help to the actor. For maximum effectiveness, however, the actor and director must be willing to explore the possibilities of garments and to allow sufficient time for rehearsal in them.

MAKE-UP

Make-up is normally used to cover all parts of the actor's body not concealed by his costume. It is, therefore, an essential part of his physical appearance. Nevertheless, the position of make-up in the theatre is ambiguous — it is acknowledged to be of great importance, but its mastery is frequently taken for granted and its planning is often left to chance.

Traditionally, make-up has been considered the actor's responsibility, and often each actor is assumed to be capable of achieving any affect. This is not always true, however, and it is especially questionable in the nonprofessional theatre. For this reason, in many organizations make-up is under the supervision of the costumer, director, or some other person specially skilled in make-up. In the professional theatre, each actor is expected to take care of his own make-up.

Make-up is discussed here in connection with costuming because of its intimate connection with the actor's appearance. Furthermore, it is desirable that make-up be planned in advance just as any other element of production. It is not entirely logical to leave each actor to decide upon his own make-up when all other elements of a production have been designed with care and after many conferences.

A make-up room showing actors in the process of applying make-up.

PURPOSES. Like the other aspects of production, make-up should aid understanding and be expressive of the play's qualities. It can establish the age of a character, his state of health, his race; within limits, it may aid in establishing profession (for example, persons who work outdoors usually have different coloration from those who work indoors), basic attitudes (a grumpy person may have different facial wrinkles and lines than a cheerful one), and his self-regard (how well he takes care of his personal appearance).

Make-up may be indicative of style. In a realistic drama, such factors as age and health are modeled as much as possible after life, whereas in an expressionistic play, more attention may be given to establishing an idea (for example, the faces of all the actors might be painted grayish-green to indicate that they are living corpses).

Make-up may be used to establish psychological qualities and to make the face more expressive. A character can be made to look the stereotype of the villain; or certain features may be emphasized to give an impression of secretiveness or of naïveté. The nose, mouth, eyes, or other facial features may be emphasized or subordinated.

Certain practical purposes are also served by make-up. For example, since stage lighting is usually more intense than normal lighting, without make-up most persons would appear too pale. Make-up restores color and form to the face. It must be applied, however, with the size of the auditorium in mind, for while it should be seen, it should not appear grotesque and distorted, unless these qualities are appropriate to production.

THE MAKE-UP PLOT. When make-up is designed and supervised by one person, a plot and sketches are normally used. A chart is made indicating basic information about the make-up of each actor: the base, liners, eye shadow, and powder; any plastic features, such as a beard; any changes to be made during the play. It serves both as a guide for applying make-up and as a check on how the make-up of each actor relates to that of all the others.

In designing make-up, the actor's facial characteristics and coloration should be analyzed and compared with the ideal for the character so that appropriate alterations can be planned.

TYPES OF MAKE-UP. In make-up, effects may be achieved in two basic ways: by painting, and through the addition of plastic, or three-dimensional, pieces. Painting involves the application of color, highlights, and lowlights on the face or other parts of the body. Plastic make-up includes such objects as beards, wigs, false noses, and warts. All make-ups use some painted effects, but plastic pieces are utilized more rarely.

Painted make-ups may be divided into a number of subcategories: various age groups; straight and character make-ups; racial types; and special effects.

If an actor is to portray a character whose age is significantly different from his own, he must alter his appearance. Like the actor, then, the make-up artist should observe the characteristic distinctions between childhood, youth, maturity, early-middle age, middle age, late-middle

493

age, and differing degrees of old age. He must study each part of the face to see the typical coloration, highlights, shadows, and lines; he should observe the forehead, eyes, nose, mouth, cheeks, jaws, and neck. He should not neglect the hands, arms, and other parts of the body, for youthful looking hands sometimes destroy the illusion created by facial make-up.

Make-ups may also be classified as *straight* or *character*. With a *straight* make-up, the actor's own basic characteristics are utilized without significant change. A *character* make-up is one in which the actor's appearance is altered. The change may be one in age, but it may involve making the actor seem fatter or coarser, more lean and wizened, or emphasizing some peculiar facial characteristic.

Frequently, scripts require a clear differentiation of races. Again, the make-up artist should observe or discover the characteristic differences between such races as Chinese, Indian, Polynesian, Caucasian, and Negro. He also needs to study the typical facial characteristics, coloration, and manifestations of age in each racial group.

Special painted effects include clown make-ups, distortions for stylistic effects, or decorative designs painted on the face (in the manner of a primitive tribe).

The number of effects which can be achieved by painting are almost limitless. Most give clear indications of age, character, and race.

While most make-up uses painting as a basis, significant transformations in an actor's appearance may be more easily accomplished with three-dimenstional elements. For example, a change in the shape of the nose and the addition of a beard and bushy eyebrows can mask an actor's features more completely than painting can.

Gauze over cotton can be glued to the actor's face to form prominent cheeks, hanging jowls, a protuberant forehead, or fleshy jaws. Warts and large scars may be used to give the actor an unsightly appearance.

A scene from Tagore's *King of the Dark Chamber.* Note the similarity of the make-up used for the figure at the lower right to that used by Kathakali dancers (see page 259). Directed by Krishna Shah; make-up by Donald Rosenberg.

Make-up and costume based on an animal. Epinard, the porcupine, in Arthur Fauquez' *Reynard the Fox. Right.* Close-up of the make-up for Epinard (played by George Bryan). Reprinted with permission from *The Mask of Reality; An Approach to Design for Theatre* by Irene Corey. Anchorage Press, 1968.

The actor may grow his own beard and mustache if he desires, but these can also be made with relative ease. Many styles of hair can be achieved only with the aid of a wig. Baldness can also be simulated with a bald wig. Much can also be done to alter the actor's own hair.

MAKE-UP MATERIALS. To accomplish effects, a variety of make-up materials are available from manufacturers and from costume supply houses. In the professional theatre and in many nonprofessional organizations the actor is expected to furnish his own make-up supplies. It is not unusual in colleges and universities, however, for the theatre to supply make-up. The following discussion indicates the principal materials most frequently used.

Most make-ups begin with a base (pigment suspended in an oily solution; most base make-up is packaged as a pastelike substance in tubes). A very wide range of base colors is available: various shades of pink, suntan, yellow, beige, brown, black and white. Each color may be used as it comes or it may be mixed with one or more additional colors to achieve the desired shade. The base color is applied over the exposed portions of the face, neck and ears. (A range of color equal to that of tube colors is available in liquid form for application to large surfaces of the body, such as the arms, legs, and torso.)

495

A base color alone is apt to make the actor's face appear flat and uninteresting. Over this base, therefore, lines, highlights, and shadows are applied. For this purpose, a thick paste is available in small tins. Normally called *liner* it comes in a wide variety of colors, such as white, light brown, dark brown, blue, green, red, gray, and black. Like the base colors, liners may be mixed to create any shade. They are used for shadows under the eyes, hollows in the cheeks or temples, for furrows in the forehead, or for creases which spread outward and downward from the nose—for any high- or low-light. Red liner may be used for lipstick or rouge.

Crepe hair is used to make beards and mustaches. It comes in a wide range of colors, which may be combined to achieve more accurate representations of human hair, which is frequently mottled. Crepe hair is sold in long, plaited strands. When unplaited it is extremely crinkled, but it may be straightened by holding it over steam or by stretching it tightly for some time.

For making beards (and similar items such as mustaches and bushy eyebrows) liquid adhesive is needed. This is a plastic substance which becomes solid, though remaining flexible, when exposed to the air. It may be applied to the face (usually several layers are built up) to form a base upon which crepe hair can be attached (with the same liquid adhesive). When a beard of the desired shape and size has been made, the whole structure, including the base and hair, can be removed. This permanent beard can be reused at each performance by reattaching it to the face with liquid adhesive.

Nose putty is used for changing the shape of the nose, chin, cheek bones, or forehead. It may be shaped as desired and then attached to the face. It is not very satisfactory when applied to flexible parts of the face, however, since it is apt to be loosened by movement and may fall off. For plastic effects on flexible parts of the face, gauze may be stretched over pieces of cotton and glued to the face with liquid adhesive. These plastic elements are then covered with the same base color as that used on the rest of the face. Liners may be used to make them more realistic in appearance.

Various materials may be employed to alter the color of the hair. A white liquid, usually called hair whitener, may be combed through the hair to make it gray. It frequently gives an unnatural appearance, however, and much more realistic effects can be achieved by combing metallic powders through oiled hair. Aluminum powder makes a convincing gray, while copper and bronze give a reddish cast.

Wigs may be made from the kind of plastic hair used on store-window models. It may be bought in a wide variety of colors and can be sewn or glued to a cloth base which has been fitted to the actor's head. The hair can then be styled. Natural-hair wigs may be rented from costume supply houses. Wigs made from anything other than plastic or human hair are seldom satisfactory if a natural appearance is desired. If naturalness is not a consideration, wigs may be made from hemp, crepe hair, or a variety of other materials.

After the make-up is complete, the painted portions must be powdered, for otherwise the actor, when seen under the bright stage lights, will appear greasy. Powder comes in the same variety of shades as base paints. It should be applied freely and the excess brushed off. Those parts of the body covered with liquid make-up need not be powdered since this kind of make-up has a low sheen. For removing make-up a good supply of cold cream and facial tissues is needed.

This brief outline does not explain the techniques needed for the proper application of make-up. These may be learned, however, from a number of textbooks.

Since the actor's physical appearance is a basic part of his characterization, he should learn as much about costume and make-up as possible. It should also be the aim of the costumer and the make-up artist to aid the actor whenever possible to transform him into the character he is playing. They must work together to make costume and make-up an integral part of the total design.

Chapter 21 THE LIGHTING DESIGNER

One of the least publicized, but most important, theatre artists is the lighting designer, for without his work that of the other artists would not be seen. Furthermore, his designs may either enhance or seriously distort the visual elements of a production – the action, scenery, costumes, and make-up.

Perhaps his work is little known because light itself is intangible, takes up no stage space, and is visible only when it strikes a reflecting surface, such as an actor or a piece of scenery. Thus, while light is present, it is usually ignored unless it is obviously inadequate or obtrusively spectacular. Since lighting also requires a knowledge of complex instruments and control boards, of electricity and electronics, of optics and physics, to many it appears more the province of the electrical engineer than that of the theatre artist. In actuality, the lighting designer must be both a sound technician and an artist of high caliber.

FUNCTIONS OF STAGE LIGHTING

The functions of stage lighting, like those of other areas of design, are to aid understanding and to express a play's values. First, and most basically, lighting aids understanding by making the other elements visible. It need not make everything equally visible, but it should reveal whatever the audience needs to see.

Lighting aids understanding in a number of other ways. It may establish the time of day (early morning, midday, late afternoon, or night), the source of the light (sun, moon, lamps, fire light), the weather conditions (a sunny, overcast, or stormy day), and it may help to identify the time of year (the amount and kind of light may vary from one season to another). The period may be established by the lighting fixtures on stage (oil

Scene from Obey's *Noah*. The stylized rainbow is in keeping with the style of the play and the scenery. Note also the cyclorama lighting.

lamps, candles, electric lights). Light may further aid understanding through special effects (such as lightning, offstage fires, flashing lights, or rainbows).

Lighting should enhance the play's mood and atmosphere, style, and themes. Brightness, color and distribution can be used to create almost any desired mood. Normally, bright, warm colors are associated with gaiety, while cool colors of low intensity may create a somber atmosphere. If a scene is lighted from the side with a single bright source, the sharp contrast between light and darkness will give a harsh quality. The intensity, color, and direction of light may be combined in other ways to create widely varying moods.

Lighting may be expressive of style and theme through its effect on form. Although the stage space, actors, properties, and furniture are three-dimensional, their shapes may be emphasized or distorted to suit the style and themes of a play. If the illusion of real people in a real environment is sought (as it often is in realistic drama), then lifelike light and shadow can reveal the scenery and the actors in all of their dimensions. On the other hand, if the designer wishes to emphasize a theme such as the emptiness of life or the shallowness of existence, everything can be made to appear two-dimensional by lighting all of the visible surfaces evenly. Distortion can be achieved in many ways. For instance, if the majority of light comes from directly overhead, unnatural shadows will be cast on the actors' faces and the entire setting may seem misshapen and sinister.

Scene from Sidney Howard's *Yellow Jack* showing the use of light to isolate scenes in space.

Lighting can also be used as a compositional element. It can reveal whatever needs emphasis; it can selectively illuminate objects, actors, or areas, focus attention upon them, or obscure them; it can let the eye see what is important and subordinate the insignificant.

THE CONTROLLABLE FACTORS OF LIGHT

To fulfill the purposes of lighting, the designer may manipulate and control four factors: intensity or brightness, color, distribution, and movement.

Intensity depends primarily upon the number and wattage of the lamps. It may be modified in several ways. If a color medium intervenes between a light source and the stage (as is typical) the amount of light is reduced, for the filter will not allow all of the light rays to pass through it. Distance also diminishes brilliance; the farther a lamp is placed from the stage the lower will be the intensity of its light on the stage. Brightness may further be controlled by the placement of lighting instruments — all may be directed at the same spot, or they may distribute the light evenly or unevenly over the stage. In addition, dimmers can vary brightness.

Intensity, thus, is principally a matter of how much light reaches the stage. It can be controlled and used in the creation of mood and atmosphere and to meet changing dramatic needs. High intensity is often associated with comedy, whereas a lower intensity is thought more appropriate to serious plays. Brightness may be adjusted according to the supposed source of the light, the hour of the day, or the psychological or atmospheric needs of the moment.

The visible spectrum of light is composed of the following colors: red, orange, yellow, green, blue-green, blue, and violet. Each color is distinguishable from the others because it is composed of light waves of a given length. Waves which create the sensation of red are the longest visible rays, while those of violet are the shortest. White or natural light is a mixture of all the visible wave lengths. Color is attributed to objects because of their capacity for adsorbing some wave lengths and reflecting others. Without light there is no color.

Each light source emits its own spectrum of color. The incandescent lamp (the most commonly used in stage lighting) tends toward yellow, with lesser amounts of other colors, while the fluorescent lamp most frequently gives a bluish light. Therefore, the apparent color of scenery and costumes is affected by the light source, even when color filters are not employed.

To prevent distortion of color in scenery, costumes, and make-up and to emphasize mood or time of day, the color of lighting should be as variable as possible. To permit control, color filters are used.

A color filter operates on the principle of selective transmission — that is, it allows only certain wave lengths of light to pass through. For example, a blue filter screens out the majority of the red, orange, yellow, and violet rays. At the same time, however, this process reduces considerably the amount of light which reaches the stage. Furthermore, if a red object

500

is lighted only with blue light, its apparent color will be changed to magenta.

To avoid such distortions, filters of different colors are placed on other lighting instruments, so that light from a number of sources may be mixed on the stage. For example, the primary colors of light—red, blue, and green—may be mixed to give white light. More frequently, however, a variety of subtle tints and shades are employed.

Color in light has three basic qualities: *hue*, *saturation*, and *brightness*. *Hue* is the name of the color (such as red, green, or violet). *Saturation* is the relative purity of the color—its concentration around a specific wave length. *Brightness* is the darkness or lightness of the color, or its component of white light. The addition of white light produces tints, while taking it away makes shades. Since the color filters available from manufacturers combine these three qualities in a wide variety of ways, it is relatively easy to obtain filters entirely appropriate to any effect.

Distribution depends upon the direction from which light comes and the way it is spread over the stage: from overhead, the front, sides, or back; covering a portion or all of the stage. Direction is determined by the position of the light source. Almost any placement is possible, for instruments may be mounted in the ceiling of the auditorium, on the front of the balcony, on pipes over the stage; they may be placed on the floor or mounted on vertical pipes or stands.

Differences in the direction of light are important in establishing mood and visibility. For example, if all the light striking a character comes from behind, his actions will be visible but his identity may remain unknown, since his face is not revealed. Such lighting can be used effectively for creating a sinister atmosphere or a mood of mystery. Furthermore, the audience's perception of dimensionality depends in large part upon the direction of the light, for illumination which strikes all surfaces of an object equally will make it appear flat, whereas that which lights some parts more than others emphasizes planes and surfaces.

Scene from Richardson's *Dark of the Moon* showing the use of lighting to establish mood.

Scene from Shakespeare's *Julius Caesar*. The manipulation of light and shadow aids in creating a sense of danger and conspiracy. Directed by A. N. Vardac; lighting by O. G. Brockett.

How much space is lighted depends upon the number of instruments used (a number of sources are normally required to light the entire stage), and upon what parts they are focused (all instruments may be concentrated on a single area or distributed over several or all parts of the stage). For example, a spotlight may be used to light the face of one character while the rest of the stage is in darkness, or the entire acting area may be lighted by a large number of spotlights. It is possible, at least in theory, to distribute light exactly as desired, both in terms of direction and area.

Movement refers to alterations in intensity, color, or distribution during a performance. The principal device for achieving the effect of movement is the controlboard. With it, lamps may be brightened or dimmed to control intensity, change color, or distribution. Movement allows the light to change in accordance with the shifting moods and dramatic events. Because it can be altered moment by moment, light is the most flexible of all elements of stage production, with the possible exception of acting.

The lighting designer should understand thoroughly the controllable factors of light—intensity, color, distribution, and movement—and how they may be manipulated to achieve his purposes.

THE PRINCIPLES OF DESIGN

Stage lighting is governed by the same principles of design employed in other visual arts: *harmony, balance, proportion, emphasis,* and *rhythm*.

The lighting for an entire production should be planned as a unit so that all the parts are harmonious. It should be entirely appropriate to the style, period, characters, actions, and ideas of the play. Unity, however, can lead to monotony if due care is not taken to ensure variety. Thus, while all the parts should constitute a harmonious whole, a wide range of appropriate devices should be employed.

Balance, proportion, and emphasis are closely related principles in lighting design, for each is achieved largely through the proper handling of the others. Lighting should be designed so that primary emphasis is placed on the acting areas. Since brightness always gives emphasis, the

502

most intense lighting is usually focused on those parts of the stage used by the actors and a proportionately lesser amount of light used for the background. Since the acting areas and the background must seem unified, proportion must be governed so that all parts blend smoothly. Furthermore, as a rule light on the acting areas should be evenly distributed so that the actors do not pass through distracting dark and bright spots as they move about the stage. This usual balance, however, may be altered as the script demands, for it is often essential that one area be more brightly lighted than another. Proportion and balance, thus, create the necessary emphases.

Rhythm is that factor which makes attention flow effortlessly from the main center of emphasis to the subordinate parts and back to the main center again. In lighting it results from gradations in intensity and the proper handling of color and distribution. Since light can reveal, conceal, or alter any of the other visual elements of a production, rhythm in lighting design is one of the most important means of welding all the parts into a unified composition.

The lighting designer, then, shapes the controllable factors of light in accordance with the principles of design so as to realize the purposes of stage lighting. In doing so, however, he must work within the limitations imposed by the script and the particular conditions in the theatre used.

WORKING PROCEDURES

The lighting designer should have a thorough understanding of the play before he searches for its specific lighting demands. He should begin, therefore, with an analysis of the action, characters, ideas, and spectacle to clarify the basic intentions of the script, its meanings, and style. After he is satisfied that he understands the play as a whole, he is ready to investigate how he may embody its qualities in light.

The designer should look for indications of the nature of the light: the sources of illumination (lamps, candles, moonlight, sunlight); changes in intensity (indications of growing darkness, of lamps being lighted or shutters opened); variations required for different parts of the stage; the direction of light (moonlight through a window, sunlight from one side of the stage); any special effects (such as lightning, rainbows, or fires); and the coloration of light (firelight, moonlight, lamplight, sunlight). Such practical considerations often need to be thought through in the design and cannot be ignored if they are essential parts of the script.

The designer should be especially concerned with mood, for lighting contributes much to the proper atmosphere of a play. Lighting may be bright or low, warm or cold; it may blend the parts of the setting or it may isolate them. Mood can be established or enhanced through varying combinations of intensity, color, and distribution.

The designer should understand the style of the play. For a realistic drama the light may appear to come from specific light sources and to change in accordance with realistic motivations. If the script is nonrealistic, light may be used more arbitrarily. It should always reflect the level of reality depicted in the script.

503

The designer should also seek to underline the structural development of the play. For example, in a play which moves from happiness to despair, lighting can help to show the change.

The lighting designer may do research to determine the typical lighting fixtures of a period, the qualities of light derived from each, and the way each fixture was used. If the production utilizes earlier staging techniques, the designer may need to study the stage-lighting practices of that time. As a rule, however, the lighting designer's work is less affected by historical considerations than that of the set and costume designers.

The lighting designer's study of the play should be reasonably complete before his first conference with the director, the other designers, the producer, and the playwright. At this meeting, he usually discusses his understanding of the play with the others and outlines his ideas for lighting the production. He must make certain that he understands the director's interpretation and the plans of the scene designer and the costumer. There may be a series of conferences before final accord is reached.

In the professional theatre, the lighting designer must make sketches showing the stage as it will look when lighted. In the nonprofessional theatre, a general (sometimes vague) agreement is reached about the qualities of the lighting to be used—its intensity, coloration and distribution—but the specific design is often left tentative.

This situation is dictated in part by the nature of light. Since much time must be spent in adjusting the lighting, it is frequently assumed that the lighting designer can make alterations to compensate for unforeseen problems in acting, scenery, or costumes. Furthermore, little can be done about carrying out the lighting designs until the theatre is available and the scenery in place. For these reasons, the major work of lighting a show is done in the last few days of the rehearsal period.

THE LIGHT PLOT AND INSTRUMENT SCHEDULE

Nevertheless, the lighting designer should be able to outline his plans by means of sketches, light plots, and an instrument schedule.

A light plot is drawn on a floor plan or on a vertical section plan. The floor plan should show, as seen from above, the layout of the entire stage, the setting, and pertinent parts of the auditorium. A vertical section plan is drawn as though one side of the theatre had been removed. It shows the vertical arrangement of the stage, the scenery, and the auditorium. In making a light plot, the following information is shown: the type, size, and position of each instrument, and the approximate area to be lighted by each. Abbreviations and symbols may be used to indicate many specifications.

It is usually necessary to make a separate light plot for each setting, since the area to be covered by the lights will vary with the scenic arrangement. It is also typical to make a composite plot which shows all of the settings simultaneously and the relationship of the lighting for each scene to that of all the others. This is especially helpful because as a rule the same equipment must be used to light more than one setting. Consequently, the areas to be covered must be worked out carefully to make effective use of the instruments in each scene.

Lighting for the stage may be divided into specific illumination, general illumination, and special effects. Specific illumination refers to lighting which is confined to a very limited area; general illumination is light which spreads over a large part of the stage; and special effects are out-of-the-ordinary demands such as fires, rainbows, and lightning. Each of these must be given proper consideration in the design and layout of the light plot.

Specific illumination is used principally for lighting the acting areas, since they need the greatest emphasis and often require much variety in intensity, color, and distribution. The spotlight, the principal source of specific illumination, has been developed especially to light the acting areas. Designed to emit a concentrated beam of light which can be confined to a restricted portion of the stage, it cannot be used efficiently for lighting the entire setting.

Since a single spotlight can satisfactorily illuminate only a small segment of the stage, the total acting space is normally divided into smaller areas, the number depending on the size of the setting. For an average-sized setting, three or four areas are needed across the forward part of the stage and an equal number at the rear. Each area may then be lighted separately. Ideally, at least one spotlight should be focused upon an area from each side so as to strike it at an angle of forty-five degrees both horizontally and vertically. The lighting for each area must overlap sufficiently to prevent unduly bright or dark spots and to achieve an even distribution of light over the entire acting area.

Since the forward acting areas cannot be lighted effectively from behind the proscenium arch, some provision must be made for hanging instruments in the auditorium. The ideal angle for light (forty-five degrees) can best be achieved from apertures in the ceiling (frequently called the *beams*) which permit instruments to be mounted across the entire width of the auditorium. Many theatres also have vertical apertures at the sides of the auditorium. Not all theatres are designed with lighting needs in mind, however, and facilities for hanging instruments may have to be improvised. In most New York theatres, for example, spotlights are mounted on the front of the balcony.

The upstage acting areas are normally lighted by instruments hung back of the proscenium arch. In most theatres a light bridge is suspended just behind and above the proscenium opening, and there may be vertical pipes on either side of the proscenium, just back of the masking pieces known as *tormentors*, to which lights may be fastened. Instruments may also be mounted on other pipe battens suspended over the stage at intervals from front to back, may be attached to the scenery, placed on the floor or mounted on stands.

In addition to the spotlights used for lighting the acting areas, others may be needed for special purposes, such as for following a ghost, achieving momentary emphasis on a doorway, or picking out the face of

505

Scene from *The Wild Duck.* Directed by John Terfloth; setting by Carleton Mollette; lighting by Ward Williamson. The light plot is shown on page 507.

one actor as the rest of the stage is darkened. These may be mounted wherever needed.

General illumination serves three basic functions. First, it is used to light all of the background elements not illuminated by the spotlights. The cyclorama, ground rows, or drops, for example, may not be lighted at all by the spots. Because it is usually desirable to light the background at a lower intensity than that used for acting areas, general illumination is sufficient for this part of the setting. Second, it is used to blend the acting areas together, and to provide a smooth transition between the high intensity of the acting areas and the low intensity of the background. Spotlight beams often produce sharp, angular lines on walls or floors. Furthermore, the brightness of the spots makes the cleavage between the acting areas and the rest of the stage conspicuous. General illumination can erase these distracting lines and blend all of the lighting into a unified whole. Third, general illumination is used to enhance or modify the color or tone of settings and costumes.

General illumination is provided primarily by striplights and floodlights, which diffuse light over a large area. Although this light cannot be confined to small areas, its direction can be partially controlled. Footlights are pointed upward and backward from the front edge of the stage. Border lights may be hung directly over the acting area and pointed downward, or they may be tilted to light the walls of the setting. Other striplights may be placed on the floor to light ground rows or the cyclorama. Floodlights may be suspended on battens or placed on stands or the floor to illuminate drops or the cyclorama.

Special effects, as the name implies, are unusual demands and, therefore, cover a wide variety of miscellaneous lighting requirements and instruments. Still or moving clouds, stars, or an entire scenic background may be projected. Prop fire logs, a machine for making bright flashes of light, or an instrument for producing realistic rays of sunlight may be needed. The demands and the solutions are many.

In making a light plot, the problems of specific illumination, general illumination, and special effects should be considered separately and then as a unit. The instruments, the placement of each, the area to be lighted by each, and the color of filters to be used must be decided and

506

CODE	AREA	INST. LOCATION	INSTRUMENT	WATTS	OUTLET	DIMMER	COLOR	NOTES
1	DL / DLC	BEAMS	8" ELLIPS.	750	B 1	A 2	62	
2	DRC	"	"	"	PROS L2	A 4	"	
3	"	"	"	1000	" L3	C 3	31	
4	DL	"	"	"	5	C 1	"	
5	"	"	"	750	6	A 1	62	
6	DC	"	"	1000	7	C 2	31	
7	DR	"	"	750	17	A 6	62	
8	"	"	"	1000	9	C 1	31	
9	DL	"	"	"	PROS R1	"	"	
10	"	"	"	750	" R2	A 3	62	
11	DC	"	"	"	12	A 5	"	
12	DLC	BRIDGE	6" FRES.	500	BR 3	D 5	70	
13	UC	"	"	"	6	B 7	62	
14	UL	"	8" OV. FRES.	1000	BR 4	D 3	31	
15	RC	"	"	"	C 6	C 6	"	
16	RC	"	6" OV. FRES.	500	8	B 3	62	
17	UC	"	8" " "	1000	15	C 4	31	
18	LC	"	6" " "	500	16	B 1	62	
19	DR SPEC.	"	"	"	17	B 5	"	
20	UL	"	"	"	19	B 6		
21	LC	"	8" " "	1000	22	C 5	31	
22	C	"	6" " "	500	21	B 2	62	
23	UL DOOR	2 ND PIPE	"	1000	BR 11	B 8	62	
24	UL BACK	"	8" "	"	TORM L1	F 3	57	
25	UC . "	"	"	"	" L3	F 2	"	
26	UL "	"	"	"	BR 1	F 3	"	
27	LC "	"	"	"	BR 28	C 8	"	
28	C "	"	"	"	DS 4	F 2	"	
29	" "	"	12" FRES.	2000	DS 2	C 9	59	
30	BACKING	3RD PIPE	8" "	1000	DS 6	E 8	20	
31	"	"	"	"	DS 7	E 7	41	

An instrument schedule.

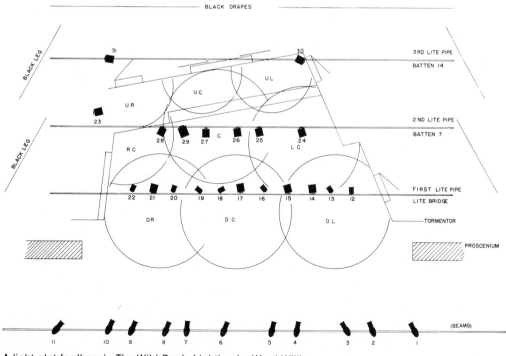

A light plot for Ibsen's *The Wild Duck.* Lighting by Ward Williamson.

LIGHT PLOT
WILD DUCK ACT II

indicated on the lighting plan. The solutions will be determined in part by the physical limitations of the theatre building, the arrangement of the settings (ceilings and walls, for example, rule out certain mounting positions), the color scheme of the settings, costumes, and make-up, and demands of the action.

It should be pointed out that many of the suggestions made here would need to be modified for an open stage or a theatre-in-the-round. In the arena, for example, no background lighting is possible or necessary. On the other hand, the acting areas must be lighted from every side. The demands made on specific illumination increase, therefore, while those on general illumination decrease. Furthermore, all of the instruments must be mounted in the auditorium. For the open stage, a scheme between that for arena and proscenium theatres is required. A larger proportion of effort will go to specific illumination than in the proscenium theatre, but some background lighting is still necessary. Nevertheless, the basic principles of light design remain unchanged.

After the lighting plots are completed, an instrument schedule is made. This is a table which lists separately each lighting instrument. It indicates specifications (wattage, lens, reflector, lamp, and any other pertinent information), the mounting position, the color filter, area to be lighted, the circuit into which it is plugged, and the dimmer to which it is connected. It provides a summary in tabular form of all the technical information needed for acquiring and setting up the lighting instruments for a production. It comprises a convenient checklist for much of the equipment.

LIGHTING INSTRUMENTS, ACCESSORIES, AND CONTROLBOARDS

To carry out his plans, the lighting designer must have at his disposal instruments, accessories, and a controlboard.

In the nonprofessional theatre, it is typical for an organization to own a supply of lighting equipment sufficient to meet the demands of its pro-

508

ductions. Also as a rule, such groups use buildings which have permanently installed electrical circuits and a controlboard. These facilities may be primitive or lavish, but the groups operate within the limitations of their resources, except in rare instances when they rent special items from a lighting supply house or borrow them from other organizations.

The same conditions apply in most cases to permanent professional groups outside of New York. Commercial theatre buildings in New York, as well as the majority of those used by touring companies elsewhere, do not have controlboards or even permanently installed electrical circuits into which lighting instruments may be plugged. Since he cannot depend upon any facilities beyond an adequate supply of electricity, the designer must list (with exact specifications) every item necessary for lighting a show. This material may be rented or bought. Because most productions tour (if only for out-of-town tryouts), the lighting equipment must be easily transportable and capable of quick installation. These requirements keep Broadway productions from using complex equipment, especially some of the more recent controlboards.

Regardless of the type of organization for which he works, the designer should be thoroughly familiar with the available lighting supplies. He should know as much as he can about the potentialities and limitations of each item so that he may plan wisely and efficiently.

LIGHTING INSTRUMENTS. Lighting instruments may be divided into a number of categories: *spotlights, striplights, floodlights,* and *special lighting equipment.* The basic characteristics of each will be discussed briefly.

Spotlights are designed to illuminate restricted portions of the stage with a concentrated beam of light. Any good spotlight has a sturdy metal housing, a lamp socket, a reflector, a lens, a color-frame guide, mounting attachments, and some device for adjusting the focus. Each of these parts may vary considerably in design from one instrument to another.

Spotlights are available in a wide range of sizes, and are normally classified according to wattage, lenses, and reflectors. They range from 100 to 10,000 watts in size. The average wattage is about 1000, although larger sizes are common.

A lens gathers the light coming from a lamp and bends it into parallel rays to create a concentrated beam. Therefore, a lens is essential if the spotlight is to fulfill its purpose. Three types of lenses, the plano-convex, the Fresnel, and the step, are used in spotlights. A plano-convex, or condensing, lens is flat on one side and convex on the other. It gives a sharp, distinct beam of light. In a Fresnel lens, one surface is plane while the other is composed of concentric rings of differing diameters. The resulting lens is ridged on its convex side, and is much thinner than a plano-convex lens. It diffuses the beam of light and prevents the sharp edges which are typical of the plano-convex lens. In the step lens, the plane surface has been treated in much the same manner as the convex surface of the Fresnel lens and produces similar optical results. Each spot-

FRESNEL SPOTLIGHT

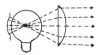

PLANO-CONVEX SPOTLIGHT

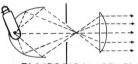

ELLIPSOIDAL SPOTLIGHT

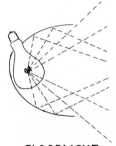

FLOODLIGHT

Diagrams showing the relationship among lenses, lamps, and reflectors in three types of spotlights and a floodlight.

A fresnel spotlight. Courtesy Kliegl Brothers.

light is designed to take advantage of the peculiar qualities of one type of lens and will not operate efficiently with any other kind.

Lenses are also described in terms of diameter and focal length. They are available in diameters from three to twenty inches, although the most common sizes are six, eight, ten, and twelve inches. The focal length of a lens (also stated in inches) indicates the distance which the filament of the lamp should be from the axis of the lens. Each spotlight is designed to use a lens of a specified diameter and focal length and it will function efficiently only with the appropriate lens.

A reflector is placed behind or around the lamp to throw light forward which would otherwise be wasted. It serves, therefore, to increase the efficiency of an instrument. (Efficiency is the ratio between the amount of light emitted by the source and that which reaches the stage.) Reflectors are made of metal and are available in a number of shapes, although those used in spotlights are either spherical or ellipsoidal. The spherical reflector is placed behind the lamp, while the ellipsoidal reflector partially surrounds the lamp. Because of its shape and placement, the ellipsoidal reflector is far more efficient than the spherical.

Spotlights are usually divided into three types: *Fresnel, plano-convex,* and *ellipsoidal.* The differences between the Fresnel and plano-convex spotlights result principally from their lenses, since otherwise their basic parts, including a spherical reflector, are similar. The ellipsoidal spotlight may be equipped with either one or two lenses of any type. Its distinctive qualities, however, are determined by its reflector.

The ellipsoidal spotlight is by far the most efficient type. It is also the most expensive and largest. It is used primarily where the distance between the instrument and the stage is great and where mounting space is not at a premium. Its primary application has been in lighting acting areas from the auditorium.

An ellipsoidal spotlight. Courtesy Kliegl Brothers.

Fresnel and plano-convex spotlights are most frequently mounted behind the proscenium for lighting the upstage acting areas, since the distance is short and hanging space is often minimal. Since it is more compact and efficient, the Fresnel spotlight is far more common now than the plano-convex.

All spotlights have a number of other features. Guides forward of the lens are used to hold color frames so that the color of the light may be controlled. All spotlights are equipped with a means of mounting which allows the instrument to be rotated from side to side and up and down. It can be pointed in any direction, therefore, and when the desired position is found, can be secured tightly. In every spotlight, the lamp, the lens, or the reflector (and sometimes more than one of these) is movable so that the focus may be adjusted.

Each of the spotlights in the wide variety now available has been designed with a specific kind of situation in mind. If the lighting designer understands the capabilities of each, he may select those best suited to his demands.

A *striplight* is composed of a series of lamps set into a narrow, roughly rectangular trough. It is used as a source of general illumination.

510

A six-foot reflector-lamp bor-
derlight. Courtesy Century
Lighting, Inc.

As a rule, each strip is wired with three or four separate circuits. Each third or fourth lamp, then, is on the same circuit and may be controlled together. All of the lamps on the same circuit are covered with filters of the same color. Thus, each strip can produce three or four different colors when each circuit is used alone or all may be combined in various intensities to produce a wide range of additional colors. Frequently, one circuit is left free of color and can be used to alter (by the addition of white light) the colors produced by the other circuits. In this way, strip-lights may be used to "tone" the settings, costumes, and make-up.

Striplights vary considerably in length. Some are very short, having only three or four lamps, while others extend the entire width of the stage. Short units are more flexible, since a number may be placed end to end to make a long section if needed and may be used individually where short units are sufficient.

Striplights also vary considerably in wattage, using individual lamps ranging from 75 to 500 watts. The size of the lamp depends upon the purpose for which the strip is being used. Most modern striplights (unlike their earlier counterparts) use a reflector, which combines a sphere and a parabola, behind and partially surrounding each lamp. The reflectors create compartments which separate each lamp from all the others in the strip. In some cases, striplights are designed to use reflector lamps (that is, the reflecting surface is a part of the bulb which surrounds the filament).

Striplights may be subdivided into three categories: *footlights, border-lights,* and *miscellaneous striplights.* Footlights are normally recessed in a slot at the front of the stage. Originally they were used to light the actors' faces from below to counteract the unnatural shadows caused by instruments placed at too sharp an angle overhead. After the development of better lighting instruments and techniques, however, footlights fell into disfavor and are now seldom employed. They may still be useful, however, for eliminating shadows cast by large hats, for blending the specific and general illumination, and for enhancing color.

Borderlights are hung from battens above the stage. They may be short or may extend the full width of settings, and may be hung in several rows from front to back. They are used more often than any other instrument for blending the acting areas and for "toning" the settings and costumes.

Miscellaneous striplights may be placed on the floor to light ground rows and drops, and around the base of the cyclorama (these are usually called "cyc foots") to create various sky effects. Small strips may be used to light backings for doors and windows and other small scenic units. Like spotlights, striplights are designed with specific uses in mind and should be selected accordingly.

511

A sixteen-inch, 750-1000-watt diffuse alzac floodlight. Courtesy Century Lighting, Inc.

The *floodlight* is also designed to give general illumination. It uses a single lamp as the light source. It has a housing with a large opening to allow light to spread over a wide area; there is no lens. Most floodlights have either ellipsoidal (the most typical) or parabolic reflectors. The wattage varies from 250 to 5000. Each floodlight is equipped to accommodate a color filter.

Floodlights may be used singly or in combination. They may be suspended above the stage to substitute for borderlights. Like striplights, they may be placed on the floor to light drops and ground rows, and they may be used to light backings and other background scenic units. Perhaps the most frequent and important use of the floodlight, however, is for lighting the cyclorama. A series may be used to achieve a smooth, even illumination over the entire visible surface; with the aid of filters, any color may be produced.

It is impossible to specify all special effects which may be needed in the theatre. Instruments have been developed, however, to meet the most frequent demands.

Projectors of various kinds are employed for many special effects. Slide projectors are often used to project rainbows, stars, clouds, still pictures or captions. With the right equipment, the entire scenic background may be projected on screens or the cyclorama. Other projectors use moving, circular disks on which images (such as clouds, waves, rain, smoke, or fire) have been painted. A motor revolves the disk at a constant speed past the projector lens to create the effect of movement.

Lightning can be produced by bringing a carbon stick, to which one electrical terminal has been attached, into close proximity with a piece of metal, to which the other terminal has been attached. As the current leaps between these two points, a bright flash of light, like that seen in welding, results.

For fireplace or campfire effects, prop logs may be constructed and painted appropriately. A lamp is then placed inside the logs and the lamp is allowed to shine through holes which have been covered with transparent red, orange, and amber material. Flames may be simulated by irregular strips of colored silk or plastic which are kept in motion by a fan or by a revolving multicolored disc moving in front of a light.

These common special effects may be supplemented by anyone with a knowledge of electricity and stage lighting instruments. Additional equipment is also available from any lighting supply house.

ACCESSORIES. In addition to instruments, a number of accessories — such as lamps, electrical cable and connectors, color frames and color media — are needed. Each instrument is designed to use a particular lamp. Similarly, each lamp is designed for specific purposes. Lamps vary in many ways, notably according to type of base, filament, wattage, shape, treatment of the glass, and position in which it should be used (such as base up or base down). The catalogues of manufacturers give complete details about lamps designed for stage use.

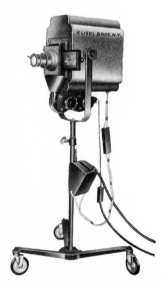

A scenic projector. Courtesy Kliegl Brothers

512

Electrical cable for the stage should be heavily insulated since it must withstand much wear (scenery may be moved over it and it is often stepped on). It is available in a number of sizes, each designed to carry a maximum electrical load. Cable should be bought with its use in mind, therefore, and the designer should make sure that no cable is overloaded, if hazards to equipment and danger of fire are to be avoided.

There are two principal types of stage connectors or plugs; the twist lock, and the pin connector. Both are of heavy-duty construction and designed for stage uses. Every theatre needs an adequate supply of electrical cable and connectors.

Almost every lighting instrument is equipped with some means for using color filters and, consequently, a supply of color frames and color media is required. A color frame is usually made of metal and has an opening of the same size and shape as that of the instrument with which it is to be used. The color medium is placed in the frame and then inserted into the color frame guides of the instrument. A rigid color medium, such as a glass roundel, does not require a color frame and is inserted directly into the guides on those instruments designed to use a glass medium.

A number of color media are used in stage lighting. The most common is gelatin, a transparent plasticlike material which is available in a wide range of hues, saturations, and intensities. Almost any color can be achieved with it, and it may be cut to any desired shape. It is fragile, however, and fades with use. Other plastic color media (such as cinemoid and cinabex) are also frequently used. They are similar to gelatin in all important respects, are thicker, more durable, and more expensive. Glass is commonly used with striplights, although plastic media may be employed. Glass is the most durable color medium, but it is available in only a limited range of colors. Each color medium has qualities, advantages, and disadvantages which should be thoroughly understood by the designer so that he may select materials wisely. Color media and color frames may be bought directly from the manufacturer or from a lighting supply house.

A number of additional accessories are available, as a glance at the catalogues from lighting equipment manufacturers will quickly reveal. Those discussed here, however, are the most common and the most essential.

Connecting Panels and Controlboards. No lighting system is complete without some means for controlling light. The type, size, and placement of instruments and the choice of color filters provide the possibilities for controlling intensity, distribution, and color, but before these opportunities can be exploited, a controlboard is needed. A board permits some instruments to be used at maximum brightness, while others are off or partially dimmed. Similarly, it allows control of color by mixing light from a number of instruments in varying proportions. In such ways, great flexibility can be gained.

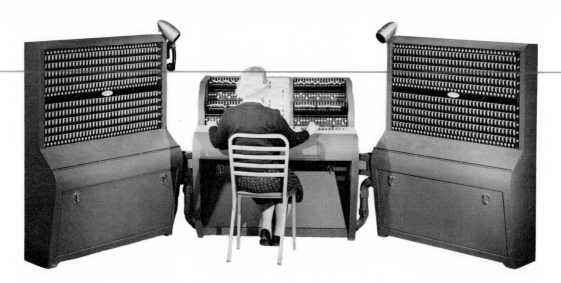

Console and preset panels for a remote control electronic dimming system. Courtesy Century Lighting, Inc.

If a controlboard is to be efficient, however, there must be some means of connecting each instrument to it. For this purpose a connecting panel is required. To this panel run all of the stage circuits, as well as all the controlboard dimmers. Consequently, any circuit may be connected to any dimmer. Complete control can be achieved if there is a sufficient number of circuits and dimmers. Since the number of both is restricted in most theatres, however, careful planning is required to arrive at an arrangement suitably flexible.

Technically, a controlboard can be merely a panel of switches for turning lights on and off. If the lights are to be controlled with any subtlety, however, dimmers are required. Each dimmer is designed to accommodate a maximum electrical load and should never be used beyond its capacity. Since the load to be placed on individual dimmers varies considerably, controlboards normally include dimmers of varying capacities.

Dimmers are of many types. The most important are the *resistance*, *autotransformer*, and *electronic*. Each works on a different principle, but each allows a gradual increase or decrease in the electrical power reaching the lamps. This results in the dimming or brightening of the lights.

Dimmers vary considerably in efficiency, compactness, and price. The electronic dimmer, for example, will dim out completely a load of any size, while the resistance dimmer must be loaded to its approximate capacity before it is entirely satisfactory. On the other hand, the electronic dimmer is very expensive, while the resistance dimmer is relatively inexpensive.

Although a large number of individual dimmers is desirable for efficient control, problems arise as the number of units increases. If each dimmer must be adjusted manually and individually, several operators will be required for a large controlboard. To overcome this difficulty, all types of dimmers are now available with master controls which allow some or all of the dimmers to be connected in such a way that a single handle can operate all. Any good board allows the dimmers to be connected in almost any combination.

514

Another problem is created by the size of a bank of dimmers. Electronic units, for example, are so bulky that it is seldom feasible to house them in the immediate stage area. They are installed in another part of the building, therefore, and a small, compact, remote-controlboard is located near the stage. This places the bulky equipment out of the way. Resistance and autotransformer dimmers must be installed in the stage area, since neither type can be operated by remote control efficiently enough for stage purposes.

The placement of the controlboard is of considerable importance. The most common locations are: at one side of the stage near the proscenium, in the orchestra pit, at the back of the auditorium, and in a booth built into the face of the balcony. The ideal arrangement is one which permits the operator to see the stage from much the same vantage as the audience. This allows him to check the lighting and to perceive immediately when something is wrong. Therefore, whenever possible the controlboard should be located somewhere in the auditorium.

With some controlboards dimmers may be preset. This means that the lighting for individual scenes, or for an entire show, may be set up in advance. Then, with a master dimming device, lights for one scene may be faded out and another brought up simultaneously, or changes within a scene may be set on the board in advance. The ability to preset controls does away with the necessity for haste in making complex changes and eliminates many mistakes.

Probably no aspect of theatrical production has undergone so many changes in recent years as lighting control. It is advisable, therefore, to make frequent inquiries about new developments.

This brief survey of lighting equipment, accessories, and controlboards does not describe all of the available equipment. It covers the most common devices and their typical uses. The lighting designer should have detailed knowledge of both the range of equipment and its possible applications so that he may select wisely and work efficiently.

REHEARSALS AND PERFORMANCES

During the period when the actors are rehearsing and the scenery and costumes are being constructed, the lighting designer must assemble his materials. If the theatre is available, many of the basic processes may be carried out at a leisurely pace. Typically, however, the theatre is not available until a few days before performances.

Regardless of time, the procedures are reasonably standard. Using the light plot and the instrument schedule as a guide, each instrument is mounted and directed toward the stage area specified by the light plot. The correct color filter is added, the instrument is plugged into the proper circuit, and connected to the designated dimmer. The instruments may be focused tentatively at this time. The work cannot be completed, however, until the scenery is in place.

The final setting and focusing of instruments is a time-consuming and sometimes disheartening task, for it is difficult to confine light exactly as envisioned. Unwanted lines, shadows, and bright areas may appear, and

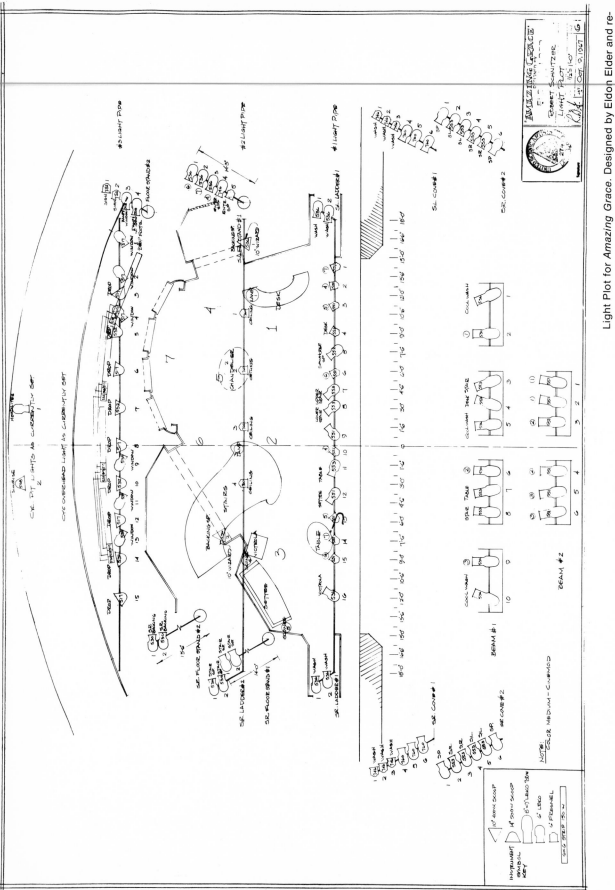

Light Plot for *Amazing Grace*. Designed by Eldon Elder and reproduced with his permission. See page 450 for design sketch.

LIGHTING DATA FOR "AMAZING GRACE"

Light Data Sheet for Amazing Grace.

an even spread of light over the acting areas may be difficult to achieve. Furthermore, when the same instruments must be used to light more than one setting, an ideal adjustment for one scene may not be right for another.

In the professional theatre, the lighting designer often sits in the auditorium (where he may see the stage from the spectator's point of view) and calls out directions over a loud speaker to the lighting crew. Sometimes as many as twenty-four continuous hours may be spent in the adjustment of the lighting. In the nonprofessional theatre, this process is seldom compressed into a continuous session of such length, but it is rarely simple.

The goal is the precise adjustment of each instrument to achieve the desired lighting effects. Accurate cue sheets must also be made. A cue sheet indicates the setting of lights at the beginning of each scene (this is done by listing the dimmers to be used, and the intensity setting of each), any changes to be made during the scene, and the cues for the changes.

If there is a technical rehearsal, the lighting may be integrated with the other elements at that time. Changes in the lights may be required because of unforeseen problems with the scenery or costumes, or because more time is required for some effects than had been envisioned. Further adjustments may be needed after dress rehearsals. Previously unnoticed shadows may be discovered or the actors may move into areas not indicated in the plans. Changes should be made as quickly as possible and recorded on the cue sheets. Changes are seldom made after opening night.

After the play is officially opened, the designer's responsibilities are over in most cases, and responsibility passes to the lighting crew.

EMPLOYMENT

Stage lighting is still viewed by some as an adjunct to scenic design. The professional lighting designer must be a member of the United Scenic Artists Union, although his entrance examination is largely restricted to skills needed in lighting. His initiation fee is $200. The demand for lighting specialists is comparatively recent. For some professional productions the scenic designer still designs the lighting, but practice is changing and the lighting designer has emerged as an artist in his own right.

In the professional theatre, the lighting designer is employed by the producer under a contract which must meet the minimum specifications of the United Scenic Artists Union. His responsibilites and his billing are specified in his contract. His fee is determined by the number of settings to be lighted and the relative difficulty of the task. He must be available for conferences throughout the rehearsal period, and his presence is mandatory for setting up and adjusting the lighting instruments. During the dress-rehearsal period, he must see that necessary changes are made and that the lighting functions as planned. His job is considered over when the play opens in New York.

Off-Broadway and resident companies do not always hire lighting designers, for lighting is usually part of the scenic designer's job. In the community theatre, the designer-technician lights productions as a regular part of his duties. Where there is no designer, the director of the theatre must assume responsibility for lighting, although the actual work may be done by volunteer helpers.

In many small educational theatres, conditions similar to those in the community theatre prevail. In organizations with a larger and more specialized staff, the technical director frequently serves as lighting designer. In larger schools, one or more staff members may devote full time to stage lighting.

THE LIGHTING DESIGNER'S ASSISTANTS

Like other theatre artists, the lighting designer depends upon a number of other persons to aid him. His principal helpers are: an assistant designer, a master electrician (or head of the lighting crew), and members of the lighting crew (including the controlboard operator).

The designer does not always have an assistant. If he does, the assistant may be assigned almost any task which the designer himself would otherwise perform. He may make the drawings for the light plots, compile the instrument schedule, find the necessary equipment, act as liaison between the lighting designer and the rest of the production staff, aid in setting up the lights and in compiling the cue sheets. In the Broadway theatre, the assistant designer must be a member of the union, but in other organizations he may be either a paid or a volunteer worker.

The master electrician (or lighting-crew head) is in charge of the lighting crew. He works closely with the designer when the lighting equipment is being installed and the instruments adjusted. After the show opens, he must see that all equipment is properly maintained, and that the lighting operates as planned during performances. He is directly responsible to the stage manager.

Outside the professional theatre, the title of "master electrician" is seldom employed. A more common term is "head of the lighting crew." This may be a paid position or it may be filled by an assigned or volunteer worker. At times, the lighting designer himself serves in this capacity. In any case, the head of the lighting crew should have sufficient knowledge and experience to supervise the work of others and to carry out plans efficiently.

Members of the lighting crew install, operate, and maintain all lighting equipment and shift any electrical equipment which must be moved during scene changes. The controlboard operator is of special importance, since he is responsible for the actual manipulation of lighting during performances. Not only must he be able to follow the cue sheets accurately, but he must be capable of meeting emergencies and adjusting to the inevitable differences between one performance and another. In the professional theatre, the crew must be composed of union members. In the nonprofessional theatre, crews are most frequently recruited or assigned.

SOUND

The place of sound in the theatre is perhaps even more ambiguous than that of make-up, for, although it is an important part of production, its planning is often haphazard and may be done by several persons. In the professional theatre, sound produced by electricity is considered part of stage lighting, while that produced mechanically is classified with properties. This division is determined by union jurisdiction rather than by the needs of the theatre, but even outside the professional theatre the responsibility for sound is often assigned at random.

Like other theatrical elements, sound makes its greatest contributions when it is designed as a unit and carefully integrated with the production as a whole. Ideally, there probably should be a separate sound crew, and the planning of sound should not be considered a mere adjunct of some other part of production. At present, however, the lighting designer, of all the usual theatrical personnel, is best qualified to cope with sound, which relies increasingly upon electrical and electronic devices. For this reason, sound is treated here in connection with lighting, although their conjunction is one of convenience more than likeness.

The total sound of a production may be divided into three main categories: the actors' voices, music and abstract sounds, and realistic noises. The first category, normally excluded in treatments of sound, has already been dealt with in chapters on acting and directing.

Music, if recorded, is relegated to the sound crew, but if played live, to the musicians. Since live music is treated in the next chapter, it will be excluded here. Abstract sound is nonmusical and nonverbal noise without recognizable origin. Realistic sound effects are those which are readily associated with a natural or man-made phenomenon, such as thunder or an airplane.

Three traditional devices for simulating thunder. *Left,* a thunder-clap device; a sharp crack is produced by pulling the Venetian-blindlike slats together. *Center,* a "rumble cart"; filled with rubble, such as broken bricks, the cart creates a low rumbling sound as the uneven wheels move across the floor. *Right,* a thunder sheet; the sound of thunder is created by shaking the thin sheet of metal. From Moynet's *La Machinerie Théâtrale,* 1893.

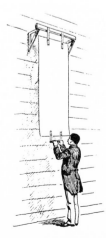

Regardless of its type, sound fulfills two basic functions: it helps to establish mood and style, and it serves as exposition. Music and abstract sound serve the first function by establishing the proper atmosphere for action and by underlining the inherent qualities of scenes. For example, strange, hollow noises may be used in a nonrealistic play to parallel the subject matter. Realistic sounds, however, may also be used for their mood value. Thunder and rain can set the background for a murder mystery, while bird songs may establish a quiet, pastoral scene. Furthermore, realistic sounds may be performed in a variety of ways to set the appropriate mood and style. For example, a prolonged and distant train whistle can produce a mournful atmosphere, while a staccato and brisk train whistle may produce a cheerful effect. In such ways, clearly identifiable sound can be altered to produce a variety of qualities.

Expository sound is most frequently realistic. Gun shots, automobile horns, crashing dishes, doorbells, and similar sounds may provide preparation for onstage action or suggest offstage happenings. Sound may identify time and place. Different noises may be associated with different times of the year and day; sound may place the action in the city or the country, near a river or streetcar tracks.

Sound for the theatre has a number of controllable properties: *pitch, quality, volume, direction,* and *duration.* Since all of these, with the exception of direction, have already been discussed as they relate to speech, they will be reviewed only briefly here.

The same basic sound may be repeated at a number of different pitches, each of which will affect an audience in a different way. Doorbells, whistles, and gunshots may be quite varied in their pitches and it is possible to select the one which seems best for the particular production.

Sounds differ in quality. Thunder is recognized in part by its rumbling, echoing quality, while an alarm clock may be distinguished by shrillness and a gunshot by sharp explosiveness. Since quality is the least understood of all the properties of sound, it is the most difficult to control. Nevertheless, it can be manipulated to achieve such characteristics as harshness, pleasantness, softness, and shrillness.

Volume is the relative loudness of sound. Any noise may be produced at any volume, although each sound may have its own characteristic loudness (thunder is normally louder than the sound of a ball being bounced). Distance, however, is also important in our perception of sound. Thunder may be so distant that it is barely audible, while a ball bounced on the side of a house may seem very loud. Stage sound must be controlled, therefore, so that the typical qualities of a sound are maintained but distance indicated. It is sometimes difficult to achieve the proper effect of distance with live sound. For example, it is often hard to find the right offstage spot from which to fire a blank cartridge to simulate a distant gunshot. On the other hand, improvements in electronic equipment have made it increasingly easy to control volume and apparent distance with recorded sound.

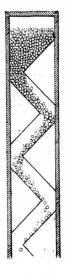

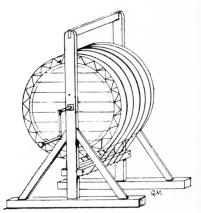

Wind and rain machines. *Top,* rain sounds are created by allowing shot or dried peas to run down a zigzag metal chute. *Bottom,* a device for creating the sound of wind; when the crank is turned, friction between the drum and the material simulates the sound of wind. From Moynet's *La Machinerie Théâtrale,* 1893.

The volume of sound must be maintained at a level consonant with stage speech and action. It should not be allowed to override the actors' voices (unless this is intended), or to become distracting.

Sound also has direction, and illusion may be shattered if sound comes from the wrong side of the stage. For example, a telephone bell may ring offstage left even though the phone is onstage right. Such a situation is sometimes created by the need to have all sound equipment in the same place.

A completely effective system permits sound from any direction: from any point in the setting, from either side, behind or above the setting from either side, the rear, or overhead in the auditorium. This requires a series of carefully placed amplifiers. With such an arrangement, a sound (such as that of a car) can begin on one side, seem to approach, pass behind the set, and out of hearing on the other side.

Sound has duration, for any noise can be prolonged or shortened. Furthermore, a sequence of sounds requires timing. For example, if thunder is to be used, a decision must be made about when it should begin, how long it should continue, when it should reach its peak, and when it should die away.

All of the controllable properties of sound—pitch, quality, volume, direction, and duration—may be varied in relation to each other and to meet the demands of a script. Careful attention to each can lead to a successful sound score for a production.

Sound may be classified as live or recorded. Since live sound is created anew at each performance, it may vary considerably from one night to the next. Its major advantage is its adaptability to the variations of individual performances. In recorded sound, effects are created and then placed on records or tape. Barring human or mechanical errors, recorded sound is the same at each performance. On the other hand, it is not adaptable to the inevitable deviations in performances or to emergencies.

Since there is scarcely a sound that cannot be produced live or by recording, a choice of method must be made. Several considerations influence choice. Among these are difficulty and efficiency. Such noises as doorbells and telephones can be produced so easily with electrical buzzers that a recording would be inefficient in most cases. On the other hand, when control of distance and volume is important (as with train noises), a recording may be preferable.

The choice may also depend upon the availability and suitability of recorded sounds. A wide variety of effects can be obtained on commercial recordings, but these are not always adapted to the specific needs of a play. Those organizations that own recording equipment can make their own effects. While almost any effect can be created live, a great deal of experimentation may be required to produce some (such as bird calls and automobile engines) and it is normally easier to use recordings.

Available equipment may also be a factor in the decision. Scratchy records and low-fidelity speakers may distort sound or call attention to the fact that it is recorded. On the other hand, tape and high-fidelity speakers are usually satisfactory.

Normally the only plan for sound is the cue sheet. It indicates each sound, when it is to begin, how it is to build, and when it is to end. It may also specify the method by which the sound is to be produced and, where electronic equipment is involved, sound levels. If elaborate and extensive sound equipment is available, it may be necessary to make a chart similar to an instrument schedule for stage lighting. It should list each piece of equipment (with adequate specifications), and should indicate for each its placement, use, and control.

As with other elements, sound must be rehearsed and integrated carefully with the production as a whole. It must be adjusted in relation to the stage and auditorium, the actors' voices, and the requirements of the script. When properly designed and executed, sound contributes much to effective theatrical production.

Elegy for Young Lovers by Hans Werner Henze at the Indiana University Opera Theatre. This multimedia production utilized film sequences and still projections. Directed by Ross Allen; designed by Andreas Nomikos. Courtesy Indiana University School of Music.

MULTIMEDIA PRODUCTIONS

In recent years, multimedia productions have attracted much attention. Combining live action with projected or motion pictures and stereophonic sound, they attempt to fuse elements drawn from the theatre, motion pictures, and music. In a multimedia production, still or motion pictures may be projected on several screens; all projections may be fragments of the same picture or each may represent a different place or object; all are chosen because of their appropriateness to the mood or dramatic action being performed by the live actors. Directional sound is used to make the audience feel at the center of events. Although multimedia productions draw materials from many sources, the techniques most nearly resemble those used in stage lighting and sound. Still in the experimental phase, multimedia productions offer considerable promise for the future.

Chapter 22 MUSIC AND DANCE

Although music and dance are independent arts, they are employed sufficiently often in present-day theatrical productions to justify treatment as dramatic elements. The following discussion, therefore, will concentrate on their stage uses, especially in musical comedy which relies so heavily upon them.

TYPES OF MUSIC IN THE
THEATRE

Music for the theatre may be divided into two major categories: *incidental* and *dramatic*. *Incidental* music accompanies a play but is not an integral part of it. It is used most frequently to set a mood, to underscore or heighten emotions, and to bridge scenes. Almost every motion picture uses incidental music extensively, just as did melodramas in the nineteenth century. In the theatre today, incidental music is normally restricted to an overture and to music between acts; its purpose is the establishment of an atmosphere proper to the play. Occasionally, such music is introduced during a scene. For example, Tennessee Williams' plays often demand background music, and Miller's *Death of a Salesman* makes effective use of musical motifs.

In addition to instrumental music, songs may also be added to scripts. Shakespeare's plays include many songs which underline the emotion of the moment or give added pleasure without forwarding the action. Most popular dramas of the nineteenth century contained several songs, the number of which might be increased or reduced as desired. Songs of this type are still occasionally employed in plays. Other incidental music may accompany dances.

Incidental music for professional productions may or may not be composed especially for the occasion, but it must be played by professional musicians, since union regulations seldom permit the use of recorded music. In the nonprofessional theatre, however, an orchestra is employed only rarely for nonmusical plays, and recorded music is customary.

Unlike incidental music, *dramatic* music is an integral part of a play. It is used most extensively in opera and musical comedy. For them, the music is written to meet the specific needs of the action, and the over-all effect is dependent upon it. The music for such works is almost always performed live. The dramatic functions of music have already been discussed in connection with *My Fair Lady.* (See Chapter 15.)

THE COMPOSER

The composer of musical comedy usually works closely with a lyricist, who writes the words of the songs. The lyricist sometimes writes the book (that is, the dramatic script) as well, though still another person may do this. Both the composer and the lyricist should keep in mind the demands of the book.

An agreement among composer, lyricist, and dramatist is normally reached as to where songs and musical interludes are needed and about the basic qualities of each scene. Either the music or the lyrics may be composed first, but they must eventually be coordinated with each other and the dramatic situation.

Man of La Mancha, a musical version of the story of Don Quixote. Music, Mitch Leigh; lyrics, Joe Darion; book, Dale Wasserman. Joey Faye, Bob Wright, and Marcia Gilford at the Martin Beck Theatre, New York, 1968. Photograph: Friedman-Abeles.

The composer of musical comedy creates the melodies (with their rhythms and tempos), but the complete musical score may require the collaboration of a dance composer, who works directly with the choreographer, an arranger and orchestrator.

The music for choreography in musical comedies is now frequently composed around the dances, rather than dances being fitted to existing music. Choreography evolves in a dance studio. Since the composer of the main score does not normally have time to work with the choreographer, someone else often does this; several persons now specialize in this field.

As the choreographer establishes time and movement patterns, the dance composer sets down rhythms and tempos. Themes and melodies from the main score may then be added or the composer may invent a melody suitable to the dance.

The work of both the main composer and the dance composer is normally given to an arranger and orchestrator, who completes the score by adding harmony, developing variations, and assigning parts to instruments. Although he must give his approval to the finished work, the composer of a musical comedy may have neither the time nor the ability to orchestrate a score.

An example should clarify the arranger's job. The composer may write a melody to serve as the basis for a ten-minute production number. Were this melody played over and over again, extreme monotony would result. The arranger achieves variety, development, and feeling through instrumentation and through modulations of key, rhythm, tempo, and volume. Much of the final texture and quality of the music, therefore, is attributable to the arranger and orchestrator.

The overture to a musical comedy is usually put together by the arranger from the melodic themes of the main score. Therefore, it is frequently the last part to be written, since the rest of the music must be set before the overture can be finished. It may also have to be tailored to fill a specified amount of time.

As a rule, more music is written than is actually used. A production may need to be shortened, a song may be discarded and another substituted, or music may be added where none was originally envisioned. Like other workers in the theatre, both the composer and the arranger must be available for making changes and alterations up to the opening night. Ordinarily, the composer is consulted about the casting of the singing roles, and he must be available to work with the singing chorus and actors during rehearsals (although he is not in charge of these rehearsals).

THE CONDUCTOR

The conductor is responsible for the actual performance of the musical score. To assure its adequate representation he must assume a number of responsibilities prior to the opening.

First, he usually makes the final selection of the singing chorus. Although preliminary tryouts may have eliminated many persons before he is brought in and although his selections must be approved by the director and producer, the conductor or musical director is asked to hear

Colasse's opera, *The Marriage of Peleus and Thetis* as staged in Paris, 1689. From *L'Ancienne France: Le Thèàtre . . . . et Musique,* 1887.

and approve each chorus member before he is employed. The conductor must also assemble an orchestra for the production; an orchestra manager usually handles contractual details, insures that the music is copied, and that parts are available to all musicians.

The conductor is in charge of all musical rehearsals and must familiarize performers – stars, chorus, and instrumentalists – with the music. These rehearsals are usually separate from acting rehearsals until late in the schedule.

A number of difficulties may arise when music and drama are brought together, for the transitions from dialogue to song and dance may be rough. Other difficulties arise when the entire orchestra is substituted for the single piano, which is usually the only accompaniment available during rehearsals. The singers may have trouble hearing the melodies at this time. It is wise, therefore, to devote as many rehearsals as possible to integrating music and dialogue. The conductor must work closely with the composer and the orchestrator, for they must agree upon tempos and interpretations.

A design of 1719 by Giuseppe Galli da Bibiena (1696-1757) for an opera. Courtesy the Metropolitan Museum of Art, Dick Fund, 1931.

Verdi's *Falstaff* at the Metropolitan Opera, New York, 1964. Production designed and directed by Franco Zeffirelli. Photograph by Louis Melancon. Courtesy Metropolitan Opera.

The conductor, unlike other supervisory personnel in the theatre, is visible during performances, since he must conduct the musical portions. He gives cues to the singers and instrumentalists, establishes the tempos, and keeps the musical interpretations as close as possible to those agreed upon during rehearsals.

In carrying out his duties, the conductor generally has an assistant to aid him. This assistant is usually a member of the orchestra and may be the pianist at rehearsals (although a special rehearsal pianist is often hired). He may be asked to assume any of the conductor's responsibilities.

The conductor is employed by the producer, although he must be acceptable to the composer and the director. He must be a member of the American Federation of Musicians.

Outside the professional theatre, the conductor's job may be divided into two—that of musical director and that of conductor. The musical director may help in casting the show and may supervise musical rehearsals, while the conductor takes over beginning with dress rehearsals.

THE ORCHESTRA MEMBERS

In the professional theatre, orchestra members are secured through a musical contractor, or orchestra manager, who receives suggestions from the conductor. All must be members of the American Federation of Musicians.

Since members of an orchestra are assumed to be accomplished sightreaders, rehearsals may not be held until shortly before the dress rehearsal. When a company travels, only key musicians go along; the rest are hired locally. This means that the conductor works with a new orchestra at each stop.

In the nonprofessional theatre, more orchestra rehearsal time may be possible, for musicians are often not members of a union. Nevertheless, the orchestra is perhaps the least-rehearsed part of any musical production.

A rehearsal of *Tosca* at the Metropolitan Opera, Lincoln Center, 1968. Gabriel Bacquier (Scarpia), Franco Corelli (Cavaradossi), Birgit Nilssen (Tosca). Courtesy The Metropolitan Opera. Photograph—P. A. Noa.

THE SINGERS

The principal (the nonchorus) roles in a musical may be cast in a number of ways. At times the musical requirements are such that only a person with a well-trained voice can be used; at others, the singing demands are slight. Sometimes a musical is written for a star and the music tailored to fit his capabilities. The producer, the composer, and the director, however, assess the various requisites and agree upon the casting of the singers. Outside the professional theatre, or where the composer is not involved in the production, the director and the musical director choose the singers.

THE CHORUS

The members of the chorus are divided into singer-dancers and dancer-singers, all-singing choruses and all-dancing choruses. Those in the first category are employed because of their singing ability (with lesser skill in dancing), while the second group is hired primarily for their dancing abilities. Here, only the singer-dancer will be considered.

In the professional theatre the chorus is employed under Actors' Equity contracts similar to those used for dramatic actors. The standard contract may be altered when bit parts are cast, for chorus members (both singers and dancers) are often assigned small singing or speaking roles after a few rehearsals. Chorus members may also be asked to serve as understudies. These additional responsibilities must be reflected in higher salaries.

Chorus members work with the conductor on the musical portions and with the stage director on the dramatic portions. Dancers work with the choreographer. Eventually all parts are combined. Since so much of the quality of a musical depends upon the chorus, it should be selected and rehearsed with care.

A ballet in a London theatre in 1791. From Vuillier's *A History of Dancing*, 1898.

DANCE

Dance has played an important role in theatrical entertainment since earliest times. An integral part of Greek drama, in later periods dance was frequently relegated to the minor dramatic forms or used as incidental entertainment between the acts of plays. It has never been absent from the theatre, and has developed into such independent art forms as ballet and modern dance.

Although dance has been an important part of musical comedy from the beginning, not until recently was it elevated from mere embellishment to an integral part of the action. The increased demands on dancers and choreographers have created a need for better training and more imaginative use of dance forms.

TYPES AND USES OF THEATRICAL DANCE

Dance in the theatre may be divided into two basic types: *incidental* and *dramatic*. *Incidental dances* are not an integral part of the dramatic action; they include ballets inserted into operas and folk dances or specialty numbers used to enliven a play or to set a mood without influencing the action. Dances are also sometimes used as between-act entertainment. Incidental dance serves principally as a diversion. It may be extended, shortened, or omitted since it is not essential to the play's development.

Suzanne Farrell and Jacques d'Amboise in *Movement for Piano and Orchestra* at the New York City Ballet. Choreography by George Balanchine. Photograph by Martha Swope.

Liebeslieder Walzer, a ballet choreographed by George Balanchine to music by Johannes Brahms and danced by the New York City Ballet. Costumes by Karinska; scenery and lighting by David Hays. Photograph—Martha Swope.

Dramatic dance, on the other hand, forwards the story, reveals character, or establishes mood and style. It cannot be left out without seriously damaging the dramatic action. It includes ballets, modern dance compositions, and danced portions of present-day musical comedy.

Theatrical dance serves a number of purposes. First, it always functions as spectacle and as entertainment with its own inherent interest. It adds movement and color which increase the audience's pleasure.

Next, dance helps to establish the proper mood. It may be carefree and comic or restrained and serious. Since the possible variations are infinite, it is possible to create sequences with qualities of mood and atmosphere appropriate to any dramatic context.

Dance may aid in characterization. The kind of movement (angular, free, awkward, graceful) may reveal essential aspects of personality, such as repressed desire or unstated feelings; it can make explicit many traits only hinted at in the dialogue.

Dance can be used in storytelling. Since realism is seldom demanded of dance, it can be used to suggest a great deal that would have to be enacted or discussed at length in a drama without music or dance. Thus, dance may condense or elaborate situations or moods. For example, if a young girl has just discovered that she is in love, a dance may expand upon the emotion more effectively than spoken words.

Dance can make an otherwise dull situation entertaining. For example, a reception or presentation can be transformed into a danced sequence which is both dramatically and esthetically effective.

Dance is an important stylistic device, since it helps to establish the level of reality, always more abstract and stylized in musical drama than in everyday life. Dance encourages the audience to accept departures

531

The City Center Joffrey Ballet's use of multimedia technique. Here, live and filmed, Maximiliano Zomosa in Robert Joffrey's "psychedelic ballet" *Astarte.* Photograph—Herbert Migdoll.

from realism. On the other hand, it may be introduced into realistic or naturalistic dramas, but its presence there usually must be motivated carefully.

Dance may help to establish themes and ideas. By providing the proper mood, by characterizing agents, by condensing action or elaborating upon emotions, it creates emphases which point up meanings.

THE ELEMENTS OF
DANCE

The choreographer works with three basic elements: *space, time,* and *intensity*. Dance, as a visual medium, is conceived in terms of line, shapes, and spatial relationships. The lines formed by the movement of the individual dancers serve to define the shape of the dance and to mark out the total space.

While most dances combine straight and curved lines, it is possible to create a dance utilizing one kind almost exclusively. Lines may also be dominantly horizontal or vertical, depending upon the physical relationship of the dancers to the stage floor. Furthermore, a dance may be confined to a small area or may utilize the entire stage. All of the visual factors are affected by the number of dancers. A single dancer creates

532

something analogous to a line drawing, while a group of dancers may be thought of in terms of areas of color or massed shapes. An analogy may also be made to music by relating the work of a principal or solo dancer to melody and the chorus to harmony. The choreographer should manipulate line, shape, and space in terms of individual dancers and the entire group. From interaction he creates the visual patterns of dance. Space in dance is dynamic, however, for the visual patterns are constantly altered by movement in time.

Three factors are involved in time: *rhythm, tempo,* and the *time consumed* by the performance. Regularly recurring pulses, or beats, combine to create *rhythm.* Beats are organized into measures, or into larger units composed of many measures. Dances are normally composed (and learned) in terms of these rhythmical units.

Tempo refers to the speed at which the pulses or beats are repeated. It may be fast or slow and may change often. A lengthy dance requires greater complexity in the handling of rhythms, tempos, and spatial patterns than a short one, and can develop more complex emotional states and ideas. Time factors, however, are flexible and allow many combinations.

A scene at the end of Gerald Arpino's contemporary ballet-parable *The Clowns,* from the repertory of the Joffrey Ballet. Photograph—James Howell.

Intensity results from the bodily attitudes, gestures, steps, and movements of individual dancers and the group as a whole. It is created by the tension and relaxation of the dancers' bodies and may be described by such adjectives as restless, concentrated, free, restrained, and tense. Spatial and time patterns may be infused with widely varying qualities through differing treatments of intensity.

The elements of dance—space, time, and intensity—should be organized according to the principles of design: unity, variety, proportion, balance, and emphasis. Since these have already been discussed extensively in Chapters 19–21, they will not be reviewed here. It is sufficient to say that the principles of design weld the elements of dance into clearly defined realtionships and esthetically pleasing patterns.

THE DANCER'S TRAINING

It is usually taken for granted that a dancer has, or will acquire, certain skills and knowledge. First, his body must be sufficiently supple and disciplined to allow him to perform and control any physical action. His body is his primary means of expression and its complete mastery comes only with years of training.

Second, the dancer should know as many different dance forms as possible. No one should need to explain to a trained dancer the distinctions among, for example, a waltz, a tango, and a minuet. In rehearsals many instructions assume the performer's acquaintance with standard dance forms and the steps which compose each.

Third, a dancer must know the basic ballet positions and movements. These are sufficiently standardized to serve as a kind of shorthand for directions in rehearsals. For example, there are five basic foot positions, designated merely as *first position, second position*, and so on. In addition, there are many types of jumps, turns, lifts, and other movements.

If dancers have well-trained bodies and are familiar with basic dance forms and techniques, much time can be saved in rehearsals. For this reason, an effort is usually made to cast dancers whose training will allow the most efficient use of rehearsal time.

THE CHOREOGRAPHER

The choreographer is a designer, or creator, of dances; his work, therefore, is analogous to that of the playwright or the composer. His working methods are such, however, that he must also fulfill functions similar to those of the play director or the musical conductor, for, since he has no universally accepted system of setting down his ideas, he must teach them to the dancers as quickly as possible. Creation and execution, thus, cannot be as clearly separated in dance as they can be in the other performing arts.

A choreographer may compose ballets, modern-dance pieces, incidental or dramatic dances for musical comedy or other theatrical forms. Here, only his work with musical comedy will be considered.

Like other theatre artists, the choreographer must understand the script as a whole, its style, mood, characterizations, its patterns of devel-

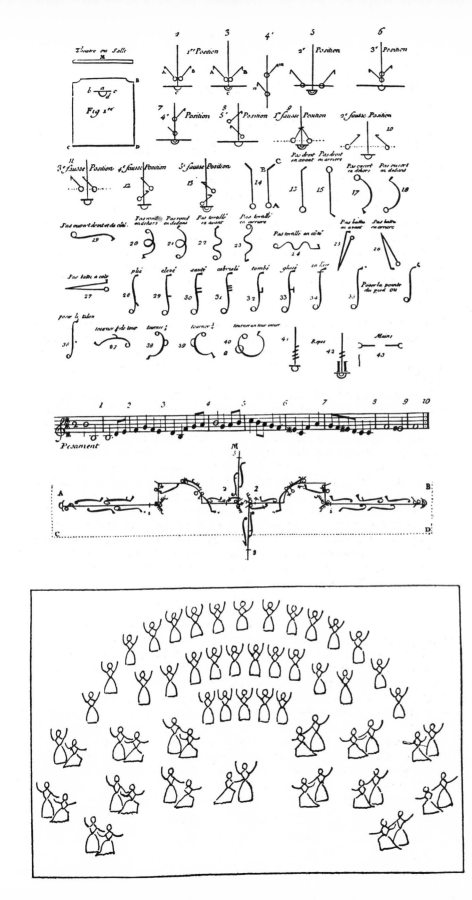

An eighteenth-century system for recording dance steps. At the bottom of the illustration, the steps are recorded in relation to the musical score. From *L'Ancienne France*, 1887.

A nineteenth-century attempt to record dance figures. From Moynet's *La Machinerie Théâtrale*, 1893.

opment, and the director's interpretation. He must seek, then, to express this understanding through dance.

Before the choreographer begins work, there should be one or more conferences with the dramatist, composer, lyricist, director, producer, and stage designers. Agreement should be reached about points in the script where dance is to be used, the length of each dance, the basic qualities to be sought, and the number of dancers to be employed in each. The choreographer must also know how much stage space is available for each dance, what parts of each setting may be used, what costumes will be worn, and how these may affect movement. He should feel free to criticize elements which affect his work and should seek changes when they may lead to adverse results. After he has clarified the conditions under which he must work, the choreographer is ready to begin the composition of dances.

The choreographer for a Broadway musical may work directly with a composer or, as is becoming increasingly common, he may design the dances apart from the music which eventually accompanies them. In this case he may employ a pianist to play a specified rhythm and tempo, without trying to fit his dances to existing music. Instead, the music is then composed around the dances after they have evolved.

The choreographer experiments with spatial relationships, rhythms, tempos, and intensities until he evolves the steps, postures, gestures, and patterns which compose the dances. Because rehearsal time must be used efficiently, he normally has the dances clearly in mind before he begins work with the chorus. Typically, he evolves the choreography by using his own body. He may work alone, or he may use an assistant choreographer or even a small group of dancers who can respond quickly and easily to directions and help him construct a highly complex dance.

Although some choreographers have devised their own notational systems for recording movement, many must remember their dances until they can be taught to the performers. It is important, therefore, that the time between the conception of the dance and its execution be short.

In addition to creating dances, the choreographer must also select and rehearse the chorus and any other members of the cast who dance. He must attend those rehearsals in which the choreography is integrated with the spoken and sung portions, and he may need to make alterations at that time to smooth out transitions or to eliminate problems not previously apparent. Adjustments may also have to be made because of the differing sizes of stages when a company is on tour. Furthermore, it is not uncommon for entire dance numbers to be eliminated and new ones substituted while a musical is on its out-of-town tryout tour.

When the show opens on Broadway the choreographer's job is finished. A dance captain, a member of the chorus, is selected and is made responsibile for seeing that the dances remain as staged. He may hold rehearsals if he deems it necessary for returning the choreography or individual performances to the original conception. For this work, he receives additional pay.

Choreographers have now joined with stage directors to form a union, the Society of Stage Directors and Choreographers. Previously there

536

A sea sprite visits a dreaming boy on a beach in Gerald Arpino's lyrical "poem-in-dance" *Sea Shadow*. Paul Sutherland and Trinette Singleton of the Joffrey Ballet company. Photograph—Fred Fehl.

were no standard fees or working conditions for the choreographer and he was forced to accept whatever terms he could negotiate with a producer. Now, provisions for standard minimum fees and working conditions are governed by the union contract. This contract also specifies his billing and duties.

Most choreographers receive their first professional training as members of dance troupes. Summer stock, resident companies, or off-Broadway productions often provide opportunities for breaking into the theatre as a choreographer.

In the nonprofessional theatre, the choreographer is most often a local dance teacher. Frequently a producer has little choice since the number of qualified persons is extremely small; in many cases neither the choreographer nor the dancers are highly skilled. Under such conditions the dances must be composed with the limitations of the dancers in mind. It is seldom possible in the nonprofessional theatre to duplicate (even if this were desirable) the dances used in the Broadway production of a musical comedy.

THE DANCERS

Of all tryouts in New York, those for dancers are most often open. Casting notices are printed in theatrical papers and posted at dance schools and studios.

Many dancers are never allowed to demonstrate their capabilities at auditions, however, for a large number are eliminated on the basis of physical appearance. This weeding out process may be conducted by an assistant who has been instructed by the choreographer and director as to the qualities they are seeking.

537

Those applicants who remain may be asked to carry out directions or to repeat dance steps and movements demonstrated to them. The instructions may become increasingly complex so that the choreographer can determine the extent of the dancers' training.

Applicants are eliminated until a reasonably small number (greater than that needed for the show) remains. Then comes the process of pairing dancers and assessing the relative merits of each. Finally the exact number of dancers needed for the production is selected. Although the choreographer must approve all dancers, the director, producer, and authors may also be consulted. Dancers in the professional theatre are employed under Actors' Equity contracts which specify rehearsal conditions and salary.

The majority of rehearsal time is spent on dance, since the choreography must be learned entirely by rote through continuous repetition. It is taught to the dancers in sections and in terms of beats (or counts) to aid memory. A lesser amount of time is devoted to dramatic and musical rehearsals. Dancers may be cast in small speaking roles and may also serve as understudies.

In the nonprofessional theatre, it is usually necessary to use those untrained or minimally trained persons who volunteer their services. Frequently the choreographer must teach the dancers the most elementary steps. Under these circumstances, dance patterns must be kept simple, although vigor and interest may still be attained within a limited range of movement. Good results are usually possible if the choreographer is willing to accept the limitations of his dancers and to capitalize upon their capabilities.

In their own right, music and dance are complex arts. When they are used in the theatre, they make production more difficult, for, like the other theatre arts, they must be conceived and rehearsed with care and integrated skillfully with the other elements. Their use in the theatre is amply justified, however, for they can heighten and project dramatic values and bring added pleasure.

Chapter 23 THE THEATRE AS A PROFESSION

The American theatre today is a mixture of professional and nonprofessional workers and organizations. Such a situation is not unusual. For example, the Greek theatre of the fifth century B.C. was largely nonprofessional. In its organization and operation it was probably closer to the community theatre than to the professional theatre of our day. In the modern era, nonprofessional organizations rose to fill the void left when the professional theatre began to disappear outside of New York. Today there are more producing groups in America than at any time in its history, although by far the majority are nonprofessional. The professional theatre is able to offer employment to relatively few persons. Nevertheless, the theatre remains a glamorous profession and numerous persons continually seek a foothold in it.

TRAINING FOR THE THEATRE

There is considerable disagreement over how the prospective theatre worker should be educated. Some argue that he should receive a liberal education first (with little or no theatre training) and then be given concentrated training in the theatre arts; others believe that professional training should be given from the beginning and that little attention need be paid to a general education; still others state that liberal arts courses and theatre training should be combined throughout the student's education. These outlooks are embodied in two types of schools: liberal arts and professional.

Although more and more liberal arts colleges give some training in theatre, many still do not include performance courses in the undergraduate curriculum. They offer work in dramatic literature and provide a sound liberal education, but leave theatrical training to professional or graduate schools.

539

Other colleges and universities combine liberal education with theatre training, so that playwriting, acting, directing, scenic, costume, and lighting design, technical production, music, and dance are regularly taught. The student is required to take a course of study designed to provide a sound liberal education, but approximately a fourth to a third of his work may be devoted to theatre arts. If there is a graduate program, an additional one to three years of training may be available.

A professional school normally allows students to devote all or most of their time to theatre training. Some do not give a certificate or degree. Rather, a student may enroll in any class for as long as he wishes. Thus, he may study acting exclusively for a number of years. Others give certificates for the satisfactory completion of a prescribed program, and still others award academic degrees (usually the BFA or MFA). The course of study may vary from one to four years and may include such subjects as history of the theatre, dramatic literature and kindred studies. If the school offers both undergraduate and graduate training, an additional one or two years of study may be possible.

Another type of training—the apprenticeship—is available to a lesser extent. In-service apprenticeships are most commonly offered by summer stock and resident companies. As a rule, formal class work is minimal and experience is the principal means of teaching. A few permanent companies provide longer apprenticeships and more systematic instruction. In most cases, in-service training is available for periods of about three months. Consequently, it is a supplementary rather than a primary means of training.

Each of these approaches has its strengths and weaknesses. Most persons will concede that a broad liberal education is of value no matter what the student's goals, and that a liberal education has special relevance to theatre and drama, since they are concerned with all aspects of human experience. A liberal education serves to broaden horizons, break down prejudices, and build inquiring and open minds.

On the other hand, the time spent in acquiring a liberal education cannot be devoted to developing professional skills. Some persons argue that the theatre arts must be studied and practiced constantly over a long period if they are to be perfected. Consequently, it is said that adequate professional training leaves little time for a full academic education. Some believe that a truly professional artist is so single minded that he has little time for anything else.

The goals of students vary widely. They may have no intention of pursuing the theatre (except as an avocation), or they may be training for a lifetime's work in the educational, community, or professional theatre.

THE THEATRE AS AN AVOCATION

The majority of students who receive theatrical training in colleges do not enter the theatre after graduation. To most, theatre is a means for acquiring a liberal education just as English, philosophy, or history

540

might be. Few persons expect students with degrees in English, philosophy, or history to become literary critics, philosophers, or historians. Similarly, a major in theatre apart from professional goals is justifiable.

Most students who major in theatre retain their theatre-going interest and many participate actively in nonprofessional productions. The opportunities for working in the theatre as an avocation are many, since the majority of theatrical organizations in America rely upon unpaid personnel. The demand for actors is great, and almost anyone with an interest in scenery, costumes, lighting, properties, make-up, sound, dance, or music can find ample opportunities.

EDUCATIONAL THEATRE

Probably the largest number of paying jobs in the theatre are in education. As a rule, theatre workers are employed in schools for two purposes: to teach and to produce plays. Occasionally, persons do only one, but typically the working hours are divided between teaching and production. A staff member may be allowed to specialize in directing, costuming, lighting, and other areas, but to be assured of employment he should be prepared to undertake almost any assignment.

The person who wishes to enter the educational theatre should have a sincere interest in teaching and be willing to spend much of his energy in preparing demonstrations, projects, and lectures. Training for educational theatre probably should be broader in scope than for other types, for a good educational theatre educates students about the history of the theatre, dramatic literature, and the theatre arts, and it produces plays representative of many periods and styles. Personnel for the educational theatre, therefore, need a varied background. Since they will be working almost exclusively with nonprofessionals who have had little training, they should also be able and willing to explain anything from the most elementary to the most complex idea or practice. They must strive simultaneously to educate students and produce exciting performances.

Achievements must be viewed differently in the educational than they are in the professional theatre. While the aim in production should always be to elicit the best possible performance, in the educational theatre accomplishments must be measured in terms of the students' development, the problems mastered, and the handicaps overcome. The teacher should set high standards, but he should not expect learners to accomplish as much as seasoned professionals.

The educational theatre may be divided in terms of levels: *children's theatre, secondary school theatre, undergraduate training,* and *graduate training.*

CHILDREN'S THEATRE

Children's theatre may operate within any framework: professional, community, or educational. Its distinguishing characteristic is its intended audience. The theatre of the past was intended primarily for adult audiences; it is only in the twentieth century, and principally since World War II, that programs have been developed to meet the needs of

541

Children's theatre production of *The Wind in the Willows* as adapted and directed by Moses Goldberg. Courtesy University of Washington School of Drama.

children. Today the children's theatre is a vigorous institution with promise of still further development. As it grows, so will the demand for qualified workers.

There are two principal types of productions: those in which children perform for other children, and those in which adults perform for children. For both, the intended audience is the same, but the first type gives experience in performance to the children in the cast.

A related area is creative dramatics, although technically it is not a theatrical activity. Rather, children are stimulated to improvise dramas out of stories, historical events, or other schoolwork. Each child is urged to express himself as fully as possible while keeping in mind the situation or story. The dialogue of the drama is improvised, and theatrical devices such as scenery and costumes are seldom used. Creative dramatics aims to develop understanding and imagination in children.

Children's theatre and creative dramatics are usually graded (or divided into levels) since the same experience will not appeal to children of all ages. Plays and approaches, therefore, may vary with the age level of the audience or participants.

While children's theatre and creative dramatics are frequently coordinated with the elementary school curriculum, theatre, as such, is seldom taught in elementary schools. Productions of children's plays are made available to children in a variety of ways. The recreation program in most large cities includes children's theatre and creative drama; many community theatres produce some plays for children each year; the Junior Leagues of America do much in this field; many high schools, colleges, and universities present one or more plays each season for child audiences; and many organizations specialize in plays for children.

Consequently, there is a fairly large demand for persons with some training in children's theatre and creative dramatics. Some colleges and universities employ specialists in these areas; school districts may hire a person who can demonstrate and supervise creative dramatics; some community theatres employ a director whose sole responsibility is the production of children's plays; and public recreation programs often

542

employ a specialist in this area. In addition, there are a number of troupes which perform only for child audiences.

The worker in children's theatre needs all the basic training in production that any other theatre worker should have. In addition, he should receive some specialized education in child psychology and the specific techniques of children's theatre. The children's theatre has an important opportunity, since it is in a position to mold future audiences, and to generate a love for the theatre and for art in general.

SECONDARY SCHOOL THEATRE

Almost every high school in the United States has some kind of theatre program. Because there are so many, secondary schools offer a major opportunity to those interested in educational theatre. Relatively few high schools, however, offer courses in theatre and drama. Since the production of plays is frequently assigned to persons who have had no theatre training whatever, the quality of production is often abysmally low. School administrators too often look upon the production of plays as a means of working off the excess energy of adolescents or as a way of raising money for the band or some other activity unrelated to the theatre program. Until such attitudes change, there is little chance of raising standards.

On the other hand, an increasing number of secondary schools have excellent theatre programs and large staffs. Many have outstanding facilities and teach a series of courses in theatre production, dramatic literature, and theatre history. Such schools are still atypical, however, and much remains to be done. Consequently, vast opportunities are open to qualified and energetic persons.

The teacher in the secondary school should have an understanding of the adolescent and usually must be certified to teach subjects other than

Billy Budd as presented at Evanston Township High School. Directed by Wallace Smith; designed by R. E. Proper.

theatre—such as speech and English, although any other subject may be acceptable. The secondary school is an important and open field, and one that must be cultivated if the majority of the population is to be reached, for most persons still receive no additional education. It is not an easy avenue to theatre work but it can be a rewarding one.

UNDERGRADUATE THEATRE IN COLLEGES AND UNIVERSITIES

An increasing number of colleges and universities are offering courses in theatre for undergraduate students. Since they seek properly qualified teachers, theatre work in colleges offers a more secure future than in secondary schools.

Because approaches to theatre training at the college level vary widely, the potential teacher should investigate the goals of a theatre program before accepting a job. In most cases, theatre courses are part of the liberal arts curriculum, while the production program is extracurricular.

Typically, students are between the ages of eighteen and twenty-two, have had little experience, and few will enter the theatre as a profession. The teacher, therefore, must be prepared to compensate for the youth and inexperience of his students, and must not expect to have classes or productions filled with persons whose sole interests lie in the theatre. Most students view the theatre as recreation. The teacher should nevertheless hold up high standards and endeavor to encourage discrimination in persons who will compose future theatre audiences.

The teacher in the undergraduate program may have a chance to specialize—for example, in directing or design—but often he must teach and supervise several areas of production. Therefore, he needs a broad background.

Working in college theatre has many rewards, but they are not necessarily those of the professional school or the professional theatre. Anyone who becomes a teacher should respect both education and theatrical production; he should not look upon his job as second best to working in the professional theatre.

THE GRADUATE SCHOOL

The graduate school is designed to give specialized training. Many of the institutions which offer undergraduate work also maintain graduate programs, but a few schools offer graduate work only.

Students in graduate school are older and more mature than undergraduates, and most are securing further education because they expect to make their living from some aspect of the theatre. Most of their course work is related to theatre or drama. Therefore, the teacher in this situation can expect greater devotion to the theatre and higher standards in production. Those who obtain graduate degrees normally go into teaching, community or children's theatre, or, to a lesser extent, the professional theatre.

Graduate education demands a staff of experienced specialists. Consequently, employment in the graduate school is usually available only to

Scene from Joseph Heller's *We Bombed in New Haven.* The original production at Yale University, 1967. Photograph by Henry Grossman. Courtesy Yale University School of Drama.

persons who have demonstrated considerable ability in specific aspects of the theatre. In many ways the graduate school is crucial for the future of the theatre, for most theatre workers now receive their basic training in colleges and universities and graduate schools supply most of the teachers.

THE COMMUNITY THEATRE

The community theatre is a product of the twentieth century. It originated between 1900 and 1920 to fill the gap left by the decline of the resident stock company and touring productions. Today, almost every town with a population of more than 30,000 has a community theatre. In number of producing organizations, the community theatre is surpassed only by the educational theatre.

Many community theatres are operated entirely by volunteers, since they cannot afford to hire anyone. Others are able to pay the director of each play a nominal fee and may provide a small sum for the designer and other key workers. Typically, however, a community theatre employs a full-time director who supervises all of the productions. The more prosperous groups also have a full-time designer-technician, and some hire a children's-theatre director as well. A few employ more than one director and may have a number of part-time employees.

Because of its purpose, however, it is undesirable in community theatres to hire persons other than in supervisory capacities. The primary function of community theatre, in addition to providing theatrical enter-

545

tainment for local audiences, is to furnish an outlet for the artistic talents of its members.

Anyone who seeks employment in the community theatre, therefore, needs to be a leader. He should be diplomatic and able to cooperate with diverse personalities. He should know a great deal about public relations and should have clearly formulated ideas about the role of the theatre in a community.

The typical volunteer in the community theatre holds a full-time job. Consequently, for him the theatre is an avocation to which he can devote only a few hours during the evening. The director and designer-technician must be willing to accept these limitations. The drawbacks are partially offset by the maturity of many volunteers.

The typical season of plays in a community theatre is composed of recent Broadway successes. Even one classic each year is unusual for most organizations. The director, therefore, needs most training in current theatre practice. On the other hand, a director probably can change the typical season by gradually introducing other kinds of plays and by demonstrating that his choices make rewarding evenings.

Like all jobs, those of community theatre director and designer-technician have their disadvantages, but they provide good opportunities for full-time employment.

STOCK COMPANIES

Since World War II, the number of summer theatres has rapidly increased. The majority are located in the eastern states, but others are scattered throughout the country.

The summer stock company usually operates from late June until early September, presenting a different play each week. During the run of a show, one or more additional scripts are being rehearsed. Under such circumstances there is little time for developing subtleties or polishing characterizations. Rather, the intensive production schedule develops techniques for working rapidly, for covering up the shortcomings of inadequate preparation, and for quick thinking in onstage and backstage emergencies. These skills, plus the experience of performing a number of plays before a variety of audiences, are the chief virtues of summer stock experience. On the other hand, shallowness and stage tricks may replace sound study and careful execution. Summer stock companies, under typical circumstances, provide valuable supplementary experience but cannot meet all the needs of the serious theatre worker.

There are many kinds of summer stock companies. Some are entirely professional and hire only professional actors, designers, and directors. Others mingle professionals and nonprofessionals. Actors' Equity classifies companies according to the number of professional actors employed, minimum salaries, and working conditions. Companies employing professional actors may hire designers and directors who are not union members. Most companies pay all members even if none is a member of a union.

546

Scene from Brecht's *Good Woman of Setzuan* at Summer Theatre '68, Newark, Delaware. Directed by James Walton. Photograph courtesy Mr. Walton.

Many summer theatres have apprenticeship programs. This means that a few inexperienced persons are taken into the company to learn while doing. Apprentices may receive room and board and even a small weekly salary; seldom is the pay more than enough for living expenses. Some organizations ask apprentices to pay a fee comparable to college tuition. This practice is generally frowned upon, and anyone interested in becoming an apprentice should be skeptical of a group which demands pay. The apprentice will learn much, but will put in long hours of hard labor and should not be expected to pay for working.

Summer stock is also being used increasingly by educational institutions as a supplement to the training offered during regular session. Many schools operate summer theatres on campus, but others maintain theatres in resort areas far removed from the campus. College credit can be earned for the work done in most of these companies. A large number offer scholarships, a percentage of the profits, or salaries as payment.

Typically, a summer theatre plays a season of recent Broadway hits. Groups affiliated with educational institutions usually mingle *avant garde* or older plays with recent successes. Some companies perform only musicals, others perform only plays, and still others do both. Occasionally a new script is tried out.

There are many variations on summer stock. Some companies perform a single work for the entire summer. Notable are those in North Carolina, Kentucky, and Virginia which produce dramatizations of local history. The experience is roughly comparable to being in a long-run show.

Other groups have turned to repertory. This means that a number of plays are readied before the season begins and that the plays are then performed in rotation throughout the summer. While the scripts may vary widely in type and period, a number of organizations specialize in the plays of a single author, particularly Shakespeare. Still other theatres employ only a nucleus company and import well-known motion picture, television, and stage actors to play leading roles. Usually the plays are rehearsed without the stars, who arrive at the last moment. Occasionally summer companies try out new plays for Broadway producers.

Since personnel for summer companies are usually hired between January and May, early application is advisable. Much of the hiring takes place in New York or other large cities. Except in a completely professional company, workers are usually expected to double in other capacities. Actors may be asked to help with scenery, costumes, or lighting; technicians may assume small acting roles.

Personnel for summer stock is drawn from many sources: Broadway and off-Broadway, radio, television, motion pictures, semiprofessional groups, community, or educational theatres. Summer stock, therefore, supplements all of the other types of theatre. Because it is seasonal, however, it does little to relieve chronic unemployment in the professional theatre or to eliminate the concentration of the professional theatre in New York. It is a temporary arrangement under which the theatre moves into the country for a few weeks without settling there.

PROFESSIONAL COMPANIES OUTSIDE OF NEW YORK

Many plans have been proposed for decentralizing the professional theatre, but little was accomplished until recently. During the 1950's resident troupes began to be established outside of New York, and in the 1960's, with the financial aid of the Ford Foundation and other groups, increased in number and prestige. In 1968 there were approximately 35 resident companies in the United States.

Most of the resident troupes produce a season of plays each year. They do not seek long runs but present each play for a limited engagement. Because they perform a number of plays, they strive for variety in programming and, like educational theatres, usually do plays from a number of periods and styles.

Normally, the same staff—designers, directors, business and promotional personnel, and, to a lesser extent, actors—continues throughout the season. Guest directors may be used for some plays, and additional or new actors may be hired for each play. Most organizations, however, seek to achieve ensemble effects which are possible only when the same persons work together over a period of time.

Most of the professional theatres outside of New York are comparatively new and are still struggling for recognition and security. Most cannot afford to employ well-known actors, designers, or directors, but they offer excellent opportunities to talented persons who are willing to work hard for limited pay. Many are willing to employ outstanding performers from colleges and universities and arrange interviews and tryouts for them. Some are affiliated with universities. Many accept apprentices. Because they are still few, however, the resident companies cannot provide employment for large numbers of persons.

548

A scene from Molière's *The School for Wives* as performed by The Actors Theatre of Louisville. This professional resident company performs in a remodeled railway station. Courtesy Actors Theatre.

It is too early to tell how successful these theatres will be, but they are among the most encouraging signs in the American theatre today. Other professional theatre outside of New York is limited primarily to touring companies. Since these productions are usually cast in New York, the road is merely an extension of the Broadway theatre.

THE PROFESSIONAL THEATRE IN NEW YORK

The conditions of employment in the New York theatre have been reviewed in Chapters 16–22. Little has been said, however, about the number of jobs available.

The situation may be illustrated by considering the actor's predicament. On March 31, 1968, Actors' Equity had 15,392 members. (This figure does not give a clear idea of the number of aspiring actors in New York, since the signing of an Equity contract is a prerequisite for admission to the union.) On the other hand, the total number of actors employed in all productions that opened on Broadway between June 1, 1966 and May 31, 1967 was approximately 1150. This figure does not include Equity members playing in long-run hits which had opened previously, nor does it include those working in off-Broadway productions, road shows, radio, television and film, or outside of New York. Nevertheless, it is safe to say that fewer than half of the members of Actors' Equity are employed at any time. Approximately twenty-five percent of the membership can fill the normal demand in New York.

As for designers, the Broadway productions of the 1966–67 season provided employment for thirty-five scene designers (some of whom did costume and lighting designs as well), twenty-five costume designers, and eleven lighting designers. The majority worked on only one show each. Forty-eight directors staged all of the plays of the 1966–67 Broadway season. Of these, forty directed only one production; none directed more than four.

The bleakness of this picture is relieved somewhat by the off-Broadway and off-off-Broadway theatres which provide as many jobs now as the Broadway stage, although the pay and the recognition are less. Off-Broadway and off-off-Broadway productions are usually housed in inconveniently located buildings, most of which have small seating capacities and poorly equipped stages. Lobby space and other audience conveniences are minimal. Such shortcomings make for low rent, while the small income potential has induced unions to lower their demands somewhat. As a result, productions can be staged much more economically than on Broadway. The smallness of the theatres also means that these groups can exist on the patronage of smaller audiences.

The off-Broadway and off-off-Broadway theatre diversify the New York stage, and offer many opportunities to lesser-known workers or to those who wish to work in a broader context than the mass-oriented Broadway theatre. The aspiring professional will find, however, that it is almost as difficult to secure employment off Broadway as on, and that the pay in most cases is as low as the unions will permit.

The outlook for the professional theatre worker in New York is discouraging. A few persons make excellent salaries and are steadily employed. Others work a few weeks each year, and still others find it impossible to secure any job in the theatre. Nevertheless, the situation does not prevent hundreds of persons from migrating to New York each year. Of these, the majority fail to achieve their goals. Enough succeed, however, to keep others hopeful.

To succeed in the American professional theatre today one needs persistence, luck, talent, and skill. A person must be willing to make the rounds and to accept rejections day after day without becoming discouraged. Unless he has faith in himself in spite of constant disappointment, he is unlikely to succeed. There are so many aspiring and talented actors in New York that a certain amount of luck is often involved: being at the right place at the right moment has started many actors on their careers. No amount of persistence and luck will keep an actor employed, however, if he does not have talent and skill. The rush of production schedules does not leave a director time to teach actors; he must assume that each already knows his trade. A knowledge of stage technique, an adequate working method, and flexibility in adjusting to a director's idiosyncrasies —all of these are essential to the actor. Designers will never have a chance to work professionally if they cannot pass the rigid examination of the union.

Almost everyone does his best to discourage would-be professionals from going to New York. Nothing that anyone can say, however, will keep many from doing so. The true professional ultimately has a single-mindedness which cannot be discouraged by hardship. But no one

550

should consider entering the professional theatre unless he is willing to make many sacrifices and to undergo many painful experiences.

SPECIAL EMPLOYMENT
OPPORTUNITIES

In addition to the more obvious opportunities already discussed, a number of related activities should be mentioned. First, television and motion pictures offer additional possibilities. Without them, many professionals would lead a difficult life indeed. But these supplementary fields have their own unemployment problems and can do no more than relieve some of the pressures.

Second, a number of industrial and commercial firms stage special shows each year to publicize their products. Frequently such a production is extremely lavish and may tour a number of major cities. These shows normally play for invited audiences only; they pay extremely well, but provide little further recognition. Most are cast in New York and are, in effect, an extension of the Broadway stage.

Third, there is a considerable demand for stagehands, electricians, and dressers. Most persons trained in colleges and universities spurn such jobs, and perhaps rightly so, but these duties must be performed, and the pay is substantial. However, admission to the unions is not easily gained.

Fourth, theatre and drama have been adapted to a number of non-theatrical uses. For example, they are being used as therapy for emotionally disturbed persons. Improvised dramas allow subjects to express their hostilities indirectly, and therapists often gain important clues about the causes of mental disorders from these sessions. To work in such a field, sound training in psychology as well as in drama and theatre is needed.

When the variety of theatrical activities—in both the nonprofessional and professional theatre—is considered, the number of employment opportunities are considerable. There are by no means as many jobs as there are applicants, especially in the professional theatre, but the situation could be worse. The theatre has never been an easy profession, and it probably never will be. There is always a demand for talented and dedicated persons, however, and the future of the theatre depends upon this select few.

POSTSCRIPT

The theatre of today is the inheritor of a tradition which began with the Greeks. Between its origins in primitive society and the present, many and complex changes have taken place, the most important of which have been surveyed in the preceding chapters. From this survey a number of conclusions may be hazarded.

First, the theatre is a vital and organic part of society. The forms it takes and the value placed upon it vary as historical and social conditions change. The theatre can remain a healthy institution only when it changes along with altering social conditions. When responsive to its age, the theatre fills a basic need in men's lives, but when it becomes static or too restricted in scope, it ceases to be important to its time.

551

Second, the theatre always reflects the ideas of its age. Each theatrical style has resulted from the attempt to find means adequate for expressing a view of reality and man's place in it. As man's conceptions about himself and his world change, his dramatic expression changes.

Third, there is always a close relationship between the drama and theatrical conventions of any age. The dramatist's conception of the theatre and its possibilities dictates in large part what demands his work makes on the theatre. The plays of any period, therefore, have many common features because they use the same conventions. Consequently, in seeking to understand a play it is important to know the theatrical conditions under which it was written.

Fourth, while historical and social conditions, ideas, and theatrical conditions are important determinants of dramatic expression, the playwright's vision is the ultimate source of greatness. A study of the Elizabethan period, for example, helps to clarify many characteristics of Shakespeare's work, but it does not explain why only one writer of Shakespeare's stature appeared.

Fifth, although every play is clearly a product of its age, the great plays are timeless. Great drama provides a means by which the present can feel its way into the past, comprehend it, and perceive the continuity of human experience.

Sixth, theatre and drama are important ways of knowing about man's ideas and feelings. Like history or science or philosophy, the theatre is a form of knowledge, but one which functions through feeling as much as through thought.

Seventh, the theatre should be studied in its total context, the scope of which is suggested in the preceding six points. A combination of the approaches outlined above yields a fuller understanding of the complex art of the theatre.

Eighth, the dramatic impulse is natural to man and cannot be eradicated. The theatre may fluctuate in popularity, and the pleasures which it offers may be fulfilled at times by other activities, but the theatre in one form or another will always be a part of human society.

Curtain call. Courtesy Repertory Theater of Lincoln Center.

BIBLIOGRAPHY

This bibliography lists some important works on the theatre—either the most authoritative or the most representative of major points of view. All are in English.

The bibliography is divided to correspond with the divisions in the text. Notes have been introduced occasionally for clarity. Additional works may be discovered easily by consulting the following bibliographical aids:

Baker, Blanch M. *Theatre and Allied Arts*. New York: H. W. Wilson Co., 1952.

Brockett, Oscar G., Becker, Samuel, and Bryant, Donald. *A Bibliographical Guide to Research in Speech and Dramatic Art*. Chicago: Scott, Foresman and Co., 1963.

Dramatic Index [1909–49]. Boston: F. W. Faxon, Inc., 1910–50. An annual list of books and articles on the theatre published in America and England.

Revue d'Histoire du Théâtre [1948–present]. This quarterly journal lists in each issue current publications on theatre throughout the Western world. English-language publications are given in English.

PART ONE

Chapter 1: *THE THEATRE AS AN ART FORM*

Beardsley, Monroe. *Aesthetics: Problems in the Philosophy of Criticism*. New York: Harcourt, Brace & World, Inc., 1958.

Bentley, Eric. *What is Theatre? A Query in Chronicle Form*. Boston: Beacon Press, 1956.

Fergusson, Francis. *The Idea of a Theater*. Princeton, N.J.: Princeton University Press, 1949.

Granville-Barker, Harley. *The Uses of Drama*. Princeton, N.J.: Princeton University Press, 1945.

Greene, Theodore M. *The Arts and the Art of Criticism*. Princeton, N.J.: Princeton University Press, 1947.

Langer, Susanne K. *Problems of Art*. New York: Charles Scribner's Sons, 1957.

553

Munro, Thomas. *The Arts and Their Interrelations.* New York: Liberal Arts Press, 1949.

Rader, Melvin M. (ed.). *A Modern Book of Esthetics: An Anthology.* 3d ed. New York: Holt, Rinehart and Winston, Inc., 1960.

Sesonske, Alexander (ed.). *What is Art? Aesthetic Theory from Plato to Tolstoy.* New York: Oxford University Press, 1965.

Vivas, Eliseo and Kreiger, Murray (eds.). *The Problems of Aesthetics; A Book of Readings.* New York: Holt, Rinehart and Winston, Inc., 1953.

Young, Stark. *The Theatre.* New York: Doubleday & Company, Inc., 1927.

Chapter 2: *THE AUDIENCE AND THE CRITIC*

Baumol, William J. and Bowen, William G. *Performing Arts—The Economic Dilemma.* New York: The Twentieth Century Fund, 1966.

Boas, George. *A Primer for Critics.* Baltimore: Johns Hopkins Press, 1937.

Crane, R. S. *The Language of Criticism and the Structure of Poetry.* Toronto: University of Toronto Press, 1953.

Daiches, David. *Critical Approaches to Literature.* Englewood Cliffs, N.J.: Prentice-Hall, Inc., 1956.

Dorian, Frederick. *Commitment to Culture.* Pittsburgh: University of Pittsburgh Press, 1964.

Hamilton, Clayton. *The Theory of the Theatre and Other Principles of Dramatic Criticism.* New York: Holt, Rinehart and Winston, Inc., 1939.

Hollingworth, H. L. *The Psychology of the Audience.* New York: American Book Company, 1935.

Littlewood, Samuel R. *The Art of Dramatic Criticism.* London: Pitman, 1952.

Munson, Henry Lee. *Money for the Arts: The What, How and Why of Government Aid to the Arts in Seven Free Countries of Europe.* New York: Harold L. Oram, Inc., n.d.

Pepper, Stephen. *The Basis of Criticism in the Arts.* Cambridge, Mass.: Harvard University Press, 1949.

The Performing Arts: Problems and Prospects. Rockefeller Panel on the Future of the Theatre, Dance, and Music in America. New York: McGraw-Hill, 1965.

Chapter 3: *DRAMATIC STRUCTURE, FORM, AND STYLE*

Archer, William. *Play-Making: A Manual of Craftsmanship.* New York: Dover Publications, Inc., 1960.

Aristotle. *Aristotle's Theory of Poetry and Fine Art.* Critical Text and Translation by S. H. Butcher. 4th ed. New York: Dover Publications, Inc., 1951.

Barnet, Sylvan, Berman, Morton, and Burto, William. *Aspects of the Drama.* Boston: Little, Brown and Co., 1967.

Bergson, Henri. *Laughter: An Essay on the Meaning of the Comic.* Tr. by C. Brereton and F. Rothwell. London: Macmillan & Co., Ltd., 1921.

Brooks, Cleanth and Heilman, R. B. *Understanding Drama.* New York: Holt, Rinehart and Winston, Inc., 1955.

Cook, Albert S. *The Dark Voyage and the Golden Mean; A Philosophy of Comedy.* Cambridge, Mass.: Harvard University Press, 1949.

Corrigan, Robert (ed.). *Comedy; Meaning and Form.* San Francisco: Chandler Publishing Co., 1965.

Corrigan, Robert (ed.). *Tragedy; Vision and Form.* San Francisco: Chandler Publishing Co., 1965.

Grebanier, Bernard. *Playwriting.* New York: Thomas Y. Crowell Company, 1961.

Heffner, Hubert. *The Nature of Drama.* Boston: Houghton Mifflin Company, 1959.

554

Kerr, Walter. *Tragedy and Comedy.* New York: Simon and Schuster, 1967.

Lawson, John Howard. *Theory and Technique of Playwriting.* New York: Hill and Wang, 1960.

Lucas, F. L. *Tragedy in Relation to Aristotle's "Poetics."* New York: Harcourt, Brace & World, Inc., 1928.

Macgowan, Kenneth. *A Primer of Playwriting.* New York: Random House, Inc., 1951.

Meredith, George. *An Essay on Comedy and the Uses of the Comic Spirit.* New York: Charles Scribner's Sons, 1909.

Myers, Henry A. *Tragedy: A View of Life.* Ithaca: N.Y.: Cornell University Press, 1956.

Nicoll, Allardyce. *The Theory of Drama.* Rev. ed. London: Harrap & Co., Ltd., 1931.

Olson, Elder. *Tragedy and the Theory of Drama.* Detroit: Wayne State University Press, 1961.

Peacock, Ronald. *The Art of the Drama.* London: Routledge & Kegan Paul, Ltd., 1957.

Prior, Moody. *The Language of Tragedy.* New York: Columbia University Press, 1947.

Rowe, Kenneth. *Write That Play.* New York: Funk & Wagnalls Co., Inc., 1939.

Shipley, Joseph T. (ed.). *Dictionary of World Literature: Criticism, Forms, Techniques.* Rev. ed. New York: Philosophical Library, 1953.

Styan, J. L. *The Elements of Drama.* New York: Cambridge University Press, 1960.

Tennyson, G. B. *An Introduction to Drama.* New York: Holt, Rinehart and Winston, Inc., 1967.

Thompson, Alan R. *The Anatomy of Drama.* 2d ed. Berkeley: University of California Press, 1946.

Weales, Gerald. *A Play and Its Parts.* New York: Basic Books, Inc., 1964.

General Works Applicable to Parts Two and Three

Altman, George *et al. Theater Pictorial; A History of World Theater as Recorded in Drawings, Paintings, Engravings, and Photographs.* Berkeley: University of California Press, 1953.

Bowman, Walter P. and Ball, Robert H. *Theatre Language; A Dictionary of Terms in English of the Drama and Stage from Medieval to Modern Times.* New York: Theatre Arts Books, 1961.

Brockett, Oscar G. *History of the Theatre.* Boston: Allyn and Bacon, Inc., 1968.

Cheney, Sheldon. *The Theatre; Three Thousand Years of Drama, Acting and Stagecraft.* Rev. ed. New York: Longmans, Green, 1952.

Clark, Barrett H. (ed.). *European Theories of the Drama.* Newly revised by Henry Popkin. New York: Crown Publishers, Inc., 1965.

Duerr, Edwin. *The Length and Depth of Acting.* New York: Holt, Rinehart and Winston, Inc., 1962.

Freedley, George and Reeves, John A. *A History of the Theatre.* 3d ed. New York: Crown Publishers, Inc., 1968.

Gassner, John. *Masters of the Drama.* 3d ed. New York: Dover Publications, Inc., 1954.

Gassner, John and Allen, Ralph (eds.). *Theatre and Drama in the Making.* Boston: Houghton, Mifflin, 1964.

Hartnoll, Phyllis (ed.). *The Oxford Companion to the Theatre.* 3d ed. London: Oxford University Press, 1967.

Laver, James. *Drama, Its Costume and Decor*. London: Studio Publications, 1951.

Macgowan, Kenneth and Melnitz, William. *The Living Stage*. Englewood Cliffs, N.J.: Prentice-Hall, Inc., 1955.

Nagler, Alois M. *Sources of Theatrical History*. New York: Theatre Annual, Inc., 1952.

Nicoll, Allardyce. *The Development of the Theatre*. 5th ed. London: Harrap & Co., Ltd., 1966.

————. *World Drama from Aeschylus to Anouilh*. London: Harrap & Co., Ltd., 1949.

Roberts, Vera M. *On Stage; A History of the Theatre*. New York: Harper and Row, 1962.

Southern, Richard. *The Seven Ages of the Theatre*. New York: Hill and Wang, 1961.

Stuart, Donald C. *The Development of Dramatic Art*. New York: Appleton-Century-Crofts, 1933.

Wimsatt, William K. and Brooks, Cleanth. *Literary Criticism; A Short History*. New York: Alfred A. Knopf, Inc., 1957.

Collections of Plays

Adams, Joseph Q. *Chief Pre-Shakespearean Dramas*. Boston: Houghton Mifflin Company, 1924.

Bates, Alfred (ed.). *The Drama; Its History, Literature and Influence on Civilization*. 22 vols. London: The Athenian Society, 1903-04.

Bentley, Eric. *The Classic Theatre*. 4 vols. Garden City, N.Y.: Doubleday & Company, Inc., 1958-61. (Vol. I—Six Italian Plays; Vol. II—Five German Plays; Vol. III—Six Spanish Plays; Vol. IV—Six French Plays.)

————. *From the Modern Repertoire*. Series 1-3. Bloomington: Indiana University Press, 1949-56.

————. *The Modern Theatre*. 6 vols. Garden City, N.Y.: Doubleday & Company, Inc., 1955-60.

Brockett, Oscar G. and Brockett, Lenyth. *Plays for the Theatre; An Anthology of World Drama*. New York: Holt, Rinehart and Winston, Inc., 1967.

Clark, Barrett H. *World Drama . . . An Anthology*. 2 vols. New York: Appleton-Century-Crofts, 1933.

Corrigan, Robert. *The Modern Theatre*. New York: Macmillan, 1964.

Dickinson, Thomas H. *Chief Contemporary Dramatists*. Series 1-3. Boston: Houghton Mifflin Company, 1915-30.

Duckworth, George E. *The Complete Roman Drama*. 2 vols. New York: Random House, Inc., 1942.

Gassner, John. *Best American Plays*. Series 1-4, and a supplementary volume. New York: Crown Publishers, 1939-61.

————. *A Treasury of the Theatre*. 2 vols. New York: Holt, Rinehart and Winston, Inc., 1960-1967. (Vol. I—*From Aeschylus to Ostrovsky*. 3d ed., 1967; Vol. II—*From Henrik Ibsen to Eugene Ionesco*. 3d ed., 1960.)

Grene, David and Lattimore, Richmond (eds.). *The Complete Greek Tragedies*. 4 vols. Chicago: University of Chicago Press, 1960.

Macmillan, Dougald and Jones, Howard M. *Plays of the Restoration and Eighteenth Century*. New York: Holt, Rinehart and Winston, Inc., 1954.

Matthews, Brander. *The Chief European Dramatists*. Boston: Houghton Mifflin Company, 1916.

Moody, Richard. *Dramas from the American Theatre, 1762-1909*. Cleveland: World Publishing Co., 1966.

Noyes, George R. *Masterpieces of the Russian Drama.* 2 vols. New York: Dover Publications, Inc., 1960.

Oates, Whitney J. and O'Neill, Eugene, Jr. *Complete Greek Drama.* 2 vols. New York: Random House, Inc., 1938.

Ottemiller, John H. *Index to Plays in Collections.* 3d ed. New York: Scarecrow Press, 1957.

Parks, Edd W. and Beatty, R. C. *The English Drama; An Anthology of Plays, 900–1642.* New York: W. W. Norton & Company, Inc., 1935.

Quinn, Arthur H. *Representative American Plays, from 1767 to the Present Day.* 7th ed. New York: Appleton-Century-Crofts, 1957.

Rowell, George. *Nineteenth Century Plays.* New York: Oxford University Press, 1953.

Stanton, Stephen. *Camille and Other Plays.* New York: Hill and Wang, 1957.

Tucker, S. M. and Downer, A. S. *Twenty-Five Modern Plays.* 3d ed. New York: Harper & Row, Publishers, 1953.

Ulanov, Barry. *Makers of the Modern Theatre.* New York: McGraw-Hill, 1961.

PART TWO

Chapter 4: *THE THEATRE OF ANCIENT GREECE*

Allen, James T. *Greek Acting in the Fifth Century.* Berkeley: Univ. of California Press, 1916.

———. *The Greek Theatre of the Fifth Century before Christ.* Berkeley: University of California Press, 1920.

Arnott, Peter D. *Greek Scenic Conventions in the Fifth Century, B.C.* Oxford: Clarendon Press, 1962.

———. *An Introduction to the Greek Theatre.* London: Macmillan & Co., Ltd., 1959.

Bieber, Margarete. *The History of the Greek and Roman Theater.* 2d ed. Princeton, N.J.: Princeton University Press, 1961.

Cornford, Francis M. *The Origin of Attic Comedy.* London: E. Arnold, 1914.

Flickinger, R. C. *The Greek Theatre and Its Drama.* 4th ed. Chicago: University of Chicago Press, 1936.

Gaster, Theodor. *Thespis; Ritual, Myth and Drama in the Ancient Near East.* New York: Abelard-Schuman, Limited, 1950.

Greene, William C. *Moira: Fate, Good, and Evil in Greek Thought.* Cambridge, Mass.: Harvard University Press, 1944.

Hamilton, Edith. *The Greek Way.* New York: W. W. Norton & Company, 1952.

Harsh, Philip W. *A Handbook of Classical Drama.* Stanford, Calif.: Stanford University Press, 1944.

Kitto, H. D. F. *Greek Tragedy.* 2d ed. London: Methuen & Co., Ltd., 1950.

Jaeger, Werner. *Paideia: The Ideals of Greek Culture.* Tr. by Gilbert Highet. 3 vols. New York: Oxford University Press, 1939–44.

Lever, Katherine. *The Art of Greek Comedy.* London: Methuen & Co., Ltd., 1956.

Murray, Gilbert. *Euripides and His Age.* New York: Holt, Rinehart and Winston, Inc., 1913.

Pickard-Cambridge, A. W. *Dithyramb, Tragedy, and Comedy.* 2d ed. rev. by T. B. L. Webster. Oxford: Clarendon Press, 1962.

———. *The Dramatic Festivals of Athens.* Oxford: Clarendon Press, 1953.

———. *The Theatre of Dionysus in Athens.* Oxford: Clarendon Press, 1946.

Rees, Kelley. *The Rule of Three Actors in the Classical Greek Drama.* Chicago: University of Chicago Press, 1908.

Webster, T. B. L. *Greek Theatre Production.* London: Methuen & Co., Ltd., 1956.

Chapter 5: *ROMAN THEATRE AND DRAMA*

Allen, James T. *Stage Antiquities of the Greeks and Romans and Their Influence.* New York: Longmans, Green, 1927.

Beare, William. *The Roman Stage; A Short History of Latin Drama in the Time of the Republic.* 2d ed. London: Methuen & Co., Ltd., 1955.

Bieber, Margarete. See under Chapter 4.

Duckworth, George E. *The Nature of Roman Comedy.* Princeton, N.J.: Princeton University Press, 1952.

Hamilton, Edith. *The Roman Way.* New York: W. W. Norton & Company, 1932.

Hanson, J. A. *Roman Theater-Temples.* Princeton, N.J.: Princeton University Press, 1959.

Harsh, Philip W. See under Chapter 4.

Lucas, Frank L. *Seneca and Elizabethan Tragedy.* Cambridge: The University Press, 1922.

Norwood, Gilbert. *Plautus and Terence.* New York: Longmans, Green, 1932.

Chapter 6: *MEDIEVAL THEATRE AND DRAMA*

Chambers, E. K. *The Mediaeval Stage.* 2 vols. Oxford: The Clarendon Press, 1903.

Craik, Thomas W. *The Tudor Interlude; Stage, Costume, and Acting.* Leicester: The University Press, 1958.

Evans, Marshall B. *The Passion Play of Lucerne.* New York: Modern Language Association, 1943.

Farnham, Willard. *The Medieval Heritage of Elizabethan Tragedy.* Berkeley: University of California Press, 1936.

Frank, Grace. *The Medieval French Drama.* Oxford: Clarendon Press, 1954.

Gardiner, Harold C. *Mysteries' End; An Investigation of the Last Days of the Medieval Religious Stage.* New Haven, Conn.: Yale University Press, 1946.

Hardison, O. B. *Christian Rite and Christian Drama in the Middle Ages; Essays in the Origin and Early History of Modern Drama.* Baltimore: John Hopkins Press, 1965.

Hunningher, Benjamin. *The Origin of the Theater.* New York: Hill and Wang, 1961.

Nicoll, Allardyce. *Masks, Mimes and Miracles.* New York: Harcourt, Brace & World, Inc., 1931.

Salter, F. M. *Medieval Drama in Chester.* Toronto: University of Toronto Press, 1955.

Southern, Richard. *The Medieval Theatre in the Round.* London: Faber & Faber, Ltd., 1957.

Stratman, Carl J. *Bibliography of Medieval Drama.* Berkeley: University of California Press, 1954.

Stuart, D. C. *Stage Decoration in France in the Middle Ages.* New York: Columbia University Press, 1910.

Weiner, Albert B. *Philippe de Mezieres' Description of the "Festum Praesentationis Beatae Mariae" Translated from the Latin and Introduced by an Essay on the Birth of Modern Acting.* New Haven, Conn.: Andrew Kner, 1958.

Wickham, Glynne. *Early English Stages, 1300–1660.* 2 vols. New York: Columbia University Press, 1959-62.

Williams, Arnold. *The Drama of Medieval England.* East Lansing: Michigan State University Press, 1961.

Young, Karl. *The Drama of the Medieval Church.* 2 vols. Oxford: Clarendon Press, 1933.

Chapter 7: *SPAIN AND ELIZABETHAN ENGLAND*

Adams, John C. *The Globe Playhouse: Its Design and Equipment.* 2d ed. New York: Barnes & Noble, 1961.

Adams, Joseph Q. *Shakespearean Playhouses; A History of English Theatres from the Beginnings to the Restoration.* Boston: Houghton Mifflin Company, 1917.

Baldwin, T. W. *The Organization and Personnel of the Shakespearean Company.* Princeton, N.J.: Princeton University Press, 1927.

Beckerman, Bernard. *Shakespeare at the Globe, 1599–1609.* New York: The Macmillan Company, 1962.

Bentley, Gerald E. *The Jacobean and Caroline Stage.* 5 vols. Oxford: Clarendon Press, 1941–56.

———. *Shakespeare: A Biographical Handbook.* New Haven, Conn.: Yale University Press, 1961.

Boas, Frederick S. *An Introduction to Stuart Drama.* London: Oxford University Press, 1946.

Brooke, C. F. T. *The Tudor Drama; A History of English National Drama to the Retirement of Shakespeare.* Boston: Houghton Mifflin Company, 1911.

Chambers, E. K. *The Elizabethan Stage.* 4 vols. London: Oxford University Press, 1923.

———. *A Short Life of Shakespeare.* Oxford: Clarendon Press, 1933.

Crawford, J. P. W. *Spanish Drama before Lope de Vega.* Rev. ed. Philadelphia: University of Pennsylvania Press, 1937.

Ebisch, Walther and Schucking, L. L. *A Shakespeare Bibliography.* Oxford: Clarendon Press, 1931. Supplement, 1935.

Ellis-Fermor, Una. *The Jacobean Drama; An Interpretation.* 3d ed. London: Methuen & Co., Ltd., 1953.

Gildersleeve, Virginia. *Government Regulation of the Elizabethan Drama.* New York: Columbia University Press, 1908.

Harrison, George B. *Shakespeare's Tragedies.* London: Routledge & Kegan Paul, Ltd., 1951.

Hodges, C. W. *The Globe Restored.* London: Ernest Benn, Ltd., 1953.

Hotson, Leslie. *Shakespeare's Wooden O.* New York: The Macmillan Company, 1960.

Joseph, Bertram. *Elizabethan Acting.* London: Oxford University Press, 1951.

Lawrence, W. J. *The Elizabethan Playhouse and Other Studies.* 2 vols. Stratford-on-Avon: Shakespeare Head Press, 1912–13.

———. *Pre-Restoration Stage Studies.* Cambridge: Harvard University Press, 1927.

Nagler, A. M. *Shakespeare's Stage.* New Haven, Conn.: Yale University Press, 1958.

Nicoll, Allardyce. *Stuart Masques and the Renaissance Stage.* London: Harrap and Co., Ltd., 1937.

Parrott, Thomas M. *Shakespearean Comedy.* New York: Oxford University Press, 1949.

——— and Ball, Robert H. *A Short View of Elizabethan Drama.* New York: Charles Scribner's Sons, 1958.

Ralli, A. J. *A History of Shakespearean Criticism.* 2 vols. London: Oxford University Press, 1932.

Rennert, Hugo A. *The Life of Lope de Vega (1562–1635).* Philadelphia: Campion and Co., 1904.

————. *The Spanish Stage in the Time of Lope de Vega.* New York: Hispanic Society of America, 1909.

Reynolds, George F. *The Staging of Elizabethan Plays at the Red Bull Theatre, 1605–1625.* New York: Modern Language Association of America, 1940.

Rosen, William. *Shakespeare and the Craft of Tragedy.* Cambridge, Mass.: Harvard University Press, 1960.

Rossiter, A. P. *English Drama from Early Times to the Elizabethans; Its Background, Origins and Developments.* New York: Hutchinson's University Library, 1950 (Reprinted, New York: Barnes and Noble, 1959).

"Shakespeare: An Annotated Bibliography," *Shakespeare Quarterly* (1924–present). [SQ was originally called *The Shakespeare Association Bulletin.*] Annual bibliography of writings about Shakespeare.

Shakespeare Survey: An Annual Review of Shakespearean Study and Production. New York: Macmillan, 1948–.

Shergold, N. D. *A History of the Spanish Stage from Medieval Times Until the End of the 17th Century.* Oxford: Clarendon Press, 1967.

Shoemaker, William H. *The Multiple Stage in Spain during the Fifteenth and Sixteenth Centuries.* Princeton, N.J.: Princeton University Press, 1935.

Smith, Irwin. *Shakespeare's Blackfriars Playhouse: Its History and Its Design.* New York: New York University Press, 1964.

Sprague, A. C. *Shakespearean Players and Performances.* Cambridge, Mass.: Harvard University Press, 1953.

Wickham, Glynne. See Chapter 6.

Chapter 8: *THE ITALIAN RENAISSANCE*

Bjurstrom, Per. *Giacomo Torelli and Baroque Stage Design.* Stockholm: Almqvist and Wiksell, 1961.

Burckhardt, Jakob C. *The Civilization of the Renaissance in Italy.* 3d ed. New York: Phaidon Publishers, Inc., 1950.

Campbell, Lily Bess. *Scenes and Machines on the English Stage during the Renaissance.* Cambridge: Cambridge University Press, 1923 (Reprinted, New York: Barnes & Noble, 1960).

Duchartre, Pierre L. *The Italian Comedy; The Improvisation, Scenarios, Lives, Attributes, Portraits and Masks of the Illustrious Characters of the Commedia dell'Arte.* Tr. by R. T. Weaver. London: Harrap & Co., Ltd., 1929.

Hathaway, Baxter. *The Age of Criticism; the Late Renaissance in Italy.* Ithaca, N.Y.: Cornell University Press, 1962.

Herrick, Marvin. *Italian Comedy in the Renaissance.* Urbana: University of Illinois Press, 1960.

Hewitt, Barnard (ed.). *The Renaissance Stage; Documents of Serlio, Sabbattini, and Furttenbach.* Coral Gables, Fla.: University of Miami Press, 1958.

Kennard, Joseph. *The Italian Theatre.* 2 vols. New York: W. E. Rudge, 1932.

Kernodle, George. *From Art to Theatre; Form and Convention in the Renaissance.* Chicago: University of Chicago Press, 1943.

Lea, Kathleen M. *Italian Popular Comedy; A Study of the Commedia dell'Arte, 1560–1620.* 2 vols. Oxford: Clarendon Press, 1934.

Nicoll, Allardyce. *Masks, Mimes, and Miracles.* See Chapter 6.

————. *Stuart Masques and the Renaissance Stage.* See Chapter 7.

Schwartz, Isidore A. *The Commedia dell'Arte and Its Influence on French Comedy in the Seventeenth Century.* Paris: H. Samuel, 1933.

Smith, Winifred. *The Commedia dell'Arte.* New York: Columbia University Press, 1912.

Spingarn, Joel E. *A History of Literary Criticism in the Renaissance.* 2d ed. New York: Columbia University Press, 1908.

Symonds, John A. *The Renaissance in Italy.* 7 vols. London: John Murray, Ltd., 1909-37.

Vasari, Giorgio. *Vasari's Lives of the Artists.* New York: Noonday Press, 1957.

Vitruvius. *The Ten Books of Architecture.* Tr. by M. H. Morgan. Cambridge, Mass.: Harvard University Press, 1914.

Weinberg, Bernard. *A History of Literary Criticism in the Italian Renaissance.* 2 vols. Chicago: University of Chicago Press, 1961.

White, John. *The Birth and Rebirth of Pictorial Space.* London: Faber and Faber, 1957.

Worsthorne, S. T. *Venetian Opera in the 17th Century.* Oxford: Clarendon Press, 1954.

Chapter 9: *FRENCH CLASSICISM*

Bjurstrom, Per. *Giacomo Torelli and Baroque Stage Design.* See Chapter 8.

Hubert, Judd D. *Molière and the Comedy of Intellect.* Berkeley: University of California Press, 1962.

Lancaster, H. C. *A History of French Dramatic Literature in the Seventeenth Century.* 5 vols. in 9. Baltimore Johns Hopkins Press, 1929-42.

Lawrenson, T. E. *The French Stage in the XVIIth Century: A Study in the Advent of the Italian Order.* Manchester: Manchester University Press, 1957.

Lockert, Lacy. *Studies in French Classical Tragedy.* Nashville: Vanderbilt University Press, 1958.

Lough, John. *Paris Theatre Audiences in the Seventeenth and Eighteenth Centuries.* London: Oxford University Press, 1957.

Palmer, John. *Molière.* New York: Brewer and Warren, 1930.

Tilley, A. A. *Molière.* Cambridge: University Press, 1936.

Turnell, Martin. *The Classical Moment; Studies in Corneille, Molière and Racine.* New York: New Directions, 1948.

Vinaver, Eugene. *Racine and Poetic Tragedy.* Tr. by P. M. Jones. Manchester: Manchester University Press, 1955.

Wiley, W.L. *The Early Public Theatre in France.* Cambridge, Mass.: Harvard University Press, 1960.

Wright, C. H. C. *French Classicism.* Cambridge, Mass.: Harvard University Press, 1920.

Chapter 10: *THE RESTORATION AND THE EIGHTEENTH CENTURY*

Beijer, Agne. *Court Theatres of Drottningholm and Gripsholm.* Tr. by G. L. Frolich. Malmo: J. Kroon, 1933.

Bernbaum, Ernest. *The Drama of Sensibility; A Sketch of the History of Sentimental Comedy and Domestic Tragedy, 1696-1780.* Cambridge, Mass.: Harvard University Press, 1915.

Boas, Frederick S. *An Introduction to Eighteenth Century Drama, 1700-1780.* New York: Oxford University Press, 1953.

Bredsdorff, Elias *et al. An Introduction to Scandinavian Literature from the Earliest Time to Our Day.* Copenhagen: E. Munksgaard, 1951.

Bruford, Walter H. *Theatre, Drama, and Audience in Goethe's Germany.* London: Routledge & Kegan Paul, Ltd., 1957.

Burnim, Kalman. *David Garrick, Director.* Pittsburgh: Pittsburgh University Press, 1961.

Campbell, Lily B. "A History of Costuming on the English Stage between 1660 and 1823," *University of Wisconsin Studies in Language and Literature,* II (1918), 187-223.

Cibber, Colley. *An Apology for the Life of Mr. Colley Cibber.* London: J. Watts, 1740. Reprinted many times.

Cook, John A. *Neo-Classic Drama in Spain; Theory and Practice.* Dallas: Southern Methodist University Press, 1959.

Dobrée, Bonamy. *Restoration Comedy, 1660-1720.* Oxford: Clarendon Press, 1924.

_____. *Restoration Tragedy, 1660-1720.* Oxford: Clarendon Press, 1929.

Downer, Alan S. "Nature to Advantage Dressed: Eighteenth Century Acting," *PMLA* (1943), 1002-37.

"English Literature, 1660-1800; A Current Bibliography," *Philological Quarterly* (1926-present). Annual list of publications.

Fitzgerald, Percy H. *The Sheridans.* 2 vols. London: R. Bentley, 1886.

Goldoni, Carlo. *Memoirs of Carlo Goldoni.* Tr. by John Black. New York: Alfred A. Knopf, Inc., 1926.

Gozzi, Carlo. *The Memoirs of Count Carlo Gozzi.* Tr. by J. A. Symonds. 2 vols. London: J. C. Nimmo, 1890.

Hawkins, Frederick. *The French Stage in the Eighteenth Century.* 2 vols. London: Chapman & Hall, Ltd., 1888.

Hotson, Leslie. *The Commonwealth and Restoration Stage.* Cambridge, Mass.: Harvard University Press, 1928.

Joseph, Bertram. *The Tragic Actor.* New York: Theatre Arts Books, 1959.

Kennard, Joseph. See Chapter 7.

Krutch, Joseph W. *Comedy and Conscience after the Restoration.* New York: Columbia University Press, 1949.

Lancaster, H. C. *French Tragedy in the Time of Louis XV and Voltaire, 1715-1774.* Baltimore: Johns Hopkins Press, 1950.

_____. *Sunset; A History of Parisian Drama in the Last Years of Louis XIV, 1701-1715.* Baltimore: Johns Hopkins Press, 1945.

The London Stage, 1660-1800. Carbondale: Southern Illinois University Press, 1960-. Not yet completed.

Lynch, James J. *Box, Pit and Gallery; Stage and Society in Johnson's London.* Berkeley: University of California Press, 1953.

Mayor, A. Hyatt. *The Bibiena Family.* New York: Bittner, 1945.

Melcher, Edith. *Stage Realism in France from Diderot to Antoine.* Bryn Mawr, Penn.: Bryn Mawr College, 1928.

Nicoll, Allardyce. *History of English Drama, 1660-1900.* 6 vols. London: Cambridge University Press, 1955-59.

Odell, G. C. D. *Shakespeare from Betterton to Irving.* 2 vols. New York: Charles Scribner's Sons, 1920.

Palmer, J. L. *The Comedy of Manners.* London: Bell & Sons, Ltd., 1913.

Pascal, Roy. *The German Sturm und Drang.* Manchester: Manchester University Press, 1953.

Scholz, Janos. *Baroque and Romantic Stage Design.* New York: Dutton, 1962.

Slonim, Marc. *Russian Theatre from the Empire to the Soviets.* Cleveland: World Publishing Co., 1961.

Southern, Richard. *The Georgian Playhouse.* London: Pleiades Books, 1948.

_____. *Changeable Scenery; Its Origin and Development in the British Theatre.* London: Faber & Faber, Ltd., 1952.

Summers, Montague. *The Playhouse of Pepys.* London: Paul, Trench, Trubner & Co., 1935.

_____. *The Restoration Theatre.* London: Paul, Trench, Trubner & Co., 1934.

Thaler, Alwin, *Shakespere to Sheridan.* Cambridge, Mass.: Harvard University Press, 1922.

Theatrical Designs from the Baroque through Neo-Classicism. 3 vols. New York: H. Bittner, 1940.

Willoughby, Leonard A. *The Classical Age of German Literature, 1748–1805.* London: Oxford University Press, 1926.

Chapter 11: *ROMANTIC DRAMA AND MELODRAMA*

Abrams, M. H. *The Mirror and the Lamp; Romantic Theory and the Critical Tradition.* New York: Oxford University Press, 1953.

Arvin, Neil S. *Eugène Scribe and the French Theatre, 1815–60.* Cambridge, Mass.: Harvard University Press, 1924.

Bernheim, A. L. *The Business of the Theatre.* New York: Actors' Equity Association, 1932.

Birdoff, Harry. *The World's Greatest Hit: "Uncle Tom's Cabin."* New York: S. F. Vanni, 1947.

Booth, Michael R. *English Melodrama.* London: Herbert Jenkins, 1965.

Carlson, Marvin. *The Theatre of the French Revolution.* Ithaca: Cornell University Press, 1966.

Clement, N. H. *Romanticism in France.* New York: Modern Language Association of America, 1939.

Coad, O. S. and Mims, Edwin, Jr. *The American Stage* (Vol. XIV of *The Pageant of America*). New Haven, Conn.: Yale University Press, 1929.

Disher, Maurice. *Blood and Thunder; Mid-Victorian Melodrama and Its Origins.* London: Muller, 1949.

———. *Melodrama; Plots that Thrilled.* New York: The Macmillan Company, 1954.

Downer, Alan S. "Players and the Painted Stage: Nineteenth Century Acting," *PMLA*, LXI (1946), 522–76.

Felheim, Marvin. *The Theater of Augustin Daly: An Account of the Late Nineteenth Century American Stage.* Cambridge, Mass.: Harvard University Press, 1956.

George, A. J. *The Development of French Romanticism.* Syracuse, N.Y.: Syracuse University Press, 1955.

Hewitt, Barnard. *Theatre USA, 1668–1957.* New York: McGraw-Hill Book Co., Inc., 1959.

Hughes, Glenn. *A History of the American Theatre, 1700–1950.* New York: Samuel French, Inc., 1951.

Joseph, Bertram. *The Tragic Actor.* See Chapter 10.

Kaufmann, F. W. *German Dramatists of the Nineteenth Century.* Los Angeles: Lymanhouse, 1940.

Lacey, Alexander. *Pixérécourt and the French Romantic Drama.* Toronto: University of Toronto Press, 1928.

Lucas, F. L. *The Decline and Fall of the Romantic Ideal.* New York: The Macmillan Company, 1936.

Mammen, Edward W. *The Old Stock Company School of Acting.* Boston: The Public Library, 1945.

Matthews, Brander. *French Dramatists of the Nineteenth Century.* 5th ed. New York: Charles Scribner's Sons, 1914.

——— and Hutton, Laurence. *Actors and Actresses of Great Britain and the United States, from the Days of David Garrick to the Present Time.* 5 vols. New York: Cassell, 1886.

Melcher, Edith. *Stage Realism in France from Diderot to Antoine.* See Chapter 10.

Moody, Richard. *America Takes the Stage; Romanticism in American Drama and Theatre, 1750–1900.* Bloomington: Indiana University Press, 1955.

Moses, Montrose J. and Brown, John M. *The American Theatre as Seen by Its Critics, 1752–1934.* New York: W. W. Norton, 1934.

Nicoll, Allardyce. See Chapter 10.

Odell, G. C. D. *Annals of the New York Stage.* 15 vols. New York: Columbia University Press, 1927–49.

———. See Chapter 10.

Peacock, Ronald. *Goethe's Major Plays; An Essay.* New York: Hill and Wang, 1959.

Quinn, Arthur H. *A History of the American Drama from the Beginning to the Civil War.* 2d ed. New York: Appleton-Century-Crofts, 1943.

———. *A History of the American Drama from the Civil War to the Present Day.* 2d ed. New York: Appleton-Century-Crofts, 1949.

Robertson, J. G. *The Life and Work of Goethe, 1749–1832.* London: Routledge & Kegan Paul, Ltd., 1932.

"The Romantic Movement; A Current Selective and Critical Bibliography," *English Literary History* (1937–49), *Philological Quarterly* (1950–present). An annual list of publications.

Rowell, George. *The Victorian Theatre.* London: Oxford University Press, 1956.

Sachs, Edwin O. and Woodrow, E. A. E. *Modern Opera Houses and Theatres.* 3 vols. London: Batsford, 1897–98.

Scholz, Janos. *Baroque and Romantic Stage Design.* See Chapter 10.

Southern, Richard. See Chapter 10.

Stratman, C. J. *Bibliography of the American Theatre. Excluding New York City.* Chicago: Loyola University Press, 1965.

Vardac, A. N. *Stage to Screen; Theatrical Method from Garrick to Griffith.* Cambridge, Mass.: Harvard University Press, 1949.

Varneke, B. V. *History of the Russian Theatre; Seventeenth through Nineteenth Century.* Tr. by Boris Brasol. New York: The Macmillan Company, 1951.

"Victorian Bibliography for /1932-/," *Modern Philology,* XXX (1932–33)-LIV (1956–57); *Victorian Studies,* I (1957–58)—.

Walzel, Oskar F. *German Romanticism.* New York: G. P. Putnam's Sons, 1932.

Watson, Ernest B. *Sheridan to Robertson: A Study of the Nineteenth Century London Stage.* Cambridge, Mass.: Harvard University Press, 1926.

Wellek, René. *A History of Modern Literary Criticism.* 2 vols. New Haven, Conn.: Yale University Press, 1955.

Willoughby, Leonard A. *The Romantic Movement in Germany.* New York: Oxford University Press, 1930.

Wilson, Garff. *A History of American Acting.* Bloomington: Indiana University Press, 1966.

Chapter 12: *THE ORIENTAL THEATRE*

Arlington, Lewis C. *The Chinese Drama from the Earliest Times until Today.* Shanghai: Kelly and Walsh, Ltd., 1930.

Bharata. *Natyasastra.* Tr. by Manmohan Ghose. Bengal: The Royal Asiatic Society, 1950.

Bowers, Faubion. *Japanese Theatre.* New York: Heritage House, 1952.

Brandon, James R. *The Theatre of Southeast Asia.* Cambridge: Harvard University Press, 1967.

Ernst, Earle. *The Kabuki Theatre.* New York: Oxford University Press, 1956.

Gargi, Balwant. *Theatre in India.* New York: Theatre Arts Books, 1962.

Gupta, Chandra B. *The Indian Theatre.* Benares: Motilal Banarasidass, 1954.

Haar, Francis. *Japanese Theatre in Highlight; a Pictorial Commentary.* Tokyo: Charles E. Tuttle Co., 1952.

Hironaga, Shuzaburo. *Bunraku, Japan's Unique Puppet Theatre.* Tokyo: Tokyo News Service, 1964.

Kawatake, Shigetoshi. *Kabuki; Japanese Drama.* Tokyo: Foreign Affairs Association of Japan, 1956.

Keene, Donald (trans.). *Major Plays of Chikamatsu.* New York: Columbia University Press, 1961.

Keith, A. Berriedale. *The Sanskrit Drama.* London: Oxford University Press, 1924.

Kincaid, Zoe. *Kabuki, the Popular Stage of Japan.* London: Macmillan and Co., 1925.

Lombard, Frank A. *An Outline History of Japanese Drama.* London: George Allen and Unwin, Ltd., 1928.

Mathur, Jagdesh. *Drama in Rural India.* New York: Asia Publishing House, 1964.

O'Neill, P. G. *A Guide to Nō.* Tokyo: Hinoki Shoten, 1953.

Pronko, Leonard. *Theatre East and West: Perspectives Toward a Total Theatre.* Berkeley: University of California Press, 1967.

Scott, A. C. *The Classical Theatre of China.* New York: Macmillan, 1957.

_____. *The Kabuki Theatre of Japan.* London: George Allen and Unwin, Ltd., 1955.

_____. *Traditional Chinese Plays.* Madison: University of Wisconsin Press, 1967.

Shaver, Ruth M. *Kabuki Costume.* Tokyo: Charles E. Tuttle Co., 1966.

Waley, Arthur. *The Nō Plays of Japan.* New York: Alfred A. Knopf, 1922.

Zucker, Adolf E. *The Chinese Theatre.* Boston: Little, Brown and Co., 1925.

PART THREE

Works Applicable to Part Three

Bentley, Eric. *The Playwright as Thinker; A Study of Drama in Modern Times.* New York: Reynal & Company, Inc., 1946.

Brustein, Robert. *The Theatre of Revolt; An Approach to Modern Drama.* Boston: Little, Brown and Co., 1964.

Cheney, Sheldon. *The New Movement in the Theatre.* New York: Mitchell Kennerley, 1914.

Clark, Barrett H. and Freedley, George. *A History of Modern Drama.* New York: Appleton-Century-Crofts, 1947.

Cole, Toby (ed.). *Playwrights on Playwriting; The Meaning and Making of Modern Drama from Ibsen to Ionesco.* New York: Hill and Wang, 1961.

Downer, Alan S. *Fifty Years of American Drama, 1900–1950.* Chicago: Henry Regnery Co., 1951.

Fuerst, Walter R. and Hume, Samuel J. *Twentieth Century Stage Decoration.* 2 vols. London: Alfred A. Knopf, Inc., 1928.

Garten, H. F. *Modern German Drama.* New York: Essential Books, 1959.

Gassner, John. *Form and Idea in the Modern Theatre.* New York: Holt, Rinehart and Winston, Inc., 1956.

_____. *The Theatre in Our Times: A Survey of the Men, Materials and Movements in the Modern Theatre.* New York: Crown Publishers, 1954.

Gorchakov, Nikolai A. *The Theater in Soviet Russia.* Tr. by Edgar Lehman. New York: Columbia University Press, 1957.

Gorelik, Mordecai. *New Theatres for Old.* New York: Samuel French, 1940.

Houghton, Norris. *Moscow Rehearsals; An Account of Methods of Production in the Soviet Theatre.* New York; Harcourt, Brace & World, Inc., 1936.

Krutch, Joseph W. *The American Drama since 1918.* Rev. ed. New York: G. Braziller, 1957.

Lumley, Frederick. *Trends in Twentieth Century Drama; A Survey Since Ibsen and Shaw*. 2d ed. London: Barrie and Rockliff, 1960.

Macgowan, Kenneth and Jones, Robert E. *Continental Stagecraft*. New York: Harcourt, Brace & World, Inc., 1922.

Mackay, Constance D. *The Little Theatre in the United States*. New York: Holt, Rinehart and Winston, Inc., 1917.

Melchinger, Siegfried. *The Concise Encyclopedia of Modern Drama*. New York: Horizon Press, 1964.

Miller, Anna Irene. *The Independent Theatre in Europe, 1887 to the Present*. New York: Ray Long and Richard R. Smith, 1931.

Moderwell, Hiram K. *The Theatre of To-day*. New York: Dodd, Mead & Co., 1925.

Moussinac, Leon. *The New Movement in the Theatre; A Survey of Recent Developments in Europe and America*. London: Batsford, 1931.

Seltzer, Daniel (ed.). *The Modern Theatre; Readings and Documents*. Boston: Little, Brown and Co., 1967.

Simonson, Lee. *The Stage is Set*. New York: Dover Publications, Inc., 1932.

Slonim, Marc. *Russian Theatre from the Empire to the Soviets*. Cleveland: World Publishing Co., 1961.

Wellek, René. *A History of Modern Criticism*. Vols. 3-4. New Haven: Yale University Press, 1965.

Williams, Raymond. *Drama from Ibsen to Eliot*. London: Chatto & Windus, Ltd., 1952.

Chapter 13: *REALISM AND NATURALISM*

Antoine, André. *Memories of the Theatre Libre*. Tr. by Marvin Carlson. Coral Gables: University of Miami Press, 1964.

Becker, George J. *Documents of Modern Literary Realism*. Princeton, N.J.: Princeton University Press, 1963.

Bradbrook, M. C. *Ibsen, the Norwegian*. London: Chatto & Windus, Ltd., 1946.

Carter, Lawson A. *Zola and the Theatre*. New Haven: Yale University Press, 1963.

Clurman, Harold. *The Fervent Years; The Story of the Group Theatre in the Thirties*. New York: Hill and Wang, 1957.

Northam, John. *Ibsen's Dramatic Method; A Study of the Prose Dramas*. London: Faber & Faber, Ltd., 1953.

Sayler, Oliver M. (ed.). *Max Reinhardt and His Theatre*. New York: Brentano's, 1926.

Sondel, Bess S. *Zola's Naturalistic Theory with Particular Reference to the Drama*. Chicago: University of Chicago Libraries, 1939.

Stone, Edward. *What Was Naturalism? Materials for an Answer*. New York: Appleton-Century-Crofts, 1959.

Waxman, S. M. *Antoine and the Théâtre Libre*. Cambridge, Mass.: Harvard University Press, 1926.

Zucker, A. E. *Ibsen, the Master Builder*. New York: Holt, Rinehart and Winston, Inc., 1929.

Chapter 14: *REVOLTS AGAINST REALISM*

Appia, Adolphe. *The Work of Living Art and Man Is the Measure of All Things*. Coral Gables, Fla.: University of Miami Press, 1960.

Bablet, Denis. *Edward Gordon Craig*. New York: Theatre Arts Books, 1967.

Balakian, Anna E. *Surrealism*. New York: Farrar, Straus & Co., 1959.

Brecht, Bertolt. *Brecht on Theatre*. Tr. by John Willett. New York: Hill and Wang, 1965.

566

Breton, André. *What Is Surrealism?* London: Faber & Faber, Ltd., 1936.

Cornell, Kenneth. *The Symbolist Movement.* New Haven, Conn.: Yale University Press, 1951.

Craig, Edward Gordon. *On the Art of the Theatre.* 2d ed. Boston: Small, Maynard, 1924.

Dahlstrom, C. E. W. L. *Strindberg's Dramatic Expressionism.* Vol. VII of *University of Michigan Publications, Language and Literature.* Ann Arbor: University of Michigan Press, 1930.

Esslin, Martin. *Brecht; The Man and His Work.* Garden City, N.Y.: Doubleday & Company, Inc., 1960.

Fowlie, Wallace. *Age of Surrealism.* Bloomington: Indiana University Press, 1960.

Lehmann, Andrew G. *The Symbolist Aesthetic in France, 1885–1895.* Oxford: Blackwell & Mott, Ltd., 1950.

Ley-Piscator, Maria. *The Piscator Experiment; The Political Theatre.* New York: James H. Heineman, Inc., 1967.

Marshall, Norman. *The Other Theatre.* London: J. Lehmann, 1947.

Samuel, Richard and Thomas, R. H. *Expressionism in German Life, Literature and the Theatre (1910–1924).* Cambridge: Heffer & Sons, Ltd., 1939.

Sokel, Walter H. *The Writer in Extremis: Expressionism in Twentieth-Century German Literature.* Stanford, Calif.: Stanford University Press, 1959.

Stein, Jack M. *Richard Wagner and the Synthesis of the Arts.* Detroit: Wayne State University Press, 1960.

Wagner, Richard. *Opera and Drama.* Tr. by Edwin Evans. London: W. Reeves, 1913.

Willett, John. *The Theatre of Bertolt Brecht.* New York: New Directions, 1959.

Chapter 15: *THE THEATRE SINCE WORLD WAR II*

Artaud, Antonin. *The Theatre and Its Double.* Tr. by Mary C. Richards. New York: Grove Press, 1958.

Bentley, Eric. *In Search of Theatre.* New York: Alfred A. Knopf, Inc., 1953.

Bowers, Faubion. *Broadway, USSR; Theatre, Ballet and Entertainment in Russia Today.* New York: Thomas Nelson & Sons, 1959.

Chiari, Joseph. *The Contemporary French Theatre; the Flight from Naturalism.* London: Barrie and Rockliff, 1958.

Donoghue, Denis. *The Third Voice: Modern British and American Verse Drama.* Princeton, N.J.: Princeton University Press, 1959.

Esslin, Martin. *The Theatre of the Absurd.* Garden City, N.Y.: Doubleday & Company, Inc., 1961.

Fowlie, Wallace. *Dionysus in Paris: A Guide to Contemporary French Theater.* New York: Meridian Books, 1960.

Gassner, John. *Theatre at the Crossroads; Plays and Playwrights of the Mid-Century American Stage.* New York: Holt, Rinehart and Winston, Inc., 1960.

Grossvogel, David I. *The Self-Conscious Stage in Modern French Drama.* New York: Columbia University Press, 1958.

Guicharnaud, Jacques. *Modern French Theatre from Giraudoux to Beckett.* New Haven Conn.: Yale University Press, 1961.

Hainaux, René (ed.). *Stage Design throughout the World since 1935.* New York: Theatre Arts Books, 1956.

Hainaux, René (ed.). *Stage Design throughout the World since 1950.* New York: Theatre Arts Books, 1964.

Houghton, Norris. *Return Engagement: A Postscript to "Moscow Rehearsals."* New York: Holt, Rinehart and Winston, Inc., 1962.

Kirby, Michael. *Happenings.* New York: E. P. Dutton & Co., 1965.

567

Magriel, Paul. *Chronicles of the American Dance*. New York: Holt, Rinehart and Winston, Inc., 1948.

Price, Julia. *The Off-Broadway Theatre*. New York: Scarecrow Press, 1962.

Richman, Robert (ed.). *The Arts at Mid-Century*. New York: Horizon Press, Inc., 1954. Contains separate chapters on the theatre in each of the following countries: France, Italy, Germany, England, and U.S.

Smith, Cecil. *Musical Comedy in America*. New York: Theatre Arts Books, 1950.

Styan, J. L. *The Dark Comedy; The Development of Modern Comic Tragedy*. Cambridge: Cambridge University Press, 1962.

Taylor, John R. *Anger and After; A Guide to the New British Drama*. London: Methuen & Co., Ltd., 1962.

Weales, Gerald. *American Drama Since World War II*. New York: Harcourt, Brace & World, 1962.

PART FOUR

General Works

Albright, H. D., Halstead, W. P., and Mitchell, Lee. *Principles of Theatre Art*. 2d ed. Boston: Houghton Mifflin Company, 1968.

Clay, James H. and Krempel, Daniel. *The Theatrical Image*. New York: McGraw-Hill Book Co., Inc., 1967.

Dolman, John, Jr. *The Art of Play Production*. Rev. ed. New York: Harper & Row, Publishers, 1948.

Gassner, John. *Producing the Play*. Rev. ed. New York: Holt, Rinehart and Winston, Inc., 1953.

Heffner, Hubert, Selden, Samuel, and Sellman, H. D. *Modern Theatre Practice*. 4th ed. New York: Appleton-Century-Crofts, 1959.

Chapter 16: *THE PLAYWRIGHT AND THE PRODUCER*

Gibson, William. *The Seesaw Log: A Chronicle of the Stage Production with the Text of "Two for the Seesaw."* New York: Alfred A. Knopf, Inc., 1959.

Plummer, Gail. *The Business of Show Business*. New York: Harper & Row, Publishers; 1961.

Savan, Bruce. *Your Career in the Theatre*. Garden City, N.Y.: Doubleday & Company, Inc., 1961.

See also those works listed under Chapter 3.

Chapter 17: *THE DIRECTOR*

Canfield, Curtis. *The Craft of Play Directing*. New York: Holt, Rinehart and Winston, Inc., 1963.

Cole, Toby and Chinoy, Helen K. (eds.). *Directing the Play; A Source Book of Stagecraft*. Indianapolis: Bobbs-Merrill, 1953.

Dean, Alexander. *Fundamentals of Play Directing*. Revised by Lawrence Carra. New York: Holt, Rinehart and Winston, Inc., 1965.

Dietrich, John. *Play Direction*. Englewood Cliffs, N.J.: Prentice-Hall, 1953.

Gorchakov, Nikolai. *Stanislavski Directs*. Tr. by Miriam Goldina. New York: Funk & Wagnalls Co., Inc., 1954.

Gruver, Elbert. *The Stage Manager's Handbook*. New York: Harper & Row, Publishers, 1953.

Hunt, Hugh. *The Director in the Theatre*. London: Routledge & Kegan Paul, Ltd., 1954.

Machlin, Evangeline. *Speech for the Stage*. New York: Theatre Arts Books, 1966.

Shaw, George Bernard. *The Art of Rehearsal.* New York: Samual French, 1928.

Sievers, W. David. *Directing for the Theatre.* Dubuque, Iowa: William C. Brown Company, Publishers, 1961.

Chapter 18: *THE ACTOR*

Albright, H. D. *Working up a Part.* 2d ed. Boston: Houghton Mifflin Company, 1959.

Blunt, Jerry. *The Composite Art of Acting.* New York: Macmillan, 1966.

Boleslavsky, Richard. *Acting; The First Six Lessons.* New York: Theatre Arts Books, 1933.

Burton, Hal (ed.). *Great Acting.* New York: Hill and Wang, 1967.

Chekhov, Michael. *To the Actor on the Technique of Acting.* New York: Harper & Row, Publishers, 1953.

Cole, Toby and Chinoy, Helen K. (eds.). *Actors on Acting; The Theories, Techniques, and Practices of the Great Actors of All Times as Told in Their Own Words.* New York: Crown Publishers, Inc., 1949.

Diderot, Denis. *The Paradox of Acting.* Archer, William. *Masks or Faces?* New York: Hill and Wang, 1957.

Funke, Lewis and Booth, John E. *Actors Talk about Acting; Fourteen Interviews with Stars of the Theatre.* New York: Random House, Inc., 1961.

Lessac, Arthur. *The Use and Training of the Human Voice.* New York: DBS Publications, Inc., 1967.

Lewes, George. *On Actors and the Art of Acting.* New York: Grove Press, 1957.

McGaw, Charles J. *Acting Is Believing.* 2d ed. New York: Holt, Rinehart and Winston, Inc., 1966.

Machlin, Evangeline. *Speech for the Stage.* See Chapter 16.

Matthews, Brander (ed.). *Papers on Acting.* New York: Hill and Wang, 1958.

Oxenford, Lyn. *Design for Movement; A Textbook on Stage Management.* New York: Theatre Arts Books, 1952.

———. *Playing Period Plays.* London: Miller, Ltd., 1958.

Rockwood, Jerome. *The Craftsmen of Dionysus; An Approach to Acting.* Chicago: Scott, Foresman and Co., 1966.

Spolin, Viola. *Improvisation for the Theatre.* Evanston: Northwestern University Press, 1963.

Stanislavski, Constantin. *An Actor Prepares.* Tr. by Elizabeth Reynolds Hapgood. New York: Theatre Arts Books, 1936.

———. *Building a Character.* Tr. by Elizabeth Reynolds Hapgood. New York: Theatre Arts Books, 1949.

———. *Creating a Role.* Tr. by Elizabeth Reynolds Hapgood. New York: Theatre Arts Books, 1961.

Strickland, F. Cowles. *The Technique of Acting.* New York: McGraw-Hill Book Co., Inc., 1956.

Young, Stark. *Theatre Practice.* New York: Charles Scribner's Sons, 1926.

Chapter 19: *THE SCENE DESIGNER*

Anderson, Donald M. *Elements of Design.* New York: Holt, Rinehart and Winston, Inc., 1961.

Boyle, Walden P. *Central and Flexible Staging.* Berkeley: University of California Press, 1956.

Burris-Meyer, Harold and Cole, Edward C. *Scenery for the Theatre.* Boston: Little, Brown and Company, 1947.

———. *Theatres and Auditoriums.* 2d ed. New York: Reinhold Publishing Corp., 1964.

Cogswell, Margaret (ed.). *The Ideal Theater: Eight Concepts.* New York: The American Federation of Arts, 1962.

Conway, Heather. *Stage Properties.* London: Jenkins, Ltd., 1959.

Friederich, Willard J. and Fraser, John H. *Scenery Design for the Amateur Stage.* New York: The Macmillan Company, 1950.

Gamble, William B. *The Development of Scenic Art and Stage Machinery.* Rev. ed. New York: New York Public Library, 1928.

Gillette, A. S. *Stage Scenery; Its Construction and Rigging.* New York: Harper & Row, Publishers, 1959.

Gillette, A. S. *An Introduction to Scene Design.* New York: Harper & Row, Publishers, 1967.

Graves, Maitland. *The Art of Color and Design.* 2d ed. New York: McGraw-Hill Book Co., Inc., 1951.

Jones, Margo. *Theatre-in-the-Round.* New York: Holt, Rinehart and Winston, Inc., 1951.

Jones, Robert E. *The Dramatic Imagination.* New York: Meredith Publishing Co., 1941.

Larson, Orville K. (ed.) *Scene Design for Stage and Screen Readings on the Aesthetics and Methodology of Scene Design for Drama, Opera, Musical Comedy, Ballet, Motion Pictures, Television and Arena Theatre.* East Lansing: Michigan State University Press, 1961.

Mielziner, Jo. *Designing for the Theatre.* New York: Athenaeum, 1965.

Oenslager, Donald. *Scenery Then and Now.* New York: W. W. Norton & Company, Inc., 1936.

Parker, W. Oren and Smith, Harvey K. *Scene Design and Stage Lighting.* 2d ed. New York: Holt, Rinehart and Winston, Inc., 1968.

Philippi, Herbert. *Stagecraft and Scene Design.* Boston: Houghton Mifflin Company, 1953.

Selden, Samuel and Sellman, H. D. *Stage Scenery and Lighting.* 3d ed. New York: Appleton-Century-Crofts, 1959.

Simonson, Lee. *The Art of Scenic Design.* New York: Harper & Row, Publishers, 1950.

Southern, Richard. *The Open Stage.* New York: Theatre Arts Books, 1959.

Chapter 20: *THE COSTUMER*

Anderson, Donald M. See Chapter 19.

Barton, Lucy. *Historic Costume for the Stage.* Boston: Baker's Plays, 1935.

Boehn, Max von. *Modes and Manners.* Tr. by Joan Joshua. 4 vols. Philadelphia: J. B. Lippincott Co., 1932–36.

Corson, Richard. *Stage Make-up.* 4th ed. New York: Appleton-Century-Crofts; 1967.

Cunnington, Cecil W. and Cunnington, Phillis. *Handbook of English Costume* [Separate volumes devoted to Medieval, 16th Century, 17th Century, 18th Century and 19th Century]. London: Faber & Faber, Ltd., 1952–66.

Davenport, Millia. *The Book of Costume.* 2 vols. New York: Crown Publishers, Inc., 1948.

Graves, Maitland. See Chapter 19.

Hiler, Hilaire and Hiler, Meyer. *Bibliography of Costume.* New York: H. W. Wilson Co., 1939.

Houston, Mary G. *Ancient Greek, Roman and Byzantine Costume and Decoration.* 2d ed. London: Black, Ltd., 1947.

———. *Medieval Costume in England and France, the 13th, 14th and 15th Centuries.* London: Black, Ltd., 1939.

Jones, Robert E. See Chapter 19.

Kohler, Karl. *A History of Costume.* Ed. and augmented by Emma von Sichart. Tr. by A. K. Dallas. Philadelphia: McKay, 1928.

Komisarjevsky, Theodore. *The Costume of the Theatre.* New York: Holt, Rinehart and Winston, Inc., 1932.

Laver, James. *Costume of the Western World; Early Tudor, 1485–1558.* London: Harrap & Co., Ltd., 1951.

Monro, Isabel S. and Cook, Dorothy E. *Costume Index.* New York: H. W. Wilson Co., 1937. Supplement, 1957.

Motley. *Designing and Making Stage Costumes.* London: Studio Vista, Ltd., 1964.

Norris, Herbert. *Costume and Fashion* [Separate volumes devoted to Earlier Ages; 1485–1603; 19th century]. London: Dent & Sons, Ltd., 1925–38.

Payne, Blanche. *History of Costume from the Ancient Egyptians to the Twentieth Century.* New York: Harper & Row, Publishers, 1965.

Prisk, Berneice. *Stage Costume Handbook.* New York: Harper & Row, Publishers, 1966.

Reynolds, Graham. *Costume of the Western World; Elizabethan and Jacobean, 1558–1625.* London: Harrap & Co., Ltd., 1951.

Strenkovsky, Serge. *The Art of Make-up.* New York: E. P. Dutton & Co., Inc., 1937.

Chapter 21: *THE LIGHTING DESIGNER*

Anderson, Donald M. See Chapter 19.

Bellman, Willard F. *Lighting the Stage: Art and Practice.* San Francisco: Chandler Publishing Co., 1967.

Burris-Meyer, Harold and Mallory, Vincent. *Sound in the Theatre.* Mineola, N.Y.: Radio Magazines, Inc., 1959.

Fuchs, Theodore. *Stage Lighting.* Boston: Little, Brown and Company, 1929.

Graves, Maitland. See Chapter 19.

Green, Michael. *Stage Noises and Effects.* London: Jenkins, Ltd., 1958.

Jones, Robert E. See Chapter 19.

McCandless, Stanley R. *A Method of Lighting the Stage.* 4th ed. New York: Theatre Arts Books, 1958.

Napier, Frank. *Noises Off; A Handbook of Sound Effects.* London: Muller, Ltd., 1936.

Parker, W. Oren and Smith, Harvey K. See Chapter 19.

Rubin, Joel E. and Watson, Leland. *Theatrical Lighting Practice.* New York: Theatre Arts Books, 1954.

Selden, Samuel. See Chapter 19.

Williams, Rollo G. *The Technique of Stage Lighting.* 2d ed. New York: Pitman Publishing Corp., 1958.

Chapter 22: *MUSIC AND DANCE*

Chujoy, Anatole. *The Dance Encyclopedia.* New York: A. S. Barnes & Company, 1949.

Dallin, Leon. *Techniques of Twentieth Century Composition.* Dubuque, Iowa: William C. Brown Company, Publishers, 1957.

Engel, Lehmann. *Planning and Producing the Musical Show.* New York: Crown Publishers, Inc., 1957.

Fleming, William and Veinus, Abraham. *Understanding Music; Style, Structure, and History.* New York: Holt, Rinehart and Winston, Inc., 1958.

Groves' Dictionary of Music and Musicians. 9 vols. 5th ed. London: Macmillan & Co., Ltd., 1954.

H'Doubler, Margaret. *Dance; A Creative Art Experience.* 2d ed. Madison: University of Wisconsin Press, 1957.

Horst, Louis and Russell, Carroll. *Modern Dance Forms in Relation to the Other Modern Arts.* San Francisco: Impulse Publications, 1961.

Jacob, Gordon. *The Composer and His Art.* New York: Oxford University Press, 1955.

Leichtentritt, Hugo. *Musical Form.* Cambridge, Mass.: Harvard University Press, 1951.

Lippincott, Gertrude (ed.). *Dance Production: Music, Costumes, Staging, Decor, Lighting, Photography, Make-up, Planning and Rehearsing.* Washington: Published for National Section on Dance by the American Association for Health, Physical Education and Recreation, 1956.

Lockhart, Aileene. *Modern Dance Building and Teaching Lessons.* 2d ed. Dubuque, Iowa: William C. Brown Company, Publishers, 1957.

Magriel, Paul. *A Bibliography of Dancing.* New York: H. W. Wilson Co., 1936. Supplement, 1941.

Melcer, Fannie Helen. *Staging the Dance.* Dubuque: William C. Brown Company, 1955.

Newman, William S. *Understanding Music: An Introduction to Music's Elements, Styles, and Forms.* 2d ed. New York: Harper & Row, Publishers, 1961.

Percival, Rachel. *Discovering Dance.* Philadelphia: Dufour Editions, 1964.

Wigman, Mary. *The Language of Dance.* Middletown, Conn.: Wesleyan University Press, 1966.

Chapter 23: *THE THEATRE AS A PROFESSION*

Benner, Ralph. *The Young Actor's Guide to Hollywood.* New York: Coward-McCann, 1964.

Davis, Jed H. and Watkins, Mary J. *Children's Theatre: Play Production for the Child Audience.* New York: Harper & Row, Publishers, 1960.

Fisher, Caroline and Robertson, Hazel. *Children and the Theatre.* Rev. ed. Stanford, Calif.: Stanford University Press, 1950.

Gard, Robert E. and Burley, Gertrude. *Community Theatre, Idea and Achievement.* New York: Meredith Publishing Co., 1959.

Harmon, Charlotte. *How to Break into the Theatre.* New York: The Dial Press, Inc., 1961.

Novick, Julius. *Beyond Broadway.* New York: Hill and Wang, 1968.

Savan, Bruce. See Chapter 16.

Siks, Geraldine and Dunnington, Hazel. *Children's Theatre and Creative Dramatics.* Seattle: University of Washington Press, 1961.

Vreeland, Frank. *Opportunities in Acting.* New York: Grosset & Dunlap, Inc., 1951.

Ward, Winifred. *Playmaking with Children.* 2d ed. New York: Appleton-Century-Crofts, 1957.

Young, John Wray. *The Community Theatre and How It Works.* New York: Harper & Row, Publishers, 1957.

INDEX

Italic numbers denote pages on which illustrations appear.

Abe Lincoln in Illinois, 412, 432
Absurdism, 29, 31-32, 50, 344, 351, 362-71, 378
Absurdist drama
  forerunners, 362-65
  structure, 29, 31-32, 34, 362-71
Academy of the Nobility, 215
Accesi troupe, 165
Acharnians, The, 81
Ackermann, Konrad, 220, 221
Act Without Words, 286
Actor Prepares, An, 304
Actor-managers, 248-53
Actors and acting
  in Absurdist drama, 368-69
  analyzing the role, 428
  and the playwright, 6
  bodily training, 421
  building a role, 433
  business, 430
  Chinese, 266-67, 269
  commedia dell'arte, 163-66
  concentration, 422-23
  conservation, 433
  creating the role, 427-35
  dress rehearsals, 434
  during Dark Ages, 102
  effect of audiences on. 20-21
  Elizabethan, 122-23, 127-28, 132-33, 137-39, 141, 144-47
  employment, 435-37, 546-51
  English, 18th century, 190, 191-94, 203, 204
  English, 19th century, 241-42, 248-53

  ensemble playing, 433-34
  French, 18th century, 206, 207-09
  French, 19th century. 241-42, 252, 253
  French, 17th century, 167, *168*, 169, 177, 179, 184-85, 186
  German, 18th century, *9*, 218-21
  gesture, 430-31
  Greek, 59, 60, 61, 62, 64-65, 66-67, 77, 78-79, 80-81, 84, 87, *96*
  imagination, 421-22
  India, 256
  Italian Renaissance, 152, 163-66
  Japanese, 271-72, 273, 275, 278-80
  line readings, 432
  means of expression, 421-23
  Medieval, 104, 105, 111-12, 114-15, 118
  memorization, 432
  modern, 420-37
  19th century, 241-42, 248-53
  observation, 421-22
  performances, 434
  professional schools, 436
  psychological and emotional preparation, 429-30
  realistic, 248-53, 351-52
  recent American, 351-52
  relationship to costumer, 491-92
  rise of professional actor, 122-23
  Roman, 90, 94-95, *96*, 97
  stage positions, 424
  style, 51
  systems of acting, 426-27
  technique, 423-26

573

training, 192, 421–35, 436
voice and speech, 421, 431–32
Actors Theatre of Louisville, *549*
Actors' Equity Association, 391, 437, 529, 538, 549
Actors' Studio, 309, 352
Adams, John Cranford, 125
Adding Machine, The, 330, *331*
Adler, Stella, 309
Admiral's Men, 129
Admission fees, 62, 90, 127
Aeschylus, 59–60, 151, *406*
Affair, The, 456
After the Fall, 347
Agamemnon, 59, 60, *406*
Agent, 385, 388
Agon, 82–83
Aiken, George L., 236
Ajax, 60
Alarcon y Mendoza, Juan Ruiz de, 148
Albee, Edward, 22, 351
Alcestis, 60
Alchemist, The, 142
Alfieri, Vittorio Amedeo, 214–15
Alice in Wonderland, 477
Alienation, 335
All for Love, 194–95
All My Sons, 347
Allegory, 38, 117–18, 144, 149, 153–54
Alley Theatre, 436
All's Well that Ends Well, 133
Alsloot, Denis von, *112*
Alzire, 205
Amazing Grace, 448–54, *516*, *517*
America, Hurrah!, *382*, *383*
American Academy of Dramatic Art, 435
American Dream, The, 351
American Federation of Musicians, 528
American Federation of Television and Radio Artists, 437
American Guild of Musical Artists, 437
American Guild of Variety Artists, 437
American Shakespeare Festival, *134*
American theatre and drama (*see* United States)
Aminta, 153
Amphitryon, 91
Anderson, Maxwell, 308, 402, *430*
Andorra, 373
Andreini, Francesco, 165
Andreini, Isabella, 165
Andrews, Julie, *357*
Andreyev, Leonid, 316
Androcles and the Lion, 296
Andromaque, 175
Andromède, 163

Angle perspective, 210–11
Anna Christie, *307*, 308
Anthesteria, 59
Antigone, 60
Antoine, André, *292*, 303
Antony and Cleopatra, 134, 195, 245
Aoi no Ue (*The Lady Aoi*), 275
Apollinaire, Guillaume, 363
Appia, Adolphe, 318–19, *319*
Apprentices, 132, 547
Apron (*see* Theatre architecture)
Architecture (*see* Theatre architecture)
Architettura (Serlio), 155
Architettura e Prospettiva, *211*, *212*
Arena Stage (Washington), *376*, 436
Arena staging, 376, 470, 472–74
Ariosto, Lodovico, 152, 155
Aristophanes, 45, 59, 76, 81–85, 151
Aristotle, 27, 30, 40, 44, 56, 151
Armat, Thomas, 361
Aronson, Boris, 309
Arpino, Gerald, *533*, *537*
Arranger and orchestrator, 526
Art
  and audiences, 17–21
  and imagination, 10
  and music, 11–12
  and painting, 12
  characteristics, 9–16
  compared with philosophy and science, 9–10, 56
  problem of value in, 14–16
  significance in, 12–14
Art of Poetry (Horace), 151
Artaud, Antonin, 270, 371–73, 392
Articulation, 408
Artists of Dionysus, 87
Arts and Crafts Theatre (Detroit), 307
Arzoomanian, Ralph, 417
As You Desire Me, 363
As You Like It, 45, 133
Asian theatre (*see* India, China, Japan)
Asides, 38, 96
Assistant director, 418
Association of Theatrical Press Agents and Managers, 389
Astarte, *379*, *532*
Astley's Amphitheatre, 47
At the Hawk's Well, 316
Atelier, Theatre de l', *364*
Atellan farce, 96–97, 165
Athalie, *208*
Atoza, 274
Atsumori, 273
Audiences
  and producers, 17–20
  and the performing arts, 17
  Chinese, 269

effect of expectations on programming, 20
effect of financial support, 18-19
effect of surroundings on response, 20-21
effect on programming, 18-19
Elizabethan, 126-27, 130, 132-33, 144-46
English, 18th century, *19*, 190, 192, 193, *200*, 204
English, 19th century, 242-44
French, 18th century, 206, 209
French, 17th century, *168*, 179, *186*
German, 18th century, 218
Greek, 62, 63, 81, 84
Italian renaissance, 152, 158-59, 165, 166
Medieval, 102, 104, 105, 111-12
psychology, 20-21
reasons for attending theatre, 17-18
relationship to art, 17
Roman, 90, 97, 99
wise use of influence, 21
Auditorium (*see* Theatre architecture)
Augier, Emile, 289-90, 297
Auto sacramentale, 109, 147, *148*, 149
Avignon Festival, 374
Awake and Sing!, 309
Ayres, Lemuel, *354*
Bacchae, The, 61
Back and Forth, 366
Back scene (*see* Scenery; Wings; Shutters)
Bacquier, Gabriel, *529*
Bajazet, 175
Bakst, Leon, 322
Balance (*see* Design)
Balanchine, George, *530, 531*
Balcony, The, 366
Bald Soprano, The, 28, 29, 48, 366
Bale, John, 118
Balinese dance, 261, 371
Ballad of Baby Doe, The, *488*
Ballad opera, 198, 207
Ballet (*see* Dance)
Ballet de la Nuit, Le, *179*
Ballets Russes, 320, *321*
Bancroft, Marie Effie, 251
Bancroft, Squire, 251
Barber of Seville, The, 206
Barrault, Jean-Louis, 316, *332*, 371
Bartholomew Fair, 142
Battles of Coxinga, The, 282-83
Baty, Gaston, 323
Bayreuth Festival Theatre, 317
Beaton, Cecil, 360
Beaujoyeulx, Balthasar, *168*
Beaumarchais, Pierre Augustin Caron de, 206, *207*
Beaumont, Francis, 143
Beaux' Stratagem, The, 196
Beck, Julian, *387*
Beckett, Samuel, 29, *286*, 365-66
Becque, Henri, 301
Beggar on Horseback, 330
Beggar's Opera, The, 198
Béjart, Louis, 179
Bel Geddes, Norman, 306
Benefit performances, 191, 194
Benny, Jack, 354
Benois, Alexandre, 322, *440*, *484*
Benrimo, J. H., 270
Bérain, Jean, *178*
Bérénice, 175
Bergson, Henri, 44
Berliner Ensemble, *335*, 373
Bernhardt, Sarah, *176*, 253
Betterton, Thomas, *191*, 193
Beyond the Horizon, 308
Bharata, 254
Bhavabhuti, 257
Bibiena family, 211-13, *446*, 527
Bickerstaffe, Isaac, 198
Biedermann and the Firebugs, 373
Billy Budd, 543
Biomechanics, 333
Birdbath, 375
Birds, The, 81
Birth of a Nation, The, 361
Birthday Party, The, 370
Black Crook, The, 353, 354
Black-Eyed Susan, 235
Black playwrights, 372
Blackfriars Theatre, 129-30
Blacks, The, 366
Blau, Herbert, *365*
Blin, Roger, 371
Blocking, 412-13
Blood Wedding, 316
Blue Bird, The, *315, 441*
Bodily attitude, 407
Bodily positions, 424
Boileau-Despreaux, Nicolas, 171
Bonarelli, Prospero, *162*
Booth, Edwin, 252, 253
Borderlights (*see* Lighting)
Borders, *160, 161*
  (*see also* Scenery)
Boucicault, Dion, 235
Box set, 246, 301
Boxes, 127, 130, 158-59, 163, 190, *200*
Boys' companies, 129-30, 132-33
Braggart Warrior, The, 91
Brahm, Otto, 303, 305
Brando, Marlon, 351-52
Break of Noon, 316

Breasts of Tiresias, The, 363
Brecht, Bertolt, *15,* 29, 33–34, 270, 331, 334–43, 344, 373, 374, 378, *547*
Breton, André, 363
Britannicus, 175
Broken Jug, The, 226
Brook, Peter, 371, *374*
Brothers, The, 91
Bruhl, Count von, 245
Brunelleschi, Filippo, 154
Buchell, Arend van, *126*
Büchner, Georg, 226, *403*
Buckingham, George Villiers, Duke of, 353
Buckstone, J. B., 235
Building a Character, 304
Bulwer-Lytton, Edward George, 235
Bunraku, 275–76, 277
Buono, Victor, *454*
Buontalenti, Bernardo, *151*
Burbage, James, 129–30
Burbage, Richard, 132
Burlesque, 198, 353, 354
Burnacini, Lodovico, *478*
Burns, George, 354
Bus Stop, 347
Business (*see* Stage business)
Butai, 274
Butchers, The, 300
Butterfly's Dream, The, 270
Byron, George Gordon, Lord, 224
Caesar and Cleopatra, 296
Calderon de la Barca, Pedro, 147–49
Caligula, 365
Callot, Jacques, *166*
Cambises, King of Persia, 124
Camelot, 355
Camerata Academy, 154
Camille (*see* Lady of the Camellias)
Camus, Albert, 364, 365
Candida, 296
Capon, William, 244
Capricci di Scene Teatrali, 211
Captives, The, 91
Caretaker, The, 370
Carnovsky, Morris, 309
Carousel, 355
Carro, *148*
Cartel des Quatre, 323
Cassaria, La, 152, 155
Castelvetro, Lodovico, 171, 173
Castle of Perseverance, The, 117
Cathleen ni Houlihan, 316
Cato, 249
Caucasian Chalk Circle, The, 336, 337
Cecchini, Pier Maria, 165
Centres dramatiques, 375
Chairs, The, 48, 366–69, 406

Chapelain, Jean, 171, 174
Character
  as organizing principle in drama, 28–29
  differentiation, 36
  methods of revealing, 35–36
Characterization
  and spectacle, 40–41
  defined, 34
  in melodrama, 36, 238–39
  in tragedy, 36
  levels of, 34–35
Chariot and pole shifting, *160,* 161
Chatterton, 228
Chekhov, Anton, 38, 297–99, 345, 346, *413*
Cheney, Sheldon, 307
Cherry Orchard, The, 38, 298, 299
Chester cycle, 110
Chestnut Street Theatre, *217*
Chikamatsu Monzaemon, 275, 277
Children's theatre, 541–43
China
  actors and acting, 266–67, 269
  audiences, 269
  conventions of drama, 264
  costume, 269
  drama, 262–66
  make-up, 267
  music in drama, 262, 266
  origins of drama, 262
  ritual dance, 262
  scenery and staging, 265
  theatre architecture, 264, 269
Chinese Wall, The, 373
Ching roles, 267
Chiton, 66, 80
Chloridia, 145
Choephoroe, 59, 60
Choregus, 61–62
Choreographer, 8, 391, 526, 534–37
Chorus, 38, 59, 60, 61–62, 64, 67–68, 77–78, 79, 80–81, 85, 87, 91, 95, 97, 125, 171, 177, 353–55, 356, 359–61, 529, 536–38
Ch'ou roles, 267
Christy's Minstrels, *240*
Church
  architecture, *103,* 104, 105
  calendar, 103
  drama in, 102–04
  opposition to theatre, 101, 102
  prohibition of drama, 121
  reasons for introducing drama, 102–03
  removal of drama, 104–05
  staging conventions in, 104
Chushingura, 277

Cibber, Colley, 193
Cid, El, 174
Cinna, 174
Cinthio, Giambattista Giraldi, 153
Cipriani, Giovanni Battista, *199*
Circe, 168
Circle-in-the-Square, 375
Circle of Chalk, The, 270
Circus Schumann, 306
City Dionysia, 59, 61–62, 80
Clairon, Claire Hippolyte, 207–09
Classical learning, revival of, 123, 150–52, 166
Claudel, Paul, 316, 371, *465*
Cleveland Playhouse, 436
Climax, 32–33
Clouds, The, 81–85
Clowns, The, 533
Clurman, Harold, 309
Cobb, Lee J., 309
Cofradías, 147
Coleridge, Samuel Taylor, 10, 224
Colleen Bawn, The, 235
College theatre, 539–40, 544–45
Collier, Jeremy, 195–96
Collier controversy, the, 195–96
Color in design, 443–44, 479–80, 500–01
Come Back, Little Sheba, 347
Comédie-en-vaudeville, 354
Comédie Française, *25, 49,* 185–86, 205, 207, 209, 210, 221, 227, *480*
Comédie Italienne, 205, 207, 210
Comédie larmoyante, 205
Comedy
  of character, 45
  characterization in, 44–46
  corrective, 46
  Elizabethan, 123–24, 125, 142–43
  emotional powers, 46
  English, 18th century, 194, 195–97, 198–204
  farce, 45
  as a form, 44–46
  French, 18th century, 205–07
  French, 17th century, 171–74, 180–85
  Greek, 62, *65, 76,* 80–87, 91–92, *97*
  of humours, 142
  of ideas, 45
  Italian, 18th century, 213–14
  Italian, Renaissance, 152, *155,* 156, 163–66
  of manners, 42, 46, 194, 195, 199–204
  Medieval, 109, 114, 119–20
  musical, 353–61, 524–38
  neoclassical, 171–74, 180–85
  of situation, 45
  principal types, 45–46
  Roman, *89,* 91–95, 96–97
  romantic, 45
  sentimental, 196–97, 199, 200–01. 205–07, 213, 214, 219
  social, 46
  of wit, 46
Comedy ballet, 180
Comedy of Errors, 133
Commedia dell'arte
  actors and acting, 163–66
  audiences, 165, 166
  character types, 164–65
  costumes and masks, 164–65
  decline, 165, 213, 214
  in France, *168,* 180, 181, 185, 186, 205, 207
  in Germany, 218, *219*
  influence, 165, 166
  scenarios, 165–66
  theories of origin, 165
  troupes, 165
Commedia erudita, 163
Commonwealth (English), 146–47, 195
Community theatre, 19, 390, 418, 468, 490, 491, 519, 545–46, 548
Company of the Holy Sacrament, 181
Company manager, 389
Complications, 32
Composer, 525–26
Comte, Auguste, 287
Condemned of Altona, The, 365
Conductor, 526–28
Confidant, 96, 171, 177
Conflict in drama, 29–30, 59, 60
Confrérie de la Passion, 167, 169
Congreve, William, 195, 429
Connelly, Marc, 330
Conscious Lovers, The, 197
Constructivism, 333–34
Contracts, 389
Contrast, The, 217, *396*
Control boards, 502, 513–15
Copeau, Jacques, *4,* 322–23
Coquelin, Benoit, 253
Corelli, Franco, *529*
Corey, Irene, *1,* 75, *476, 495*
Corneille, Pierre, *163,* 174–75, 180, 185, 186, 204
Corpus Christi festival, 110, 147–49
Corrale, 147, *148*
Corsican Brothers, The, 235
Cost of production, 386
  (*see also* Finances)
Costume design
  elements and principles, 478–82
  purposes, 475–78
Costumer

and the actor, 491–92
assistants, 490–91
drawings and plans, 482–85
employment, 489–90, 549–50
functions, 8, 475–78
relationship with other artists, 475, 483–84
working procedures, 482–89
Costumes
  borrowing, 486
  Chinese, 269
  commedia dell'arte, 164–65
  crew, 489
  as an element of spectacle, 40–41
  crew, 489
  Elizabethan, 131–32, 141, *145*
  English, 18th century, *191, 193, 200*
  French, 18th century, 207–09
  French, 17th century, *178,* 179
  Greek, 61, 62, *65,* 66–67, 78, *79,* 80–81, 85, 87, *96, 97*
  India, 256
  Japanese, 273–74, 278–79
  and make-up, 492   ⸺7
  making, 486–89
  Medieval, *107,* 108, 112, 116
  modern, 359–61
  parade, 489
  patterns, 487, 489
  rehearsal and performance, 489
  renting, 486
  Roman, 90, 91, 95, *96, 97*
  sources of, 486–89
  and style, 51
Cothurnus, 67
Council of Trent, 121
Count of Monte Cristo, The, 228
Counterweight system, 463–64
Court entertainments, 144–46, 151–52, 154, 163, *168, 178, 179,* 180, 218
Covent Garden Theatre, *188,* 189, *199,* 243, *244,* 477
Coventry cycle, 110
Craig, Gordon, 318–20, 392
Crawford, Cheryl, 352
Creating a Role, 304
Creation of Noah's Ark, The, 109
Creative dramatics, 542–43
Crisis, 33
Critic, 21–26
Critic, The, 199, 353
Criticism
  basic problems, 23–26
  desirable characteristics, 21–22
  meaning and purposes, 23
Cromwell, 227
Cross-Purposes, 365
Crucible, The, 347

Curtain, The (London), 126
Cushman, Charlotte, 253
Cycle of Spring, The, 260
Cyclops, The, 61, 79
Cyclorama, 458–59, *465, 499*
Cymbeline, 134
Czechoslovakia, 370, 377
Dadaism, 362, 363
Daijinbashira, 274
D'Amboise, Jacques, *530*
Damn Yankees, 355
Dance
  in America today, *379,* 530–38
  casting, 529, 534, 536, 537–38
  choreography, 8, 391, 526, 534–37
  composer, 526
  elements of, 532–34
  employment, 534, 536–38
  French, 17th century, *168, 179,* 180, 186
  functions in theatre, 530–32
  Greek, 65, 70, 77–78, 80, 85
  Hindu, *11,* 259–60
  Italian, 154
  in multimedia productions, 532
  in musical comedy, 353–55, 356, 359–61
  notation, 534–36
  rehearsals, 534, 536, 538
  theatrical types, 530–31
  training, 534
Dancers, 8, 529, 534, 536–38
Daniel, Samuel, *145*
Danton's Death, 226, *403, 434*
Dark ages, 102, 165
Dark at the Top of the Stairs, The, 347
Dark of the Moon, 501
Darwin, Charles, 288
D'Aubignac, Abbé, 171
Daumier, Honoré, 7
D'Avenant, William, 187
De Architectura (Vitruvius), 151
Death of a Salesman, 14, 42, 347–51, 433, 441, 524
Deceiver of Seville, The, 148
Décor simultanée (*see* Simultaneous settings)
Decorum, 171–73, 174, 177, 178, 202–03
Dekker, Thomas, 143
Delicate Balance, A, 351
DeLoutherbourg, Philippe Jacques, *8,* 190–91
DeMille, Agnes, *354*
Demi-Monde, The, 290
Denmark, 215–16
Denouement, 33–34
Design

elements of, 442–44, 478–81, 500–02
principles of, 445–46, 481–82, 502–03
purposes of, 439–41, 475–78, 498–500
(*see also* Costumes; Lighting; Scenery)
Desire under the Elms, 308
Destouches, Philippe-Néricault, *480*
Deus ex machina, 64
Devil and the Good Lord, The, 365
Devine, George, 352, *353*
Devotion to the Cross, The, 148
Devrient, Emil, 253
Devrient, Ludwig, 253
DeWitt, Johannes, *126*
Diaghilev, Sergei, 320
Dialogue
desirable characteristics, 40
functions of, 38–39
imagery in, 39–40
in nonrealistic drama, 39–40
in realistic drama, 38
Dibdin, Charles, *199*
Diderot, Denis, 205–06, 209, 247
Dimmers (*see* Lighting)
Dionysus, 56, 62, 88
Dionysus in 69, 377
Director
in America today, 392–419
analysis of script, 393
in arena theatre, 417
basic conceptions of, 392
casting, 397–400
emergence of, 301–02
employment, 417–18
English, 18th century, 192–93
functions, 8, 392
Greek, 61–62, 81, 87
interpreting the script, 393–95
means, 400–10
special problems, 415–16
and style, 51
working with actors, 400
working with designers, 393–97, 447–50, 483–84, 504
working with playwright, 395
(*see also* Rehearsal)
Direzioni a'Giovani studenti nel disegno, 446
Discourse on . . . Viet Nam, 373–74
Discovery, 32–33
Discovery space, 127, *128*, 140
Dithyrambs, 59, 62, 80
Doctor Faustus, 29, 125
Doctor in Spite of Himself, The, 180
Don Carlos, 226
Don Juan, 479
Door Should Either be Shut or Open, A, 228

Dorset Gardens Theatre, *189*
Double casting, 399
Drama
conflict in, 29–30
criteria of success, 18
historical, 10
parts of, 30–41
probability in, 28
relationship to theatre, 6–8
significance in, 12–14
Dramatic action
characteristics, 27–28
climactic order, 30
methods of organizing, 28–30
Dramatic form (*see* Form in drama)
Dramatic structure
beginning of a play, 30–32
character and characterization, 34–36
climax, 32–33
complications, 32
crisis, 33
dialogue, 38–40
discovery, 32–33
end of a play, 33–34
exposition, 30–31
inciting incident, 31
major dramatic question, 31
methods of organizing plays, 28–30, 31–32
middle of a play, 32–33
obligatory scene, 33–34
spectacle, 40–41
thought or theme, 36–38
Dramatists (*see* Playwrights)
Dramatists Guild, 389
Drame, 43, 46, 205–06
Dream Play, The, 324, *325*, *508*
Dress parade, 414
Dress rehearsal, 414–15, 434, 467–68, 489, 515–18
Drolls, *146*
Drops (*see* Scenery)
Drottningholm, 216
Drury Lane Theatre, *8*, *188*, 189, *243*
Dryden, John, 194–95
Duchess of Malfi, The, 143, *441*
DuCroisy, Philibert Gassot, 184
Duerrenmatt, Friedrich, *31*, *372*, 373
Dullin, Charles, 323
Dumas, Alexandre *fils*, 289–90, 297
Dumas, Alexandre *pére*, 228, 245
Dumb Waiter, The, 370
Dumesnil, Marie Françoise, 207–09
Dunlap, William, 217
Durante, Jimmy, 354
Duration, 409
Duse, Eleanora, 253

Earl of Leicester's Men, 123
Earth, The, 300
Earth Spirit, 325
Eastman, George, 361
Ecclesiazusae, 81
Eccyclema, 64, 84
Eclecticism, 305, 306
Edison, Thomas A., 361
Educational theatre, 19, 390, 418, 436, 468, 469, 490, 491, 519, 539–45
Edward II, 125
Edwardes, George, 354–55
Egan, Pierce, 235
Egypt, 56
Eighteen Happenings in Six Parts, 376
Ekhof, Konrad, 220, 221
Elder, Eldon, *86, 448–54, 456, 488, 516, 517*
Electra (Euripides), 61
Electra (Sophocles), 60, 75
Elegy for Young Lovers, 523
Elektra, 321
Elevator stage, 246, 466–67
Elizabeth the Queen, 402, 430
Elizabethan Stage Society, 305
Emotion memory, 304
Empathy, 10
Emperor Chia Ching, *263*
Emphasis in directing, 401–04
Emphasis (*see* Design)
Empress of Morocco, The, 189
Endgame, 366
Enemy of the People, An, 290
England
    Commonwealth, 146–47
    cycle plays, 110–16, 120
    Elizabethan
        actors and acting, 122–23, 127–28, 132–33, 137–39, 141, 144–47
        audiences, 126–27, 130, 132–33, 144–46
        closing of theatres, 146–47
        comedy, 123–24, 125, 133–34, 142–43
        compared with Greek and Roman, 130–31
        compared with Medieval, 116, 131
        compared with Spain, 147
        costume, 131–32, 141, *145*
        dramatists, 123–25, 133–34, 142–43
        finances, 132–33, 144
        Italian influence on, 146
        licensing of plays and players, 122–23, 133
        lighting, 131
        machinery, 129
        masques, 142, 144–46

        music, 127, 141, 144–46
        objections to theatre, 123, 146–47
        private theatres, 125, 129–31, 132–33
        public theatres, 125–29, 132–33, 146
        repertory, 132
        scenery, 129, 140–41, 144–46
        sound effects, 129, 141
        stage, 127–28, 130, 144–46
        theatre architecture, 125–31, 140, 144–46
        tragedy, 124–25, 133–41, 143
    Master of Revels, 122–23, 133
    Medieval drama, 110–16, 117–18, 119–20
    19th century
        actors and acting, 241–42, 248–53
        audiences, 242–44
        dramatists, 224–25, 235, 253
        scenery, 244–48
        theatre architecture, 243–44
    pageant wagons, 105–07, 110–12, 115–16
    prohibition of religious drama, 120
    realism, 296
    since 1945, 352, *353*, 370, 371, *374*, 375
    1660–1800
        actors and acting, 190, 191–94, 203, 204
        audiences, *19*, 190, 192, 193, *200*, 204
        costume, *191, 193, 200*
        directing, 192–93
        dramatic forms, 194–99
        dramatists, 192–93, 194–99
        finances, 191–92, 194
        lighting, 190–91, 192
        managers, 191–92, 193, 199
        production procedures, 192–93, 194
        puritan opposition, 195–96
        reopening of theatres, 187
        repertory, 192
        scenery, 190–91, 199, 200, 203–04
        special effects, 190, 199
        theatre architecture, *188*, 189–90, *200*
Entr'actes, 354
Environmental theatre, 376
Epic theatre, 29, 50, 331, 334–43
Epidaurus, Theatre at, *68, 69*
Epilogue, 201
Equestrian drama, 47
Erasmus Montanus, 216
Essai sur l'Histoire du Theatre, 229
Esthetic distance, 10
Etherege, George, 195

Euminides, 59, 60
Eunuch, The, 91
Euripides, 31, 42, 59, 60–61, 79, 95, 151
Everyman, 38, 117–18
Everyman in His Humour, 141
Exaustra, 64
Existentialism, 364–65
Exposition, 30–31
Expressionism
    decline of, 330
    in scene design, 5, 50
    in theatre and drama, 29, 323–31, 334, 343
    influence of, 330
Extravaganza, 353
Fabula Atellana, 96–97
Fabula crepidata, 95
Fabula palliata, 95
Fabula praetexta, 95
Fabula togata, 95
Fair theatres, 207
Faithful Shepherd, The, 153
False Antipathy, The, 205
False Confidences, 205
False Delicacy, 197
Falstaff, 528
Fan, The, 214
Farce
    Elizabethan, 124, 125, 133
    French, 17th century, 167, *168*
    as a form, 38, 45, 367
    Italian, 152, 163–66, 213
    Medieval, 114, 119, 120, 152
Farquhar, George, 196
Farrell, Suzanne, *530*
Fashionable Prejudice, The, 205
Father, The, 324
Father of a Family, The, 206
Fauquez, Arthur, *495*
Faust, 225, 228–33, *229*, *230*, 349
Favart, Charles Simon, 207
Faye, Joey, *525*
Feast of Fools, The, 109
Federal Theatre project, *342*, 342–43
Fehling, Jurgen, 330
Fernald, John, *456*
Festivals
    Greek, 59, 61–62, 80, 87, 116
    Medieval, 110, 147–49
    Roman, 88–90
Fielding, Henry, 198
Finances
    effect on programming, 18–20
    Elizabethan, 132–33, 144
    English, 18th century, 191–92, 194
    French, 17th century, 178–79, 185–86
    in New York theatre, 386
Fitzball, Edward, 235

Flashback, 349
Flats (*see* Scenery)
Fletcher, John, 143
Flies, The, 365
Floodlights (*see* Lighting)
Floor plan, 413
Flying (*see* Machinery)
Focus, 402–03
Fokine, Mikhail, 320
Folk play, 118
Footlights (*see* Lighting)
Ford, John, 143
Ford Foundation, The, 548
Forest, The, 297
Forestage (*see* Theatre architecture)
Form in drama
    classification of, 42–43
    comedy, 44–46
    determinants of, 42
    drame, 43, 46
    epic theatre, 29, 50, 331, 334–43
    fixed, 42
    labels used by contemporary dramatists, 48
    melodrama, 48, 233–35
    mixed forms, 48, 233–35
    organic, 42
    tragedy, 43–44
    tragicomedy, 46
Forrest, Edwin, 252, 253
Fort, Paul, 318
Fortune, The, 126, 127, *128*
Fountain, The, 308
Fourth wall, 206, 247
France
    18th century
        actors and acting, 206, 207–09
        audiences, 206, 209
        comedy, 205–07
        costume, 207–09
        dramatists, 204–09
        fair theatres, 207
        Italian troupe, 205, 207
        music, 207, 209
        scenery, 206, 209, *210*
        theatre architecture, 209, *210*
        tragedy, 204–05
    Medieval drama, *104*, 105, *106*, 107, 109, *117*, 119, 121, 167, 169
    19th century
        actors and acting, 241–42, 252, 253
        dramatists, 227, 235, 253
        scenery, 245–58
    prohibition of religious plays, 121, 167
    17th century
        actors and acting, 167, *168*, 169, 177–79, 184–85, 186

audiences, *168*, 179, 186
comedy, 171–74, 180–85
commedia dell'arte, *168*, 180, 181, 185, 186
costume, *178*, 179
dance, *168*, *179*, 180, 186
development of neoclassical ideal, -171–74
dramatists, 169, 174–75, 179–80, 185, 186
farce, 167, *168*
finances, 178–79, 185–86
forces shaping drama, 170–74
introduction of proscenium arch, 170
Italian influence on, 169, 170, 171–74, 179
managers, 167, 169, 178–79, 185–86
monopolies, 185–86
opera, 170, 185, 186
production procedures, 178–79
scenery, *168*, 169, 170, 179, *180*, 185
theatre architecture, 167, *168*, 169, 170, 179, *180*, *185*
tragedy, 171–78, 180
since 1945, 362–63, 364–69, 370, 371, 373, 374, 375
Frankenstein, 383, *387*
Freie Bühne, 303
French Academy, 171, 174, 185
French Revolution, 210
Freud, Sigmund, 309, 346
Frisch, Max, 373
Frogs, The, 81
From Morn to Midnight, 325–30, *327*, 406
Fry, Christopher, 424
Fuchs, Georg, 320
Fuebashira, 274
Furniture, 467
Furttenbach, Joseph, *153*, *159*, *160*
Gaiety Theatre (London), 354
Galileo, 15
Galleries, 127, 130, 159, 163, *168*, 190
Galliari family, 213
Galloway, Pat, *181*
Galsworthy, John, 296
Game of Love and Chance, The, 205
Garden Party, The, 370
Garfield, John, 309
Gamester, The, 198
Gammer Gurton's Needle, 124
Garcia Lorca, Federico, 316, *425*
Gardener's Dog, The, 147
Garrick, David, 190, *191*, *193*, 194
Gas, 325–26
Gas lighting, 247–48
Gauguin, Paul, 323
Gaultier-Garguille, 167, *168*

Gay, John, 198, 207
Gedatsu, 278
Gelosi troupe, 165
General Lien P'u, 268
Genet, Jean, 365, 366
Germany
   beginnings of theatre, 218
   18th century, 218–21
   epic theatre, 334–43
   expressionism, 324–30
   19th century, 225–27, 245–48, 253
   since 1945, 373–74
Gesture, 405–07
Ghelderode, Michel de, 48
Ghosts, 290, *291*, 303
Gidé, Andre, 332
Gilford, Marcia, 525
Giraldi Cinthio, Giambattista, 153
Giraudoux, Jean, *459*
Giunio Bruto overa la Caduta de Tarquinii, 481
Glass Menagerie, The, 345, 346
Globe Theatre, 125–26, 133
Glories, 163
Goethe, Johann Wolfgang von, 225, 228–33
Gogol, Nikolai, 297
Golden Boy, 309
Goldoni, Carlo, 213, 214, 219, *440*, *484*
Goldsmith, Oliver, 199
Good-Natured Man, The, 199
Good Soldier Schweik, 336
Good Woman of Setzuan, The, 337, 337–42, 547
Gorboduc, 124
Gottsched, Johann Christoph, 218, 219
Götz von Berlichingen, 225
Gozzi, Carlo, 213, 214
Graduate schools, 544–45
Great God Brown, The, 330
Great World Theatre, The, 148
Greece
   actors and acting, 59, 60, 61, 62, 64–65, 66–67, 77, 78–79, 80–81, 84, 87, *96*
   admission prices, 62
   audience, 62, 63, 81, 84
   beginnings of drama, 56–59
   chorus, 59, 61–62, 64, 67–68, 77–78, 79, 80–81, 85, 87
   comedy, 62, *65*, 76, 80–87, 91–92, 97
   compared with Elizabethan, 130–31
   compared with Middle Ages, 116
   contests and prizes, 62, 80, 87
   costumes, 61, 62, *65*, 66–67, 78, *79*, 80–81, 85, 87, *96*, *97*
   dance, 65, 70, 77–78, 80, 85
   directing, 61–62, 80–81, 87

dithyrambs, 59, 62, 80
drama and religion, 56-57
dramatists, 59-61, 81, 85
festivals, 59, 61-62, 80, 87
Hellenistic period, 63, 68, 69, 85-87, 96
machinery, 64, 84-85
masks, 59, 66-67, 77-78, 79, 80-81, 85, 87, 96, 97
mime, 97
music, 65, 70, 77-78, 80, 84-85, 87
playwrights' working conditions, 61-62, 87
process of producing plays, 61-62, 80, 87
raised stage, 64, 87
relationship to Roman theatre, 87-88, 91-92, 96, 97, 98-99, 101
satyr play, 60, 61, 62, 78-79, 80
scenery, 58, 61, 63-64, 77-78, 84
theatre architecture, 57, 58, 62-64, 84, 86, 87, 98-99, 101
tragedy, 59-61, 62, 64-65, 66-78, 80, 85, 87, 154
value placed on drama, 61-62, 87
Greek Theatre (Ypsilanti), 86
Green, Paul, 464
Grein, J. T., 303
Griffith, D. W., 361
Groove shifting, 161, 190
Gros-Guillaume, 167, 168
Grosses Schauspielhaus, 306
Grouch, The, 85
Ground plan (see Scenery)
Ground rows, 190
Group Theatre, 308-309
Guarini, Giambattista, 153
Guthrie, Tyrone, 53
Guys and Dolls, 355
Hairy Ape, The, 308, 330
Hallam, Lewis, 216
Hamburg Dramaturgy, 220
Hamlet, 14, 37, 40, 125, 134, 191, 250, 394, 395
Hammerstein, Oscar II, 354, 355
Hanamichi, 280, 281
Handel, George Frederick, 198
Hanswurst, 218, 219, 220
Happenings, 344, 376-77, 378
Happy Days, 366
Hardy, Alexandre, 169
Harlequin, 164-65, 199, 218
Harmony (see Design)
Harrison, Rex, 357
Hasenclever, Walter, 323
Hashigakari, 274
Havel, Vaclav, 370
Haymarket Theatre, 189

Heartbreak House, 296
Hebbel, Friedrich, 226-27
Hebrew Actors Guild, 437
Heckart, Eileen, 346
Hedda Gabler, 291
Heffner, Hubert, 34
Hell Mouth, 106
Heller, Joseph, 545
Hello, Dolly, 355
Henry III and His Court, 228
Henry IV (Pirandello), 363, 364
Henry IV (Shakespeare), 133, 245
Henry V, 133
Henry VI, 133
Henry VIII, 41, 133
Henslowe, Philip, 129
Henze, Hans Werner, 523
Herman, Jerry, 16
Hernani, 25, 227-28
Heroic tragedy, 194
Heywood, John, 119
Heywood, Thomas, 143
High school theatre (see Secondary schools)
Hindu dance, 11, 259-60
Hindu drama (see India)
Hippolytus, 61
Historical accuracy in costuming and scenery, 245-46
Historical Register of 1736, The, 198
Historification, 335
History of the American Theatre, 217
History play, 125, 133
Histriones, 102
Hodges, C. Walter, 128
Hofmannsthal, Hugo von, 118
Hogarth, William, 19
Holberg, Ludwig, 216
Holland, Betty Lou, 346
Holm, Ian, 370
Home on the Range, 372
Homecoming, The, 370
Hope, The, 126
Hôpital de la Trinité, 167
Hopkins, Arthur, 5, 308
Horace, 151
Horace (Corneille), 174
Hotel de Bourgogne, 167, 168, 169, 170, 179, 185, 209
House of Bernarda Alba, The, 309, 316, 426
House of Connelly, The, 464
Householders, 132
How to Succeed in Business Without Really Trying, 355
Howard, Sidney, 308, 499
Hsiung, 270
Hugo, Victor, 25, 227-28, 245

Humours, 142
Hunchback, The, 225
Hunger and Thirst, 49, 366
Hurry, Leslie, *138*
Hutt, William, *181*
Ibsen, Henrik, 20, 30–31, 38, 290–96, 345, 347, 349
Iliad, The, 336
Illegitimate Son, The, 206
Illusionism, 245–47
Imagery, 39–40
Imitation, 56
Impressionism, 310
Improvisation, 163–64, 383, 430
Incident at Vichy, 347
Inciting incident, 31
Independent Theatre (London), 303
Independent theatre movement, 302–05
India
  acting, 256
  costumes and make-up, 256
  dance drama, 259–60
  drama, 254–60
  dramatists, 254–60
  music in drama, 256
  origins of drama, 254
  staging, 255
  theatre architecture, 255–56
Indonesia
  puppet theatre, 262
  shadow plays, 260–61
Industrial shows, 551
Inflection, 409
Inge, William, *346,* 347
Inner below (*see* Discovery space)
Inns of Court, 124, 144
Inspector General, The, 297
Intermezzi, 144, 153–54
International Alliance of Theatrical Stage Employees, 469
International Phonetic Alphabet, 409
Investigation, The, 373
Ioculatores, 102
Ion, 61
Ionesco, Eugène, 28, 29, 39, 48, *49,* 365, 366–69
Iphigenia in Tauris, 225
Irving, Henry, 251
Italian Actors Union, 437
Italy
  18th century
    comedy, 213–14
    dramatists, 213–15
    scenery, 210–13
    theatre architecture, *213*
    tragedy, 214–15
  Medieval drama, 109

19th century, 253
Renaissance
  academies, 152, 156, 163
  actors and acting, 152, 163–66
  audiences, 152, 158–59, 165, 166
  beginnings, 150–52
  costume, 164–65
  comedy, 152, *155,* 156, 163–66
  commedia dell'arte, 163–66
  dance, 154
  dramatists, 152–53, 165
  influence on England and France, 152, 165, 166, 170, 171–74, 179
  intermezzi, 144, 153–54
  lighting, 159
  machinery, 159, 161–63, 166
  music, 154, 166
  opera, 154, 158–59, 166
  perspective scenery, 154–63, 166
  scene shifting, 159–63, 166
  scenery, 151, 152, 154–63, 165, 166
  special effects, 162–63, 165, 166
  theatre architecture, 151, 152, 154–63, 166
  tragedy, 153, 156
  20th century, 363–64
Jackknife stage, 464
Jacobean (*see* England, Elizabethan)
Janauschek, Fanny, 253
Japan
  Kabuki
    acting, 278–80
    costume and make-up, 278–79
    drama, 276–83
    music, 279–80
    origins, 276–77
    scenery and staging, 277, 278, 280–82
  Noh
    acting, 271–72, 273, 275
    costume, 273–74
    dramatists, 272–73
    production, 273–75
    scenery and stage, 274–75
    theatre architecture, 272, 274–75
    puppet theatre, 275–76, 277
Jarry, Alfred, 362, *363*
Javanese drama (*see* Indonesia)
Jeppe of the Hill, 216
Jessner, Leopold, 330
Jesuit drama, 121
Jerrold, Douglas William, 235
Jew of Malta, The, 125
Jidaimono play, 282
Joel Brand, 374
Joffrey Ballet Company, *379, 532, 533, 537*
Jolly, George, 187

Jonathan Bradford, 235
Jones, Henry Arthur, 296
Jones, Inigo, 144, *145*, 146, *483*
Jones, LeRoi, 372
Jones, Robert Edmond, 5, 307, 308
Jonson, Ben, 46, 141–43, 144, *145*
Jouvet, Louis, 323
Julius Caesar, 134, *502*
Junior Leagues of America, 542
Just Assassins, The, 365
Justice, 296
Juvarra, Filippo, 213, *481*
Kabuki (*see* Japan)
Kafka, Franz, 332
Kaiser, Georg, 325
Kalidasa, 257
Kamerny Theatre, 320, 322
Kamimono, 272
Kamishimo, 279
Kanami Kiyotsugu, 271
Kaprow, Allan, 376
Kathakali, 259–60, *494*
Kaufman, George, 330
Kawatake Mokuami, 277
Kazan, Elia, 309, *348*, 351–52
Kazuramono, 272
Kean, Charles, *41*, 250
Kean, Edmund, *249*, 250
Kelly, Hugh, 197
Kemble, Charles, 245
Kemble, John Philip, 249–50
Khorev, 215
Killer, The, 366
Killigrew, Thomas, 187
King of the Dark Chamber, The, 260,
    494
King Dies, The, 366
King Harsha, 257
King John, 118, 245, *477*
King Lear, 12–13, 37, 134–41, *191*, *251*,
    433
King and No King, A, 143
King Shudraka, 257
King, the Greatest Alcalde, The, 147
King's Men, 130, 133, 144
Kippardt, Heinar, 373, 374
Kirinohmono, 272
Klabund, Alfred H., 270
Kleist, Heinrich von, 226
Knights, The, 81
Knowles, James Sheridan, 224–25
Kokata, 273
Komos, 82, 83
Kotzebue, August Friedrich Ferdinand
    von, 234
Krapp's Last Tape, 366
Kumano, 273
Kuruimono, 272

Kyd, Thomas, 124–25
Kyogen, 275
La Chaussée, Pierre Claude Nivelle de,
    205
La Scala opera house, *213*
Lady in the Dark, 355
Lady of the Camellias, The, 289–90
Lady of Lyons, The, 235
Lady's Not for Burning, The, 424
Lady Precious Stream, 270
Lahr, Bert, 354
LaMama Experimental Theatre Club,
    375
Lansbury, Angela, *16*
Later Story of Rama, The, 257
Laughter, 44
Lazzi, 165
League of New York Theatres, 389
Legal restrictions, 122–23, 146–47, 187–
    89, 205
Leigh, Mitch, 525
LeKain, Henry Louis, 207–09
Lenaia, 59, 80
Lerner, Alan Jay, 355–61
LeSage, Alain-René, 207
Lessing, Gotthold Ephraim, 219–20
Lesson, The, 366
Licensing Act of 1737, 187–89, 198, 243
Licensing of plays and troupes, 122–23,
    133, 187–89
Liebeslieder Walzer, 531
Life is a Dream, 148
Life of Man, The, 316
Lighting
    arena stage, *473*, *474*
    color in, 500–01, 513
    connecting panels, 513–14
    control boards, 502, 513–15
    controllable factors, 500–02
    crews, 519
    dimmers, 514–15
    Elizabethan, 131
    English, 18th century, 190–91, 192
    equipment, 508–15
    floodlights, 512
    functions, 40–41, 498–500
    gas, 247–48
    general illumination, 506
    instrument schedules, 504, *507*, 508,
    517
    Italian Renaissance, 159
    19th century, 247–48
    open stage, 472
    plot, 504–08, *516*
    projections, 377, *508*, 512
    rehearsals and performance, 515–18
    special effects, *499*, 506, 512
    specific illumination, 505–06

spotlights, 509–10
striplights, 510–11
style and mood, 499, 501
20th century, 318, 498–519
Lighting designer
assistants, 519
employment, 518–19, 549–50
functions, 8, 498–500
relationship to other artists, 504
working plans and procedures, 503–08, 515–18
Lillo, George, 197–98
Lincoln Center for the Performing Arts, 5, *15*, *365*
Lincoln cycle, 110
Line (*see* Design)
Lines of business, 192
Little Clay Cart, The, 257
Little Theatre of Chicago, 307
Littlewood, Joan, 374
Liturgical drama, 103–04, 116
Living Newspaper, 342–43
Living Theatre, The, *372*, *375*, *383*, *387*
Livius Andronicus, 88
Local color, 190, 209, 213, 245–46
Loewe, Frederick, 355–61
Logan, Joshua, *346*
London Merchant, The, 197–98
Long Day's Journey into Night, A, *345*
Look Back in Anger, 352, *353*
Lorca (*see* Garcia Lorca)
Lord Chamberlain's Men, 133
Lords' rooms, 127
Lorenzaccio, 228
Lost Princess, The, 257
Louis XIV, *178*, *179*, 180, 181, 186, 205
Love for Love, 195, *429*
Love in a Tub, 195
Love in a Village, 198
Loyalties, 296
Ludi (*see* Rome, festivals)
Lugné-Poë, Aurélien-Marie, 318
Luke the Labourer, 235
Lully, Jean Baptiste, 185
Lyly, John, 124, 125
Lysistrata, 76, 81
Ma Fu-lu, 268
Macbeth, 5, 43, 134, *193*
McDevitt, Ruth, *346*
Machiavelli, Niccolo, 152
Machina, 64, 84–85
Machine Wreckers, The, 325
Machinery
Elizabethan, 129
Greek, 64, 84–85
Italian Renaissance, 159, 161–63, 166
Japanese, 276, 280
Medieval, 106–07, 111

modern, 463–67
19th century, 246–47
Mackaye, Steele, 247
Macklin, Charles, 193, 194
Macready, William Charles, 249–50
Madison Square Theatre, 247
Maeterlinck, Maurice, 310–16, *311*, *313*, *315*, *441*
Magee, Patrick, *374*
Mahabharata, 254, 261
Mahagonny, 337
Mahelot, Laurent, 169
Maid of the Mill, The, 198
Maid of Orleans, The, 225, 226, 245
Maid's Tragedy, The, 143
Maids, The, 366
Maintenon, Mme. de, 186
Major Barbara, 296
Major dramatic question, 31
Make-up
based on Medieval sculpture, *476*
based on mosaics, *1*
designing, 493
as element of production, 492
materials, 495–97
in Oriental theatre, 256, 267, 278–79
purposes, 493
types, 493–95
Malina, Judith, *387*
Mame, *16*, 355
Man and the Masses, 325
Man and Superman, 296
Man of La Mancha, 525
Man of Mode, The, 195
Managers
England, 1660–1800, 191–92, 193, 199
France, 17th century, 167, 169, 178–79, 185–86
Roman, 90
(*see also* Actor-managers; Producer)
Mandragola, 152
Mankind, 117
Mansions, 104, 105, 106, 107, 110–12, 115–16, 129, *168*, 169
Manual for Constructing Theatrical Scenes and Machines (Sabbattini), 160
Marat/Sade (*see The Persecution and Assassination of Jean-Paul Marat . . .*)
Maria Magdalena, 227
Maria Stuart, 226
Marionette, 319
(*see also* Japan, puppet theatre)
Marivaux, Pierre Carlet de, 205
Marlowe, Christopher, 29, 124, 125
Marriage of Figaro, The, 206, 207
Marriage of Peleus and Thetis, 527

Married Philosopher, The, 480
Martinelli, Tristano, 165
Mask, The, 320
Masks, 55, 59, 66-67, 77-78, *79,* 80-81, 85, 87, 91, 95, *96,* 97, 164-65, 273
Masques, 142, 144-46
Mass (*see* Design)
Massinger, Philip, 143
Master Builder, The, 291
Master of Revels, 122-23, 133
Matthews, Charles, 250
Mauro family, 213
Mayakovsky Theatre, *394*
Mazarin, Cardinal, 170
Mazzi, Vincenzo, *211*
Measure for Measure, 133
Medea, 43, 60
Medieval (*see* Middle Ages)
Meeker, Ralph, *346*
Meeting of the League of Heroes, 268
Mei lan-fang, 267
Meilziner, Jo, *346, 348,* 351-52
Melodrama
  character in, 36, 46-48, 238-39
  characteristics of, 46-48, 233-35
  emotional powers, 46-48, 238
  equestrian, 47
  as a form, 46-48, 233-35
  language, 239
  music, 239-40
  spectacle, 239-40
Memorandum, The, 370
Menaechmi, The, 91, 92-95, 133
Menander, 59, 85
Merchant of Venice, The, 194, 394
Merchant, Vivian, *370*
Meredith, Burgess, *456*
Mermaid Theatre, *109, 113,* 394
Merrick, David, 388
Merry Wives of Windsor, The, 133
Mertz, Fritz, 72
Metaphor, 40
Metropolitan Opera Company, *528, 529*
Metsukebashira, 274
Meyerhold, Vsevolod, 270, 332-33, *333, 334,* 392
Michael and His Lost Angel, 296
Middle Ages
  actors and acting, 104, 105, 111-12, 114-15, 118
  audiences, 102, 104, 111-12
  beginnings of drama, 102-03
  comedy, 109, 114, 119-20
  compared with Elizabethan, 116, 131
  compared with Greece, 116
  control over plays, 105, 110, 120-21
  conventions of thought, 108-09
  Corpus Christi festival, 110
  costumes, *107,* 108, 112, 116

cycle plays, 105-06, 109-16, 120
decline of drama, 120-21
dramatic types, 103-04, 109-10, 116-20
farce, 114, 119, 120
financing productions, 105, 110
machinery, 106-07, 111
miracle plays, 116, *117*
morality plays, 117-18, 120
music, 115-16
mystery plays, 109-16, 120
processional staging, 110
production arrangements, 105, 110-12
removal of drama from church, 104-05
scenery, 104, 105, 106-07, 111, 115-16
secular interludes, 120, *121*
special effects, 106-07, 111
staging conventions, 104, 105-08, 110-12, 115-16
symbolic devices, 107-08, 116
theatre architecture, *103,* 104, 105, 110-12, *120, 121*
types of stages, 105-08, *120, 121*
Middle genres, 205-06
Middleton, Thomas, 143
Midsummer Night's Dream, A, 133
Miller, Arthur, 347-51, 524
Mime, 97, 98, 102
Minna von Barnhelm, 219
Minotis, Alexis, 70
Minturno, Antonio, 171
Miracle of Notre Dame, The, 117
Miracle plays, 116, *117*
Miracle, The, 306
Mirame, 170
Mirra, 215
Mirror, The, or Harlequin Everywhere, 199
Misanthrope, The, 180
Misanthropy and Repentance, 234
Miser, The, 180
Miss Julie, 324
Miss Sara Sampson, 219
Mixed dramatic forms, 48, 172
Modjeska, Helena, 253
Moliere, 45, 166, *168, 170,* 179-85, 186, 199-200, 202, 204, 205, 283, 440, *479, 549*
Molina, Tirso de, 148
Monopolies, 167, 185-86, 187-88, 205, 207, 210
Mons Passion Play, 107
Montaigu, Rene Magnon de, 216
Month in the Country, A, 297
Moore, Douglas, *488*
Moore, Edward, 198

Morality play, 117–18, 120, 124
Moscow Art Theatre, 76, 303, *304, 315, 441*
Mother Courage, 335–36, 337
Mother-in-Law, The, 91
Motion pictures, 354, 361, 377, 523, 548, 551
Motokiyo, Zeami, 275
Movement, 405–06, 426, 430–31
Movement for Piano and Orchestra, 530
Mrozek, Slawomir, 370
Mrs. Dane's Defense, 296
Much Ado About Nothing, 394
Multimedia productions, 377, *379*, 523, 532
Munich Art Theatre, 320
Music
  arranger and orchestrator, 527
  composing for musical comedy, 525–26
  conductor, 526–28
  Elizabethan, 127, 141, 144–46
  as a form of art, 11–12
  French, 18th century, 207, 209
  Greek, 65, 70, 77–78, 80, 84–85, 87
  Italian, 154, 166
  Medieval, 115–16
  in multimedia productions, 523
  in Oriental theatre, 256, 260, 261, 262, 264, 265–66, 274, 275, 276, 279
  rehearsals, 527–28, 529
  Roman, 90, 91, 95, 97
  types of theatrical, 524–25
Music Man, The, 355
Musical comedy
  in America today, 355–61, 524–38
  casting, 526–28, 529
  chorus, 529, 537–38
  composing, 525–26
  dance in, 526, 529, 530–38
  orchestra members, 528
  origin and development, 353–55
  (*see also* Opera)
Musicians, 8, 526–29
Musset, Alfred de, 228
My Fair Lady, 355–61, 525
My Life in Art, 304
Mysteries and Smaller Pieces, 372
Mystery play, 109–16
Myth, 55–56, 81
Nagananda, 257
Nathan the Wise, 219, 220
National Council of the Arts, 19
National theatres, 185, 221
Naturalism, 50, 287, 299–302, 331, 362
Natyasastra, 254
Naumachia, 98

Nemerovich-Danchenko, Vladimir, *76*, 303
Neoclassicism, 50, 151, 171–74, 190, 202–03, 204–05, 210, 214–15, 218
Neoromanticism, 310
Nesbitt, Cathleen, *454*
Neuber, Carolina, 218–19, 220
New stagecraft, 307
New Tenant, The, 366
New York City Ballet Company, *530, 531*
Newington Butts, 126
Night of the Iguana, The, 345
Nilssen, Birgit, *529*
Noah (Medieval cycle play), *394*
Noah (Obey), *403, 499*
No Exit, 365
No Trifling with Love, 228
Noh drama, 271–75
Norton, Thomas, 124
Norway, 215–16, 290–96
Nudity, 373
Oberon, 144
Obey, André, *403, 499*
Objections to theatre, 123, 146–47
Obligatory scene, 33
O'Connell, Arthur, *346*
Octoroon, The, 235
Odets, Clifford, 309
Oedipus (Seneca), 96
Oedipus at Colonus, 60
Oedipus the King, 31, 32, 53, 60, 61, 63, 69, 70–78, 137, 349, 406
Of Love Remembered, *456*
Of Thee I Sing, 355
Off-Broadway, 375, 376, 468, 490, 519, 537, 548, 549, 550
Off-off-Broadway, 375, 377, 550
Oh, What a Lovely War, 374
Oklahoma, 354, 355
Okuni, 276
Old Vic, *138*
Olympic Academy, 156
Olympic Theatre (London), 250
On Baile's Strand, 316
On Germany, 227
Ondine, *459*
One Third of a Nation, 342
O'Neill, Eugene, 307–08, *345*, 351
Open stage, 376, 471–72, *473*
Open Theatre, *382*
Opera
  ballad, 198, 207
  beginnings, 154, 158–59, 166
  comic, 198, 199, 207, 213
  in England, 190, 198, 199
  French, 17th century, 170, 185, 186
  in Germany, 218
  Italy, 18th century, 210, 213

Peking, 263–70
  (*see also* Music *and* Musical comedy)
Oppenheimer Case, The, 374
Orange, Theatre at, *100*
Orbecche, 153
Orchestra (architectural), 62, 90
  97–98, 99, 155
Orchestra (musical) (*see* Music)
Oregon Shakespeare Festival, *130, 135*
Oresteia, 59, 60
Oriental theatre (*see* China; India;
  Indonesia; Japan)
Origin of the Species, The, 288
Origins of theatre, 55–56, 102–03
Ornament (*see* Design)
Oropos, Theatre at, *86*
Orphan, The, 194
Orphan of China, The, 208
Osborne, John, 352, *353*
Ostia, Theatre at, *99*
Ostrovsky, Alexander, 297
Othello, 134, *249*
Otway, Thomas, 194
Our Town, 29, 401
Pagan rites, 55–56, 102, 118
Pageant wagons, 105–07, 110–12,
  115–16, *148*, 159
Paint Your Wagon, 355
Pajama Game, 355
Pal Joey, 355
Palais Royal, 170, 179, 185, 209
Palladio, Andrea, *4*, 156
Pandora's Box, 325
Pantalone, 164
Pantomime, 97, 98, 190, 198, 199,
  405–07, 430–31
Parabasis, 82, 83
Paradox of the Actor, The, 206
Paraskenia, 63–64
Parigi, Alfonso, *162*
Paris Opera, 209, 210
Parisienne, La, 301
Parodos, 63, 64, 72, 77, 82–83
Pasquin, 198
Pastor, Tony, 354
Pastoral drama, 125, 153, 156
Patents, 187–89
Patin, Jacques, *168*
Peace, 81
Pearl Necklace, The, 257
Peer Gynt, 290
Peking Opera, 263–64, *270, 271*
Pelléas and Mélisande, 311–16, 318,
  368, 406, 477
Penthesilea, 226
People's Theatre, 332
Performance Group, *377*
Periaktoi, 64, 159–60
Pericles, 134

*Persecution and Assassination of
  Jean-Paul Marat as Performed by
  the Inmates of the Asylum of
  Charenton under the Direction of
  the Marquis de Sade, The,* 371,
  373, *374*
Persians, The, 59
Perspective scenery, 154–56, 158,
  159–62, 166, 210–11, *446*
Petit Bourbon, *168*
Phaedra, 28, 175–78, 207
Philaster, 143
Philoctetes, 60
Philosophy and art, 9–10, 56
Phlyakes, *97*
Phormio, 91
Physicists, The, 31, 373
Picnic, 346, 347
Pièce à thèse, 290
Piermarini, Guiseppe, *213*
Pierre Patelin, 119
Pillars of Society, The, 290
Pinero, Arthur Wing, 296
Pinter, Harold, 48, 370
Pirandello, Luigi, 363–64
Piranesi, Gian Battista, *212, 213*
Piscator, Erwin, 336–37, 343
Pit, 126–27, 130, 159, 163, 190
Pitch (*see* Voice and speech)
Pitoëff, Georges, 323
Pixérécourt, René Charles Guilbert de,
  234–35
Place, unity of, 173–74, 177, 185, 202
Planché, J. R., 245, 477
Planchon, Roger, *183,* 374
Platea, 104, 105, 111, 116, 127, *168,*
  169
Plautus, 88, 89, 90, 91–95, 98, 101, 123,
  150, 151, 165, 180
Playboy of the Western World, 407
Playwright
  and audience, 18, 20
  contemporary working conditions,
    384–88
  methods, 383
  out-of-town try-outs, 385–86
  relation to producer, 385–86
  rewriting, 385–86
  use of group improvisation, 383
  (*see also* China, Dramatic structure;
    England; France; Germany;
    Greece; India; Italy; Japan; Nor-
    way; Rome; Russia; Sweden;
    United States)
Plot, 30–34
Plutus, 81
Poel, William, 305
Poetic justice, 171–72, 173
Poetics (Aristotle), 44

Point of attack, 30
Poland, 253, 370
Polyeucte, 174
Pompeii, 213
Poquelin, Jean Baptiste (*see* Molière)
Positivism, 287–88
Possession of parts, 192
Pot of Gold, The, 91
Press agent, 389, 391
Preston, Thomas, 124
Price, The, 347
Pride of Life, 117
Primitive drama, 55–56
Prince of Homburg, The, 226
Prince Igor, 321
Prince of Wales' Theatre, 251
Princesse d'Elide, La, 180
Prise de Marsilly, La, 169
Pritchard, Hannah, *193*
Private Life of the Master Race, The, 29
Probability in drama, 28
Processional staging, 110
Producer
  in American theatre today, 385, 388–91
  and audience demands, 17–20
  in community theatre, 390
  in educational theatre, 391
  financing productions, 389
  in resident company, 390
  in summer stock, 390
  and unions, 389
  (*see also* Actor-managers; Finances; Managers)
Projection (vocal), 409
Projections, 377, *508*, 512
Prologue, 71–72, 82, 201
Prometheus Bound, 59
Prompt book, 413, 414
Propaganda drama, 37–38
Properties, 40–41, 467
Property men, 265
Proportion (*see* Design)
Proscenium arch
  functions, 158
  introduction in France, 170
  origins, 158
Proscenium doors, 189–90, 200, *203*, 204
Proscenium stage, 156, 157–58, 159, 163, 470–71
  (*see also* Theatre architecture)
Provincetown Players, 307, *308*
Psychoanalytic theory, 309
Puccini, Giacomo, *13*
Puppet theatre (*see* Japan; Indonesia)
Purgatory, 316

Puritan opposition, 146–47, 195–96
Pygmalion, 296, 355–61
Quaglio family, 213
Quality (vocal), 408
Quem Quaeritis trope, 103
Quin, James, 193, 194
Rabinovitch, Isaac, *76*
Rachel, 253
Racine, Jean, 28, 175–78, 180, 185, 186, 204, 205, *208*
Ralph Roister Doister, 123–24
Ramayana, 254, 261
Rasa, 255
Realism, 50, 247–48, 287–302, 305, 309, 344–52
Reconciliation between the General and the Minister, 268
Recreational Architecture (Furttenbach), *160*
Recruiting Officer, The, 196
Red Army Theatre (Moscow), *466*
Red Bull, The, 126
Reformation, The, 109, 118, 120–21
Regiebuch, 306
Rehearsal
  blocking, 412–13
  dress, 414–15, 434, 467–68, 489, 515–18
  integrating, 414, 527–28, 536, 538
  reading, 412
  schedule, 411–12
  secretary, 418
  space, 410–11
  technical, 414–15, 467–68, 515–18
Rehearsal, The, 353
Reinhardt, Max, 305–07
Renaissance (*see* England; France; Italy)
Renoir, Pierre Auguste, 360
Repertory companies, 18, 192, 241–42, 386, 548–49
Repertory Theater of Lincoln Center, *397*, *403*, *434*, 552
Resident companies, 390, 418, 548–49
Resolution, 33–34
Restoration (*see* England)
Revenge play, 125
Revolution in the Theatre, 320
Revolving stage, 246, 276, 465–66
Reynard the Fox, 495
Rhinoceros, 366
Rhythm (*see* Design)
Rice, Elmer, 308, *331*
Rich, John, 199
Richard II, 133
Richard III, 8, 23, 43, 133
Richards, Inigo, *199*
Richardson, Howard, *501*

Richardson, Ian, *374*

Richelieu, Cardinal, 170, 174, 179, 235

Right You Are, if You Think You Are, 363

Ring of Rahshasha, The, 257

Ristori, Adelaide, 253

Ritual and theatre, 55-56, 102-04

Rivals, The, 199

Robbers, The, 225

Rodgers, Richard, *354, 355*

Romance of the Three Kingdoms, 264

Romans of St. Paul, 476

Romantic movement (*see* Romanticism)

Romanticism, 25, 50, 222-28, 287

Rome
    actors and acting, 90, 94-95, *96,* 97
    audiences, 90, 97, 99
    beginnings of theatre, 88
    chorus, 91, 95, 97
    comedy, *89,* 91-95, *96*-97
    compared with Elizabethan, 130
    contests and prizes, 90
    costumes, 90, 91, 95, *96,* 97
    curtain, 101
    decline of theatre, 101
    dramatists, 88, 91, 95-96
    festivals, 88-90
    gladiatorial contests, 97
    increase in theatrical activity, 88-89
    influence in Renaissance, 95-96, 101
    managers, 90
    masks, 91, 95, *96,* 97
    mime, 97, 98
    music, 90, 91, 95, 97
    naumachia, 98
    pantomime, 97, 98
    playwrights' working conditions, 90
    production arrangements, 90
    relationship to Greek drama and theatre, 87-88, 91-92, *96,* 97, 98-99, 101
    rise of church, 101
    scenery, 90, 94-95
    theatre architecture, 90, 94-95, 98-101
    tragedy, 88, 95-96
    types of drama, 95-98

Romeo and Juliet, 134

Room, The, 370

Ropes and pulleys (*see* Machinery)

Rose, The, 126

Rose Tattoo, The, 345

Rosmersholm, 291

Rossballet, Das, 152

Royal Court Theatre (London), *353*

Royal Shakespeare Company, *370, 374*

Royalties, 253

Rueda, Lope de, 147

Rule, Janice, *346*

Rural Dionysia, 59

Russia
    constructivism, 333, *334*
    dramatists, 297-99
    18th century, 215
    Medieval drama, 215
    naturalism, 298-99
    19th century, 253
    nonrealistic staging, 320
    realism, 297-99
    theatre of social action, 331

Saarinen, Eero, 5

Sabbattini, Nicola, 159-160

Sackville, Thomas, 124

Sacre rapresentazione, 109

Sadovsky, Prov, 253

Saint Joan, 296

Saints and Sinners, 296

Salvini, Tommaso, 253

Salzburg Everyman, The, 118

Samisen, 276

Samurai, 271

Sanskrit drama, 254-59

Santa Fe Opera Company, *488*

Sardou, Victorien, *13*

Sartre, Jean-Paul, 364-65

Satin Slipper, The, 316, 317

Satyr play, 60, 61, 62, 78-79, 80, 153

Saxe-Meiningen, George II, Duke of, 301-02, 303

Saul, 215

Scaenae frons, 90, 94-95, 99-100

Scala, Flaminio, 165

Scaliger, Julius Caesar, 171

Scamozzi, Vincenzo, *4,* 156

Scene designer
    assistants, 468-70
    employment, 468-70, 489-90, 518, 549-50
    function of, 439, 447-55
    relationship with other artists, 447-50, 475
    working procedures, 447-55, 468-70

Scene shifting, 159-63, 166, 246-47, 276, 280, 462-67

Scenery
    arena stage, 472-74
    assembling, 459-60 467-68
    basic units, 455-59
    Chinese, 265
    crews, 469-70
    Elizabethan, 129, 140-41, 144-46
    English, 1660-1800, 190-91, 199, *200,* 203-04
    French, 18th century, 206, 209, *210*

French, 17th century, *168*, 169, 170, 179, *180*, 185
functions of, 40–41, 439–41
Greek, *58*, 61, 63–64, 77–78, 84
hanging units, 458–59
influence on acting, 440–41
Italian Renaissance, 151, 152, 154–63 165, 166
Italy, 18th century, 210–13
Japanese, 277, 278, 280–82
Medieval, 104, 105, 106–07, 111, 115–16
19th century, 244–48
open stage, 472
painting, 460–62
at rehearsals, performance, 467–68
Roman, 90, 94–95
set decoration, 467
shifting, 159–63, 166, 246–47, 276, 280, 462–67
standing units, 455–58
and style, 51, 441
20th century, 344, 345, *348*, 355, 359–61, 369, 439–74
working plans, 447–55
Schiller, Friedrich von, 225–26, 301
Schinkel, Karl Friedrich, 225, 245
Schneider, Alan, 22
Schönemann, Johann Friedrich, 220, 221
School drama, 123–24, 215, 216
School for Scandal, The, 199–204, 206, 406
School for Wives, The, 180, *549*
Schroeder, Friedrich Ludwig, 220, 221
Schroeder, Sophie, 220, 221
Science and art, 9–10, 56
Science of Dramaturgy, The, 254
Scornful Lady, The, 143
Scott, A. C., 270
Screen Actors Guild, 437
Screen Extras Guild, 437
Screens, The, 366
Scribe, Eugène, 289
Sea Gull, The, 298, 413
Sea Shadow, 537
Seale, Douglas, *138*
Second Mrs. Tanqueray, The, 296
Second Shepherd's Play, The, 112–16
Secondary Schools, Theatre in, 543–44
Sedes, 104
Self-Tormentor, The, 91
Sellner, G. R., 72
Seneca, 88, 95–96, 101, 123, 124, 125, 134, 150, 151, 153
Sententiae, 96
Sentimental drama, 196–99, 200–01, 205–07, 213, 214, 219
Sentimentalism, 197, 199, 205–06

Serlio, Sebastiano, 155–56, 169
Servandoni, Jean Nicolas, *209*
Servant of Two Masters, The, 214
Set Decoration, 467
Settle, Elkanah, *189*
Seven Against Thebes, 59
Shakespeare, William, *8*, 30, *41*, 46, 50, 124, 132, 133–41, 143, 144, 146, 147, 194, 195, 202, 221, 283, 301, *376*, 440, 476, 477, 502
Shakuntala, 257–58, 283
Shape (*see* Design)
Sharing companies, 132–33, 178–79, 185–86
Shaughraun, The, 235
Shaw, George Bernard, 38, 45, 296, 355–61
Shchepkin, Mikhail, 253
She Stoops to Conquer, 199
She Would if She Could, 195
Sheep Well, The, 147, 425
Shelley, Mary Wollstonecraft, *387*
Shelley, Percy Bysshe, 224
Sheng roles, 266, 267
Sheridan, Richard Brinsley, 199–204, 353, 440
Sherwood, Robert, *412*, *432*
Shibaraku, 279
Shimpa, 283
Shingeki, 283
Shirley, James, 143
Shite, 273
Shitebashira, 274
Shock techniques, 373
Shogun, 271
Short View of the Immorality and Profaneness of the English Stage, A, 195–96
Shuramono, 272
Shutters, 160, 161
Significance in drama, 12–14, 36–38
Siddons, Sarah, 249
Silent Woman, The, 142
Similes, 40
Simonson, Lee, 307
Simultaneous settings, 104, 105, 106–07, 111, 115–16, 169, 170
Singleton, Trinette, *379*, 537
Six Characters in Search of an Author, 363
Skene, 62–64, 84, *86*, 87
Slapstick Tragedy, 345
Snow, C. P., *456*
Social problem plays, 37–38
Socialist realism, 332
Society of Stage Directors and Choreographers, 417, 536–37
Sofonisba, 153
Soliloquy, 38, 96, 171, 177

Solimano, I1, 162
Son, The, 323
Song of the Lusitanian Bogey, The, 373
Sophocles, 31, 42, 50, 59, 60, 61, 67, 70–78, 79, 151
Sound
  controllable properties, 521–22
  cue sheets, 523
  equipment, *520, 521*, 522
  in motion pictures, 361
  in multimedia productions, 377, 523
  position in the theatre, 520
  purposes, 520–21
  and style, 51
  types, 520–21
South Pacific, 355
Spain
  comparison with England, 147
  dramatists, 147–49
  religious drama, 109, 121, 147–49
  theatre architecture, 147, *148*
Spaniards in Peru, 234
Spanish Tragedy, The, 124–25
Special effects
  English, 1660–1800, 190, 199
  Italian Renaissance, 162–63, 165, 166
  Medieval, 106–07, 111
  (*see also* Lighting; Machinery)
Spectacle, 40–41
  (*see also* Actors and acting; Costumes; Director; Lighting; Scenery)
Spectators (*see* Audiences)
Spectators on stage, 179, *186*, 190, 204, 209
Spirit House Movers, 372
Spook Sonata, The, 324
Spotlights (*see* Lighting)
Spring's Awakening, 325
Ssu Lang Visits his Mother, 270
Staël, Mme. de, 227
Stage, (*see* Theatre architecture)
Stage areas, 402
Stage business, 408, 430–31
Stage directions, 35, 38, 40
Stage fright, 20
Stage machinery (*see* Machinery)
Stage manager, 415–19
Stage picture (*see* Director)
Stage positions, 424–25
Standby, 399
Stanislavsky, Constantin, 206, 303–05, 308, 332, 352, *413*
Steele, Richard, 197
Stolen Marriage, The, 257
Story of the Great Hero, The, 257
Stowe, Harriet Beecher, 235

Strand Theatre (New York), 361
Stranger, The, 234
Strasberg, Lee, 309, 352
Stratford (Canada) Shakespearean Festival, *53, 131, 181*
Streetcar Named Desire, A, 345, 346, 351–52, *423*
Strife, 296
Strindberg, August, 216, 324, *325,* 346, 508
Striplights (*see* Lighting)
Structure of drama, 27–41
Style, 48–51
Stylization, 51
Subsidies, 18–19, 178, 186, 221, 375
Suddenly Last Summer, 345
Sumarokov, Alexei Petrovich, 215
Summer and Smoke, 345
Summer stock, 390, 418, 436, 468, 490, 519, 537, 546–48
Summer Theatre '68, 547
Sun and the Moon, The, 263
Sundgaard, Arnold, *456*
Suppliants, The, 59
Surprise of Love, The, 205
Surrealism, 363, 368
Sutherland, Paul, *537*
Svoboda, Josef, *35,* 377
Swan, The, 126
Sweden, 216
Symbol, 38
Symbolic devices, 107–08, 116
Symbolism, 50, 310–21, 323, 345, *441*
Synge, John M., *407*
Systems of acting, 426–27
Tagore, Rabindrinath, 260, *494*
Takeda, Izumo, 277
Takemoto Gidayu, 275
Tairov, Alexander, 322
Talma, François-Joseph, 252, 253
Tamburalaine, 29, 125
Taming of the Shrew, The, 133, 376
Tan roles, 266–67
Tango, 370
Tartuffe, 180–85, 199–200
Tasso, Torquato, 153
Teatro Farnese, 157, 158
Teatro Olimpico, *4,* 156–57
Technical director, 469
Television, 361, 548, 551
Tempest, The, 146
Terence, 88, 89, 90, 91–92, 98, 101, 123, 150, 151, 154, 165, 180
Terence stage, 154
Terkel, Studs, *448–54*
Terry, Ellen, 251
Terry, Megan, 383, *384*
Tethy's Festival, 145
Texture (*see* Design)

Theatre
  avocational, 540–41
  characteristics of, 3–8
  as a form of art, 9–16
  general conclusions about, 551–52
  origins of, 55–56
  as a profession, 539–51
  as recreation or relaxation, 17–18
  relationship to drama, 6–8
  as stimulation, 18
  training for, 539–40
Theatre, The (London), 126, 130
Théâtre Alfred Jarry, 371
Théâtre Antoine, 300, *363*
Theatre architecture
  and audience response, 21
  China, 264, 269
  effect on staging, 470–74
  England, 125–31, 140, 144–46, *188*, 189–90, *200*
  France, 167, *168*, 169, 170, 179, *180*, *185*, 209, *210*
  Greece, *57*, *58*, 62–64, 84, *86*, *87*, 98–99, 101
  India, 255–56
  Italy, 151, 152, 154–63, 166, *213*
  Japan, 272, 274–75, 276, 280–81
  Medieval, *103*, 104, 105, 110–12, *120*, *121*
  19th century, 243–44
  Roman, 90, 94–95, 98–101
  since 1945, 376, 377, 463–467, 470–74
  Spanish, 147, *148*
  work space, 474
Theatre Arts Monthly, 307
Théâtre d'Art, 318
Théâtre de France, 371
Théâtre de la Cité, 374
Théâtre de l'Oeuvre, 318
Théâtre du Marais, 170, 185
Théâtre du Vieux Colombier, *4*, 322
Theatre Guild, 308, *327*, *328*, *346*, 388
Théâtre Illustre, 179
Theatre and Its Double, The, 371
Théâtre Libre, 303
Théâtre Marigny, 371
Theatre of Dionysus, *57*, *58*, 62–64
Theatre of the Future, The, 320
Theatre of Social Action, 331, 334–43
Theatre Workshop, 374
Theatrical production (*see* Actors and acting; Costumes; Director; Finances; Lighting; Scenery)
Theatrical Syndicate, 242, 307
Theatricalism, 333
Theatron, 62
Thébiade, La, 175
Their Day, 35

Theme (*see* Thought)
Therapeutic drama, 551
Thérèse Raquin, 300
Thesmophoriazusae, 81
Thespis, 59
Thirty Years' War, 218
Thought
  clarity of, 37–38
  devices for projecting, 38
  and meaning in drama, 36–38
  in Medieval drama, 108–09
  as organizing principle in drama, 28–29, 34, 36–37
  and universality, 37
Three Musketeers, The, 228
Three-Penny Opera, 337
Three Sisters, The, 298
Thrust stage (*see* Open stage)
Thunderstorm, The, 297
Thyestes, 96
Thymele, 62
Tidings Brought to Mary, The, 316, 465
Time, unity of, 173–74, 177, 185, 202
Tiny Alice, 351
'Tis Pity She's a Whore, 143
Titus Andronicus, 134
Toller, Ernst, 325
Tom and Jerry, 235
Topol, Josef, *35*
Torelli, Giacomo, 161–62, *163*, *168*, 170
Tosca, *13*, 529
Total theatre, 371–73
Tourneur, Cyril, 143
Tower of Nesle, The, 228
Toy Theatre (Boston), 307
Trachiniae, 60
Trackers, The, 60, 79
Trade guilds, 105, 109, 110–12
Traditional Chinese Plays, 270
Tragedy
  characterization in, 36, 43–44
  domestic, 197–98, 199, 205–06
  Elizabethan, 124–25, 133–41, 143
  emotional powers, 44
  England, 1660–1800, 194–95, 196, 197–98, 199
  as a form, 43–44
  French, 18th century, 204–05
  French, 17th century, 171–78, 180
  Greek, 59–61, 62, 64–65, 66–78, 80, 85, 87, 154
  heroic, 194
  Italian, 153, 156, 214–15
  neoclassical, 171–78, 180
  Roman, 88, 95–96
Tragedy of Tragedies, The, 198
Tragicomedy, 46, 134, 143, 169, 174
Transfiguration, 325

Trap doors (*see* Machinery)
Tree, Ellen, 250
Trespassers, The, 417
Trial, The, 332
Trissino, Giangiorgio, 153
Triumph of Isabella, The, 112
Troilus and Cressida, 133–34
Trojan Women, The, 61
Tropes, 103–04
Tryouts, 385–86, 397–98
Turcaret, 207
Turgenev, Ivan, 297
Turlupin, 167, *168*
Twelfth Night, 45, 133
Twice a Bride, 270
Tyler, Royall, *217*, *396*
Tyrone Guthrie Theatre, 376, 436
Tzara, Tristan, 362
Ubu Roi, 362, *363*
Udall, Nicholas, 123–24
Uncle Tom's Cabin, 235–41
Uncle Vanya, 298
Understudy, 399
Unions, Theatrical, 389
United Scenic Artists Union, 468, 469,
    490, 518
United States
    beginnings of theatre, 216–17
    18th century, 216–17
    Expressionism, 330
    little theatre movement, 307
    new stagecraft, 307
    19th century, 235–41, 247, 252, 253
    realism, 288–302, 309
    since 1945, 345–52, *372*, 375–77,
        379–551
Unities, 173–74, 177, 185, 202, 238
Universality, 37
University theatre, 539–40, 544–45
Vakhtangov, Eugene, 334
Valenciennes Passion Play, *104*, *106*
Valleran-Lecomte, 167, 169
Van Gogh, Vincent, 323
van Itallie, Jean-Claude, *382*, 383
Variety show, 353, 354
Vaudeville, 354
Vega, Lope de, 147, *425*
Venetian opera houses, 158–59, 161
Venice Preserv'd, 194
Verdi, Giuseppe, *528*
Verfremdungseffekt, 335
Verisimilitude, 171–74, 177
Versailles, *180*
Vestris, Lucia Elizabeth, 250
Victims of Duty, 366
Victor, or the Child of the Forest, 235
Viet Rock, 383, *384*
Vieux Colombier (*see* Théâtre du Vieux
    Colombier)

View from the Bridge, The, 347
Vigny, Alfred de, 228
Vilar, Jean, 364
Virginius, 225
Vishakhadatta, 257
Visit, The, 372, 373
Vitruvius, 151, 152, 154, 155, 156
Vivian Beaumont Theater, 5, 376
Voice and speech, 408–10, 421, 431–32
Volkov, Fyodor, 215
Volpone, 46, 142–43
Voltaire, 204–05, 207, *208*
Volume, 408, 521–22
Vultures, The, 301
Wagner, Richard, 316
Wagner, Robin, 365
Wagon stages, 246, 464–65
Waiting for Godot, 29, 33, 365, *366*, 371
Waiting for Lefty, 309
Wakebashira, 274
Wakefield Cycle, The, *109*, 110, 112
Waki, 273
Wakinomono, 272
Wakiza, 274
Wallenstein trilogy, 226
Wardrobe mistress, 489, 490–91
Washington Square Players, 307–08
Wasps, The, 81
Wasserman, Dale, 525
Water's Edge, The, 264
Watteau, Jean Antoine, 7, *178*
Way of the World, The, 195
Wayang kulit, 261
We Bombed in New Haven, 545
Webster, John, 143, *441*
Wedekind, Franz, 324–25
Weiss, Peter, 371, 373–74
Welded, 308
Well-made play, 289
West Side Story, 355
When We Dead Awaken, 291
White Devil, The, 143
White, Miles, *354*
Who's Afraid of Virginia Woolf?, 22,
    351
Wild Duck, The, 291–96, *292*, 299, 440,
    477, *506*, *507*
Wilder, Thornton, 29, 401
William Tell, 225, 226
Williams, Tennessee, 345–47, 351–52,
    423, 524
Wind in the Willows, The, 542
Wings (*see* Scenery)
Winter's Tale, The, 134
Wits, The, 146
Woman of Andros, The, 91
Wordsworth, William, 224
Would-Be Gentleman, The, 180
Woyzeck, 226

Wright, Bob, 525
Yard (*see* Pit)
Yeats, William Butler, 316
Yellow Jack, 499
Yellow Jacket, The, 270
Yerma, 316
York cycle, 110
Yoshitsune Sembon Zakura, 277

Zaïre, 205, 208
Zanni, 164
Zeami Motokiyo, 271
Zeffirelli, Franco, 528
Zola, Emile, 299–300, 303
Zomosa, Maximiliano, 379, 532
Zoo Story, The, 351